THE CIVILIZATION OF THE AMERICAN INDIAN SERIES

PEYOTE RELIGION

Peyote Religion

A HISTORY

By Omer C. Stewart

UNIVERSITY OF OKLAHOMA PRESS : NORMAN AND LONDON

BY OMER C. STEWART

Ethnohistorical Bibliography of the Ute Indians of Colorado (Boulder, 1971)
Indians of the Great Basin: A Critical Bibliography (Bloomington, 1982)
As Long as the River Shall Run: An Ethnohistory of Pyramid Lake Indian Reservation (coauthor) (Berkeley, 1984)
Peyotism in the West (coauthor) (Salt Lake City, 1983)
Peyote Religion: A History (Norman, 1987)

Library of Congress Cataloging-in-Publication Data

Stewart, Omer Call, 1908–
  Peyote religion.

  (The Civilization of the American Indian series;
v. 181)
  Bibliography: p. 389.
  Includes index.
  1. Peyotism—History.   2. Indians of North America—
Religion and mythology.   I. Title.   II. Series.
E98.R3S79   1987   299'.78   87–5941
ISBN 0–8061–2068–1

The paper in this book meets the guidelines for permanence and durability of the Committee on Production Guidelines for Book Longevity of the Council on Library Resources, Inc. ∞

To my wife, Lenore

Contents

Illustrations

Maps

Preface

THE title, *Peyote Religion: A History* indicates my aim to relate in chronological order the known facts about the development and spread of the peyote religion. The subject, however, is too complicated for a simple chronology. It also seems necessary to try to explain the events as much as possible. As I do so, I will not be oblivious to the theories and controversies that have characterized discussions of why new religions are accepted or rejected, but my consideration of peyotism rests primarily on ethnographic interviews and participant observations, both my own and those of many others, and not on theories.

There is little difference of opinion about the time, ca. 1880, or the place, western Oklahoma, where the modern peyote religion became formalized, but there is considerable controversy about the content of that early cult and even more difference of opinion about the manner of the growth of the religion up to the time of its discovery in Oklahoma. Some of the questions I will deal with revolve around the influence on the peyote ritual of the old red bean or mescal bean cult, and the effect on peyotism of Christianity, geography and economics, personalities and laws, education, and American non-Indian culture. I will consider throughout the opposition to peyotism and the stubborn fight for what Americans generally take for granted: religious freedom. I will consider the physical and psychological effects of eating the peyote cactus, *Lophophora williamsii,* and especially the differences of opinion concerning its effects. I hope this history will be read by Indians as well as non-Indians, and I have tried to write in a simple style that any interested reader can understand.

I would like to highlight here two conclusions I have reached about peyotism as part of a cultural and historical process. First of all, peyotism has been a unifying influence in American Indian life, providing the basis for Indian friendships, rituals, social gatherings, travel, marriage, and more. It has been a source of comfort and healing and a means of expression for a troubled people. And it has resulted in one of the strongest pan-Indian movements in the United States. But at the same time that it has been a unifying force, it has also been divisive. Factionalism—splitting, feuding, fighting, quarreling—has troubled peyotism just as it has other religions. At least from the 1880s (and one assumes long before that), when the Big Moon ritual of John Wilson began competing with the traditional Half Moon ritual of Quanah Parker, peyotism has been characterized by divisiveness as well as acceptance. Often this division has been only a matter of a strong preference for a leader who has introduced a minor innovation in ritual; occasionally it has been significant enough to divide the international church and separate large segments of the great body of Navajo peyotists. In this counterpoint of unification and divisiveness peyotism has shown its psychic unity with other religions.

In evaluating this ambivalent history, while I regret the factionalism, I do not feel that it diminishes the place of peyotism as a unique, original, and unifying phenomenon, peculiar and indigenous to these Indians, through which they have been able to learn some answers to their condition in new white America in their own way, at their own pace, and on their own ground. Through peyotism, the majority of adherents have been able to grow in understanding and strength to meet the demands of everyday life. Moreover, it is worthwhile to note in regard to the pull between factionalism and cooperation how often peyotists, though deeply divided, have been able to put aside their differences in order to participate in the unifying experience of a peyote meeting which did not quite meet their preference and how reluctant they have been to criticize one another's differences. If this is a peculiarly Indian characteristic, it suggests a tolerance and patience which we all would like to have.

Second, I wish to stress the importance of the individual in the diffusion of culture. The history of peyotism is the history of people of many kinds in various situations with different talents. As they have met together in the context of peyotism, they have become leaders and followers, advocates and opponents, fascinated observers and manipulators of public opinion. These individuals determined the course of peyotism. Many were Indians of unusual intelligence and enterprise who had the advantage of education at Carlisle, Haskell, or other Indian schools, where they learned English, Christianity, and something about white culture. Some others, equally or perhaps specially endowed, found inspiration within themselves. Such a one was John Wilson. But in every case it was an interested person here, an inspired one there, and so on, who spread peyotism throughout Oklahoma and then beyond. Some were self-seeking as well as religious, like Sam Lone Bear and Ben Lancaster; others, like Jim Blue Bird and Truman Daily, were men of integrity and deep religious conviction. But they all contributed to the spread of peyotism and what it came to be. There were the non-Indians, too—outsiders like James Mooney, John Collier, and J. Sydney Slotkin—who encouraged and valued it, and those others who tried to stamp it out, such as "Pussyfoot" Johnson, Major Pratt, and Mabel Luhan. And of course there were those many nameless ones, those who remained indifferent to peyotism, for it was almost always a minority religion. They, too, should be considered.

I have been dependent, of course, on the wide range of published sources and extensive unpublished materials as well as a lifetime of personal experience and research to aid me in writing this history. I feel obligated to go into some detail concerning the latter. My interest in peyote

began in 1937, when, on a field trip to the Ute Indians in Utah and Colorado, I attended three peyote meetings (Stewart 1948). In 1938, a chance
attendance at a peyote meeting with the Northern Paiute and Washo Indians at Mono Lake, California, convinced me to make a study of peyotism
among those people for my Ph.D. thesis (Stewart 1944).

The war years interrupted my research into peyotism, but after the
war, while engaged in teaching anthropology at the University of Colorado,
Boulder, I again had the opportunity to exchange views and information regarding peyote. I soon gained a reputation as a friend of peyotists. For example, one well-attended lecture in Denver in 1948, in which I explored
some of the misconceptions concerning peyotism, led to criticism in the
Rocky Mountain News but attracted the attention of many Indians, including
Jim Blue Bird, longtime leader of Sioux peyotism, who appreciated my defense of peyotism and became a valuable personal contact for me over two
decades.

In 1948, J. Sidney Slotkin, anthropologist at the University of Chicago,
became involved in an intensive study of Menominee peyotism and shared
my concern to disabuse the public conerning the evils of peyote. Articles on
peyote containing false information had appeared in several national maga-
zines, such as *Time* and the *Journal of the American Medical Association*.
Feeling that they called for concerted scholarly refutation, Slotkin prepared
a statement of facts about peyotism to be submitted to *Science* and asked
for the signatures of Weston La Barre, David P. McAllester, Sol Tax, and
myself. We were all glad to sign, and the statement was published on November 30, 1951. For the next seven years, until his death in 1958, Slotkin
devoted nearly all his time to research and activity concerning the Native
American Church, collecting a massive file on every aspect of peyotism, but
especially on the church organization. At his death, his widow presented
me with his peyote archive and library, and my research has been greatly
facilitated by that gift.

In a sense, I not only inherited Slotkin's files but also his place as defender of peyotism in court. Slotkin had appeared in court in 1956 in behalf
of a Winnebago peyotist, and in 1957 he defended Navajo peyotists in court
in Arizona. Since 1960, I have appeared in court in behalf of peyotists in
Arizona, California, Colorado, New Mexico, Washington, South Dakota,
and North Dakota. In or out of court, I have considered it a privilege and an
obligation to use my special knowledge of peyotism and the Native American Church to educate students and the general public concerning peyotism
whenever the opportunity presented itself.

To maintain and broaden my knowledge, I have read extensively, interviewed many peyotists, and attended as many different ceremonies of the
Native American Church (NAC) as possible. In 1972, I spent nearly the
whole year traveling to tribes not before visited to add personal knowledge

of their ceremonies and to renew my understanding of familiar groups such as the Ute, Washo, and Northern Paiute, who had initially introduced me to peyotism. A travel grant from the American Council of Learned Societies allowed me to visit and talk to peyotists among the Taos Indians, Arapaho, Kiowa, Comanche, Kickapoo, Sac and Fox, Pawnee, Osage, and Oto. In Oklahoma I attended peyote meetings with hosts from the Kiowa, Sac and Fox, and Oto tribes. At each meeting peyotists of many other tribes were present. In South Dakota, Wyoming, and Montana I attended peyote ceremonies with the Sioux, Northern Arapaho, Wind River Shoshone, and Northern Cheyenne. Long and free discussions with a dozen or so Crow peyotists were very helpful. In Nevada I not only found members from the groups I had known in 1938, but also was able to participate in a peyote meeting with the Northern Paiute on the McDermit Reservation. Finally, in Arizona, Colorado, Utah, and New Mexico I attended meetings with the Navajo, the Ute Mountain Ute, the Uintah-Ouray Ute, and the Taos. In 1978, I attended a meeting on the Colville Reservation in Washington after assisting three NAC members to be cleared of any offense for transporting peyote to an NAC ritual.

Recognizing the value of government documents as well as unofficial archives in the research of Indian affairs has led me to accumulate material on peyote in Washington, D.C., from the National Archives, the Smithsonian Archives, and the Library of Congress. Traveling in my camper bus with a portable microfilm camera enabled me to copy hundreds of pages of manuscripts. In Oklahoma, both the university collections and those of the state library were useful, as were the files at Fort Sill Museum. Hundreds of documents have been obtained from various branches of the National Archives. For instance, in Kansas City I obtained information dealing with peyotism among the Winnebago, the Omaha, the Prairie Potawatomi, and the Sac and Fox. My card file of members of the NAC, copied from all types of records, contains more than ten thousand names and is still growing.

I wish to take this opportunity to show my appreciation to certain of my professional colleagues whose work and concern over the years have aided this research. Besides J. Sidney Slotkin they are David F. Aberle, Garrick A. Bailey, Kenneth L. Beals, Warren L. d'Azevedo, James H. Howard, Weston La Barre, Sven Liljeblad, Nancy O. Lurie, Carling Malouf, David P. McAllester, J. Gilbert McAllister, George R. Morgan, Morris E. Opler, the Reverend Peter J. Powell, Paul B. Steinmetz, S. J., Melburn D. Thurman, Erminie W. Voegelin, and Roland M. Wagner. William B. Taylor, my former neighbor and colleague at the University of Colorado, now professor of Latin American history at the University of Virginia, helped me initially with contributions from his research in Mexican archives and read the entire manuscript, giving editorial help, comments, and suggestions. It is impossible to evaluate his assistance in the preparation of this book.

I find it impossible to select a few among the Indians who have aided me. There are just too many who have given me their time and knowledge. I can only hope this book will reward them a little.

My wife, Lenore, must be especially thanked. Without her help in re-writing my manuscript, this book would never have appeared in its present form.

OMER C. STEWART
Boulder, Colorado

PART ONE

Peyote and Its Early Use

FIG. 1. Earliest known botanical illustration of *Lophophora williamsii,* peyote. *Botanical Magazine,* 1847, tab. 4296.

CHAPTER 1

The Plant

THIS book is about peyote, a small, spineless cactus having psychedelic properties which grows in a limited area principally in northern Mexico and southern Texas. It is also about the peoples and ceremonies concerned with the use of peyote over the last four hundred years, culminating in the present-day Native American Church, the members of which number perhaps two hundred thousand and the territory of which extends from Alberta, Canada, to west central Mexico and from Wisconsin to the Pacific Coast states.

The plant is light green and segmented, about one to two inches across, growing singly or in clusters close to the ground from a long taproot (Fig. 1). It is harvested by cutting off the exposed tops of the clusters, leaving the root to produce more "buttons," as the tops are usually called. The buttons are generally dried before being eaten, and they are extremely bitter to the taste, frequently producing vomiting. However, they also produce a warm and pleasant euphoria, an agreeable point of view, relaxation, colorful visual distortions, and a sense of timelessness that are conducive to the all-night ceremony of the Native American Church. To the church's members, peyote is the essential ingredient, the sacrament, in their well-established, unique ceremony. Peyote is not habit-forming, and in the controlled ambience of a peyote meeting it is in no way harmful.

Since earliest recognition of use of peyote on Indian reservations (Clark 1888), it has been assumed by BIA officials and missionaries and later by most psychological, pharmacological, and medical researchers, that peyote was a habit-forming and dangerous drug (Braasch, et al 1949: *Arizona Republic* March 23, 1971). Nevertheless, the U.S. Congress did not declare peyote a dangerous drug until 1965, except in a back-handed way in the Narcotic Farms [hospitals] Act of January 19, 1929. The act of 1929 included peyote among the "habit forming drugs," but in 1949, I was informed by Dr. Harris Isabell (personal communication) that of 18,000 admissions for drug addictions by that time none had been admitted for addiction to peyote. Researchers at the "narcotic farms" A. B. Wolback, Jr.; Harris Isabell; and E. J. Miner reported full "Cross tolerance between Mescaline [the major alkaloid in peyote] and LSD-25." Both LSD-25 and mescaline were chemically produced and became available in quantities in the United States in the 1960s, when experimentation with psychedelic drugs became popular. It was probably the excesses of the "hippies" that prompted the U.S. Congress in March 1965 to amend the Federal Food, Drug, and Cosmetic

Act (21 U.S.C. 321) to place controls on several "depressant and stimulant drugs, including peyote (mescaline)," except "its use in connection with the ceremonies of a bona fide religious organization" (Congressional Record— House, March 10, 1965, pp. 4571–75). The Controlled Substance Act of 1970, Section 202, includes "peyote as a Schedule 1, hallucinogenic substance," meaning it had a "high potential for abuse" (Myers, 1975, p. 41).

The scientific name for peyote (or *peyotl,* as it was called by the Aztec) is *Lophophora williamsii,* the name given to it by John Coulter in 1894. It has been analyzed extensively since then and has been found to contain the alkaloids mescaline, anhalamine, anhalonidine, peyotine, anhalonine, lophophorine, and possibly others. Pharmacologists of more than twenty countries have been involved in analysis of peyote in the hope of finding significant medical and pharmacological uses for it, but it has not proved valuable for medical purposes. Mescaline, by far the most important alkaloid in the plant, is produced in the laboratory, and its effect, physiologically and psychologically, is almost identical with that of peyote.

In the United States there has been a persistent misunderstanding of the use of the terms *mescal bean* or *mescal button* for peyote. Mescal beans are the hard red seeds, ranging from 0.8 cm to 2 cm in length and 0.5 cm to 1.5 cm in breadth, that are found in the woody, indehiscent pods of the evergreen bush *Sophora secundiflora* (Fig. 2; Merrill 1977*a*). Like peyote, the *Sophora* bean, called by the Mexicans *frijolillo,* is an intoxicant but, unlike peyote, it is not a mild intoxicant but is extremely powerful. The two plants grow in about the same area. The superimposition of a map published by Anderson (1969) showing the natural range of *Lophophora* on another by Merrill (1977*a*) showing the natural range of *Sophora* indicates that nearly all of the peyote area was shared by the mescal beans (Map 1).

Dr. Valery Havard, captain and assistant surgeon, U.S. Army, learned of both peyote and mescal beans while he was stationed near Presidio, Texas, in 1880, and was one of the first in the United States to describe them. Of peyote Havard wrote (1885: 470, 521):

Of the abundant Cacti the most remarkable species . . . (Pellote) bearing a beautiful flower and used medicinally by Mexicans . . . was not before observed on this side of the Rio Grande. . . . The fleshy part of the plant is used, and pieces are found in most Mexican houses. An infusion of it is said to be good in fevers. It is principally as an intoxicant that the Peyote has become noted, being often added to "tizwin" or other wild fermented native drinks to render it more inebriating. If chewed, it produces a sort of delirious exhilaration which has won for it the designation of "dry whiskey."

Havard (1885: 500) cited a Mr. Bellanger on the use and intoxicating properties of *Sophora:* "The Indians near San Antonio used this bean as an intoxicant, half a bean producing delirious exhilaration followed by a sleep which lasts 2 or 3 days, and it is asserted that a whole bean would kill a man."

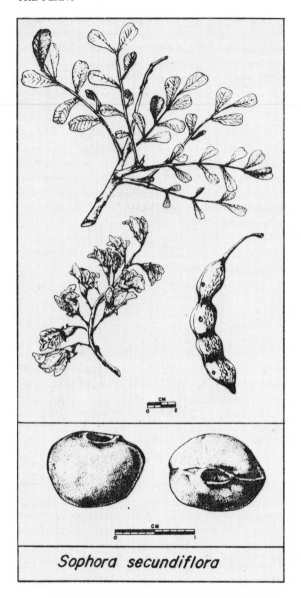

FIG. 2. *Sophora secundi-flora,* "mescal." After Merrill (1977).

Possibly because both were intoxicating and both grew in the same area, the nomenclature of the two plants became confused in American minds. However, the two plants were never confused in the minds of the Indians, the Spaniards, or, later, the Mexicans. In Mexico, "mescal" is the name for the agave plant used either as a food or, fermented or distilled, as an intoxicant, and the red beans are *frijolillos*. Unfortunately, when peyote came to

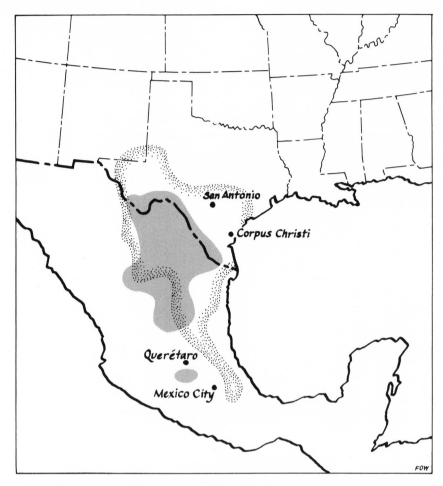

MAP 1. Natural range of *Sophora secundiflora* ("mescal," dotted area) (after Merrill 1977A) and *Lophophora williamsii* (peyote, shaded area) (after Anderson 1969).

popular and then official attention in the United States, the term *mescal* was used for all three plants: peyote, agave, and *frijolillo.* To the best of my knowledge, there are no reports from Mexico at any time down to the present using any form of the word *mescal* to designate peyote.

Reference to peyote is found in the *Reports of the Commissioner of Indian Affairs* for 1886, in which Agent J. Lee Hall describes a narcotic cactus called *wocowist* by the Comanche and *hoas* or *hose* by the Apache. In his 1888 *Annual Report,* Agent E. E. White wrote of *woqui* and its use among the Comanche and added, "Its common name here among the whites is mescal bean."

At about the same time, J. R. Briggs, M.D., of Dallas, Texas, ate some peyote and reported his experience in the *Medical Register* of April 7, 1887. This was reprinted in the *Druggists' Bulletin* under the title, "Muscale Buttons—Physiological Action—a Mexican Fruit with Possible Medicinal Virtues." In July, 1887, Briggs sent five bushels of peyote, which he called "muscale buttons," to Parke Davis Pharmaceutical Company in Detroit. The next year, Parke Davis sent some of these to Louis Lewin, a pharmacologist in Germany, who shared them with a friend, botanist Paul Hennings. This led to an article in the *Therapeutic Gazette* by Lewin (1888) in which the scientific name of "muscale buttons" was given as *Anhalonium lewinii hennings;* both terms were eventually proven to be inaccurate.

The confusion in terminology was spread further into the scholarly and popular literature by Smithsonian ethnologist James Mooney, who was a participant-observer in a Kiowa peyote meeting in early 1891. Writing about it in a letter in April, 1891, he called it "the mescal ceremony." Appearing before the Anthropological Society of Washington, D.C., and reported in the *Washington, D.C., Evening Star* of November 4, 1891, Mooney spoke on the "Kiowa Mescal Rite." The *Augusta* (Georgia) *Chronicle* of January 24, 1892, carried a copyrighted story by Mooney under the headline, "Eating the Mescal." The *American Anthropologist* published a short article by Mooney (1892b) with the title, "A Kiowa Mescal rattle," accompanied by a photograph of a peyote rattle.

Mooney appears to have been aware of the multiplicity of terms for peyote. In his article, "The Mescal Plant and Ceremony" (1896b), the names for *Anhalonium williamsii,* that is, peyote, were explained as follows:

Among the Kiowa it was *seni;* among the Comanche, *wokowi;* with the Mescalero, *ho;* and with the Tarahumara, *hikori.* The traders of the Indian Territory commonly called it *mescal,* although it must not be confounded with another mescal in Arizona, the *Agave.* . . . The local Mexican name upon the Rio Grande is *peyote* or *pellote,* from the old Aztec name *peyotl.* . . . The Mescalero Apache take their name from it.

In a footnote, Mooney reported: "Mr. Colville, botanist of the Agricultural Department, has made a distinct genus of the mescal plant, calling it *Lophophora williamsii lewinii.*" By 1897, Mooney seems more confused than ever about the proper terminology, for he wrote an article for *Der Urquell* entitled, "The Kiowa Peyote Rite."

Officials of the U.S. Indian Service continued to refer to peyote as "mescal" until 1907, when their confusion of terms led them to lose a lawsuit against the use of peyote by the Indians of Oklahoma. Nevertheless, the confusion still appears from time to time, indicating that, no matter how false or misleading, once a term becomes common usage, it is very hard to dislodge.

Serious anthropologists, long disabused of the confusion of terms, have occasionally speculated about the possibility that a "red bean" or "mescal bean" cult, in which *frijolillos* are eaten or made into a tea for drinking, preceded and led to the peyote cult, but there is little solid evidence that such was ever the case. *Frijolillo* is too lethal to be ingested without serious consequences, and there have been no significant studies of such a cult. Such studies as have been made are based mostly on supposition. However, the red beans are used often by peyotists and others for decorative purposes. A red bean necklace has frequently been made to be worn especially during a peyote meeting. That Indians have for centuries found some use for mescal beans as well as for peyote was clear when archaeologists found mescal beans and peyote in a number of prehistoric sites. Thomas N. Campbell (1958) reported many finds of mescal beans and two of peyote in Texas caves. J. M. Adovasio and G. F. Fry (1976) reported hundreds of mescal beans in a number of deposits dating back to 7500 B.C. and peyote in a few sites but no further back than A.D. 810–1070.

For nearly half a century following its publication in 1926, Alexandre Rouhier's map and description of the natural growth area of peyote were accepted as correct and regularly served as the basis for anthropologists writing about peyote. He wrote as follows (my translation):

> Peyote is native to Mexico and the extreme south of the United States, and we do not know at present whether it has been found elsewhere. Its area of growth, clearly defined, fits into a diamond-shape quadrilateral of which the main axis, from northwest to southeast, is inclined about 45 degrees from the Tropic of Cancer, which cuts off approximately its lower third. The sides of this figure are as follows: from Deming (New Mexico) southeast to Corpus Christi (Texas); from Corpus Christi south to Puebla; from Puebla northwest to Sombrerete (Zacatecas); Sombrerete north to Deming.
>
> . . . this lozenge coincides in its major features with the form of the Mexican plateau and the area it occupies. . . .
>
> Peyote is found on the two banks of the [Rio Grande], on the rocky cliffs of the canyons as well as on the slopes of the hills and mountains, more or less on the edges of the river valley. From El Paso, it is found on all of the left bank up to 150 kilometers of its length. It grows in the sandy and rocky soil of the desert in the region of Presidio County; then south to Laredo on the Texas side of the river; and on both shores of its lower reaches. Indians of the United States harvest it in south Texas where it abounds. Some specimens in our possession

came from the vicinity of Aguilares [Texas] and from the hilly zone which extends between Laredo and Rio Nueces. All of the region of the Salt Plains Mountains and the Apache Mountains situated between the Pecos River and the Rio Grande above the Big Bend is rich in Peyote. The plant has been harvested also near the mouth of the Pecos.

In 1969, new information about the natural habitat of peyote has made it necessary to question Rouhier's map and findings. An article that appeared in *Brittonia* under the title, "The Biogeography, Ecology, and Taxonomy of Lophophora (Cactaceae)," by Edward F. Anderson (1969), summarized the results of data collected during seven field trips to Texas and Mexico from 1957 to 1961 and from a review of published reports for a 1961 Ph.D. thesis at Claremont Graduate School under the direction of Dr. Gordon A. Alles. Data from H. Halia Bravo (1967) and from laboratory and herbarium research were also included. Anderson's map reduces considerably the growth area of peyote, especially in West Texas, when compared to the map of Rouhier (Map 2). The following is from Anderson's article of 1969:

Extensive studies were not possible at every collection site, so ten were selected to represent *Lophophora* localities throughout its natural range. These sites not only include the geographical extremes but also represent various locations along the Rio Grande . . . , in the low hot basin of northern Mexico . . . , in the intermediate areas around Saltillo . . . , on the higher central plateau . . . , and the somewhat unique zone in Querétaro. . . .

Distribution. *Lophophora* has a latitudinal distribution of about 1200 km from 20° 54' to 29° 47' North Latitude. It is found along the Rio Grande drainage basin and southward into the high central plateau of northern Mexico lying between the Sierra Madre Oriental and Sierra Madre Occidental. Generally the elevation of the localities increases to the southward. Those along the Rio Grande near Reynosa, Tamaulipas, are less than 50 m, while localities in San Luis Potosi exceed 180 m in elevation.

Ecologists describe this large desert area of Texas and northern Mexico as the Chihuahuan Desert. . . .

In his book *Peyote, the Divine Cactus,* Anderson (1980:137) is less technical but equally specific: "*Lophophora williamsii,* the commonly known peyote cactus, comprises a large northern population, extending from southern Texas southward along the high plateau land of northern Mexico. This variable and extensive population reaches its southern limit in the Mexican state of San Luis Potosi where, near the junction of federal highways 57 and 80, for example, it forms large, variable clumps. The second species, *L. diffusa,* is a more southern population that occurs in the dry central area of the state of Querétaro, Mexico."

The peyote-growing zones Rouhier designated, although generally similar, are about two hundred miles of additional country on both sides of the Rio Grande in Mexico and Texas and west of the Pecos River in West Texas. Anderson (1969:209) disagrees: "Of the locations reported earlier in the

MAP 2. Natural growth of peyote (after Rouhier 1926, solid line, and Anderson 1969, shaded area).

literature or on herbarium specimens, only two were visited that failed to yield peyote—Big Bend National Park and the region along the Pecos River. *Lophophora* was collected in Big Bend National Park by Barton R. Warnock in 1961, but my search of the locality in 1967 was unsuccessful. . . ."

Also in his book, *Peyote, the Divine Cactus* (1980: 151–52), Anderson gives a good description of the plant and its characteristics:

Peyote consists of populations that are not only wide ranging geographically, but which are also variable in topographical appearance and methods of reproduction. Commonly peyote is found growing under shrubs. . . . at other times, however, it grows in the open with no protection or shade of any kind. In some areas, such as in the state of San Luis Potosi, peyote sometimes grows in silty mud flats that become temporary shallow fresh-water lakes during the rainy season. In west Texas peyote has even been found growing in crevices on steep limestone cliffs.

The appearance of peyote also varies widely. . . . In some cases the plants occur as single-headed individuals and in others they come caespitose, forming dense clumps up to two meters across with scores of heads. Plants in Texas do not seem to form clumps as often as those in the state of San Luis Potosí but plants with several tops can arise as the result of injury by grazing animals or other factors. Many-headed individuals are also produced by harvesting the tops. In Texas, for example, collectors normally cut off the top of the plant, leaving the long, carrot-shaped root in the ground. The subterranean portion soon calluses and in a few months produces several new tops rather than just a single one like that which was cut off. . . .

Reproduction occurs mainly by sexual means. The plants flower in the early summer, and the ovules, which are fertilized during that season mature into seeds a year later. The fruit which arises from the center of the plant late in the spring or early in the summer rapidly elongates into a pink or reddish cylindrical structure up to about one-half inch in length. Within a few weeks these fruits mature; their walls dry, become paper-thin, and turn brownish. Late in the summer, usually as a result of wind, rain, or some other climatic factor, the fruit wall ruptures and the many small black seeds are released. The heavy summer rains then wash the seeds out of the sunken center of the plant and disperse them.

Another method of reproduction in peyote is by vegetative or asexual means. Many plants produce "pups" or lateral shoots which arise from lateral areoles. After these new shoots have attained sufficient size they can often root and survive if broken off. If these new portions successfully grow into new plants, they are genetically identical to their parents. Surprisingly, peyote plants rarely rot if injured or cut, so excised pieces will readily form adventitious roots and can become independent plants.

There are others who have written about the growth area of peyote, generally extending the area of growth beyond Rouhier's and especially beyond Anderson's. Vincenzo Petrullo (1934: 129) reported that "Quanna Parker drifted down into Old Mexico and also traveled in Arizona and New Mexico. He became acquainted with the peyote leaders in that part of the country. . . ." Regarding John Wilson, Petrullo wrote (1934: 440: "As a young man, he went to Arizona and New Mexico, and it was there that he had some experience with Peyote." Sidney Cohen (1964: 21) was explicit: "The peyote cactus (*Lophophora williamsii*) . . . grows in the watershed of the Rio Grande. . . ." Richard E. Schultes (1937*d*: 131) wrote: "In Ward County, Texas, the town of Peyote [Pyote] takes its name from the trade in mescal i.e., peyote buttons, gathered in Ward and Winkler Counties." Pyote is twenty-three miles east of the Pecos River on U.S. Highway 20 and about fifty miles south of the southeast corner of New Mexico. Winkler County lies between Ward County and New Mexico, actually being both south and east of the corner of New Mexico. Inasmuch as the town of Pyote is not within the area of peyote growth described by Rouhier and is over one hundred miles outside of the peyote growth areas shown by Anderson, I have tried to discover the basis for Schultes's statement. In a letter written in 1927, which Schultes may have seen, the manager of the Pyote Chamber of Commerce wrote:

The town of Pyote is named after the plant, which the Indians call Pe-o-ta, but how it came to be so called, we are at a loss to understand, unless it may be from the fact that there are several spots in Ward and Winkler counties where this wild plant is found. And a further explanation may be found in the legend that generations ago, the various tribes using this plant would come here stated times during the year to gather the plant. These seasons of harvest were always marked by strict truces. . . . The center of the Pe-o-ta harvesting seems to have shifted of recent years to localities closer to the Mexican Border. . . . The plant is gathered by Mexicans. . . .

This letter established, in my opinion, only that there was a local legend about the name.

In order to broaden my information about the natural range of peyote in the past as well as the present, in 1971 and 1972 I wrote to the editors of local newspapers in Las Cruces, Deming, and Carlsbad, New Mexico, and to sixteen editors of local newspapers in West Texas from El Paso east to San Angelo and from Midland south to Del Rio. I also wrote to botany departments at two universities in the same region and to Sul Ross State College at Alpine, Texas. Letters were sent to the botany departments in twenty-one high schools and to twelve county agricultural agents in the area, and a letter went to the chief park naturalist of Big Bend National Park. All letters asked for information concerning the growth of peyote in the area, particularly whether past growth was in sufficient quantity for one or more peyote meetings, which would have required one hundred to two hundred buttons. I received twenty-three replies.

A short summary of the responses to my inquiries follows: In the vicinity of Columbus, New Mexico, eighty miles west of El Paso and thirty miles south of Deming, peyote was "scarce and hard to find," but it "can be bought in a little Mexican town just south of Columbus . . . sold by the Indians of Mexico as a medicine." Botanists at New Mexico State University, Las Cruces, forty-five miles north of El Paso and sixty miles straight east of Deming, wrote that peyote did not grow "in our area," and the botanist at the University of Texas, El Paso, reported, "I have not collected or observed peyote in El Paso County." The most explicit information from the vicinity of El Paso came from John W. Green, "A botanist/horticulturalist, employed by the U.S. Customs Service as a plant inspector on the International Bridge, El Paso, and a member of the El Paso Cactus Club." Mr. Green wrote: "There is only one place in West Texas where I have seen peyote growing in a natural state and that was at Shafter, Texas. . . . I only saw a few plants but I understand from others that it grows elsewhere in the area. . . . As far as I know there is no record of the plant occurring in New Mexico. Dr. Castetter [botanist, University of New Mexico, Albuquerque] has never found it there."

From high school botany teachers within a fifty-mile radius of Pyote, Texas, came the comments: "The old settlers in Pyote tell that there was peyote there 60 or 70 years ago (ca. 1900). But Indians came from the West [direction of the Mescalero reservation] and gathered all of it. About 30 years ago one plant was found, and since then none. . . . I have never seen a plant growing," and, ". . . It does not grow in the area." From Lampasas, Texas, about 140 miles east-southeast of San Angelo and about 70 miles northwest of Austin: "In the 1920s a man collected peyote plants in the vicinity of Big Bend National Park and replanted them at Lampasas. The plant would survive for a while, then . . . die." Professor J. Gilbert McAllister in Austin reported that peyote planted in his cactus garden did not survive many winters. These statements confirm the difficulty peyote would have in spreading to areas outside its own particular ecological zone.

Langtry, Texas, on the Rio Grande east of the Big Bend country was mentioned several times as a place where peyote grew. The county agricultural agent from Pecos, Texas, wrote that peyote is "known from Chinati Mountains and Chilicotal Mountains in the Big Bend National Park, and near Langtry in Caliche soils." From Jack R. Skiles, supervisor of the Judge Roy Bean Visitor Center, Langtry, came the following:

Your letter . . . has been referred to me, since I have degrees in botany and maintain a cactus garden. . . . Peyote is not commonly found throughout the region northwest of Eagle Pass, but is found in isolated areas in that section. . . . It is found in the Langtry area on only one ranch, but is fairly abundant there. . . . Indians from Oklahoma made trips to Langtry for many years gathering peyote for use in their religious ceremonies. . . . In the 1930s Indian men with their long hair were quite an attraction when they came to this area. . . .

In the end my research simply confirmed the limits of the natural habitat of peyote given by Anderson. Extending peyote beyond those limits seems mostly speculation, hearsay, and often carelessness. At best, the evidence is scant and unreliable. That a peyote plant should occasionally appear somewhat beyond the usual habitat of peyote is natural, and that a fairly healthy growth should disappear entirely near the edges of usual growth over a period of years as the result of normal climatic or other change is also to be expected, but these occurrences do not define the area of natural growth. I believe we are justified in assuming that the area of natural growth of peyote extends only about twenty miles on the north side of the Rio Grande, from Presidio, Texas, downstream to McAllen and into Mexico, embracing the Chihuahuan Desert south to San Luis Potosí and with interruption to an area around Querétaro, where Anderson found a different species of *Lophophora*.

Only a small area of the natural habitat of peyote is in the United States, and that is in the state of Texas. George R. Morgan, of Chadron State College, Nebraska, has clarified the natural growth area in Texas in his Ph.D. dissertation on the economic geography of the plant in the United States. His maps and explanation are useful in placing peyote in Texas (Map 3). In an article in the *Southwestern Historical Quarterly* for January, 1984, entitled "Peyote Trade in South Texas," he wrote:

Southern Texas, lying within the semiarid to subhumid subtropics, is the northern optimum environment for peyote north of Mexico. The commercial range of peyote in Texas, which is coextensive with high densities of the plant, is a north-south belt extending about ninety miles north from the Rio Grande at Roma to a few miles north of Oilton; the east-west dimension of the range is less than twenty miles. . . . Virtually all peyote harvested in Texas by *peyoteros* and Indians grows in four counties of South Texas: Starr, Jim Hogg, Webb, and Zapata. Areas of harvesting occur along the margins of the western-facing Bordas Escarpment, the adjacent Aguilares Plain, and the Breaks of the Rio Grande.

This fact of very restricted natural growth of the plant north of the Mexican border became all-important in the development and diffusion of peyotism in the United States.

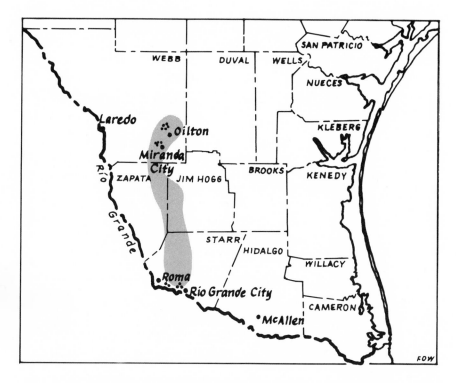

MAP 3. Commercial peyote range (shaded area) and location of registered peyote dealers in South Texas. Dots indicate dealers (after Texas State Board of Pharmacy).

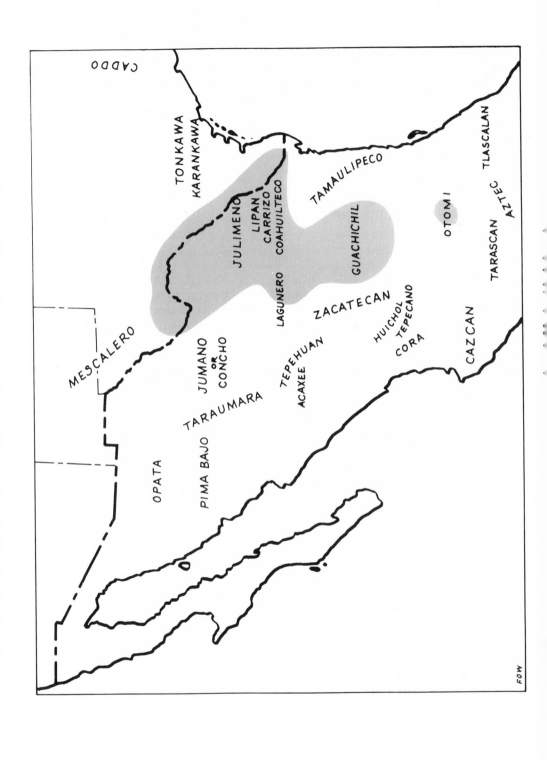

CADDO

TONKAWA
KARANKAWA

TAMAULIPECO

TLASCALAN

AZTEC

JULIMENO
LIPAN
CARRIZO
COAHUILTECO

OTOMI

TARASCAN

GUACHICHIL

MESCALERO

LAGUNERO

ZACATECAN

HUICHOL
TEPECANO
CORA

CAZCAN

JUMANO
OR
CONCHO

TEPEHUAN
ACAXEE

TARAUMARA

OPATA

PIMA BAJO

FOW

CHAPTER 2

Peyote Eaters and Their Ceremonies

IT is generally agreed by ethnologists that hunting and gathering people, dependent on the produce of their natural environment, learn the properties of all plants that grow where they live. For perhaps ten thousand years before the discovery of America, the aborigines living in the area of peyote growth, along the lower Rio Grande and south into Mexico as far as Querétaro, were undoubtedly familiar with peyote and its psychedelic properties. We can assume with assurance that for millennia they used it in the same manner they used it in early historic times: as a medicine to be taken internally or as a poultice on sores; to foretell the future; to find lost objects; as a stimulant during strenuous activity, such as travel or war; and in group religious ceremonies when supernatural aid was sought through group participation. At the time of the Spanish Conquest of Mexico and our first written records of its use, peyote was known far beyond its natural habitat. The more advanced farming cultures of Mesoamerica in Classic and Post-Classic times were as well versed in the uses of wild plants as were the simpler cultures where it grew, and although there is no record of peyote being cultivated by the Aztec, dried peyote was offered for sale in Mexican drug markets (Reko 1928; Kelly 1965) and must have formed part of drug inventories and been an item of commerce in pre-Conquest times. In the next three centuries, records from Catholic missionaries and from the Inquisition show that peyote was known as far south as Oaxaca, throughout central Mexico, and as far north as Santa Fe, New Mexico, although most early references are from the large area north of the Valley of Mexico, occupied by unconquered tribes known in the beginning as the Chichimec.

PEYOTE IN MEXICO

Today, with knowledge of tribal distinctions and histories, it is possible to say that from pre-Conquest time to the early nineteenth century, the following groups of Mexico and Texas were familiar with peyote, and some still are: Aztec, Zacateco, Tarascan, Cazcan, Guachichil, Huichol, Lagunero, Tepehuan, Tepecano, Cora, Acaxee, Tamaulipeco, Coahuilteco, Tarahumara, Opata, Pima Bajo, Jumano or Concho, Julimeno, Lipan Apache, Carrizo, Tonkawa, Karankawa, Mescalero Apache, Caddo, Otomi, and Tlascalan. Map 4 is based on information from Ralph L. Beals (1932), modified to include data from James Mooney (1898b), from J. Sidney Slotkin (1955b),

17

and from myself. The growth area from Edward F. Anderson (1969) is also shown. The distribution of peyote use has been described by Manuel Urbina (1903), Alexandre Rouhier (1926), and Weston La Barre (1938), among others. In nearly all cases the same historical documents have been cited by several of these authors, and in several instances the same region has been cited in Inquisition documents and other more recently discovered historical documents.

The area of early use includes almost all of northern Mexico from the Aztec, Tlascalan, and Tarascan in the south to the Mescalero Apache in the north and the Caddo along the northern Gulf Coast. There is little evidence of early peyote use along the coast west of the Sierra Madre in the north, but it was reportedly known to the Cora and Cazcan farther south, to the mountain tribes such as the Tarahumara, Huichol, and Zacateco in the western mountains and among the Tamaulipeco along the Gulf Coast. Beals named eleven of the twenty-six shown on Map 4: Aztec, Acaxee, Tarahumara, Opata, Pima Bajo (Beals calls these Sonora), Tamaulipeco, Huichol, Lagunero, Tepehuan, Zacateco, and Coahuilteco (he calls these Nuevo León). Slotkin (1955b) repeated the same list as Beals, only omitting Tepehuan and adding seven new names: Tarascan, Cazcan, Jumano or Concho, Lipan Apache, Tonkawa, Caddo, and Cora. I would keep both lists and add the Carrizo, Karankawa, Julimeno, Tepecano, Otomi, and Tlascalan. In support of the Tepecano we have a citation of Urbina (1903: 26) from Arlegui (1737) that the "guazancoros, tepecanos, coras, y nayaritas" were peyote users. These last, following Beals, I interpret to be Huichol.

Regarding the Otomi, whose tribal region surrounds the isolated peyote area of Querétaro, records of the Inquisition archives have yielded eight trial records that were held in Otomi territory from 1644 to 1779, and one must assume that at least some of these concerned Otomi or mestizo Otomi and that therefore Otomi territory should be included in the aboriginal cult area. The Tlascalan were not specifically documented in early Spanish records as peyote users, although peyote was used by their neighbors, the Aztec. Rouhier (1926: 12) gives some authority for including them as peyotists when he states, "the ancient Tlaxcaltecs made the same use of this plant [peyote] as did the Tarahumaras and the Huichols. . . . [It was used] by the auxiliary forces of the conquistadores in order not to feel fatigued on marches" (my translation). But Rouhier gives no source for his statement. La Barre, too (1938: 37), mentions the Tlascalan: "The Cazcan used the peyote ceremonially . . . but the Tlaxcaltecans' use points again, though uncertainly, to war." Given these references and the many Inquisition trials near the state of Tlascala, I suspect that the Tlascalan aboriginally ate peyote.

The earliest historical reference to peyote is that of the Franciscan missionary Bernardino de Sahagún. In his *Historia general de las cosas de Nueva España* he wrote:

The peyotl [peyote] is white and grows only there in the north region called Mictlan. On him who eats it or drinks it, it takes effect like mushrooms. Also he sees many things which frighten one, or make one laugh. It affects him perhaps one day, perhaps two days, but likewise it abates. However, it harms one, troubles one, makes one besotted, takes effect on one.

He described in some detail the use of peyote in its native habitat north of Mexico City in Chichimec country, saying that the Chichimec

were the first to discover and use the root which they call *peiotl*, and those who are accustomed to eat and drink them used them in the place of wine. . . . Those who eat or drink it see visions either frightful or laughable. . . . It is a common food of the Chichimecas, for it stimulates them and gives them sufficient spirit to fight and have neither fear, thirst, nor hunger, and they say it guards them from all danger. [Safford 1916: 401]

Fernando Hernandez, making a study in 1577 of plants used by the Aztec, included peyote (*peyotl*) among other intoxicating plants: tobacco (*picietl*), narcotic mushrooms (*teonancatl*), and psychedelic morning glory (*ololuiqui*). He wrote:

Wonderful properties are attributed to this root (if any faith can be given to what is commonly said among them on this point). It causes those devouring it to be able to foresee and to predict things; such, for instance, as whether the weather will continue favorable; or to discern who has stolen from them some utensils or anything else; and other things of like nature which the Chichimecas really believe them have found out. On which account this root scarcely issues forth but conceals itself in the ground, as if it did not wish to harm those who discover it and eat it. [Hernandez 1628; Safford 1916: 401]

Other early writers who wrote of peyote in a similar vein were Diego Muñoz Camargo (ca. 1590) and Juan Cardenas (1591), writing on Tlascala and the Valley of Mexico, and the authors of the *Primeras misiones de la Viscaya* (1598), describing the Zacateco.

Before 1600 it is not certain whether the Indians who used peyote were already Christianized or were still for the most part pagans. We do know, however, that the Spaniards started the task of conversion as soon as they gained control of an area. The wild Chichimec had been under pressure to become Christian for over thirty years by the time Father Sahagún compiled his information from survivors of the Conquest in the Valley of Mexico. Bancroft (1883: 12) summarized the conquest of the southern section of peyote country:

To the west and inland was the territory comprising the present states of Querétaro, Guanajuato, San Luis Potosí, and Aguas Calientes; the home of the wild Chicimecs, never permanently subjugated to the Aztecs. The Chichimec country proper extended indefinitely northward . . . but the name applied commonly to this region as the home of the only Chichimec with whom the Aztecs or earliest Spaniards came in contact. . . . Converted native chieftains . . . fur-

nished with ammunition, material and spiritual, gunpowder and crucifixes . . .
set forth to Christianize their rude brethren on several occasions between 1521
and 1525.

From the beginning, the Catholic church found in peyote another evil to
be rooted out of the New World. Norman Taylor (1944:176) describes the
dilemma of the Church:

Scarcely forty years after Montezuma lost his empire to Cortez, the Church in
Mexico began to worry about two rather disturbing phases of what the priests
called Aztec idolatry. The Spaniards had been . . . horror-stricken by the heca-
tombs of "ritual murders" on the *teocalli*. . . . While the Conquest had stopped
this atrocity, the Church was still disturbed.

It soon found that the beautiful symbolism of the mass was being horribly
distorted by other, if less bloody, examples of Indian perversity. The good
padres feared for the souls of their flock, if not for the prestige of the Church
itself. . . . They were talking against a graftage of Aztec lore upon Roman lit-
urgy . . . particularly in the case of two plants—*ololuiqui* and *peyotl*. . . . The
persistence of these Aztec cults is matched only by their extraordinary hold on
the Indians and by their antiquity. . . . In its desire to purge the Indians of the
black magic of *ololuiqui* and *peyotl,* the Church left us the only writing we possess of the early use of either plant.

In an effort to purge their new Christian converts of the use of *peyotl*
and *ololuiqui* the Church prepared a catechism to be used by priests conducting confessionals. One can appreciate just how evil peyote was considered to be by the Church by reading a few lines of this catechism (Taylor
1944:176–77):

Hast thou eaten the flesh of man?
Hast thou eaten the peyote?
Do you suck the blood of others?
Do you adorn with flowers places where idols are kept?

That the use of peyote was pervasive throughout central and northern
Mexico and deeply engrained in the lives of those who used it can be judged
by the radical efforts of the Catholic church to stamp it out. The Church,
afraid that peyote was spreading among converted Christians, and possibly
to some Spaniards as well, took its strongest measures to fight it. In 1620,
it brought the Inquisition to bear against peyote and issued the following
edict (Ramo de Inquisición, tomo 289, Archivo General de la Nación, Mexico City, quoted in Leonard 1942:324–26):

We, the Inquisitors against heretical perversity and apostasy in the City of
Mexico, states and provinces of New Spain, New Galicia, Guatemala, Nicaragua
Yucatán, Verapaz, Honduras, Philippine Islands and their districts and jurisdic-
tions, by virtue of apostolic authority. . . .

Inasmuch as the use of the herb or root called peyote has been introduced
into these Provinces for the purpose of detecting thefts, of divining other hap-

penings, and of foretelling future events, it is an act of superstition condemned as opposed to the purity and integrity of our Holy Catholic Faith. . . .

Said abuse has increased in strength and is indulged in with the frequency observed. As our duty imposes upon us the obligation to put a stop to this vice. . . . We order that henceforth no person of whatever rank or social condition can or may make use of the said herb, peyote, nor any other kind under any name or appearance for the same or similar purposes, nor shall he make the Indians or any other person take them, with the further warning that disobedience to these decrees shall cause us . . . to take action against such disobedient and recalcitrant persons as we would against those suspected of heresy to our Holy Catholic Faith.

Inasmuch as the said vice has been so widely introduced and practiced . . . and as our intention is both to ban it, and to remedy this evil henceforth and to ease the conscience to those who have been guilty, we . . . do hereby grant pardon and remission of all past sins in the said vice up to the day of this our edict and ban; and we confer upon any confessor whatsoever, whether of the secular or the regular clergy duly approved by his Superior, the right and power to absolve from the said sin any person who may have committed it up to now, but with the proviso that this abolution shall not be extended to the future, nor (apply) to other misdeeds, abuses, sorcery and acts of superstition enumerated in the General Edict of Faith. . . . Given in the Hall of our Court on the 29th day of June, 1620, Licenciado D. Pedro Nabarre de Isla (Rubric).

It is doubtful if the Inquisitors in New Spain would have bothered to publish the prohibition against peyote throughout the full range of their jurisdiction if the use of the cactus had been limited to pagan or gentile Indians in remote mountain villages or on the frontiers. Such documents were to guide faithful Catholics away from error as well as to warn neophytes against sin. The promulgation of such an edict is prima facie evidence that the aboriginal practices of using peyote for "the purpose of detecting thefts, of divining other happenings, and of foretelling future events' had been continued by many Catholic converts. As inhabitants of the peyote growth area were brought into missions and taught how to be Catholics, it must have been obvious to the Church fathers that many maintained ancient beliefs and practices.

The hearings resulted from the prosecution of this edict occupied the Church for much of the next two centuries. The Mexican scholar Gonzalo Aguirre Beltrán (1963) reports that seventy-four Inquisition court cases were heard in thirty-nine Spanish settlements, the earliest in Cuautla, Morelos, in 1614, actually before the formal edict, and the latest in Guanajuato in 1779. William B. Taylor, professor of Latin American history at the University of Colorado, working in Mexican archives, found eighteen additional hearings and added six new towns to the locations of the trials. We have, then, ninety cases for forty-five locations extending over a period of 265 years. In addition to places near the natural growth area, hearings occurred in three distant towns: Santa Fe, New Mexico; Antequero, Oaxaca, and

Manila, Philippines. Only two towns where Inquisition hearings took place were within the boundaries of native growth of peyote: Saltillo in the district of Coahuila and Guadalcazar in the district of San Luis Potosí. Generally, for convenience's sake, the hearings took place in larger populated areas, such as Mexico City, but the wide area covered is an indication of the extent of traffic in and of the influence of peyote in the Spanish Colonial period (Map 5).

Map 5 shows the distribution of Inquisition hearings involving peyote. The numbers refer to the towns where investigations were conducted for possession of peyote. The first thirty-nine numbers are for towns named by Aguirre Beltrán (1963: 309); numbers forty to forty-five are additional sites located by William B. Taylor (personal communication). The citations are all from the Archivo General de la Nación: Inquisición (AGN: Inq), and the date indicates the year each investigation was held. Three places, Manila, Antequero, and Santa Fé, do not appear on the map.

1. Acambaro 792.400 (1724).
2. Antequero (Oaxaca) (1621).
3. Atlixco 342.3 (1622).
4. Chalco 360.314 (1627).
5. Chihuahua 116.5 (1726).
6. Cholula 435.335 (1650).
7. Cuautla 302.8 (1614).
8. Cuitzeo 486.417 (1621).
9. Guadalajara 486.43 (1620).
10. Guadalcazar 757.149 (1716); 894.88 (1759).
11. Guanajuato 811.15 (1725); 1110.17 (1779).
12. Hurepitio 380.535 (1634).
13. Ixmiquilpan 727.9 (1704).
14. León 687.1 (1692).
15. Manila (Philippines) 293.73 (1617); 388.17 (1639).
16. Mexico City 314.388, 317.21, 317.22, 333.35, 335.89, 335.96, 341.4, 373.4, 360.159, 380.320, 520.55, 534.8, 758.105, 1019.1 (1617–1762)
17. Pachuca 419.250 (1644).
18. Puebla 335.104 (1622).
19. Querétaro 841.7 (1733).
20. Salamanca 844.6 (1733).
21. Saltillo 912.72 (1742).
22. San Luis de la Paz 872.113 (1737).
23. San Luis Potosi 604.2 (1665); 1168.7 (1776).
24. San Juan del Río 746.12 (1713); 757.20 (1716).
25. San Pedro Piedras Gordas 826.8 (1729).
26. Santa Ana Maya 380.536 (1634).
27. Santa Fé (New Mexico) 304.26 (1632).
28. Sinola 789.10 (1721).

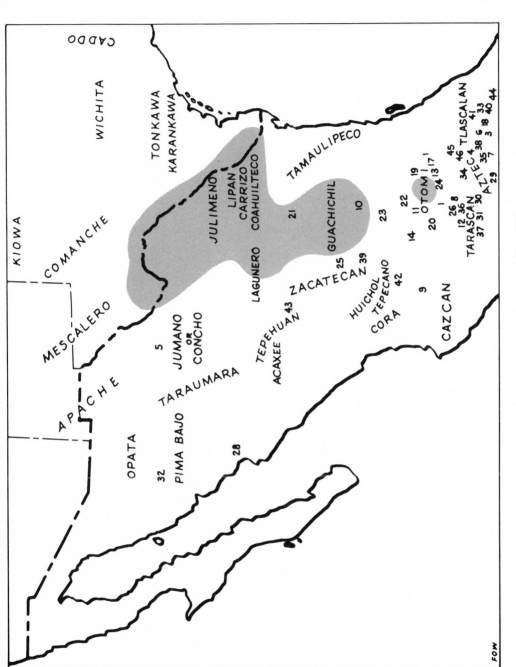

MAP 5. Locations of Inquisition hearings, 1614–1779.

29. Taxco 339.33–34 (1621).
30. Tarimbaro 668.6 (1684).
31. Taximaro 340.4–5 (1630).
32. Tecoripa 1104.24 (1776).
33. Tepeaca 356.II.83, 356.II.108 (1626); 872.4 (1716).
34. Texcoco 335.6 (1622); 373.3 (1632).
35. Tepoztlan 301.10 (1614); 342.10 (1622).
36. Tlalpujagua 674.12 (1689).
37. Valladolid 346.11, 376.31, 388.12, 510.23, 668.5 (1623–84).
38. Zacualpa 363.9 (1628).
39. Zacateca 356.126, 363.30, 513.31, 600.28, 697.13, 746.500, 781.54, 812.19 (1626–1725).
40. Acahuato 332.2 (1620).
41. Huejotzingo 377.155 (1633).
42. Tlaltenango 510.112 (1625).
43. Nombre de Dios 799.613 (1723).
44. Tehuacán 1328.357 (1713).
45. Tlalmanalco 360.314 (1627).

The seventeenth-century confessionals during the Inquisition centered attention on individual sin and suggested little about collective rituals. They suggested that peyote had been used for such reasons as detections, divinations, and forecasting future events. In 1629, Hernandez Ruiz de Alarcón wrote: "If the consultation is about a lost or stolen article or concerning a woman who had absented herself from her husband, or some similar thing, . . . the divination is made in one of two ways, either by means of a trance or by drinking peyote or ololuiqui . . ." (La Barre 1938: 24).

Two Inquisition hearings in Santa Fé, New Mexico, five hundred miles from peyote's northernmost habitat, establish individual use and divination by Indians there. These accounts also indicate that peyote had become an item of contraband commerce by Indians, mestizos, and soldiers who participated in the colonization of New Mexico. In 1631, Friar Esteban de Perea, commissioner of the Inquisition in Santa Fe (Slotkin 1955b: 213–14) reported that "Ana Cadimo [a mestiza] . . . says that it was about a year ago that the Indians [around Santa Fé, i.e. Tewa, Tano, or Queres] . . . were telling her that she [Ana] was bewitched, and that she should take peyote (*peiote*) and that with it she would see [by means of a vision] the person who had bewitched her and done her evil. . . ." Another testimonial concerns a soldier:

Luis Pacheco, [Spanish] soldier and citizen of the city of Santa Fé, . . . declared . . . that on the 10th of December of the past year of 1631 . . . in the house of Juan Anton . . . there being present Jusepe [de la Cruz], a *ladino* Indian of the Queres tribe, . . . a servant of this declarant [Pacheco] having fallen and broken an arm, and that cooking a poultice [?; *bilma*] to put on him, that said declarant said: "If we had here a little peyote (*peiote*), it would be very good for this." And that the said Juan Anton answered, "Peyote is not only good for this, but to find stolen things [as well]. That when I was in the Mines of Mapimi [Durango] in New Spain [i.e., Mexico], there having been stolen from my servant and from an Indian . . . an undershirt and other clothing, and from the Indian some blankets—and going to look for it and not finding it, I took six or seven heads or roots of peyote and, ground, drank it. And afterwards I went into a private room and there appeared to me an old man and an old woman. And he asked what was my difficulty, and I answered him that they had stolen that clothing. And he answer me, 'Don't worry; go to a certain place; you will find it there.' And I and the Indian went there, and we found an Indian who had the clothing, and we took it away from him." [Perea 1632: 181r]

There are many similar accounts of the magical use of peyote in the records of missionaries and church officials of the seventeenth century. For instance, Domingo Lazaro de Arreguí, in his *Descripción de la Nueva Galicia* (1621), reported that peyote in central western Mexico was used to induce visions for purposes of supernatural revelation (Slotkin 1955*b*: 209); Andrés de Estrada y Flores (1659) reported the use of peyote by the Cazcan of the Sierra Madre Occidental as a medicine and to obtain visions (Slotkin 1955*b*: 209); in 1672, Antonio Arias y Saavedra made the same charge regarding the tribes of the Sierra del Nayarit (Slotkin 1955*b*: 209). Father Andrés Perez de Ribas (1645: 486) visited the Acaxee and related a story about a priest who discovered a peyote plant and an image in human form placed atop the ball court wall as good luck fetishes. He lectured the Indians so forcefully against peyote that not only was the cactus destroyed along with the idol, but the ball court was destroyed as well. Father Perez de Ribas wrote: "Although it is medicinal, yet in its use there are many superstitions, which the Holy Tribunal of the Inquisition had at times punished." Father de Ribas also reported the use of peyote among the Indians known as the Lagunero who lived near Mapimi (Durango) (Schultes 1938: 705).

Although most of the records of peyote use during the 1600s were for individual charms, visions, or healing, some peyote ceremonies were observed, and a few of the early rituals have been described. These ceremonies include all-night dancing and singing with the participants arranged in a circle and following an established beat, bloodletting, prophesying, and passing out. In 1649, Alonzo de León described a ritual among the Coahuiltecan Indians in the peyote region of north central Mexico:

The Indian men and women begin to dance in one or two circles around the fire . . . until the night is already dark, singing in their fashion whatever words they want, without having meaning, only harmony, and they sing them so harmoniously that one is not discordant from another, but it seems a single voice. Everyone who wants to joins in this group, sometimes a hundred, at other times more or less. They drink the peyote ground up and dissolved in water; this drink intoxicates in such a manner that it makes them lose consciousness and they remain, from the movement and the wine, on the ground like dead persons. They choose among two or three of such as these, and with some beaks from a fish called *aguja* . . . they scratch them from shoulders to ankles and to the wrists, from whence flows a quantity of blood, and with it they smear it all over their bodies. They leave them in this condition until they are over their drunkenness. [Troike 1962: 934]

Padre Jacinto de la Serna observed and reported a less bloody ceremony in July, 1626, near Toluca, at which time narcotic mushrooms were also eaten:

At dawn when a certain little breeze known to them begins to blow, they would gather the narcotic, attributing to it deity, with the same properties as *ololuiqui* or *peyote*, since when eaten or drunk, they intoxicate those who partake of them, depriving them of their senses. . . . This man . . . brought these . . . one night to a house where there was a gathering for the celebration of a saint's feast. [Safford 1915: 309–10]

Padre José de Ortega described a Cora peyote meeting in his *Historia de Nayarit*, written in 1690:

Close to the musician was seated the leader of the singing whose business it was to mark the time. Each of these had his assistants to take his place when he should become fatigued. Nearby was placed a tray filled with peyote which is a diabolical root that is ground up and drunk by them so that they may not become weakened by the exhausting effects of so long a function, which they began by forming as large a circle of men and women as could occupy the space of ground that had been swept off for this purpose. One after the other went dancing in a ring or marked time with his feet, keeping in the middle the musician and the choirmaster whom they had invited, and singing in the same unmusical tune . . . that he set them. They would dance all night, from five o'clock in the evening to seven o'clock in the morning, without stopping nor leaving the circle. When the dance was ended, all stood who could hold themselves on their feet; for the majority, from the peyote and the wine which they drink, they were unable to utilize their legs to hold themselves upright. [Safford 1916: 402]

In spite of the efforts of the Catholic church to eradicate peyote, its use continued to flourish, especially among the tribes where it grew and farther north. Records in the eighteenth century show that it was still used individually and ceremonially as it spread northward into Texas beyond the limits of its natural growth. By the eighteenth century, Mexico, including the peyote-growing area of Texas, was under the political, economic, and religious control of Spain. Every town had its church and every village its mission. The church consolidated its position wherever it could, and missionaries continued to press farther into the uncivilized areas and to the north. Inevitably, as the church spread Christianity and civilization, it spread knowledge of peyote. It is probable that at times the two went hand in hand. Missionaries used converted Indians from peyote areas to help start new missions in areas beyond peyote's natural habitat, thereby acquainting new groups with the magical new herb. Indians, mestizos, and soldiers accompanied missionaries back and forth in their travels from peyote growing

areas to areas where it was less well known, and it is probable that sometimes they carried contraband peyote. At the same time in the wild area
beyond Texas, Plains Indians acquired the horse, enabling them to begin
their frightening raids into northern Mexico, where they began to learn of
new things, such as peyote.

In northeastern Coahuila, extending from the northwest to the southeast along the Río Salado and parallel to it for about a hundred miles, is an
area known since it was first explored as "Peyotes." There a mission founded
in 1688 by Jaliscan friars came to be named Nombre de Jesús de Peyotes
(Bancroft 1883: 378); in 1698 it was renamed Misión del Dulce Nombre de
Jesús de Peyotes by Franciscans. Also in Coahuila is the district known as
"Lomeria de Peyotes," described by Max Sorre (1928: 56) as hills extending from the Río Grande southeast to become the mountains of Lampozas
and the Sierra Madre Oriental. It is in this area during the eighteenth and
early nineteenth centuries that one expects the peyote ceremony of the Indians of Oklahoma to have developed. Bancroft (p. 606) was referring to
the peyote area of northern Coahuila when he wrote:

But it was only in comparison with one or two other provinces and taking into
consideration the difficulties encountered by a small and indolent population
constantly exposed to the attacks of savage hordes, that Coahuila could be
called flourishing; and mission work was almost a complete failure. The number
of mission Indians was about 1,800 in 1786, and 1,600 seven years later; but
two-thirds of the number were Tlascaltecs [Christianized Indians serving as
soldiers for New Spain]. The total population of neophytes and *gente de razon*
. . . was estimated in 1780 at about 8,000.

An early-eighteenth-century statement of the use of peyote in this area
comes from Padre Antonio Olivares, who in 1700 moved from his assignment at the Misión del Dulce Nombre de Jesús de Peyotes to help start a
mission along the Río Grande near Laredo which came to be known as the
Presidio de San Juan Bautista (Bancroft 1883: 379). In 1709 he wrote of his
experiences at his new location (Slotkin 1955b: 220),"I noted that only on
the occasion of a *mitote,* or general dance, do they (i.e., the Indians of the
Province of Texas) drink peyote and (the juice of) other herbs which cause
a disturbance of senses, producing visions and apparitions." Later, in 1718
he transferred some of his neophytes from his mission on the Rio Grande
to the mission at San Antonio, 150 miles north of the peyote area (Bancroft
1883: 379). Among them there may well have been some Indians carrying
contraband peyote for personal use or for sale. One supposes, also, that
among the Indians moved to San Antonio were Coahuiltecan-speaking Indians, such as the Carrizo and possibly some Caddo, Tonkawa, and Karankawa, although he does not name them.

In 1709, visiting the Caddo near what is now the Texas-Louisiana border, Padre Isidro Felix de Espinosa (Swanton 1942: 51–52) learned that a
Caddo chief had visited the Spanish mission near Laredo and had returned

home with two Indians from there. They or others on similar journeys may have been carriers of contraband peyote. In 1716, Padre Espinosa was assigned to the Caddo and stayed two years, returning again in 1721. He wrote extensively of Caddo religion, but did not mention their use of peyote. Since he was well acquainted with peyote and its use, having previously served at the missions in Coahuila and Laredo, his failure to mention its use in eastern Texas, some three hundred miles from the peyote fields, suggests that its use was not great among the Caddo at that time.

On the other hand, Padre Francisco Hidalgo, who worked alone among the Caddo from 1709 to 1714, returning in 1716 for a longer stay, wrote that the Caddo "are very much perverted and in their dances they have Indian braves or Indian women who get drunk on peyote or *frixolillo,* which they made for the occasion and the people believe everything these persons tell them they have seen" (Swanton 1942:219).

The best description of a peyote ceremony of this period comes from Vicente Santa María, who in 1760 told of a peyote ceremony of Tamaulipecan Indians (La Barre 1938:36):

A Tamaulipecan group often in these orgies was wont to impose silence, at the height of their drunkenness . . . prognosticated to the future events. . . . One of the Tamaulipecan tribes would usually hold feasts for only those of its own community, or it would invite some of those that were neighbors and friends. They took place generally by night. Devoting two or three previous days to the preparation of a sufficient quantity of peyote and the gathering of fruits of the season, and in allotting certain fruits of the chase, which, broiled on the hearth that illuminated the feast, were served as a common banquet. The feast always had an object among these peoples. With feasts they celebrated the beginning of summer, which was the season least rigorous for those nude people, or the abundant harvests of corn, or of forest fruits, or their victory in some attack on their enemies. When these feasts were held for one tribe alone they took place commonly in the rancherias where they lived permanently. But when one who was promoting the feast invited some of his neighbors, then he chose an intermediate point between the two places that they inhabited, and that was picked out generally in the most inaccessible or hidden places in the mountains. As soon as everything was prepared for the banquet and the guests had collected, a great bonfire was lighted. They placed around it the fruits of the hunt prepared before hand. Those that took part in the dance immediately formed a circle around the fire, and to the measured beats of the drum (the drum was made of an arc of wood over which they attached the parchment of a deer or a coyote) which, united with the voices, composed the music. They took part in the dance alternately raising one foot and then the other, or the whole circle started circling around the fire. During the dance dancers and spectators broke out in discordant howls, each one reciting in his own strophes, alluding to the cause that was motivating the feast. Of this versification I have already previously given you an idea: relative to the celebration of some triumph gained in their skirmishes; and in the same way they directed their phrases to the sun, to the moon, and to the clouds, when they were enjoying good weather; to the earth and to the rain when they had an abundance of fruit; and finally to their strength and bravery when they recalled their hunts in the mountains or their wars. The poetic enthusiasm of the guests became more animated with the first fumes of the peyote, which, placed on a counter that was improvised on the trunk of a tree, was served to them by young Indian girls and the old men, and in the same gourds, jars, or rude baked clay vases. This class of feast always used to end with the complete drunkenness of all the guests, who, exhausted moreover by the dance, fell asleep around the almost burnt-out fire.

Elsewhere in Mexico reports of peyote use continued to appear throughout the eighteenth century. In 1737, Padre José Arleguí wrote of the use of peyote by the Zacateco, describing a ceremony in which one person, "a father," made senseless by peyote, is wounded successively by each member of the group, a rite similar to an earlier Coahuilteco ceremony described by Alonzo de León. He also reported that the Zacateco used peyote to foretell the future, saying;

The use of peyote for cures would not be so bad if they did not abuse its virtues, for, in order to have knowledge of the future and find out how their battles will turn out, they drink it brewed in water, and, as it is very strong, it intoxicates them with a paroxysm of madness, and all the fantastic hallucinations that come over them with this horrible drink they seize upon as omens of the future, imagining that the root has revealed to them their future. [La Barre 1938:23]

In another mid-eighteenth-century account, Matias de la Mota Padilla reported that Indians in Nayarit (the Huichol) had used peyote as a stimulant for greater exertion in war and had thereby inhibited the Spanish conquest of their area (Schultes 1938:704). Francisco Javier Alegre, writing of the Zacateco also, said that they revered peyote above all other remedies. He also reported the use of peyote by the Opata and the Pima, which indicates that peyote was transported a great distance from its natural habitat, probably by soldiers and retainers of missionaries (Schultes 1938:705; Slotkin 1955b:209). Toward the end of the century, in 1770, the Lipan Apache became identified with the peyote area in northern Coahuila. Padre Luis de Lizarraras wrote: "I have also frequently seen the Apache Indians go to where the Julimenos are to attend their fairs or exchange, but the Apaches also go to places called Gigedo [Xigedo] and San Fernando and to the Mission Pellotes and Bizarron." In the same year, Father Antonio Lorenzo de la Peña wrote concerning local Julimeno neophytes:

All the rest of the day they waste in gambling, and most of the nights of the year they pass in dancing [mitote], drinking pellotes and other drinks like patalillo which inebriate like the best wine. They make use of these drinks in their sorcery. A great disaster can occur because of their undisciplined mode of living and their association with the Mescaleros. [Stewart 1948:34]

In summarizing the early history of peyote to the end of the eighteenth century, one can say that peyote was probably used by the people inhabiting the area of its natural growth in the Chichimec zone north to southern Texas during prehistoric times, perhaps as remote as ten thousand years ago. It spread north, south, west to the high Sierras, and east to the Gulf as the movement of people carried it. At the time of the Spanish Conquest, it was well known and valued several hundreds of miles beyond its native habitat. It was used individually and ritually, with Indian ritual use documented mainly for areas of peyote's natural growth northward, and it persisted and spread during three centuries of Spanish rule in spite of the efforts of the Catholic church to discourage it. With the coming of the Americans in the nineteenth century and the consequent increase in the movement of the native inhabitants of the southwestern United States and northern Mexico, we can expect further diffusion of peyote and changes in its use.

MEXICAN AND AMERICAN PEYOTE CEREMONIES IN
THE LATE NINETEENTH CENTURY

The nineteenth century brought many changes to the area of the natural growth of peyote. Spain, which had held the area since the sixteenth century, lost control to Mexico in 1821. There followed a century of unrest in Mexico: revolution, wars with the United States and France, more revolution, weak republics, and dictatorships. Many Indian tribes disappeared or lost their identity with the inroads of civilization, peaceful as well as otherwise. In the territory which became the Mexico we know today, Catholicism was well established as the religion of the people, replacing most aboriginal religions. Peyote continued to some extent to be a valuable folk medicine but ceased to exist for ceremonial use except among a few tribes who lived in remote areas and were able to keep their tribal identities and aboriginal religions. Those Mexican tribes that survived to the end of the century and into the twentieth and maintained and further developed distinct peyote ceremonies are the Huichol, the Tarahumara, the Cora, and to a lesser degree the Tepehuan and the Tepecano. All now live in the western mountains of the high Sierra Madre Occidental, far outside the natural growth area of peyote. To understand fully the roots of the peyote ceremony as it finally developed in the United States, it is pertinent to understand also the peyote ceremony that persisted in the mountains of north central Mexico. Each ceremony is unique, but each has a common heritage.

In the last hundred years, many scholars have studied the peyote ceremonies of the Mexican Indians. One who wrote early and extensively of both the Huichol and the Tarahumara is Carl Lumholtz. In 1894 he published in *Scribner's Magazine* a brief account of the Tarahumara peyote rit-

ual. His more comprehensive reports appeared in the American Museum of
Natural History series and in 1902 in a two-volume work entitled *Unknown
Mexico*. He described one of the most important aboriginal aspects of the
Huichol and the Tarahumara to be the long, sacred pilgrimage to harvest
peyote. In the 1890s the Huichol traveled some 250 miles from their villages in the mountains to Real del Catorce, San Luis Potosí, to gather
peyote. Although ancient Tarahumara territory was actually in the peyote
growing area of southeastern Chihuahua, the Tarahumara withdrew into the
mountains as the Spanish conquered, colonized, and exploited the mines at
the eastern edge of the mountains of Chihuahua, and at the end of the century they were ten days' travel by foot from the peyote fields. Other Mexican tribes requiring peyote, such as the Cora, Tepehuan, and Tepecano, all
now living in the western mountains, generally received peyote from the
Huichol or the Tarahumara.

    Although the peyote ceremonies in these different tribes vary in detail,
the essential spirit and ingredients of all are similar. The following is from
the account of the Tarahumara ceremony as described by Lumholtz (1902,
2:359–72):

The effect of the plant [*hikuli,* peyote] is so much enjoyed by the Tarahumaras
that they attribute to it power to give health and long life and to purify body and
soul. The little cacti, either fresh or dried, are ground on the metate, while
being mixed with water: and this liquor is the usual form in which it [peyote] is
consumed.

    [Peyote] is also applied externally for snake-bites, burns, wounds, and
rheumatism: for these purposes it is chewed, or merely moistened in the mouth,
and applied to the afflicted part. Not only does it cure disease, causing it to run
off, but it also so strengthens the body that it can resist illness, and is therefore
much used in warding off sickness. Though not given to the dead, since the
dead are no longer in need of remedies, [peyote] is always partaken at feasts of
the dead.

    Moreover, [peyote] is a powerful protector of its people under all circum-
stances, and it gives good luck. If a man carries some [peyote] in his belt, the
bear cannot bite him and the deer cannot run away, but become quite tame and
can easily be killed. Should he meet Apaches, [peyote] would prevent them
from firing off their guns at him. It gives good luck in footraces and all kinds of
games, in climbing trees, etc. [Peyote] is the great safeguard against witchcraft. It sees even better than shamans, and it watches that nothing bad is put
into the food. The Christian Tarahumares, when they partake of [peyote], think
that the devil runs out of their stomachs. [Peyote] purifies any man who is willing to sacrifice a sheep and to make native beer. There is, however, no remedy
for a murderer; not even [peyote] can cure him.

    The Christian Tarahumares make the sign of the cross when coming into
the presence of the plant, and I was told to lift my hat to it. It is always saluted
in the same way as a man, and is supposed to make the customary responses to
the salutations. [Peyote] is not as great as Father Sun, but sits next to him. It is
the brother of Tata Dios; and the greatest [peyote] is his twin brother. . . . Ac-

cording to tradition, when Tato Dios went to heaven in the beginning of the world, he left [peyote] behind as the great remedy of the people. [Peyote] has four faces and sees everything. . . .

Upon arriving at the spot, the pilgrims erect a cross, and near it they place the first plants taken up, that these may tell where others may be found in plenty. The second batch of plants gathered is eaten raw, and makes the men drunk. As speech is forbidden, they lie down in silence and sleep. The following day, when perfectly sober again, they begin early in the morning to collect the plants, taking them up with utmost care, by means of sticks, so as not to touch or injure them, because [peyote] would get angry and punish the offender. . . .

In the field in which it grows, it sings beautifully, that the Tarahumara may find it. It says, "I want to go to your country, that you may sing your songs to me." It also sings in the bag while it is being carried home. One man, who wanted to use his bag as a pillow, could not sleep, he said, because the plants made so much noise.

When the [peyote]-seekers arrive at their homes, the people turn out to welcome the plants with music, and a festival at which a sheep or a goat is sacrificed is held in their honour. On this occasion the shaman wears necklaces made of the seeds of *Coix Lachryma-Jobi*. In due time he takes them off, and places them in a bowl containing water in which the heart of the maguey has been soaked, and after a while everyone present gets a spoonful of this water. The shaman, too, takes some, and afterward wears the necklaces again. Both plants, the *Coix Lachryma-Jobi* as well as the maguey, are highly esteemed for their curative properties; and in his songs the shaman describes [peyote] as standing on top of a gigantic seed of the *Coix Lachryma-Jobi*, as big as a mountain.

The night is passed in dancing [peyote] and *Yumari*. The pile of fresh plants, perhaps two bushels or more, is placed under the cross, and sprinkled with *tesvino* [maize beer], for [peyote] wants to drink beer, and if the people should not give it, it would go back to its own country. Food is also offered to the plants and even money is placed before them, perhaps three silver dollars, which the owner, after the feast, takes back again.

During the year, the feasts may be held especially in honour of [peyote], but generally the [peyote] dance is performed simultaneously with, though apart from the *rutuburi* or other dances. On such occasions some shamans devote themselves exclusively to the [peyote] cult, in order that the health of the dancers may be preserved, and they may have vigour for their work.

The [peyote] feast consists mainly in dancing, which, of course, is followed by eating and drinking, after the customary offerings of food and *tesvino* have been made to the gods. It is not held on the general dance-place, in front of the Tarahumara dwelling, but on a special patio. For the occasion a level piece of ground may be cleared of all stones and rubbish, and carefully swept with the Indian broom. . . .

The shaman (sometimes there are two) takes his seat on the ground to the west of the fire, about two yards off. On the opposite side of the dancing-place, toward the east, the cross is placed. The shaman's male assistants . . . at least two in number, seat themselves on either side of their principal, while the women helpers take a position to the north of the fire. . . . Close by the shaman's seat a hole is dug, into which he or his assistants may spit, after having drunk or eaten [peyote], so that nothing may be lost. After this improvised cuspidor has been used, it is always carefully covered with a leaf.

As soon as the shaman has seated himself, he takes a round drinking-gourd, and by pressing its rim firmly into the soil and turning the vessel round, makes a circular mark. Lifting up the bowl again, he draws two diametrical lines and right angles in the circle, and thus produces a symbol of the world.

In the centre he puts a [peyote], right side up. . . .

The notched stick, as well as the rasping-stick, is made of heavy, hard Brazile-wood, brought from the vicinity of San Ignacio, the [peyote] country. The shaman holds the notched stick, a little away from himself. . . .

Presently the shaman's assistants, men and women, arise. They carry censers filled with burning charcoals and copal, and emitting a heavy smoke, and proceed toward the cross, to which they offer the smoking incense, kneeling down, facing east, and crossing themselves. This feature, if not wholly due to Catholic influence, is at least strongly affected by it. . . .

[The shaman's] songs describe how [peyote] walks with his rattles and with his staff of authority; he comes to cure and to guard the people and to grant a "beautiful" intoxication. To bring about the latter result, the brownish liquor is dispensed from a jar standing under the cross. A man serves it in small quantities from a gourd, which he first carries around the fire on a rapid run, making three circuits for the shaman, and one for the rest of the assemblage. The spirits of the feasters rise in proportion to their potations. Sometimes only the shaman and his assistants indulge in the drinking; on other occasions all the people partake of the liquor. . . .

Just as daybreak, as the fire is dying out, the shaman gives the welcome signal that the dance is over, by the three final raps on his notched-stick. Then the people gather at the eastern end of the dancing-place, near the cross. The shaman rises from his seat, carrying in his hands his rasping implements, and, followed by a boy who carried a gourd with water, he proceeds to confer upon everybody present the benediction. Stopping in front of each one, he solemnly dips the point of the rasping-stick into the water, and after touching the notched-stick lightly with the wetted end, first in the middle, then on the lower end, and finally on the top, he daubs the head of the person three times with it. Then he rests the end of the notched-stick against the man's head and rasps three long strokes from end to end, throwing out his hand far into the air after each stroke. . . . Now he turns toward the rising Sun, holding out his implements to him; and, quickly rubbing up and down a few times at the lower end of the notched-stick, he makes a long stroke from end to end, passing the hand far out from the stick toward the Sun. By this act, three times performed, he waves [peyote] home.

While the ceremony of the Tarahumara Indians just described was being practiced in the mountains of north central Mexico, something different was happening to the peyote ceremony among the Indians living in the rich peyote area near the Rio Grande in south Texas. When Spain lost control of its territories in the New World, the area of the Rio Grande river was politically one of the most volatile spots on earth. Not only was it subject to the

political upheavals in Mexico, but it was beset by the political uncertainties
of the United States, and particularly of Texas, where for a time it was
simply illegal to be an Indian of any tribe. The Indians living in the area of
the northernmost peyote growth, along the Rio Grande, at that time were
the Mescalero to the west, the Lipan in the center, and the Carrizo to the
east and south. Not far from the peyote fields to the north of the Carrizo
were the Karankawa and Tonkawa, and north of these two small tribes were
the Caddo; north of the Mescalero and Lipan were the Comanche and a
small group of Wichita. And still north of these in what is now Oklahoma
were the Kiowa (Map 6). Among these people in the eighteenth and nineteenth centuries, another ceremony centering around peyote began to develop, culminating in the peyote ceremony described by Mooney in 1891. It
is the history of this ceremony and its adherents that are the greatest concern of this book.

In 1885, James Mooney, age twenty-five and a reporter for the Rich-
mond, Indiana, newspaper *Palladium,* decided that his fascination concerning the American Indians could be satisfied only by studying them in person. That year he presented himself to Major J. W. Powell, director of the
newly organized Bureau of American Ethnology of the Smithsonian Institution, and was hired as an ethnologist. He was sent out to study the Cherokee and started his work in North Carolina. In 1890 and 1891 he was in
Oklahoma, then Indian Territory, interviewing the Cherokee there when
the excitement created by the Ghost Dance led to his assignment by the
bureau to study that new religious movement.

Mooney's conviction that he must be, as far as possible, a full participant-
observer with the Indians he was studying led him to attend performances
of the Ghost Dance and to identify and later question its leaders. He soon
discovered that another new religious movement was taking place in Indian
Territory: the peyote or mescal religion. Some participants in the Ghost
Dance were leaders in this other religion. In some ways the two religions
seemed to be rivals. At least it seemed that the rejection of the Ghost
Dance by the powerful chief of the Comanches, Quanah Parker, was because of Parker's belief that "their own mescal [peyote] rite was sufficient
to all their needs" (Mooney 1896a: 902).

Although busy with his research and the writing of his large monograph
on the Ghost Dance, Mooney managed to participate in several all-night
peyote rituals. His notes and photographs are the first objective description
of the peyote ceremony in the United States. He wrote a number of articles
about peyote over the next few years, describing in detail the ritual and
theology of this new Indian religion. These articles present a ceremony essentially different from that in Mexico (though having some basic similarities); a ceremony essentially Indian, but not of any particular tribe; a
ceremony having overtones of Christianity, but so different from all Christian sects that it would provoke them all to do their best to eradicate it.

MAP 6. Locations of Southern Plains tribes, 1832 (after Mooney 1898) and source
areas of peyote (shaded area) (after Anderson 1969).

Central to the ceremony was the plant peyote and the experience of eating it. Furthermore, the ceremony as Mooney described it was so well defined, so established in traditional practice, that it has not changed greatly from that day to this, nearly a hundred years later. Meanwhile, it has spread widely. Just how this dissemination happened, with what first people, first prophet or genius, we can only speculate. The following is a composite account taken from several articles by Mooney of the myths, beliefs, and rituals of the peyote religion:

One of the most interesting and impressive religious ceremonies of the Kiowa Indians of Oklahoma is that in connection with the eating of the peyote or mescal plant. The ceremony usually takes place every Saturday night in the various camps, whenever a sufficient quantity of the plant can be procured.

The peyote [*Lophophora williamsii*] is a small turnip-shaped species of cactus which grows in the desert region along both sides of the Rio Grande. It possesses tonic and stimulant properties, and produces an especially wonderful mental effect. . . . The dried top, commonly known as the mescal [or peyote] button, is the part eaten, and the quantity varies according to the individual, 8 to 10 being considered the minimum.

[The Kiowa origin myth of the peyote religion relates that] "two young men" [tribe and date unspecified] had gone upon a war expedition to the far south. They did not return at the expected time, and after long waiting their sister, according to Indian custom, retired alone to the hills to bewail their death. Worn out with grief and weeping, as night came on she was unable to get back to the camp and lay down where she was. In her dreams the peyote spirit came to her and said: "You wail for your brothers, but they still live. In the morning look, and where your head now rests, you will find that which will restore them to you." The spirit then gave her further instructions and was gone. With the daylight she arose, and on looking where she had slept, she found peyote, which she dug up and took back with her to camp. Here she summoned the priests of the tribe, to whom she told her vision and delivered the instructions which she had received from the spirit. Under her direction the sacred tipi was set up with its crescent mound, and the old men entered and said prayers and sang the songs and ate the peyote—which seems to have been miraculously multiplied—until daylight, when they saw in their visions a picture of the two young warriors, wandering on foot and hungry in the far off passes of the Sierra Madre. A strong party was organized to penetrate the enemy's country and after many days the young men were found and restored to their people. Since then, the peyote is eaten by Indians with song and prayer that they may see visions and know inspiration, and the young girl who first gave it is venerated as the "Peyote Woman."

The greatest of the Kiowa gods is the sun . . . while the peyote [button], with its circular disk and bright center, surrounded by white spots or rays, is its vegetal representative. [Mooney, 1898b: 327]. . . .

Briefly stated, it may be said that the Indians regard the . . . [peyote] as a panacea in medicine, a source of inspiration, and the key which opens to him all the glories of another world. Saturday night is now the time selected, in deference to the white man's idea of Sunday as a sacred day and a day of rest. . . .

There is no preliminary preparation, such as by fasting or the sweat-bath, and supper is eaten as usual before going in. [Mooney, 1896a: 7–8]. . . .

The ceremony begins about 9 o'clock at night; after the devotees have spent an hour or so painting and decorating themselves, for everyone must wear his finest paint, feathers, and buckskin dress on this occasion. . . . Many of the mescal [peyote] eaters wear crucifixes, which they regard as sacred emblems of the rite, the cross representing the cross of scented leaves upon which the consecrated mescal [i.e., Peyote Chief] rests during the ceremony, while Christ is the mescal goddess [i.e., the Peyote Woman], the presiding goddess of the ceremony. [Mooney, 1892b: 65]. . . .

No women are admitted, except for special reasons, and then they are only allowed to eat one or two peyotes prepared for them by one of the leaders but not permitted to take an active part in the proceedings. A tipi has been erected for the ceremony in the afternoon with a shallow fire-hole in the center, around which is built a low crescent-shaped mound, with the horns pointing to the doorway at the east. The . . . [leader] now produced a package of mescals [peyote] and selecting the largest one deposited it carefully upon the top of the mound upon a bed of fragrant herbs arranged in the form of a cross. Around the sides of the tipi are laid bunches of fragrant wild sage for the worshippers to sit upon. Just inside the doorway is a pile of broken sticks for the fire. . . . A Kiowa came to announce that the ceremony was about to begin in the sacred lodge, and warned us that before entering we must remove our hats. [Mooney, 1892a]. . . .

When all is ready the fire tender [fireman] enters and lights the fire in the fire hole, piling the sticks in a v-shape, with the opening toward the east and the rising sun. The others then approach, led by the priest, and making a complete circuit around the tipi, enter at the east and take their places one after another until the circle is filled, sitting cross-legged upon a blanket spread over the wild sage. The chief priest sits at the west, directly opposite the door, while the fire tender sits at the right of the door with the pile of sticks beside him.

The chief priest opens the ceremony with a prayer, after which he hands to each man four peyotes from a bag beside him. Each man takes his share, and selecting one first, picks out the tuft of down from the center of the peyote and then chews up the button with a crunching sound until it is reduced to a paste. Now taking it out upon his hand he rolls it into a ball about the size of an ordinary marble. Holding it in his open right hand, he passes this three times through the blaze of the fire, and then, with a fourth similar motion, swallows it whole, rubbing his throat and breast to assist its passage. Each one eats the first four thus as rapidly as possible, after which the chief priest takes a gourd rattle while the man on his left [chief drummer] takes a small drum, and together they sing the opening song, which, like all the songs of the ceremony, is repeated four times over. These songs have a peculiar lullaby effect, which intensifies the dreamy condition produced by the drug, at times rising into a note of wild triumph and then again sinking into wailing sadness. The peyote itself has an extremely bitter and nauseating taste and usually produces vomiting in those unaccustomed to it. Like strong liquor, it is used, not for the taste, but the effect.

After the first song, the drum and rattle are passed to the next two men on the left of the chief priest, who sing four other songs, and so it goes round and round the circle until midnight. Until their turn comes to take up the song, the devotees sit quietly with blankets drawn up over the head, with eyes closed or looking into the fire, occasionally holding out their hands in prayer toward a sacred peyote placed in the center of the crescent mound. . . . [The neophyte is constantly exhorted not to allow his eyes to wander, but to keep them fixed upon the sacred mescal in the center of the circle (Mooney, 1896a: 11).] As the fire burns down, it is replenished by the fire tender who carefully piles up the sticks as already described and gathers the ashes into a white crescent mound just within the higher mound of earth.

After midnight there is a pause [up to this hour no one has moved from his position, sitting cross-legged upon the ground and with no support for his back, but now any one is at liberty to go out and walk about for a while and return again. Few, however, do this, as it is considered a sign of weakness [Mooney, 1896a: 8]. . . . At a signal from the chief priest, the fire tender rises and goes out of the tipi, taking a bucket which he fills with water from the nearest spring. Returning through the darkness, he stands outside at each of the four cardinal points in turn and at each blows four times upon an eaglebone whistle in imitation of the scream of the eagle. On hearing this whistle from the outside, the chief priest and his assistant again take the drum and rattle and sing the "Midnight song," four times repeated. The fire tender then enters with the water, which he passes to the chief priest, who places it between himself and the crescent mound upon which is the sacred peyote.

Now raising up the eaglebone whistle the priest blows four times upon it, after which he draws it twice through the water at right angles, making a cross. Then taking a fan made of eagle feathers, he dips it into the water and sprinkles the drops as in baptism upon the worshippers around the circle.

At this point prayers are said for any sick woman or child who may be in the camp, and for whom prayers have been requested. A sick woman usually enters with her husband or brother at the beginning and sits beside him to the close. A sick infant is handed in by the mother and taken in the arms of the father, who passes it out again to the mother after the blessing.

The sick child is handed over by its father to the priest. Holding it high in his arms he imitates the cry of the eagle, after which he passes the infant rapidly four times above the blaze of the fire, taking care not to hold it too near the blaze. Then taking it upon his lap, with the fan he sprinkles it with the sacred water, and makes a fervent prayer for its recovery or growth, after which the child is handed back to its father to be put to bed.

A sick woman sits beside her husband, near the doorway, and is allowed to eat one or more peyotes which have been consecrated by the priest with prayers in her behalf. Her husband makes request for these prayers by lighting a cigarette at the fire, and, after taking a puff himself, handing it to the one whose prayers he desires. [Everyone smokes hand-made cigarettes, the smoke being regarded as sacred incense (Mooney 1896a: 80)] . . . This one takes it, and after a preliminary puff, begins a prayer, taking a puff at each paragraph until the cigarette is consumed to a stump, which he throws into the fire. The woman remains until the close of the ceremony next morning, but is allowed to lie down or even sleep if too weak to sit up so long.

After the midnight baptismal ceremony the water is passed around and each one takes a drink. Each man then calls for as many peyotes as he desires to eat, and the songs are resumed, increasing in weird power as the effect of the drug deepens. So it goes on until daylight begins to glimmer through the canvas, and sounds outside tell that the camp is awakening.

As the first clear beam of light shines from the east, the rattle and drum, wherever in the circle they may be, are passed again to the chief priest and his assistant, who together sing the wonderful Wakaho song, that rouses every dreamer to instant alertness like the sound of a triumphal march. At its close there is a pause and the women who have been waiting outside for this signal, hand in the four vessels of sacred food and water: parched corn, hashed and sweetened beef, and stewed fruit. These are placed in a line between the fire and the doorway.

Still the song goes around until the sun is well up in the heavens, about 9 or 10 o'clock or even later, when the priest and his assistant again take the drum and rattle and sing four times the final song, the Gayatina. As the last echo dies away the buckskin head is taken from the drum. The drum kettle, rattle, rattle stick, and fan are then passed from hand to hand around the whole circle to the firekeeper, who puts them outside the tipi, each man in turn taking a sip of the water in the bottom of the kettle, tapping a few times on the sides of the kettle with the drumstick and shaking the rattle once or twice, before handing it to the next.

As soon as the instruments are outside the religious ceremony is over, and the company assumes the air of good-natured jollity as the water, corn, meat, and fruit are sent around the circle one at a time. Each man in turn helps himself, first offering a small libation to the earth or fire. When the last morsel is consumed they file out of the tipi, which is then quickly taken down by the women, while the recent worshippers sit about to gossip or sing their new songs until their wives announce that dinner is ready, when the whole company partakes of the best feast the host can provide before dispersing to their homes. . . . They go to bed at the usual time, and are generally up at the usual time the next morning. No salt is used in the food until the day after the ceremony.

Before the ceremony just described had begun, Mooney wrote:

[The leader] delivered an earnest address . . . [including] a special word to me to the effect that they had permitted me to be present that I might note everything, so that on my return I could tell the government and the white men that it was all good and not bad, and that it was the religion of the Indians in which they believed, and which was as dear to them as ours is to us.

And the ceremony concluded with another plea that he should "go back and tell the whites that the Indians had a religion of their own which they loved." For the rest of Mooney's life, he was much involved in explaining the peyote ceremony to the government and to the whites and supporting the Indians in the practice of the peyote religion.

It must be borne in mind that the two tribal ceremonies just described, that of the Tarahumara and the Kiowa, are only representatives of two ritu-als and not the entire picture. Yet we can have confidence in this picture. Lumholtz wrote of the Tarahumara in the 1880s; forty years later, a study by Zingg and Bennett corroborated his findings. The objective of Zingg and Bennett was to continue and bring up to date the research of Lumholtz and Hrdlicka, that is, to illuminate the culture history of the Uto-Aztecan-speaking peoples, who extend more or less continuously from Wyoming and Idaho to south of the Valley of Mexico. In Mexico each started with the Tarahumara and then devoted months of field work to the Huichol, with only incidental references to neighboring tribes. It was both the size of the Tara-humara and Huichol populations as well as the preservation by each of abo-riginal pre-Conquest elements of culture which prompted Lumholtz and Zingg and Bennett to concentrate on those two tribes. It was a coincidence that the people of both tribes used and continue to use peyote for cere-monial and medicinal purposes. The reports of the peyote ceremony by these scholars, and others as well, justify the present description. As for the Kiowa ceremony reported by Mooney, the continued history of the peyote ceremony in the United States bears evidence to its authenticity.

As the Lumholtz and Mooney descriptions suggest, the peyote com-plexes of Mexico and the Kiowa ceremony of the United States are vastly different; yet a detailed analysis of the two reveals many parallels. (See ap-pendix A for a comparative list of elements.) The smoking of tobacco in the form of cigarettes and the consideration of fire as an agent of purification are elements common to each. There is a certain similarity in the collecting of holy water at a special spring in San Luis Potosí and the attitude toward water as a sacred element used in the water-drum in the United States. Shaman curing by sucking, which occurs during the Huichol pilgrimage, has its counterpart in the Kiowa sucking shamans who take their patients into peyote meetings. Four as a sacred number is implied in the Huichol shoot-ing of four arrows over the first peyote found at Real del Catorce, and it finds its parallel in the idea of four as a sacred number among peyotists everywhere in the United States. Although the Huichol peyotists do not construct a shelter for their ritual, they do have an all-night ritual of singing and eating peyote while seated around a fire, as in the United States, and they also pour holy water on the fire in the morning. Another similarity is at the end of the all-night ritual when the leader is thanked and the partici-pants are told that "peyote teaches."

There are additional areas of accord between Mexican and U.S. peyo-tism that are found in other feasts not specifically designated peyote feasts. Lumholtz (1900: 155–57) wrote of the "feast of the green squash." At this feast are used peyote, a drum, and a gourd rattle, three elements of the peyote ritual of the United States:

. . . the shaman, seated in his arm chair, facing as usual the door-opening of the temple [east], beats his drum and sings from early morning until sunset.

On the same day the women bring the children. . . . They carry rattles. . . . [After the children are taken home] singing and dancing continue in the temple all night. . . . At this festival the adults drink *hikuli* [peyote]. . . . It is note-worthy that the feast is accompanied by much noise of the drum and rattle. . . .

Both Lumholtz (1900:193) and Zingg (1938:508–509) describe a peyote dance-staff or wand. It is carved with a rattlesnake symbol and is "1.1 m. average length." Although it is used differently, its length and its careful preparation and treatment as a sacred object are like that of the staff employed in peyote ceremonies in the United States. Huichol plumes and feathers used in the peyote ritual as well as a special fire brush of maguey fibers gathered in the peyote country have their counterparts in the feath-ers and special firestick in the United States.

The fire itself is an important element in both rituals. The connection between fire and peyote among the Huichol was explained by Zingg (1938: 368): "Grandfather Fire was the first and greatest shaman who successfully led the first peyote pilgrimage. . . . Since all Huichol shamans derive their power from having hunted and eaten peyote, Grandfather Fire is considered the particular god of shamans. It was Grandfather Fire who established the—peyote ceremonies."

Finally, the meat and maize of the United States peyote cult ceremonial breakfast may be related to the eating of deer meat and parched corn in the Huichol peyote rite. In writing of the parched-corn ceremony, Zingg wrote:

The floor had been wet and cleanly swept. The wall facing the door formed the family altar. . . . There were two pictures of Guadalupe [the Virgin of the In-dians] and a crucifix all covered with curtains. . . [There were] three shaman's wands [beautifully worked sticks with eagle feathers attached]. . . . The go-bernador entered, knelt before the altar and crossed himself, and took a seat near the shamans [who] roll cigarettes of corn husks . . . shaman's "plume" moistened with sacred water from peyote pilgrimage . . . tamales eaten. . . . The tamales, the food given away in the ceremony, are associated with peyote.

In conclusion, it seems to me that there are enough features of the old Mexican peyote complex present in the modern American peyote religion to support a theory of at least partial continuity of many ideas and prac-tices: the gourd rattle, the ritual number four, the dedication to the four directions, the cleansing in fire, smoke and incense, the all-night ceremony, cigarette smoking, and so forth. But most significant of all is the ancient, persistent belief in the supernatural power of the peyote plant common to both rituals. Peyote is a sacred medicine; peyote protects; peyote allows one to see the future, or to find lost objects; peyote gives power to the user that may be manifest in various ways; peyote teaches; peyote may be used by Christians or may be incorporated with Christian ideas; a pilgrimage to gather peyote plants is viewed as an act of piety to be undertaken if pos-sible, and so on.

Nonetheless, the differences, too, are significant and are sufficient to cause us to conclude that neither the number of similar individual elements nor the likeness of the overall pattern of belief in both Mexico and the United States justifies the conclusion that the peyote religion in the United States is a direct diffusion of an entire complex.

PART TWO

The Beginnings of Peyotism in the United States, 1885–1918

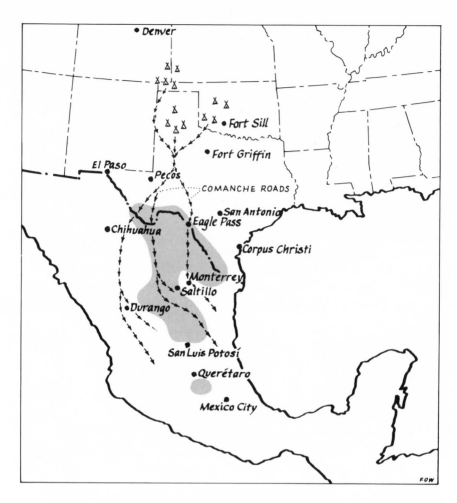

MAP 7. Source areas of peyote (shaded area) (after Anderson 1969) and Comanche roads from the Southern Plains into Mexico, 1840–70 (after Ralph A. Smith 1961).

The Nineteenth Century

How did the Kiowa and other Oklahoma tribes learn the complex religious ritual described by Mooney in 1891? Where did it come from? Through which channels did it travel? What circumstances hindered or aided it? What personalities were involved? To answer such questions, one must return again to northern Mexico and southern Texas, to the native habitat of the plant. We find that some of the tribes who were settled in Oklahoma in 1890 had once lived in or very near the area of natural growth of peyote along the Rio Grande during the century and a half preceding 1890; and those tribes that had not actually resided in the peyote growth area were strongly associated with the tribes that had, making it probable that they learned from them the religious ritual as well as the medicinal, magical, and stimulative qualities of peyote. The Oklahoma tribes most closely associated with the area of natural growth of peyote were the Carrizo, the Lipan Apache, the Mescalero Apache, the Tonkawa, the Karankawa, and the Caddo. Unfortunately, few details are known of events among these people in the early part of the nineteenth century, so we will never know exactly the answers to our questions. We can only conjecture with the little we do know and arrive at possible conclusions.

THE ROOTS OF PEYOTISM

For centuries the Carrizo had occupied the peyote growth area of the United States from Laredo east to the Gulf of Mexico. According to the *Handbook of American Indians North of Mexico* (Hodge 1907: 209) the Carrizo were "Coahuiltecan Indians between Camargo and Matamoros and along the Gulf Coast in N.E. Tamaulipas, Mexico, including remnants of the Comecrudo. . . . The Carrizo are known . . . as the 'shoeless people' because they wore sandals instead of moccasins." The linguistic family known as Coahuiltecan to which the Carrizo belong was given a number of different names in the past, but Carrizo came to be designated as the generic term, and, with Comecrudo, the only name to survive to modern times. One might apply to the Carrizo the references to Coahuiltecans in early Spanish documents in the absence of other distinguishing names. For example, the peyote ceremony desribed by Alonso de León (1649, cited in Troike 1962: 954) and in chapter 2 could have been a Carrizo rite.

Another tribe that occupied the peyote-growing area around the turn of the century was the Lipan Apache. The first mention we have of the Lipan comes with the establishment of the San Saba mission in 1757, about a hundred miles northwest of present-day Austin, Texas, and well outside the natural area of peyote growth. Later, between 1762 and 1771, the Lipan moved a hundred miles south to the San Lorenzo de la Santa Cruz mission near present-day Camp Wood, Real County, Texas, which meant that they were only about a hundred miles from the Rio Grande and the peyote gardens near Eagle Pass and about the same distance from Carrizo Springs, Texas. By 1830 the Lipan Apache and the Carrizo Coahuilteco were reported together in the town of Laredo.

A book edited and published by John C. Ewers (1969), entitled *The Indians of Texas in 1830,* by Juan Louis Berlandier, contains a good deal of information about the Lipan Apache. Berlandier was a Swiss botanist who came to Texas in 1826 with a Mexican government exploring expedition and stayed until his death in 1851. Based on Berlandier's data, Ewers (1969: 32) prepared a map which differs from Mooney's, showing only Lipan Apache and Carrizo in the peyote growing area of the lower Rio Grande in 1830. Berlandier wrote (1969: 131): "For more than ten years the Lipan have found refuge from ceaseless Comanche persecution behind the line of presidios and the populated areas along the Rio Bravo del Norte [Rio Grande]." He considered the Lipan an important tribe in Texas between 1770 and 1819 (1969: 182), saying the Mexican government wooed the Lipan as allies against the Comanche. Moreover, in 1822, Lipan Chief Castro of Laredo was invited to the Mexico City coronation of Emperor Agustín de Iturbide as an honored guest. Concerning peyote, Berlandier wrote (1969: 62):

Lipans, the Carrizo, and almost all the rest of the people who live along the Rio Bravo del Norte are ones who consume the most hard liquor. . . . Before the time of the conquerors . . . [they] got drunk by chewing a plant known in Mexico as *peiotl,* and in Creole as peyote. . . . The Lipans, and several other native groups of the northern reaches of Tamulipas still use this . . . plant. . . .

According to Mooney, the third tribe living in the area of peyote growth early in the century may have been the Mescalero Apache. Mooney shows the Mescalero occupying a large area both in the United States and in Mexico, encompassing the peyote growing area of West Texas as well as that of Chihuahua, including part of the Bolson de Mapimí. On the other hand, Ewers places the Mescalero in 1830 to the west of the Pecos in Texas, north of the Big Bend area and thus beyond the extreme northern and western limit of abundant growth. In any case, the Mescalero must have known of peyote for decades. For at least a century they had occupied peyote lands or raided into them. They were in contact with peyote-using groups from the Huichol and Tarahumara in Mexico to the Lipan and Carrizo in southern Texas. The Mescalero raided primarily in Chihuahua, but were also reported in the area of Coahuila in 1770 (Stewart 1948: 34–35).

Two other tribes close to the area of peyote growth, familiar with peyote and with a history of having been in the area for a long time, are the Tonkawa and Karankawa. Berlandier wrote that the Tonkawa used peyote back in 1830 in company with the Lipan and Carrizo. Herbert E. Bolton wrote of Tonkawa relations, alternately friendly and hostile, with French, Spanish, Comanche, and Apache in Texas from 1691 to 1857. During that century and a half the Tonkawa were frequently in or near the growth area of peyote. Little is known of the Karankawa, but that tribe is found on Mooney's map. Some pertinent information about these Indians comes from Elizabeth A. H. John, working in the Spanish Archives of Bexar (San Antonio), who reported that in 1816, Fray José Manuel Gaitán of the Refugio Mission near Corpus Christi was asked to explain why "his" Karankawa were associated with the Lipan in the vicinity of Laredo. Fray Gaitán replied (April 20, 1816): "A short time ago my Karankawa Indians . . . told me there had been at the Sierrita about fourteen of their men, only for the purpose of getting a supply of peyote for the year, and therefore taking their women and children." Indians from Refugio were permitted to go to the Laredo area, a distance of between 165 and 176 miles, depending on the route taken, to collect "la yerva nombrada pellote."

Finally, the Caddo had used peyote over a long period of time, at least since the early eighteenth century. The reports of Padre Francisco Hidalgo, Padre Isidro Espinosa, and Padre Antonio Olivares, briefly reviewed in the last chapter, show that the Caddo were users of peyote at least since the early eighteenth century.

It is within these six tribes—the Carrizo, the Lipan Apache, the Mescalero Apache, the Tonkawa, the Karankawa, and the Caddo—that we should find the origin of the peyote ceremony of the United States. These are the tribes in or nearest the growth area at the beginning of the nineteenth century. All were familiar with the ritual use of peyote. All other southern Plains tribes shown on Mooney's map are located well outside the area of natural growth of peyote, and though they may have known of the peyote plant and some of its properties and uses, it was not of general use to them until the latter part of the century, when it did become important to many. The Kiowa, Comanche, and Kiowa-Apache raided extensively in Mexico. It was commonly said that the range of a Comanche war party was limited only by light to ride by and feed for horses, and that with grass high and a full moon they could range a thousand miles. These raids would have acquainted them with peyote and may have helped prepare the way for their later acceptance of it, but the primary source for the peyote religion must be found among those living in the growth area, with long familiarity and use.

It is fairly easy to eliminate three of these tribes—the Caddo, the Tonkawa, and the Karankawa—as the probable originators of the Oklahoma ceremony. Although the Caddo were familiar with the plant and some rituals concerning it at least from the early part of the eighteenth century, they had never lived in the area of abundant growth, and while they visited in the area, there is no record of regular pilgrimages to get peyote, which would have been necessary to supply themselves with a sufficient amount to develop and practice a complex ceremony. The Karankawa did make pilgrimages to secure peyote, so they must have been early users and probably required peyote for ritual purposes. But they, too, did not reside directly in the area of natural growth, and ethnographic reports do not suggest that they were either originators or teachers of the peyote ritual. As for the Tonkawa, they were early practicers and teachers of the peyote ritual to other tribes, yet there is no evidence that they either lived directly in the growth area or made pilgrimages there to get peyote. Moreover, the Tonkawa had a reputation of cannibalism and were generally disliked by other Indians. It does not seem that they would have originated a ritual such as the peyote ceremony or that other groups would have followed their lead.

Nor does the peyote religion seem to have come originally from the Mescalero Apache, even though Mooney thought it did, and for some time others, following Mooney, thought so, too. In 1896, Mooney (1896b: 7) wrote: "The Mescalero Apache take their name from it [peyote called mescal]." Again, he wrote (1897b: 330): "The Kiowas have come from the north and first learned of the plant from the southern tribes, particularly the Mescaleros of New Mexico, who are regarded by all their neighbors as the high priests of the ceremony." And in 1915 he testified before the Board of Indian Commissioners and his testimony was inserted in the record of a congressional hearing on peyote held on February 22, 1918, on H.R. 2614 (p. 70): "The Kiowa say the Comanche knew of it before they did. Both tribes say they got it from the Mescalero and Tonkawa."

In his belief that the Mescalero were the originators of the peyote ceremony, it is possible that Mooney was influenced by his association with Andele or Andrés Martínez, who was his informant and interpreter in 1891 and 1893 and who was his companion when he first participated in a peyote meeting. Andele was a Mexican youth when, at the age of about seven, he and another boy were captured by the Mescalero Apache and taken from their homes in Las Vegas, New Mexico, in 1866. They witnessed a peyote meeting shortly thereafter. Rev. J. J. Methvin (1899: 37), who recorded the life story of Andele, described the experience: "But as he [Andele] anxiously watched, he discovered the [Mescalero] Indians, painted in most fantastic style, were gathering around a tepee. . . . The tom-tom, the rattle-gourd, and the discordant song began in earnest, and the Indians were indulging in a . . . [peyote meeting]." The ceremony lasted all night.

Andele later became a Kiowa captive, which explains how he came to know Mooney. He may very well have informed Mooney of his early experiences with the Mescalero and convinced him that the Mescalero had indeed brought peyotism to the Oklahoma tribes.

But though the Mescalero had occupied peyote lands or raided into them for decades, peyotism never seems to have been well rooted in the tribe, and in 1890, at the time peyotism was flourishing in Oklahoma, it was actually on a decline in New Mexico among the Mescalero, a situation one would hardly expect of the tribe that gave it birth. A report on Mooney's activities for the year 1893, included in the account of research for the Bureau of American Ethnology (Mooney 1900: xvi–xvii), stated:

The Mescalero Apache, numbering 450 . . . were next visited. These Indians, whose popular name is derived from their use of the "mescal" or peyote, are regarded by the Plains tribes as masters in all that concerns the plant; but from information received through their best informants, as well as from actually witnessing the ceremony, Mr. Mooney found the rite to be declining among them, largely through the difficulty of procuring the plant in their isolated condition, as it requires five days' journey on horseback to obtain a supply. Mr. Mooney discovered a number of Lipan and a few Kiowa-Apache living with the Mescalero. . . ."

It will be remembered that others traveled even longer distances to procure peyote where its use was considered important.

Others have been even less able to find peyotism among the Mescalero. Opler (1936b: 191) observed in his major report on Mescalero peyotism: "It is evidently not generally known the Mescalero Indians ate peyote. They are not represented on Shonle's (1925) map of the distribution of the use of peyote in the United States." In a much-consulted booklet compiled under the aegis of the Bureau of Indian Affairs (Newberne 1925), they are listed as "non-users." Neither the full-length history entitled *The Mescalero Apaches,* by C. L. Sonnichsen (1958), nor the one entitled *The Apache Frontier,* by Max L. Moorhead (1968), mentions Mescalero peyotism. And, finally, there is the report (Opler 1936b: 191) of June 22, 1909, by James T. Carroll, superintendent of the Mescalero Agency, who stated that "the Mescalero Apache . . . have never become addicted to the use of . . . [peyote]." If the peyote ceremony had originated among the Mescalero Apache, surely it would have left a greater impression on the tribe than it did. That it was known and practiced among them at the time it flourished in Oklahoma is beyond doubt, but it was not important to the tribe as a whole, and it did not persist.

This brings us to the Carrizo and the Lipan Apache, and of these two the evidence is strongly in favor of finding the Carrizo to be the originators of the peyote ceremony. Coahuiltecan-speaking people were the original inhabitants of the growth area and were probably using peyote before the arrival of the first Spanish explorers. At least as early as 1649 (A. de León, cited by Slotkin 1955b: 205) the Carrizo were engaged in the ritual use of peyote involving an all-night ceremony, singing and drumming around a circle. The Lipan, on the other hand, were newcomers to the area after 1770, only really becoming firmly established there after 1800. As they became friends with the Carrizo after 1770, they would have learned from them of the local wild foods and stimulants—and rituals.

Furthermore, early ethnographic accounts confirm the Carrizo as having taught peyotism to the Lipan, the best known being an article by Morris E. Opler entitled "The Use of Peyote by the Carrizo and Lipan Apache Tribes" (1938). From interviews with Lipan informants living on the Mescalero reservation in 1935, Opler reported that "the use of peyote had diffused from the Carrizo Indians to the Tonkawa and Lipan Apache. . . . it is plain that with Lipan and Carrizo peyote we are close to the source of this interesting cult within the present boundaries of the United States. . . ." His informant told him (Opler 1938: 273): "The Lipan learned it from these people, the Carrizo. . . . The Lipan learned it from the Carrizo before they had any experience with white people or Mexicans." In 1939, Opler published an account of Tonkawa peyotism in which the Tonkawa expressed their belief that they, too, had learned of peyote from the Carrizo.

For the most part La Barre used Opler's research to establish the origin of peyotism, but added (1938: 111): "One is not at all inclined to discount the vague information from Kiowas that they knew of peyote from Cayeso, the Zebakiene of 'Long Arrows,' the Yaeki (a loose designation for various north Mexican tribes) and the Kwonhego. These last so-called 'bare-footed' people are probably the Carrizo. . . ." La Barre concluded that the Carrizo were the group responsible for the original diffusion of peyote to other tribes by placing the beginning with the "Tamaulipecan-Carrizo (pre-Columbian)" (1938: 122). He drew a line from the Carrizo to the Tonkawa, then a separate line from the Carrizo to the Lipan, and then one from the Lipan to the "Mescalero (before 1870)." Finally, he drew a line from the Mescalero to the Kiowa and Comanche. My own reconstruction has the Lipan teaching the Mescalero and also, at the same time, teaching the Comanche.

David P. McAllester's *Peyote Music* (1949: 13–17), cited and summarized by Ernest Wallace and E. Adamson Hoebel (1952: 333), stated that the Carrizo were the people through whom the use of peyote was transmitted to both the Apaches and the Comanches, and he presented a full and detailed version of the acquisition of peyote from the Carrizo. J. Gilbert McAllister (1952: 370) follows Opler in stating: "The Carrizo and Lipan Apache . . . knew of [peyote's] . . . use before historic records."*

In 1954, Professor William E. Bittle of the University of Oklahoma published an article, "The Peyote Ritual: Kiowa-Apache," in which he stated (1954: 70): "The Tonkawa . . . received peyote from the Carrizo, or Barefoot Indians. . . . The Carrizo are . . . known to have used peyote at an

*McAllester, however, erred in interpreting the term *kariso* given him by his Comanche informants as "Carrizo Apache." The southern Texas Carrizo were Coahuiltecan-speakers, while the Carrizo Apache were a small band of Apachean speakers living in northeastern Arizona. The error was repeated by Wallace and Hoebel (1952: 333) and by J. Gilbert McAllister 1952: 370) in his article on peyote in the *Handbook of Texas*.

early date. The date of adoption of peyote by the Lipan is probably around 1850, or perhaps, somewhat earlier."

For the Oral History Project of the University of Oklahoma, two old Kiowa-Apache reported their tradition of the origin of peyotism in the United States. Alfred Calepah was unsure whether to say the Keresos (that is, Carrizos) or the Lipan had peyote first. Calepah spoke of one Carrizo, Jim White, who "died a long time ago" but whose tribe "used to live in Mexico." Ray Blackbear appeared to indicate that the Barefoot Indians or the Carrizo transmitted peyote to the Tonkawa and to the Lipan. And finally, David Aberle, in a personal communication, wrote: "An old Kiowa-Apache peyotist, Tennyson Berry, since dead, told me firmly that the Carrizo brought it to the Apaches. . . ."

But if the Lipan Apache were not the originators of the peyote ceremony in the United States, they were undoubtedly the principal purveyors of the ritual that they had learned from the Carrizo to the Kiowa, Kiowa-Apache, and Comanche in Oklahoma, and through them to many other tribes. Unfortunately, most of the Carrizo died in Texas before the end of the century, as did the Karankawa, but the Lipan Apache moved northwest and found refuge with their linguistic kin, the Mescalero in New Mexico, and with the Kiowa-Apache on the reservation in Oklahoma, where the large Comanche and Kiowa tribes came to live. The Caddo and Tonkawa in different directions also arrived in Oklahoma before the end of the century, and some became teachers of the peyote ritual.

When attempting to answer the questions surrounding the origin of the peyote cult, one should bear in mind the larger picture, beyond any particular tribe to the total environment. We know that the movement of people for food gathering; for conquest, war, or plunder; for indoctrination; for friendship and curiosity—or for whatever reason—leads to new ideas, new inventions, new problems, new institutions. For three hundred years in the area of the Rio Grande the movement of people had been gathering momentum. The peyote religion was a result of this acceleration; a result, albeit small, of the conquest of the New World.

One of the participating groups in this movement, and probably the most important, was the Catholic church. Spanish missions had been in the area for three hundred years, accelerating their growth in the eighteenth century. One will recall the Misión del Dulce Nombre de Jesús de Peyote, the Presidio and San Juan Bautisto, the missions at San Antonio and at Santa Fe, the mission on the San Saba for the Lipan Apache, and many more. One will recall as well the generations of Catholic padres and their accompanying soldiers and retainers. The establishment of missions spread knowledge of peyote—sometimes, first knowledge. The missions also promoted and facilitated trade in peyote.

The spread of Christianity by the Catholic church had another influence, a civilizing influence which perhaps had an effect on the ceremony itself.

The peyote ceremony in Oklahoma was different from earlier Mexican peyote ceremonies. There was no blood-letting; there was almost never any dancing; people sat as in a meeting; there were no drunken stupors. It was an affair of family and friends, with singing and praying, and for all its strangeness to outsiders, to its participants it carried a high moral tone, such as might characterize a mission service. While no Christian symbol, with the possible exception of the cross, can be found in early peyote ceremonies, they might be said to have had a certain Christian ambience. This is not to say that aboriginal or earlier Mexican peyote rites were not gatherings of friends and families and of a serious nature; it is only to say that it was the civilized manifestations of the aboriginal ceremonies that were integrated into the Oklahoma ceremony and not the primitive, uncivilized aspects.

The southern Plains tribes who swept down upon Mexico on their horses were part of this movement of people, and they, too, had their effect on events. Berlandier reports on the friendship and enmity between the Lipan and the Comanche to the north of them: "The Lipans, after living at peace with the Comanches for many years, have since sworn eternal warfare against them . . ." (p. 62). The Comanche were particularly famous for their raids. The journals of William Bollaert (1956) for the period from December, 1841, to April, 1844, report that the Comanche spent months in southern Texas living on the wild mustangs of the region, which they killed in great numbers. Vivid accounts of Comanche raiding into Mexico are found in an article, including a map, by Ralph A. Smith (1961) entitled, "Comanche Roads from the South Plains into Mexico, about 1840–1870" (Map 7). Smith describes roads from 1834 to 1844 into the Mexican states of Durango, Chihuahua, Coahuila, Nuevo León, and Tamaulipas. He wrote (1961:54ff.):

The demands for Mexican livestock, captives, and plunder increased after American commissioners made treaties of amity and trade with the Indians of the South Plains in the 1830's. The Comanche and Kiowa consequently stepped up their predatory raids below the Rio Grande. . . . Their deepest penetrations of Mexico put the Indians at points a thousand miles straight south of their home range in Kansas and Oklahoma. . . . Plains Indians might spend an entire winter in the Bolson [de Mapimí], enjoying the climate, rounding out herds for the long drives, and giving grass time to grow out along the trail northward.

One suspects the warriors also experimented with peyote, which grew abundantly in the area.

The Kiowa provided documentation of Kiowa, Comanche, and Kiowa-Apache raids into Mexico between 1834 and 1874 on their picturesque calendar history painted on buffalo hides. Of special significance is the raid during the winter of 1844–45, when the Comanche, Kiowa, and Kiowa-Apache were together on the Salado River, called "Sen P'a," meaning "Cactus River," which flows through the "Lomerias de Peyotes," or "Peyote

Hills." According to Mooney (1898b: 164), in about 1790 the Kiowa made a lasting peace with the Comanche, an alliance which he thought could be considered as a confederation of the two tribes. The effect of this alliance was considerable. "The raids of the Kiowa on the Mexican settlements, hitherto desultory and ineffective, now became constant and destructive and continued until both tribes were finally subjugated and confined to their reservations after the outbreak of 1874."

Not only did groups of people influence the beginning and spread of the peyote ceremony at that time, but individuals were influential as well. There are few individuals mentioned in this part of this history of peyotism, whereas there will be many as the details unfold in later chapters. The number of characters in later chapters should give an idea of the many and varied personalities that went into the creation and development of peyote in its formative time—people we can never know, shrouded as they are in prehistory. Individuals certainly were of utmost importance in the beginning, for they have been ever since.

Finally, we come to the influence of the Americans, who forced the "wild Indians of the Plains" to settle on reservations and to give up their horses, their arrows, their guns, their traditional food—their independence. We have the pragmatic, far-off U.S. government trying to find short-term, easy answers for monumental human problems. We have determined pioneers and desperate Indians meeting head-on in southern Texas. Eventually, all of the Indians on Mooney's map who still lived joined hosts of other Indians in Oklahoma, Indian Territory, far from the peyote fields.

OKLAHOMA: THE CRADLE OF PEYOTISM

The peyote religion developed in the United States after Indian reservations were established by the U.S. government. It was one of the results of the confluence of peoples, cultures, and conflicts that the U.S. government created when it established the "Indian Territory" in Oklahoma.

Summing up the policy of the U.S. government concerning the Indians in the nineteenth century, the *Handbook of American Indians* contains the following (Hodge 1910, II: 373):

The idea of removing the Indians residing E. of the Mississippi to reservations W. of that river was a policy adopted at an early date. The first official notice of it appears in the act of Mar. 26, 1804. . . . In 1825 President Monroe reported to the Senate a formal "plan of colonization or removal . . ." of all tribes then residing E. of the Mississippi, to the same general western region. In accordance with the plan present Oklahoma, with the greater portion of what is now Kansas, was soon after constituted a territory, under the name of "Indian Territory," as a permanent home for the tribes. . . . Before the close of 1840, almost all of the principal Eastern tribes and tribal remnants had been removed to the "Indian Territory." . . . By subsequent legislation Kansas was detached from the Territory, most of the emigrant tribes within the bounds of Kansas being again removed to new reservations S. of the boundary line. . . . The Indian population of the Territory comprised some forty officially recognized tribes.

In the beginning, the tribes forced to settle in Indian Territory were the so-called Five Civilized Tribes—the Cherokee, the Choctaw, the Chickasaw, the Creek, and the Seminole—and the remnants of other eastern tribes, a total of about 100,000 people. They were given all of what is now Oklahoma and a somewhat greater area where, after immeasurable hardship, they settled themselves in towns with schools, churches, and other refinements of civilization to which they had been accustomed. Very soon, however, the government found itself in trouble with other Indians, the "wild Indians" of the Plains, and in an effort to confine some of them, the government leased back from the settled Indians the western quarter of the lands comprising "Indian Territory" for places to confine various of the troublesome Plains tribes.

At the time of exploration, the Indians of the High Plains were roaming bands, sometimes settling for a time in one place, but moving freely otherwise, without hard and fast territorial boundaries. Among them were the Apache (Kiowa, Lipan, Mescalero, and others), the Comanche, the Caddo, the Wichita, the Osage, the Arapaho, and the Cheyenne. Some were large and aggressive tribes, others small; some were related linguistically, others not; some lived in friendly association, and others were at war with one another. By the nineteenth century, many of these Indians had horses and sometimes raided from the Mississippi to New Mexico and from Colorado to Texas, crossing the Rio Grande and traveling deep into Mexico. With the coming of immigrants in trains of covered wagons and the consequent disappearance of game, the Plains Indians saw their way of life increasingly threatened. They became more aggressive against the white settlers, who became more frightened and appealed to Washington.

Settlement of the eastern Indians in the Indian Territory was apparently a success, so the policy of government was to settle the "wild" Indians as soon as possible on specified tracts of land in or near "Indian Territory." Thus, it became a time of treaty-making. In 1835, the U.S. government signed its first treaty with the free-roaming tribes of the Plains. The treaty was called the Comanche and Wichita Treaty, but it included many other tribes, including the Five Civilized Tribes and other eastern tribes already located in Indian Territory, all concurring in the pledge of peace among tribes and with the United States. Soon after Texas joined the United States in 1846, the Wichita, the Caddo, the Tonkawa, and seven other tribes signed the Treaty of Council Springs near the Brazos River in Texas, where a reservation on the Brazos was given them. The treaty was ill-fated; in 1858, Texans attacked the Indians, and during the next year all the

Indians in Texas were removed to an area in what is now southwestern Oklahoma (Bolton 1910: 782).

The Civil War brought more changes in Oklahoma. The eastern Indians, most of whom had come from the Southern states, had elected the Southern cause, and after the war the government meted out punishment to them by taking away, with only slight compensation, their autonomy on the land that had been given them. That land then became the government's to give away again. In 1867 came the Treaty of Medicine Lodge. Mooney says of it:

On October 21, 1867, . . . the Kiowa, Comanche, and Kiowa-Apache were officially confederated and agreed to come upon their present reservation. . . . This treaty merits extended notice, inasmuch as it changed the whole status of the Kiowa and their allies from that of independent tribes with free and unrestricted range over the whole plains to that of pensioners dependent on the government, confined to the narrow limits of a reservation and subject to constant military and civilian supervision. For them it marks the beginning of the end.

This was true of others as well. The Cheyenne and Arapaho signed treaties about the same time. Within about a year treaties were signed which provided reservations for the Texas tribes—the Caddo, Delaware, Tonkawa, and Wichita—on the Wichita reservation, (treaty of July 4, 1866) which was bounded on the west by the Cheyenne and Arapaho reservation and on the south by the Kiowa and Comanche reservation, which also included the Kiowa-Apache (see Map 8).

In 1869, President U.S. Grant initiated the Indian Peace Policy. Wallace and Hoebel (1952, 313–14) write of that event:

Congress in an effort to correct some of the abuses charged against the Indian administration, authorized the President to organize a board of Indian commissioners, who were to exercise joint control over appropriations with the Secretary of the Interior. This new body became at once a dominant force in determining the Indian policy of the government. Simultaneously, President U.S. Grant made another important change in Indian administration by appointing Quakers as Indian agents and employees. Other denominations were, however, allowed to participate in the Indian work, and most agents, teachers, and employees at the Indian agencies came to be nominees of some church or religious society. This was the era of the Peace Policy, and on July 1, 1869, Lawrie Tatum, an unimaginative but courageous and sensible Quaker, took up his duties at Fort Sill as the agent of the Comanche, Kiowa, and Kiowa Apache reservation.

As far as bringing hostile Kiowa and Comanche warriors to settle on reservations is concerned, the Indian Peace Policy was a failure. It required a large and multipronged military operation directed by Generals William T. Sherman and Philip H. Sheridan in the field with such famous Indian fighters as Generals John W. Davidson, Ranald S. Mackenzie, and Nelson A. Miles.

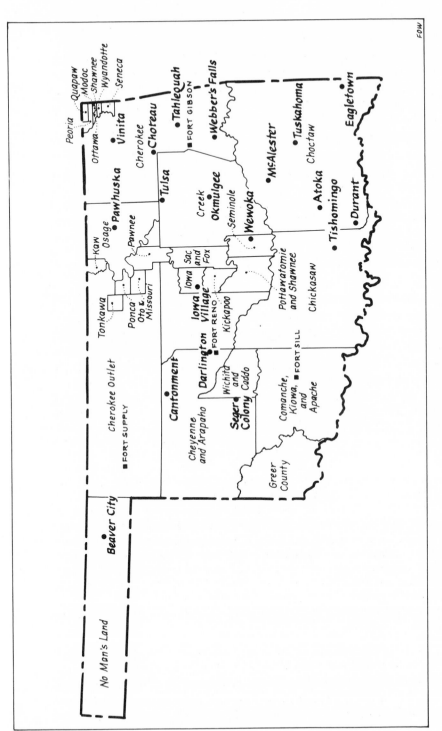

MAP 8. Locations of Indian tribes in Indian Territory, 1866–1889 (from John W. Morris, Charles R. Goins, and Edwin C. McReynolds, *Historical Atlas of Oklahoma*, 2d ed. [Norman: University of Oklahoma Press, 1976], map 33).

Finally, the capture and destruction of the Indians' horses, in addition to the great reduction of the buffalo herds, forced even the Antelope band of Comanche to submit to life on a reservation. During the military campaigns of the summer and fall of 1874, leaders of Indian raids were identified and imprisoned in preparation for their removal from the reservations and placement in a prisoner-of-war camp. The prison selected was Fort Marion, Florida, on the site of historic fortifications near Saint Augustine, and the officer put in charge of the seventy-two warriors (and a Comanche woman and child who insisted on going along) was Lt. Richard Henry Pratt.In his *Memoirs* (1964: 138–44), Pratt gives the names, ages, crimes, and other pertinent data concerning the entire group.

Thus, by 1874, the "wild Indians of the Plains," or what was left of them, had joined the civilized tribes in Oklahoma. Peyote would have been known to many of these people. The Caddo and Tonkawa, as well as any Karankawa and Carrizo who remained, would have known peyote; the Lipan and Mescalero Apache, some in nearby New Mexico and some in Oklahoma, would have known of it. All of these southern tribes probably would have experienced the southern Texas Carrizo peyote ceremony. The Comanche, the Kiowa, the Cheyenne, and others would have had some knowledge and experience of peyote from their years of raiding into Texas and Mexico. The present closeness of their lives and their common difficulties should have made them ready for the diffusion of a new religion. At first, however, diffusion was slow, for in the 1870s all of these Indians were living far from the peyote gardens and were, for the most part, unhorsed. Without the essential ingredient, the sacrament, peyotism was likely to become just a memory.

One feels that the peyotism of earlier, better days must have been a strong, healthy product, because it did not fade away. Its growth was slowed because peyote was in extremely short supply, but still some Indians managed to acquire it. Gathering peyote was from early time the province of *peyoteros,* the Mexican or Hispanic collectors in the growth areas. George Morgan (1976: 60–61) recorded a statement of a contemporary *peyotero,* one Arnulfo Canales, who said that his grandfather, Francisco Canales, started selling peyote to Indians in 1870 or 1872 in the vicinity of Los Ojuelos. If indeed peyote was traded in the 1870s near Laredo, the social unrest of the period made travel to the area by Indians a hazardous activity. In his history of the area, J. B. Wilkinson (1975: 331–61) characterized the decade of the seventies in Laredo as the most violent in the history of a violent town, years in which Indians from the United States raided from strongholds across the border in Mexico. This was the period when no Indians were officially located or allowed in Texas, and in all of southern and western Texas an active war against Indians was being waged by Texas Rangers and forces of the U.S. Army. The hostility towards Indians in Texas would certainly have inhibited most from traveling to the area to collect peyote.

Still, there were some bold young men who did hazard the journey for a few hundred buttons of peyote. They lived in Oklahoma and traveled five hundred miles by horseback to the peyote gardens and five hundred miles back, always on the alert for Texas Rangers or U.S. troops. It might have been worthwhile at that if, as one report claimed (Clark 1888), in 1878 Indians were willing to pay one dollar for one peyote button.

Two who dared to collect peyote in Laredo and to enter Texas in the seventies were Lipan Apaches named Pinero and Chiwat (Chivato or Civato). Their story comes to us because in 1870 they captured an eleven-year-old boy named Henry Lehmann in the vicinity of Fredericksburg, Texas, about ninety miles west of Austin. That boy lived with them until 1879 and later told of the circumstances of his capture and of his life among the Lipan, and of Comanche and Kiowa raids into Texas and Mexico. There are two descriptions, one published by J. A. Jones in 1899 and the other by J. Marvin Hunter in 1927, the latter edited and republished by A. C. Greene in 1972. The two accounts differ somewhat, but in both Lehmann tells of eating a cactus found in old Mexico, which he referred to as "hoosh," and which he identified as peyote. He stated that one of the Lipans who captured him became an important tribal leader (Greene 1972: 89): "I want to say that one of the Apaches who stole me . . . afterward became a chief of his tribe. . . . This chief's name is Chiwat, and he now lives among the Comanches at Indiahoma, in Oklahoma." His account included a photograph of Chiwat which, with others, is preserved in the Fort Sill Museum; it shows Chiwat in a peyote tipi with two early Comanche leaders of peyotism (Fig. 3).

Lehmann's other captor, Pinero, identified himself as a peyotist in the *American Indian YMCA Bulletin* (November, 1918):

I am a Lipan Apache. I live five miles northeast of Indiahoma, Oklahoma, on my allotment. I am 57 years old. I knew about peyote before any of these Indians in Oklahoma country knew about it. I first ate peyote in Mexico. My great-grandfather was the first [Lipan] to make use of it in Mexico; it was brought among the Indians here years after. It was used as a medicine at first, and no woman or young people ate it as they do now. It is called mescal-peyote in Mexico; here in Oklahoma it is called peyote. . . .

Confirmation that the Lipan in general, and Chiwat and Pinero in particular, were primary teachers of peyotism to Indians in Oklahoma comes from a number of different sources. There are many first-hand accounts by old-time members of the Comanche, Kiowa, and Kiowa-Apache tribes. Guy Quoetone, a Kiowa born in 1884 who was an interpreter for Mooney in 1918, claimed to be quoting Pinero exactly when he said: "I was fleeing for safety and Quanah Parker [Comanche leader] took me in. I learned Comanche. I married a Comanche. I was the first to teach the peyote cere-

FIG. 3. Billy Chiwat (Lipan Apache), one of the first peyotists in Oklahoma, about 1915. Fort Sill Museum, Fort Sill, Oklahoma, #P–2290.

mony to Quanah Parker." He further reported that Pinero and Chiwat together ran meetings for Quanah and that among the features of the peyote
meeting taught to Quanah were worship in a big tipi, the fire in a pit in the
center,* the roadman sprinkling cedar, water at midnight, feathers, the entrance to the east, cigarettes smoked, and everything done by fours. In
1967, Cecil Horse, age seventy-six, son of Hunting Horse, described the
beginning of peyotism in Oklahoma:

Pinero killed another Apache man, a Mescalero, so they were going to kill him.
So he took out of that New Mexico and came into Oklahoma. . . . That's why
this peyote came from Old Mexico into New Mexico and this man Pinero
took this peyote . . . over to the Comanche. . . . They began to use it, not
knowing exactly what it was till another man, Pinero's brother, named Chivato,
came in and also brought this peyote among the Comanches. . . . And that's
how, by these two men, Pinero and Chivato brought this peyote . . . into the
Comanches.

As with any cherished institution, myths and stories abound regarding "the
beginning." One with several versions relates the story that Lipan Apache
women were menaced by soldiers (sometimes Mexican, sometimes U.S.)
and were saved by supernatural guidance leading them to eat peyote.

Other stories state that the Lipan, and particularly Chiwat and Pinero,
brought peyote not only to the Comanche, but also to the Kiowa and the
Kiowa-Apache. Modern Kiowa tradition regarding the origin of peyotism on
the Kiowa-Comanche reservation was recorded from two Kiowa peyotists,
each about fifty years old. Nelson Big Bow, who lived near Fort Sill and was
questioned the morning following a peyote meeting held at his place, said:
"Quanah Parker brought Lipan back from Mescalero to run peyote meetings." David Apekaum, an Indian student advisor at the University of Oklahoma, told me in Norman: "The Lipan, Chivato, taught peyotism to the
Kiowa." One other Kiowa peyotist who remembered Chiwat in 1972 was
James Auchiah. His version was that Quanah paid a fine for Chiwat in
Laredo and thus got him freed from jail, after which Chiwat and Pinero
came to Oklahoma to run meetings for Quanah.

Anthropologists, as well, have recorded that they have found the Lipan
to have been the primary teachers of peyote to the Indians of Oklahoma.
McAllister (1952:370) stated: "The Kiowa-Apache say they obtained the
plant and its ritual from the Lipan in the 1880's and then introduced it to the

---

The "roadman" is the leader of the all-night peyote ceremony, the "peyote meeting."
The name refers to "the peyote road," a line incised along the crest of the half-moon altar on
which ritual participants are asked to concentrate in the belief that "the road" will lead their
thoughts and prayers to the supernatural—in modern times often designated as "God the
Father."

Other officials in a peyote meeting are the Chief Drummer, who sits on the right of the
roadman; the Cedarman, who sits on the left of the roadman and sprinkles sagebrush "incense" on the fire; and the Fireman, who tends the fire and sits near the opening or door.

Kiowa and Comanche." William E. Bittle wrote (1954: 70): "From the Lipan, the Mescalero obtained the plant in 1870. . . . The Kiowa-Apache . . . claim to have obtained peyote directly from the Lipan, though probably no earlier than the Kiowa, around 1870." Despite the differences in dates and routes, researchers usually agree that the Lipan were the first teachers to tribes settled in Oklahoma.

Finally, musicologists, studying peyote music, have found reason to believe that the Lipan were first in the early diffusion of peyotism. Bruno Nettl (1954: 306) wrote: "The songs of the peyote cult . . . are related in musical style to those of the Navajo and Apache. This may be due to the fact that the style could have spread. . . from the Lipan Apache." David P. McAllester recorded ninety Comanche peyote songs in 1940. He wrote (1949: 32–33): "We were told that one singer . . . specialized in a particular subject matter for his songs. Civato, an Apache . . . was known for singing songs about the wind . . . 'those . . . songs of Civato's . . . seem to fit in well, they seem to point to the peyote meeting.'"

The diffusion of peyotism accelerated in the eighties, which were different in two ways. First, the Indians had been conquered and confined as a group to the Indian Territory, and no longer posed a threat to the peace of the area. This meant that from then on, individual Indians could make ordinary business trips to bring back peyote to the reservations. More important for the supplying of peyote from the vicinity of Laredo to the Kiowa-Comanche reservation was the completion of railroads linking Los Ojuelos with Wichita Falls and Vernon, Texas.

The Texas-Mexican Railroad, connecting Corpus Christi with Laredo, was completed in December, 1881. The narrow-gauge line crossed the northern end of the most productive peyote-growing zone, and two railway stations were established close to Los Ojuelos, the home village of the first *peyoteros*. Almost immediately, boxes and barrels of dried peyote were shipped on the Texas-Mexican Railway to Laredo. Once in Laredo, the peyote could be trans-shipped, because in late December, 1881, the regular-gauge line of the International and Great Northern Railroad was completed, connecting Laredo to Austin and beyond. Also in 1881, the International and Great Northern and the Missouri, Kansas and Texas railroad companies had merged, so there was continuous rail service from Laredo across Texas to enter Indian Territory at Denison. At the same time, the Fort Worth and Denver City Railway was under construction, and it reached Wichita Falls in late 1883. By October, 1886, traffic was open to Vernon, Texas, only about ten miles from the edge of the Comanche section of the Kiowa-Comanche reservation. Also in 1881, the line from San Antonio to Eagle Pass, Texas, was opened by the Galveston, Harrisburg and San Antonio Railway, operating over the Mexican and Pacific rails part of the way (Poor vols. 9–23, 1876–1890).

With the coming of the railroads, peyote was in abundance in Oklahoma, and diffusion of peyotism increased rapidly. The first published reference to the use of peyote by Indians in the United States was by J. Lee Hall, agent of the Kiowa-Comanche Agency, Anadarko. In his annual report of 1886, Hall said little beyond the fact that "the Comanches and a few of the Kiowas secure the tops of a kind of cactus that comes from Mexico, which they eat, and it produces the same effect as opium. . . . suggest that the same should be made contraband. . . ." By 1886 there was plenty of peyote to be had on the reservation. Agent Hall passed along to Washington a letter he had received from one E. L. Clark, whom he recommended as "a gentleman who has lived among the Comanche many years and knows their habits and language probably better than any person on the Reservation. He is a truthful man. . . ." Clark wrote, in part:

The Spanish name is piote or peotah. . . . The Indians of this reservation have used very little of [it] prior to four years ago except a few of the Quahadis [Comanche of Quanah Parker's band] who happened to be associated with the Lipan Apaches. These Apaches having practiced the use of the Wok-wave for the last 20 or 30 years . . . it is kept by almost all of the little stores in Greer County near the border of this reservation, also . . . at Doran's Store. . . . Four or five years ago [that is, 1883 or 1884], a Mexican named Sit-chees-toque or Che-wow-wah, having been a captive of the Comanche . . . escaped punishment by remaining with the Apache in New Mexico. He returned to this reservation during P. B. Hunt's term of office [1878–85], bringing with him quite a sack full of these Opium Buttons (as I call them) and traded them to the Comanches for several head of horses and cattle. . . . He is still one of the ring leaders in the use of the Medicine. . . . The usual dose of these Buttons some four years ago [1884] were from 4 to 6 per night. . . . Now they use from 20 to 50 per night . . . seeing or imagining all kinds of things. These visions . . . were communicated to them through the Wok-Wave and they come direct from the Great Spirit (they said).

Another, or perhaps the same, Mexican connection appears in an account by Dr. J. R. Briggs, of Dallas, that was published in the *Medical Register,* April 8, 1887. Dr. Briggs was experimenting with peyote himself and recording his own physiological reactions. He stated that he had never seen Indians using peyote, but his second-hand account seems authentic, based on the amount of peyote eaten and the arrangement of Indians in the tipi. In June, 1887, he reported that Kiowa Indians were using peyote and he could obtain the cactus from a Mexican for fifteen dollars a bushel of dried buttons, approximately thirty-five hundred buttons in all. In August, 1887,he identified the Mexican as E. A. Paffrath, an associate of J. R. Wood, a general wholesaler of Vernon, Texas.

Paffrath would not reveal the source of his supplies to Parke, Davis and Company, when requested, and after some delays the drug company established contact with another source of peyote buttons, Anna B. Nickels of Laredo, Texas. A collector and dealer in cactus, Nickels informed the Detroit company on May 29, 1888, that she had three thousand plants growing in her garden and could collect all she could "find sale for." In a letter dated July 11, 1888, Mrs. Nickels volunteered the information that "the Mexicans here in Laredo buy [peyote buttons] off me at 5 cents each, 1 or 2 at a time to make a drink (they say for headache). They pound fresh ones and soak them in water, then strain and drink the water. They use the pulp left to bind on any sort of sores" (Bender 1968:164). William E. Safford (1915:309) published a photograph of Mrs. Nickels in her cactus garden. As to the use of peyote by the Indians, Mrs. Nickels wrote: "I am certain the Mescal buttons are the real ones used by the Indians as a drink because the same man that goes with me collecting them gathered 30,000 of the same last fall [1887] for a Mexican Merchant of this place and he sliced and dried them here in Laredo and shipped them to some Agency. . . . I am also sure 'tis Anhalonium williamsii."

Another event which influenced its spread and undoubtedly in some manner its direction was the establishment of the prisoner-of-war camp at the termination of the Indian wars. The Indians sent to that camp were young leaders from several tribes who were kept at the camp at Fort Marion for four years and were given intensive training in the English language, in the American work ethic, in Christianity, in a number of practical trades, and, of great importance, in intertribal friendship and understanding. Many of the friendships that were formed lasted lifetimes and helped to smooth lives when the prisoners returned to Oklahoma.

The role of Lt. Richard Henry Pratt, later to become General Pratt, who was put in charge of the prisoner-of-war camp, is significant. He had come early onto the scene in Oklahoma. Shortly before the signing of the Medicine Lodge treaty, he was ordered to Fort Arbuckle, about seventy miles south of present-day Oklahoma City. Fort Arbuckle was one of the most western military posts in Oklahoma until 1869 and the establishment of Fort Sill, about sixty-five miles farther west. Lieutenant Pratt was in command of a detachment of Negro troops of the Tenth U.S. Cavalry as well as the American Indian scouts recruited to aid U.S. Army soldiers. He reported of reservation life in 1867 (Pratt 1964:9):

The twenty-five Arbuckle scouts were Caddoes and Wichitas from along the Washita River, northwest of Arbuckle. Very few could speak any English, but there was an interpreter, Horace P. Jones, speaking Comanche, employed by the government to enable intercourse between the military and the Kiowas, Comanches, Cheyennes, Arapahoes, Apaches, and affiliated bands of Caddoes, Wichitas, Keechies, and others. There were individuals in all of these tribes who could speak Comanche, that having become the court language of our southwest Indians.

The problem of intertribal communications can be realized when one contemplates that on the three reservations in western Oklahoma there were speakers of at least eight languages from five distinct linguistic families. These were (Driver 1969:43–45) Caddo, and Wichita languages of the Caddoan family; the Comanche language of the Uto-Aztecan family; Delaware, Cheyenne, and Arapaho languages of the Algonquian family; Kiowa-Apache of the Athapascan family; and Kiowa of the Kiowa-Tanoan family. In addition, hundreds of Mexican captives among the Kiowa and Comanche may have retained a knowledge of Spanish, and Spanish may have been used at times for intertribal communications. English-speaking captives would have added some English words. The Plains Indians had developed their sign language for intertribal communication between people of distinctive speech, but the Plains sign language was not universally known and was probably not known in the 1860s by the Texas tribes speaking Caddoan languages. With such diverse languages, the need of a *lingua franca* for intertribal communication was apparent to everyone, and the value of English for that purpose as well as to talk to agency officials, traders, soldiers, and so on soon was recognized.

The need for the Indians to learn English was uppermost in Lieutenant Pratt's mind when he was assigned to be director of the prisoner-of-war camp. He described (1964:121) his policy and practice for prisoner education:

Promoting English speech was among the earliest and most persistent of our efforts in order to bring the Indians into best understanding and relations with our people. Trading and talking with visitors was valuable help in forwarding this purpose. Excellent ladies, who had in their earlier years been engaged in teaching, had volunteered to give daily instructions to the prisoners in classes. . . . Most of the young men learned to write fairly intelligent letters during the three years of their imprisonment and the English language became the common tongue among them, thus breaking down the wall of language which separates the tribes as fully as between them and our own people.

Christianity was taught also. According to Bishop H. B. Whipple, who visited the fort in 1876, the "discipline, kindness, and Christian teaching" gave the Indians "manhood and the Gospel of Jesus Christ" (Pratt 1964:164).

When the prisoner-of-war camp was disbanded in 1879, Pratt was put in charge of Carlisle Indian School, which was established at his urging in the town of Carlisle, Cumberland County, Pennsylvania, eighteen miles southwest of Harrisburg. This school was under the auspices of the army and lasted until 1918, when the barracks were needed for soldiers of the World War. Though the Indians who attended this school were no longer prisoners, the same philosophy, discipline, and motivation prevailed. It was Pratt's idea (and the army's) to make Indians into "white men" as quickly as possible. He saw no virtue in Indians preserving any of their own culture— their languages, their customs, styles of dress, religions. The sooner they became civilized and forgot all about being Indians, the better. And to some extent he was quite successful. Those who attended the prisoner-of-war camp and, later, those hundreds who spent some years at Carlisle did learn English (some very well); they also learned the basic beliefs of Christianity, especially the Protestant variety; they often learned a trade and something about farming; and they learned the culture essentials of white society. When they returned to the reservation, as most of them did, they often became leaders of their people and influential in tribal affairs.

There were other schools that attempted to civilize the Indians as Carlisle did. One was Hampton Institute, a private institution located at Fort Monroe, Virginia, which was started in 1868 for blacks. After 1879 it was opened to Indians, and by 1908, eleven hundred Indian girls and boys received training there. Another school was Haskell Junior College near the University of Kansas, at Lawrence, Kansas, which opened in 1900. And still another, principally an agricultural and industrial school, was Chilocco Indian Industrial School, established in July, 1880, on 8,320 acres on the Oklahoma-Kansas boundary in central Oklahoma.

Those who came together at these schools learned English, Christianity, and the rudiments of white civilization, but they probably learned some things that might have surprised and dismayed Pratt, for they were Indians of different tribes and backgrounds, and they certainly would have learned from each other certain Indian lore. One bit of information passed about must have been of peyote. It is not likely that peyote was discussed at the prisoner-of-war camp at Fort Marion, but by the time Carlisle and Hampton were established in 1880 and peyote was abundant and peyotism flourishing on the reservations, it is reasonable to assume that peyote was a topic of conversation among the young Indians fresh from Oklahoma who were acquiring a common language and learning about Christianity. It is also quite possible that peyote itself found its way into the schools as an individual's protective fetish, since that has been one of the uses of peyote from earliest times to the present. But whether or not students learned of peyote at school, many did become peyotists after they returned home and were outstanding members of their tribes as well. The list of Carlisle graduates who became peyotists is well over a hundred.

While the educational opportunities in the schools brought many Indians together in 1890, another event occurred which, for a brief time, had social and religious importance to all those living in Indian Territory: the Ghost Dance came to Oklahoma. This was the movement that resulted from the teaching of Wovoka, a Northern Paiute of western Nevada who directed his first Ghost Dance in January, 1889. A convert of Wovoka, one Northern Arapaho named Sitting Bull, but not to be confused with the Sioux medicine man of the same name, arrived on the Cheyenne-Arapaho reservation in the summer of 1890 and by September could attract as many as three thousand people to one Ghost Dance. Everyone living on the reservation of western Oklahoma—Kiowa, Comanche, Wichita, Caddo, Kiowa-Apache, Cheyenne, and Arapaho, with a few Delaware and Lipan Apache—had a chance to learn the Ghost Dance doctrine and dance procedure by the fall of 1890. Ghost Dances were held among other Oklahoma tribes in 1891 and 1892.

The Ghost Dance doctrine was compounded of an ancient Northern

Paiute and Northwest Plateau belief in a periodic world renewal that could be brought about by ceremonies (usually group dancing), combined with Christian teachings of the second coming of Jesus Christ. The dance taught by Wovoka was the ordinary Paiute round dance, performed by individuals holding hands and circling by stepping sideways. According to Wovoka, instructions were received from supernatural powers, especially Jesus, during periods of trance or unconsciousness. Faithful dancing, clean living, peaceful adjustment with whites, hard work, and following God's chosen leaders would hasten the resurrection of dead relatives and the desired restoration of the "good old days" of Indian prosperity. During world renewal, whites would be quietly removed. Although variations on the above doctrine later developed, those basic Ghost Dance teachings have remained stable.

It was probably the idea that "whites would be quietly removed" and the large crowds that the Ghost Dance attracted that worried the army and the general white population. The army reacted with force on the Sioux reservation, and the massacre at Wounded Knee resulted. In Oklahoma, the story was different, thanks to Lt. Hugh L. Scott, who was put in charge of Ghost Dance management. He supported a policy of noninterference, and the Ghost Dance ran its course for two or three years, thereafter being of only sporadic interest until finally almost dying out.

Scott's account in *Some Memories of a Soldier* (1928) gives an indication of the interest and feeling aroused by the Ghost Dance in Oklahoma at the time.

The excitment became as great among the white communities as among the Indians, the former expecting an uprising, a feeling that was greatly intensified by news of the battle of Wounded Knee in South Dakota with the Sioux. . . . The press called for the disarming of the Indians all over the Plains. Some of the agents, notably the agent in charge of the Kiowas and Comanches at Anadarko, were insistent upon the troops to bring about disarmament and the stopping of the dance, a policy I resisted with all my force." [Hugh L. Scott 1928:147]

Though short-lived, the Ghost Dance brought many Indians together to consider a new and exciting Indian-Christian religion. Without doubt, it made many question, as well as defend, beliefs already held. Some peyotists, like Quanah Parker, disavowed it and tried to discourage attendance. Some Christian Indians, like those belonging to the long-established communities of the Five Civilized Tribes, did likewise. But many Indians experimented with it. The excitement of the Ghost Dance between 1890 and 1893 increased intertribal visiting. A trip halfway across the state of Oklahoma might be undertaken primarily in order to observe and judge the Ghost Dance, yet it also brought individuals in contact with peyotism. Many of the curious found no great conflict between the two religions, experimenting with both at the same time. It is characteristic of Indians not to reject necessarily something old in order to accept something new. Thus it was possible for peyotists like Caddo John Wilson and Pawnee Frank White to become Ghost Dance leaders for a time and to remain peyote leaders after the Ghost Dance movement had ended. Arapaho Sitting Bull, the very Ghost Dance leader who brought the Ghost Dance to Oklahoma, became a peyote leader.

But soon the excitement was over. Wovoka was largely forgotten. Though he lived for a long time, maintaining to the last his prophetic role, he was no longer important. In Oklahoma, it had been a few years of heightened religious fervor that had helped to spread the new religion of peyotism as well as the Ghost Dance.

CHAPTER 4

The Kiowa-Comanche Agency, Locus of Peyotism and the Two Ceremonies

In the treaty of 1867, the U.S. government set aside a large tract of land in southwestern Oklahoma for the Kiowa, Kiowa-Apache, and Comanche Indians, some of the tribes that had been most difficult to subdue. The reservation had good grassland, suitable for farming but particularly adaptable to grazing. It was centered about the evergreen-forested Wichita Mountains, which rise to a height of twenty-four hundred feet. Fort Sill was on this reservation. A smaller tract, contiguous with the first on the northeast along the Washita River, was reserved for the Caddo, the Wichita, and a group of Delaware, three tribes which for some time had been associated in Texas. They had shared the experience of the ill-fated reservation on the Brazos River and then had moved or been moved as one group. After 1878 these two groups of tribes were administered by the government as one agency, called the Kiowa-Comanche Agency because of the larger numbers of those two tribes. Headquarters were at Anadarko, near the Caddo tract. In 1890, the population figures show 1,590 Comanche, 1,140 Kiowa and Kiowa-Apache, 538 Caddo, 381 Wichita, and 95 Delaware. It was at this agency that the peyote ceremony first found wide acceptance.

In 1880, with the availability of peyote and the new stability of life on the reservation, peyotism spread rapidly. It spread in the natural course of daily life. Someone who had learned the ceremony was asked to conduct a meeting, probably for a reason such as an illness, and people came. Frequently, a person from another tribe or reservation attended such a meeting and stayed to learn how to be a roadman himself and how to get peyote for a meeting, and then returned home to teach the methods to his people. Generally, the person who wished to become a roadman was already distinguished as a medicine man. Often he was a tribal leader or chief who had attended one of the schools or the prisoner-of-war camp, who understood English and something about white culture and religion, or who was otherwise outstanding. Most of these leaders were members of a Christian mission and sometimes were active participants. Later, many were active, also, in the Ghost Dance. Few found conflict in participating in shamanistic curing practices, ancient Indian ceremonials such as the Sun Dance, peyotism, and Christian Sunday schools.

As peyotism developed, some roadmen devoted themselves exclusively to it, becoming avowed missionaries. There could be many rewards to a missionary life. There was, of course, the feeling of being important and of doing good. Also, there was economic opportunity. Throughout the Plains culture, payment was the rule for shamanistic services or instruction in ritual, so it was assumed that some sort of payment would be given to a roadman who gave a meeting or instructed another in the ceremony. There was not a set fee, and payment was always viewed as a gift. There is an "article of faith," an idealism, in the peyote religion that roughly says that since peyote is a divine plant, it should not be corrupted by commercialism, but should be distributed freely, as an act of religious charity or as a sacred duty, to anyone who desires to use it as a sacred medicine. Therefore, a price was not put upon it. It was freely given by the host or leader of a meeting. However, it was appropriate, and even expected, that one would give a present to the host or roadman in appreciation of his kindness; and presents were made to roadmen of money, jewelry, ponies, blankets, and the like. A talented missionary could profit well. Still, he should not be ostentatious about his wealth or seem avaricious or he might receive criticism.

In the 1880s on the Kiowa-Comanche reservations there came to be two peyote roadmen of great importance whose influence on the peyote religion extends to the present day. One was the Comanche chief Quanah Parker; the other was a Caddo-Delaware medicine man named John Wilson.

THE COMANCHE

Although Quanah Parker was by far the most important Comanche roadman in the early history of peyotism, he was not the first or the only peyote leader. The Comanche had known of peyote for many years from their raids into Texas and Mexico. They had learned to use peyote in shamanistic rites and had had instruction in the peyote ceremony from such Lipans as Pinero and Chiwat. The first documentation of Comanche peyotism is found in the letter from agency farmer E. L. Clark to E. E. White in June, 1888, which named Old Man Paddy Qull and Sit-chees-toque (Chew-wow-wah) as Comanche peyote leaders. Of Old Man Paddy Qull, he wrote:

This Old Man Paddy Qull never has attempted to work. He is a big fat fellow about 50 years of age. He calls himself a medicine man and makes all the weak-minded Indians believe it. He has two young men and a boy 15 years-old in his family and not a stroke of work going on. His whole attention is directed toward the [peyote] button, calling a party of young men numbering from eight to fifteen together for that purpose as often as twice or three times a week.

He referred to Sit-chees-toque as "a Mexican . . . captive of the Comanche" who had lived for years with the Apache in New Mexico, but had returned and established himself among the Comanche as a peyote supplier and was becoming wealthy. Possibly, this is Chiwat, the Lipan Apache who brought peyote to Oklahoma during the perilous seventies.

La Barre (1938: 112) called Buiwat the first Comanche user of peyote, saying Buiwat said he had learned it from the Mescalero, and La Barre named Desode and Tasipa as early leaders. Wallace and Hoebel (1952: 335) said that Charcoal (Kuaheta) was the first Comanche roadman, 1860–70, and that the Comanche Mumshukawa said he had been given the first Chief Peyote used in the first Comanche peyote meeting and that it had been presented to him by Charcoal as a gift for serving as fire tender. A "chief peyote" is an unusually large peyote "button" that is placed on the center of the half-moon altar to serve as a focus for worshipers during the peyote ceremony. Chief peyotes are often cherished and reused many times or presented as valuable fetishs to friends or students of the ritual.

Comanche Jack was also said to have tended fire for Charcoal, to have been a subchief to Quanah Parker, and to have been the first to use the name of Jesus in peyote meetings.

But Quanah Parker was the most important peyotist among the Comanches, and possibly the most important early peyotist on the entire Kiowa-Comanche reservation. He was leader of a large tribe with an extensive reservation which Texas cattlemen were eager to use for a small fee. He was an integrationist; he believed Indians and whites should live and work together. He introduced peyote into his tribe, protected its use from those who would have banned it, and missionized in its favor, all the while continuing to be a friend and collaborator with white Christian missionaries and businessmen. He was characterized by personal ambition and motivation to leadership; desire for wealth and power; friendliness toward Christian missionaries and openness to their ideals and moral teachings; eagerness to learn English and American cultural patterns; and willingness to adjust to legal requirements. Yet he was anxious to protect personally selected Indian customs and values and skillful in making friends among both whites and Indians and was able to call on friends for guidance, support, and aid. His great contribution to the spread of peyotism was threefold: First, through his position as chief of the Comanches and as a man of substance and leadership, he was able to influence and attract others to his form of belief. Second, through tact and diplomacy he was able to protect the use of peyote for the Indians when great effort was being made to stamp out its use, and he was ready to stand outright for its use when dissembling and agreeableness did not prevail. And finally, he was the apostle of the Half Moon peyote ceremony and stood for this version of peyotism against the innovations of others.

Much has been written about Quanah Parker, so it is possible to have a detailed picture of his life and personality. According to a footnote by Robert M. Utley, editor of Major Pratt's memoirs (Pratt 1964: 84), one Cynthia Ann Parker was twelve years old when she was captured by Indians in Texas in 1835. She became the wife of a Comanche chief and gave birth to Quanah in 1845. Quanah was fifteen when his father was killed and

FIG. 4. Quanah Parker, Comanche leader, about 1908. Fort Sill Museum, Fort Sill, Oklahoma, #P3248. Original photograph owned by Quanah's son, Tom Parker.

his mother recaptured (Jackson and Jackson 1963: 42–43). Quanah apparently remained with the Comanches, but it is not inconceivable that Cynthia Ann Parker had taught her son some of the religious ideas she herself had been taught as a child.

As a young warrior, Quanah refused to abide by the Treaty of Medicine Lodge of 1867 and led Kwahadi Comanche raids into Texas when other

Comanches had agreed to settle on the reservation, but when he finally saw the handwriting on the wall and that he must capitulate to white military might, he did so in a spirit of full cooperation. He told Mooney (1898*b*: 203), who called him "the present noted head chief of the Comanche," that he had had seven hundred warriors in the fight "at Adobe Walls in June, 1874," and that "the (unfavorable) result convinced him of the falsity of the claims of the medicine men, against whom he has ever since used his powerful influence in his tribe."

He became a close friend of white Americans of all types as soon as he was settled on the reservation in June, 1875. The reason may lie in his interest in his ancestry (Jackson and Jackson 1963: 157): "Quanah immediately began to search for someone who knew about his mother. Upon hearing the true story, he immediately changed his name to Quanah Parker in memory of his white mother."

Further family ties brought him additional contact with peyote: "He soon decided to visit his mother's brother, John Parker, in Chihuahua, Mexico. . . . A Spanish bull attacked him and left him with the largest wound he ever suffered. A burning fever of blood poisoning set in and the Indians gave Quanah 'woqui,' which was a strong drink made from boiled green cactus (peyote juice)." There is some resemblance between this account and one reported by La Barre (1938: 85): "Quanah Parker, the great Comanche proselytizer of peyote, at first opposed to it, was cured of a stomach ailment in 1885 and became one of the most enthusiastic proponents of the herb." Regardless of the exact circumstances, about that time Quanah became involved with peyote.

Regarding Quanah's attitude toward Christian religion, Jackson and Jackson (1963: 152–56) wrote: "he was not blind to the good points of Christianity, but he was never convinced that monogamy was one of them. Mrs. Lee Hall, wife of Captain Hall, the Indian agent at Fort Sill (1885–86), told Quanah about his grandfather Elder Parker's religion. Quanah listened very attentively and then asked what he must do to embrace it. She told him that he must give up all of his wives but one. Quanah argued back that Hall should take another wife, and added, 'In that case, I keep my religion.'"

Pratt (1964: 98–99) recorded a similar story:

When the tribes finally settled down and accepted the situation, Quanah became quite a cattle baron among them and was most powerful with his people in favoring the cattle interests of the Southwest by arranging consent of the Indians for the leasing of large sections of their reservations to cattlemen for grazing. He lived in a large frame house built for him on his allotment by the cattlemen. . . . In his later years he often visited Washington on tribal business. . . . He had three wives but on these trips took with him his youngest, who was, like Quanah, an attractive personality. During this time the Government was trying to end the Indian custom of plurality of wives, and the Secretary of the Interior urged Quanah to conform to the rules. Quanah asked how he was to proceed. The Secretary told him to select the wife he wanted to keep and provide for the others as best he could, and then tell them that they were no longer his wives. Quanah said, "Mr. Secretary, you tell them."

Quanah favored education and early sent his children to the Carlisle school. He had three daughters and a son by his Indian wives. I was at the Comanche agency (1879) with Mrs. Pratt, making up a party of pupils for Carlisle, and Quanah gave me all four of his children. . . . Quanah insisted that his children should go in the sleeper, for which he would pay.

Education and friendly relations with Christians went hand in hand for Quanah (Jackson and Jackson 1963: 154–56:

Quanah had the greatest respect and appreciation for the religious bodies that endeavored to teach and train the Comanche children. Among them was Rev. J. J. Methvin, who organized the Methvin Institute two miles south of the agency headquarters. This Methodist school had a meager beginning with only fifteen students enrolled in 1890. The second year the attendance was doubled and soon after there were seventy-five pupils enrolled. Quanah had a deep feeling for this school because of his confidence and love for Rev. Methvin. He could see the great need for this type of instruction for the young Comanches, for he felt it would not only train them in the arts but would teach them how to live under their difficult circumstances on the reservation. . . .

The two branches of the Presbyterian church were among the first to enter into a contract with the government to make religious education available for all Indian children. It agreed to pay a certain amount of tuition on a monthly basis from year to year so long as the government felt it was a blessing to the reservation. The Northern Presbyterian Church established the first mission school under this cooperative movement. Joshua Givens, a converted Kiowa, the son of Satanta, had been educated in the East with the help of this church. He returned to the reservation in 1889 to join with Rev. S. V. Faith, missionary of the Northern Church body. In the same year, this group began operating the Mary Gregory Memorial School of Religious Education. It was located south of the Washita River, four miles from the Indian agency. It grew in one year from 50 pupils to one hundred.

The Reformed Presbyterian Church sent W. W. Carrithers in 1889 to procure a tract of land for a mission school. He opened the Cache Mission School of Religious Education the same year. It was located on Cache Creek, twenty-five miles from the agency near the Kiowa-Apache village. Rev. Carrithers gained the confidence and respect of both the Indian parents and the pupils. Quanah was a great friend of Carrithers and held him very highly in his appreciation. The School of Religious Educaton had the facilities for only fifty pupils but usually ran over its capacity each year. . . .

Quanah was always ready to tell the people everywhere how proud he was of his missionaries. Although he never made an open profession of Christianity, he realized its value and had the deepest respect for those who embraced it.

In addition to the Methodist and Presbyterian schools, the Catholic church and the Reformed Church of America also had mission schools on the Comanche reservation.

The Ghost Dance made little headway among the Comanche, mostly because of Quanah's opposition to it. Mooney wrote (1896a: 901–902):

The messiah doctrine never gained many converts among the Comanche, excepting those of the Penataka division and a few others living on the Little Washita and other streams on the northern boundary of the reservation, adjoining the tribes most interested in the Ghost Dance. These Comanches held a few Ghost Dances and made a few songs, but the body of the tribe would have nothing to do with it. This lack of interest was due partly to the general skeptical temperament of the Comanche, evinced by their carelessness in regard to ceremonial forms, and partly to their tribal pride which forbade their following after the strange gods of another people, as they considered their own mescal [peyote] rite sufficient to their needs. Quanah Parker, their head chief, a shrewd half-breed, opposed the new doctrine and prevented its spread among his tribe.

Quanah enjoyed considerable success in business, mostly based on the leasing of tribal grasslands to cattlemen. For his aid to large Texas cattle ranchers, Quanah received both cash and gifts. At the time of his death in 1911, he owned forty thousand dollars' worth of stock in the Quanah, Acme, and Pacific Railway (Jackson and Jackson 1963: 141). The Kiowa maintained a picture calendar of paintings on skins of specific events of importance, and Quanah's business pursuits were described in three entries. According to Mayhall (1962: 176–80), these are:

Winter, 1882–83: Quanah Parker . . . persuaded the allied tribes to lease their grassland to the cattlemen. . . . Summer, 1890: A Sun Dance started . . . Quanah Parker sent word to Stumbling Bear to advise the Kiowa to stop the dance or the soldiers would kill them and their horses. . . . they dispersed. Summer, 1892: Grass money was received during the summer. . . . Quanah, Lone Wolf, and White man were chosen to represent the Comanche, Kiowa, and Kiowa-Apache respectively. Permissions were granted and leases were made producing for the three tribes about $100,000 a year. . . . sixty homes were built that year.

Nor, according to Mooney (1896b: 9–10), did Quanah's peyote use impair his ability to do business:

As to the mental effect of the habitual use of the plant, it may be sufficient to say that the great high priest of the rite among the Comanche is Zuanah [Quanah], the half-breed chief of the tribe, and any who have known him at home or in Washington will admit that there is no more shrewd or capable businessmen in the Southwest. On one occasion I was with him when he sat up all night leading the ceremony, eating perhaps thirty mescal [peyote buttons]. Coming out in the morning he found two cattlemen awaiting him on important business, which occupied him and his white secretary all that afternoon. Next day he was up before daylight ready for an early breakfast before starting for

Texas to conclude the deal. This after eating a large quantity of the cactus and losing a night's sleep; and Zuanah is entirely too smart a man to attend to business when his brain is not in working order.

It was in dealing with the opposition that Parker's tact and ability to get along with and persuade others was most useful. When the Indian agents and missionaries became aware of peyote, they quite naturally sought to suppress it. In 1888 an order was posted on the Kiowa-Comanche reservation prohibiting the use of peyote. Special Agent E. E. White, who was responsible for the order, wrote to the Commission of Indian Affairs: "At first the Comanches declaimed that they would rather die than give up the use of [peyote]. . . . They said plural wives and . . . [peyote] were two things they would not give up," but "yesterday Quanah Parker, the Principal Chief of the Comanche, was in the office and saw for himself and delivered a message to me from the other Chiefs and headmen that they had concluded that I had taken the step solely for their own good and they had almost entirely quit using [peyote]." However, in less than two months White reported an agreement he had reached with the Comanche that he "would permit them to eat their [peyote] one night at each full moon for three or four months . . . and that they would not eat any at any other time. They also agreed that when their present supply of . . . [peyote] gave out they would quit entirely" (White 1888d: 95). Through diplomacy, he had received permission to continue his religion. A soft word and friendly approach had succeeded in changing an absolute prohibition against the use of peyote to a general permission which might easily be extended indefinitely.

Fruitless efforts to control the use of peyote continued for a number of years. Those who would ban it needed legislation.

Whenever he could, Parker fought opposition to peyote with behind-the-scenes diplomacy, with dissembling, and with pretending to go along while in reality encouraging its use. But he fought in the open, too. When it was proposed to add "peyote" to the law against "mescal" in the territorial legislature, he and others were organized. He was asked to testify along with other chiefs who came with a large delegation of Indian leaders, all anxious to speak against the proposed prohibition of the use of peyote. He was received with honor and respect, and his words were well chosen and convincing. When the law came to a vote, the legislature accepted Quanah's plea: "I do not think this Legislature should interfere with a man's religion; also, these people should be allowed to retain this health restorer. . . . I do think peyote has helped Indians to quit drinking." The legislature did not prohibit the use of peyote, even after the courts had ruled that "mescal" was a misnomer and was not used in the peyote religion.

The opposition was aware of the strength of Quanah Parker. Special Agent Johnson, who led the fight against peyote at that time, wrote the commissioner of Indian affairs: "The first difficulty in the way will be Quanah Parker who is exceedingly potent in democratic councils down in that country. Quanah defeated our attempt to get the provision in the Constitution."

And again: "We would have had trouble on our hands even if the bill had come up for action, for the reason that the Indians, under the leadership of Quanah Parker, were preparing to fight the measure. Inasmuch as the Indians have votes, the legislators would be prone to listen attentively."

Not able to get legislation to outlaw peyote as a drug, the opposition to peyote sought to ban its importation and sale, claiming legality under the law prohibiting the selling of intoxicating spirits to Indians. Special Agent Johnson bought the entire crop of peyote at its source in Texas and burned it, and he prohibited all merchants from selling peyote to Indians. However, within a year Quanah had sent Kickapoo Henry Murdock and Comanche medicine man Marcus Poco to Mexico to obtain peyote, and they were reported to be bringing dried peyote buttons by the trunkful through customs at Eagle Pass. Quanah was using his political influence, lulling certain officials with soothing promises and using intimidation where it might prove most effective. Johnson wrote to the Bureau of Indian Affairs:

It appears that Quanah Parker, under cover of an intimation that the Office had no objection to his getting a little peyote for his own use, sent a representative to Mexico and brought in 8,000 peyotes. . . .

In order to give the old Indians an opportunity to taper off, I have instructed my officer at Eagle Pass to permit Indians to bring in as baggage, not to exceed 500 peyotes. . . . In return for this concession, Congressman Ferris undertakes to dissuade Quanah Parker and his friends from the traffic. . . .

Agent C. C. Brannon, involved with stopping peyote, wrote: "I also learn that Quanah Parker furnished peyote for Indians all through this section and that he tells the Indians that he has a right to get them and that pretty soon he will go into Mexico and bring them back for his people." And again Officer C. C. Brannon wrote: "Quanah Parker, who is the chief grand chief of all the Indians of Oklahoma, and this is true, they all believe in him [when he] tells them that Valentine the Commissioner gave him the right to go to Mexico or [to have] his Indians to go and get all the peyote they wanted . . ." (Brannon to Russell, February 17, 1910). Finally, Special Agent Johnson wrote to Hon. Scott Ferris, U.S. congressman from Oklahoma, on February 21, 1910: "I am somewhat impatient with Quanah Parker. We tried to fix it so they could get in a little for their own use but Parker deliberately sends a man down there and brings in 8,000 peyotes."

Not only was Quanah Parker outstanding as a leader of men and a defender of peyote, but he was also the apostle of a certain kind of peyote ceremony. The ceremony that Quanah Parker conducted as roadman had been taught to him by the Lipan-Apaches Chiwat and Pinero, and it was this ceremony that was taught to the Kiowa and that was described by Mooney in chapter 2. This version of the peyote ceremony was considered the old way, the most traditional way, and was called the Half Moon ceremony, taking its name from the shape of the altar whereon rested the Chief

Peyote. An individual learned to be a roadman by having been taught by another roadman, and by attending meetings and observing how it was done. He needed to have experiences and emotions that impelled him to believe that he, too, could serve in such a capacity. And, finally, someone had to request that he lead a meeting.

If these things happened and a man was asked to give a meeting, he could ask others to assist him, but he himself was expected to run the meeting as he saw fit, adding this or changing that. By the time the peyote ceremony came to Oklahoma, its general pattern was well established, and a roadman would not be able to change that pattern, but he could vary it in the context of the established pattern. So there were differences in the arrangement of the altar, new songs, the amount of sagebrush for seating, whether to admit women or not, the use of tobacco in the ritual, the presence of the Bible, emphasis on Indian legends, and so forth. During his lifetime and after his death, many peyotists referred to the Half Moon ceremony as the Quanah Parker Way. It has also been called the Comanche way or the Kiowa way. It was characterized by the half-moon-shaped altar, emphasis on Indian legends in prayers, the use of tobacco, and sagebrush all around the tipi for participants to sit on. A description of Quanah Parker as roadman is found in an account by a white peyotist and employee of Parker, who described a meeting held in Parker's house. C. S. Simmons, in a manuscript entitled "The Peyote Road" (1913), wrote:

One of the best meetings that I ever attended was at the home of Quanah Parker about four years ago [i.e., 1909]. The surroundings were noticeably clean and pleasant, the participants earnest and well-behaved, and the spirit of harmony pervaded all. At about three o'clock in the morning, the "silent hour" and the time of the greatest manifestation of power, Quanah, the leader, knelt before the altar and prayed earnestly. Then, taking the eagle feathers in both hands, he arose to his feet. I saw at once he was under great inspiration. His whole personality seemed to change. His eyes glowed with a strong light and his body swayed to and fro, vibrating with some powerful emotion. He sang the beautiful song "Ya-na-ah-away" (the eagle's flight to the sun), in a most grand and inspiring manner. Then all sang together in harmony. They prayed to God and to Jesus, and sang of a "narrow way." [Ch. 8, p. 3]

There is no documentation of the financial reward that Quanah received for his involvement in peyotism, but it could have been considerable. Quanah was an astute businessman, and it is not unreasonable for us to think of him to some degree as investing capital in a risk venture when he sent his agents to Mexico to obtain peyote. Without the full details of the commercial arrangements which were made secretly, one cannot fully appreciate the special privilege Quanah had set up for himself, but it appears that there may have been a near monopoly in the peyote business in his hands, at least for a few years.

Petrullo (1934: 129–30) reports his death in a way that leads us to conclude that he received remuneration for his services and that receiving large fees for bestowing "medicine" was not wholly without sin. Petrullo writes:

A young man was taken very sick. He was of a different tribe, which was very poor. Having heard of the great healing power of Parker, they sent a messenger to interview him and to see what it would cost to have this great doctor treat the sick man. Parker informed the messenger that it would cost the tribe $225.00 to cure the man. This created great consternation, because the Indians are well aware of the fact that any man who is possessed of power to heal through the gift of the Great Spirit will have his power taken away from him if he charges a fee for his services.

As a consequence of his disregard of this rule, Parker lost his life. Although the young man's relatives and parents had been able to raise only $75.00, the chief accepted this and agreed to give three meetings for the boy. Each meeting proved to be effective and the young man improved. He fully recovered from his illness, and his tribe was so well pleased with this that they agreed to pay the rest of the money as soon as they could get it.

Unfortunately, the old chief fell ill himself. He called the best leaders of the tribe and they held a series of meetings. Finally, he was told that his case was hopeless. Before dying, he said, "I have made a great mistake to demand a fee for helping the meek and poor. For this I must pay the price by giving up my own life."

There is another account of the death of Quanah. Jackson and Jackson (1963: 164–65) wrote:

Quanah had been invited to the Cheyenne's medicine feast. On February 11, 1911, word was sent by telephone that the great chief had taken sick . . . and was returning by train to his home. Arriving at Cache, he was taken to his ranch, four miles distant. . . . Taupay, one of his wives, asked him if he had any objection to a white man's doctor, to which he replied, "No, it's good. I am ready." [By the best estimate of Mooney (1918a: 145) he would have been between seventy-two and seventy-five years old.]

The Indian women seemed to know that death was near and they motioned the white doctor away. As a last resort they had one of the Indian medicine men minister to him. The chief asked the medicine man to pray to God, and he began, "Father in heaven, this, our brother is coming." Then, placing his arms about the chief's body, he flapped his hands and imitated the call of the great eagle, the messenger of the Great Father. . . .

His death attracted some two hundred whites and Indians from all over the United States. Indian representatives from almost every tribe in the country came to pay their last tribute to the Comanche chief. There were politicians, ranchers, financiers, and religious groups from far and near. . . . It was believed by doctors and others that Quanah had succumbed to an attack of asthmatic rheumatism. . . . Rev. A. J. Becker, who had charge of the funeral, read Psalm 90. Rev. Deyo led the congregation in a touching prayer. . . . Rev. Becker, a close friend of Quanah's, delivered the message. . . . The American government placed a red granite monument over Quanah's grave as an appreciation of the great chief.

In 1918, at a congressional hearing on a bill to ban peyote, the oldest daughter of Quanah Parker, who had been married to a white cattle rancher for thirty-five years and did not share her father's beliefs, testified that it was addiction to peyote that led to her father's death. James Mooney, who also testified at this hearing, pointed out that Quanah had been a warrior for many years and that in living to the age of approximately seventy-five years he had surpassed U.S. Generals Ulysses S. Grant, Philip Sheridan, William T. Sherman, and others.

Quanah's influence beyond his own tribe included the Delaware and Caddo (Petrullo 1934), the Kansas Potawatomi (Howard 1962b: 170), and the Cheyenne, Arapaho, Ponca, Oto, Pawnee, Osage, and others (La Barre 1938: 113). But it is difficult really to evaluate the influence of Quanah Parker because, like other important people whose lives have touched intimately the lives of many others, he has become something of a legend among his people and among peyotists.

Although Parker outshines his Comanche contemporaries, a few others, particularly Marcus Poco, his henchman, especially in fighting the ban of peyote at the Texas-Mexico border, are worthy of note. Another was Otto Wells, who accompanied Parker to the territorial legislative hearings in defense of the right to use peyote. Two more early leaders were Jim Tinaquah, whose "father brought peyote from Mexico," and Jim Pebo, a "peyote leader for about 50 years" (Slotkin's notes in possession of O. C. Stewart).

THE KIOWA

We must assume that the Kiowa learned about peyote and began to use it in ritual concurrently with the Comanche. Notwithstanding the sharp and complete linguistic separation of the Kiowa from the Comanche, their confederation after about 1790 and their decades of raiding together in Texas and Mexico united and integrated them. However, it must be stated that most authors have nevertheless separated these tribes in the chronology of peyote and usually they attributed first knowledge of the peyote ritual to the Kiowa. Rouhier, Wissler, Cline, Havard, La Barre, and Mooney have all done so. I believe that it is impossible to divide clearly the Kiowa, the Kiowa-Apache, and the Comanche into tribal groups reacting to the peyote religion.

The Kiowa were familiar with peyote before they settled on their reservation. Havard (1896: 39) wrote: "The Kiowa Indians were formerly much addicted to the use of this plant [peyote] in their religious ceremonies when dwelling on the Rio Grande. . . ." In summarizing the early history of Kiowa peyotism, La Barre (1938: 111) wrote: "Most Kiowa agree that they got peyote and the accompanying ritual from the Mescalero Apache." Cline

(1904:5–7, 28–29) reported: "The Kiowa adopted the custom [peyote ceremony] from the Apaches about fifty years since [1854]."

Perhaps the earliest recorded leader of the Kiowa ceremony may have been Satanta (White Bear), a Kiowa warrior who spent much of the seventies in prison, where he finally committed suicide (Howard 1967). It is assumed by Howard that Satanta was a peyotist. His companion in war and part of his imprisonment was Big Tree, who did become a peyote leader.

Like Parker, Kiowa peyote leaders were often men who were willing to adjust to new cultural patterns and were ambitious for both honor and wealth. Many accepted the opportunity to learn both English and Christianity and showed ability to syncretize Indian and white religious patterns. One of these men was Apiaton (Wooden Lance). Mooney (1896a:908, 912) wrote of him:

About this time [summer 1890] a Sioux chief High Wolf, came down from the north to visit the tribes in that section. He remained some time among them, and on his return to the north invited a young Kiowa, Apiaton, "Wooden Lance," whose grandmother had been a Sioux captive, to come up and visit his relatives at Pine Ridge. The invitation was accepted by Apiaton, partly for the pleasure of seeing a new tribe and meeting his mother's kindred, but chiefly for the purpose of investigating for himself and for the Kiowa the truth of the messiah story (the Ghost Dance]. Apiaton, who speaks but little English, and who was then about 30 years of age, had recently lost a child to whom he had been very much attached. He brooded over his loss until the new doctrine came with its promise of a reunion with departed friends and its possibility of seeing and talking with them in visions of the trance. . . . He determined [to go] on this long journey in search of the messiah. . . . the Chiefs . . . decided to send him as a delegate.

In October, 1890, "Apiaton went first to Pine Ridge, where he was well received by the Sioux . . . hurried on to Fort Washakie, where he met northern Arapaho and the Shoshoni." After a short visit with Wovoka in Mason Valley, Nevada, Apiaton, "Saddened and disgusted," returned home to report "the utter falsity of the pretension of the messiah." Mooney did not identify Apiaton as a peyotist, but in 1902 and later he was often identified with other peyote leaders and was called a director of the peyote religion. Whether he was an earlier leader of peyotism we do not know, but peyotism may have been a reason why he rejected the Ghost Dance, as was the case with Quanah Parker.

The Methodist minister, Rev. J. J. Methvin (1931:535) wrote:

An interesting chapter in the history of the Kiowa tribe clusters around the life of Ahpiatone, the late Kiowa chief. . . . he was born back in 1856. . . . after the capture [1866] of "Andele" (Andres Martinez), he and "Andele" grew up together in the same environment and were constant and lasting friends.

And such was his confidence in Martinez that he called for him during the past few months to hold prayer services at his home, he being unable to get out to church. . . .

Such was his influence among his tribe, that it could not be broken by any opposition brought against him, and both Indians and white people had confidence in his ability and integrity, and together with Quanah Parker he was always called upon to represent affairs in Washington.

In 1907, writing of Apiaton, Natalie Curtis (1907: 222–23) said: "As . . . [peyote] leader, Apiaton receives a loyalty from his people that is second only to their faith in his judgment and his ability to guard their welfare."

Agency officials, too, appreciated the ability of Apiaton, for they made him a judge of the Court of Indian Offenses. However, again paralleling Parker's case, he was dismissed for polygamy.

Another early peyotist of distinction among the Kiowa was Lone Wolf, so identified by Francis E. Leupp in 1903 in a special investigation of Kiowa financial dealings. Mooney said of him (1898b: 233): "The present officially recognized head chief is Lone-wolf, the adopted son of the hostile leader of the same name in the last outbreak. The elder Lone-wolf formally bestowed the name upon the younger man in 1879, thus publicly recognizing him as his successor."

Still another Kiowa leader was Setkopte. Because of ill health, Setkopte probably was never a roadman, but his experience and activity and support of peyotism were extraordinary. He appears several times in Mooney's monograph "Calendar History of the Kiowa" (1898b). First, he serves as an example of "Method of Fixing Dates [1898b: 147]:" "Paul Setkopte first saw light among the Cheyenne the winter after the 'showery medicine dance' (1853), and joined the Kiowa in the autumn after the 'smallpox medicine dance' (1862)." Setkopte had been a warrior in the "outbreak of 1874, and became a prisoner of war in 1875." Mooney wrote (1898b: 216):

The prisoners while in Florida were merely kept under surveillance and were not subjected to close confinement. Philanthropic white people took an interest in them . . . and undertook to give them rudimentary instruction in civilization and Christianity. When they were finally released in May, 1878, a number of the young men consented to remain a few years longer. . . .

Several of the young Kiowa were received in refined and philanthropic families in the north, with the purpose of educating them to be missionaries among their people on their return. . . . Paul Setkopte after . . . careful training in a refined family . . . returned . . . [and] later nearly died from consumption contracted in the east.

Also, in an article in the *Therapeutic Gazette* (1896b: 9) Mooney tells how Setkopte became a peyotist:

He had . . . contracted consumption in Florida, and during the whole of his four years in New York he was stretched upon a sick-bed, racked with a cough and frequent hemorrhages, until at last, as there seemed no chance for life, he was sent back . . . to die among his own people. He arrived completely prostrated, and being strongly urged by his Indian friends, he ate a few . . . [peyote] with such speedy relief from the cough that he continued the practice. That was thirteen years ago, and he is still alive and in fairly good health. . . . He is a leader in the ceremony, and defends it in eloquent English, because, as he says, the . . . [peyote] keeps him alive. . . .

On one occasion, when I was present alone in a camp where they were preparing to eat . . . [peyote] that night, he rode in late in the evening, through a cold drizzling rain, and told me that he had been eating . . . [peyote] the previous night at a camp about twenty miles away, and hearing that they were going to eat in our camp that night and that I had no interpreter with me, he had come to stay with me and explain the ceremony. . . . On hearing the signal, about 11 o'clock at night he came into the tipi and bent over the fire to warm himself, when he was seized with such a fit of coughing that it seemed as if his lungs would be torn to pieces. . . . He then took and ate four . . . [peyote buttons], stepped to his place, and when it was his turn then and throughout the night sang his song like the others, and came out as fresh as they in the morning. . . . There was no coughing after the first four [peyote].

Jim Aton was another early Kiowa peyotist and shaman. He claimed (La Barre 1938:52) to have "doctored in peyote meetings of the Yuchi, Shawnee, Kickapoo, Creek, Caddo, Osage, Comanche, Kiowa Apache, Kiowa, Mescalero Apache and Quapaw; also whites and Mexicans." Belo Kozad was an early peyotist who had attended Carlisle from October, 1889, to September, 1890. A letter to Congressman J. V. McClintic, inserted in the *Congressional Record* of January 6, 1923 (p. 1383), described him: "It might be that Belo . . . could furnish evidence of the healing qualities of peyote; he is an educated Indian of more than average intelligence and has studied and used peyote for 30 years; he is the leading doctor in this locality." James Waldo had long experience in Carlisle, from September, 1888, to June, 1894. Sometime before 1902 he became a peyotist, and in his testimony before the Oklahoma territorial senate in January, 1908, he declared peyotism to be "worship of the Lord" and said that peyote reminded him of "Lord Jesus." Still another early Kiowa peyotist was Delos Lonewolf, who was at Carlisle from July, 1892, to March, 1896. He was officially recognized as tribal chief for many years and as a peyotist although, according to La Barre (1938:102): "Delos Lonewolf (Kiowa) quit peyote and became a preacher again. . . ." La Barre (1960:55) quotes Lonewolf's widow as saying that "sometimes in the old days, toward morning, if a man had great reverence, he might dance in a peyote meeting."

Finally, an important early Kiowa peyotist was a man named I-See-O. His story is told in an article entitled "I-See-O, 'Stone-Age Product' Bridged White, Indian 'Gap,'" by Jan Jacobs in the *Lawton Constitution Morning Press,* January 5, 1969. I-See-O had served as a scout under the name Tahbone-mah from the time the Kiowa settled down near Fort Sill about 1874, but in 1891, in order to enlist in Troop L, he changed his age from forty-two to twenty-nine and took the name I-See-O. He was selected by Lt. H. L. Scott to serve as horse wrangler, guide, helper, and informant on Scott's assignment to learn everything possible about the Ghost Dance religion.

In 1915, having been discharged from the army scout troop because of old age, I-See-O again met Scott, then a major general and chief of staff of the army, who arranged for him to have a lifetime enlistment as senior duty sergeant in the army. In the unique request to the secretary of war, General Scott said:

It has long been the custom of the white man to employ a native against his own people, then when the war or other trouble is over, to cast him aside like a sucked lemon, with the rankest ingratitude. Look at this old Kiowa. He is down and out—broken in the service of the United States. There is no more work in him, the Army cannot use him. Yet there are Indians and whites alive today who would not be alive were it not for the fidelity of I-See-O.

With the help of his Indian Scout, Lieutenant Scott had observed and understood the Ghost Dance in Oklahoma and had convinced the army to allow it to run its course peacefully to avoid bloodshed.

An old Kiowa peyotist, James Auchiah, told me in 1972 that I-See-O was known as a peyotist before 1890. It is thus probable that I-See-O was a peyotist before and during the Ghost Dance as well as after. In 1923 he was honored when the commanding general of Fort Sill, Maj. Gen. Ernest Hinds, with M. Sgt. Morris Swett and Capt. A. R. Ginsburgh, attended a peyote meeting in his tipi at Fort Sill. Chief Delos K. Lonewolf was interpreter; Hunting Horse, age 77, was roadman. James Auchiah was also present and showed me a newspaper clipping with photographs verifying this remarkable event. I-See-O was buried with full military honors upon his death in 1927. The roadman of I-See-O's famous peyote meeting, Hunting Horse, who also had been a scout for the army, was also buried in the post cemetery with honors when he died in 1953 at the age of 107 (Corwin 1958: 43).

THE KIOWA-APACHE

Although the Kiowa-Apache Indians spoke an Athapascan language which related them to the Navajo and other Apache tribes of the southwest, they were never identified politically with other Apache, but rather were identified with the Kiowa, whose customs and characteristics were similar and with whom they had long been associated. At the time of the gathering of the tribes in Oklahoma, the Comanche, Kiowa, and Kiowa-Apache were closely associated and therefore located together on the reservation.

Concerning the early spread of peyote to the Kiowa-Apache, we have Kenneth Beals (1967: 15, 17, 20):

Although the prototype of the peyote ritual came to the Kiowa-Apache about 1875 or 1880, some informants believed that tribal knowledge of the plant preceded this. One peyote chief claims that the Kiowa-Apache had, on occasion, obtained the cactus from the Tonkawa and used it as a medicine and as a part of shamanism prior to 1875, and perhaps prior to the time of reservationism in 1868. . . .

The use of peyote as a focus of a religion is said to have originated with a visit of Dayugal, who was either Mescalero or Lipan. Informants say that this person demonstrated "the right way to use peyote" to at least four prominent Kiowa-Apache men. These four men—Saddle Blanket, Old Man Architah, Daveko and Apache John—became the first four peyote chiefs of the tribe. . . . The four chiefs were divided, with the shaman Daveko representing the conservative faction; and the remaining chiefs, particularly Old Man Architah, being responsible for the elimination of shamanism and the incorporation of God and Jesus into the cult. . . .

Of the four, Daveko was most famous. Born in 1818, he had gained fame as a medicine man long before peyotism became a force in Oklahoma in 1880, and he continued to be an active shaman, as well as a peyote leader, until his death in 1898. Apache John was also important. He served for a time as judge of the Court of Indian Offenses, and he was one of those leaders who met with the Oklahoma Medical Committee to testify in favor of peyote before consideration of peyote legislation.

J. Gilbert McAllister (1952:370) described the introduction of peyote to the Kiowa-Apache in this way: "The Kiowa-Apache say they obtained the plant and its ritual from the Lipan [Apache] in the 1880s and then introduced it to the Kiowa and Comanche."

This seems probable. Moreover, being related linguistically, the Kiowa-Apache may have been able to converse with, and even to serve as interpreters for, the Lipan when the Kiowa and Comanche met the Lipan in southern Texas during the century before the reservations were imposed in 1875. La Barre (1969:199) agrees with the transmission of peyote from the Apache, whether Lipan or Mescalero, to the Kiowa and Comanche and also believes that the Kiowa-Apache may have aided the transfer.

Ray Blackbear, a Kiowa-Apache informant for the University of Oklahoma Oral History Project, has contributed a good deal of information regarding early Kiowa-Apache peyotists. He said (1968:25) that his grandfather, Old Man Blackbear, "recalls every meeting with those Apaches and those of Saddle-blanket and Daveko and Apache John." He claimed that Old Man Blackbear "used to carry drum for Daveko and Apache John . . . [and] Saddleblanket. . . ." He also described another Kiowa-Apache peyotist, one Apache Ben Chaletsin, who claimed he learned to run peyote meetings when relatively young by assisting Apache John. Ray Blackbear also said that Apache Ben was really a Lipan who knew Chiwat well. He said (1968:31): that "I began to hear about him—Chivato. He used to come down and he used to run meetings for Ben over here at Ben's house. . . . Ben, he took

FIG. 5. Three early peyote leaders on the Kiowa-Comanche Reservation. Left, with drum: Big Looking Glass (Comanche); center: Apache John (Kiowa-Apache); right: Apiatan (Kiowa). Photograph by John K. Hillers, Bureau of American Ethnology, 1894. Courtesy Smithsonian Institution, National Anthropological Archives, Washington, D.C.

him for a brother. . . ." Apache Ben himself told McAllister (1938:35) that "[Chiwat] died two years ago [that is, about 1932], an old man, one of the oldest members of peyote. He died of old age. . . . He used peyote about 50 years."

Tennyson Berry seems to have been the only early Kiowa-Apache peyotist to have been a student at Carlisle, and like many other former students, he served as an informant and interpreter for ethnologists. When Ray Blackbear was asked about the origin of peyotism among the Kiowa-Apache for the Oral History Project, he said: "I want to read this letter from Tennyson Berry so I'll get it down: . . . 'My people Lipan, Mescalero and Kiowa-Apache inform the young generation that peyote herb (waisi) was first begun or originated by the southern ocean coast by following Indians. 1st the Barefoot Indians; 2nd Kordosos [Carrizos]; 3rd Tonkawas, and 4th the Apache mentioned above.'" Ray Blackbear had preserved that letter for twenty-six years.

Tennyson Berry was over ninety when he died in 1971. His obituary in *Prairie Lore,* by Paul McClung (1971: 89–93) states that

Tennyson prided himself on the fact that he never drank and never gambled. He was a member of the Methodist Church and was a member and leader in the Native American Church. . . . When he was a young man at the beginning of the century, he accompanied three chiefs to Washington to act as their interpreter. The Chiefs, long deceased, were Ahpeaton (Apiaton) of the Kiowas, Quanah Parker of the Comanches, and Apache John of the Kiowa-Apaches. Tennyson later succeeded Apache John as leader of his tribe.

THE CADDO

In the northeast corner of the Kiowa-Comanche reservation was the smaller area designated for the Caddo, Wichita, and Delaware and a few scattered remnants of tribes who had been moved together from one place to another for about fifty years. One Caddo medicine man was John Wilson. He was one-half Delaware, one-fourth Caddo, and one-fourth French (Mooney 1896a: 903), but he considered himself a Caddo and spoke only Caddo. The group of Caddo and Delaware to which he belonged was still in northeastern Texas in 1840, the presumed date of his birth. In 1859, when the Tonkawa, Wichita, Caddo, Shawnee, and Delaware were driven from the reservation on the Brazos River, John Wilson would have been nineteen years old.

Wilson seems to have had a flair for religion. Before 1880 he was undistinguished except as a medicine man. But in 1880 he became a peyote roadman with a unique ceremony and attracted a considerable following. He was then forty years old. When the Ghost Dance came to Oklahoma, it, too, interested him, and for five or six years he was one of the most active leaders, although he seems to have maintained involvement in peyotism at the same time. As interest in the Ghost Dance waned in Oklahoma, he became again a full-time peyote roadman. Unlike Parker, he never seems to have been important except as a religious leader. He was never among those who defended peyote against the government's efforts to ban it. His importance is simply as a roadman, and through his spiritual experience and exceptional qualities as a leader and missionary he added a special variation to the peyote ritual. It is not easy to account for the fact that references to either Quanah Parker or John Wilson so seldom mention the other. They were near neighbors, living for twenty-five years of adulthood less than fifty miles apart, and for most of that time they were administered

FIG. 6. John Wilson (Caddo), originator of the Big Moon Ceremony, about 1900. Copy of photograph in Osage wooden peyote church of Fred Lookout by O. C. Stewart, 1972. Pawhuska, Oklahoma.

by the same agency. Peyotism was the primary interest of both. Wilson died at age sixty-one in 1901; Parker, at age sixty-six in 1911. Perhaps it was jealousy and religious and economic competition that kept these two peyote leaders almost completely apart in the official reports and ethnographic research studies covering the period from 1875 to 1901. For in one respect, John Wilson does seem to resemble Quanah Parker; there seems no doubt that Wilson, too, used his ability as a peyote roadman for personal gain. For twenty years he lived on the fees, collections, and gifts or "free will offerings" of his patients, students, converts, and followers.

The fascinating thing about John Wilson's peyotism is that he claimed to have learned the ceremony through divine revelation. However, since the basic structure of his ceremony does not depart radically from the Lipan ceremony taught to the Comanche and Kiowa, one must conclude that he had become familiar with the same ceremony sometime in his earlier life. He would, of course, have had such opportunity when the Caddo and Delaware were associated with the Tonkawa in Texas, or from certain Caddo themselves, or even from Lipan.

All scholars accept the year 1880 as the year that Wilson ate eight to fifteen peyote buttons a night a number of times during a two-week period while "learning from the peyote" how to direct a peyote ritual (Speck 1933:540–41; Petrullo 1934:79–86; La Barre 1938:153–56; Newcomb 1956b:202). None of these writers attribute Wilson's ritual or theology to any other tribe. Speck (1933:540) wrote: "At about this time [1880] he [Wilson] happened to be attending a dance in a Comanche village. Before he left the dance, one of the Comanche men presented him with a peyote 'button' and told him to give it a trial." The occasion was a Comanche dance, not a Comanche peyote ceremony. There was apparently no instruction as to the manner of the trial or the results that might be expected. Other scholars tell a similar story.

Speck (1933:540–56) reported John Wilson's conversion to peyotism as told by his nephew, George Anderson:

Wilson took it [the peyote] away with him and began to think over the circumstance. Before long he concluded to adopt the advice given and retire from worldly companionship, to make the trial and to study its outcome. With this objective in mind, he informed his wife, secured provisions for a few weeks' stay in camp and together they drove away in a wagon to a little creek where an abundant supply of fresh drinkable water might be had. The place he selected was a secluded, "clean and open place," where they would be alone, free from intrusion and worldly distractions. Anderson thinks that Wilson remained there about two or three weeks but does not remember hearing him say just how long. When all was ready, he began his innovation into the mysteries of Peyote the first night by eating eight or nine "buttons." We learn that during the period of self-exposure to the power of Peyote he took the medicine at frequent intervals during the day or night as the impulse prompted him, using about the same quantity each time it was taken.

As soon as he began, using the words of the informant, "Peyote took pity on him" for his humble mein and sincere desire to learn its power. During the whole period, he allowed nothing to distract him, giving his entire thought and wish to learn what Peyote might teach him. The outcome was the revelation that motivated him for the rest of his life and made him a teacher of the Peyote doctrines, which he himself exclusively evolved through the revelations given him at this time.

During the time of his sojourn, Wilson did not fast or undergo other abnegations but lived normally. It was during the periods when he took peyote that he experienced the contacts with the supernatural which we are now to record as they were given by Anderson. Each time Wilson took peyote during these days and nights of seclusion, he ate about fifteen peyote "buttons." He ate them in the natural state. During the two weeks or so of his experimental seclusion, Wilson was continually translated in spirit to the sky realm where he was conducted by Peyote. In this estate he was shown the figures in the sky and the celestial landmarks which represented the events in the life of Christ, and also the relative positions of the Spiritual Forces, the Moon, Sun, Fire, which had long been known to the Delawares, through native traditional teachings, as Grandfathers and Elder Brothers. Here, too, he was shown the grave of Christ, now empty, "where Christ had rolled away the rocks at the door of the cave and had risen to the sky." He was shown, always under the guidance of Peyote, the "Road" which led from the grave of Christ to the Moon in the Sky which Christ had taken in his ascent. He was told by Peyote to walk in this path or "Road" for the rest of his life, advancing step by step as his knowledge would increase through the use of the peyote, remaining faithful to its teachings, using the plant with a desire to learn and benefit by the knowledge that would come to him when under its influence, he would finally, just before his death, reach to the door of the moon one step beyond which, at the moment of his death, would bring him into the actual presence of Christ and Peyote. The "Road" referred to Wilson was accustomed to denote as "Our Creator's Road." During these revelations in the realm above, while under the guidance of Peyote, he knew that Peyote was a person, that it had human form, of great size, but he never actually saw him, nor did he see Christ. These sights were reserved for him "when the time had come to him to leave the place," meaning the realm of the living. The details of construction of the earthworks to form the "Moon" which he was to construct in the Peyote tent were all revealed to him with their meanings as Peyote continued his instructions to Wilson during his visits to the sky. And of especial importance was the emphasis placed by Peyote upon the details of construction of the sacred paraphernalia which Wilson was taught to make and use when he returned to earth and performed the Peyote rites. He was first shown how to make the drum stick and then followed the details of the Peyote worshipper's water drum. Next followed the details of as to how the "feathers" (fan) should be made, the gourd rattle, and the prayer staff. These objects completed the worshipper's required equipment. Also, came revelations as to how the face should be painted, the hair dressed. Of major importance, however, was the complete course of instruction given to Wilson by Peyote in the singing and syllabization of the numerous Peyote songs which were to form the principal parts of the ceremony of worship. Anderson felt certain that Wilson possessed and used no less than two hundred of these songs, of which Anderson has knowledge of about one hundred. Without going into further detail in his explanations to me, Anderson summarized the character of the knowledge revealed to Wilson as including instruction in every detail as to how the tent of Peyote worship should be made, the "Moon" or floor shrine, the conduct of the meeting with its particular rules, the duties of the officers and participants, the mental attitude, in fact everything which formed the body of his teaching as revealed to this Delaware Indian Dante, or should I liken him to Swedenborg, while conducted by the spirit Peyote through the heights beyond. Wilson was also given moral teachings to promulgate among his followers, and not least of all, the assurance that sincere devotion to the sacred rites and teaching then revealed would result in the curing of disease by the administration of Peyote when taken in the right spirit during the meetings by believers sincere in purpose and observant of the regulations imposed upon them.

Each day while under the spiritual guidance of Peyote during his seclusion, Wilson worked out the instructions given him in regard to the construction and furnishings of the Peyote tent and the "Moon," the Wilson "Moon" which has become typical of his followers.

At the termination of his period of seclusion, Wilson was released by Peyote, his spirit control, and told that as he progressed in age and experience Peyote would reveal more and more to him and increase his power to cure and regenerate the more he gave himself up to spiritual influence. And the same he was told would apply to the spiritual education of his followers.

Wilson then returned to Anadarko and began to teach his spiritual rules and philosophy to several followers among whom Black Wolf was prominent.

Although the published reports to the Bureau of Indian Affairs during the 1890s do not mention John Wilson's role as peyote proselytizer, three unpublished letters to the bureau, as well as Mooney's Ghost Dance monograph (1896a) do so identify him. In 1895, Agent Adams wrote that "John Wilson . . . has been doing missionary" work for peyotism. In 1896, Agent Smoot was more descriptive: "John Wilson . . . has been . . . gathering crowds of Indians, Mexicans, white men, and sometimes Negroes, at his place for as many as ten days eating mescal." And in 1899, a letter from the Osage Agency to the commissioner of Indian affairs is indicative of John Wilson's activities:

Sometime early last spring it was reported to me that one of the Osage boys . . . went down to the Anadarko country, among the Caddos, for the purpose of obtaining and bringing to the Osage reservation a lot of Mescal Beans [peyote buttons], and also to take instruction from one John Wilson, a medicine man among the Caddos, in the science of "medicine men" or "dreamers."

In 1898, one of the "spies" for the Indian agent at Anadarko gave this vivid, but obviously biased, account of a peyote meeting at the home of John Wilson:

I have been inquiring about the mescal eating at John Wilsons. He has been away doing missionary [work] and on his return called his mescal eaters together for a good time, regardless of orders to the contrary.

He told the police that they intended to continue and if the white men did not like it they could come and kill him, as he would then go to heaven. Wilson is their "king bee." What he says is law and gospel and is regarded as equal to a divine. He age 60 [written over 50] or about is a conceited and stubborn old fellow so there is no use of argument with him. The mescal eaters planted and cared for 3 or 4 acres of corn for him while he was away. I believe Saturday and Sunday were the only days they were together this time. More often 3 or 4 days and every 3 weeks during this time their stock at home must suffer as well as any crops they may have. All that they teach is superstition and intensify prejudice. At the entrance of the tepee is a half blob of baked clay and horseshoe shape is claimed to be the earth. They talk to a crows hide that hangs on the wall when they want a rain.

They paint and dress in blankets when they go to eat, and it is claimed virtue is not much respected in such cases. . . . [Ijams 1898]

Wilson may not have figured prominently in agency reports, but in ethnographic literature he is a well-documented leader. Mooney (1896a), Speck (1907, 1933), Petrullo (1934), La Barre (1938), Swanton (1942), M. R. Harrington (1921), Slotkin (1956b), Newcomb (1956), and Thurman (1973) have all written about John Wilson. The definitive work on Wilson and the special ritual he invented, by Vincenzo Petrullo (1934), entitled *The Diabolic Root: A Study of Peyotism, the New Indian Religion, among the Delawares* is based on field work in Oklahoma in 1929–30. A most important source is the article by Speck (1933: 539–56) entitled, "Notes on the Life of John Wilson, the Revealer of Peyote, as Recalled by his Nephew, George Anderson."

The ceremony of John Wilson is generally called the Big Moon ceremony and later is identified with the Cross Fire ceremony. It is also called the Moonhead ceremony, which is a name also identified with John Wilson himself. The main difference between John Wilson's ceremony and the Half Moon ceremony of the Comanche was the shape of the altar; Wilson's was larger and in the shape of a horseshoe rather than a crescent. The ceremonial arrangement was also more complex. A mound representing the sun was constructed immediately opposite the door to the east of a heart and a cross. From the center of the doorway and through "the sun" a line was either imagined or drawn to the center of the altar where the Chief Peyote was placed, sometimes surmounted by a crucifix. This line was called the Peyote Road. The gathering of the ashes to form a heart-shaped mound was also a feature of the Wilson moon.

The theologies of both ceremonies were similar. Peyote is good; peyote comes from God; peyote heals. Peyote teaches one to think good thoughts; it teaches one to know good from evil. It can cure anything, if one is sincere, if one concentrates, if one is full of devotion. Both ceremonies were strongly opposed to the use of liquor and claimed that peyote destroyed the taste for alcohol. Generally, a peyote meeting was called for a special purpose, for some person who was ill or for some other trouble. In both ceremonies it was reiterated that peyote was eaten not for visions, but to concentrate and learn from peyote. Visions and nausea were an indication that the mind was wandering from devotion to peyote, or that the body was trying to rid itself from some bad thing.

The two ceremonies differed in that the Half Moon ceremony referred more frequently to Indian legend, to Indian stories regarding the origin of peyotism, to the Great Spirit, Mother Earth, and so on, whereas the Big Moon ceremony mixed Jesus, the crucifix, the Bible, and the like, into the ceremony more often. However, neither ceremony ignored references to

Indian legend and lore or to Christianity—it was simply a matter of degree. The heavier influence of Christianity in the Wilson rite may have been a result of the fact that John Wilson was of mixed Caddo-Delaware-French ancestry, and both the Caddo and the Delaware had been under the influence of Christianity for a very long time. Wilson appears actually to have been a Catholic in addition to his other religions. Thurman (1973: 282) cited a letter by Wilson to the Bureau of Indian Affairs in 1893 requesting that Caddo children be allowed to attend Catholic schools because "most of us Caddo believe in the Catholic Church."

Not everyone was happy with the more heavily Christian ceremony of Wilson. Some of the Delaware in particular were hostile to the Wilson moon, according to Petrullo (1934: 31–32), who stated that they had "taken up an Indian product which they know to be ancient and free of European defilement, namely peyotism," and that they had sought a second form of the peyote ritual directly from the Kiowa and Comanche because Wilson had included "some Christian concepts."

Wilson seems to have been aware that his ritual was different and was content that it should be so. Speck (1933: 556) wrote: "According to Anderson, his uncle did not make a practice of reciting . . . [origin] legends when conducting meetings." It was inferred by Anderson that his uncle was not particularly concerned with how the Comanche had peyote revealed to them (as recounted in a legend), because it was upon his own revelations that he wished to lay stress. Thus it may be understood that Wilson claimed that he was not promulgating an already established religious observance, but rather founding a sect upon the authority of his own revelation.

Still, Wilson's teachings were not very different from those of other peyote roadmen of the Half Moon way. He taught that it was peyote itself who was the teacher. Revelation was a matter of direct communication between peyote and the suppliant. It was up to each person to find the peyote way for himself. According to Wilson's nephew (Speck 1933: 546), Wilson's instructions were: "Keep your mind on peyote [sic] and don't think anything about the people around you or anything outside. Look at Peyote and the fire all the time and think of it. Sit quiet and do not move around or be uneasy. Then you will not get sick (nauseated) or see visions. Visions and nausea are signs of bad self-adjustment to the proper religious attitude."

Wilson would not allow anyone who had been drinking to attend his meeting, saying he should come another time when he had not been drinking. He also exhorted his followers to practice sexual restraint and marital fidelity, and he strongly advised against fighting and violence, angry speech, getting even. Wilson, like the others, believed peyote could cure anything if one tried hard enough in proper spirit to learn and to live what peyote was teaching.

Wilson died on April 16, 1901, at about the age of sixty, after having been struck by a train at a railroad crossing near the Quapaw reservation in the extreme northeastern corner of Oklahoma. Some said that he, like Quanah Parker, brought about his own death through avarice. Let Petrullo (1934: 45–46) tell the story:

He went to the Quapaws to conduct a meeting. In addition to charging a fee for conducting the meeting, and receiving rich presents, he asked the Quapaws to give him a woman. He then started for home, driving a two-horse wagon. His wagon was filled with presents given to him by the Quapaws, and in the wagon with him there was a Quapaw woman and another Quapaw. A string of ponies were tied to the buckboard, and they caused his death. When he came to a railroad crossing the ponies pulled back, and the horses in front pulled forward and he was hit by a train. He was instantly killed, as well as his two companions. The Indians say that he was killed because he violated the laws of the Great Spirit.

Among the groups other than the Caddo who became converted to Wilson's Big Moon brand of peyotism, the most notable are the Delaware and the Osage. Speck (1933: 553) reports that in 1891 Wilson was holding Big Moon ceremonies for Delaware and Osage Indians. Black Wolf, John Wilson's first convert and adopted son and heir, continued to proselytize among the Osage. Speck names only the Caddo, Delaware, Osage, and Quapaw as having been converted by Wilson personally, but adds that George Anderson, Wilson's nephew, took the Wilson moon to the Seneca of Oklahoma in 1907. Petrullo (1934: 79) and La Barre (1938: 151–61) added the Wichita as Wilson's personal converts and expressed the opinion that the Winnebago, Kickapoo, Omaha, and Potawatomi "patterned their peyote creeds and ceremonies after those of Wilson."

In time, Wilson's Big Moon style for conducting peyote ceremonies became also known as the Cross Fire ritual and was particularly characterized as banning the use of tobacco in the ritual. Since about 1900, the Cross Fire ritual has been an alternate form of peyotism among the Chippewa, the Menominee, the Sioux, the Shoshone, the Ute, the Gosiute, and, most recently, the Navajo.

Although John Wilson overshadowed other Caddo leaders during his lifetime, there were others who carried on after his death. One was Enoch Hoag, at one time John Wilson's assistant and drummer, a leader who developed an original variation of Wilson's Big Moon ceremony. Information about Hoag comes from the interviews of Elsie Clews Parsons (1941). She constructed fairly complete genealogical charts for the families of three people, all early peyotists: Enoch Hoag, John Wilson, and Ingkanish. The charts required more than two hundred positions to trace these three families over four generations. As might be expected, family connections, like friendships, were often a means to the spread of peyotism. An example of this is found in the chart of Enoch Hoag, who had three sisters. Each sister had two husbands, and four of them became peyote leaders: Bob Dunlap, Sorrel (Kahkish), Worthless (Habana; Frank Sargent), and Alfred Taylor.

Since Parsons (1941: 10) reported that the Caddo consider a man under forty too young to assume the office of chief, we might be safe in assuming that Hoag was at least forty in 1896, the year he became tribal chief. Before that, for a number of years he had been an apprentice chief to his predecessor, Chief Whitebread. He continued to be chief for thirty years. Like John Wilson, he was at one time prominent as a leader of the Ghost Dance.

As the Kiowa-Comanche Agency officials became concerned about the effect of peyotism on the Indians under their charge, they carried on various investigations. In 1898, in an effort to find out just who the peyotists were and what went on at meetings, they employed two white men, agency farmers J. W. Ijams, cited above, and Jim Deer, to be spies and informants on peyote meetings. Ijams and Deer sent in handwritten reports, which now are located in the Oklahoma Historical Society. They questioned participants at peyote meetings in the Caddo area on Sugar Creek, about fifteen miles from Anadarko, and furnished the names of thirty participants. We learn from them, also, something of the frequency of peyote meetings on that reservation at the turn of the century. On October 12, 1898, Ijams wrote: "The same night of the eating at Big Tree's [a Kiowa chief] a big meeting was in progress at John Wilson's and I understand one at Enoch Hoges [Hoag's]." Thus, three meetings were being held simultaneously in a Caddo neighborhood. Big Tree would probably have represented the traditional Kiowa or Comanche "moon," while John Wilson would, of course, have conducted his Big Moon ceremony and Enoch Hoag would have directed his own variation on the Wilson moon.

THE WICHITA

Although early reports from the Kiowa-Comanche Agency do not specify which peyotists belonged to which tribe, and little is made of Wichita peyotists, nonetheless it seems logical to assume that the Wichita shared in the establishment of peyotism among the other tribes of the agency. In his earlier writings on the subject, Mooney does not mention the Wichita, but later in the *Handbook of American Indians North of Mexico* (1910, II: 949) he asserted: "Within recent years they [the Wichita] have taken up the Ghost Dance and peyote rite. . . ." They did not acquire both at the same time, for we know that the Ghost Dance became available to the Wichita in 1890, whereas the peyote religion was probably among them at least ten years earlier.

La Barre (1938: 120) provides the following interesting material regarding early Wichita peyotism:

The Wichita, like the Shawnee, claim to have had peyote long before they learned to eat it in meetings. In one of their rain ceremonies they used a medicine bundle containing four objects: feather, a little buckskin doll, a piece of flint and peyote. The ceremony was called hactias, "fire-people-around," and they sang all night for four nights to bring rain. The coming of the peyote ritual, therefore, aroused no hostility:

"No Wichita was ever against it (Sly Picard says); they couldn't be, as all our medicine men and women had peyote in their medicine."

Yellow Bird (Wichita-Kichai) may have eaten peyote as early as 1889 . . . and Sly's father used it in 1892, learning it from the Caddo. . . . Old Man Horse (Kiowa) is usually credited, however, with bringing peyote to the Wichita about 1902.

Although in the above La Barre names only one Wichita informant, in his preface he also names George May and Henry Hunt as Wichita peyotists who were of particular help in gathering data.

THE DELAWARE

There were two groups of Delaware Indians living in Oklahoma in 1874. The largest group was the Registered Delaware or Eastern Delaware, who in 1866–67 had been moved from a reservation in Kansas to Oklahoma to become incorporated into the Cherokee Nation. In 1890 there were 754 Eastern Delaware living among the Cherokee, and they were considered Cherokee citizens.

The other group had left the main body of Delaware about a century earlier and had shared the fortunes of the Caddo, the Wichita, the Comanche, the Kiowa, and the Kiowa-Apache. By 1890 they numbered only 87 and were located on the Kiowa-Comanche reservation in its northeast corner along with the Caddo and Wichita. They were known as the Anadarko Delaware, and about two hundred miles separated them from their tribal relatives.

Anthony F. C. Wallace, who wrote a summary (1956) of the religions of the Delaware Indians from 1600 to 1900, considers 1880 to be the date the Delaware were converted to peyotism by John Wilson. This is certainly possible for the Anadarko Delaware, since they lived with the Caddo and John Wilson himself was half Delaware. His conversion of the Anadarko Delaware would have taken place at the same time he became roadman for the Caddo—that is, 1880. His conversion of the Eastern Delaware must have occurred five or six years later and was complicated by a rival missionary, the Eastern Delaware tribal chief Elk Hair.

In 1930, Petrullo talked with Chief Elk Hair, as well as with his nephew Joe Washington, about the conversion of the Eastern Delaware to peyotism. Washington provided the following account of the origin of peyotism among the Eastern Delaware (Petrullo 1934: 41–49):

About fifty years ago [that is, 1880] Elk Hair, who is my uncle and who is now chief of the Delaware, had many misfortunes. His wife died and he himself became desperately ill. He no longer wanted to live. . . . However, he had a friend, also a Delaware, who was living with the Anadarko band. His name was Johnson Bob and he had known the use of peyote for many years, having learned it from the Comanche. Hearing that his friend Elk Hair was desperately ill, he came to see him. He talked to the sick man about peyote . . . but he was not able to convince Elk Hair. . . . [Elk Hair] thought of this all day and night, and by the following morning he had made up his mind to use peyote.

Johnson Bob gave a "little meeting" for Elk Hair, who was cured. Soon after, Johnson Bob cured Elk Hair's sister, and in 1885, Joe Washington, age ten, was taken by Elk Hair the two hundred miles to Anadarko to hunt in Comanche territory and to learn more about peyote. It was while they were visiting in Anadarko that Elk Hair first learned of John Wilson's Big Moon ritual. And it was while they were in Anadarko that Wilson himself traveled to the Eastern Delaware with the purpose of proselytizing his Big Moon ritual. Joe Washington spoke disparagingly of Wilson's "mixing two things: Christianity and peyote." He continued: "When we returned we found that Wilson brought the Big Moon meeting to our band. Many Delaware worship peyote that way and also many other tribes who don't know the original rite."

Thus, while John Wilson played a role in the introduction of peyotism to the Eastern Delaware, he was preceded by Johnson Bob (another Anadarko Delaware), who taught the Comanche Half Moon ceremony to Elk Hair, who was probably the first Eastern Delaware to become a peyote leader.

Elk Hair was a typical peyote leader in that he was both a political and a religious leader of his people and cooperative with white Americans. He was an informant for ethnologists from 1910 to 1930. Petrullo (1934: 46–48) reported the creed of Elk Hair at the age of seventy: "I have been using peyote for forty-five years [since 1885]. I have had my own experiences with peyote. It has given me a clear mind and good health. . . . I pray to the Great Spirit and to Peyote. . . . I pray to peyote. It was put here by God for me to use. It is good for sickness and to cleanse the soul before death."

We leave now the six tribes administered by the Kiowa-Comanche Agency at Anadarko to see what is happening to peyote among the other Indians in Oklahoma, but we will take with us our two strong leaders, Quanah Parker and John Wilson, and our two rituals, the Half Moon and Big Moon ceremonies. The influence of these two men will be felt by every tribe in Oklahoma and beyond, and the two ceremonies will continue and sometimes compete for adherents.

CHAPTER 5

The Spread of Peyote in Indian Territory

AT the same time that peyotism was being developed on the Kiowa-Comanche and Wichita reservations by such able missionaries as Quanah Parker and John Wilson, it was also being introduced to other Indian tribes in Oklahoma and elsewhere in the West. Many tribes were quick to accept it, but others rejected it altogether. The varied and broken histories of tribes, the varieties of languages and customs, the efforts of the Christian missionaries and government authorities to suppress it, as well as the abilities of peyote missionaries influenced its acceptance. It never gained more than 90 percent acceptance on any reservation at any time, and usually the percentage of peyotists was more likely to be from 35 to 50 percent. Its appeal was greatest among the newcomers to Oklahoma—among the young, newly educated Indians who found in it a form of Indian Christianity and often became its leaders. It was a ceremony they felt comfortable with, in which they could celebrate the Christian ideas they had recently learned at school in a setting that was familiar and indigenous. For all it was a curing ceremony, and the newcomers to Oklahoma had need of many cures. The serious but controlled ambience of the ceremony together with the euphoria produced by the plant brought about many miracles. When one considers the physical, psychological, and social problems of these early peyotists, when entire tribes were dying out from depression as well as from disease, one can sympathize with a ceremony and a sacrament that gave emotional strength and were followed with a good breakfast.

Although one cannot always say why anyone accepts or rejects an idea, it seems probable that those newly arrived to Oklahoma who rejected peyote were strongly influenced by the Christian missionaries and government officials who tried in every way to suppress it. The religious and civil authorities exhorted and threatened the Indians under their jurisdiction concerning the evils of peyote and at times punished those who were known to use it. Peyote was said to be illegal by most. It was not even available to all.

But the majority of Indians in Oklahoma rejected peyote for the same reasons that white people rejected it. By far the greatest numbers of Indians in Indian Territory were members of the Five Civilized Tribes: the Cherokee, the Choctaw, the Seminole, the Creek, and the Chickasaw. None of these tribes accepted peyotism. They had been exposed to Christianity for several generations, and before being moved to Indian Territory in 1835, many of them had been landowners living in towns with good schools

97

and prosperous churches. Some had been educated at universities in the East, such as Harvard and Princeton. They looked down upon and denigrated the primitive beliefs and practices of the "wild tribes" of the western part of Indian Territory. From childhood, members of the Five Civilized Tribes were conditioned to take pride in their special status and to reject anything native from the western Prairie and Plains Indians. Moreover, like white Christians, they felt that whatever Christian denomination they espoused, be it Baptist or Methodist or any other sect, warranted exclusive participation. For most believers, Christianity does not now allow for multiple religions. For the members of the Five Civilized Tribes, many of whom were devoutly religious in some sect of Protestantism, it did not either. To them there was no question that peyotism was an evil, heathenish business to be shunned and stamped out. In time an individual from the Five Civilized Tribes might join peyotists of some other tribe in a meeting, just as an occasional white or black man might do, but especially in the early history of peyotism this was rare.

One exception to the complete rejection of peyote by the Five Civilized Tribes came in 1919 when it was reported that a small band of Yuchi had developed a peyote ceremony. The Yuchi, long associated with the Creek Indians, lived in the Creek Nation. They had moved with the Creek from the southern states when the Five Civilized Tribes were forced to leave their homes east of the Mississippi, and there is no reason to think they were less civilized than the others of the Five Civilized Tribes. But in 1919, replying to a request for information by the Bureau of Indian Affairs, Gabe E. Parker, superintendent for the Five Civilized Tribes, wrote that it was indeed true that 10 percent of the four hundred Yuchis were "occasional users of peyote. . . . I have been informally advised that the Euchees [Yuchis] began using the drug through their associations with the Shawnee Indians. This is the first intimation I have had that any Indians of the Five Civilized Tribes use of peyote. . . . It is used in a so-called religious ceremony. However, it is only copied from the ceremony of the western tribes as: Cheyennes, Arapahoes, Shawnees. . . . Jeanette Tiger and John James, Depew, Oklahoma, are credited with being the first users among the Euchees [Yuchis]."

Several small tribes on separate reservations in the extreme northeastern corner of Indian Territory in what is now Ottawa County were variable in their attitudes toward peyotism. The Quapaw accepted it enthusiastically, but there was no acceptance among the Wyandotte, Modoc, Peoria, or Ottawa, and little acceptance by the Eastern Shawnee and Seneca. These groups were accidental, heterogeneous mixtures of several groups, remnants of once powerful tribes, or awkward offshoots of tribes, the majority of whose members were located elsewhere, as was the case with the Modoc and Seneca. These tribes had weaker tribal identity, and when they did participate in peyotism they were more likely to do so in meetings with the Quapaw. In particular, the Seneca and Eastern Shawnee were influenced by the Quapaw.

The other newly arrived Indians in Oklahoma were interested enough in peyotism soon to have active ceremonies. They were the Cheyenne and the Arapaho, who shared a large reservation north of the Kiowa-Comanche reservation; the Osage, who first were located on the Cherokee reservation but who soon had their own reservation west of the Cherokee; the Quapaw, whose reservation was east of the Cherokee in the northeast corner of the Indian Territory; the Oto, Pawnee, Tonkawa, Ponca, and Kaw on reservations west of the Osage bordering the Cherokee Strip; and the Sauk or Sac and Fox, Shawnee, Kickapoo, Citizen Potawatomi, and Iowa on reservations in the center of Oklahoma, west of the Creek and south of the Osage.

THE CHEYENNE AND ARAPAHO

North of the Kiowa-Comanche reservation was the Cheyenne-Arapaho reservation, with agency headquarters at Darlington. It was appropriate that these two tribes should share the same reservation, since they had jointly occupied hunting territory on the High Plains for a century or longer. Certainly, the two tribes were together on the High Plains between the Black Hills and the northern Rockies at the beginning of the nineteenth century and were considered to be closely associated. Generally, the Arapaho, who seemed to have an affinity for the mountains, were west of the Cheyenne, who were usually on the plains. With the acquisition of the horse many Cheyenne and Arapaho began traveling south far from their traditional hunting grounds, while others, perhaps the more conservative remained in the north around the headwaters of the Platte and Yellowstone rivers, from time to time travelling east to the Black Hills of South Dakota.

The Arapaho and Cheyenne who were on the move began exploring southern hunting grounds as early as 1830. Mooney (1907a) wrote: "They [the Cheyenne] made their first treaty with the Government in 1825 at the mouth of the Teton (Bad) r. on the Missouri about the present Pierre, S.D." According to Mooney, it was in consequence of the building of Bent's Fort on the upper Arkansas, in Colorado, in 1832 that a large part of the tribe decided to move down and make permanent headquarters on the Arkansas, while the rest continued to rove about the headwaters of the North Platte and the Yellowstone. In 1837 and 1839 the southern Cheyenne and Arapaho fought notable battles with the Kiowa, Kiowa-Apache, and Comanche, but in 1840 they made peace with the southern plains tribes and in 1853 made their first raid into Mexico in company with the Kiowa.

In 1851, the Cheyenne and Arapaho signed the Treaty of Fort Laramie, which assigned them all of eastern Colorado between the North Platte and the Arkansas rivers plus six to ten thousand acres in each of Wyoming, Kansas, and Nebraska. However, the U.S. government soon thought better of this action and in a treaty signed at Fort Wise, Kansas, in 1861, the Cheyenne and Arapaho ceded back all these lands except a tract in eastern Colorado south from Big Sandy Creek to the Arkansas and Purgatory rivers. It was this treaty which marked the most definite break between the northern and southern divisions of these two tribes. Those who accepted the land on the Arkansas and settled there were henceforth considered Southern Arapaho and Southern Cheyenne as opposed to those of each tribe who eventually settled with others of their kin to the north and became known as the Northern Arapaho and Northern Cheyenne.

The southern divisions suffered greatly at the hands of the U.S. Army. In 1864, in the Sand Creek Massacre, Colorado Volunteers, led by Col. John M. Chivington killed many, including women and children; in 1868, many more lost their lives when Gen. George Armstrong Custer, commanding the U.S. Seventh Cavalry, attacked their village on the Washita. In 1869, by presidential proclamation, a reservation for the Southern Arapaho and Southern Cheyenne was established in Oklahoma north of their allies, the Kiowa and Comanche.

The Arapaho who did not settle on the Arkansas roamed northern Colorado and Wyoming, moving from place to place, never given a permanent settlement, joining the Sioux and others in their warfare against the whites, until finally in 1878 the government arranged for them, along with those Arapaho who had remained north from the beginning, to occupy a portion of the Shoshone reservation at Wind River, Wyoming, where they have lived to the present.

The Cheyenne who did not settle on the Arkansas also turned north. They were involved in much of the warfare between whites and Indians in the sixties and seventies, and some were involved with the Sioux in the Battle of the Little Bighorn, where Custer was killed. As a result, the army transported all of the Northern Cheyenne it could collect to Oklahoma, where they were ordered to stay with their southern relatives. They were most unhappy there and refused to remain. In the fall of 1878, about 250–300 of the followers of Chiefs Morning Star (Dull Knife), Wild Hog, and Little Wolf, in spite of the best efforts of the U.S. Army to stop them, escaped north to Montana, where eventually a reservation was established for them on the Tongue River. Peyotism among the Northern Arapaho and Northern Cheyenne will be considered in a later chapter.

THE SOUTHERN CHEYENNE

It can be assumed that the Southern Cheyenne learned of peyote and the peyote ceremony in the early 1880s. La Barre (1938:114) says: "In the diffusion of the standard rite the Arapaho and the Cheyenne perhaps come next after the Kiowa and the Comanche."

The bitter history of the Cheyenne before they settled on their third reservation left them with a deep distrust and anger toward Americans, and that was perhaps the reason for the bitter fighting to the very end against the government's efforts to force them onto a reservation. Also, the emphasis on the glory of warfare in Cheyenne tradition may help to explain why the Cheyenne particularly distinguished themselves in battle. At any rate, when the fighting in Oklahoma ceased in 1874 and a number of the warriors were rounded up and sent to the prisoner-of-war camp in Florida, there were thirty-three Cheyenne warriors among them, outnumbering those from any other tribe.

This may have been an advantage for the spread of peyote among the Southern Cheyenne, for it meant that many of their young men would receive early training in the English language and indoctrination into Protestant Christianity, two positive influences toward peyote's diffusion. La Barre (1938:113n) put it this way: "In modern times the use of English as a lingua franca is an enabling factor of great importance in the diffusion of the [peyote] cult." In truth, special ability in the use of English characterized the early Cheyenne peyotists. Four peyote leaders who underwent English-language training and Christian religious instruction during the three-year imprisonment at Fort Marion were Co-hoe, age twenty-four; Howling Wolf, age twenty-seven; Roman Nose, age twenty-two; and Little Chief, age twenty-one. All four, after outstanding careers as warriors against the invading white population, learned to accommodate themselves to the conquerors and to use the experience of imprisonment to acquire new skills.

While in prison, Cohoe distinguished himself by painting excellent scenes of Cheyenne life, which in 1964 were published in a volume entitled *A Cheyenne Sketchbook,* with a commentary by E. Adamson Hoebel and Karen Daniels Petersen. Hoebel and Petersen write that Cohoe remained in the eastern United States to further his education in language and religion after most of the prisoners had returned to Oklahoma. He went first to Hampton Institute, where he "became an apprentice tailor among fifty Negro girls," and "in March, 1879, he and twelve other former prisoners were baptized and accepted into the brotherhood of Christianity."

After Hampton, Cohoe was transferred to the new Indian boarding school at Carlisle. In 1880 he returned home to the Cheyenne and Arapaho Agency, and the next year Agent J. D. Miles wrote to Pratt at Carlisle: "Cohoe is hard at work, exemplifying his faith in civilization . . . and working as white men do" (Cohoe 1964: 14). From 1881 to 1888, Cohoe had a number of jobs around the Cheyenne and Arapaho Agency and with a local trading post, but he then became a farmer on his allotment.* He also became a peyote leader.

Hoebel and Petersen (Cohoe 1964:18) concluded: "Cohoe's life of ill-rewarded effort held some relief in the color that survived in the readapted remnants of the life that once was. He found solace and vision in membership in the peyote cult, the Native American Church, that developed among the Plains tribes in the days after defeat. He put Christianity behind him. And in his last years he was head chief of the Onihanotria, or War Dancers Society. . . ."

Little Chief was a companion of Cohoe in the internment camp in Florida and remained close to him upon their return to Oklahoma, perhaps because the two had married sisters. They also attended Carlisle Institute together in 1879–80. After returning to Oklahoma, Little Chief was employed for ten years in the Indian Police and for five and a half years as a scout for the U.S. Army. Later, he was for four years an interpreter and assistant in a white doctor's office. Indian Agent Shell identified him as a peyotist, and in answering a questionnaire sent to all former Carlisle students, he himself said: "I am an officer of the [peyote] church."

Howling Wolf returned directly to the Cheyenne-Arapahoe reservation following his internment. Agent J. D. Miles mentioned him in his annual report for 1878: "On the 27th of April, 1878, all but eleven of the Cheyenne and Arapahoe prisoners for the past three years held as prisoners at Fort Marion at Saint Augustine, Florida, were returned to the agency. . . . The exertions of one of these returned prisoners (Howling Wolf) have resulted in more than twenty of his friends and relatives adopting the dress, habits, and ways of whites."

Indian agent Lawie Tatum, of the Kiowa-Comanche Agency, was also impressed with Howling Wolf:

When on one of my visits to the Cheyenne and Arapahoe Agency in 1878, "Howling Wolf" of that Agency . . . related to me some of his experience . . .: "When a young man . . . I used to sometimes think about God, but I did not think it wrong to raid and fight, which I now believe to be wrong, for I was an Indian and thought and acted as an Indian. I wanted to be a leader and went into sin, for which I was taken prisoner, and with others sent to St. Augustine. There I learned much more about the Great Spirit, who caused me to realize that I had done very wrong. I wanted to throw away all of my bad deeds. I asked God to take away my bad heart and give me a good heart. The Great Spirit heard me,

---

*This was the time of the Dawes Severalty Act (1887), which provided that lands belonging to certain Indian tribes should be allotted in severalty; that is, individual Indians would be given an allotment from tribal lands which they would own and use or sell as each saw fit. It was the end of the tribal life of the past, as it gave rise to an influx of whites who were permitted to settle on the unassigned lands after all allotments had been made.

and gave me a good heart. . . . I sometimes took the Bible and held it open before me, and that gave me comfort, although I could not read it."

Like Cohoe, Howling Wolf was talented as an artist. In her biography, *Howling Wolf: A Cheyenne Warrior's Graphic Interpretation of His People* (1968), Karen Daniels Petersen included twelve colored plates of pictures painted by Howling Wolf between 1878 and 1881, soon after his return from Florida. She also included a black and white portrait of him holding the staff, fan, and rattle of a peyote roadman with the caption: "By the end of his life, Howling Wolf had returned to the ways of an Indian—with certain changes. While at a Sun Dance ceremony in 1913, he was painted carrying the symbols—gourd and feathers—of the new Cheyenne religion, the Native American Church, which combined elements of Christianity with the use of the hallucenogenic drug peyote."

Roman Nose, after his three years in the Florida prisoner-of-war camp, first went to Hampton Institute and then to Carlisle for an additional two years of English, Christianity, and tinsmithing. In 1879, at Hampton, he was baptized Henry Carruthers, taking the name of the doctor from Tarrytown, New York, who had befriended him in Florida (Petersen 1964: 465). In a letter to Agent John D. Miles before his return to the reservation, he wrote: "When I come home to Indian Territory . . . I am sure I would be anxious to help you make good Indians, and give them a good road of the whiteman's ways. . . . I will pray to God to help each one of us. . . ." And according to one biographer, Ellsworth Collings, in an article entitled "Roman Nose: Chief of the Southern Cheyenne," in the *Chronicles of Oklahoma* (1965: 420, 448): "For the next eighteen years, Chief Henry C. Roman Nose devoted his efforts and time to assisting the Cheyennes and Commissioner of Indian Affairs to improve the living conditions among the Indians."

But Roman Nose, too, again practiced some Indian ways. According to Karen Daniels Petersen:

In the decade following allotments (1890–1900), Roman Nose achieved two more of his early goals. The Native American Church, the third religion he espoused after his native Sun Dance, brought him into praying fellowship that stressed brotherhood and peace. [He had also espoused the Ghost Dance.] Lastly, he was recognized as a leader of his people. He became a chief. Around the neck of Roman Nose, Chief Big Jake [Little Big Jake] hung the Chief's medal bestowed years before by George Washington. In return Roman Nose gave Big Jake a spotted horse, indicating appreciation of the honor done him. . . . Roman Nose kept the title of chief until his death.

Because the canyon near Watonga, Blaine County, Oklahoma, where Roman Nose accepted an allotment in 1890 had valuable gypsum deposits, he became relatively wealthy, being paid as much as thirteen dollars per month from 1903 to 1927. He maintained his interest in ancient Cheyenne culture and in 1901 and 1903 took an active role in a Cheyenne Sun Dance, described by George A. Dorsey for the Chicago Field Museum. He accompanied Dorsey throughout the Sun Dance, explaining everything to him, including how a dancer was to be skewered as in ancient times (Dorsey 1905 (2): 177–78).

Roman Nose was well known as a peyotist by the people at the Cheyenne-Arapaho Agency, but when he died in 1916, he was "buried . . . at the Baptist Indian Mission near Watonga. The ceremonies are to be strictly after the manner of the Christian Religion. Roman Nose believed that it was best for the Indian to follow the white man's way and take up the obligation of civilization" (Collings, quoting a newspaper clipping, 1965: 454). Roman Nose, in fact, died while participating in a peyote ceremony at the home of his former prison mate, Cohoe (Petersen 1964: 477). A park was named in his honor.

Southern Cheyenne Reuben Taylor was not an internee or Carlisle student but studied English and theology at a Kansas institute. That he became accomplished in both subjects is clear inasmuch as he became a Christian minister and interpreter, once accompanying a delegation of Indians to Washington as interpreter. He told a congressional committee in 1918 that he had used peyote since 1886 when it had cured his leg and allowed him to walk without crutches. A Cheyenne Indian informant for the reservation agency reported that Reuben Taylor had led a meeting at his home in 1899. The same informant also reported on the peyote meeting in 1907 which led to Reuben Taylor's arrest and trial, along with that of Howling Wolf and Percy Kable, for breaking the narcotic law by eating "mescal beans." Taylor was also said to have been a peyote missionary to the Ponca.

Another well-known early peyotist was Percy Kable, who had been a student at Carlisle from 1883 to 1888, followed by a few months at Haskell. He, too, was proficient in English. Besides testifying that "mescal" was not "peyote" in the trial mentioned above, he was one of those who defended peyote before the territorial legislature in 1908. He was also said to be a supplier of peyote.

Southern Cheyenne peyotist Leonard Tyler was also a student at Carlisle and Haskell as well as a successful farmer and businessman. In 1909, the *Indian Helper,* the Carlisle student paper, reprinted an item from the *Calumet* (Oklahoma) *Chieftain:*

Leonard Tyler, a fancy stock raiser and one of the large land owners of this country, is one of the real pioneers of this section. He is a Cheyenne, and knows every foot of ground for miles around. Mr. Tyler is a well-read man, posted on topics of the day and a student of stock and stock-breeding. Thus far he has met with phenomenal success and has a state-wide reputation as a fancy breeder and an authority on stock.

Mr. Tyler has 620 acres of the finest land in Oklahoma. Last year $2,800 worth of corn alone was harvested on this farm. The stock-breeding industry in Oklahoma is still in its infancy and none know this better than Mr. Tyler. With advanced methods in the care and wider knowledge of their qualities the stock-raising business will become one of the most important activities in the State. Mr. Tyler is well-versed in the business and has ample facilities to enable him to raise the very best. The next few years will doubtless see a great increase in this branch of his business.

La Barre (1938:115), too, wrote of Tyler and some other Cheyenne peyotists: "Leonard Tyler and John Turtle went to the Kiowa country in 1884–85 and learned the ceremony. A little later, in 1889–90, Henry White Antelope and Standing Bird visited the Comanche and learned Quanah Parker's 'way'. Tyler later got a 'heart moon' of his own (Caddo influence?) some time after the allotment of lands."

One Louis L. Meeker, Darlington, Oklahoma, wrote to the Bureau of Ethnology in 1896 concerning Leonard Tyler, saying: "I succeeded in getting into the good graces of Leonard Tyler, a chief and medicine man." He further said that Tyler claimed he had been cured of consumption by peyote and considered himself "the great Cheyenne apostle" of peyotism. Rev. G. Elmer E. Lindquist (1937:3), quoting an old missionary who had met Tyler in Montana, said "he [Tyler] had just come to introduce peyote among the Northern Cheyenne. That was in 1899." In 1899, Agent A. E. Woodson said Tyler was one of the delegates sent to Washington who were guilty of eating peyote. In 1906, Special Agent Connell complained to Cheyenne-Arapaho agent White that Leonard Tyler was supplying peyote to the Osage Agency, and it is possible that Tyler may well have supplemented his income for many years as a peyote missionary and supplier. In 1911 he was reported traveling into Mexico by way of Eagle Pass to obtain peyote, and Special Agent Johnson claimed that he was in the peyote supply business.

On January 2, 1913, the Carlisle Indian School published an obituary of Leonard Tyler taken from the *Calumet* (Oklahoma) *Chieftain*. It reported that he was born in 1864, the son of "a prominent Cheyenne chief . . . and was among the first party of Indian boys to enter Carlisle." Ignoring his peyotism, the article continued:

Early in life he adopted the white man's ways, to which he always adhered. He was of a very religious nature and constantly exhorted his tribesmen to follow in the "Jesus Way."

In October of last year he was baptized into the Reorganized Church of Jesus Christ of Latter Day Saints, and was later made an elder.

A short time ago he made his will, and planned his funeral arrangements, requesting that he should be buried as he had lived, like a white man.

He was buried April 4, 1913, at Darlington.

Kish Hawkins, born in 1866, attended grade school on the reservation for four years and a Methodist school in Indiana for one. Then he went to Carlisle, where he stayed for five years, the last two as an "assistant disciplinarian." Returning to the reservation, he became an employee of the Bureau of American Indians as clerk, teacher-farmer, and policeman. He was well known as a peyotist, the superintendent of the agency referring to him as a noted peyotist. He owned a peyote fan that had been blessed by Quanah Parker; when it was used, "it was supposed that the spirit of Christ was there" (Densmore 1936: 85).

In summary, the Southern Cheyenne early peyote leaders were characterized by their ability to communicate well in English, having gained a better than average Indian education. They were usually peyotists of the "old way," the Quanah Parker Way, and many of them became missionaries to other tribes and were importers of peyote, particularly when peyote was hard to get.

THE SOUTHERN ARAPAHO

The Southern Arapaho, like the Southern Cheyenne, were followers of the Quanah Parker Way of peyotism. They possibly received first instruction directly from him or through one Medicine Bird, an Arapaho who some say learned it from the Comanche and Apache but others say learned it from the Caddo. At all events, according to La Barre, Quanah Parker "led meetings among the Southern Arapahoes and Cheyennes in 1884" (1938: 113).

Cleaver Warden, who attended Carlisle from 1880 to 1887, was the Southern Arapaho to whom Medicine Bird was said to have taught the peyote ritual (Trenholm 1970: 296–97). After leaving Carlisle, he spent one year as a U.S. Army scout out of Fort Reno, two years as an employee of a stage company, and four years as a clerk in a hardware store. He farmed, and he was on call and devoted considerable time working for the Field Museum in Chicago, the American Museum of Natural History in New York, and the Smithsonian Institution in Washington, in the last case as Mooney's informant and interpreter. In a 1910 report to the Carlisle Indian School he stated: "[I] was baptized in Protestant Episcopal Church in Wyoming, by Rev. Sherman Coolidge, an Arapaho Indian. . . . I am member of Arapaho Business Committee . . . have voted at county and state elections. . . ."

In 1918, in Washington, when questioned before a congressional committee about the fate of the Arapaho Indian named Sitting Bull, who had been the leader of the Ghost Dance of the southern Plains and who had later been converted to peyotism, he said that Sitting Bull suffered a "partial stroke of paralysis." A congressman asked, "What happened to Sitting Bull" after he started eating peyote? Warden said (U.S. Congress, House, Committee on Indian Affairs 1918a: 191):

He came out of it. He is there now, well, perfectly well. He can smile, he can tell how he came out, how he conquered. He is there now a Christian. He is home in all peace and contentment of Godliness. There is no such thing as immorality surrounding his house. He is there listed as a Mennonite member now. That is the work of peyote.

Paul Boynton, half Cheyenne and half Arapaho, lived on that part of the reservation dominated by the Arapaho and was therefore considered to be Arapaho. He, too, had attended Carlisle and became sufficiently proficient in English to be an informant and interpreter for Mooney, who considered him "particularly bright" (1896a: 923). He was one of those to testify in defense of peyote before the Oklahoma legislature in 1908, and again in 1918 before a congressional committee in Washington. To the congressmen he said: "Through . . . this peyote I was made well. . . . I could see that there was something greater than the medicine itself. I saw that God planted the herb . . . God planted this herb and blessed it, and I am going to take God's blessing."

Jock Bull Bear was an early peyotist who defended the right to use peyote before the congressional committee in 1918. He wrote a statement of his early life and conversion to peyote which he submitted to the *Washington Times* of March 23, 1918:

I was a student at Carlisle Indian Training School, Carlisle, Pa., from 1880 to 1883, and was baptized as a Presbyterian church member. When I returned to my home among my tribesmen on the Cheyenne and Arapaho reservation in Oklahoma, I joined the commonly called Peyote society. I joined this society, however among the Comanches in 1884. I have used the peyote bean for the last 32 years, and am now 54 years old, and I have six children, all grown and married, and I am the grandfather of ten grandchildren. I live in a nice little home with a small farm of my own. All of my children have good homes. I believe I have all of these things becaue of what my religion has done for me. And I do not use any intoxicating liquor of any kind nor indulge in gambling. And my sons, daughters and sons-in-law all have had experience with this little herb called the peyote bean, or mescal button, that has been so much talked about and against by the inexperienced persons who know nothing about it except what they have heard. I speak from experience, having been a leader in this religious society for 28 years. . . . Our religion, peyote members, as we might express it, are not against anything that is good, or in truth of worshipping, or Christianity.

We try to be friendly with all, and Christianity is our motto through life, and so we teach our children. . . .

We are living uprightly under the United States flag, and helping to improve the condition of our Indian race, make them better Christians, and to live the real civilized life.

Bull Bear's dedication to peyotism included missionizing among other tribes, to the Winnebago of Nebraska and the Shoshone of Wyoming. If we believe that the meeting which Bull Bear said he led among the Winnebago in 1913 is the same meeting that Paul Radin describes wherein one "Arapaho Bull" led a ceremony for the Winnebago that same year (and I believe it is), we have insights into the missionary process as well as into theological variations. Radin (1920: 415) describes this ceremony through Jesse Clay's account of it: "I went to Oklahoma once as a guest of an Arapaho Indian [Jock Bullbear?]. . . . A year later this Arapaho came to visit me in Winnebago, and while he was with us a few of my friends urged me to hold the peyote ceremony according to the Arapaho method. I held several meetings at which my Arapaho friend led." Clay attributed a few of the ideas regarding peyote theology to his Arapaho teacher (Radin 1923: 415, 418):

The reason for drinking water at midnight is because Christ was born at midnight and because of the good tidings that he brought to the earth, for water is one of the best things in life and Christ is the savior of mankind. . . . The purpose of going to the Four directions and blowing the flute [that is, the eagle bone whistle] is to announce the birth of Christ to all the world. . . . The meat represents the message of Christ and those who accept it will be saved.

Jesse Rowledge was another Southern Arapaho who attended Carlisle and became an early peyotist. He held a position with the Bureau of Indian Affairs as farmer-teacher at Geary, Oklahoma, which required him to visit and talk to fellow tribesmen about how to improve farming methods while maintaining his own farm as an example and demonstration of good farming procedures. He maintained that peyote had been known to the Southern Arapaho from 1884, and two other educated early peyotists, Frank and Carl Sweezy, concurred. Carl Sweezy was something of an artist, having been taught by Mooney to draw pictures of museum specimens being collected for the U.S. National Museum. A collection of his designs from Arapaho and Cheyenne shields, robes, leggings, tipis, bags, and so on, with text has been published by Althea Bass. She writes (1966: ix): "He remembered the Ghost Dance and Sun Dances and peyote meetings, and Christian services of many sects." He said (1966: 76): "Left Hand spoke the truth. There are many ways to God."

THE OSAGE

The ancestral home of the Osage was in the vicinity of Missouri along the Mississippi River, where they lived in villages and subsisted on game and some products of agriculture. Even before 1700 they had become acquainted with Europeans, particularly with French traders and a few Catholic missionaries with whom they were friendly. After the Louisiana Purchase, the westward push of colonizers made game scarce, and the Osage, too, moved west into Kansas. Like other displaced Indians, they endured many hardships during the 1800s, but somehow they managed to avoid the extreme reduction suffered by many tribes. In 1821 they numbered fifty-two hundred, and they have managed to maintain about that number to the present although thousands have left the tribal roles to join the regular citizenry of the United States. In 1872 the Osage were given a reservation in northeastern Oklahoma next to the Cherokee Nation.

The Osage had been cooperative in their dealings with the U.S. government and had proved shrewd and tough bargainers in negotiating nine treaties which were ratified by Congress and signed by presidents from 1803 to 1871. From 1872 to 1881 these treaties were supplemented by four acts of Congress concerning the Osage, and in each case the Osage profited. Osage wealth came as interest on Osage funds in the U.S. Treasury which totaled $8,562,690. It amounted to per capita payments of over two hundred dollars per year for every man, woman, and child beginning in 1878. The discovery of valuable minerals on their reservation further increased the wealth of this fortunate tribe, and in the 1890s oil was discovered on the reservation, making the Osage wealthy indeed.

But in one respect wealth was not an advantage to the Osage. They, like others, were easily seduced by whiskey, and, being wealthy, they attracted a large number of whiskey peddlers, who established themselves on the borders of the reservation and helped the Indians evade the federal liquor prohibition, which applied to Indians but not to whites.

On August 20, 1877, Osage agent Cyrus Beede reported to the Bureau of Indian Affairs (1877:90):

There is another class of irresponsible traders and dealers in whiskey who infest the border, and offer their inducements, more potent with Indians than bread and clothing. . . . The demoralization to Indian tribes consequent upon the liquor traffic among them gives grave apprehension to the propriety to too friendly relations between Indians and whites.

In 1888, Osage acting agent Carroll H. Potter wrote (U.S. Bureau of Indian Affairs 1888:101): "The traffic in whiskey by peddlers on the reservation is, in my opinion, alarmingly on the increase. . . ." A year later, Agent L. J. Miles, who had earlier spent six years with the Osage, reported: "The presence of numerous vagabond white people on the reservation is a detriment to the welfare of the Indians. Many of them prove to be gamblers or whiskey peddlers. . . . The Indian, like too many of his white neighbors, will drink when he can get it. . . ."

Frank F. Finney devoted an article in the *Chronicles of Oklahoma* (1957:462–63) to "The Osage Indians and the Liquor Problems before Statehood," in which he wrote:

The run in 1889 of white settlers and the creation of the Territory of Oklahoma brought the beginning of a drastic change in the lives of the Osages. One of the first acts of the Oklahoma territorial legislature legalized the use and trade of liquor. The law took effect Christmas Day, 1890. . . . The lands opened for settlement were not contiguous to the Osage reservation but near enough to provide a base from which whiskey peddlers . . . could cross the border at night, dispose of their liquor poison . . . and be safely with their friends in Oklahoma by daylight.

With the opening of the Cherokee Outlet and the surplus lands of Tonkawa and Pawnee reservations, conditions went from bad to worse. It was not until then that liquor could be legally disposed of on any borders of the Osage reservation. Almost overnight the little towns . . . sprang up across the Arkansas

River from the Osage reservation which were filled with saloons. . . . Once again the use of whiskey spread among the Osages like a deadly epidemic. . . .

One influence had appeared to displace the liquor habits of some of the Indians. More Osages were turning to the peyote religious cult which had been introduced among the Osages by John Wilson. . . . The adherents drink no alcoholic liquor. . . . Peyote induced a beautiful state and behavior of adherents was as different from that of whiskey drinkers on a spree as that of peaceful sheep and rampant lions.

When John Wilson left the Kiowa-Comanche reservation to vist his eastern Delaware relatives living among the Cherokee, he had to pass through the Osage reservation. It was this circumstance that probably brought peyotism early to this tribe. In 1885, five years after his conversion to peyotism, we know that Wilson visited Dewey and Copan on the Cherokee reservation. It is possible that he could have begun to proselytize among the Osage any time after this date.

There are two dated accounts for the conversion of the Osage, one by Frank G. Speck and the other by John J. Mathews. It is important to say something about Mathews. He was an Osage Indian who excelled in scholarship; he was educated at Oxford, England, and wrote three books on the Osage, one of which, an ethnohistory, *Wah'Kon-Tah: The Osage and the White Man's Road,* was a Book-of-the-Month Club selection in 1932. As a sensitive, observant scholar, reared among the Osage and accepted as one of them, he had many advantages as recorder of Osage cultural values and individual and group relations to their adjustment to conquest by Amer-Europeans, as he called white Americans.

Mathews wrote that the conversion of the Osage to peyotism by John Wilson occurred after interest in the Ghost Dance had waned, which would have been after 1893. Wilson, he said, was looking for new ways to enhance his image as his position as Ghost Dance leader lost importance. He therefore sought a leadership position through peyotism. It is difficult, however, to believe that Wilson would not have sought to establish peyotism among the Osage whenever he had the opportunity, before, as well as after, the Ghost Dance.

Mathews (1961: 744–46) in *The Osages: Children of the Middle Waters,* found ideas in native Osage traditions that contributed to the acceptance of peyotism. He described the Osage conversion as follows:

This is the way Victor Griffin, the Quapaw, explained the peyote dreams of John Wilson to . . . Black Dog . . . and . . . Claremore. . . . He told them how he had been instructed to build fireplaces which were called "Moons" which would symbolize the grave of Christ.

This was the sort of thing they could believe, and they would not find it too difficult to relegate the Moon Woman to a messenger's role under the Creator who was still Wah'kon-tah. Grandfather the Sun must now be a messenger of the ruler also, and the Morning Star degraded, but still the lightning and the thunder could be messengers and manifestations as they had always been. All this had been indicated to them through the later years, and now this Caddo had discovered to them what had happened through peyote.

Victor Griffin went down to the Caddo country to get Wilson to come to the Quapaws and the Osages. Wilson was not prepossessing, and Agent Pollack had him run off the reservation several times, but finally he got permission to come to the Upland Forest People at Hominy and built two fireplaces, two moon altars. . . . The Osages called him . . . Moonhead, because of his obsession with the moon.

Victor Griffin . . . recalled: ". . . one nice morning he [Wilson] wanted to take a walk, told him alright. We was in house where I lived. On a hill there nice trees, no grass or nothing, horses been rolling around. 'Nephew [courtesy from older man to younger]' he said, 'this is sure a good place to have a meeting here, a good place for fireplace.' Just listen to him. Never thought anything about it. I just listened. Sure enough two or three days after that some of the old chiefs came over, he said, 'You chiefs, my nephew has found good ground up here, take you up there.' We all went up there and he said, 'Sure good place to have meeting.' They didn't know what he meant. No one knew what up to, but he know what we are to do. 'What do you say, let's fix a place here.' He laid down, hands out like that (extending his arms), said: 'Make mark where hands extended, and head here, now, nephew make marks there.' In two, three days we had meeting there."

Wilson had difficulty with the Osage when it came to placing the altar facing east, as was traditional with both his ceremony and that of the Half Moon. Mathews wrote:

When he went over to the Upland-Forest People at Hominy to build an altar for Black Dog and one for Claremore, he came face to face with Osage resistance. No matter what invisible person had instructed him, Black Dog would not have his altar facing east. This was the Heavy Eyebrows way; all Osage know that one traveled to Spiritland with Grandfather Sun, starting at noon; therefore that altar must face west. Two hundred dollars and some very fine horses and other gifts from Black Dog and Claremore submerged whatever scruples Moonhead might have had about west-facing altars, but he told Victor Griffin later: "But this here what you see, this does not belong here. . . . God didn't authorize me to build this. Christ didn't authorize me to build this. None of the employees of God. I done this on my own free will, done it to get through, to get by. When build four, ready. I am going home." He seemed to have built four "West Moon" altars, one for Griffin, one for a man called Frank Williams in the Caddo country, one for Black Dog, and one for Claremore.

The account of Osage conversion by Speck (1933:533) is probably more accurate as to date. Again, it is Wilson's nephew, George Anderson, who provides the story:

Anderson's narrative of his uncle's mission to the Osage is given as he recalled it. I take no responsibility for its accuracy. It is a native oral document. The event is staged about 1891. John Wilson was on his way from Anadarko to conduct meetings among the Delawares around Copan. While passing through the Osage nation, he visited Tall Chief, a Quapaw married to an Osage woman. While here, Wilson was stopped by an Osage who had previously attended peyote meetings among the Delawares and requested him to meet a group of Osage and tell him about his revelations and convictions and instruct them in his rules. He consented and complied with their wishes. The Osage in attendance at his meeting were convinced and converted. He accordingly stayed on with them about three weeks. Black Dog was at the time Chief of the Osage. His tribe were won over in force to the Wilson sect of peyote worshippers. John Wilson then returned to Anadarko, leaving behind him among the Osage two young Delaware who were attracted by the prospects of fortune offered by the wealthy Osage. Wilson had received presents from the tribe of new converts amounting to considerable value, a wagon, a carriage, a buggy and teams of good horses and harness for each and other horses, fourteen in all, not to mention blankets, goods, and money. He was unable to induce his Delaware companions to help him back to Anadarko with his gifts so he sent for his nephew, George Anderson, our informant, to help him drive the stock home. Anderson did go and then remained with Wilson for some time. The Osage have elevated Wilson almost to the station of a saint. . . .

With the conversion of the Osage, we probably have come to the construction of the first peyote church building. The peyote meeting place was traditionally, and still is, a tipi erected at a convenient place especially for the occasion, and the altar was dug into the ground, the earth removed being used to form the crescent or horseshoe shape of the altar. In time, more permanent altars have been made of concrete and have been used repeatedly and even "handed down" from one generation to another. Such concrete altars became characteristic of the Osage and were housed inside an eight-sided, roofed building. It was, of course, necessary for all peyotists to hold meetings in houses in winter or when the weather was very bad. In such cases a fire was made in the yard near the building to be used, and live coals were brought inside from time to time and placed on a mound of earth shaped to form the altar.

Attention to education by the Osage contributed to and gave strength to peyotism. In 1881 the Osage voted to accept the Osage Tribal Constitution, modeled on that of the Cherokee, which not only provided for popularly elected representative government, but also "included a provision for compulsory education of Indian children, with penalties of withholding annuity payments for the failure of attendance at school. . . . During the first year, 120 boys and girls were sent from the reservation and distributed among the Indian schools" (Finney 1962: 8–9). Undoubtedly, the emphasis on "Christian" education was strong at whatever schools these young Indians attended and during the 1880s and '90s many young adults must have returned to the Osage reservation as Christian converts with some ability to speak and understand the English language, qualities which would have facilitated their conversion to the Christianized peyote religion of John Wilson.

THE QUAPAW

When John Wilson made the acquaintance of the Osage, he also became acquainted with the Quapaw, most of whom, destitute, starving, and unwanted, were living among the Osage. The Quapaw had had a particularly difficult time since the Louisiana Purchase, when they, too, found it necessary to move from their home along the Mississippi about fifty miles north of the Arkansas. Like the Osage, they cooperated with the U.S. government, but unlike the Osage, they never seemed to benefit from their treaties. They were uprooted time and again, and the difficulties of their uncertain life, together with disease, reduced their numbers. In 1852, 314 Quapaw were given a reservation in the extreme northeastern corner of Indian Territory, beyond the Cherokee reservation, but they abandoned it during the Civil War because of the fighting there and were reluctant to return. For a time they were tolerated on the Osage reservation. About 1887 they at last began returning to their own reservation and eventually improved their life by alloting themselves two hundred acres for each member of the tribe and acquiring a tract of four hundred acres for schools and forty acres for churches. When lead and zinc were discovered on their land in 1895, the Quapaw became quite prosperous.

Ethnologists believe that John Wilson brought peyotism to the Quapaw between 1888 and 1891. Petrullo thought that it could have been as early as 1885; La Barre cited a manuscript by Voegelin to the effect that peyotism was taught to the Quapaw in 1889; Slotkin, quoting McKern, said it happened in 1891–92. Wilson's Big Moon ceremony was certainly well established among the Quapaw by 1900, the time of his last visit. He was by then very popular. According to his nephew, George Anderson, the Quapaw loaded Wilson down with gifts on his last visit because they hoped to persuade him to stay in their midst and make his home with them (Speck 1933:544). When he was killed at a railway crossing, they brought his body back to the reservation, where he is buried on the allotment of Peter Clabber.

The Christian training of the Quapaw and of Wilson himself was Roman Catholic. It may have been this circumstance that accounts for the rapport between them. In 1740 a Roman Catholic mission had been established among the Quapaw; in 1853, young Quapaw attended the Osage Manual Labor School run by Jesuits in southeastern Kansas; and the eleventh U.S. census for 1890 (U.S. Department of Commerce 1890:247) reported: "The Quapaws are Catholics, and a priest visits them once a month for spiritual instruction, which is mostly given at their residences." A Carmelite nun, Sister M. Laurence, attended a peyote meeting in Quapaw in 1903 (Laurence 1953) and recorded the event in her journal. The editor of that journal, Velma Neiderding, further commented on early Quapaw peyotism:

FIG. 7. Quapaw peyote church, Quapaw, Oklahoma, sketched by Charles Banks Wilson in 1954. Courtesy Thomas Gilcrease Institute of American History and Art, Tulsa, Oklahoma.

"Peyote worship was introduced to the Osage in 1898 by Moon Head a Caddo-Delaware. The Quapaws, according to Victor Griffin, their present Chief and a 'peyote priest,' were using peyote 'ten years before the Osages'" (that is, 1880). Moreover,

The Quapaws . . . having been Christianized by Catholic missionaries, adopted many sacramentals of the Catholic Church into the ritual of the native church. The crucifix is used today [1953] according to Indians who attend the peyote rites. Another use of a Christian symbol is the cross surmounting the "Medicine house" where peyote rites are held.

Early Quapaw peyote leaders were John Quapaw, Victor Griffin, and Peter Clabber.

THE SENECA

With the Quapaw in the northeastern corner of Indian Territory were also located several small groups of Indians of different backgrounds pragmatically settled there at various times in the interest of expediency. One of these tribes, the Seneca of Ohio, had been there since 1832 at the time when all Indians east of the Mississippi were asked to migrate to territory west of that river. A few of these Seneca became peyotists about 1907.

La Barre (1938: 119) reports: "George Anderson (Delaware) brought the Wilson moon to the Seneca in 1907, when eighteen men and women became members. One of the Seneca had a Quapaw wife, who gave him the idea of obtaining the moon; they were too poor to pay Anderson's usual fee, and merely gave him carfare home." Concerning the Seneca, Petrullo (1934: 103) wrote that the primary missionary to the Seneca was Charles Tyner (a Quapaw). He further said:

The Griffin Moon was established about 1906 or 1907 by a Quapaw, Victor Griffin. . . . He was greatly instrumental in inducing many to follow Wilson when he introduced his cult to the Quapaw and the neighboring Seneca. . . . With his influence over the Quapaw and the Seneca (his first wife belonged to that tribe), he has been successful in creating a following.

Ethnologist William C. Sturtevant, who studied Seneca peyotism in 1961, informed me in a personal communication that

according to Ernest Whitetree (Seneca, born 1892), peyote was introduced to the Seneca-Cayuga in 1907 by Delawares Tom, John, and Sam Anderson. The tipi they introduced had 21 poles, with the door at the east. Peyote meetings ceased around 1920. . . . He and a few others still consider themselves peyotists and attend meetings elsewhere when they can. . . ."

Thus, whether the Seneca learned of peyotism first from the Anderson brothers, who were Delawares, or from Victor Griffin, who was a Quapaw, or from someone else, it is quite clear that the Big Moon ceremony came to them about 1907 and flourished for a time.

THE PONCA

In 1877 the Ponca were moved from their homeland along the Missouri and Niobrara rivers in northern Nebraska and extreme south central South Dakota and were given a reservation in Indian Territory. However, about a third of the tribe, unable to endure their new location, returned to the Niobrara River of Nebraska. Peyotism of the Northern Ponca will be considered in chapter 7.

The Oklahoma or Southern Ponca numbered six hundred in 1880, and their reservation was located west of the Osage's along the Arkansas River. Although they were close neighbors of the Osage, the Kaw, the Oto, and others, they found more congeniality with the Cheyenne, about two hundred miles southwest. Ponca dances and a Ponca powwow were popular as early as 1880, and as many as two hundred Cheyenne visited the Ponca on those occasions. Such events furnished opportunity for the spread of peyotism.

The earliest actual report of peyotism on the Ponca reservation is the report of July 31, 1906, of Special Agent R. S. Connell to the Bureau of Indian Affairs in which he reported arresting Ponca peyote leader Robert Buffalohead and forcing six Cheyenne peyote missionaries to leave the Ponca reservation. In a letter to the superintendent of the Cheyenne-Arapaho Agency that same month, he noted that "Leonard Tyler, a Carlisle graduate of your Agency" was a supplier to the Poncas; also, he judged that Oto peyotism was more religious than the Ponca's ritual, which he branded "more of a drunk and carousal."

It is almost certain that the Ponca learned of peyote much earlier. Visiting back and forth as well as contact with neighboring tribes already involved in the peyote ceremony would suggest that the Ponca were familiar with the ceremony at least by 1900. It is even recorded that Quanah Parker once visited the Ponca. In 1916, Ponca Agency superintendent Charles E. Norton estimated that 50 percent of the Poncas were peyotists out of a total population of 630 and reported that Laraie Deere and Ed, Thomas, and Louis Primeaux were Ponca peyote leaders.

In 1923, Ruth Shonle conducted a survey of early peyotism on the Ponca reservation by way of a mailed questionnaire. She asked the date of first use, from whom peyote use was learned, circumstances of that introduction, and how peyote was used. Three sets of answers were returned from two Ponca Indians—Louis McDonald and Frank Eagle—and one set from an Oto, Charles Moore. All were officials of the Native American Church. Moore said the Cheyenne brought peyote to the Ponca in 1904, and

Moore stated that Reuben Taylor was the missionary. McDonald and Eagle said that peyote was introduced in 1902 and that Robert Buffalohead had learned of peyote while visiting the Cheyenne in Kingfisher County; there he had learned the ritual and from there he brought it home to the Ponca. They said that Reuben Taylor came later and conducted meetings.

THE KAW (KANSA)

In 1873, the Kaw (Kansa), a Sioux-speaking tribe linguistically close to the Osage and Omaha, were moved from central Kansas just over the border into Oklahoma. By 1881 they had purchased the northwest corner of the Osage territory just east of the Arkansas River. They were thus close to the Oklahoma Ponca, and their affairs were administered by the Ponca Agency, which also was in charge of the small Tonkawa group southwest in the same vicinity. Although the distance from their old reservation to their new one was not as far as many tribes had had to travel, the effort was hard on the Kaw, and their numbers decreased from 533 when they arrived in Oklahoma to 194 in 1889. Since then the tribe has shown a healthy growth, partly because of the particular interest that was taken in it by its most distinguished member, Charles Curtis.

Charles Curtis was one-eighth Kaw. He was born in Topeka, Kansas, in 1860 and lived and went to school during his childhood on the Kaw reservation. As an adult, he studied law, was elected to the House of Representatives, then to the Senate, and eventually became vice president of the United States. He was always interested in Indian affairs and was prominent in a good deal of legislation having to do with Indians. Quite naturally, he was particularly interested in helping the Kaw profit in their business affairs with the U.S. government. When in the Congress he was besieged with letters both for and against peyote; he became convinced that it should be banned, even for religious purposes and introduced a bill into Congress to that effect; fortunately for peyotism, it was defeated.

It is likely that the Kaw learned of peyote before the end of the nineteenth century, but the first report of its use is contained in a letter to Chief Special Officer Johnson from Almond R. Miller, superintendent of the Kaw Training School, dated June 21, 1909. Miller wrote: "There are only five members of the Kaw Tribe who use the peyotes. . . . As used by the Kaw Indians . . . I do not believe that they have been injured."

In June, 1914, Alanson Skinner interviewed several Kaw regarding peyotism, and his short report constitutes the entire ethnological data on Kaw peyotism. He wrote (1915b: 745, 758):

The peyote religion and the acquisition of considerable wealth (many Kansa have automobiles, telephones, and other luxuries) have broken down old customs. . . . The peyote cult while very strong here, having apparently superceded all of the old Kansa beliefs, has been in vogue, it is said, 7 or 8 years. It probably came from the Ponca. None of the teachings of the cult, as practiced by the Kansa, have any Biblical foundation. The ceremonies are held in a large conical tipi, and the usual rattles are made of small gourds and eagle feather fans and other paraphernalia occur. The effect of peyote-eating on the Kansa has been to abolish drunkenness among its followers.

It is quite possible that the Ponca were the first teachers of peyotism to the Kaw, but without definite information, the teachers might also have been the Tonkawa, the Oto, or others in the vicinity.

In 1916 farmer J. E. Goss reported to Superintendent Norton of the Ponca Agency that a majority of the Kaw full-bloods used peyote and that the leaders were Harry Stubbs, Barclay DeLano, and Jesse and Ed Mohojah. Another time he wrote that having been with the Kaw from 1912 to 1916, he could say that during that time they had a peyote meeting nearly every Saturday night.

THE TONKAWA

West of the Ponca and not far from the Kaw was the small reservation of the Tonkawa. As we know, the Tonkawa had been familiar with peyote at least since 1830 and probably much longer, sharing the knowledge with the Carrizo, the Lipan Apache, the Karankawa, and the Mescalero Apache. By the 1880s, the Carrizo, the Karankawa, and the Lipan Apache had ceased to exist as tribes. The Mescalero Apache lived on a reservation in New Mexico and seemed to have given up peyote. In Oklahoma a few Tonkawa managed to hang on, in company with an even fewer Lipan.

Tonkawa were cooperative with the U.S. government, serving well as army scouts, but for this same reason, and because they were suspected of cannibalism, they were generally disliked by other Indians. Moreover, they were linguistically isolated. No other tribe understood Tonkawa, and this language was for long thought to represent a separate language family, although it is now grouped, distantly, with Sioux.

The Tonkawa had had a violent history after 1830. Herbert E. Bolton, who wrote the article on the Tonkawa for the *Handbook of American Indians North of Mexico* (Hodge 1910, II: 778–83), relates the events which reduced the Tonkawa tribe from about a thousand in 1830 to ninety-two, including seventeen Lipan, in 1880:

In the fall of 1855 the Government settled them [the Tonkawa] together with the Caddo, Kichai, Waco, Tawakoni and Penateka Comanche, upon two small reservations on the Clear Fork of Brazos River, Texas. In consequence of the violent opposition of the Texans, culminating in an attack upon the agency, the Indians were removed to Washita River, Oklahoma, the Tonkawa being temporarily camped about the mouth of Tonkawa Creek, just above the present Anadarko.

In the confusion brought about by the Civil War, the other tribes saw an opportunity to pay off old scores against the Tonkawa, who were generally hated for their cannibalistic practices as well as for serving as government scouts against the more western tribes. On the excuse that the Tonkawa and their agent were in alliance with the Confederacy, a body of Delaware, Shawnee, and Caddo attacked the Anadarko agency and the Tonkawa camp on the night of October 25, 1862, killing two of the agency employees and massacring 137 men, women, and children out of a total of about 300 of the Tonkawa tribe. The survivors, after some years of miserable wandering, were finally gathered in at Fort Griffin, Texas, to save them from complete extinction by their enemies. In 1884, all that were left—92, including a number of Lipan—were removed to Oklahoma, being assigned the next year to their present location at Oakland Agency, near Ponca.

That the Tonkawa maintained their use of peyote and perhaps even further developed their own peyote ceremony is evidenced by the fact that all reports claim that peyotism among the Oto, whose reservation was located southeast of the Tonkawa, was brought by the Tonkawa. Charles Whitehorn, the Oto first to learn peyotism and to teach it to his people, wrote to Ruth Shonle (1925:54): "Peyote was first among the Oto in 1896. The use of peyote was first acquired from the Tonkawa. It was with this tribe that we first learned of the use of peyote and learned of them that it was of God and it was given to use in the name of our Lord Jesus Christ."

THE OTO

The Oto moved from their home along the Platte River in Nebraska to Oklahoma in 1880, with the official resettlement in 1881 and 1882. Like the Ponca, the Osage, and the Kaw, they spoke a dialect of Sioux. Their reservation was located just south of the Ponca and west of the Pawnee, with the Tonkawa, Kaw, and Osage as near neighbors.

Since the peyote ceremony of the Oto came directly from the Tonkawa, who only arrived in Oklahoma in 1884, one might expect a somewhat different ceremony from the Kiowa-Comanche Half Moon or the Caddo-Delaware Big Moon. However, the unique features of this old Oto ceremony are few. As described by James H. Howard, it is essentially the same as the Kiowa-Comanche ceremony, with only a slight alteration indicative of Wilson influence: a heart under the fire and a line crossing from horn to horn of the moon.

Charles Whitehorn, the first Oto roadman, who attributed his knowledge of peyotism to the Tonkawa, was born about 1865, so he would have been a young adult when the Tonkawa settled on a reservation near his home in Red Rock, Oklahoma. He was "uneducated" according to the superintendent of the agency, and we must assume that his knowledge of English was limited. No Tonkawan is given as his teacher, and we have no account of the Tonkawa ceremony as it was practiced in the 1880s. The Tonkawan language should also have given him some difficulty. These facts tend to draw one to the conclusion that perhaps he only received his first peyote buttons from the Tonkawa, and feeling grateful and indebted, forever after attributed his knowledge of peyote to that tribe.

Whitehorn had ample opportunity to learn the Kiowa-Comanche moon from members of those tribes. Bela Kozad, a Kiowa, and Reuben Taylor, a Cheyenne, were known to hold meetings on the Oto reservation. Although the ceremony was characterized by a number of Christian symbols which are suggestive of the John Wilson influence, Whitehorn never mentioned Wilson or the Caddo-Delaware Big Moon. If Whitehorn did indeed learn his peyote ceremony directly from the Tonkawa, without attending other meetings from the tribes in the vicinity, the fact that his ceremony and that of the Kiowa-Comanche are so similar is again evidence of the strength of the ancient ceremony.

One unique feature of the Oto ceremony as described by Howard (1956: 435) was a specially decorated tipi in which to hold meetings: "This is brown or gray, and has a green band around the bottom which rises to form a 'hill' in the rear. Upon this hill a white cross is painted. The hill represents Calvary and the cross that upon which Christ was crucified." Obviously, though "uneducated," Whitehorn had picked up some knowledge of Christianity. This tipi, along with Whitehorn's other peyote paraphernalia, was ceremonially transfered by him to his son-in-law, Omaha Cyrus Phillips, and from Cyrus Phillips to his son George Phillips. Wrote Howard (1956: 443): "George Phillips was present, as a child, at the ceremonial transfer of the fireplace [ceremony] to Cyrus Phillips, his father. George thinks this was about 1904 or 1905. . . . At the transfer ceremony . . . Whitehorn recounted his vision." This vision was said to have inspired the fireplace, and George Phillips described it (Howard 1956: 433):

Whitehorn said that when he was younger he had been a cowboy and that one night when he was rolled up in his blanket on the prairie, he heard a voice speaking to him. It told him that if his people ever wanted to talk with God, they had the privilege to do so: God would listen to whatever they had to say if they talked to him at a sacred altar.

Another Oto peyotist, George Daily, referred to this vision when he told W. Whitman (1937: 82, fn. 1): "The late Charles Whitehorn . . . was the last one to have had a vision during his puberty fast. He later became the leader of a peyote 'fireplace' founded on this vision."

In 1906, Special Agent R. S. Connell commented on the early Oto ceremony in a report to the Bureau of Indian Affairs: "It is coupled with a very elaborate and artistic exercise. I attended one of their meetings held in a large tepee with a wing audience tent. A large cross was painted on the altar tent, and they had a big picture of Christ hung up in a prominent position."

THE PAWNEE

The Pawnee, Caddoan-speaking, originally a strong, clever, agricultural tribe of the lower Mississippi Valley, remembered for the men's picturesque dressing of the scalp lock with ochre and buffalo grease so that it stood erect and then curved backward, suffered the fate of other Plains Indians. From an energetic tribe of perhaps 10,000 in 1838, they were reduced to 1,306 in 1875 when they moved from their first reservation in Nebraska to one in Oklahoma. They were given a reservation between the Oto and the southern end of the Osage reservations. The Ponca were to the north, and the three tribes—the Oto, the Ponca, and the Pawnee—were administered from the same agency.

James Mooney, Alexander Lesser, and James R. Murie say that Frank White was the first Pawnee peyote leader. He was also the Pawnee leader of the Ghost Dance, which was very popular on the Pawnee reservation for a few years. Lesser wrote (1933: 60):

The Pawnee tell of White's learning the Ghost Dance among the southern tribes in the following way: "One time Frank White went over to the Comanche, who were dancing the Ghost Dance. . . . He ate peyote a great deal. . . . Then he left them and went to the Wichita. He ate peyote there, and watched them dance the Ghost Dance and learned it. . . ." In 1892 to keep the Pawnee quiet for a while, they say the agent had White arrested. A United States marshal and three Indian policemen arrested White. . . . [P. 66] "All this time White drank peyote, which made him wise." [P. 76]

James R. Murie (1914: 636–37) has this story:

About 1890, two Pawnee youths visited the Quapaw where they learned something of the peyote cult. They brought back with them some of the peyote buttons but a very meager knowledge of the ritual. . . . Later on, a visiting Arapahoe taught them the ritual. . . . At once this member [Frank White] became leader and gradually elaborated the ritual into which he introduced many Christian conceptions, because in the induced visions he frequently saw and talked with Christ. . . .

La Barre (1938: 118) received still a different story of the origin of peyotism among the Pawnee. He wrote:

Eagle Flying Above, who later became oil-wealthy, was the first Pawnee user of peyote, obtaining it from an Arapaho friend, about 1890 or a little later. Several months later Sun Chief, the writer's informant, took it up. At the death of Eagle Flying Above, Sun Chief was the only Pawnee leader, and all the others learned the rite from him; he has eaten peyote since 1892–94, but only later became a leader. A still earlier source appears to be the Quapaw, whom two Pawnee youths visited in 1890. . . . Pawnee peyote was early involved in the Ghost Dance excitement.

La Barre (1938: 113) also reported that Quanah Parker visited the Pawnee, and it is probable that the peyote ceremony first practiced by the Pawnee was the Comanche Half Moon ceremony, but soon the ceremony was influenced by John Wilson through the Quapaw or the Wichita, or perhaps it was the Ghost Dance that brought elements of Christianity to the Pawnee peyote ceremony. Frank White died in 1893, but there were others to carry on. In 1916, Chief Special Officer Henry A. Larson reported that forty-five Pawnee adults used peyote and the "leaders in such practices are Thomas Morgan, Sherman Keller, Henry Minthorn, James Murie, and Thomas Yellow Horse."

THE SAC AND FOX OF OKLAHOMA

The Sac and Fox, two tribes of Algonquian-speaking people, long allied and affiliated, formerly lived near the Great Lakes. By 1869 they had split into three groups: one lived on the Neosho Reservation in northeastern Kansas with small groups of Kickapoo and Iowa; another lived on their own land at Tama, Iowa; and a third were given a reservation in central Oklahoma, this last being the remnants of a group known as the Mississippi Sac and Fox. Those groups not in Oklahoma will be considered in a later chapter. From 6,400 Indians in 1825, the number of Sac and Fox had greatly shrunk by 1880, when the Oklahoma tribe could count only 441. The Sac and Fox reservation was located between the Iowa and the Creek lands. To the north were the Pawnee, Osage, Oto, Ponca, Kaw, and Tonkawa.

La Barre relied on Truman Michelson's account of Sac and Fox peyotism for his data on the early diffusion of peyote to this tribe. He wrote (1938: 119): "Ed Butler brought Sac peyote directly from the Tonkawa." Others confirmed this. The first official acknowledgment by the agency of Sac and Fox peyotism came in the annual report of Indian agent W. C. Kohlenberg for the year 1906, but it must have been well established before that. Inasmuch as the Oto also claimed to have been taught about peyote by the Tonkawa, it may be that the Sac and Fox were proselytized at about the same time, probably in the 1890s. In 1916, Superintendent Horace J. Johnson wrote to Chief Special Officer Henry A. Larson that Ed Butler, George Butler, Harding Franklin, and Dickson Mokokoko (one of the last great Sac and Fox chiefs) were among nine Sac and Fox who had "used the drug for a period of from 15 to 20 years" among a total of about sixty users. In 1972, in Stroud, Oklahoma, Tom Morris, age ninety-seven, told me that Ed Butler had learned peyotism from the Tonkawa "down in Ponca City."

Variety characterized peyotism on the Sac and Fox reservation. La Barre continued: "The Sac have been tenacious of their older religion and its fetishes, though peyotism is now strong among them; indeed, about 1923, attempted affiliation with the Native American Church failed because five rival chiefs ran different meetings." One can imagine the five variations of peyotism to have been the Tonkawa ceremony of Ed Butler, the Caddo Big Moon, the Comanche-Kiowa Half Moon, the Oto Whitehorn moon, and perhaps the ceremony of Johnathan Koshiway, a Sac and Fox leader from the Kansas Sac and Fox reservation. Since it is not unusual for peyotists to be active members of Christian churches, I was not surprised to hear that this was true of the Oklahoma Sac and Fox when, in 1972, I visited that tribe and attended a peyote meeting with them. However, I was some-what taken aback when ninety-seven-year-old Tom Morris informed me that George Butler, brother of Ed, had been a peyote roadman at the same time he was minister in charge of the Baptist church in Cushing, Oklahoma. Carl Butler, roadman of the meeting I attended and son of George, said: "Father was a Baptist minister and peyote roadman at the same time. Many times I attended peyote meetings with dad on Saturday night; then left with him Sunday morning and helped sing in the Baptist Church service, and then returned and ate the noon peyote feast with the Indians."

THE IOWA OF OKLAHOMA

By 1836, the Iowa, Sioux-speaking, formerly living in the area of the pres-ent states of Iowa, Illinois, and Minnesota, were settled on the Great Nemeha Agency in southeastern Nebraska, their total number being 470. In 1876, unhappy with the idea of allotments, about one-half of their num-ber, then 224, moved to Oklahoma. They camped on the Sac and Fox reser-vation until 1883, when they were assigned a small reservation west of that of the Sac and Fox, with whom they had been historically congenial.

Joseph Springer was probably the first Iowa peyotist, and he may have learned the ceremony as early as 1879 from none other than Quanah Parker. Certainly, by 1908 he had become a successful roadman and an elo-quent one. We have no record of his education, but he was chosen to speak in defense of peyotism before the Oklahoma legislature in 1908 with Parker, Arapaho Paul Boynton, and Kiowa James Waldo, the last two being Carlisle graduates. At that time, he said: "We are learning. . . . we know who Jesus is. We are trying to take the road to Jesus Christ, and we take up this little medicine called Peoti. . . . We are trying to reach Jesus Christ. . . . We have done lots of crimes and we ask the Great Spirit to forgive them. He says to 'ask with all your heart' and then He helps us."

In 1972, I obtained from the Library of Congress a mimeographed pub-lication entitled "The Raven Speaks" (vol. 4, no. 10 [January 7, 1972], Dallas, Texas) containing an article, "The Peyote Ceremony," by one Dan Murray, who identified himself as "an Oto Indian from Perkins, Oklahoma," but later confirmed that he was more Iowa than Oto. The ceremony he described was principally that of the Iowa. I corresponded with Murray and over the period of a year, he sent me fifty-four pages of data on the history of Iowa peyotism, with a detailed description of the peyote ritual as he had observed it and the changes that had been made in it, as related by some of the old Iowa. He asserted that Kirwin Murray, his ancestor, was a collaborator of Joseph Springer and that he had become an Iowa roadman of the Kiowa-Comanche Way by 1880. He further said that Joseph Springer had learned of peyote from Quanah Parker by 1879. Also, he emphasized that neither Delaware-Caddo John Wilson nor Kansas Sac and Fox Johnathan Koshiway had influenced Iowa peyotism. He described the importance of intertribal marriages in binding together peyotists of various tribes, this being the case between the Oto and the Iowa.

Skinner (1915: 724–28) published a statement on peyote by Joe Springer:

Some southern peoples have used it for many years before it came to us. . . . Now a great change has taken place, and it is used to worship Jesus Christ and God, the Father. It is only those who do not yet know Jesus and have not seen his light who utilize peyote for heathen practices. . . . The peyote chief sees to the seating of guests and members, and leads in the preaching and Bible reading. . . . [The] cane . . . represents the staff of the Saviour. . . . Throw away liquor, tobacco, stealing, lying and gossip. The Bible teaches us to do as we would be done by, and to love our neighbors. . . . The peyote chief himself carries the water to show his humility, because of Biblical references as to the washing of the feet, etc. . . . Typical songs of the Peyote society are "Jesus way is the only way," "Saviour Jesus is the only Saviour."

Although the Iowa ceremony was essentially the Kiowa-Comanche Half Moon, the many Christian ideas expressed by roadman Springer indicate how Christianity was affecting this ritual. If they hadn't been so opposed, Christian missionaries, school teachers, agency officials, and others might have rejoiced at the success of their efforts to teach Christian principles as manifested in the peyote religion in all its variations. But they continued to be blind to their successes and opposed peyotism vigorously. Nevertheless, according to Skinner, by 1914 the peyote religion of Joe Springer was "in full swing" among the Iowa, and in 1919, Robert E. L. Newberne's statistics of peyotism indicate that 60 percent of adult Iowa Indians adhered to it.

THE KICKAPOO

The Kickapoo, like the Iowa and the Sac and Fox, were Algonquian-speaking and originally lived near the Great Lakes in Wisconsin and Illinois. They were a close-knit tribe of agriculturalists living in neat villages of bark houses. From one group of about 2,200 in 1825, the vicissitudes of civilization soon resulted in three far-flung bands from Kansas to Mexico. In 1819, when their lands in Illinois were ceded to the United States and a reservation in northeastern Kansas was assigned to them, some of the Kickapoo left the others and went to Texas. Eventually they joined a group of Seminole and were induced to establish themselves in the border area of Coahuila, Mexico, on a reservation given them by the Mexican government. After the Civil War, Texans complained of Kickapoo raids from Mexico into Texas, and the United States sought the return of the Kickapoo in order to better control them. In 1870 an illegal raid by the U.S. Army into Mexico and a specially appointed U.S. commission partially succeeded in bringing the Mexican Kickapoo back to the United States and locating them on a reservation in central Oklahoma, near the Iowa and the Sac and Fox, where they became known as the Mexican Kickapoo. Some Kickapoo, however, still live in Coahuila, Mexico, and all three groups maintain contact through marriage and visiting. In 1876 there were 312 Kickapoo living in Oklahoma, 252 living in Kansas, and 100 living in Mexico.

There is no peyote ceremony among the Kickapoo who stayed in Mexico. No doubt they were familiar with the plant, since it grew in their midst. And they were certainly aware of the ceremony, since many peyotists visited the area to obtain supplies. When they could, they probably visited relatives and friends in Oklahoma and Kansas, and likewise they were visited by their northern relatives. At such times they would surely have observed peyote ceremonies. But a peyote ceremony did not develop among them, perhaps because of their isolation or the fact that the lack of opposition made it less appealing.

Among the Mexican Kickapoo in Oklahoma there did flourish a peyote ceremony, and although there are a few contradictory reports about who introduced it and when, it seems clear that it probably began before 1900 and that the primary teacher was Henry Murdock (Kickapoo). Murdock was informant for La Barre, who wrote (1938: 116):

Henry Murdock brought the new religion from Quanah Parker and the Comanche in 1906; but he had personally known of peyote before, having gone to Mexico in 1864. Quanah had known Murdock before the peyote religion began spreading and Quanah invited his friend by letter to visit him. He put on a meeting in his honor, taught him the ceremony and presented him with peyote paraphernalia. The set songs in the Kickapoo rite are Comanche, and the custom of making the ashes into a bird likewise indicates a Comanche provenience for the ceremony.

In 1909, Murdock said he had been using peyote for ten years, which would have put the introduction of peyote to the Kickapoo before 1900. This was the occasion when the Indians were having trouble procuring peyote because of the efforts of Chief Special Officer Johnson to stop all peyote traffic. Henry Murdock, with a number of others of his tribe, prepared and presented a signed statement regarding peyote to Superintendent Frank A. Thackery of their agency. The statement asked the agent to help them continue to use peyote, arguing that its use cured all kinds of sickness, that it was important in the practice of their religion, which was a sincere form of worship including Jesus and the Bible, that it helped them to avoid drinking, that it was definitely not "mescal," that one of them (Murdock) had used it for ten years, and that he had benefited in many ways.

The plea probably fell on deaf ears, but Murdock and other Kickapoo continued to be active in transporting peyote from Mexico during the difficult years when Johnson was trying to stop the traffic. Murdock was an educated man, having spent six years at Carlisle. In 1910, when that school sent out a questionnaire to graduates, he described himself: "I am a Christian man. I don't smoke, drink whiskey or play cards or use bad language. . . . We had a good meeting Saturday on my place telling them about God and Jesus. I am glad I went to Carlisle and learned lots of things."

THE SHAWNEE

In prehistoric times the Shawnee, another Algonquian-speaking tribe, lived along the Ohio River. During the first three centuries of history, wars, displacements, and wanderings took the great tribe of Tecumseh to practically every section of the United States east of the Rocky Mountains before finally they were settled in Oklahoma in three small groups. The Shawnee were in South Carolina and Georgia when the colonists arrived. At different times they were in Alabama, Kentucky, Pennsylvania, Ohio, and, later, in Kansas, Louisiana, and Texas. After the Civil War, the main body of Shawnee relinquished their reservation in Kansas, and, in agreement with the Cherokee, settled on the northern part of the Cherokee Nation in Indian Territory as Cherokee citizens. Earlier, in 1832, a smaller group had been settled in the extreme northeastern corner of Oklahoma with the Quapaw, Seneca, and others. A third group, known as the Absentee Shawnee, had earlier become associated with the Caddo, Tonkawa, Delaware, and others, sharing their fortunes on the Brazos River in Texas and later on the Wichita reservation in Oklahoma. In 1872, all of the Absentee Shawnee were officially settled on part of the Potawatomi reservation in central Oklahoma. In 1890 there were 820 Cherokee-Shawnee, in 1891 there were 563 Absentee Shawnee, and in 1893 there were 84 Eastern Shawnee.

Almost anytime from 1830 to 1862, the Absentee Shawnee could have learned of peyote directly from the Tonkawa even though they were anything but friendly. There is no doubt that the Shawnee despised the Tonkawa, inasmuch as they led the massacre of them at Anadarko in 1862, yet as long as tribes live close to one another, there has usually been an exchange of cultural knowledge, especially of medicine said to have supernatural qualities. Suggesting that the Shawnee had learned of peyote while in Texas before 1859 is the fact that "war bundles of the Shawnee [contained peyote], long before they knew the generalized peyote ritual" (La Barre, 1938: 26).

Erminie Voegelin has done extensive research among the Shawnee and has shared her "notes" generously. In a letter to me in 1940, she wrote: "Peyote among the Absentee Group is said to have been introduced ca. 1900, from the Kickapoo, who learned it from the Comanche. The meetings mainly follow the Kiowa-Apache procedure." However, La Barre reported that Jim Clark, an Absentee Shawnee, brought peyotism directly from the Comanche in the 1890s (1938: 119 and 153–3).

Voegelin stated that the Wilson Big Moon ceremony was also known among the Absentee Shawnee, with Ernest Spybuck as roadman. Spybuck was also an artist of ability who produced a number of paintings of the peyote ceremony. Made about 1910, his paintings leave no doubt that by that time the Absentee Shawnee did indeed have a Big Moon, as well as a Half Moon, ceremony, although the former was thought to be of secondary importance.

Officially, the Cherokee Shawnee were considered, like the Cherokee, to be nonpeyotists, yet anthropologists have found ample evidence of the ceremony among them. They and the Eastern Shawnee, who lived nearby, seem to have been as one as far as peyote is concerned. The ceremony of both was the Big Moon rite, and Wilson himself was probably the proselytizer. La Barre wrote (1938: 153): "Early peyotism occurred among the [Cherokee] Shawnee when Wilson came to them about 1889," and he reported that Wilson came again in 1894 and that George Foreleaf (Delaware) brought peyote from Mexico to the Cherokee Shawnee about 1898. His Cherokee Shawnee informants, Tom and Collins Panther, reported the making of chewed peyote into poultices for sores and snake-bites and eating it for colds, pneumonia, rheumatism, aches, and pains.

SUMMARY

By 1910 peyotism had become well established among the Indians of Oklahoma, with the exception for the most part of the Five Civilized tribes. Nearly all of those arriving after 1874 had taken it up to some extent. It spread by word of mouth, from person to person, as well as deliberately by a few dedicated believers and some self-seeking missionaries. It survived the early antagonisms of the establishment. And it changed a little as each new roadman expressed his personality in guiding the ritual, but it remained basically true to the form and spirit of its beginning.

We have only touched on the antagonism to peyotism that was felt by government officials, teachers, missionaries as the white establishment became aware of the new Indian religion. The violence of the opposition to peyotism will be our next consideration.

CHAPTER 6

Early Efforts to Suppress Peyote

WHEN the use of peyote became apparent to missionaries and Indian agents of the U.S. government, they immediately sought to suppress it. To them, as to the Catholic fathers in Mexico some two hundred years earlier, the plant and the peyote ceremony seemed the very essence of heathenish Indian practices, a veritable "root" of all evil.

In 1886, J. Lee Hall, agent of the Kiowa, Comanche, and Wichita Agency, reported the use of "a kind of cactus that comes from Mexico. . . . the Comanche call it wo-co-wist. The Apaches ho-as or ho-se." Hall (p. 130) added: "I would respectfully suggest that the same be made contraband." A year later, a Bureau of Indian Affairs attorney and special agent, one E. E. White, replaced Hall, who had been dismissed for drunkenness (White 1888d: 98). White soon learned of peyote and of its bad reputation. One source might have been E. L. Clark, who had lived among the Comanche many years and later wrote to White of "Many cases [in which] men went mad and killed their own people; their own families, and others" (Clark 1888). Probably other sources were missionaries, Episcopalian J. B. Wicks among the Comanche since 1881 and Methodist J. J. Methvin, who arrived early in 1887. In a letter included as part of the annual report of Agent George D. Day, 1892, Rev. Methvin wrote: "Gambling and mescal-eating are common among the Indians, and if some wholesome law against these could be enacted and enforced so as to make these evils among them disreputable it would be a wise step."

White was a man of action. Although he remained at Anadarko, Indian Territory, only from October 19, 1887, to September, 1888, during those eleven months he originated an order which was to be repeated many times on a number of different Indian reservations during the next half-century. On June 6, 1888, he posted the following (1888a):

Being convinced from what I learn from various sources, which I deem reliable that many Indians on this Reservation are using Mescal Beans to the extent of impairing their minds and physical strength: that some Indians have died from the excessive use of these beans: that they are in fact distructive to both the health, and mental faculties of the Indians and will soon greatly decimate them, if this is not checked. . . .

Wherefore all Indians on this Reservation are hereby forbidden to eat any of said beans, or to drink any decoction for fermentation thereof, or liquor distilled therefrom, or to sell or give to any Indian or have in his possession, any of these beans. Any Indian convicted of violating this order will be punished by the cutting off of his annuity goods and rations according to the aggravation of the case. And in extreme cases the grass money will be cut off. . . .

This order is for the good of the Indians—many of whom are being destroyed by the use of this bean. And I hereby call all chiefs and head men and all good Indians of every class to aid and assist me in enforcing this order. It is solely for their own welfare.

In the covering letter transmitting a copy of the order to the commissioner of Indian affairs (1888*b*), he wrote:

I have the honor to transmit herewith a copy of an order which I have assumed to issue in reference to the use of the Mescal Beans [Peyote] by the Indians on this Reservation and respectfully request your approval of the same. . . . In my judgment there should be legislation to prevent whites from selling or giving these beans to the Indians either on or off the Reservation. . . .

This action was received favorably by the Bureau of Indian Affairs (BIA) and became the guide for bureau instruction to all agencies. The following letter to S. L. Patrick, U.S. Indian agent, Sac and Fox Agency, July 31, 1890, from T. J. Morgan, commissioner, found in a BIA letter book in the National Archives, shows that E. E. White's "order" had become general:

I am not informed as to whether this habit has taken any hold among the Indians of your agency. If it has, the following instructions issued to the Kiowa and Comanche Agency you will enforce among the Indians under your charge.

"It is the duty of the government preemptorily to stop the use of this bean by Indians. You will direct the police of your agency to seize and destroy the mescal bean, or any preparation or decoction thereof, wherever found on the reservation. The article itself, and those who use it are to be treated exactly as if it were alcohol or whiskey, or a compound thereof; in fact it may be classified for all practical purposes as an 'intoxicating liquor.'

"Licensed traders are, of course, prohibited from selling this article to Indians, and I have no reason to suppose that they have done so. . . . The Indians will be less likely to get an article which they are to be punished for using and which is liable to confiscation wherever found in their possession.

"The Court of Indian Offenses at your agency shall consider the use, sale, exchange, gift, or introduction of the mescal bean as a misdeameanor punishable under Section 9 [re. intoxicants] of the Rules governing the Court of Indian Offenses."

You will please take some pains to inform yourself whether the Indians of your agency are using mescal or "woqui" in any of its forms, and if so, I hope you will be prompt, energetic, and persistent in your efforts to stamp out among them this evil practice.

The Court of Indian Offenses had been established in 1883. On December 2, 1882, the secretary of the interior, H. M. Teller, recommended to the commissioner of Indian affairs, Hirman Price, that he prepare "Rules Governing the Court of Indian Offenses." These rules were finalized by March 30, 1883, and copies were sent to all Indian agencies. Each court of

Indian offenses was authorized to have as judges three Indian police officers or cooperative tribal chiefs or leaders. The offenses the Indian judges were to stop or to punish were performances of "old heathenish dances" or ceremonies such as the Sun Dance and the Scalp Dance; plural marriage; the usual ritual practices of so-called medicine men; destruction of property at a burial; or use of any intoxicants. The rules governing the Court of Indian Offenses could, of course, be applied by superintendents of reservations and agencies if the courts were not functioning. In fact, each agent was to "see to it that the requirements are strictly enforced, with the view of having the evil practices mentioned by the honorable Secretary ultimately abolished" (Price 1883: 5).

In spite of the ban, peyote was easily available during the 1890s. Mooney (1897a: 329–30) wrote:

The . . . [peyote rite] was noted by the Spanish missionaries very soon after they had established themselves in Mexico. Recognizing in it one of the most important of the native rites, they endeavored to suppress it, but with little result. Later on it fell under the ban of the American missionaries and officials, so that the eating of peyote is prohibited and the trade in it is contraband on all the southwestern Indian reservations. Notwithstanding all this, the use of the plant is spreading and the Indians find no difficulty in procuring all they can pay for.

Mooney (1896a: 7) had earlier reported that "severe penalties have been threatened and inflicted against Indians using it or having it in their possession." Peyote meetings were being held increasingly, and the ceremony spread to new tribes. Oddly, there were no reports of agencies seizing quantities of peyote. Perhaps one reason for lack of success in enforcing the order was the fact that, at least on the Comanche-Kiowa reservation, the Court of Indian Offenses was dominated by peyotists, notably the very clever Comanche chief and peyote roadman Quanah Parker.

Aware that peyote had not been wiped out, the Indian bureau in Washington periodically prodded the agencies. For example, on August 4, 1896, Commissioner D. M. Browning wrote to Acting Agent Capt. F. D. Baldwin in Anadarko:

It has recently been reported to this office that some of the Indians of the Kiowa, etc. Agency are again indulging in the use of "mescal," and reviving the "ghost dance," and that these two destructive influences . . . are interfering quite seriously with the work of missionaries among them.

I would therefore be glad to have you make a careful and thorough investigation in the matter, and if you find that such reports are true, you will use your best efforts to stamp out these evils.

The Court of Indian Offenses was to be used.

The Indian prohibition was made more explicit under the act of January 30, 1897 (29 Stat. 506), which made it an offense "to furnish any article whatsoever under any name, label, or brand which produces intoxication to any Indian ward of the Government." Some believed that this legalized the suppression of peyotism, and there was a slight attempt by the federal special agent to use it to limit and stop the distribution of peyote. But generally law enforcement officials were uneasy about its application to peyote. It had not been tested in court, and more specific federal and state laws were sought.

The first statute law enacted specifically to control the use of peyote occurred in the Territory of Oklahoma in 1899, stimulated by a federal official, A. E. Woodson, agent of the Cheyenne and Arapaho Agency at Darlington. In his annual report, he wrote:

At the last session of the Territorial legislature I procured the passage of a law prohibiting medicine men from practicing their incantations among allotted Indians under penalty of fine and imprisonment. . . . With the abolition of medicine men and the adoption of legal marriages, these people will have taken an advanced step in their civilization.

The use of the mescal bean was also declared to be unlawful. [Woodson 1899:284]

The statute read:

Section 2652—That it shall be unlawful for any person to introduce on any Indian reservation or Indian allotment situated within this Territory or to have in possession, barter, sell, give, or otherwise dispose of, any "Mescal Bean," or the product of any such drug, to any allotted Indian in this Territory. . . . Any person who shall violate the provisions of this Act in this Teritory, shall be deemed guilty of a misdemeanor, and, upon conviction, thereof, shall be fined in a sum not less than twenty-five dollars, nor more than two hundred dollars, or be confined in the county jail for not more than six months, or be assessed both such fine and imprisonment in the discretion of the court. [Oklahoma, *Session Laws,* 1899, pp. 122–23]*

In an effort to find out who the peyotists were, where and when meetings were held, who were trading in peyote, and so on, Indian agents employed nonpeyotist Indians and white "farmers" (the name given to Indians or whites teaching farming to the Indians and supervised by the government to do so) to spy on peyote gatherings. Even before the territorial prohibition against peyote had been enacted, intelligence reports were ac-

---

*It appears significant that this first statute law, like the first administrative order to prohibit the Indian use of peyote in ceremonies or otherwise, came about through independent action of a U.S. Indian agent, without explicit instruction from the central headquarters in Washington, D.C. It is also noteworthy that at the time use of peyote for Indian rituals was outlawed, peyote was being offered for sale by pharmaceutical firms such as Parke, Davis, and Company of Detroit. As late as the 1920s peyote was considered of therapeutic use, with dosage given in the *United States Dispensatory,* nineteenth edition, although it was not recognized by the *United States Pharmacopoeia* (Newberne 1925:22–23).

cumulating in the agency offices in Anadarko, Darlington, and other agency headquarters. White Indian farmer J. W. Ijams in 1898 sent to the Cheyenne Agency more than fifty names of Indians who attended meetings. White farmer James H. Deer informed the same agency that stores near Oak Dale, Oklahoma Territory, were selling peyote. He wrote (Deer 1898): "In Cheyenne County near the line of this reservation, a White man has a store in which he keeps mescal [peyote] by the cases . . . to sell to the Indians. . . . He offered a large case . . . for $30. . . ."

Agency officials tried to enforce the law but were often confused and doubtful how to do it. On September 22, 1899, U.S. Indian Agent W. J. Pollack wrote to the BIA asking what might be done with an "Osage boy by the name of Arthur Bonnicastle: who disobeyed his order and used his annuity money to travel to Anadarko to visit with John Wilson in order to be instructed in Peyotism." After threatening to punish Bonnicastle for going to visit Wilson, Agent Pollack was uncertain about the legal justification for his threatened actions. He wrote:

I therefore ask instructions as to what punishment, if any may be inflicted upon Mr. Bonnicastle and his friends who went with him to Anadarko without permission, and what penalty, if any, may be imposed upon him for bringing the mescal Bean [peyote] into this country; also whether or not it will justify the withholding from Mr. Bonnicastle and those who went with him their annuity money.

Arthur Bonnicastle was sent to Carlisle Indian School in October, 1899, even though he was, at age twenty-two, several years older than the average male students at that time. In 1900 he ran away and enlisted in the U.S. Army and was soon sent to China, where he became an American hero during the Boxer Rebellion (U.S. Congress, House, Committee on Indian Affairs 1918a: 84).

At about the same time that Bonnicastle was fighting to protect Christians in China, Agent O. A. Mitschet at the Osage Agency forbade an Osage chief to invite a Caddo peyote leader to visit the Osage reservation (Mitschet 1900). Since there was no law justifying such an order, the Osage ignored it.

In 1903 the Reverend B. F. Gassaway wrote to the BIA to complain that Comanche-Kiowa agent Col. J. F. Randlett was not active enough in suppressing Kiowa and Comanche peyotism. He said that Kiowa chief Horse and Comanche chief Quanah Parker encouraged their fellow tribesmen to participate in peyote ceremonies which run "all Saturday night and up to 9 or 10 o'clock Sunday morning; leaving the devotees in such a state of stupefaction that it is utterly impossible to teach them anything from the word of God. . . . The Sabbath is the principal day for our preaching services and if the Indians are first made drunk on mescal [peyote] they cannot then be benefitted by the gospel." Reverend Gassaway also wrote that peyotism "is perhaps the chief hindrance to the efforts of the missionaries. . . . In talking to an educated Comanche yesterday on the subject, he said that the Comanche would never cease the practice unless the Government would positively prohibit it."

The law against mescal (peyote) continued to be poorly enforced. Quanah Parker, active peyote proselytizer, lost his position as judge of the Court of Indian Offenses because he took a new wife, his seventh, not because of his peyotism (Hagan 1962), and he continued to be retained on the federal government payroll because of his importance to the local agent in the management of Indian affairs. In 1905, besides Parker there were five well-known peyotists on the BIA payroll at Anadarko: Otto Wells, farmer; Willie Ahdozy, assistant farmer; Stanley Edge, blacksmith; Pe-wo, private of police; and Marcus Poco, private of police. At the same time, Charles W. Daily, a leader of Oto peyotism, was private of police at the Ponca Agency (U.S. Bureau of Indian Affairs 1905).

One attempt to enforce the antipeyote law was reported by BIA special agent R. S. Connell to the commissioner of Indian affairs:

The second night here [Ponca Agency] Supt. Noble; the Deputy U.S. Marshal and myself, pulled a Mescal [peyote] meeting. Six Cheyennes, who seemed to be the leaders, were sent home, and Robert Buffalo Head, the leader here, was sent to jail. He was afterwards released, after giving the enclosed affidavit before the U.S. Commissioner, as to where he obtained the . . . [peyote] buttons. . . . [Connell 1906b]

The suppression of peyote had been, and continued to be, closely involved with the prohibition against the Indian use of alcohol. Alcohol was a terrible problem among the Indians in Oklahoma, and Agent Connell had been hired to arrest whiskey sellers. Since some people said that peyote was worse than whiskey, he considered prohibition of peyote also his duty. Yet he, too, was at times uncertain about legal authority. "I am not familiar with these eastern Indians," he said. Yet he wrote: "Under Territorial law its sale is prohibited under penalty of $200.00 fine. I am not familiar with U.S. Statutes on the subject, but its importation should be made to come under heavy interstate Commerce penalty and its sale be made a penitentiary offence."

In 1906, Congress passed a new law against the sale of liquor to Indians (34 Stat. L. 328) with a special appropriation to employ detectives to obtain evidence required to prosecute the violators. Frank F. Finney (1957: 464), writing of the wealthy Osage, reported:

All of these changes brought no improvement in the enforcement of the liquor laws on Indian lands, and the resulting lawlessness had finally become a national scandal. With characteristic vigor President Theodore Roosevelt decided to do something about it. He obtained a special appropriation from Congress and specified W. E. Johnson, who became known as "Pussyfoot," as a special officer to enforce the prohibition laws in the Indian country. Johnson, with fanatical zeal, and with about one hundred deputies and helpers, arrested whiskey peddlars [*sic*], confiscated their horses and wagons, smashed kegs and bottles and burned gambling paraphernalia wherever he found it. He had some narrow escapes and a reward was offered by outlaws for his assassination. Christmas, 1906, during his crusade was said to have been the driest the Indian Territory had seen since the white people had first begun making their homes here.

W. E. Johnson, born in New York state in 1862, attended the University of Nebraska, and in Nebraska he became a newspaperman active in the prohibition cause. Later he moved to New York City and became associate editor of the *New York Voice,* a national prohibition organ (1895–99). In 1901 he investigated liquor conditions in the Philippines as managing editor of the *Manila Freedom.* He was the nominee of the Prohibition party for the Maryland House of Delegates in 1903, and the next year he was a candidate for Congress from the Fifth Maryland District. From 1906 to 1911 he was appointed a special officer for the BIA to suppress liquor on Indian reservations. He effected more than forty-four hundred convictions. From 1912 to his death in 1945 he worked against alcohol in the United States and internationally, serving ten years (1922–32) as director of the World League against Alcoholism, with headquarters in London (National Cyclopaedia of American Biography 1949, 35: 161).

When Johnson arrived in Oklahoma to enforce the Indian liquor laws, he met Charles E. Shell, the new superintendent for the Cheyenne and Arapaho Agency at Darlington, who indoctrinated him into the equal evil of peyote. Together they began a vigorous campaign to suppress peyote as well as whiskey. Being new to the region deterred neither Johnson nor Shell from quick action, just as lack of familiarity had not inhibited Agent Connell from raiding a Ponca peyote meeting on his second night in Oklahoma. Missionaries and established employees might have persuaded Johnson and Shell against using extreme measures, if given a chance. They had influenced Connell, who later wrote:

It is but fair to state, however, that the use of whiskey has been greatly decreased; the craving for the . . . [peyote] seeming to supersede the desire for whiskey, the substitution appearing to an impartial observer, to be a case of "jumping from the frying-pan into the fire." . . . One drunk on it, injures the nervous system more than a dozen consecutive drunks on bad whiskey.

It was Shell who finally brought the territorial law against peyote to be tested in court. Within a month after arriving in Oklahoma, Shell, on the information from a white farmer working with the Cheyenne and Arapaho, sent police to raid a peyote meeting on Saturday night, February 9, 1907. Reuben Taylor, Howling Wolf, and Percy Kable were arrested and charged with willfully and unlawfully having "Mescal Beans in their possession." All three were educated Indians. Reuben Taylor had been at Haskell; Howling Wolf had been in Florida at the prisoner-of-war camp, followed by a period at Carlisle; and Percy Kable had attended both Carlisle and Haskell. These men had all experienced intensive training in English, Christianity, and other aspects of white culture. They did not take their arrests "lying down."

Two days later, attorney D. K. Cunningham of Kingfisher, Oklahoma, wrote to Superintendent Shell, at the request of Reuben Taylor and twelve other peyotists, complaining that their religious service had been disrupted. The communication said peyote was used and that the drum was used in "singing praises to God." The Indians reported that they "acted as Christian Indians and did nothing which is disrespectful to the civilized Christian religion" (Cunningham 1907). Shell sought help from George L. Bowman, county attorney, who notified him that

the evidence that we will need will be a proof that this bean that you have that was secured that night from these parties is the "Mescal Bean." If we can't prove that I doubt very much if we can make a case. As I wrote to you, I had a talk with their attorney and he claims that this bean is not "Mescal" but "Pyota" or some such name, and that it is not against the law for Indians to use "Pyota." The case is set for February 26th at 2 o'clock P.M.

Shell wrote to Rev. C. C. Brannon, a local BIA anti-alcohol agent in Guthrie, for proof that "peyote" and the "mescal bean" are one and the same thing and asked him to get help from Johnson (Shell 1907a). Johnson's reply was: "Peyote and mescal bean are one and the same thing. I could probably arrange to have some one from another agency, who is personally familiar with these things, go down and testify to that fact if it is necessary. My experience with these things is not extensive but I know this to be the fact."

The probate judge convicted Reuben Taylor, Howling Wolf, and Percy Kable on March 1, fined each twenty-five dollars and costs, and sentenced each to five days in the county jail. The attorney for the Indians appealed, and an appeal bond of five hundred dollars was secured by John W. Block and three Cheyenne peyotists, John Red Wolf, Clark Starr, and Leonard Tyler. Appeal was heard in district court in July, and after written briefs, the case was dismissed. The court found that the Indians had had no mescal; they had had peyote. Mescal and peyote were not the same thing (Kingfisher County, Okla., District Court 1907).

To the commissioner of Indian affairs, Special Officer Johnson wrote:

The smart lawyers for the medicine men set up the defense that this particular thing used was not . . . a mescal bean but a "peyote plant." This confused the situation. . . . I testified in the case that the peyote and mescal bean were one and the same thing and was supported in this testimony by Professor John F. Nichelson, botanist of the Oklahoma Agricultural and Mechanical College.

Meanwhile, on April 6, 1907, R. C. Preston, superintendent of Seger School at Colony, Oklahoma, raided a "mescal meeting" in Custer County. In his letter to Johnson naming the nine Cheyenne and Arapaho "violators" and the seven Indian "witnesses," Preston admitted he was not familiar with the law and legal procedure, but wished to press the prosecution "on

account of the injury that this drug does the Indians." The case was brought
to trial at Arapaho in Custer County, also in July, 1907, and the Indian defense was the same as that at Kingfisher: mescal is not peyote. There was
no conviction. In a letter to Shell dated July 27, Johnson explained the failure to obtain a conviction: "We fell down on our mescal cases at Arapaho. I
am satisfied that we were euchred by the interpreter. According to the interpreter, the Indians all testified that none of the witnesses had any of the
mescal beans. This, of course, killed our case." To the Custer County attorney he wrote that the Arapaho "cases fell flat, owing, I think, to the
eloquence of the interpreter in translating testimony." The interpreter was
Paul Mouse, a devout peyotist, who had written Mooney on May 20 to
come to Oklahoma and help the Indians. "We have been troubled here in
Clinton of using peyote. You know all about what we are doing in the peyote
tipi. We all pray just the same like white people" (May 20, 1907, BAE Ms.
2537). After August 21, 1907, Shell and Johnson had no excuse for confus-
ing the terms "peyote" and "mescal," for Special Agent R. S. Connell, then
at Rosebud, South Dakota, brought to their attention the difference between the mescal bean, *Sophora secundiflora,* also called *frijolillo* or carol
bean, and peyote, *Lophophora williamsii.*

Call it what you will, Johnson and Shell were bound to get a law prohibiting its use by the Indians. Early in September, they circulated a petition to
be sent to Congress "to prevent the introduction of peyote (Mescal Bean)
or use thereof by Indians" which was signed by ten superintendents of Indian agencies in Oklahoma. In December, Johnson had second thoughts
about Indian agents making a direct appeal to Congress, and each agent was
told instead to write to the commissioner of Indian affairs so that he could
"have Brosius, of the Indian Rights Association, look after the matter in
Congress."

Superintendent Shell, at the same time, promoted a state law. Oklahoma was applying for statehood, and he wanted to be ready with an antipeyote state law. Peyotists, too, were not without forethought at this important time. Leading peyotists, who were often tribal leaders, met with
the Medical Committee of the Constitutional Convention in February, 1907,
and at that meeting "Chief Quanah Parker explained that mescal beans
were poison and peyote is an herb learned from the Mexican Indians to the
Lipan Apache, then Comanche, Kiowa, etc." Furthermore, the Medical
Committee was sympathetic to the Indians, impressed by their demeanor
and intelligence, and "told the chiefs that 'This is your religion like my white
church. Keep it for your younger children that they too will preserve it for
the future generations'" (Fig. 8).

Superintendent Shell informed Johnson of his efforts to get a state law:

I have quite a number of friends in the legislature of Oklahoma and through
them have succeeded in getting an amendment introduced into both branches
to amend section 2652 so that it becomes a misdeameanor to introduce into the

FIG. 8. The delegation of peyotists with the medical committee who met before the Oklahoma Constitutional Convention in 1907 and decided the legality of peyote in Oklahoma. The peyotists are, left to right, front row: Tennyson Berry (Kiowa Apache); Codsy (Kiowa); Apache John (Kiowa-Apache); Otto Wells (Comanche); Quanah Parker (Comanche); Apeatone (Kiowa); Little Bird (Cheyenne); Young Calf (Cheyenne); second row: Ned Brace (Kiowa); far right: Joseph Blackbear (Cheyenne); Leonard Tyler (Cheyenne). Fort Sill Museum, #P–4868.

state or have in possession any Mescal Bean, also known as Peyote, etc. . . . I have no doubt that it will pass and if it does, it is all we need. I was assured by Lieutenant Governor Bellamy who is a mighty good friend of mine and who was the author of the original Mescal Bean statute and that he did not doubt that it would pass.

As the time for the constitutional convention approached, Johnson learned of the efforts of the peyotists and warned Shell: "I understand from dispatches in the newspaper that Quanah Parker is going up to Guthrie to fight your proposition. . . . I would suggest that the letters from Indian agents be addressed to the one who has charge of this bill, showing the necessity for such a measure. I would be glad to write such a letter if you think it best."

Shell heeded the advice of Johnson, and not only were letters from Indian agents written to the appropriate members of the legislature showing why certain legislation prohibiting the use or possession of peyote or mescal bean should be enacted, but Shell also encouraged the agents themselves to go to the constitutional convention in Guthrie and lobby personally for the legislation. Moreover, when Shell and agency superintendents asked for official permission to leave their respective reservations in order to do so, official permission was granted by the commissioner of Indian affairs in Washington, the time spent not to be charged as annual leave.

We do not know how many Indian Service employees went to Guthrie to lobby for the prohibition of peyote. Only Superintendent Shell testified, and the attorney for the Indians, D. K. Cunningham, spoke to refute his arguments. But it was the Indians themselves who were most important in bringing about the repeal of the law against mescal bean and in defeating a new law to outlaw peyote. As early as January 7, 1908, sixteen peyotists had registered as lobbyists against legislation to interfere with the peyote religion. Three Southern Cheyenne peyotists who had attended Carlisle were among them: Kish Hawkins, Percy Kable, and Leonard Tyler. Arapaho Paul Boynton, also a Carlisle graduate, and Kiowa James Waldo made eloquent statements in favor of religious freedom. Chief Joseph Springer (Iowa) spoke of using peyote to find "the road to Jesus Christ." Osage Chief Black Dog said: "I use the peyote in my religious ceremonies. We use it in our meeting same as you white people worship God in your churches."

One member of the legislature was so moved by the arguments of the Indians that he said: "I have been almost overcome by the talk of these Indians and I do not believe any legislature wants to rob these Indians of their religious rights. If I have regard for any person on earth, it is for the aborigines of our country. It is our duty to protect their rights—religious or otherwise" (Hearings on Mescal Bean Bill 1908, Oklahoma Historical Society).

It would be good to be able to say that this was the end of efforts, legal and otherwise, to suppress peyote, but such was not the case. Those who felt it should be outlawed sought other means to forbid its use. They fell back on the argument that since eating peyote causes intoxication, it could be outlawed under the liquor prohibition law of 1897. Though some had considered use of that law earlier, it was never seriously applied to peyote until 1909. Then it was all the antipeyotists had, and they worked it energetically.

During 1909 there was the greatest effort to deny peyote to Indians and thus to put an end to the peyote religion. Prohibitionist Johnson gave peyote his full attention. His training and experience as a newspaperman and prohibitionist were put to use writing hundreds of letters and reports against peyote. He conducted a campaign against peyote addressed to superintendents, Indian agents, and BIA officials in Washington. Immediately he attempted to stop, and for a time succeeded in stopping, shipments of peyote at its place of origin, Laredo, Texas. On April 28, 1909, Johnson pressured the superintendent of Wells, Fargo Express, Houston, Texas, to refuse shipments of peyote to Indians because shipping peyote "becomes liable to prosecution." During that April, Johnson sought the names of peyote suppliers and then personally visited them in Laredo. Using threats of prosecution, he bought the entire supply of peyote from the seven companies who sold it in Laredo and vicinity. From each shipper he also exacted a promise that no more peyote would be sent to Indians anywhere. He reported to the commissioner of Indian affairs that he had "purchased and destroyed by burning, 176,400 peyotes, for which I paid $443.00."

There was real doubt that the 1897 law against furnishing Indians intoxicating liquor should cover peyote. Acting Commissioner R. G. Valentine informed Representative John J. Esch of Wisconsin on January 20, 1909: "It is doubtful . . . whether there is any Federal law or state law . . . under which the sale . . . of Peyote to any Indians can be prevented." Nevertheless he sent Special Officer Johnson to Wisconsin to take such action as may be appropriate against peyotists.

Johnson frequently suggested ways to deter peyotism. On May 4, 1909, he proposed to the Bureau of Indian Affairs that a "prohibitive tariff be imposed upon peyotes" to insure that they would not be imported from Mexico. As strategy, he "suggested . . . coupling of peyotes with Marihuana and Hashish, chiefly as a matter of expediency, and an easy way of getting what we desire." He had evidence that peyote was shipped from Allende, Coahuila, Mexico, to Comanche peyotists Marcus Poco, Willie Adhossy, George Cable, and Po-ah-wa-ke, and wrote to Agent Shell to threaten express agents with prosecution if packages from Mexico were delivered to those Indians. On his own authority he wrote to superintendents of nine reservations where peyotism was known to exist, directing them to "take special pains to look out for shipments or movements of the peyote beans. If you locate shipments, I request that you seize and hold them and telegraph me. . . ."

Johnson was his own judge of whether white people should be allowed to buy peyote. On May 14, 1909, he wrote to Wormser Bros., dealers in peyote in Laredo, Texas, who had stopped shipments of peyote to Indians under his threat:

I have to acknowledge the receipt of your letter of May 5 stating that certain druggists have written to you [white people] stating that they wish to purchase these peyotes to manufacture into a medicine. The peyotes have no medicinal qualities whatever. . . . Outside a few ignorant Mexicans along the border, there is absolutely no demand for these articles except from Indians who want it for a dope. It is a cinch, therefore, that any druggist who claims to want to manufacture a medicine is faking and that he really wants them for an illicit traffic.

Suppliers of peyote in Laredo not only refused to ship peyote to anyone during most of 1909, but also furnished Johnson with copies of the orders and their letters of refusal. However, Wormser Bros. came to question the legality of the complete ban on peyote shipments and wrote to the secretary of the interior for a citation of the law. Acting Commissioner of Indian Affairs F. Abbott replied, in part: "The law referred to by Mr. Johnson relates solely to intoxicants and narcotics being sold to Indians and necessarily sales to whites are not prohibited by the law mentioned."

When furnished a copy of this letter, Johnson wrote to his informer and representative in Laredo:

There is no market whatever for these articles [peyote] among white men and this stuff about drug stores writing Wormser Bros. for peyote is a "fake." Wormser Bros. promised to "cut this business out" and if I find that they have not "cut it out," I will dig up all the old cases I can find against them and present them to grand juries in several different states. I am tired of this "monkey business" on the part of Wormser Bros. They seem to have no regard for their promise.

Reporting to the Bureau of Indian Affairs of his threat to Wormser, Johnson wrote on November 18, 1909: "This bluffed the Wormser people out and they still have the peyotes. I anticipate, however, that sooner or later they will break loose again somewhere."

Threats were not limited to the Laredo merchants who had shipped peyote, but each Indian who visited Laredo or who tried to purchase peyote by mail received a personal threatening letter from Chief Special Officer Johnson. Following a trip to Laredo accompanied by Attorney D. K. Cunningham of Kingfisher, Oklahoma, and Comanche peyotist Marcus Poco, James Waldo, also a Comanche peyotist, received the following in a letter from Johnson:

I am informed by my agents that during the month of August you were visiting in Laredo, Texas, in company with the quack lawyer from Kingfisher, Okla., trying to find some way of getting peyotes for the use of the Indians.

You are hereby informed that the furnishing of peyotes to the Indians directly or indirectly is a violation of the act of 1897 and subjects the offender to a punishment as high as two years in the penitentiary. You are notified that you will be prosecuted to the fullest extent of the law in case you undertake any such thing. You are advised to disregard any statements of tricky lawyers as to this matter, for such men only want to skin the Indians out of their money. If you wish advice upon these matters, you should consult with your agent or superintendent.

Letters to Delaware John Drum of Copan, Oklahoma, and to Sac and Fox peyotist Ed Butler of Avery, Oklahoma, put the warning in another way: "Now that we know what you have been trying to do we are keeping a special watch of your movements and you are hereby notified that if you furnish or cause to be furnished to the Indians any peyotes that you will be prosecuted to the fullest extent of the law. You will subject yourself to the punishment of up to two years in the penitentiary for such offense." Throughout 1909, such letters were sent to peyotists on nearly every reservation where the peyote religion had become established.

Distinguishing harassment from administration of the law was not easy. Indians seldom had the resources available to determine whether an order from a supervisor was in fact a legal order. If a federal police officer made a request or issued an order, Indians and whites generally felt they must act as if there was proper authority for it. Frequently the Bureau of Indian Affairs acted on the most slender legal base. Often it was simply that they had been commissioned to promote and protect the welfare of the Indians.

Another device employed to discourage peyotism in 1909 by the Bureau of Indian Affairs with the blessing, if not the inspiration, of Johnson was a questionnaire. It was obviously not so much for information as to influence public opinion as to the evils of peyote. In May, 1909, the bureau sent Johnson a questionnaire for distribution to all reservations where peyote was used because "the Office has discovered that the scientists who have written on the subject of the peyote and its effects have lacked opportunity to observe the results of its continued use because they have had no contact with persons who have acquired the habit." Then followed eighteen questions based on the assumption that peyote was harmful and habit-forming. For example: "It is possible for a maximum dose to cause death without previous use? If so, how large dose? how soon does habitual use prove fatal? Just how does it cause death?" The questionnaire was sent to nineteen Indian agencies; only four replies are available.

Superintendent Frank A. Thackery, reporting on the Kickapoo, gave a middle-of-the-road opinion: "With the peyote there is very rarely any violence shown from its use while quite the reverse is the case with alcohol." He reported that deaths did occur and that the peyotists were less energetic, but he also said the Indians claimed peyote was used in religious ceremonies and that peyotists stopped the use of alcohol. Superintendent A. R. Miller, reporting on the Kaw, wrote: "There have been no deaths from its use in this tribe. . . . The Indians of this tribe who use peyotes were formerly hard drinkers, but claim that now they have no appetite for alcohol. . . . It is used here, I am informed, in connection with religion."

From the Kiowa Agency both Superintendent Ernest Stecker and physician R. L. Russell wrote letters. Wrote Stecker: "I have lived for more than 16 years among the Indians of this section and although I have known them to use the peyote . . . during all that time I do not recall any instance where there was a fatal or serious effect from its use." Dr. Russell wrote: "In all my experience I have never seen a case of acute peyote poisoning, nor have I ever known any of the many confessed habitues of it to develop symptoms which could be charged to the constant use of the drug. . . ." He considered it was used in religious ceremonies.

The most surprising response came from Superintendent Shell of the Cheyenne and Arapaho Agency, longtime opponent of peyote. Apparently he had decided to find out first-hand what peyote was like, and he replied to the questionnaire mostly on the basis of his own sensations after consuming a rather large amount of peyote while under observation of a medical doctor. Whereas Thackery had reported peyotists became inactive and unfit to discharge ordinary industrial and business functions, Shell wrote that the persons he had observed who had used peyote at regular intervals for an extended period were "no more or no less progressive and accumulative than other Indians." He said "that a habit is not formed" by use of peyote. Although he wrote that he knew of two deaths caused by use of peyote, he added: "Both of these cases were in the last stages of tuberculosis," and he said that he knew of no healthy person dying from use of peyote. He also reported peyote was used "in connection with religious rites." During his own intoxication resulting from partaking of peyote in his own home, Shell experienced thoughts "along the line of honor, integrity, and brotherly love." He also wrote: "I seemed incapable of having base thoughts. . . . I do not believe that any person under the influence of this drug could possibly be induced to commit a crime. . . ." J. S. Lindly, M.D., who examined Mr. Shell before and during his intoxication, reported dilated pupils and increased heart beat, little else. He added that Shell's description of his reactions to peyote "differs very little from the crude descriptions given by the Indians of their experience . . . under its influence."

Perhaps the other replies, which seem to have disappeared, were more disparaging. At any rate the only reaction from this campaign against peyotism was a reprimand from the Bureau of Indian Affairs to Superintendent Stecker for his not working vigorously enough to suppress the use of peyote and liquor among the Kiowa and Comanche (letter from Chief Clerk Hauke to Johnson, December 6, 1909).

The year 1910 was one of great frustration for the Indians as well as for the officers of the Bureau of Indian Affairs trying to stop the growth of peyotism. Their easy access to peyote interferred with, their supplies perhaps gone, the Indians began to apply their own pressures on the bureau. The commissioner of Indian affairs began to doubt whether it was proper to prohibit use of peyote on the untested interpretation that peyote was an intoxicant and thus came under the prohibition of liquor to Indians of the act of 1897. On January 11, 1910, Assistant Commissioner F. H. Abbott sent to Johnson the text of a petition from the Osage declaring that peyotism reduced the use of whiskey, that peyote was good medicine, and that in peyote services, held once a week, God was worshiped in proper fashion. The Osage asked for just enough peyote to conduct their religious services. Johnson replied that peyotism was "practically dead" and asked for a continuation of the ban, ending: "In the meantime I will keep the source shut off and the Osage and other Oklahoma Indians will eventually forget all about their desire for peyote just as the Nebraska, Wyoming, Iowa and Wisconsin Indians have."

Most opponents of peyote assumed that it was attractive only because of its ability to cause physical and psychological sensations which, once tried, were greatly desired and soon necessary. The idea that old habitual users should be allowed limited amounts of peyote to "taper off" from the habit had led Agent E. E. White (1888) to relax his ban against peyote, and the same reasoning appeared again. Quanah Parker began "bombarding Washington with appeals for special permission," and he must have received it from someone, because by February 12, 1910, Deputy Special Officer C. C. Brannon at Darlington wrote to Johnson that the "peyote traffic" was in full swing in western Oklahoma. "I came to Geary to look after that druggist selling peyote" he wrote:

There are three stores side by side, two of them sell, one does not. . . . I also learn that Quanah Parker furnishes peyote for Indians all thru' this section and he tells the Indians that he has a right to get them and that pretty soon he will go into Mexico and bring them back for his people.

I send you a clipping of the paper in which the medicine man of the Comanche came to the Mexican border at Eagle Pass, Texas, and was there told by the custom house officers that he could not take it farther. He wired Congressman Ferris to help him get this peyote into Oklahoma. . . .

This medicine man at Eagle Pass has the following name: S. O. S. Marcus Poco. He has several thousand of these beans at the border.

Johnson wired Brannon to "seize and destroy Marcus Poco's peyotes. There has been a little mix-up in the Indian Office regarding our policy about peyotes but this is all straightened out now. Better destroy everything you get." Poco had eight thousand buttons.

But Johnson must have received some new instructions, for he wrote to F. W. Carothers at Eagle Pass that Carothers was henceforth to allow Indians to bring into the United States as baggage "not more than 500 peyotes." He explained:

It is the desire of the Office to give the older Indians a chance to taper off on this peyote habit. Of late, they have gotten out of peyotes and some of them are employing lawyers and doing other foolish things to restore their supply of peyotes. In order to permit these old men to have a very limited number of peyotes for religious purposes and not enough for purposes of debauchery [limited amounts are permitted].

Then Johnson wrote to Brannon:

I have your letter from Darlington about the peyote business and also have your telegram of Saturday from Lawton, stating that you had gotten Marcus Poco's peyotes away from him and destroyed them.

So far as the legal phase of this situation is concerned, we are proceeding under the Act of 1897 which forbids the furnishing to an Indian or introducing upon an Indian allotment of "any article whatsoever which produces intoxication."

I feel that we would have difficulty in proceeding under this Act except for selling to an Indian who is not a citizen and who is a ward of the Government. . . .

The Osages have gotten their lawyer busy and the Quanah Parker outfit has gotten their Congressman busy. I prefer to keep the matter out of the courts. I have, therefore, arranged a temporary settlement of this matter by instructing my agent in Eagle Pass to permit Indians to bring in as personal baggage not to exceed 500 peyotes. I am sending you a copy of my instructions to Carothers. In return for this concession, Congressman Ferris has promised to hold down his Indians and Attorney Kappler for the Osages has promised to hold them down to this program.

It will cost about $100 for an Indian to get to Mexico and get his 500 peyotes. I hope by this proceeding that the practice will die out in a year or so. I want you to impress upon these Indians that if they play any tricks or attempt to get by express or attempt to sneak in this stuff in quantities or engage in the traffic of it in any way that we will be compelled to shut off the peyote entirely and prosecute them besides.

I note the cases that you have against the druggist at Geary. If the Indians are citizen Indians, I do not think that we can do anything. If they are not citizen Indians, use your judgment about taking it up with the United States Attorney at Guthrie.

I am not entirely satisfied with the arrangement . . . but it seemed the best that I could do under the circumstances.

To U.S. congressman from Oklahoma Scott Ferris he wrote:

I am enclosing you a copy of instructions just given to my deputy at Eagle Pass.

Now if you will impress it upon your Indians that they must not play tricks upon us, that they must not engage in the traffic of peyote and undertake to get in large amounts, I think that the problem will be solved. I am somewhat impatient with Quanah Parker. We tried to fix it so they could get in a little for their own use but Parker deliberately sends a man down there and brings in 8,000 peyotes. My representatives have seized and destroyed all of them except 500 and if Parker tries any job of this sort again I shall institute prosecution against him and put it to the limit. I do not like to do it but I will do it and do it with a vengeance if Parker makes it necessary.

Protest came from another reservation. The Winnebago Indians on their reservation in northeastern Nebraska had learned of peyote about 1889 and soon had developed an active ceremonial organization on the model of the Osage and Oto. John Rave was the local peyote leader in the beginning, but in 1908 Albert Hensley was one of the most active leaders. He was a well-educated Indian, having spent nearly seven years at Carlisle. His concern about peyotism led him, in October, 1908, to write to the commissioner of Indian affairs through the agency superintendent, A. H. Kneale, sending some samples of peyote, explaining the religious value of peyotism, and offering to help the commissioner understand this valuable Indian religion. During the first three months of 1909, Winnebago Indians in both Nebraska and Wisconsin received supplies of peyote by railway express or by parcel post, but in May, shipments had been stopped by Johnson. In March, 1910, Hensley again wrote to the Bureau of Indian Affairs, this time assisted by two other peyotists, Oliver Lamere and John H. Clay. Commissioner Valentine seems to have been somewhat impressed for he replied: "You are advised that for the present I have decided to permit any Indians who may wish to secure a supply of the beans [peyote buttons] to purchase a small quantity for his personal use, but any traffic therein will be promptly suppressed." He wrote Johnson that he had decided to allow each Indian five hundred "peyotes" but did not wish to tell the Indians, since he was "sure with such information they will abuse the privilege."

Rather than abuse the privilege, the Indians promptly wrote Valentine the following plan:

Your letter of March 30th, 1910, to the Superintendent of Indian Schools, received and contents noted. In your letter . . . you advised us as follows: "You are advised that for the present I have decided to permit any Indian who may wish to secure a supply of the beans to purchase a small quantity for his own use, but any traffic therein will be promptly suppressed." After reading, and having the Superintendent in charge here read the above letter, we are unable to decide just how you intend us to be able to procure the peyote.

You advise that we may purchase and have in our possession a small quantity of peyote; you also advise that any traffic will be suppressed. We understand by traffic the sale of. Unless someone is permitted to sell without violating the order of your office you can readily see that it will be impossible for us to purchase it without directly violating the law and the orders, but we desire to be able to procure the same in reasonable quantities and to do the same in accordance with law and the rules of your office.

Peyote is grown in Texas and Mexico, and there is no other place that we know of that it can be procured, if traffic of the same in any form of quantity is prohibited, the only means, lawfully, thereby we could procure peyote would be by making a personal trip to Mexico or Texas at a time of the year that the same could be gathered and there and then gather such a quantity as we could lawfully have in our possession, therefore, a strict compliance with the letter of the regulations as we are able to interpret, the same would practically mean a prohibition. As the traveling expense to and from Texas and Mexico, for one person, including railroad fare is about $125.00 or about $5.00 a peyote, for we suppose that about twenty-five peyotes, which is enough for a meeting for five persons, would be considered a reasonable quantity for any one person to have in his possession at one time. We are, therefore, writing you for more specific regulations, or an interpretation of the regulations already made and hope that you will be willing to give us more particulars concerning the sale and purchase of peyote.

Could we without violating the order or spirit of the order relative to the purchase and sale of peyote, send a representative to Texas or Mexico and there without violating either the law or the regulations have such representative purchase and ship to Winnebago, Nebraska, of say about twenty-five peyotes for each member of our church?

Or could we, each making an order for himself of twenty-five peyotes, put all of the orders in one inclosure and send the same by United States mail to a dealer in peyotes and have him ship us, in separate packages, but all in one shipment?

Could we have dispensed to us by the Superintendent through the doctor here, a reasonable amount of peyotes, we having each and every member of our church receipt for the same and not allowing any member to have more than twenty-five at a time nor oftener than once in five weeks?

Our members use on an average about five peyotes at a meeting, twenty-five peyotes would therefore, last about five weeks; considering the distance the peyote has to come, a five weeks' supply would be about as small as would be practical for one order. We have made every effort to follow your wishes relative to the (procurement) and use of peyote and have practically abstained from the use thereof during the investigation concerning the same by your office and we desire to live up to the spirit as well as the letter of all regulations thereto made by you, hoping that in the end the department will see and appreciate that it is the means of a benefit rather than an injury to us and to our people. . . .

Respectfully submitted through A. H. Kneale, Superintendant. Signed: Oliver Lamere, John Clay, and Albert Hensley.

The full story of Winnebago difficulty in obtaining peyote is not easily reconstructed. Correspondence in the National Archives reveals that Oliver Lamere was apprehended by an operative of Chief Special Officer Johnson at Sioux City, Iowa, with two thousand "peyote beans," all of which were ordered destroyed. However, the Bureau of Indian Affairs responded to the Winnebago letter and asked Oliver Lamere to send the names of all adult peyotists among the Nebraska Winnebago. Commissioner Valentine then sent this list, which contained 243 names, to Johnson and instructed him that the Nebraska Winnebago were to be allowed five peyote buttons per week for each member, or 6,075 buttons every five weeks, or 63,180 per year.

The reasonableness of the Winnebago request and Valentine's acquiesence did not please Johnson. He recommended:

The arrangement that I have with the Osages [which] is that only one man of the congregation shall be become intoxicated each week, and he will report the visions that he sees to the others. If the idea is a purely religious one, that of communing with their God, it seems to me that it is sufficient for one member of the church to become intoxicated each week.

The policy of the bureau became increasingly inconsistent and uneasy. Commissioner Valentine allowed Winnebago and Omaha "to purchase a supply of 500 beans or less but [argued] that no shipments of peyote will be permitted" (Valentine 1910). At about the same time, C. D. Hilles, assistant secretary of the Treasury Department, on May 20, 1910, informed Oklahoma Senator T. P. Gore that "there is no provision of law specifically prohibiting the importation of peyote" (1913: appendix).

In December, 1910, when Superintendent H. W. Wadsworth, Wind River, Wyoming, reported to Johnson that he had confiscated a package of peyote addressed to Black Sleeper, an Arapaho of Darlington, Oklahoma, visiting in Wyoming, and offered to help on the case, Johnson replied:

Since the receipt of your letter regarding the matter [of peyote], my attention has been called to the fact that appropriation under which I am operating is for the purpose of suppressing the "traffic in intoxicating liquors," and that peyote is not a liquor, which is true. I am asking Washington for a little money out of some other fund to enable me to continue looking after peyote. In the meantime it will be necessary to cut out operations as to this thing. . . .

Undoubtedly the publication in 1910 of the article on peyote by James Mooney in the *Handbook of American Indians,* reporting that peyote "possesses varied and valuable medicinal properties" and that it is used in "a ceremony of prayer and quiet contemplation," contributed to the problems of "Pussyfoot" Johnson. In February, 1911, he reported to the Bureau that Cheyennes Leonard Tyler, Bushyhead, and Roland Coyote had gone to Eagle Pass to obtain peyote and further that Wormser Bros. were shipping peyote and complained: "I had no funds available to assist in this matter."

In 1911 there was a lull in the harassment of peyotists. Church groups and the chief special officer sent to R. G. Valentine, commissioner of Indian affairs, strong recommendations to support explicit laws against peyote, but nothing was done. On August 29, 1911, Johnson sent a fifteen-page argument against peyote as his last communication with the Bureau. In 1912 he joined the forces of the Anti-Saloon League of America (*National Cyclopaedia of American Biography* 1949, 35: 161).

CHAPTER 7

The Spread of Peyotism Beyond Oklahoma

SINCE peyotism spread by personal contact through chance visits, as well as by confirmed missionaries, some diffusion beyond Oklahoma took place at the same time as diffusion within the state. By 1914 it had spread to the Sac and Fox, Prairie Potawatomi, Kickapoo, and Iowa of Kansas; the Winnebago of Nebraska and Wisconsin; the Omaha of Nebraska; the Fox of Iowa; the Menominee of Wisconsin; the Chippewa of Minnesota; the Northern Ponca of Nebraska; the Sioux of South Dakota; the Northern Cheyenne and Crow of Montana; the Northern Arapaho and Shoshone of Wyoming; the Ute of Colorado and Utah; and the Taos of New Mexico. As it spread, it was colored by each new environment and the personality of each new prose-lytizer. Tribal similarities in language and habits played a part in its ac-ceptance. Also, education, both formal and practical, was influential in its diffusion. Christianity played an increasing role. And wherever it spread, opposition to peyote continued from Christian missionaries, agency offi-cials, the Bureau of Indian Affairs, and well-meaning whites as well as from some Indian nonpeyotists.

THE WINNEBAGO

By 1889 peyotism had diffused beyond Indian Territory to the Winnebago of northeastern Nebraska. The Winnebago were first known in Wiscon-sin near Lake Winnebago and although they were closely associated with Algonquian-speakers, such as the Potawatomi, Chippewa, and Kickapoo, they were themselves Siouan-speakers. They had suffered as others had in the thrust of civilization, their numbers being greatly reduced in the middle of the nineteenth century as a result of disease, warfare, and continual dis-placement by the U.S. government. After giving up their lands in Wiscon-sin, they were forced for a time to live in various places in Iowa, Minnesota, and South Dakota, where they were usually so unhappy that they were only kept on their reservations by the use of troops. Finally, in 1863, most Win-nebago accepted a reservation in northeastern Nebraska next to that of the Omaha, who sold part of their reservation to accommodate the Winnebago. The two tribes were usually administered by the same agency.

Some Winnebago, however, refused to settle in Nebraska and found their way back to their original homeland in northern Wisconsin, where they lived, and still live, on their own farms. We therefore have two groups

148

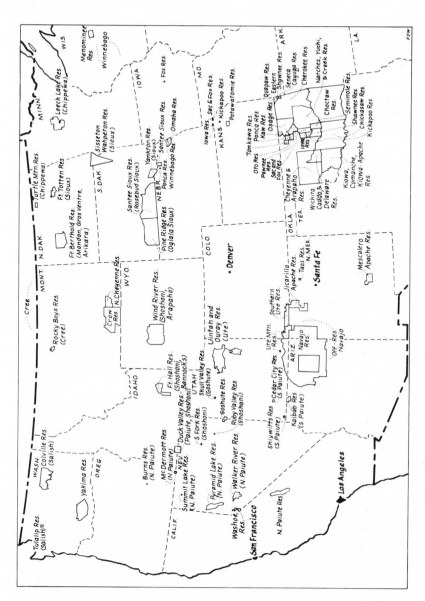

MAP 9. The western United States and Canada showing distribution of peyotists as of 1985.

of Winnebago to deal with: the Winnebago of Nebraska and the Winnebago of Wisconsin, for both groups adopted peyotism. In 1886 there were 1,222 Winnebago in Nebraska and 930 in Wisconsin.

With the Winnebago we come to the variation of the peyote ritual called the John Rave Cross Fire ritual (named after the first Winnebago roadman). It is not so much a new ritual as it is the Wilson Big Moon ritual under a new name. With the Winnebago the characteristics of the Big Moon cere-mony—Christian symbolism, altar style, nonsmoking, and so on—became more firmly established, with additions and elaborations.

The development of the Rave Cross Fire ritual from the earlier Wilson Big Moon ritual was not a clear case of transference by one man of one tribe to another man of another tribe. Although John Rave may have known John Wilson and may even have attended meetings conducted by him, we have no record of that. What did happen was that one John Rave, a Win-nebago of Nebraska, went to Oklahoma about 1889 at the earliest, and at least by 1893–94, where he ate peyote many times. Among the people he visited were the Oto, who were closely related linguistically, and it was to the Oto that he attributed his knowledge of peyote.

The major early ethnographic research on the Winnebago is Paul Radin's "The Winnebago Tribe," published as an accompanying paper to annual re-port no. 37 of the Bureau of American Ethnology, 1923. The field work was done in 1908–12. Radin included in his book an account of the peyote reli-gion among the Winnebago, and John Rave was one of his informants. Rave told Radin (1923: 389): "During 1883–94 I was in Oklahoma with peyote eaters," and (1923: 393): "It is now 23 years since I first ate peyote, and I am still [1912] doing it." This last quotation would place the date of his conversion in 1889. That he soon brought peyotism to the Winnebago is indicated by a letter from Louis L. Meeker, Darlington, Oklahoma, dated December 28, 1896, to the Smithsonian Institution, stating that he had learned about "the mescal bean" while studying Winnebago folklore in northeastern Nebraska.

Rave described for Radin his early experiences while eating peyote. Re-counting an initial, frightening experience in 1893, he said (Radin 1923: 390):

Then we breakfasted. . . . Then I said, "Let us eat peyote again tonight." That evening I ate eight peyote. In the middle of the night I saw God. To God living up above, our Father, I prayed. "Have mercy upon me. Give me knowledge that I may not say or do evil things. To you, O God, I am trying to pray. Do thou, O Son of God, help me, too. This religion, let me know. Help me, O medicine, grandfather, help me. Let me know this religion." Thus I spoke and sat very quiet. And then I beheld the morning star. . . .

Another account of Rave's conversion comes from Nancy Lurie as told to her by Mountain Wolf Woman (Lurie 1944–49):

John Rave's whole family died and he felt ready for death himself and left Win-nebago, Nebraska, to go to Oklahoma. There he met a friend or relative who took pity on his plight and said he would give him something to make him see what he should do. The two men went into the man's house in an upstairs room, drew the shades and ate peyote. Although they were indoors, John Rave could see the out-of-doors and the morning star. It was like the story of Abraham and the stars in the Bible. Then Rave knew he had to take back the new knowledge. . . . The rite introduced by Rave . . . requires an altar of sort of a horseshoe shape of concrete with a cross of the same material and a fire at the junction of the two arms of the cross, hence, the name, "Cross Fire," sometimes called "old man fire," because it was introduced by Rave and is followed by the older peyote people. . . .

Other ethnologists corroborated that the Oto were the source of Winnebago peyotism. La Barre (1938: 170) accepted a different date ("In 1897 the Oto brought the new religion to the Omaha and Winenbago of Nebraska . . ."), basing his belief in a 1909 letter to Emma Helen Blair (Blair 1912, II: 283) from one Thomas R. Roddy, a white man of Black River Falls, Wisconsin, who recruited Indians for Wild West shows (Lurie 1961: 129). In 1907, Natalie Curtis in *The Indians' Book* wrote that peyote "rites are performed as far north as the Winnebago, in Nebraska" (p. 163).

There is reason for confusion regarding the date of introduction of peyote to the Winnebago, because Charley Whitehorn, the first Oto roadman and the one likely to have been Rave's teacher, stated that peyotism was first brought to the Oto by the Tonkawa in 1896. In view of the many claims that peyote was also known among the Winnebago by that time and that they had received peyote from the Oto, we must assume that Oto peyotism was in fact earlier, and that the date given by Charley Whitehorn was inaccurate.

There is another confusion concerning the transference of the Oto ceremony to the Winnebago, and that is the nature of the ceremony itself. The Oto ceremony was said by La Barre (1938: 167) to have been originally essentially the Half Moon ceremony of the Kiowa-Comanche, rather than the Wilson Big Moon ceremony, although at some time Whitehorn added a few Big Moon elements—slight change of altar to include a hearth under the fire and a line from the tips of the horn, and later, the near elimination of tobacco. However, the John Rave Cross Fire ritual is so close to the Wilson ceremony that one must conclude that it was indeed the Wilson Big Moon ceremony which John Rave brought to the Winnebago. He was in Oklahoma for a number of years with the peyote eaters, and it seems inevitable that he experienced peyote, not only with the Oto, but also with the Quapaw, the Osage, the Pawnee, the Delaware, and possibly even the Caddo, where he might have picked up much of the Big Moon ritual.

Silvester Brito (1975: 172–78) quotes Eagle Claw as saying, "A very wise old man who was about eighty years old [Eagle Claw] said 'At one time for many years they who used that Cross Fire place of that Oklahoma man, Moonhead Wilson.'"

The number and nature of the similar elements in the Wilson Big Moon and the Rave Cross Fire rituals are such that only a theory of diffusion can account for them. To begin with, there is the similarity of the altar or fireplace. Whether we use Petrullo (1934: 179–82), with his eight Big Moon variants of the Wilson moon, or La Barre (1938: 154–55 and Pl. 2), with two designs and a photograph of various Wilson moons, the Winnebago Cross Fire altars fit the descriptions of the Wilson fireplaces. Radin (1923: 389) described the altar as being "in the shape a horseshoe. . . . At one end . . . is placed a small mound of earth, called by Rave 'Mount Sinai.'" Densmore (1931: 4) reported that her informant described Rave's moon "was more like a mule-shoe." The unusual mound, Rave's "Mount Sinai," is duplicated in La Barre's photograph of a "Quapaw permanent cement altar of the John Wilson Big Moon Rite." Rave's altar as described above by Lurie (1944) was a rough description of the Osage altar illustrated by La Barre (1938: 154).

There are many Christian elements in both the Big Moon and Cross Fire rituals that are either absent or weak in the Half Moon ceremony. There was preaching in the Cross Fire meetings as in the meetings of Wilson. Peyote was said to teach how to be good. Oliver La Mere, a Winnebago peyotist contemporary of Rave, said (Radin 1923: 394): "About four or five years ago the membership in the peyote religion began to increase, for many people now noticed that those connected with the peyote culture were the only people in the tribe leading a Christian life."

The Cross Fire ceremony also had a kind of baptism. Oliver La Mere describes it (Radin 1923: 396): "John Rave baptizes by dipping his hand in a dilute infusion of peyote and rubbing it across the forehead of a new member, saying, 'I baptize thee in the name of God, the Son, and the Holy Ghost, which is called God's Holiness.'"

The songs of the Cross Fire ceremony are characterized by Christian texts (Radin 1923: 395): "Ask God for life and he will give it to us," "God created us so pray to him," and "Come ye to the road of the Son of God; come ye to the road." Other titles recorded by Frances Densmore (1931) are also of Christian origin or implication: "Let there be light," "This is God's way," "Our Heavenly Father, we want everlasting life through Jesus Christ," "Christ is the way of Life. He is the only way," "The Lord's Prayer," "Jesus, how do we know, We think of Jesus wherever we are," and "How did I know, How did I know Jesus."

A new element which may have been introduced into the peyote ritual by the Winnebago Cross Fire peyotists is the presence of the Bible. In the Cross Fire ceremony the Father, or Chief, Peyote is placed directly on an open Bible. Radin stated that "the use of the Bible is an entirely new element introduced by the Winnebago." He also stated, "Hensley [Winnebago peyotist and influential disciple of Rave] introduced a large number of Christian elements in the ceremony, the principal one being the Bible" (Radin 1923: 397). La Barre seems to concur (1938: 73): "Peyote-users have also taken over the typical Protestant fetishism of the Bible, but this Christian element in peyote meetings is confined exclusively to Siouan-speaking groups (Winnebago, Oto, etc.)." Thomas R. Roddy wrote to Emma Helen Blair in April, 1909 (Blair 1912, II: 282–83):

In talking with Albert Hensley . . . he said: "The . . . [peyote] was formerly used improperly, but since it has been used in connection with the Bible, it is proving a great benefit to the Indians." The Winnebagos have the credit for being the first to use the Bible in conjunction with this medicine. . . . God is their guide, and they use the Bible and quotations from it all through the services. . . . It is very surprising, the way the Indians have become familiar with the Bible, and how closely they try to follow the teaching of Jesus. By using the medicine in connection with the Bible they are able to understand the Bible.

By 1909, fourteen Winnebagos had spent up to five years each at Carlisle, which may account for their interest and knowledge of the Bible.

There were others who laid claim to being the first to introduce the Bible into the Cross Fire rite. There is an interesting affidavit signed by Harry Rave, brother to John, on October 11, 1911, during a period of disaffection, stating:

John Rave, my brother, went up to Oklahoma, and ate . . . Peyote at Oto Indian Tribe, and he ate with the Pawnees also. . . . They worship that . . . Peyote— I am next leader to John. I thought if I pray God will hear me so we ought to have a Bible, so I went to Sioux City and got a Bible and I told him to learn the Bible and I said, "If you pray you must pray to the Father and to the Son and to the Holy Ghost, and not to anything else."

Another claimant was one Henry Johnson, who, in 1949, told Lurie that he himself "had been partly responsible for the church aspect of adding the Bible to the cult," although he was reminded that "Albert Hensley was in that too" (Lurie 1949).

There are other ritual characteristics that are common to both the Cross Fire ceremony and the Wilson moon. To begin with, in both the three leaders of the ritual—the roadman, the drummer, and the cedarman—are said to represent the Father, the Son, and the Holy Ghost. In both there is the absence of the midnight water call; the absence of the ceremonial breakfast *inside* the meeting place; and the absence of the eagle bone whistle. In both there is a rule to keep the staff standing "up-right in a hole" (Praus 1944). La Barre (1938) mentioned several other items common to the Winnebago and the Wilson moon tribes: preaching in meetings (p. 88), prophecy (p. 90), and baptism (p. 91). He also mentioned fanning of persons who reenter as practiced by the Delaware, Caddo, Osage, and Quapaw (La Barre 1938: 70).

Another practice which characterizes both the Winnebago Cross Fire ritual and the Wilson Big Moon is the limitation or prohibition of tobacco in the peyote ceremony. In 1938 La Barre wrote (p. 78): "In the Wilson rite . . . only the leader smoked, and 'show-offs' who made requests for tobacco were frowned upon." Radin described that Winnebago Crashing Thunder (Radin 1923:409) took a vow of nonsmoking during his conversion about 1908. It is not clear whether it was Crashing Thunder's vow not to use tobacco which started Winnebago peyotists to prohibit tobacco in the peyote ceremony or whether his vow was simply an expression of a rule already established and seldom mentioned. Nevertheless, in both rituals the use of tobacco was discouraged, limited, or prohibited. In 1939, Praus (in Stewart 1944) noted that the Winnebago Cross Fire ritual lacked smoking, and in 1971, I learned the Dakota Cross Fire members strongly opposed the use of tobacco at any time. This rule is found elsewhere, among the Ute, for example, and is considered part of the "Old Sioux Way." We can only guess the reason for the antismoking rule. The influence of all Protestant missions against tobacco could account for it. It hardly seems possible that one single Protestant sect, such as the Russellites (Jehovah's Witnesses), would account for it, as La Barre supposed, inasmuch as all were strongly against it.

Another peculiarity of both the Cross Fire and Big Moon rituals is the construction of permanent church buildings and permanent concrete altars in the floors. La Barre (1938:165) said this was true for the Osage and Quapaw Big Moon rituals, and Radin (1923:388) reported that the Nebraska Winnebago of Rave's branch also had a permanent wooden church. Two similar wooden churches were reported to exist for Wisconsin peyotists (observation and personal communication, 1971), and I have photographed a Sioux Cross Fire church building at Potato Creek, South Dakota.

Whether or not Albert Hensley was responsible for introducing the Bible into the Cross Fire ritual, he was, after Rave, surely its most important early leader and missionary. He was a good deal younger than Rave and could not have participated in its beginning, but the ceremony became stronger and more Christianized under his influence, and he defended and encouraged it all his life. It is generally agreed that the two together established the northern extension of the Big Moon or Wilson way, which we call Cross Fire, among the Sioux and Chippewa.

In 1916, Hensley wrote a brief account of his early life for Miss Mollie Gaither, superintendent of the Indian School in Sioux City, South Dakota, where his little daughters and nieces were attending school. It is an extraordinary document which illuminates the abilities of an extraordinary man. It follows:

My mother died while I was yet a baby so my grandmother (my father's mother) raised me on gravy and she also died when I was five years old, then I was kicked here and there in different families, and when I was seven years old my father took me and made me work for him what little I could do til I was

FIG. 9. Albert Hensley (Winnebago), with his two daughters and two nieces, who were being delivered to boarding school. From National Archives Record Group 75, Carlisle Indian Industrial School, Record No. 2144, Washington, D.C.

sixteen. The Allotting Agent Miss Alice Fletcher came, year 1887, and she saw me twice, and both times she said to me, I ought to be in school, we talked through an interpreter, and I told her, I have tried to go to school, even at Agency school my father would not let me, and I told her if she can obtain permission from my father, I would go anywhere to school, but she failed, and I supposed she was very sorry for me, and next time I saw her, she asked me if I would run away from my father, if she get me the ticket to Carlisle, Pa. and I told her I would, so she arrange certain night and certain place to meet, so we carried out and I was taken to Bancroft, Nebr. Thirty two miles from the Winnebago Ag'cy.

I started to run away from father, Dec. 18th, 1888, and I got to Carlisle Dec. 22nd 1888, and in April 24th 1889, I went out in the country. Rushville, Bucks Co. Pa. and I happen to struck a very mean man to work for, but I stayed there for two seasons getting only ten dollars a month, but I worked just as hard as though I was getting $40.00 a month. And went back to Carlisle Sept. 12th 1890, and I was out again April 14th 1892 at Bryn Mawr, Montgomery Co. Pa. At last I worked for very kind man and he gave me $35.00 a month, and I only worked there five month and went back to Carlisle Sept. 12th, 1892, and stayed til I was send back to Nebraska to die, they thought I was consumped, I left Carlisle, June 15th 1895. I never graduate, although I was in the senior class for three month, and I learn to be a steam-plumber, including carpentering and blacksmithing, when I came back to Winnebago Agency, I was well in side of two month and I was offered the position of chief of police and beside I was promise a better place later on and I gladly accepted it, and about two months later I was promoted to be the Agency blacksmith, and three years later I was promoted again as a Agency interpreter and again eighteen months later, I was given a better place, I worked with John K. Ranking an Allotting Agent.

I worked with him three years and then I was elected as a county commissioner, in our county, (Thurston Co., Nebr.) and I serve one term and refuse the second term, and in meantime I got married to Martha Henry, she never have any schooling because her parents were oppose of schooling, there were five girls and two boys that never went to a day to school, but she was a good worker.

And then we move on farm of one hundred and sixty acres. Near Thurston, Nebr.

We now got five healthy children and we are always happy and made good living on farm and independent.

Hensley did not report that he was leader of the peyote religion, but in 1910 he had reported to Captain Pratt at Carlisle in answer to the request to "tell me anything else of interest connected with your life": "I am doing my best to teach my people both young and old, and they are learning, too, about God and Jesus. The people are calling us 'mescal eater,' for nickname. I suppose you hear good deal about it."

Albert Hensley was similar to Quanah Parker in that he was a man of affairs, a leader in economics and politics as well as in religion. He wrote many letters to the Bureau of Indian Affairs on a wide range of subjects from rules of inheritance and leasing of lands to interference of the agency superintendent in an Indian fair. His defense of peyote was strong and unfaltering. In 1908 he wrote an instructive letter to the bureau:

Sir: Having read in some of the state newspapers that you are about to investigate "Mescal" and its use by Indians I wish to do everything that lies in my power to assist you in this investigation. I am the leader of the "Mescal" Winnebagos, who number probably three hundred, and in this letter I speak not only for myself but also for all of those who believe as I believe.

As you are doubtless aware, the term "Mescal" is a misnomer. The correct name for the plant is Peyote, the same growing in New Mexico and Arizona, but it may be that you are not aware of the veneration in which we hold it. We do not call it mescal, neither do we call it peyote. Our favorite term is "Medicine," and to us it is a portion of the body of Christ, even as the communion bread is believed to be a portion of Christ's body by other Christian denominations.

We read in the Bible where Christ spoke of a Comforter who was to come. Long ago this Comforter came to the Whites, but it never came to the Indians until it was sent by God in the form of this Holy medicine. We know whereof we speak. We have tasted of God and our eyes have been opened.

It is utter folly for scientists to attempt to analyze this medicine. Can science analyze God's body? No White man can understand it. It came from God. It is a part of God's body. God's Holy Spirit enveloped in it. It was given exclusively to Indians and God never intended that White men should understand it, hence the folly of any such attempt. It cures us of our temporal ills, as well as those of a spiritual nature. It takes away the desire for strong drink. I, myself, have been cured of a loathsome disease, too horrible to mention. So have hundreds of others. Hundreds of confirmed drunkards have been dragged from their downward way.

Proof of any statement I have made, or will make, is not wanting. In the face of all this, is it any wonder that the use of this medicine is increasing? Is it any wonder that our ranks are constantly increasing in number?

You know better than I, although I know well enough, what has been the result when any man or body of men have endeavored to oppose God's will; and I know, whether you do or not, what will be the result if any man or body of men attempt to oppose the onward march of this movement. It will not cease nor falter 'till every Indian within the boundaries of our great country has learned the truth, and knows God as God intends they should know him.

I am forwarding this through our Superintendent, who is also sending you a sample of the medicine.

Within two years after Hensley wrote this letter, there commenced an active exchange of letters between the Bureau of Indian Affairs and the Winnebago peyotists because of the activities of Chief Special Officer William E. Johnson to "suppress the peyote traffic" under the extension to peyote of the law prohibiting the sale of alcohol to Indians (see chapter 6). Albert Hensley was involved along with Oliver La Mere and John H. Clay in the correspondence which resulted in the request for permission to import five buttons a week for each of the 243 adult members of the Nebraska Winnebago tribe.

In November, 1911, Albert H. Kneale, agency superintendent, compiled a list of three hundred Winnebago adult males from twenty-one to eighty years old to show religious affiliations. The results indicated 37 percent of the tribe to be peyotists, 41 percent to be Medicine Lodge members, and 21 percent to belong to Christian organizations. The list was then graded to show how many in each group were self-supporting, and 83 percent of the Christians, 54 percent of the Medicine Lodge members, and 61 percent of the peyotists were found to qualify as such. Needless to say, these statistics were widely quoted to show that Christian Indians adjusted better than non-Christians to civilized life.

In 1912 the Half Moon peyote ceremony was introduced to the Winnebago through the efforts of Winnebago Jesse Clay. Jesse Clay was also an informant for Radin, whom he told that he had visited the Arapaho as a guest of a friend and there had learned the Half Moon ritual. The friend had then visited him in Nebraska and while there he had been encouraged to hold a Half Moon meeting, which he did with the assistance of his Arapaho friend. Radin calls the Arapaho, "Arapahoe Bull," but it seems obvious now that this missionary was Jock Bull Bear, who testified before a congressional committee in 1918 that about in 1913 he had been in charge of a peyote meeting for Indians in Nebraska. The Half Moon ceremony introduced by Jesse Clay had considerable acceptance among the Winnebago without, however, taking the place of the Cross Fire ritual. In 1931, when Densmore studied the Winnebago, she found

two branches of the peyote cult, one derived from John Rave, and the other from Jesse Clay. [P. 2] . . . There seems entire accord between the two branches but the differences are recognized. In general, the branch led by Jesse Clay is more native in its customs, while that led by John Rave shows more resemblances to the churches of the white race. The followers of Rave were said to use songs and customs derived from the Quapaw and Oto tribes while Jesse Clay followed the Arapaho customs.

An outstanding difference between the two branches is in respect to the outline which encircles the fire in the ceremonial tipi. [P. 4]

Radin had found that the ceremony introduced by Jesse Clay had "none of the characteristics of the Winnebago [that is, Cross Fire] ceremonial" (Radin 1923: 422). Other ethnologists, however, have found as many similarities as differences (see Appendix A). Petrullo, comparing the Wilson Delaware Moon (Big Moon) with the Elk Hair Delaware Moon (Half Moon), tabulated 70 "Doctrinal and Ritual Traits" for both, and all but 20 were held in common. A comparison of the Winnebago Cross Fire ritual (Praus 1944) and the Northern Cheyenne Half Moon (Hoebel 1944) shows about half of 265 traits to be the same.

Though the Jesse Clay Half Moon ritual was said to be "more native," it still has been greatly Christianized since 1880. The account by Jesse Clay of the Half Moon ceremony as he described it for Radin abounds with Christian ideas and explanations. Consider the explanation of the midnight water ceremony (Radin 1923:417): "The reason for drinking water at midnight is because Christ was born at midnight and because of the good tidings that he brought to the earth, for water is one of the best things in life and Christ is the savior of mankind." Or consider the reasons for the eagle bone whistle (Radin 1923:417):

The purpose of going to the four directions and blowing the flute [eagle bone whistle] is to announce the birth of Christ to all the world. . . . At daybreak . . . the staff, drum, etc., is now passed to the leader, who as soon as he has received everything takes his . . . [whistle] and blows on it. The purpose of blowing . . . [the whistle] just at that time is to represent the trumpet of the Day of Judgement, when Christ will appear wearing His crown in all glory. The putting on of the otter-skin cap represents the crown.

Clay described the ceremonial breakfast inside the meeting-place (Radin 1923:418):

During the evening the leader represents the first created man, the woman dressed up is the New Jerusalem, the bride waiting for the bride-groom. The cup used by the leader and the woman is supposed to symbolize the fact that they are to become one; the water represents God's gift, His Holiness. The corn represents the feast to be partaken of on the Day of Judgment and the fruit represents the fruit of the tree of life. The meat represents the message of Christ and those who accept it will be saved.

Clearly, by 1912, Christianity had become as much a part of the explanation of the Winnebago Half Moon ceremony as it was a part of the Big Moon. Jock Bull Bear, like many others of the Half Moon way, had spent a number of years at Carlisle and other schools, and by this time there was hardly an Indian anywhere who had not been subjected to considerable Christian indoctrination. It was to be expected that the ideas of Christianity would find an increasing place in both variations of peyotism.

In 1931, Frances Densmore was told by James Yellowbank, who had been drummer for Jesse Clay, that the staff

used by Clay was plain, even lacking the decoration of feathers. This represents Moses' staff, and the informant called attention to the fact that Moses' staff was not decorated. [Pp. 4–5] . . . The leader represents the Almighty . . . the men . . . sit at his right and left, representing Jesus Christ and the Holy Ghost. [P. 7]

Among the Half Moon songs which Yellowbank sang for Densmore were "God's Son Says, 'Get up and follow Me,'" "Jesus said, 'You shall enter into the kingdom of God,'" and "Jesus said, 'Whoever asks Me for water, I will give the water of life.'"

In 1949, Nancy Lurie participated in a Half Moon peyote ritual and was told that the three leaders represented the trinity—God, Jesus Christ, and the Holy Ghost. The leader carried a small pocket-sized Bible in his equipment box and said to Lurie: "This is the Bible, we read this, we believe this," although it was not used in the peyote ritual Lurie observed.

The Winnebago of Wisconsin were closely associated with friends and relatives of the tribe in Nebraska. As a matter of fact, all Winnebago seem to have changed residence frequently between Wisconsin and Nebraska or at least to have made months-long visits back and forth. Conversion of the Wisconsin Winnebago began early. A letter from Chief Special Officer Johnson to the Bureau of Indian Affairs in 1909 stated:

You will recall that the Winnebago Indians have been the chief propagators of the Peyote. . . . It was the Winnebago who organized the first Mescal church and sent out missionaries to the Indian tribes in the neighboring states and the Winnebagos have been largely responsible for the spreading of these practices.

And in the letter by Thomas R. Roddy, Black River Falls, Wisconsin, May 14, 1909, to Emma H. Blair (1912, II: 298), we learn:

In regard to the "mescal [peyote] eating" among the Winnebagos, those in Nebraska sent [in the summer of 1908] a delegation of about one hundred persons to Wisconsin, to introduce the new religion among their brothers there. They held three or four meetings, and made fifteen or twenty converts; but there was so much opposition to the movement that most persons held back from joining.

Some opposition was from the Reverend J. Stucki, whose mission church was in the Indian community of Black River Falls.

This incident was remembered as an important event in the life of Mountain Wolf Woman, who described it in 1957 for Nancy Lurie (1961: 47–49):

Mountain Wolf Woman and her husband had learned of peyote among the Nebraska Winnebago earlier that year, and had even held meetings with Oglala Sioux while working near Martin, South Dakota, before returning to their home in Black River Falls. She recalled: "Every Saturday we used to have a peyote meeting. We had a gunny-sac full of peyote and that is why we were able to have meetings every Saturday. My husband did not know the songs very well. . . . Only older brother (Radin's *Crashing Thunder*) knew them. . . . that must have been 1908. . . .

"At that time the Nebraskans had a lot of money from selling their land and they were enjoying themselves. They filled two train coaches with Indians. They even had their drums and they sang in the train, drumming loudly. They got off at Black River Falls. We went there with our wagons. . . . There were a lot of them. They used all the wagons and then filled a big hay rack. . . . Eventually, we were going to have a big peyote meeting. They came to us and brought a big teepee. Previously brother and others had cut big poles and trimmed them and covered over with canvas. . . .

"There were all kinds of Winnebago, Nebraskans and a lot of Wisconsin Indians. It was very pleasant. . . .

The first peyote ritual known to the Wisconsin Winnebago was, of course, the Cross Fire ritual of John Rave, but after the Half Moon ceremony was introduced by Jesse Clay, it, too, became familiar to the Wisconsin tribe. Mountain Wolf Woman described the differences (Lurie 1961: 50–51):

They all made a big building in Nebraska for their meeting place. . . . They used to preach to one another there. They chose twelve men who were educated and there they used to read. They used to tell what God did when he came to earth. They used to preach in their group.
Over at John Rave's meeting place it was called the Cross Fire rite. That group preached among themselves. . . . Over there at the Half moon place all they did was sing.

In 1915, Superintendent E. J. Bost wrote to the Bureau of Indian Affairs that Will Boyce and Ed Littlewolf, Wisconsin Winnebagos, had bought peyote near Wittenberg. The next year, 1916, Frank T. Thunder wrote that he was denouncing peyote after having used it for ten years. Also in 1916, Superintendent S. J. Steinstra, in answer to a Bureau of Indian Affairs questionnaire, reported: "Perhaps one third of our Indians are addicted to the use of peyote to some extent. The number of Indians enrolled is approximately 1,250." The leaders he named were Ed Greengrass, Albert Big Thunder, Tom Prescott, and nine others. In reply to the same questionnaire, Superintendent O. L. Babcock reported 250 Winnebago peyotists in Nebraska and wrote: "The leaders are John Rave who is 'High Priest,' his sons, Late Rave, Harry Rave, and Charles Rave, all more or less active. Charles Raymond and possibly one or two others might be called leaders."

In 1923, Radin (p. 419) reported that Albert Hensley had led a separatist movement in 1908 to establish himself as a leader equal with Rave, but by 1913 no rift existed between them. Rifts and rivalries do not seem to have characterized Winnebago peyotism, either in Wisconsin or Nebraska. There was no great rift between the members of the Cross Fire and the Half Moon sects. The Cross Fire ritual maintained its strength, while the Half Moon became a strong alternative ritual. Individuals usually preferred one or the other, but most Winnebago attended services—and still attend services— of either sect. Even officials participate in the services of either sect, so that being designated as a member of Cross Fire or Half Moon seems to be determined by chance factors such as who happened to have enough peyote, or what neighborhood one happened to be in when a meeting was held, or which roadman was a close personal friend of the family sponsoring a particular meeting.

In 1917, John Rave died at sixty-two years of age after having been committed to an insane asylum. He may have been only senile, but it gave the agency officials and the leaders of the Christian missions opportunity to decry peyotism.

THE OMAHA

The Omaha were not displaced by white immigration as severely as were most other tribes. Since they were first identified, they had ranged the country of the upper Missouri. Therefore, their reservation on the west side of the Missouri near present-day Omaha, Nebraska, was familiar territory. They spoke a Siouan language, and to other Siouan-speakers of the Mississippi Valley they were mutually intelligible—to the Oto and Winnebago as well as to those of the same linguistic family, the Dhegiha: the Kaw, the Quapaw, the Osage, and the Ponca. In 1906 the Omaha numbered 1,228. They shared their agency at Macy, Nebraska, with the Winnebago.

The Omaha had early access to Christian education. In the introduction to the autobiographical book of Francis La Flesche (1963), entitled *The Middle Five,* David Barreis wrote:

Missionary work among the Omaha was initiated in 1846 by the Board of Foreign Missions of the Presbyterian Church when agency headquarters for the Oto and Omaha tribes was at Bellevue, south of the city of Omaha in Sarpy County. . . . A new mission headquarters and school was constructed in 1857 at the agency headquarters in Thurston County on a terrace overlooking the Missouri. . . . The school continued in operation until 1869. . . . In keeping with the mission sponsorship of the school, the students were treated as members of a Christian family and had their meals and worshipped with the members of the mission staff.

And Christian education was not limited to that provided on the reservation, for many went to such schools as Carlisle. In 1891, twenty-two were enrolled there.

The proximity of the Winnebago and their common language brought knowledge of peyote to the Omaha about the same time as to the Winnebago, and indeed Roddy stated that peyote had come to both tribes about 1897 (Blair 1912, II: 282). Other Omaha have usually given the year as 1906, and we can assume that by then peyotism was fairly flourishing under the leadership of John Rave, with his Cross Fire variation. In 1919, Gilmore (p. 163) described the process:

The [peyote] was introduced into the Omaha tribe in the winter of 1906–7 by an Omaha returning from a visit to the Oto of Oklahoma. He had been addicted to alcohol, and was told by an Oto that this plant and the religious cult practised therewith would be a cure. On his return he sought the advice and help of the [Peyote] Society of the Winnebago, next neighbors tribe of the Omaha. He and a few other Omaha, who also suffered from alcoholism, formed a society which has since increased in numbers and influence against much opposition, till it includes about half of the tribe. . . . No doubt the fundamental rites antedate the coming of the white man . . . but since then Christian ideas have been added together with original religious ideas. . . . The fireplace . . . is usually an excavation, eight to twelve inches deep, and in the shape of a heart to represent the heart of Jesus. . . . at the west side . . . a . . . [peyote] button is placed upon a cloth worked with symbolic figures, as upon an altar. Near this is placed an open Bible and there is set up a staff about three feet in height. . . . [There is] a symbolic fan made of twelve eagle feathers, representing the twelve apostles of Christ. . . .

By 1908 official correspondence to the Bureau of Indian Affairs, as well as missionary reports, indicated that an active peyote ceremony existed among the Omaha, and the agency and churches exerted themselves to eradicate it. It was a time when efforts were being made to destroy peyote at its source, so the Indians were hard-pressed to obtain it. In 1909 an attorney for the Omaha obtained twenty-five pounds of peyote so that one Dr. Harvey W. Wiley might carry on an experiment as to the toxicity of peyote. Also that same year Omaha Indians were successful in receiving shipments directly from L. Villegas and Wormser Bros. of Laredo.

In 1912 the Omaha sent a delegation to Washington to testify for the right to use peyote. To introduce the first delegation, attorney Harry L. Keefe of Walthill, Nebraska, wrote the following to the BIA:

Daniel Webster, Harry Lyon, and Parish Saunsoci called my office and asked me to make a statement to you in regard to an organization known as the Mescal Society among the Omaha Indians. I asked them to hand me a list of Omaha Indians who belonged to this Society so that I might consider their condition as I originally knew them and see if the changes which they claim for their Society to the betterment of these people were general and also whether they were due to the influences of the Society.

I have a list of ninety-seven members of the Society. Some have belonged for five years, others have joined since that time. Of these ninety-seven, over sixty of them I knew as habitual drunkards. Some ten or twelve of them got drunk every time they came to town. Of this ninety-seven I have seen fully one-half of them under the influence of liquor on election day. With hardly an exception the whole list of ninety-seven members are now total abstainers. I consider that this has been brought about entirely through the influence of the Society.

About four years ago a member of the Board of Indian Commissioners wrote me in regard to the Mescal Society and the influence of the peyote. He stated that experiments were then being conducted in the Department of Agriculture to determine the effect of its use. I wrote him at that time that the direct effect of the use of the drug could not be determined satisfactorily by such experiments; that at least the effect upon the Indians would be materially different from its effects upon a "poison squad." At his request I visited the meetings of this Society regularly every Saturday night for several weeks and have been a frequent visitor since that time, solely for the purpose of determining the physical and psychological effect.

The ceremony is an extended one; the Bible is read, prayers are offered;

the most intense and reverential spirit prevails at the meetings; the members give an account of their past sins and several of the members sing in a minor strain a very weird chant. During the singing, a number of the members hold a gourd in their hands which is shaken to the time of the singing, and a little drum is beaten to rapid time. The singers and members sit and gaze upon this highly colored gourd. This singing continues for hours. The peyotes or mescals are distributed around and a few of them are eaten. They use them in very limited quantities.

From my own personal experience in tasting and eating these peyotes, I am convinced that without the ceremony and the singing, the effect of the peyotes is very slight. I have never been able to observe any effects one way or the other and that has been the experience of a number of white people who visited with me. These people believe fervently that the effect of the peyote makes them see their past errors and brings about the reform. I think the effect is somewhat of a hypnotic nature coupled with some narcotic effect which the peyote may produce. I have seen very little if any evil influence of it, and I have seen a great amount of good. I am not prejudiced in the matter, because I am not a member of the Society, and have no personal interest in it whatever except for the good that it may do. . . . They are intensely earnest in their desires and consider their request as one of their religious rights.

In 1915 and again in 1916 the Omaha petitioned the Bureau of Indian Affairs for permission to practice peyotism. The delegation carried many petitions. Hiram Mitchell wrote: "I am of the first who used the peyote root (about eight years ago). . . . Ever since I have used Peyote I think about God. . . ." Peter Blackbird emphasized his personal reformation: "I drank whiskey. I was bad. I almost murdered a man and they arrested me. And even I almost accidentally killed myself with a revolver. Finally, I found out about Peyote and joined the society. . . . I found that their belief is that this Peyote and the Bible are the same thing." Sam Gilpin wrote: "It has been seven years since I joined them [the Peyote Society]. Since then I have spent no money for whiskey. I believe this Peyote is good. . . ." Thomas Walker, who had attended Carlisle, wrote: "This religious use of Peyote is on the same line as the white people's use of the Bible. What we learn from the Bible is true in Peyote." Simon Hollowell had been an important leader of the Omaha. He wrote: "They gave me a job as councilman and later as judge and then as assessor." But he was ruined by drink until rehabilitated by peyote. He said: "When we eat Peyote we think about it in the Bible. There is a God, Christ, Holy Ghost we pray to." And so on.

The Omaha continued to defend their right to use peyote as the opposition grew. When the attempt was made to pass a federal law banning peyote, they were again in Washington to try to prevent it, and they were among the most eloquent and persuasive.

At some time the Half Moon ceremony was also introduced to the Omaha. Whether it was early or late is not known, but perhaps we can assume that it, too, came to the Omaha at about the same time it came to the

Winnebago. In any case, on December 21–22, 1962, in a series of articles for the *Lincoln Star,* there is a photograph of Mr. and Mrs. Alfred Wayne Gilpin, Omaha Indians, with the ritual paraphernalia of the Half Moon ceremony, and the ceremony described in the article is the Half Moon ceremony.

THE KANSAS TRIBES

In the first ten years of the twentieth century, peyote meetings began to be held in Kansas in four small tribes, related to tribes living in Oklahoma: the Prairie Potawatomi, the Sac and Fox of Kansas, the Kansas Kickapoo, and the Iowa of Kansas. All lived in the northeastern corner of the state on adjoining reservations, and usually they were administered by one agency, situated at Mayetta, on the Prairie Potawatomi Reservation.

The Prairie Potawatomi were descendants of Algonquian-speaking people, mostly from Michigan, who acted on provisions of treaties and in 1846 moved west of the Mississippi River to a reservation in Kansas. Other Potawatomi remained in Michigan, and a large group, after several displacements, settled in central Oklahoma and were known as the Citizen Potawatomi. Peyotism did not attract the Potawatomi of Michigan or the Citizen Potawatomi of Oklahoma. Of the last group, La Barre (1938:119) wrote briefly that "The [Citizen] Potawatomi first had peyote sometime between 1908 and 1914, but little else is known about it there." As far as I know, no other person has added to our knowledge of peyotism among the Citizen Potawatomi.

The Prairie Potawatomi, on the other hand, stayed in Kansas after 1846, refusing to relocate again, and they had a fairly eventful history of peyotism. In 1923, Skinner wrote (1924:232): "The Prairie Potawatomi declared that the peyote ceremonies in the form which they practice, were obtained by them from the Comanche," and he described their typical Half-Moon ritual. In 1961, while interviewing old Potawatomi about the mescal bean ritual, James H. Howard (1962b:120) was told that Quanah Parker had brought both the Red Bean cult and the peyote religion to northeastern Kansas about 1908. Wrote Howard:

When Quanah Parker introduced the Red Bean ritual among the Prairie Potawatomi, he told them that it should not be used in conjunction with peyote. . . . He demonstrated how the mescal bean should be drilled at both ends and the meat dug out from the inside. Parker cautioned them to use the bean sparingly because it was . . . "about five times as powerful as peyote."

Quanah Parker, of course, would have taught the Potawatomi the Comanche Half Moon rite.

The Christianized Big Moon sect also soon found its way to Mayetta. Skinner had described the Potawatomi Half Moon ceremony as typical, but he included in his account (1924:241) that his informant, Sam Bosley, had told him that "The Kansas Potawatomi use the Bible and its teachings, and are said to be much less strict in their rules." Petrullo expressed the opinion (1934:79) that "the Potawatomi are among others that seem to have patterned their Peyote creeds and ceremonies after those of Wilson." La Barre wrote (1938:158): "The Potawatomi may have been influenced by the teachings of Wilson. . . ." Ruth Landes (1970:303) provided additional evidence: "In 1936, the band's cult pioneer, Bill Skishkee, was still around and was reputed to be in his late sixties. He had led the peyotists for some time after introducing the 'buttons,' a Christian-like cross, and dogma from the Oklahoma Osage to the Band's reservation, about 1910. . . ."

The Prairie Potawatomi were engaged in early importation of peyote. William Skishkee, Mayetta, Kansas, sent an order to L. Villegas, Laredo, Texas, dated September 20, 1909, for a shipment of peyote. He wrote: "Sir. You will find five dollars for peyote and send to the above address and if you can't send it to me, please forward the money back. I just got out [of Oklahoma] last week and the rest of the Indians in Oklahoma has been getting it right along from what I learn." This letter was given to the detectives of the Bureau of Indian Affairs and thereby found its way into the National Archives. Another letter from Mayetta ordering peyote was from one Claudio Borrego, who said he was ordering directly on the advice of his friend, Ed Butler, and wanted to know the cost of a thousand buttons. Superintendent A. R. Snyder, Mayetta, reported that there were about one hundred peyotists on the Potawatomi reservation, and that shipments of peyote from Aguilares, Texas, were being received in a number of small towns in the vicinity of Mayetta. Tom Herrick received over a hundred pounds during the first four months of 1915. Others (some of whom may have been Kickapoo, just twenty-five miles away) were receiving shipments. From Tom Herrick, Snyder seized a half-bushel sack of peyote, out of which a small boxful was sent to the state university at Lawrence, Kansas, "for the purpose of having it analyzed with a view of determining whether or not its use might come under the federal Harrison Act which has to do with 'dope.'"

In 1919, in response to a questionnaire, Snyder reported;

there are probably now 125 who are regular devotees at these meetings. . . . The cult is organized along the lines of a church, there being a peyote preacher who does the preaching. . . . An Indian by name, Oliver Marshall, holds the honorable position of preacher for this tribe and he is generally seen out on the reservation traveling around from house to house with a Bible under his arm. . . .

The Sac and Fox of Kansas, the Kansas Kickapoo, and the Iowa of Kansas seem to have shared the same experience of peyotism. They could hardly have avoided knowledge of peyote through their near neighbors, the

Potawatomi, and through relatives and friends in Oklahoma. But the principal teacher of these three tribes was a young man born on the Sac and Fox reservation of Kansas of a Sac and Fox father and an Oto-Iowa mother. His name was Johnathan Koshiway, and he came to be an exceedingly important peyote proselytizer and roadman. He taught the Oto ceremony of Charles Whitehorn, which had elements of both the Comanche Half Moon and the Wilson Big Moon.

Johnathan Koshiway was born on the Kansas Sac and Fox reservation on November 20, 1886, and he probably lived most of his early life there. In 1899 he attended Chilocco Industrial School, and in 1903, at the age of seventeen he was on the Oto reservation, where he married an Oto girl and ate peyote for the first time. He seems to have been unusually curious about religion, for it was said that he went to Bible school, that he took Bible classes, that he was at one time associated with the Russellites (Jehovah's Witnesses), that he was a missionary for the Reorganized Church of Jesus Christ of Latter Day Saints, that he became a Presbyterian minister, and that withal he became a sucking shaman. He also attended Haskell for a time.

Sometime before 1910 he learned the Oto Whitehorn peyote ceremony well enough to take it back to his people in Kansas, and it was then that the Sac and Fox, Kickapoo, and Iowa of Kansas learned the ceremony. Agency superintendent L. S. Bonin, answering an all-agency questionnaire, wrote: "I understand that John Koshaway [*sic*], a member of the Sac and Fox tribe first introduced its use among these tribes about 1910. . . . He is a man of some education." Further, Bonin stated that about 40 to 50 percent of the Indians were peyote users. Koshiway maintained an interest in the Kansas reservations, returning again and again, according to his daughter. However, he did not confine his interest to Kansas. When he died in 1971 at the age of eighty-five on the Navajo reservation, he had also been influential in the development and spread of peyote among the Winnebago and Omaha, the Menominee, and the Navajo and, through the Native American Church, to all other peyote groups in the United States and Canada.

THE FOX OF IOWA

The Fox of Iowa, like the Winnebago of Wisconsin, are among those few Indians who rejected the care and control of the Bureau of Indian Affairs to purchase their own land and live by their own efforts. In 1859, averse to allotments and reservations, some Fox left Kansas and purchased land near Tama, Iowa, where they established their own cooperative farming venture. It was an independent Algonquian-speaking community of 350 in 1905.

Lloyd A. Fallers (1960: 77) is responsible for dating the introduction of peyotism to the Fox of Iowa as 1904, but he gives no evidence supporting that date, nor does he say who were the leaders, who brought the ritual, or which one was practiced. One of the first roadmen, however, must have been Harry Davenport, a Fox tribal member and one who practiced the Cross Fire ritual (personal communication from Jim Bluebird, 1971). This suggests that peyotism came to the Iowa Fox by way of the Winnebago, which would have been natural as the Winnebago traveled through Iowa back and forth between Nebraska and Wisconsin.

In 1909, Harry Davenport became irrational and died in a public and much publicized suicide. The story is best told in a letter from one of the United Presbyterian missionaries, a Miss Smith:

I have to tell you of the sad fate of our beloved Harry Davenport, whose infatuation for the Mescal [peyote] I told you of in my last letter. We had seen for some time that his mind was not just right. He would fall into such violent fits of laughter when I would tell him some little thing. This was so unlike him, for he was so dignified when he was himself. A week ago last Friday he went to Marshalltown and stayed till Sabbath afternoon. Went to a church there and was baptised again. Came to Tama on the 4 o'clock train and went to evening service and Epworth League in the evening, stayed at the hotel all night, went to the bank Monday a.m. drew his money, paid his bills, kept looking at his watch, and when it was ten o'clock he walked out in a square made by the inter-sections of two streets, drew a revolver from his pocket and shot up in the air, described a circle with his hands, brought the revolver down to the middle of his forehead and fired. He died almost immediately. . . . Miss Hapt and I were teaching out here at the mission when the postman came and brought me a letter from him. This was the way it ran.

Marshalltown, Iowa, Jan 31st 1909.
At office and clerks desk to report for witness fees. I tried to tell you some things Miss Smith—I like you very much, you like me to.
Well I am going home, the Indian call me like crazy. I am poor boy, I never get talk to me good any Indian any white to Harry Davenport. I was born at here Dec. 9, 1877 and I got died and the same place January 31, 1909, aged 32 years and fifty days. All paid. Goodby.
I am very glad going home. Goodby.
    Your friend,
    Harry Davenport.
    Goodby

It goes without saying that such a spectacular suicide was cited time and again as proof of the evils of peyote. Indian agent O. J. Green characterized Davenport as "the leader of the [peyote] society," when he reported the death, stating also that "the society seems at a standstill, and it may be has begun to die out."

Peyote may have received a blow with Davenport's suicide, but it was not a death blow. In 1916 two new leaders, George Green and Percy Bear, came to the fore, and it was estimated that "the peyote society here is composed of about twelve members" (Russell 1916). Peyote was supplied by Nebraska Winnebagos, and consumption of alcohol was greatly reduced. R. L. Russell, superintendent of the Sac and Fox Sanatorium, Toledo, Iowa, which also served the Tama Fox community, wrote:

In so far as I know the use of this drug has had no visible effect on its users most of them being just now in excellent health, nor has it had any bad effect on the social condition of those participating, for I am quite sure that the users of it will rank with the better class of our Indians. These people seem to be sincere in its use, and do not indulge in peyote debaches. . . .

George Green is not identified in other documents, but Percy Bear was listed on the 1906 tribal roll as born in 1892, and in 1916 he was reported as a peyote leader by Officer Larson in an interview with the *Denver Times*. Larson said, "At the Sac and Fox Agency, Toledo, Iowa, twelve Indians under Percy Bear's pious leadership are members of the cult." Thirty-four years later Percy Bear, at age fifty-one, was still leader and president of the Tama group, which legally incorporated themselves as the Native American Church, the "object" of which was to be: "the practice and promotion of religious worship founded on the four great primal laws of God, to-wit: Love, Faith, Hope and Charity, to include the recognized sacramental use of tobacco and peyote." The other officers were Mike Wanatee, William Poweshiek, John Papakee, and Walter Wabaunasee.

THE MENOMINEE

The Menominee, an Algonquian tribe of northern Wisconsin, clung to part of its aboriginal territory in spite of decades of pressure to move. They probably learned of peyote and the peyote ritual from the Wisconsin Winnebago shortly after it became known to them, about 1900, but peyotism did not then take hold strongly. It probably did not completely die out, though, and in 1914 it was introduced again by a Potawatomi, one Medicine (or Mitchell) Neck, who was arrested for doing so by the superintendent of the reservation and brought to trial in U.S. district court in Milwaukee for violating the 1897 federal law prohibiting introduction of any intoxicating substance onto Indian reservations. Medicine Neck was found not guilty by the federal judge, who declared without qualification that existing federal laws against furnishing Indians intoxicants clearly meant prohibition against alcoholic beverages and did not apply to peyote.

Although there came to be a vigorous and dedicated group of peyotists among the Menominee, it has never been a large group, never involving more than 3 percent of the tribe. Still, Menominee peyotism is of particular importance to the history of the cult because, as a result of two thorough investigations, so much is known about it as it does exist. One of these investigations is that of J. Sidney Slotkin. He and his wife spent three summers from 1949 to 1951 on the Menominee reservation studying peyotism at the request of the Menominee peyotists themselves, who wished to have a printed record of the history, ritual, and theology of their religion. The bulk of the research was verbatim quotations, often in question and answer form, by the Indians. The study was published by the American Philosophical Society in 1951 under the title "Menomini Peyotism." The other study is that of George and Louise Spindler, who spent each summer from 1948 to 1952 on the Menominee reservation—at the same time as the Slotkins, but a little longer. Spindlers' book, *Dreamers Without Power,* is a study of the entire Menominee community among which the peyotists formed a distinctive and interesting minority.

Slotkin found two peyote sects among the Menominee: the Cross Fireplace or Old Man's Meeting and the Half Moon, or Boy's, Meeting. Slotkin wrote (1952:574–75): "In general, the Half Moon is more like traditional Indian rites, while the Cross Fireplace has adopted many more details from white Christian rituals. The missionary's [Medicine Neck's] version of Peyotism seems to have been a variant of the Cross Fireplace. The rites are always held in a house." The Old Man's Meeting would have come either directly or indirectly from Winnebago John Rave and would have preceded the Half Moon ritual. Slotkin continued (1952:575): "In the beginning the Peyote missionary alone acted as leader. But after a few years John Neconish (now dead) became the first Menominee Peyote leader. Dewey Neconish was chosen next. Other knowledgeable and commanding personalities were George Neconish, Mitchell Weso, Howard Rain, and Louis Thunder."

Slotkin was told that about 1918, "Nat Decorah, a Wisconsin Winnebago peyote leader [introduced] . . . the Half Moon version, with use of the tipi. . . ." (Here it might be mentioned that in the western states the Half Moon sect is often designated the Tipi way.) It is logical to assume that the Half Moon version of Nat Decorah would have been much the same as Winnebago Jesse Clay's version of the Half Moon ceremony with its many Christian overtones.

Slotkin (1952:678) supplemented his informants' information regarding the Cross Fire ceremony by printing a 1917 interview with A. S. Nicholson, superintendent of the Menominee reservation, the man who had previously brought Medicine Neck to trial. Nicholson described the ceremony thus:

It has, however, been masked around with certain Christian symbols and Christian elements. . . . There is a chief priest. . . . there is a large altar cloth spread . . . bearing Christian symbols. . . . He has also an ordinary Bible, which he uses at times. . . . The whole Christian element of the ceremony is on the strictly Catholic order. . . .

While he is making this speech, he carries in his left hand a gourd rattle, in his right hand a peculiar, long lance inscribed with a Biblical inscription and bearing certain Biblical devices. . . .

A new feature of the Menominee peyote ceremony is the altar cloth. Exactly when and where the altar cloth originated is not known, but it is generally thought to have been the inspiration of the Sioux leader Sam Lone Bear, who is said to have been converted to peyotism on the Nebraska Winnebago reservation by John Rave about 1910 or 1912. Although Radin does not mention an altar cloth, it must have been used about that time, or a little later, by the Winnebago, for Albert Hensley once presented an altar cloth of black velvet with painted Christian-peyote symbols to Jim Blue Bird with instructions to use it instead of a sand altar. Through the Winnebago it would have arrived among the Menominee. When used, the altar cloth was spread west of the crescent altar, or it could take the place of the altar, and on it was put the Bible. The Spindlers (1971:107) published a photograph of an elaborate Menominee altar cloth with "embroidered peyote buttons on the corners and the crown of thorns, the crown and cross and insignia, and the lamb of peace." The altar cloth came to be particularly useful for meetings held inside a house or a wooden church, although it also was used, though not essential, in tipis and in both the Cross Fire and the Half Moon rituals.

Another unusual feature of Menominee peyotism is the absence of tobacco from the Half Moon ceremony as well as from the Cross Fire. I believe this is a simple carryover from the earlier form of the ritual to the later. Among the Menominee with a limited number of adherents, it was convenient to have limited distinction in the two rituals. Nearly everyone attended rituals of either sect, and when a meeting was announced, participants would not know before arrival at the service whether it was to be in Cross Fire or Half Moon style (Slotkin 1952:640).

Slotkin reported (1952:578): "essentially, the religion is Christianity adapted to traditional Indian beliefs and practices." And again (p. 578):

On the whole, to the Menomini, Christianity means Catholicism. For the last three hundred years there have been Catholic missionaries among them. About 93 per cent of the Menomini on the reservation are now Catholic. . . . Protestant missionaries have given English translations of the Bible to literate Peyotists. . . .

The Menomini Peyotists call themselves Christians. They consider themselves to be such because they have adopted the Trinity. For example, prayers are said in Menomini, and almost invariably terminate with, "In the name of the Father, the Son, and the Holy Ghost. . . ." Jesus is considered as a kind of culture hero who gave the white version of Christianity to the white man, and Peyotism to the Indian; . . . a few people accept Jesus' role as an intercessor spirit between God and man. . . . Some speak of the second coming of Christ. . . ."

The Spindlers wrote that the Menominee believe peyote cures the sick and that it teaches. They wrote (1971:102):

Christian symbols are apparent in the material structure and paraphernalia, as well as in the prayers and speeches. The tepee's poles represent Jesus Christ and the disciples. The staff is carved with crosses. Sometimes ten carefully selected sticks used to start the fire are regarded as representing the Ten commandments. Many prayers and songs are directed to Christ by name. . . .

Finally, the Spindlers wrote (p. 109): "It is clear that Menomini Peyotism is more nativistic than Whiteman-Christian in its orientation, however much of it is a response to the impact of Whiteman culture."

THE CHIPPEWA, OR OJIBWA

Like the Menominee, the Chippewa, or Ojibwa, never completely lost their aboriginal location in the north central United States. Today they are still situated on reservations along the northern border in North Dakota, Minnesota, and Wisconsin, although many thousands have left to become a part of the general population of the United States. La Barre wrote (1938:131): "In 1903 or 1904, Rave went to South Dakota, Minnesota and Wisconsin to preach the new religion." I find no other detail or confirmation of Rave's visit to Minnesota, but peyotism did eventually reach the Chippewa, if not quite that early, at least by 1914.

In an interview with Peter Rave, Winnebago of Nebraska, in 1972, I was told that the first Chippewa peyotist was Jacob Morgan of Cass Lake Reservation, who came to the Nebraska Winnebago reservation before 1912 as a boy of sixteen and was more or less adopted by Late Rave, brother of John and father of Peter. Peter had heard of Jake Morgan as long as he could remember. Sometime after 1912, probably two or three years, Jacob Morgan took peyote to his own people at Cass Lake and ran peyote meetings for them. This agrees with information in a letter from Morgan to Allen Dale in 1954, in which he said: "I have used this medicine for over 40 years now."

In 1916, the superintendent of the Red Lake Chippewa Agency reported that peyote had recently appeared at Red Lake and that it had been suppressed by confiscating the peyote and frightening away the peyote leader with threats of arrest. In 1919 a deputy special officer at Bemidji, Minnesota, reported that Late Rave of Thurston, Nebraska, was jailed in Bemidji for furnishing peyote to Chippewa Indians of the vicinity. Said to have received peyote from him were Dan Taylor and others. In his summary list of peyotists by states, Newberne (1922) gave a total of 89 Chippewa peyotists in Minnesota in 1919; they were 5 percent of the population of 1,789 at Leech Lake–Cass Lake Agency, but only 0.7 percent of the total Indian population of Minnesota, then 12,003.

Benny White, a Chippewa from Cass Lake, told me in 1976 that he believed Dan Taylor should be given equal credit with Jacob Morgan for the introduction of peyotism to the Chippewa. Dan Taylor had been a professional baseball player in Oklahoma and Kansas, where he had learned the ceremony. Benny White thought he may have led ceremonies among the Chippewa even before Morgan.

The ritual introduced by Jacob Morgan was the Cross Fireplace ritual, so it did not include tobacco. Later, according to Benny White, the Winnebago Half Moon ritual, which did include tobacco, came to Cass Lake. Benny White, who at the time of my interview with him was president of the Native American Church of Minnesota, mixed the two rituals, saying that he conducted the Half Moon ritual but omitted tobacco and also placed a Bible before him, two elements of the Cross Fire rite. Another peculiarity of the Chippewa ritual was remarked by an amateur anthropologist, Fred K. Blessing, in an article in the *Minnesota Archaeologist* for January, 1961. He wrote that during the peyote ceremony there was dancing by the male members. They did not move about the room, he said, but danced in place. James Howard, commenting on this, said that he had observed that members sometimes stood up when they prayed in peyote meetings at Ryan's village, a Chippewa settlement, and thought that this may have been what Blessing had observed as "dancing."

In 1960, Howard learned that Clarence White and his wife Mary were two of the leaders of peyotism at Ryan's village. Mary later was interviewed on the Leech Lake Reservation in 1968 for the American Indian Research Project of the University of South Dakota at Vermillion. She said that peyotism had begun in 1916 at Leech Lake, and that she herself was the first "of all my people" to be baptized into the Native American Church. It took place while on the visit to the Winnebago reservation.

Winnebago Peter Rave and his wife Lucy became prominent in later Chippewa peyotism. They had found work near Albert Lea, Minnesota, in the early 1940s and remained there for over thirty years. With other transplanted Winnebago and visitors from Wisconsin and Nebraska they made canvas tipis and held peyote meetings during all holidays. Chippewa from Minnesota as well as Sioux from the Dakotas and Minnesota were in attendance at the Albert Lea meetings.

THE NORTHERN PONCA

The Ponca who refused to stay in Indian Territory and returned to their old home in Nebraska were eventually granted allotments there, and their affairs were administered by the Yankton and Santee Sioux Agency. Visits from relatives in Oklahoma brought knowledge of peyote soon after it became accepted by the Southern Ponca. James H. Howard in *The Ponca Tribe,* Bulletin 195 of the Bureau of American Ethnology, wrote (1965: 125):

The peyote ritual is the only religious ceremony of an aboriginal nature still performed by the Ponca. As noted earlier, it came to the Southern Ponca from the Cheyenne in 1902. Shortly thereafter, the Southern Ponca carried it to the

Northern band of the tribe. EBC [Edward Buffalo-chief or Buffalo chip] . . . came from a long line of Ponca chiefs and was himself a peyote chief or road-man. . . . [He] contributed valuable original material on the Northern Ponca religion. . . . [He] died in 1950 at the age of 80.

Howard stated (p. ix) that the Northern Ponca had one fireplace of a Cross Fire or Big Moon type, which was introduced by the Winnebago peyote leader John Rave. The usual early ceremony brought by the Southern Ponca would have followed the pattern of the Comanche moon, since it diffused from the Comanche through the Cheyenne.

The Bureau of Indian Affairs confirmed the presence of peyote among the Northern Ponca when, in 1908, Acting Commissioner C. F. Larrabee replied to a report concerning the use of peyote "by the Indians of the Winnebago, Omaha and Santee Agencies." The peyote users on the Santee Agency would have been Ponca, for there are several reports that the Santee Sioux were not peyotists.

Early Northern Ponca peyote leaders besides Edward Buffalo Chief were James Roy, who applied to the Bureau of Indian Affairs for a license to become a peyote missionary, and Alfred Larvie, a successful farmer. Like many other peyotists, Larvie was an educated and outstanding man who had attended Carlisle Indian School for nearly four years, from October 23, 1889, to April 4, 1893.

THE SIOUX

The Sioux (Sioux being the common name for the Dakota) are the largest division of the Siouan linguistic family (Hodge 1907: 378). A number of sub-divisions have been maintained, such as the Yankton, the Santee, the Teton, the Oglala, the Sisseton, and the Yanktonai. Most now live in South Dakota on seven reservations, in North Dakota on two, and in towns off the reservation. The *Handbook of American Indians* (Hodge 1907: 378) combined Assiniboin and Dakota for a total of 28,780 in 1904, and the tribe has grown considerably since then. Sol Tax et al. (1956) found there were 34,644 Sioux in North and South Dakota in 1950. In 1974 there were 35,799 listed (U.S. Department of Commerce).

Although the Sioux are perhaps the best known tribe in the United States in popular literature, being the stereotype for everything Indian, and are the most fully documented in scholarly publications, little has been written of Sioux peyotism. This may be because of uneven and sometimes weak acceptance of peyotism among them. It never found early, widespread acceptance at the Lower Brule, Sisseton, or Standing Rock agencies. It has been strongest at the Yankton Agency, with 20 percent, or 623 peyotists out of a total of 3,117 Indians. There were 40 peyotists on the Rosebud Reservation out of a total of 5,521, or 0.7 percent. At Pine Ridge there

were 367 peyotists, or 5 percent, out of a total of 7,340 Indians. These are
Newberne's statistics for 1919 (1922:34–35), and the percentages were
approximately the same in 1955. But though a minority, Sioux peyotists
have been an important, as well as a controversial, segment of Sioux society since the early days of this century.

All evidence indicates that the Winnebago and Omaha were the teachers of peyotism to the Sioux. Densmore (1931, II:14) quoted her Winnebago informant, John Bearskin, as saying: "In 1903 or 1904, John Rave and
some others came to South Dakota, Minnesota, and Wisconsin and instructed the people in the peyote religion." Jim Blue Bird, of Allen, South
Dakota, one of the prime movers of South Dakota peyotism for many years,
wrote me on January 13, 1948: "I became a member of the peyote religion
in July, 1902, at Calumet, Oklahoma. Pine Ridge Sioux in South Dakota
commenced to use Peyote in 1904." Lurie (1961:44–45) quoted Winnebago Mountain Wolf Woman as saying that she and her husband went to
work in 1908 at Martin, South Dakota, not far from Allen and that Sioux
"Peyotists used to come to us. We used to eat with them." Other early
Sioux peyotists who considered that John Rave and Albert Hensley were
the first to bring peyote to the Sioux and to instruct them in the peyote
ceremony were Ed Richards, born in 1890; Sam Kills Crow Indian, born in
1894; and Tom Bullman, born in 1904. They also remembered other early
Winnebago proselytizers: Joe Brown, Henry White, Moses Hensley, and
Abraham Priest. Since Rave and Hensley were the first proselytizers, the
Cross Fire ritual was the ceremony first learned by the Sioux. The Half
Moon sect came later—some say in 1914, others in 1924—and again it was
a Winnebago, James Seymour, who introduced it.

Like the Winnebago, Sioux peyotists freely attend either Half Moon or
Cross Fire service. They are fully aware of the differences between the two
and are often very sectarian in discussions, but they tolerate their differences and enjoy each other's meetings. From 1908 to the present, most
reports lump all Sioux peyotists together, and to outsiders it is not always
clear if a particular group is actually of the Cross Fire or the Half Moon
ritual.

Wissler's first mention of peyote was in a monograph on Oglala ceremonies. He wrote (1912:99):

The mescal [peyote] has a firm hold among the Oglala notwithstanding official
efforts to suppress it. The usual form of rattle and drum is used. It was said
that a dream eagle appears to the devotees, sounding a whistle and giving instructions. Some of the songs seem to be of Christian origin. Though but recently introduced, and not generally recognized as a cult by the Indians themselves, the underlying conceptions of sanction and sources of power seem
about the same as in the case of typical dream cults.

In a general book (Wissler 1926:190) he assigned the date 1909 to Sioux
acceptance of peyote.

The earliest official report of Sioux peyote use is typical of agency attitudes toward peyotism. On March 31, 1911, Superintendent Walter Runke reported from Greenwood, South Dakota, concerning the Yankton Sioux:

A number of the Indians of this reservation have recently taken it upon themselves to introduce the use of . . . [peyote] among the people of this agency. In the past, the Indians here have been practically free from the use of this drug. . . . I am putting forth all possible effort to prevent the use thereof by the Indians under the jurisdiction of this Agency. It will be much easier at this time to prevent the introduction and general use of . . . [peyote] on this reservation than it will be later to stamp out its use. I have taken drastic measures with the ring-leaders of our new so-called Mescal [Peyote] Society and have them now lodged in the Agency jails.

Further correspondence did not reveal how long Superintendent Runke kept the Indians in jail, but since there was no law at that time against peyote in South Dakota or anywhere else, any imprisonment would have been illegal.

When Harry Black Bear, Willie Red Nest, and Charles Red Bear sought permission to use peyote from Assistant Commissioner of Indian Affairs C. F. Hauke, they received a rejection dated October 11, 1911:

Concerning your letter of July 24, wherein you request permission to secure peyote for use in connection with the services to be held in one of your Churches, you are advised that the Department has under consideration the question of whether or not these buttons can be lawfully supplied to Indians and until this matter has been settled, the Office withholds its permission to use them.

The three suppliants in this case were all dedicated peyotists of the Pine Ridge Reservation and did not knuckle under to the attitudes of Washington or the agency officials. Charles Red Bear was distinguished as the first home-grown Sioux to conduct peyote meetings at Pine Ridge. William Red Nest was pointed out by Superintendent John R. Brennan in 1916 as one of five Oglala peyote leaders and was said to be the one to have conceived the idea of a Cross Fire cemetery, donating the land for it. Harry Blackbear was brought to trial in 1916 in Deadwood, South Dakota, for giving ten peyote buttons each to Jacob Black Bear, Paul Black Bear, Jr., John Black Cat, and James Real Bull. The action of arrest and trial was under the act of 1897 to prohibit the sale of intoxicating drinks to Indians, and as in the case of Menominee Mitchell Neck, the judge found that the law did not apply to peyote.

Superintendent Brennan, who signed the complaint and testified against Black Bear, was much disturbed at the outcome of the case. He wrote to the Bureau of Indian Affairs: "It is to be regretted that Judge Elliott overruled the verdict of the jury. . . . It is hoped that your office will urge early legislation making it a crime to sell . . . [peyote] to Indians. The Pine Ridge Indians secure their supply of [peyote] . . . from the Omaha and Winnebago Indians." Judge Elliott summarized the case for the *Deadwood News:*

Robert Ogden, Jr., . . . quotes the testimony of witness Sloan, a gentleman prominent in reservation affairs and one who has used . . . [peyote] in its various forms, to the effect that it is not an intoxicant, that its effects after long usage are not bad on the system, and that it really does have an elevating effect upon its users: that it has cured people addicted to the use of intoxicants. . . .

Sioux peyotists continued to be plagued by antipeyotists, who were unusually well organized. In addition to the bureau in Washington, Christian missionaries, and the schools, the Lake Mohonk Conference of Friends of the Indians, of Lake Mohonk, New York, launched a national campaign against peyote and concentrated attention on the Sioux. One of its leaders, Reverend Dr. Edward Ashley, spoke to the conference (Daiker 1914: 76):

It is only recently that . . . [peyote] has been introduced among the Sioux. . . . the religious aspect has been adopted through the influence and suggestion of a returned student living in Nebraska. The other day on Pine Ridge . . . I listened to stories of how he had received $100 which had been raised to be used in interceding for assistance at Washington. I also saw . . . a petition from that society . . . asking that they should not be interfered with or prosecuted or arrested. . . . The Indian Office did not acquiesce. . . . [They] say they desire to put down this evil, but are up against the fact that it is a religious institution and comes within the Constitution of the United States. . . . the case looks to me like that of a second Benedict Arnold—a returned student coming back and betraying his people, the whole Indian people. . . .

The "returned student" could have been Albert Hensley, Jim Blue Bird, or Sam Lone Bear, or any number of others who had been educated at Carlisle.

In 1916, Representative H. L. Gandy of South Dakota introduced into the Sixty-fourth U.S. Congress a bill to outlaw peyote, and a number of Indian organizations were persuaded to support it. One of the leaders against peyote was a Yankton Sioux, Gertrude Bonnin, secretary of the Society of American Indians, an Indian-white organization which petitioned in favor of the Gandy bill. Twenty-three members of the Rosebud Tribal Council also supported it. The Indian Student Conference passed a resolution: "We view with alarm the pernicious effects of the use of the drug Peyote by our Indian race. . . . (resolution printed in 1916 Report of Lake Mohonk Conference). At a meeting of the Sioux tribe, held at Mitchell, South Dakota, during the summer of 1916, seven hundred Indians voted to oppose alcohol and peyote (report in *American Indian Magazine*). Nevertheless, in spite of opposition almost approaching hysteria, peyote meetings continued to be held at Pine Ridge, Rosebud, and Yankton, with no lack of leadership—or of peyote, which was available from the Aguilares Mercantile Company, Aguilares, Texas, at $2.50 per thousand.

Among the Sioux peyote leaders were some who had had, in addition to education at Carlisle, some years of education and experience as members of Wild West shows, which were popular for a number of years in both the

United States and Europe. Appearance of Indians in Wild West shows and similar exhibitions was strongly condemned by the Bureau of Indian Affairs (1890*b*), which warned:

... giving exhibitions of frontier life and savage customs, has been very harmful in its results. . . . Agents fully confirmed my . . . impressions that the practice is a most pernicious one, fraught with dangerous results, economically, physically, and morally. . . . [Indians] are frequently brought into association with some of the worst elements of society. . . . [The Indians] become self-important. . . . Their surroundings in these tours are generally of the worst, and they pick up most degrading vices. . . . [Indians] frequently return home . . . wrecked morally and physically, and, in such cases, their influences and example among other Indians is the worst possible.

In spite of such official discouragement, many Indians did participate in Wild West shows, among them peyotists Jim Blue Bird, William Black Bear, and Sam Lone Bear. Upon returning home, the first two of these Indians lived useful but unspectacular lives on the reservation. Sam Lone Bear was different.

Sam Lone Bear was born in 1879 to Oliver Lone Bear and Alice Plenty Brothers, of the Oglala tribe, living on Lone Bear Creek in South Dakota. He was at Carlisle five and one-half years from February, 1892, until July, 1897. In 1899 he joined Buffalo Bill Cody's Wild West Show, and in 1902 he went with the show to Europe, where it toured until 1906. Back in the states, he continued to travel with the show in the summers, at least some of the time. He was an exceptionally attractive young man at this time, according to William H. Powers, who knew him in the summer of 1908 when both were employed on the railroad in Eli, Nebraska. Fifty-four years later Powers wrote of his friendship with Sam that summer, of Sam's fascinating life, of his years at Carlisle and in Europe with Buffalo Bill, and of Sam's marriage to a Santee Sioux girl named Sophie. He remembered that Sam was always pleasant, friendly, interesting, exciting, and instructive.

Nevertheless, time has proved Sam Lone Bear to be lawless, immoral, exploitative, overbearing, acquisitive, and dishonest—a real scalawag. Among his sins were the exploitation of many young women and girls; the use of his position as roadman and supplier of peyote to extract money and goods from peyotists; nonpayment of debts; the sale of cheap, ten-cent-store articles at inflated prices, claiming them to be possessed of magical properties; the performance of sleight-of-hand tricks in peyote meetings, claiming them to be manifestations of the supernatural; and just plain stealing and lying. He was a restless man, traveling throughout the West for twenty-five to thirty years, teaching peyotism, living by his wits, satisfying a lustful appetite, and fooling a gullible public. Many honest Indians were taken in by him, and there were those who defended him to the extreme. There were others who saw through him, and while Indians in general were loathe to discredit him entirely, many came to distrust him. He hurt the

FIG. 10. Sam Lone Bear (Sioux). Photograph taken at Cardiff, Wales, about 1904, when he was a member of Buffalo Bill's Wild West show. Buffalo Bill Museum, Denver, Colorado.

cause of peyotism because whites, who were suspicious of peyote anyway, had in him a character completely unscrupulous whom they could use effectively as an example of the evils of peyote. Readers will meet up with him often in this account as he spreads the gospel of peyotism throughout the West, accompanied by an unmistakably bad odor.

Sam Lone Bear was an early missionary to the Sioux, according to Jim Blue Bird. Shortly after 1910, when Jim left his job with Miller's 101 Ranch Wild West Show, he and Sam went to the Winnebago in Nebraska, where they participated in Cross Fire peyote meetings with John Rave presiding. At that time Sam had an illegitimate son by a white woman in Chicago, Esther Demarest. Jonas Walker of Wounded Knee, a Half Moon peyotist, remembered that Sam Lone Bear had brought peyote to Pine Ridge in 1912. Sam's sister, Susie Lone Bear Iron Rope, thought the year was 1914. By that time, Sam had already begun proselytizing among the Ute, and some were beginning to question his morals. As the antipeyotists geared to enact state and federal laws prohibiting peyote, the character of Sam Lone Bear was cited as an argument against peyote, particularly by his fellow tribeswoman Gertrude Bonnin.

Jim Blue Bird, as honest as Lone Bear was devious, became one of the earliest and most influential peyote leaders among the Sioux and other northern tribes. In 1971, at age eighty-two, still vital, in good health, and possessing a remarkable memory, Jim supplied me with details of names, places, and dates concerning the spread of peyote among the Sioux. He had first learned of peyote when he was fourteen at a meeting led by Quanah Parker at Calumet, Oklahoma. From 1904 to 1907 he participated in meetings held on the Pine Ridge Reservation led by John Rave and Albert Hensley. From 1907 to 1911 he attended Carlisle, where he was subjected to the usual Christian influences, but he attributed his faith in the Bible to the early teachings of his father, who had become an Episcopal minister in 1892 when Jim was five. At Carlisle he met many people from many tribes who later became, if they were not already, peyotists.

After Carlisle he spent a number of years with Wild West shows, but in 1916 he again attended peyote meetings in Nebraska with John Rave and Albert Hensley, and it was from them that he learned to be a roadman. His form of peyotism was, of course, the Cross Fire ritual, and like the Winnebago teachers, he was much against the use of tobacco. He later had to compromise about this with the Half Moon members of the Native American Church, but he left no doubt about his sentiments. He said: "The Bible says 'No Smoking' and I made a rule against it." When Jim returned home in 1916 to become the acknowledged leader of the peyote religion among the Sioux, his father did not attempt to dissuade him, recognizing that in the Cross Fire church one prayed to Jesus Christ and preached clean living.

In Nebraska, Jim not only knew John Rave and Albert Hensley, but also came to know Harry, Late, and Pete Rave, younger brothers of John, and

Moses Hensley, son of Albert. He knew that both Harry and Late Rave had defected from peyotism for a while for personal reasons, but said both had returned. He attended Wisconsin Winnebago meetings with Henry White-thunder, Angelo La Mere, and others.

Jim attributed the Sioux Half Moon ritual to Willie Running Hawk and his brother, who lived on the northwest part of Pine Ridge; they had learned it during a long stay in Oklahoma, but Jim said that Winnebago Half Moon peyotists Jim Seymour and Joe Brown had also contributed to the Sioux Half Moon ritual along with Omahas Peter Blackbird, Leonard Springer, Allen Dale, and Charlie Cox.

When Jim traveled south of Pine Ridge to peyote meetings, he was usually in the company of established peyotists, and his role was that of "learner." On the other hand, when he traveled north, he was usually the teacher, if not innovator. Direction was also significant when people visited Allen, South Dakota, determining whether they were to be leaders or followers. The Cross Fire church at Allen was the first established in the state, and learners and teachers came from east, west, north, and south. Without claiming to be the original or only teacher of the Yankton peyotists, Jim pointed out that Samuel B. Necklace, Johnson Goodhouse, Charles Jones, and Charles Iron Hawk, the incorporators and first members of the Native American Church for the Yankton Sioux, had often visited Allen before they incorporated, and he could vouch that they were solidly Cross Fire.

As Sioux peyotism developed, some new elements were added and others received emphasis. The Cross Fire was the strongest sect, but people participated freely in both. Meetings were often held in a special building constructed for the purpose. Often an altar cloth was used, and sometimes there was a concrete altar. The most original development was the setting aside of special cemeteries for peyotists, characterized by head-stones bearing designs taken from peyote paraphernalia, such as peyote buttons and birds, as well as crosses.

In 1926, Yankton Sioux Johnson Goodhouse visited Devil's Lake, North Dakota, and the Canadian Sioux at Griswold, Manitoba, where he held enough peyote meetings to feel that the peyote religion was somewhat established in both places. Jim visited the same groups in 1928. Four meetings were held at Devil's Lake. In Griswold, Manitoba, Jim worked in the harvest for a month and directed peyotism there. In both places the Cross Fire ritual was practiced. Then he attended meetings at Red Lake and Cass Lake, Minnesota, with the Chippewa. Following that trip, a Chip-pewa peyotist of the Turtle Mountain Reservation in North Dakota visited Pine Ridge for instruction, but Jim could not say if regular meetings were held there.

For three years, beginning in 1928, Jim Blue Bird drove a truck for the South Dakota Highway Department in the vicinity of Sisseton, South Da-kota. While he was there, ten Sisseton Sioux families joined together in a

Cross Fire peyote church of which Jim was the roadman. In 1939 the Native American Church of Sisseton was separately incorporated.

Jim was familiar with peyotists from the Wind River Shoshone and Arapaho Reservation of Wyoming, as well as the Northern Cheyenne and the Rocky Boy's reservations of Montana. Eventually he came to know practically every peyote leader. He became the organizer and director of the Native American Church of South Dakota, with headquarters at Allen, and kept the job for fifty years, no matter who was elected to the other offices. His letterhead listed sixteen local chapters. In letters and conversation he was most helpful to me. His experiences made me sensitive to the importance that Carlisle graduates and Wild West show performers played in the diffusion of peyote.

Some of the ideas that Jim emphasized in his prayers and sermons were:

The old time Sioux went out to get visions so that they could go and scalp their enemies, but I am against all killing because I believe in the Bible. . . .

My boys in the Korean War carried Peyote all the time. . . .

The Cross Fire has the Bible and so has rules of conduct all the time, whereas Half Moon has no guide outside of meetings. . . .

The Bible guides us in life just like doctors' instruction—it is our prescription for life. . . .

We put the staff in a hole in front of the altar so that it stands upright and points to heaven. . . .

Peyote is an awful wonderful thing. When you eat peyote you feel guilty in your conscience for being a sinner. You think about yourself and try to lead a better life and be a brother to all. . . .

Something around us tells us how far we stand from God. Then it is revealed to us what we should do and what we should not do. . . .

We don't try to convert. . . . Let them come themselves.

Two early Sioux peyote leaders were remarkable for their friendship. They were Sam Kills Crow Indian and Charles Spotted Eagle. As young men they studied together a mail-order Bible course, prepared in English and Sioux by the Santee Normal School, which they both had attended. They did the lessons together regularly, thoroughly, and punctually each two weeks over a period of two years. After completing the course, they continued to read the Bible together and to attend peyote meetings. Charles Spotted Eagle had become a convert to peyotism among the Winnebago and Omaha in Nebraska. He introduced peyotism to Sam Kills Crow Indian, and the two drummed for each other and practiced peyote songs together between meetings. They conducted Cross Fire rituals in Norris, Porcupine, Rosebud, Saint Francis, Brennan, and Allen, South Dakota, and in Alliance and Scottsbluff, Nebraska, and later spent a number of years in Denver, Colorado, where they also conducted peyote meetings.

THE NORTHERN CHEYENNE

The Northern Cheyenne on their reservation at Lame Deer, Montana, received frequent visits from friends and relatives among the Southern Cheyenne in Oklahoma. One such visit is described in a publication by Rev. G. Elmer E. Lindquist, as recounted by Mennonite missionary the Reverend Rodolphe Petter:

When I first came to the Cheyenne and Arapahoe (Oklahoma) in 1890, they all had embraced the so-called Messiah religion; it was later that the peyote cult found entrance among them. While in Montana I met Leonard Tyler, a young educated Indian from Oklahoma, who told me he had just come to introduce the peyote among the Northern Cheyenne. That was in 1889.

In 1934, Petter also wrote to Commissioner John Collier of the BIA, saying:

In the course of my 43 years among the Cheyenne . . . the Cheyenne cults have undergone not inconsiderable changes. . . . In 1890 came the "Messiah" cult, introducing songs and prayers unknown before. Soon after, a former YMCA Indian worker brought the peyote, adding to its medicinal use a cult . . . mixture of the old religion, the "Messiah's" teachings and Christian views. A few years later I met him here in Lame Deer, bringing the "new doctrine" to the Northern Cheyenne.

Since then, the peyote cult has grown apace and at the present [1934] boldly claims it will displace both the old Indian cults and Christian religions.

Again, the missionary and YMCA worker to whom he made reference was Leonard Tyler.

The first Northern Cheyenne peyotist to be identified by name was Thaddeus Redwater, who had attended Carlisle from 1896 to 1900 and later spent two years at Haskell. When he returned to the reservation, he was employed as the official interpreter for the Northern Cheyenne Agency at Lame Deer. Six other Northern Cheyenne peyotists attended Carlisle. A group of three young men went together in 1907: Willis Medicine Bull, William Little Wolf, and Albert Monothy. Others were John Russell, Sr., Jerome Bear Tusk, and Marion Mexican Cheyenne. Willis Medicine Bull, who collaborated with Father Peter Powell on his study of aboriginal Cheyenne religion entitled *Sweet Medicine* (1969), said that he had used peyote since about 1903, before attending Carlisle. Furthermore, he had eaten peyote and practiced peyote songs and drumming with a Kiowa fellow student at Carlisle, and the Kiowa had given him fifty peyote buttons to bring home when he left Carlisle because of the illness of a sister.

When the Native American Church was established, many Northern Cheyenne were active in both the national and state divisions.

THE CROW

The Crow Indians, a part of the Sioux linguistic family, live on a large reservation in Montana, which is part of their ancient territory and is contiguous to the reservation of the Northern Cheyenne. The Crow Agency is located only forty miles from Lame Deer, Montana, headquarters of the Northern Cheyenne, and it is this closeness to the Cheyenne which led to the early diffusion of peyote to the Crow, in spite of the fact that the two tribes were often unfriendly.

Early official documents and ethnographic accounts of peyotism among the Crow are scarce. Perhaps in the beginning the officials on the Crow Agency were indifferent or the Crow peyotists were particularly circumspect in the practice of their new religion. In any event the earliest report of Crow peyotism is in a 1916 letter from Superintendent Evan W. Estep of the Crow Agency to H. A. Larson, chief special officer for the Bureau of Indian Affairs, which stated:

As far as we are able to learn, there is only one Indian on the Crow Reservation who is addicted to the use of this drug [peyote]. He has been using it for some years, but does not appear to be spreading its use among the other Indians of the tribe. His name is Frank Bethune and he lives on the eastern side of the reservation along one of the usual routes to the Tongue River [Northern Cheyenne] Reservation. It is believed that he learned the use of the drug from the Cheyenne Indians. The Cheyenne Indians from the Oklahoma Reservations frequently visit their relatives and friends on the Tongue River Reservation, and it is believed that the latter Indians receive their supply from Oklahoma in this manner. Frank Bethune doubtless gets his supply from passing Cheyennes.

In 1972 at the Crow Agency, Edison Real Bird told me: "My grandfather, Frank Bethune, put up the first peyote tipi on the Crow Reservation about 1910. Before that he had brought Peyotism from the Northern Cheyenne."

By 1919 the Crow Agency had become alert to the problem of peyote, for Superintendent C. H. Asbury added the name of Albert Anderson to that of Bethune as leading Crow peyotists who "are trying hard to spread the use among the people at Reno and Black Lodge communities." Reverend G. A. Vennink, missionary, who supplied data to Superintendent Asbury, was of the opinion that in addition to use in worship, peyote was used "as a medicine, and as a means of warding off disease." He reported that "Anderson comes now rarely to YMCA or Church," and "they believe when using it, they can see Christ, sometimes the Devil." The 1919 questionnaire of Newberne (1922) indicated that there were 34 Crow peyotists out of a population of 1,703, or 2 percent.

The reason for the lack of early ethnological reporting of peyotism among the Crow was the peculiar bias of the most important ethnologist to visit the Crow, Robert H. Lowie. Lowie first visited them in 1907. In 1910 he returned and "was allowed to spend at least part of every summer for seven consecutive years—through 1916—on the Crow Reservations" (1959: 41). In 1931 he returned again to collect more data on the Crow language. From the ethnographic and linguistic notes he made during nine summer visits to the Crow reservation he published thirty monographs and articles on the Crow and one hardcover book, *The Crow Indians* (1935). One large monograph was entitled *The Religion of the Crow* (1922) and a smaller one, *Minor Ceremonies of the Crow Indians* (1924). Yet in not one of them is it recorded that the peyote religion was present among the Crow. He was quite familiar with the peyote phenomenon, having published an item on the "Peyote Rite" in the *Encyclopedia of Religion and Ethics* (1917, IX: 815) and a section on "The Peyote Cult" in his textbook *Primitive Religion* (1925: 200–205).

In 1957, just before he died, Lowie finished a little book entitled *Robert H. Lowie, Ethnologist: A Personal Record* (1959). In it he discussed his two outstanding Crow interpreters: Robert Yellowtail (who became superintendent of the Crow Agency and in 1950 a delegate to the national convention of the Native American Church), and James Carpenter, of whom Lowie wrote: "I have had many other interpreters among Indians, some good ones among them; but I have never had another like Jim" (p. 50). While writing of Jim Carpenter as a marginal man, Lowie disclosed that Jim had tried to help him learn about Crow peyotism. It may have been as early as 1910, but it certainly was before 1916. Lowie continued:

An older cousin of his had become a devout adherent of the peyote cult. He assured me vehemently that this was a truly native Indian faith which owed nothing to white influence. A little later he declared with equal vigor that the Peyote was the tree of knowledge in Genesis and that twelve decorative appendages of a ritual object in his cult represented the twelve apostles.

Lowie said no more on the subject, and one must only conclude that peyotism among the Crow was too new, too much influenced by Christianity, for him. He was not interested in the Crow as he found them but only in the more aboriginal Crow.

The first ethnologist to mention peyotism among the crow was Ruth Shonle (1925: 58), who gave the date of 1912 when peyotism diffused from the Northern Cheyenne to the Crow. Other ethnologists have accepted that date. In 1939, Fred Voget, then a graduate student in anthropology, was living and working on the Crow reservation and at my request marked a peyote element distribution list for the Crow which I used in comparing the Washo–Northern Paiute peyote ritual with others. Voget was able to confirm that Frank Bethune was the first Crow leader, that he was said to have introduced it about 1915–16, and that Sam Lone Bear, an alien missionary, brought a "new way" to the Crow in the 1920s.

Hoping to fill in a few gaps in the history of Crow peyotism, I visited the Crow reservation in the spring of 1972. Fortunately, some of the older Crow Indians I talked with were able to supply a remarkable amount of data regarding the beginning of peyotism among the Crow. Martin He Does It, born in 1901, who had lived all his life near Saint Xavier, Montana, and at age seventy-one was an active tribal game warden, told me he remembered peeking into a peyote tipi before 1912, although he did not participate fully in a peyote ritual until 1916. He confirmed that Frank Bethune and Albert Anderson had learned to conduct the peyote ceremony while visiting with Northern Cheyenne and were running meetings among the Crow before 1912.

Martin He Does It had a good memory. He said Sam Lone Bear was in Montana after the Big Sheep case (1924), and he remembered that Lone Bear had been there again in 1926 when he left with a teenage girl, Julie, and her younger brother Mike, whom they "ditched" in Douglas, Wyoming. Martin had accepted Sam's "new way" of conducting meetings, which employed an altar cloth, the Bible, and candles and prohibited smoking. Martin told me he had made an altar cloth following the design of Lone Bear. It was a square of blue plush with a white dove painted at either corner at the top, and in the center were a white cross and two U.S. flags, crossed. Just above this was written "Jesus Only," and below it "Love One Another."

Martin He Does It reported that he had been cured of diabetes by peyote and that several doctors of medicine certified this remarkable cure. He said that everyone considers him a miracle. At Christmastime in 1970 during a peyote meeting put up for him, he saw the star that appeared at the birth of Jesus. After conducting rituals in the manner of Lone Bear for about five years, Martin abandoned the Cross Fire way for the Tipi way of the Cheyennes. Still he invited Paul Spider, a Pine Ridge Sioux Cross Fire roadman, to hold a meeting for the Saint Xavier area Crow. The Tipi way leaders whom Martin remembered as visitors to the Crow were Baldwin Parker (Comanche), Bill and Joe Kaulaity (Kiowa), Alfred Wilson (Southern Cheyenne), and Allan Dale (Omaha). Martin had traveled to Laredo, Texas, twice to obtain peyote, each time performing the ritual of praying and smoking in the peyote area before cutting.

Another Crow peyotist informant of about the same age as Martin He Does It was William Russell of Lodge Grass, who served as judge of the Crow Indian court for many years. During an evening in May, 1972, Judge Russell confirmed early reports that the Crow first learned peyotism from their neighbors the Northern Cheyenne. He added that a white man, Tom Morgan, was the first regular supplier of the dried peyote buttons to both the Northern Cheyenne and the Crow. In 1919 dried peyote was for sale over the counter in a drugstore in Ashland, Montana, on the eastern edge of the Northern Cheyenne reservation (Ketcham 1919). Russell said that Lone Bear introduced the second type of peyote meeting, the Cross Fire. He recognized that Lone Bear's ritual was like that of Albert Hensley, who came to the Crow in 1927 and actually stayed as a guest in his home. A year or so later, Hensley returned to conduct Cross Fire meetings for the Crow, and this time he was accompanied by his son, Moses. The Sioux Cross Fire roadman, William Black Bear, also had conducted meetings for the Crow.

In spite of knowledge and reinforcement of the Cross Fire ritual, the Crow had more attention from alien members of the Half Moon ritual, variously referred to as Tipi way, Kiowa way, and Comanche way. Seven different Northern Arapaho leaders from the Wind River Reservation had been visitors among them: Charlie Bell, George Behan, Gregory Blackburn, William Shakespeare, and Sherman Welch. Shoshone who came from the same reservation were Marshall and Charlie Washakie and Gilbert Day. Kiowa-Apache peyotist Apache Ben had visited and directed ceremonies for the Crow several times. Three visiting peyote roadmen who had come to supply and conduct peyote ceremonies had married Crow women and stayed on the reservation. These were John Horse Chief (Pawnee), Ed Hummingbird (Kiowa), and Quinten Anquoe (Kiowa).

As a calm, judicious, friendly devotee, William Russell had visited with nearly all tribal groups having peyote meetings. His first visit to a peyote group in Oklahoma took place while he was a student at Haskell Indian School, Lawrence, Kansas, when he was about twenty years old. Henry Lookout, Osage peyotist, had taken Russell home with him, where he had had an opportunity to participate in one of the oldest Cross Fire peyote churches, the round, wooden one started by John ("Moonhead") Wilson about 1890.

Other Crow peyotists I interviewed in 1972 were James Big Lake, Ellsworth Little Light, Joe Ten Bears, Jr., and Henry Old Coyote.

James Big Lake had attended his first peyote meeting in 1923 at the age of fifteen. He did not remember having seen Sam Lone Bear, but he remembered that Lone Bear often stayed in the home of his wife's father, Archie White Clay, when he visited the Crow reservation. He said, "Sam Lone Bear came about 1920 . . . [and] stressed medicinal use of peyote. . . . The Crow in time offered him their very best things . . . [but] the government had gotten after him for selling peyote." Big Lake did not say that the reason the government "had gotten after" Lone Bear was for taking Julie, a girl of fifteen, from Montana to New Mexico for immoral purposes, but he knew all about it. He was close kin of Julie, "who went on a trip with Lone Bear." He further said: "There is no more 'new way' among the Crow. After Sam took that girl away I didn't like his ways of running meetings."

James Big Lake had become the official supplier of peyote to the Crow, going every year to Roma, Texas, where the Crow had an agreement with a Texan who owned seven sections of peyote-producing land, giving them the exclusive right to harvest his peyote at five dollars a sack. The previous year he had brought back to Montana ten thousand green peyote plants to clean and dry. James Big Lake had attended meetings with the Kiowa-Apache, the Kiowa, the Sac and Fox, the Taos, the Fox of Iowa, the Navajo, the Comanche, the Bannock, and the Southern Cheyenne. But, he maintained, most peyotists "are also members of other Churches—especially for education. I regularly go to Baptist, Catholic, and Native American Churches."

Ellsworth Little Light had been taken by his six older brothers to his first peyote meeting in 1922 at the age of ten, when Austin Stray Calf was roadman. He knew the first peyote roadman, because Frank Bethune was his father-in-law. Like Judge Russell he had attended meetings with the Osage in the round wooden church built by John Wilson, and he recognized many similarities between the Osage ceremony and the Cross Fire ritual introduced by Sam Lone Bear and carried on among the Crow by Chester Medicine Crow and Xavier Flower. Victor Griffin (Quapaw) had been road-man when he had visited the Osage. He also had attended meetings with Jim Blue Bird and William Black Bear in South Dakota, and once he had attended a peyote meeting with the Cree in Hobbema, Alberta, Canada. Peyotists he knew who had conducted meetings on the Crow reservations were Jim Silverhorn (Kiowa), John Padapony (Comanche), Herman Haury (Arapaho), and Tom Morgan (Pawnee).

Joe Ten Bears, Jr., had attended the University of Chicago and "nearly graduated." He, too, was of an old peyote family. His grandfather, Charlie Ten Bears, had attended Hampton Institute when it was a boarding school for Negroes which accepted a few Indians, who were segregated but stud-ied manual training and agriculture with the blacks. Joe Ten Bears, Sr., had been appointed chaplain of the Native American Church of the Crow, and now Joe, Jr., held elective office in that group.

Joe spoke of the close association between the Crow and the Kiowa. In addition to those Kiowas named by others as visiting peyotists he added the names of Oscar Tsoodle, Charlie Anko, Bert Giacomo, Clyde Ahtape, James Auchiah, David Apekaum, and John Little Chief. One Kiowa not named by Ten Bears but who said he once lived three months on the Crow reservation conducting peyote meetings was Emmet Tsatigh. Ten Bears claimed that peyotism was stronger and attracted more participation than in the past, and he agreed with the others that many peyotists were also ac-tive in the Christian missions. He said the Pentecostals spoke out strongest against peyote; the Mormon church did not say much against it, but the Baptists were most tolerant and "paid no attention."

Finally, Henry Old Coyote talked to me about peyotism on the Crow reservation. His ancestor Barney Old Coyote had welcomed Sam Lone Bear onto the Crow reservation because they had been together in Wild West shows. Barney Old Coyote was active in the Saint Xavier Catholic Church, being a catechist for the mission, explaining Catholic lessons in the Crow language to young and old. Yet he frequently participated in peyote rituals and spoke out in defense of peyotism, although he was not an official.

Henry had attended peyote meetings with at least a dozen different tribes. He had participated in both Cross Fire and Tipi way services with the Winnebago and the Omaha. He said the Crow had swung entirely to the Tipi way and now used tobacco in nearly all meetings. He added the name of Truman Daily (Oto)to those of visiting roadmen. In 1970 he had the good fortune to be a member of a large group of American Indians taken to fourteen European countries on a six-month "good-will tour."

All of the Crow Indian peyotists who talked to me in May, 1972, except Chester Medicine Crow, who was old, deaf, and feeble, were active in both tribal and Native American church affairs. Most were employed by the U.S. government or the Crow tribe. They were sophisticated and knowledgeable and functioned well as Crow Indians and as American citizens. They were obviously proud to be Crow Indians and peyotists.

Frank Takes Gun, elected president of the Native American Church of North America in 1956, will be discussed in following chapters.

THE NORTHERN ARAPAHO

According to Virginia Cole Trenholm (1970: 296–97):

The Northern Arapahoes give William Shakespeare credit for bringing the peyote cult to Wind River, Wyoming about 1895. While in school, Shakespeare became seriously ill and his father sent him south in the care of White Antelope to learn about peyotism. . . . He was directed . . . to take peyote to his people and teach them how to worship. Shakespeare taught the ritual to John Goggles, who later went to Indian Territory, where he studied under Cleaver Warden.

Shakespeare was a student at Carlisle from 1881 to 1883 and later worked as a policeman, farmer, and herder.

John Goggles was the principal informant for Molly Peacock Stenberg in 1944. He was then sixty-one years old, having used peyote for forty-seven years, beginning at the age of fourteen. Goggles justified almost every Northern Arapaho use of peyote as an attempt to cure some illness. He said (Stenberg 1946: 143ff.):

My father told me because I was hurt when a horse fell on me . . . "I'd like to have you try this medicine. . . ."

So I asked my cousin, Shakespeare; told him what my father said. I wanted to try it, and asked if it would be alright for me, a boy. So he told me it didn't make any difference, old or young. "You can come. . . ."

I went in and I done everything just like the rest. I began to feel changed. I felt the feelings that I never felt before. I didn't get tired; I just enjoyed listening to the singing and drumming. I forgot the pain here and never had it again after that. So it seemed like after I got started he wanted to keep me around, more close than before.

. . . he began to make me do some thing in the meeting. . . .

So I finally ask him; he answered in kindly way, "My brother, reason why I do this, I know you well and I think you can be trusted and will be honest man when you grow up. . . . That is why I'm teaching you this. You might become a leader of this worship some day."

. . . I started conducting when 28 years old.

At start this meeting was left with just me and my brother, Michael, when old man passed on. I thought I should go to Oklahoma and see how they use it. So I went down there to learn, attended meetings, learned more things they did when they had this worship. Attended Kiowa, Cheyenne, Comanche meetings. Kept doing this . . . five trips. . . . Spent my own money trying to learn this.

Had a friend there, Cleaver Warden, well-educated [Carlisle] man, Arapahoe. . . . He told me he was going to teach me. . . .

He was the man that teach on how to conduct this meeting. Put up tipi for this purpose, invited leaders from neighboring tribes to witness this meeting so they can see that the worship is passed on to me correctly, to bring to my people. So the time came I went through the meeting; many tribes represented: Kiowas, Comanches, South Cheyenne, South Arapahoes, and a few Otoes.

When the meeting was over each tribe was asked to say something. They would talk and say they were glad to see young boy from Wyoming learning to be a leader from those people down there. Had seen me many times going to meetings, and they thought I had really learned this Peyote meeting right. I was first one in state of Oklahoma where this meeting was passed on in the right way. Told me not to be afraid of anything and go ahead and when people wanted me to conduct their meeting to go ahead and do it. When I got back I was 28 [i.e., about 1911] and I started to run these worship meetings here. . . .

There are other Arapahoe leaders now. I have passed it on to my friends. There is Joe Duran; he came as a school boy. After meeting he went to church in early morning [Catholic]; he went to church and then came back. . . .

These are the ones who have it right way. Some others have come from Oklahoma without authority and introduced the worship. . . .

Charlie Washakie was first [Shoshone] to start going to meetings. . . .

When I see that Marshall Washakie stayed on with it I had a chance to teach him just as I had learned it from my friends. . . .

It was eight years before Marshall felt ready.

The earliest agency document from Wind River concerning peyote known to me is a letter from Superintendent H. R. Wadsworth to the Bureau of Indian Affairs, dated August 21, 1908: "I learn that visiting Indians from some of the southern reservations have introduced among the Indians here, principally Arapaho, the use of . . . [peyote], and the same seems to be a great rage among them. . . ." Two years later, he wrote: "One of our Indians, Frank Armejo, bought his peyote from Henry Rowledge." He also reported that one Black Sleeper, an Arapaho from Darlington, had been in Wyoming several months and was selling peyote at Wind River. In 1909, Charles W. Bell of Arapaho, Wyoming, was trying to purchase peyote by mail from L. Villegas and Co., Laredo, Texas.

In *Acculturation in Seven American Indian Tribes* (1940), edited by Ralph Linton, the peyote religion of the Northern Arapaho of Wyoming was discussed by Henry Elkin:

The disappearance of the society lodge dance has confined the younger men to a meagre role in the traditional ceremonial life. This has facilitated in the spread of the peyote cult, introduced to the reservation about twenty-five years ago [1910]. In contrast to the Ghost Dance, which never gained a firm place, the "Peyote Brotherhood" has steadily grown and now includes a large number of young and especially middle-aged men. It is a religion of "good thoughts" and mutual help, and has taken over a number of Christian symbols and be- liefs. . . . A decided break has occurred between the peyote members and the old medicine-men. The latter, having a vested interest in the traditional reli- gious forms, and deriving material gain from their treatment of disease, are antagonistic to the peyote cult, and cast aspersions on the medicinal value of the peyote which apart from the regular ceremony is widely eaten as a curing device.

Like Kroeber (1907), La Barre (1938) does not distinguish between the Northern and Southern Arapaho, except to say that peyote was directly transmitted from the Southern Arapaho to the Northern Arapaho about the year 1903. The form of ceremony followed the Comanche or Kiowa Way, since that was the form of ceremony followed by the Southern Arapaho. Still, Kroeber found many Christian ideas incorporated in the rite. In the monograph by Kroeber and Dorsey, entitled *Traditions of the Arapaho* (1903), Kroeber does not specifically name his peyotist informant but there is this acknowledgement: "The greater part of the material recorded by both authors was obtained through Cleaver Warden, a full-blood." They might have added, "Cleaver Warden, active peyote missionary."*

---

*I have observed no antagonism between peyotism and traditional Indian curing cere- monies either among the Northern Arapaho or any other tribe, and traditional curing rites have taken place in peyote meetings both by the roadman and peyotist medicine men (Morris E. Opler 1938:284; Lumholtz 1902). It happened that I observed such a practice among the Northern Arapaho. During a Northern Arapaho peyote meeting I attended at Ethete, Wyo- ming, on the night of June 25, 1971, the roadman and another regular shaman both practiced old-fashioned shamanistic sucking on a patient. It was the roadman of the meeting, Ben Fri- day, Sr., who first called for a glass of water and a paper plate to be brought into the tepee at about 3:00 A.M. The patient was a World War II veteran who had previously been treated at a veterans' hospital. The pain was in the back of the patient's head, and the roadman placed his lips directly over the spot and began sucking. He repeated it several times. Water seemed to be held in the mouth during the sucking and was then spit into the paper plate. Ben Friday was helped by a younger man, Richard A. Willow, who repeated the sucking performance a couple of times in the same way. A white object was extracted, but exactly what it was was not obvious. The paper plate with water and the object were burned on the fire in the center of the tepee. Except for the sucking interlude, the ceremony that night was a typical Half Moon ritual.

THE WIND RIVER SHOSHONE

The Wind River Shoshone are part of the northern division of the large Shoshonean linguistic family which includes the Comanche and the Ute. They occupy a reservation in central Wyoming just east of their ancient territory. This group was formerly known as Washakie's band, referring to their long-enduring and last great chief. In 1909 there were 816 Shoshone at Wind River, Wyoming, and at the request of the U.S. government they shared their reservation with the Northern Arapaho, through whom they first learned of peyote.

By 1908 the use of peyote by the Wind River Shoshone had come to the attention of the Bureau of Indian Affairs. At that time Acting Commissioner C. F. Larrabee wrote to Wyoming and also to Chief Special Officer William E. Johnson in Salt Lake City, suggesting that Shoshone Indians be arrested to provoke a court test of the 1897 antiintoxicant law to see if it would apply to peyote. He wrote:

It is therefore suggested that in order to test the question in the courts you take appropriate steps to obtain the prosecution in one or two cases on different reservations of persons guilty of introducing the mescal [peyote] on the reservations or selling it to non-citizen Indians.

In this connection there is herewith transmitted to you a copy of a letter of the 21st ultimo from the Superintendent of the Shoshone Indian school concerning the introduction of mescal [peyote] among the Indians of the Wind River Reservation.

Johnson communicated with Superintendent H. E. Wadsworth of the Shoshone Agency, saying: "From my knowledge of . . . the peyote plant, I am persuaded that there will be no difficulty whatever in proving the intoxicating qualities of this article. . . ." However, no record that a trial took place has come to light.

The next document regarding Shoshone peyotism was the reply to the 1916 Bureau of Indian Affairs questionnaire seeking information about the use of peyote on resevations. The reply from Fort Washakie enclosed a letter from Reverend J. Roberts, who had been a missionary on the Wind River Reservation for thirty years. For a change, it did not condemn peyote. Reverend Roberts wrote:

I beg to state that I am informed that about thirty of them use the peyote on this Reservation. They use it, they tell me, only in their lodge meetings, never outside.

The late Dr. C. I. Smith, resident Agency Physician, and the late Mr. Richard Morse, Chief of Police here, both attended one of the local lodge meetings. They told me that they admired the ritual of the lodge and that they saw nothing reprehensible at the meeting.

This was followed in 1919 by a similar report from Superintendent A. L. Corey. He had attended meetings where peyote was used and had tried the buttons himself. He estimated that 2 percent of the Shoshone were peyotists and that the Shoshone had peyote ceremonies independent of those of the Arapaho. He believed the Arapaho, who instructed the Shoshone in peyotism, had practiced the religion for over twenty years. Corey asserted: "They do not . . . use the peyote for other than religious meetings," and "the members of the peyote lodge refuse to use whiskey, refuse to gamble, and altogether are among the better members of the tribe."

Peyotism on the Wind River Reservation was the subject of the research of Molly Peacock Stenberg, wife of an Indian Service employee, who spent seven years on the Wind River Reservation. Her master's thesis was published in 1946 by the University of Wyoming. Stenberg participated in rituals of the Shoshone and Northern Arapaho, interviewed leaders, searched out old documents and letters, and accumulated statistics to give a complete picture of peyotism on the Wind River Reservation up to 1944. According to Stenberg, John Goggles, a Northern Arapaho, acquired peyote from friends and relatives in Oklahoma on the Cheyenne-Arapaho reservation in 1897. Soon he brought peyotism to his own tribe and also taught his Shoshone friends, Charlie and Marshall Washakie, to conduct meetings. Charlie Washakie told Stenberg (1946: 146): "I've been using it [peyote] for 34 years, longer than anyone else. . . ." Although he had first learned peyotism from John Goggles, Charlie Washakie continued to seek instruction. Stenberg wrote:

Jock Bull Bear, medicine man of the Southern Arapaho . . . came to Wyoming to lead meetings and invited Charlie to come to Oklahoma and learn the Peyote "Right Way." Charlie went December 1916 to Oklahoma to get instruction, stayed till March . . . (Charlie keeps a journal or diary of his doings, to which he referred constantly, he has a complete record of his trip to Oklahoma and record of his first use of Peyote in 1909).

Anthropologist Demitri Shimkin, on the Wind River Reservation to study the Shoshone Sun Dance, also learned much about the Shoshone peyote cult. In a letter to me in 1938, he wrote:

Peyote was and is associated almost entirely with members of Washakie's band, and the Episcopal Church. Two men brought it in; both are still living, although one is very old. The other is the official head of the cult here. The first of these men, Tassitsie, was one of Washakie's warriors. He was one of the first to adopt Christianity. Shortly afterwards he went to the Comanche with his son and brought back the peyote cult. He has also been influential in the Sun Dance, and was probably one of the chief factors in its Christianization. . . . The other man, Charlie Washakie (one of Chief Washakie's sons) brought the cult from the Arapaho. . . . Generally speaking, there is no conflict internally when the same person is a good Episcopalian, a good Peyotist, and a leader of the Sun Dance.

Another early Shoshone peyotist was Jesse Day, whose son Gilbert also became a peyote leader. When interviewed on August 19, 1944, by Stenberg, Jesse Day said:

The Barefooters (Carrizo) . . . were the first to use the Peyote; second were the Apache, and third the Comanches. . . . Quanah Parker, chief of the Comanches, introduced it to the other tribes. . . . I went to Oklahoma and took it with the Comanches. . . . Before Shoshones had used it there was a man who had rheumatism—Iowa Jackson. . . . I said let's go to Oklahoma to the Comanche to see about that good medicine they have. . . . That was thirty-five years ago [1909].

Iowa Jackson was said to have been so impressed by Quanah Parker that he never ceased to talk about his encounter with him, and for that reason the Shoshone called him "Little Quanah Parker."

And finally, perhaps the earliest Shoshone peyotist of all may have been one White Saint Clair, whom George Wesaw, a Wind River Shoshone living in Idaho, remembered hearing had gone to Lawton, Oklahoma, and had eaten peyote with the Comanches even before Jesse Day and Iowa Jackson.

In the beginning the peyote ritual of the Wind River Shosone was that of the Comanche and the Arapaho, the Half Moon way, but the Cross Fire ritual was introduced at least by 1918 and by none other than Sam Lone Bear. One of Stenberg's informants, Bat Weed, related, "That boy, my son, Starr, he was pretty sick boy already when we went to Casper and Sam Lone Bear put up a meeting for him in 1918 when he was five. He got well."

In 1971, I was directed to Crowheart, Wyoming, to talk with Sam Nipwater, who was said to be one of the oldest living Shoshone peyotists. Sam calculated that it was about 1902 when he was a small boy that he first heard drumming and singing coming from a tipi where an Arapaho peyote meeting was in progress, but he thought a number of years passed before Shoshone had such ceremonies. He thought Lone Bear first conducted peyote meetings among the Shoshone about 1918, although Nipwater himself did not participate until 1921. Tom Wesaw and Jesse Day convinced him to go to a meeting with Sam Lone Bear. Sam Lone Bear and Nipwater were friends for the next ten years and met for peyote ceremonies whenever Lone Bear came to Wind River or Casper, Wyoming. The ritual was Cross Fire. There was "just a cloth" instead of the sand crescent altar, but there were feathers, gourds, and a drum. Nipwater believed Lone Bear was special:

Lone Bear prophecied that the Tipi Way [Half Moon] could replace his way. . . . He could read any man's mind. . . . He was my friend—always talked good . . . got on knees and prayed . . . talked to Peyote. . . . I thought Sam Lone Bear was a good man, but I found out that he used Peyote bad. He used it to get game while hunting. Peyote helped him get girls, to win horse races, to win bucking contests. Sam said that was his way, but he said that way was not for me.

Sam had married a Ute girl, Ella Sirawap, in 1914, and her brother Archie said that he had lived with them in Casper for at least three years, about 1917 to 1920. Sam came to be well known around the reservation and disillusioned more than Sam Nipwater. Arapaho peyote roadman George Behan said that Lone Bear once brought a hundred head of horses from Montana and changed the brands on them. Behan also knew him to be a sleight-of-hand artist.

Whether it was Sam's behavior that made the Cross Fire less attractive to the Shoshone or something else, the Cross Fire was never as popular among the Shoshone as the Half Moon ritual. Jim Blue Bird and other Cross Fire leaders did conduct meetings at Wind River, but most Shoshone held with the Tipi way of the Comanche. Besides Charlie and Marshall Washakie and Jessie Day, leaders were Gilbert Day and others.

In 1919, Newberne gave statistics for peyotism on the Wind River Reservation, including the Northern Arapaho, as 127 peyotists out of a population of 1,696, or 7.5 percent. In 1944, Stenberg (1946: 116) found that "of the 182 families of the Shoshone tribe, 138, or seventy-six percent, are in the [peyote] cult," with an equal percentage of Arapaho families.

THE UTE

The Ute Indians are part of the Shoshonean linguistic family and formerly occupied all of western Colorado and eastern Utah, from the Salt Lake valley to the Rocky Mountains and south into New Mexico. Today they live on three widely separated reservations on part of their ancient land: the Uintah-Ouray Reservation in northeastern Utah; the Ute Mountain Reservation in southwestern Colorado at Towaoc, near Cortez; and the Southern Ute Reservation at Ignacio, east of Durango.

Early records show that the Ute of Colorado began visiting the Cheyenne and Arapaho Agency in Oklahoma, where they would have had contact with peyotism, at least by 1896. A letter from the Cheyenne and Arapaho Agency in 1896 to Ute agent David F. Day reported "the arrival of Buckskin Charlie's party. . . . The Indians are gathering in camp at the Red Hills to entertain them in their usual way. . . . The civil officers are searching for James Frost . . . who is reported to have returned with Buckskin Charlie's party." In 1949, I was told by Tony Buck, son of Buckskin Charlie, that Buckskin Charlie was the "first leader [of southern Ute Peyotism] . . . who had been visited by Cheyenne Indians who taught him." The Cheyenne Indian who taught Buckskin Charlie may well have been James Frost, who seems to have spent a good deal of time on the Southern Ute reservation. For a while he was married to a Ute girl and made himself disagreeable to the Indian agent, Joseph Smith (1900–1905), who complained to the Bureau of Indian Affairs: "Your office has from time to time been informed of the presence on this reservation of a renegade Cheyenne Indian who goes by the name of Jim Frost. . . ."

The Ute continued to visit the Cheyenne and other Indians in Oklahoma. Only a few days after his complaint to Washington, Smith wrote the following pass: "To Whom It May Concern: The bearer of this letter, Buckskin Charley, is one of the Chiefs of the Southern Ute Indians. He with a band of about 16 Indians and squaws are on their way to the Cheyenne, Arapaho, Comanche and Kiowa agencies. . . ." Letters of introduction were also sent to the Indian agents of those tribes. Peyotism may well have been on the minds of this party of Indians. In my interview with Tony Buck, he also reported that one Henry Lincoln, an Arapaho, had conducted peyote meetings in Ignacio in 1900.

Coming from the Cheyenne, the style of peyotism first known by the Southern Ute would have been the Half Moon ceremony of Quanah Parker. Given the Indian habit of visiting, we can expect that some knowledge of this form of peyotism was soon known at Towaoc among the Ute Mountain Ute, one hundred miles to the west, and among the Uncompahgre Ute on the Uintah-Ouray Reservation in Utah, some five hundred miles north. Moreover these Ute reservations were convenient stopping places for Oklahoma peyote missionaries on their way to and from the Shoshone and Northern Arapaho reservations in Wyoming and the Crow and Northern Cheyenne reservations in Montana. One of these roadmen, Alfred Wilson (Southern Cheyenne), later president of the Native American church, was said by Clifford Duncan of White Rocks, Utah, and Jacob Lopez of Towaoc to be one of the earliest missionaries of the Tipi way. There may well have been others.

Later, John Peak Heart (Southern Cheyenne) became noted as a missionary to the Ute. About 1916 or 1917 he began coming to Towaoc every summer to conduct peyote meetings. Although he usually stayed with Walter Lopez, a Towaoc shaman and sheepman, he seems to have conducted Half Moon meetings on all three reservations. Marvin Opler, who studied the Southern Ute in 1936, was told (1940a:464): "John Peehart taught us, coming down from the Northern Ute country. . . . John Peehart was our first teacher." In an interview in 1972, Amos Prank, an elderly Utah Ute peyotist, said that John Peak Heart was one of the first Oklahoma missionaries to the Northern Ute. James Mills, a Towaoc Ute, was Heart's disciple and accompanied him back to Oklahoma for several years to receive further instruction. Another early Oklahoma missionary was Albert Hoffman (Southern Cheyenne), seventy-nine years old when I interviewed him in 1972, who said he had been a missionary and supplier to the Ute. Ute informants agreed that he had been taking peyote to the Ute "for a very long time."

In spite of early knowledge of it, peyotism did not seem to maintain a strong hold among the Colorado Ute. In answer to the Bureau of Indian Affairs questionnaires of both 1916 and 1919, the agencies reported that peyote was not known at either Ignacio or Towaoc. It is hard to understand how peyote could have completely escaped the attention of the agency officials. Perhaps they were unusually indifferent to tribal activity, or it may have been the relative isolation of the Ute reservations, or perhaps it was simply that the Indians involved were not aggressive personalities.

However, on the Uintah Reservation in Utah it was a different story. By 1916 about 50 percent of the Indians were peyotists, and the agency officials were only too well aware of it. It was in 1914 that Sioux Sam Lone Bear decided to bring the Cross Fire ritual to the Ute. He selected as the place to begin his missionary work the tiny community of Dragon, Utah, an isolated terminal of a narrow-gauge railroad seventy-five miles from agency headquarters at Fort Duchesne. He immediately charmed everyone with his ability as a trick roper and bronco buster. The Ute had an old culture pattern of allowing successful men to take several wives, a custom that appealed to Sam. He joined the household of Dick Sirawap, who had two teenage daughters, Ella and Sue. Sam was soon considered to be married to Ella, and in the next few years she bore him three children. Sue was said to have had two children by Sam also, one when she was thirteen. And one summer, while still living with the Sirawaps, Sam took a young girl, Mary Guerro, to Chadron, Nebraska, where he kept her a virtual prisoner all summer and got her with child, too. For this, the Utah courts put him in jail and tried to convict him in the U.S. district court under the Mann Act. But Sam seems to have had the Indians under a spell, for they refused to testify against him, and he was freed.

His actions, however, colored his success as a missionary. In 1916, Uintah Ute chief John Duncan wrote to Standing Bear at Oglala, South Dakota,

to find out about the peyote medicine. . . . We don't know about this medicine but we are afraid of it but this fellow is fooling lots of my Indians. . . . They say it is something about God. . . . He has been here two years now. . . . The Sioux fellow told the Utes that if any of them are sick or poor . . . if they eat this medicine they will get well and fat again.

The agency officials were concerned, too. The superintendent of the Uintah Agency was Albert H. Kneale, who for fifteen years previously had been superintendent of the Nebraska Winnebago Agency, where he had fought a losing battle against peyotism. In answer to the 1916 questionnaire, he wrote:

I would say that possibly 40 to 50 percent of the Indians on this reservation are, or have been, partakers of this drug. . . . This drug was introduced into this reservation in 1914 by a Sioux Indian. He interested some of our very best men, particularly, McCook, Witchits, Monk Shavanaux, Captain Jenks, Grant, Corass, and William Wash. These men were all leaders among their people. . . . The drug is used at meetings held every week. . . . They are supposed to be of a religious nature.

That Kneale was doing his best to stamp out peyote is evident from his report that same year to the Bureau of Indian Affairs: "I have the assurance of the State Senator representing this district that the next session of the State Legislature will provide legislation [on peyote]."

In 1916, Sioux Gertrude Bonnin, secretary of the Society of American Indians, already a veteran fighter against peyotism in general and the loose-living Lone Bear in particular, was living on the Ute reservation with her husband, Raymond. She sent a letter to S. M. Brosius of the Indian Rights Association on the subject of Ute peyotism which brought him to Utah, and after a short visit, he was able to include in the thirty-fourth annual report of his association:

Among the latest victims succumbing to this enchantment are the Uintah and Ouray Indians of Utah. It is alleged that secret agents visit this reservation for the purpose of introducing the use of the drug, and derive financial contributions from their victims. So successful have they been in their efforts that the postmaster located in a town near the reservation is reported to have stated that in his opinion not less than $800 were forwarded to the headquarters of promoters and agents from disseminating propaganda favorable to peyote by the traveling representative of the Indians. . . . Dr. Lloyd cites instances in which the use of Peyote has undermined the health. Several deaths are reported as directly traceable to the habit. . . . Many Indians are appealing for legislation restricting the importation and use of peyote. Mr. and Mrs. R. T. Bonnin, intelligent and educated Indians, located at the Uintah and Ouray Agency, have joined in a statement reciting the evil effects of the use of the drug.

The evils, as stated by the Bonnins, were:

1. It excites the baser passions and is demoralizing—similar in its abnormal effects to that of opium, morphine, and cocaine.

2. It creates false notions in the minds of the users, preventing sound logic and rational thought with which to meet the problems of their daily lives. Believing that peyote is the comforter sent by God, they reject the teachings of Church. . . . Believing peyote a cure-all for every human ailment, they ignore the advice and aid of physicians. Attending the weekly peyote meetings, they waste time, strength, and money.

3. It has spread with alarming rapidity within the last two years. . . .

4. It appears to have been the direct cause of the deaths of 25 persons among the Utes within the last two years.

5. . . . it appears to us that an unscrupulous organization, through its agents, is promoting the Peyote Cult, under a religious guise, solely for the easy money gotten from their superstitious victims. . . .

6. Since the use of peyote is spreading rapidly . . . we do implore all earnest citizens of America for a Federal law to protect us against the traffic in and the indiscriminate use of peyote.

This eloquent plea was presented to Don B. Colton, state senator of the district nearest the reservation, who presented it to the governor. The state pharmacist was asked to do an analysis of peyote and found it to contain an alkaloid, among other things. He recommended it be placed on "the

FIG. 11. Gertrude Bonnin (Dakota Sioux). Reproduced from the Collections of the Library of Congress. Frontispiece, *American Indian Stories*, by Gertrude Bonnin, 1921.

list of prohibited narcotics, as no doubt, its indiscriminate use by the Indians and the laiety produces a demoralizing, harmful, and a depraved condition." All this led to the passage in February, 1917, of a state law prohibiting the use of peyote.

Mrs. Bonnin was already in action in Colorado, attempting to bring about a similar law there. In January, 1917, the *Denver Post* carried an article with the headline "Denver Women Fighting to Stop Dope Leaf Trade Among Colorado Indians," with pictures of two Denver society women. The article said that members of the National Mothers Congress, the Parent-Teacher Association, the Women's Christian Temperance Union, the Ministerial Alliance, and the Women's Clubs backed a bill "to check the peyote habit among the Indians." The Colorado antipeyote law was also enacted in February, 1917, and Sam Lone Bear, who happened to be in Grand Junction, Colorado, was arrested for possession of peyote, tried, convicted, and obliged to spend fifteen days in jail. The law did not stop peyotism in either state, inasmuch as it could not be applied on an Indian reservation, but it was an inconvenience and it frightened some.

That peyotism was as popular as ever in 1919 is clear from Superintendent Kneale's reply to the questionnaire of that year. He wrote:

In response to the above cited Office letter I have to state that the Indians of this jurisdiction do not use peyote for sacramental purposes in the sense in which the word is ordinarily used. It may be used ceremonially on occasions however it is used a hundred times without ceremony and for no purpose other than to get the kick which it contains to one that it is used ceremonially. It is a vicious drug, used precisely as other drugs are used by the ignorant and viciously inclined and with the same object in view.

When he returned the questionnaire, he included statements from Wallace Stark, a carpenter from Ouray, and Henry B. Lloyd, agency physician. Stark wrote that peyote was "introduced by a Sioux Indian, known by various names, Pete Phillips or Phelps, Cactus Pete, and Sam Lone Bear. . . . About 50 percent [of Ute] use Peyote." Dr. Lloyd wrote that peyote was used by about 50 percent and results were "degrading and degenerating to an extreme extent. Weakens them mentally and physically; yet acts as an aphrodisiac while it causes a shamelessness and lack of restriction in sexual matters, causes self abuse and sexual perversions. . . ." In a final burst of frustration, Kneale answered the question, "Through what agency is the peyote buttons distributed?" by stating, "Through the agency of the *almighty dollar.*"

Sam Lone Bear did not remain long on the Uintah-Ouray Reservation. He came and went for a period of ten years and never returned after 1926. At least twice he took his message to the Ute of Towaoc and Ignacio, but he seems not to have stayed long. On the Uintah-Ouray Reservation he was, with all his faults, a noteworthy leader, the first proselytizer of the Cross

Fire way. Though he appeared at one time or another on nearly every reservation in the Rocky Mountains, sometimes bringing peyote, sometimes leading a few meetings, he was never again so important. He never stayed long enough in one place to be influential because he was always avoiding the law. But if he was not influential, he was nevertheless remembered. The stories about him are many: of miraculous cures, of shady dealings, of large meetings, of tricks, of kidnappings, of rape, of theft, of lies, and so on. He went by a number of names besides Sam Lone Bear: Cactus Pete, Peter Phelps, Sam Loganberry, Pete Phillips, Chief S. C. Bird, Leo Old Coyote, Leo Okio. Eventually he served a year and a half of a three-year sentence in a federal prison in Washington state for taking the Crow girl to New Mexico.

The Cross Fire ritual of Sam Lone Bear among the Ute was partially described by James Monaghan, an interviewer for the federal Civil Works Administration, who, in 1934, reported his experience at a Ute peyote meeting:

I have only attended one peyote religious meeting and that was some twenty-years ago [that is, 1914] when the cult was first introduced to the Utes. At that time we met in a small wall tent and sat on blankets on the ground. At the head of the tent was a large sheet of brown paper on which was drawn, with crayon, a picture of Christ on the cross. . . . A small, earthen-ware crock, probably six inches across the top, served for a drum. This crock was partly filled with water and over the head was stretched a covering of buckskin. The drummer would shake this crock at intervals to keep the drum-head saturated. The drum tone was very clear and resonant.

Tobacco was not used. There were Bible reading, baptism, and statements concerning the resurrection of Christ. The staff was planted in a hole to stand upright and point the way to heaven.

There were others to carry on the Cross Fire way when Lone Bear was gone, but in time the Tipi way became more popular with the Ute. Perhaps Lone Bear's shady dealings somewhat discredited the Cross Fire. Orin Curry, one of the leaders of the Uintah-Ouray Reservation, spoke in 1925 at the sixth annual meeting of the Native American church:

I came a long ways to attend this conference, I came on my own accord to represent my people and to benefit them some way in the line of this organization. I heard talk of Indians having hard times in other states. We are the one having the hard times. We have been thrown in jails for using peyote for religious purpose and fined without being brought to courts and it appears now that we cannot use it much longer so I have come here to see what can be done to give us assistance so that we can continue the use of the peyote in our worships. This is my main object at this time. The peyote was introduced to us by a man whom we came to find out was doing it for his own gain. Hence the trouble came upon us because he did not . . . guide us in the right."

THE TAOS

The Taos Indians are of the Tanoan linguistic family which comprises many of the Pueblo Indians of the American Southwest. They still live in their ancient pueblo village in northern New Mexico which is now part of their reservation. Taos is the most northern pueblo and is near the reservation of the Southern Ute, with whom they have been neighbors, and sometimes enemies, for centuries.

Although the Taos Indians had had a few experiences with peyote in the early days of the Spanish occupation of New Mexico,* their knowledge of modern peyotism probably began about 1896. That year "a party of Taos men went with a small company of Utes into what was Indian Territory," according to Merton Leland Miller (1898: 26–27). On July 13, 1896, Captain Woodson of the Cheyenne-Arapaho reservation near Darlington, Oklahoma, wrote a letter to David F. Day, superintendent of the Southern Ute reservation at Ignacio, Colorado, stating that Ute Chief Buckskin Charlie and his party had arrived and would depart for home in about ten days. "The party appears to be very much pleased at the reception given them by the Arapahoes and myself." We are justified in thinking that this trip was motivated by peyotism because among the names of the party are two well-known early Taos peyotists, Lorenzo Martinez (Martina) and Frank Marquez.

The next evidence of peyotism at Taos comes from informant recall during ethnological interviews. In 1926, E. S. Curtis (1907–30, XVI: 53) was told: "The [peyote] cult was introduced about 1910 by certain young men who had been initiated in Oklahoma by Cheyenne Indians. The drug is ordered by mail from a certain Texas trader and is shipped by express. . . ."

Elsie Clews Parsons (1936: 62) quoted her Taos informant, in part, as follows:

At school [Carlisle] I made the acquaintance of some Plains Indians, so in 1907 I proposed to take a Taos party of twelve to visit in Oklahoma. . . . I saw nothing of peyote. But Geronimo Gomez was along and went into the meeting, and on his return to Taos taught his son John. . . . Later his son Joe went to Oklahoma. . . . [In 1910] . . . I went to Oklahoma again with some southern Utes. . . . In 1915 I went to Oklahoma and . . . went into meeting. . . .

Harold D. Lasswell (1935: 236) received similar information: "Young men from Taos who visited among the Plains Indians of Oklahoma [about

---

*One such experience occurred in 1720 when Antonio Quara and Aristoval Teajaya, Taos Indians, ate peyote, had visions under its influence, and tried to arouse the population of Taos to accept as true their vision, revolt against the Spanish, and prepare for an attack from the Ute. The Taos tribal leaders rejected the prophecies, declared Quara and Teajaya out of their minds, and delivered the two peyote eaters to Spanish authorities for trial (Slotkin 1951: 421–27).

1909–10] were invited to eat peyote, and some of them introduced the practice to Taos. The principal carrier of the new trait was Antonio Gomez, now deceased."

In 1916, in response to the questionnaire sent out by the Bureau of Indian Affairs, the deputy special officer assigned to Taos Pueblo reported that there were twelve peyotists at Taos, that the leaders were Antonio Lujan and Jose Ignacio Bernal, and that they received peyote by mail and from visitors.

The experience with peyote at Taos was different from that of any of the Plains tribes, because Pueblo culture was different from that of the Plains. Among the Indians discussed heretofore, the chief of the tribe was more or less simply a distinguished citizen. He led (and sometimes he was a great leader), but only as long as he was followed. Tribal organization was loose. While among the Plains Indians there were many nonpeyotists—the peyotists were nearly always a minority—and peyotism was often denigrated, peyotists were never persecuted by fellow tribesmen. The Pueblos, on the other hand, were tight theocracies which ruled with an iron hand. The governor and his council, chosen by kiva* members each year, had complete religious and political control over life in the Pueblo, and this they had had for centuries. Tribal authority was accustomed to being obeyed, almost without question, and likewise tribal members were used to obeying. In the case of peyote, this led to trouble, because when the governor and his council were not peyotists (and this was usual inasmuch as peyotists never numbered more than 10 percent of the tribe), tribal authority against them was often harsh.

Antipeyote feeling began at Taos almost as soon as peyote began to be used. The Catholic church was by far the principal source of Christianity for the Pueblo Indians, and by 1910 correspondence from the director of the Catholic missions, William H. Ketchum, to the Bureau of Indian Affairs indicates that the Catholics were aware of peyote and eager to have it declared illegal. Nonpeyote tribal leaders also were upset. In 1917, the governor of the Taos Pueblo, Domención Córdova, ordered a peyote meeting to be raided, and peyote fans, a drum, a staff, a gourd rattle, and a Chief Peyote were confiscated. A fine of two hundred dollars in cash was assessed on the Monday following the Saturday night raid against Gerónimo Gómez, the roadman. In 1936, Gerónimo ("Star Road") Gómez described the event to United Pueblos superintendent S. D. Aberle:

The Lieutenant Governor said to me, "Last Saturday night you have had a meeting in which the peyote herb was used, which you are not supposed to do. For that reason, you pay $200 fine to this court. I want it in cash." Then I told him, "I am not doing anything wrong. Only thing I do, as far as I know, I pray to the Great Spirit or the same God that intelligent white men pray to today. Now

*Kivas are underground ceremonial chambers of Pueblo Indians.

we have a Catholic Church here. The same church that is used among the white people. This Native American Church is the same thing, only we do this in our own simple way of believing in God so that we shall be better men to mankind. Is there going to be the same fine put on the Catholic group that is put on us who practice in the Native American Church?" Then several of the Council said to me, "You have no respect for your people or for the Governor. We have not time to discuss all this matter with only one man. It is better to stop him from talking. Therefore, in order to be through with you, just cover up the $200 fine in this court." Then I told the Council, "I am not going to pay you a cent, because I am not doing anything wrong or hurting any one in the community or the community itself." Then the Council told me, "Whether you want to or not, you have to pay this fine," and they told me to get out. I went out.

Tribal authority was very strong at Taos, and tribal authority continued to be against peyote. Before 1918, "Three peyote men were turned out of their kiva memberships—Lorenzo Martínez from Big-earring kiva, Jose Romero from Water kiva, and Teles Rena from his Kuyukana society in Feather kiva" (Parsons 1936: 66).

The national survey of peyotism in 1919 (Newberne 1925: 34) described 33 Taos Indians affected by peyote out of a population of 8,896. The report from Taos also stated that peyote was supplied by Cheyenne and Arapaho Indians, by mail, and by Taos men going to Oklahoma. Although the questionnaire asked for accounts of possible pueblo factions or village splits resulting from the use of peyote, no mention was made of the fine imposed on Star Road Gómez in 1917, or of the removal of peyotists from their kivas. Nevertheless, a cleavage was developing at Taos—a bitter and long-lasting one—and government officials and Pueblo "friends" became involved and were at least partly responsible for it.

In 1921, Horace J. Johnson became superintendent of the Northern Pueblos, which included Taos. He had formerly been in charge of the Sac and Fox reservation and was already convinced that peyote was worse than whiskey and would do permanent injury to anyone who used it. He found many, both Indian and white, to support his antipeyote campaign at Taos. A letter from J. J. Bergman, the government physician, informed him about the peyote situation: "In a special council meeting of the principals of the Pueblo of Taos, in which I was asked to be present, and which was called for such purpose, it was decided to bring to your attention through me the necessity of suppressing the use of . . . Peyote. . . ." He went on to report that there were twenty "habitual users," that peyote "addicts . . . prove to be a public nuisance" by singing all Saturday night," that peyote was imported from the Cheyenne and Arapaho; and that the council voted to suppress importation of peyote. Superintendent Johnson replied: "The action of the Indians meets with my approval. . . . The disturbances which you mentioned . . . may be suppressed, however, by the Governor and his council and the Governor already has information to that effect."

Assistant Commissioner E. B. Merritt wrote from Washington, stimulated by a letter from the Catholic mission: "The enclosed communications show that an alarming situation exists in the Pueblo and that immediate steps should be taken to eliminate the use of this drug and prosecute those who are responsible for its introduction." Johnson requested the legal citations to be used in prosecuting peyotists. The bureau did not furnish any.

Walter L. Bolander, BIA farmer assistant for Taos, answered a letter from Johnson:

. . . referring to the Peyote situation at Taos. . . . The drug was first used in the pueblo about 1910 but no organization then existed here. It was about 7 yrs. ago that some Oklahoma Indians organized a small band here and from that band the habit has grown until today there are 59 addicts. As to the time and place of meeting, there are no set dates nor places. They meet just when they want to and where it is convenient. I presume when their appetite for it calls. . . . It is usually eaten, but sometimes they make a tea. . . . The council at its meeting said that the addicts claimed to know from day to day what their next days provisions would be and as a result of this view they did not put out very much crops and did not cultivate what they did put out. The opinion of the principal men of the pueblo is that it affects not only their usefulness as people of the community but affected the mentality of the addict. . . . In the accompanying sheet I will give the story of an exaddict that will tell more than the council could give me.

The story of the "exaddict," Alberto Martínez, was given in the handwriting of Bolander:

Hoping that some effort will be made to save the children as well as older ones from the dangers of peyote, I will give an account of my experience with it. I believe I was the first Taos Indian to use it. I first learned it in 1910 in Oklahoma. I met with them in a Cheyenne tepee, Arapaho tepee, and a Pawnee Tepee. I used it about 4 years, quitting it about 7 years ago. There is no regularity about their meeting places or times. They meet just when and where they want to and as often as they see fit. . . . It is not a religion, but a habit. They claim it to be a religion only to be able to get by with it. As the habit grows on them, they eat it more frequently.

It has an influence on them that saps their energy and they do not want to work, hence their claim that they do not have to work. I have been under its influence many a time and I never saw Jesus yet nor any of my dead relations as they claim to be able to do. God never told me I did not need to work. I did not want to as long as I ate it.

While I was under the influence of the drug, I had no desire for work and hence I acquired nothing. . . . Since I quit it . . . I have acquired farming tools and furnishings for my home and been able to furnish my family with necessities of life. . . . I would like very much if the U.S. Government would help my pueblo to get rid of the drug.

In a letter to the BIA, Johnson reviewed his efforts to suppress peyotism. Regarding the noise made by peyotists, he wrote:

I told him [the Governor] he had authority to regulate that and that I would stand behind him in a reasonable exercise of his authority. I further told him that he might give them notice that unseemly disturbances or disturbances at an unusual hour would not be tolerated within the Pueblo walls nor adjacent thereto, and that if they persisted in making common nuisances of themselves, he should punish them. I also told him if officials caught them in act of doing this, he might have them arrested as disturbers and bring them before the Pueblo Council for punishment as he saw fit. . . .

"Recently the Peyote Eaters have come back to the Pueblo with their performances and only a few nights ago the Governor sent out his officials with instructions to seize their drums and other paraphernalia and arrest the chief disturbers. I am told he fined them and that they paid their fines without question.

In 1922, one J. Marie Richeson wrote to the bureau on behalf of Joe Bernal, head of the peyotists:

The Governor has seized the blankets, drums, paint, and other various instruments used by these Indians in their ceremonies and is threatening to burn same in the Plaza of Taos. He has thrown some of these Indians into jail and torn their blankets. . . . What the Peyote Indians wish to know is whether he has the authority to do this or not.

The bureau asked the new superintendent, A. W. Leech, who asked Bolander to explain. Bolander obliged, as follows:

About March 4th the Governor ordered certain Peyote fiends before the council to answer charges of misconduct while under the influence of Peyote as well as for violating the Pueblo law against the traffic in and the use of this drug; found them guilty and fined them; they refused to pay their fines and the officers seized their blankets, etc., to hold as security until fines were paid. . . .
    On behalf of the Pueblo Council I will say that I believe them to be right and just . . . in their efforts to suppress the Peyote traffic and habit.

Superintendent Leech added:

We are fortunate in having an Indian Governor in this Pueblo who is in sympathy with the suppression of this vice. . . . I have no sympathy whatever with any person or clan who countenances the use of peyote with its attendant ceremonies, for these ceremonies are nothing more than a cloak to hide the evil practices. . . . I do not care to interfere with the Governor of the Pueblo in his endeavors to suppress these practices.

It was probably this incident which prompted the statement made by John Collier to a House Committee on Indian Affairs on March 4, 1922 (Collier 1923: 302):

My contact with peyote has been on the Pueblo of Taos, and there I think I know personally all the members of what they call the peyote church. . . . The orthodox group of Indians on the Taos Pueblo—that is, the old men who represent the old magical, pagan religion of the Pueblos—were very bitter against the Peyote people, because the peyote church was like a heresy brought into the pueblo. . . . The peyote chief . . . said this, "Last spring very unpleasant things happened to us because we were using peyote; that is, the old men jumped on us and they even beat us."

In 1923, according to Parsons (1936:67), who was at Taos at the time, peyotists Juan Gómez and Gerónimo Sandoval were publicly whipped twenty-five lashes at the order of Lieutenant Governor Anton Mirabel, and later three peyotists were fined seven hundred, eight hundred, and one thousand dollars by the tribal council.

Taos peyotists were much in need of an influential friend, and they found one in Oklahoma. Friends there had told them about Senator Robert Owens of that state, who kept watch to see that antipeyote bills did not become federal laws. They wrote to him:

Dear Sir: For the last fifteen years about fifty members of the Taos Pueblo which has a total population of about six hundred and fifty have been using to a limited extent peyote for religious and medicinal purposes.

This use has not interferred with the work or regulations of the Pueblo and has been carried on in a quite harmonious way. It has not been used to excess.

As there are no laws restricting the use of this plant we do not know why when we are quietly in our tepee observing our ceremony why we should be swooped down upon by the Officials of the Pueblo and our blankets and shawls and other property confiscated.

We are being persecuted without law or authority and hope that you will be interested enough in us to see that we are protected, and our property returned.

Thanking you in advance for anything you can do in our behalf, we are, respectfully, Gerónimo Sandoval, Don Marcus, John Gómez, Joe Gómez, Taos Pueblo.

When asked by the bureau about this letter, then Superintendent C. J. Crandell wrote:

The Governor and his Council have a number of drums and a few cheap shawls and blankets. . . .

I discussed the question of returning them to the offenders, but the Council is very much opposed to same, and I did not insist, as I feel that the governor and his Council have a perfect right to prohibit their people from using peyote, even if there is no law governing the use of this drug. . . . I believe it best to allow the pueblo authorities to try to stamp it out and also that we should give them our support. . . . The Catholic Church does not approve of this practice any more than we do.

It was in 1924 that E. S. Curtis (1926, XVI:53, 59) wrote on Taos peyotism: "Taos priests strongly oppose the cult because it threatens the integrity of the old ceremonial system. The United States Government too at one time seemed likely to ban the drug, but in 1924 it ruled that there were no grounds for restricting its use." After a long description of the peyote ritual at Taos, Curtis concluded:

A ceremony of this kind was held in the spring of 1924, but for a time thereafter they refrained from public ceremony because of the hostility of the majority, meeting only by twos and threes to sing quietly. About the first of August . . . they built a booth in the canyon and held a ceremony, and the village officers went up with the avowed intention of tearing down the lodge. Following their rule of passive resistance, the devotees simply sat motionless and sang on, and the officers withdrew without taking action. The peyote adherents are instructed not to retaliate if anyone uses force, no matter how great the provocation.

In 1928, in a letter to T. F. McCormick, then superintendent of the Northern Pueblos, Commissioner Charles H. Burke stated his unchanging position regarding peyote: "It is suggested that said Taos council make appropriate ordinances to prevent the introduction of peyote into the pueblo. . . ." A year later, Superintendent McCormick wrote to Ed Safford, state legislator for New Mexico:

You will recall my speaking to you a few days ago about a bill which I would like to have introduced at this session of the State Legislature. . . . There is really only one pueblo that is affected by it and that is the pueblo of Taos where there are at least eighty people or 10 per cent of the pueblo that are using this bean. It has demoralizing effect on them and if allowed to continue the users will undoubtedly increase. There is no federal law at the present time and all we can look for is what help the state can give us.

In 1929 a law was duly enacted, and possession of peyote in New Mexico became illegal for all purposes.

Difficulties continued for peyotists in New Mexico until 1934, when a new administration in Washington put a rein to antipeyotism both at Taos and elsewhere.

SUMMARY

In summarizing the diffusion of peyotism beyond Oklahoma up to 1918, we can observe some changes and additions. Most important is the increasing distinction between the two forms of the cult. The Wilson Big Moon ritual and the Comanche Half Moon ritual have acquired two new names (without, however, losing their old names): the Cross Fire way and the Tipi way. The Cross Fire way, coming from Wilson, has practically eliminated tobacco from the ritual. The staff has become implanted so that it stands erect; the eagle-bone (sometimes wooden) whistle ceremony has usually been eliminated, as has the ceremonial partaking of food inside the tepee in the morning, that is, the ceremonial breakfast. The altar continues to be more elaborate, with the addition at times of an altar cloth on which is placed the Bible and the Chief Peyote. The ashes are formed into a ceremonial design, sometimes elaborately worked out. Preaching from a Bible text and frequent references to the Bible are characteristic. There are baptisms, marriages, and funerals. Wooden houses built for the purpose of holding peyote meetings are more frequent, and there are a few cemeteries.

The Tipi way, too, has changed, but it is more conservative, and changes in it are not as noticeable. Christianity has become emphasized, although not as much as some of the explanations of the ceremony by Tipi way adherents would suggest. It must be borne in mind that since there was no written ceremony, there were no hard and fast rules. Exceptions were frequent and noted as such. For example, the Menominee Cross Fire ritual did use tobacco; the Jesse Clay Tipi way gave elaborate Biblical explanations for the ritual, even though the ceremony itself was still nativistic.

But with all the changes, the basic peyote ceremony remained the same. It was still the all-night (usually Saturday night) ritual observed by Mooney: the circle around the sacred fire and sand altar; the four officials; the singing, drumming, praying, in turn, following a clockwise direction; the eating of peyote; the sacred number four; the gourd rattles; the feather fans; and, finally, the breakfast and social gathering following the meeting. The meeting remained dedicated to curing, to sobriety, and to Christian ideals. Peyote members, although well aware of the two types of ritual and sophisticated in the observance of the distinctions, nevertheless participated in both as the opportunity presented itself. Also, they continued to participate in tribal societies such as the Sun Dance, in Christian churches, and in shaman curing ceremonies. Anxiety on the part of nonpeyotists, agency officials, and the Bureau of Indian Affairs continued to bring about the harassment of peyotists, causing a regrettable schism on some reservations.

PART THREE

The Later Twentieth Century:
Politics and Consolidation

FIG. 12. James Mooney (1861–1921), of the U.S. Bureau of American Ethnology. Courtesy Smithsonian Institution, National Anthropological Archives, Bureau of American Ethnology Collection.

CHAPTER 8

Efforts to Pass a Federal Law

FROM the beginning, those in charge of the Indian, both those in Washington and those on the reservations, officials as well as those in the capacity of teachers, Christian religious leaders, and just farmers, blacksmiths, and other supervisors, felt the need for a federal law to prohibit the use of peyote. At first the antipeyotists of Oklahoma had used the 1897 Prohibition Law, adding, without authority, the prohibition of peyote. Uneasy that the 1897 law did not really cover peyote, the Oklahoma antipeyotists in 1899 succeeded in getting passed a territorial law prohibiting the use of the "mescale bean." An attempt to amend this law so that it referred to "peyote" was roundly defeated in 1907 by the state of Oklahoma. But peyotism seemed so strange, frightening, and downright sinful to the antipeyotists that they continued to forbid its practice and to harass its adherents under the old 1897 law or simply by an order from the Indian agents. We have seen arrests, confiscation of property, fines, jail terms, and verbal abuse on nearly every reservation that dared experiment with the new religion.

In 1912 the Board of Indian Commissioners, that group of prestigious citizens appointed to oversee the Bureau of Indian Affairs, began to lobby in earnest for a strong federal law against peyote. In their 1912 annual report they stated: "We are convinced . . . that the Commissioner . . . has not overstated the serious effect of the use of Peyote. The danger of the rapid spread of the habit, increased by its so-called religious associations, makes the need of its early suppression doubly pressing." Their lobby was directed by Robert D. Hall of the YMCA. On January 12 he sent to the Bureau of Indian Affairs a twenty-three-page report against peyote, including two affidavits by Winnebago Indians denigrating peyotism as well as anti-peyote statements by Reverend Walter C. Roe and a white farmer, Charles J. Palmer, of the Winnebago reservation. He also sent reports against peyote from psychologist Professor Roswell P. Angier, Yale University; chemists E. F. Ladd and E. B. Putt, North Dakota Agricultural College; Reverend G. Elmer E. Lindquist, missionary to the Mescalero Apache and later chaplain at Haskell Indian School; and Superintendent A. H. Kneale of the Winnebago Agency and later of the Uintah-Ouray Agency.

In March, Father William H. Ketchum, director of the Bureau of Catholic Indian Missions, sent to the Bureau of Indian Affairs a nine-page file and memorandum including a request to "rid the Reservations of the Mescal [peyote] evil."

The Society for American Indians was organized in 1912 and soon became the American Indian organization most actively and persistently opposed to peyotism. Composed mostly of Indians, it proposed both federal and state laws to stop the transportation and use of peyote. Also in 1912, the Bureau of Indian Affairs sent out to all reservations Circular 598, which asked for information regarding peyote with questions phrased to bring out the worst. Among other questions, it asked: "What is the moral, mental, and physical effect produced by the use of Peyote?" "Through what agency is this button or bean distributed among the Indians addicted to its use?" "Have any court cases determined whether Peyote is in fact an intoxicant?" Although no answers to this questionnaire have come to light, it was probably inquiries such as these which caused reservation peyotists to realize that they might have a fight on their hands if they wished to maintain their religion.

In defense of the right to use peyote, Charles Kappler and Charles Merillat, Washington attorneys for the Osage, wrote to the commissioner of Indian affairs on behalf of their clients, saying peyote was not harmful as used by the Osage in religious ceremonies and requesting that they be informed if legislation dealing with peyote were contemplated so that the Osage could be notified, inasmuch as they wished to come to Washington "to give their views of the subject." Even without notification, on February 12, Osage chiefs Edgar McCarthy and Roman Logan prepared a petition with twenty-one signatures from Osage peyotists which requested assurance from the commissioner that their supply of peyote would be protected, enabling them to continue in the practice of their religion.

The next month, attorney Harry L. Keefe of Walthill, Nebraska, wrote to the commissioner on behalf of Omaha peyotists. Keefe assured the commissioner that the peyote ceremony was a serious religious ritual at which "the Bible is read, prayers are offered," and that peyotism opposes use of alcohol and helps believers refrain from drinking. He asked that the supply of peyote be allowed to continue "as one of their religious rights," and he included a letter from a general merchandizer of Macy, Nebraska, G. C. Maryott, who shared his point of view. These letters were meant as an introduction to a delegation of Omaha Indians including Daniel Webster, Harry Lyon, and Parrish Sansouci, who went to Washington and testified in favor of peyotism before Assistant Commissioner Abbott. A similar delegation of Cheyenne and Arapaho Indians visited Washington the following July to express opposition to legislation designed to prohibit free access to peyote for religious purposes. The delegation talked with the congressmen from their areas, who wrote to the Bureau of Indian Affairs on their behalf. Nevertheless, the commissioner remained unconvinced that peyote was harmless. He answered Representative Dick T. Morgan of Oklahoma: "I firmly believe that the use of Peyote is injurious to the health and welfare of the Indians and, therefore, shall do everything within my power to prevent its use among the Indians."

No bill to outlaw peyote was introduced in 1912. In March, 1913, anti-peyotists, through members of Congress, attempted a quiet, roundabout legal maneuver to stop the use of peyote by means of the Indian appropriation bill. Since 1897, with the passage of the Indian Prohibition Law, a provision to finance activities of the Bureau of Indian Affairs specified an amount "for the suppression of the traffic in intoxicating liquors." In 1913 both the House of Representatives and the Senate approved an amendment to add "and peyote" following "intoxicating liquors." The device was not successful, and in June, 1913, on the advice of the Senate Committee on Indian Affairs, the Senate voted to strike the words "and peyote" from the bill. This attempt failed largely because the congressmen from Oklahoma had been pressured to protect peyote by their many Indian constituents, who instructed them by means of petitions, delegations to Washington, and a multitude of letters. The Osage accumulated and published a pamphlet of documents to establish that peyotism was a good influence on Indian behavior and not harmful to health (McCarthy 1923). The Indians of Oklahoma had not forgotten the experience they had had in the Oklahoma State Legislature in 1907. They had learned then that in a democracy you have a chance to secure your just rights, but you must fight for those rights and you must be heard.

The opponents of peyote were not ready to give up, and they, too, knew the rules of the game. Each year they continued to try to include peyote among the narcotics suppressed by the Indian appropriation bill. They also prepared to present new legislation. And they continued to attempt suppression of peyote under the 1897 Indian Prohibition Act, arresting users and suppliers of peyote in the hope that if the arrests were challenged in the courts, a court opinion would support their bluff. The first of several court cases occurred in Wisconsin on April 2, 1914, when the U.S. marshal arrested a Potawatomi Indian, Mitchell Neck, for introducing peyote on the Menominee Indian reservation and giving it to members of the Neconish family. Mitchell Neck was tried under the Indian Prohibition Act of 1897, and the federal judge in Milwaukee declared without qualification that the law clearly meant prohibition against furnishing Indians alcoholic beverages and that the Bureau of Indian Affairs could not legally interfere with the use or shipping of peyote anywhere.

On September 11, 1915, a South Dakota grand jury indicted a Sioux Indian, William Red Nest, of Pine Ridge Reservation, "Under the Act of January 30, 1897, for selling and giving intoxicants to Indians." The case was not immediately brought to trial, and later, in 1917, it was dismissed by the U.S. attorney. While it was in recess, another peyote case came to trial in the U.S. district court in Deadwood, South Dakota. Under the same act, Harry Black Bear of Pine Ridge Reservation was indicted on May 19, 1916, and stood trial on September 7 and 8, 1916. Two news items in the *Deadwood Daily Pioneer-Times;* a report of the trial by the supervisor in charge,

Charles W. Davis, to the Bureau of Indian Affairs; and a letter from Superintendent John R. Brennan have furnished good coverage of the event. The
U.S. attorney for South Dakota, R. P. Stewart, was praised for his thorough preparation and skill in arguing the case. The defense of Black Bear
was handled, in part, by "a mixed-blood Indian of the Sisseton tribe, who is
practicing law at Martin, South Dakota." Attorney Thomas L. Sloan of the
Omaha tribe was present as a witness and as an advisor to the attorneys
for the defense. Attorney Stewart introduced chemist E. B. Putt of the
North Dakota Agricultural College and Indian Agent Charles E. Shell, who
had collaborated with Special Agent "Pussyfoot" Johnson in Oklahoma for
several years before he was transferred to California in 1910. Both Putt
and Shell had eaten peyote under doctors' observations and both declared it
harmful and dangerous. The jury convicted Black Bear, but upon the defense attorney's "motion in arrest in judgment" that the 1897 law did not
apply, Judge Elliot studied the case, granted the motion, and then dismissed Black Bear. He ruled that the wording and history of the 1897 Indian Prohibition Law indicated that it was designed for the control of alcoholic beverages exclusively and could not be extended to peyote, even
though Shell and Putt had testified that it was intoxicating.

Government officials, church groups, and other antipeyotists had hoped
that peyote would be found illegal because it was intoxicating if the question
was clearly at issue in a U.S. federal court. The cases of Medicine Neck,
William Red Nest, and Harry Black Bear plainly showed that it would not
be. Something more needed to be done.

In the meantime, Indians were petitioning harder than ever for the right
to use peyote. In February, 1915, it was the Omaha tribe of Nebraska that
petitioned Cato Sells, commissioner of Indian affairs, to protect their religious freedom to use peyote in their ceremonies. Fifty-four Omaha Indians
signed the petition, and seven sent individual statements from one to five
pages long. Hiram Mitchell wrote: "I am one of the first who used the
Peyote root (about eight years ago). . . . Ever since I have used Peyote I
think about God. . . ." Peter Blackbird emphasized his personal reformation: "I drink whiskey. I was bad. I almost murdered a man and they arrested me. And even I almost killed myself with a revolver. Finally, I found
out about Peyote and joined the Society. . . . I found that their belief is that
this Peyote and the Bible are the same thing." Sam Gilpin wrote: "It has
been seven years since I joined them [the Peyote society]. Since then I have
spent no money for whiskey. I believe this Peyote is good. . . ." Thomas
Walker wrote: "This religious use of peyote is on the same line as the white
people's use of the Bible. What we learn from the Bible is true in Peyote."
Stewart Walker reported that peyote helped Indians to stop drinking whiskey and then said: "When we are in a meeting we eat peyote which gives us
the spirit of comfort and we would sit there and pray to God and his son
Jesus. It would make me think about God, Jesus. . . . Here I am I don't

understand the Bible, still I believe in it." Edward Cline wrote: "When I eat the peyote I pray to God and I believe the religion we get from the Bible is the same with Peyote." Simon Hollowell had been an important leader of the Omaha. He wrote: "They gave me a job as councilman and later as judge and then as assessor." But he was ruined by drink until rehabilitated by peyote. He said: "When we eat peyote we think about it in the Bible. There is a God, Christ, Holy Ghost we pray to."

Pressure such as this from Indian tribes, the failure of the 1897 Indian Prohibition law to apply to peyote, the lack of success in amending the Indian appropriation bill to include peyote—these gave urgency to the antipeyotists in their efforts to persuade the U.S. Congress to enact a law explicitly prohibiting the use of peyote. The first bills were introduced by Representative Harry L. Gandy of South Dakota and Senator W. W. Thompson of Kansas. Following successful efforts by Senator Owen of Oklahoma to block Senate action on the Thompson bill (S. 3526), efforts to procure a 1916 law against peyote focused on the Gandy bill (H.R. 10669), which sought to prohibit "traffic in peyote, including its sale to Indians, introduction into the Country, importation and transportation," and provided penalties for that trafficking: "imprisonment for more than sixty days and less than one year, or by a fine of not less than $100 nor more than $500, or both."

Support for the Gandy bill was sent from Utah in letters by Mr. and Mrs. R. T. Bonnin; Dr. Henry B. Lloyd, resident physician at Fort Duchesne Indian Agency; Reverend M. J. Hersey, missionary of the Episcopal Church; Governor Spry; and the Utah state chemist, Herman Harms, who produced a five-page report concluding that peyote "produces a demoralizing, harmful, and depraved condition." Support came also in published reports from the National Indian Association, the Society of American Indians, the National Indian Student Conference, the Lake Mohonk Conference, and the YMCA. Charles M. Siever, M.D., of Holton, Kansas, joined L. E. Sayre, dean of the University of Kansas School of Pharmacy, and A. R. Snyder, superintendent of the Potawatomi Agency, in collecting antipeyote opinions. Assistant Commissioner E. B. Merritt of the Bureau of Indian Affairs coordinated the materials against peyote in Washington, and S. M. Brosius of the Indian Rights Association appears to have been the leader of the nongovernmental antipeyote lobby.

Indian opposition to the Gandy bill was carried in person to Washington by Omaha Indians Harry Lyon, Silas Wood, and Noah Leaming. Francis La Flesche, Omaha Indian ethnologist of the Smithsonian Institution, served as interpreter. The hearing was held on April 1, 1916, before Chief Special Officer Henry A. Larson, an outspoken, active antipeyotist. A twenty-four-page transcript of the hearing was supplied to the Indians and to Larson's Denver office. The Indians had made a strong statement to the effect that peyotism was a sincere religion which helped them resist liquor.

On October 28, the antipeyote forces, over the signature of Larson, sent to 136 superintendents of Indian agencies, schools, hospitals, and the like nationwide a letter of inquiry asking for the most up-to-date information about peyote. Like the 1912 questionnaire, the 1916 letter was worded to elicit pejorative answers. It read, in part:

Please let me have a report from you, immediately, giving the number of Indians addicted to its [peyote's] use, and the extent and frequency of its use. Who are the leaders? Where do they get their supply from, and how? What is its effect on the users as shown by your own observations and from the reports of employees, missionaries, and others? . . . What is the physical condition of users during and after its use? What is its effect on the moral and social relations? What proportion of the users of peyote use intoxicating liquors?

Replies were received from twenty-five reservations, where peyote was used by an estimated six thousand Indians. Most condemned peyote. C. J. Green, superintendent on the Shawnee reservation, wrote: "I am convinced in my own mind that the use of this drug, medicine, dope, or whatever it ought to be called has a weakening influence on both mind and body of the Indians who use it." W. W. Mace, superintendent on the Cheyenne reservation, wrote: "I am of the opinion that the peyote is completely ruining the Indian people . . . physically, morally, and spiritually." Willis E. Dunn, superintendent at Red Moon School, Harmon, Oklahoma, wrote: "The effect is a deadening of the senses and the principal users do not seem willing to undertake any mental or physical labor." Some answers, however, were favorable to peyote, such as that of Reverend J. Roberts, missionary to the Wind River Shoshone, who wrote that his white colleagues, who had attended a peyote meeting, "admired the ritual and . . . saw nothing reprehensible at the meeting." R. L. Russell, superintendent of the Sac and Fox Sanatorium at Toledo, Iowa, wrote that "the members of the society are among our better Indians and in so far as I know but few of them are given to the use of intoxicating liquors."

The Gandy Bill was not enacted in 1916; consequently, in 1917 it was resubmitted as H.R. 4999. In the Senate the Thompson bill was replaced by Senate Bill 1862, sponsored by Senator H. F. Ashurst of Arizona. Nothing happened to these bills in 1917, but in Utah, Nevada, and Colorado, state laws prohibiting peyote were enacted.

In 1918, congressional action against peyote was contained in H.R. 2614, presented by Representative Carl Hayden of Arizona at the request of the Indian Office. Extensive hearings were held before a subcommittee of the House of Representatives (1918a) under the chairmanship of John H. Tillman of Arkansas. Testimony was taken February 21 to 25 and again on March 23, 1918. Numerous documents and reports were submitted, and, together with a transcript of the oral statements of all who wished to be heard, these were published in a document of 193 printed pages. Simply titled *Peyote,* it includes many of the antipeyote reports submitted to the

Bureau of Indian Affairs in earlier years, some dating back to 1909.

The defense of peyote was led by James Mooney, who had witnessed his first peyote ceremony in 1891, and was supported by two other ethnologists from the Bureau of American Ethnology of the Smithsonian Institution, Francis La Flesche and Truman Michelson, and by economic botanist William Safford of the Department of Agriculture. Peyotist leaders from the Arapaho, Cheyenne, Comanche, Osage, and Omaha tribes testified at length and were cross-examined. Mooney gave a history of peyote, an analysis of the plant, described the ceremony, and explained the Indian attitude toward peyote. During the years between 1891 and 1918 he had spent months at a time among the western Plains Indians, particularly on the reservations in Oklahoma, and had been a participant observer in several peyote rituals. The Ghost Dance and peyote had been his chief concerns. He knew well many peyote tribal leaders. He answered patiently and fully all questions put to him. His explanation for the recent rapid spread of peyote was:

The Indians now are largely civilized; they are becoming citizens; they are educated, and they travel about and take an interest in each other. A great many of the young men who have been sent to eastern schools, in a climate damper than the one to which they have been accustomed, come back with weakened lungs, coughs, and hemorrhages, and they are told by their Indian friends at home that if they use the peyote it will relieve the coughs and check the hemorrhages, and they have found that to be true. That is the universal testimony of the Indians. . . . The result is that the young men, not the older uncivilized ones, but the younger, middle-aged, and educated men, have taken up the peyote cult and organized it as a regular religion, beyond what they knew before among the various tribes.

When the morality of the peyotists was challenged, he said:

I shall describe the ceremony briefly as conducted among the Kiowas and Comanches, whom I know best. The Indians of the same neighborhood assemble at the home of one of their number—whole families together—late Saturday afternoon. They come in wagons or now even in automobiles. They have their supper together in picnic fashion, the women doing the cooking while the men prepare the peyote tipi and the children play about. Only the men take part in the ceremony, excepting when a sick woman or child is brought in to be prayed for. The men go into the tipi or church, set up for this purpose, about nine o'clock at night. The meeting is opened with prayer, after which four peyotes are handed around to each participant and eaten. After that they take a small drum and rattle, the usual Indian accompaniment to singing, and sing hymns, and at intervals say prayers in which they mention quite frequently the name of Jesus and their Indian name for God, both which names they now know well. They keep that up through the greater part of the night. At intervals there is a break in the ceremony, especially at midnight when they have a sort of baptismal performance. Then they go on with other prayers and other singing until almost daylight when they have a ceremonial refreshment of dried meat and fruit, after which they come out; and the women who have been asleep with their children in the other house prepare dinner. They all eat dinner together— their Sunday dinner—and have a sociable time throughout the afternoon, and when it is time in the evening they get their wagons ready and go back to their homes. A camp or settlement will have such a meeting usually about every two weeks. I know they have brought about modifications in some respects since, but I am speaking now of the ceremony as I knew it for a number of years. After having spent the afternoon thus with their friends they go back to their homes and their farms talking about the news and discussing religious questions. I have seen it many times in a number of tribes and there is nothing that can be called an orgy, there is nothing that can be called immoral, and in the tribes that I know, women and children were never present except when they were brought in to be prayed over as sick persons. . . . I understand that in the tribes which have adopted it more recently women take part with the men, the result probably of the spread of education.

Francis La Flesche, himself an Omaha Indian, in an extended testimony told the committee that peyote had done much good. Although he had not eaten peyote and was not a member of the peyote religion, he had observed its effect on the people of his tribe and he had nothing but praise for it. He said:

It may be a very strange thing for me to say, but I cannot talk about peyote without a feeling of gratitude, and I will tell you why. In 1884 the allotment to the Omahas of their lands in severalty was completed, and a few years after the completion of that allotment some of the white neighbors who had dealings with the Indians said to them: "You people are citizens of the United States; therefore you can drink all the whiskey you want." . . . To justify their drinking they would say, "The white people drink, and why should not we?" Matters began to grow from bad to worse, and it was simply a continuous drunken orgy for several years. After a while white men became afraid to travel the roads on the reservation in the night, and the Indians themselves were afraid to travel on the roads for fear of meeting drunken men. Murders and rape were committed and lawlessness had sway, and the Indians needed help in all this trouble. The agent who had charge of these Indians was aware of the condition, the Indian Office was aware of the condition, and I think the Indian Rights Association and the missionaries were aware of this desperate situation. What did they do? Nothing. They did absolutely nothing. Poor little children became afraid of their mothers because they drank. They became afraid of their fathers, and when they heard them coming home from town they ran into the ravines, into the bushes, so as to avoid getting hurt.

But suddenly there came a lull in all this drunkenness and lawlessness. I had a sister who was a physician, and her practice was mostly among the Indians, and she wrote me regularly about the conditions of the Omaha people. She was interested and one day I got a letter from her in which she said: "A strange thing has happened among the Omahas. They have quit drinking, and they have taken to a new religion, and members of that new religion say that they will not drink; and the extraordinary part of the thing is that these people pray, and they pray intelligently, they pray to God, they pray to Jesus, and in their prayers they pray for the little ones, and they ask God to bring them up to live sober lives; they ask help of God."

She regarded that as something very strange, because the Indian, although they had missionaries for many years, could not understand the white man's religion; it was too intricate a thing for them, and they could not understand it. But the teaching of this new religion was something they could understand. In connection with this new religion they used a plant called peyote as a sort of sacrament. This peyote, they said, helped them not only to stop drinking, but it also helped them to think intelligently of God and of their relations to Him. At meetings of this new religion is taught the avoidance of stealing, lying, drunkenness, adultery, assaults, the making of false and evil reports against neighbors. People are taught to be kind and loving to one another and particularly to the little ones.

The persons who are opposed to the use of peyote by the Indians in their religion say that it makes them immoral. That has not been my observation. The Indians who have taken the new religion strive to live upright, moral lives, and I think their morality can be favorably compared with that of any community of a like number in this country.

When all the testimony for the defense of peyote had been heard from Mooney, La Flesche, Michelson, and Safford, and from the lawyers and Indians, and all the testimony against peyote from S. Brosius of the Indian Rights Association, Gertrude Bonnin of the Society of American Indians, General R. H. Pratt of Carlisle Indian School, agency officials, missionaries, teachers, and others under the Bureau of Indian Affairs, the bill to outlaw peyote was passed by the House of Representatives but was rejected in the Senate. Again, the senator from Oklahoma responded to pressure from his Indian constituency and persuaded his colleagues in the Senate to vote against it. Thus ended the most serious attempt to get a federal law explicitly prohibiting the use of peyote. Although a similar law was introduced every year for a number of years, it never had another full hearing until 1937.

An unfortunate and bitter schism developed during the 1918 hearing between the Bureau of American Ethnology and the Bureau of Indian Affairs. Those testifying for the legislation at the instigation of the Bureau of Indian Affairs accused the ethnologists of encouraging Indians to maintain old, heathenish, unhealthy, uncivilized customs so the scientists could write books, take pictures, and thus exploit the Indians with cheap publicity while doing nothing to help them become civilized. General R. H. Pratt, testifying for the Bureau of Indian Affairs, was largely responsible for this. He was an important witness. He had been involved in the civilization and education of Indians from their wild days, he had been in charge of the prisoner-of-war camp in Florida, and he had organized and directed the Carlisle Indian School for twenty-five years. In his own way he was dedicated to the welfare of the Indians. But he had no sympathy for ethnologists. He felt that they were worse than useless; that they were an impediment to the civilization of Indians. He accused Mooney of specific disgusting exploitation and considered all ethnologists like him.

Mooney defended himself and his profession by saying:

Now, in regard to an ethnologist never having helped the Indians: as a matter of fact anybody who knows anything about ethnologists knows that is not true. The Indians look upon ethnologists as their best friends. Ethnologists . . . have always endeavored to help the Indians, as is born out by hundreds of letters from representative Indians showing to what extent they appreciate the work of the ethnologists. We have helped them in Congressional matters and have been delegated to help in matters of allotment; some of us have been sent out to make allotments for them; that is, to help choose the best land, and avoid being victimized by the white settlers. We have helped them to civilization in every way; we have helped them in the choice of schools, in the choice of education; we have helped them to raise cattle and to build houses; we have gone into their tepees and shown them how to cook and live decently. All these things have been done by the ethnologists, both men and women. . . .

If you want to get at the truth . . . have the Indians come from the tribes that are concerned. An Indian delegate from a sectarian body of an alleged up-lift organization is not a delegate for his tribe. The tribes have councils elected by themselves, and they elect those council men year after year to come here and appear for them. . . . The men are there; you can send for them.

As for the specific accusation against him, he said: "I denounce that as an absolute falsehood."

After the hearings were over, Mooney went again to the Kiowa reservation, but the commissioner of Indian affairs requested the director of the Smithsonian Institution to recall him because he was "interfering" with the administration of the Bureau of Indian Affairs. Specifically, Mooney had participated in peyote ceremonies and had consulted with and encouraged peyotists to incorporate their religion under the laws of Oklahoma as the Native American Church. To the shame of the Bureau of American Ethnology and the Smithsonian Institution, Mooney was recalled and was never again allowed to return to Oklahoma to continue his study of peyotism. He died a few years later of a heart attack.

The Indians who had defended peyotism in the hearings of 1918 had had a vivid education in American government. They had heard the case against peyote argued by their powerful white adversaries, and they had defended it with the help of white scholars from the Smithsonian before the high court of the U.S. House of Representatives. It had been a tough fight, and this time they had won a close victory. But they were aware that the fight was not over, and they realized that in order to prevail again, they must learn to conform to the other religious institutions of the country. They had said their religious ceremony was the same kind of thing as the Presbyterian, the Mormon, the Catholic, or any other church. But in the eyes of the world it was not the same because it was not organized. It needed a name and needed to be known by that name; it needed a set of rules, officers, stated responsibilities; it needed to be "incorporated." In August, 1918, at El Reno, Oklahoma, peyotists from Oklahoma met to establish a peyote church.

The idea was not entirely new. The first record of an organized church of peyotism is so slight as to be negligible. It was mentioned in a U.S. court hearing in March, 1914, as "a regularly organized association among the Indians called the Peyote Society, also known as the Union Church Society of which [the witness] had been a priest for seven years" (Safford 1915: 306). Almost nothing more is known of the Union Church, and it was probably not legally incorporated. The second peyote church to be organized, the first to be legally incorporated, was stimulated by Johnathan Koshiway (Sac and Fox of Kansas) when, at the age of twenty-eight, he was living on the Oto reservation with his wife's people. Koshiway described the founding of the First Born Church of Christ on December 8, 1914, for Slotkin:

We were having trouble way back as long as I remember. I thought there must be a way to defend our religion; so a few leaders went to a lawyer [Henry S. Johnston of Perry, Oklahoma]. He helped us write up the Articles of Incorporation; so we got a charter; the name came from the Bible, Hebrs. 12: 28. . . . I was sent to Washington, D.C., for a hearing on the peyote bill. . . . 1914 . . . I was told to come home [and help] the Indians to organize a church.

Koshiway also described the beginning of the First Born Church of Christ to La Barre, who wrote (1938: 168):

First of all, he [Koshiway] consulted White Horn, leader of the native peyote rite, and gained his support. Koshiway generously states that White Horn was the co-founder of the Church of the First Born, but the fact appears to be that the latter's role consisted in giving the official approval of the older established peyote cult. Koshiway also visited many white ministers to get their advice on organization. . . . Koshiway went to a lawyer in Perry, Oklahoma, H. F. Johnson [sic] and sought legal advice. . . . The articles of incorporation were signed by Johnathan Koshiway and four hundred [sic] and ten other names.

An official copy of the articles of incorporation indicates that the first named officer was "Charley Whitehorn," designated "Deacon," followed by the ten directors, starting with Johnathan Koshiway. The certifcate verifying the meeting and election of directors is signed by "Charley White Horn, Pastor, Presiding Officer."

The statement of purpose was strongly Christian:

The purposes for which this Corporation is formed are to give legal corporate entity to an association of persons having for their purpose and ideal the founding and establishment of a church organisation embodying the conception found in the King James Version of the Holy Bible in Ephesians, fourth chapter, verses 5 and 6, as follows: "One Lord, One Faith, One Baptism, One God and Father of all." And Hebrews, twelfth chapter, verse 23, "One Church of the Firstborn . . . and to Evangelize and spread Scriptural Holiness over all lands and to all people."

Probably for diplomatic reasons peyote is nowhere mentioned in the articles of incorporation. And it is interesting that tobacco was specifically omitted from the ceremony. Not all Oto peyotists supported the First Born Church, objecting to the prohibition of tobacco. Louis McDonald talked about this troublesome issue:

I have seen that the big problem arises about the smoking among the Oto tribe. . . . During my school days, I learned that on the line of Christianity smoke was filthiness or foulness. We may call it on the grounds of filthiness that smoke was disapproved; but still I cannot be convinced that the old Indian natural tobacco would be wrong; I want to say this, I am not a smoker. . . . you don't see me carrying tobacco of any kind. The only time I smoke is during the ordinance of the Peyote meeting, and I have never heard among the average preacher today condemn the natural Indian leaf tobacco.

The Church of the First Born had not sought a wider following or larger jurisdiction than the Oto tribe. The group that met in El Reno in August, 1918, to establish the Native American Church were representative of most Oklahoma peyotists and were ambitious to include all Oklahoma peyotists in their church. They did not equivocate about the use of the word *peyote,* realizing that this was the issue and that it must be openly acknowledged. The articles of incorporation of the Native American Church, signed October 10, 1918, are as follows:

KNOW ALL MEN BY THESE PRESENT, That we, Mack Haag, and Sidney White Crane of the Cheyenne Tribe of Indians, Charles W. Daily, George Pipestem and Charles E. Moore, members of the Otoe Tribe of Indians, Frank Eagle of the Ponca Tribe of Indians, Wilbur Peawa and Mam Sookwat, members of the Comanche Tribe of Indians, Kiowa Charley of the Kiowa Tribe of Indians, and Apache Ben of the [Kiowa-] Apache Tribe of Indians, all residents of the State of Oklahoma, do hereby associate ourselves together to form a religious and benevolent association under the laws of the State of Oklahoma, and do hereby certify:

ARTICLE I.

The name of this incorporation shall be and is "NATIVE AMERICAN CHURCH."

ARTICLE II.

The purpose for which this corporation is formed is to foster and promote the religious belief of the several tribes of Indians in the State of Oklahoma, in the Christian religion with the practice of the Peyote Sacrament as commonly understood and used among the adherents of this religion in the several tribes of Indians in the State of Oklahoma, and to teach the Christian religion with morality, sobriety, industry, kindly charity and right living and to cultivate a spirit of self-respect and brotherly union among the members of the Native Race of Indians, including therein the various Indian tribes in the State of Oklahoma.

ARTICLE III.

It is the purpose of this organization to establish one central church to be known as "Native American Church" with branch churches subject to the jurisdiction to the General Church to be organized in each of the Indian tribes in the State of Oklahoma.

ARTICLE IV.

The principal church with its seat of government and principal place of business is hereby established at El Reno, Canadian County, Oklahoma; each of the subordinate churches to establish by vote of the members the location of the various churches and branch churches in the territory of each of the Indian tribes in the State of Oklahoma, respectively.

ARTICLE V.

The term for which this organization shall exist is perpetual.

ARTICLE VI.

The principal churches shall be governed by trustees, the same to be called "The General Council of the Church" to consist of two members to be elected by the local Church established in each Indian tribe in the State of Oklahoma that may desire to become affiliated with this church and for the time being, shall consist of Mack Haag, and Sidney White Crane of the Cheyenne Tribe of Indians; Charley W. Dailey and Geo. Pipestem of the Otoe Tribe of Indians; Frank Eagle and Louis McDonald of the Ponca Tribe of Indians; Wilbur Peawa and Mam Sookwat of the Comanche Tribe of Indians; Kiowa Charley and Delos Lone Wolf of the Kiowa Tribe of Indians; Apache Ben and Tennyson Berry of the [Kiowa-] Apache Tribe of Indians, being fourteen trustees, which for the time being, shall constitute the Board of Trustees or General Council of the Main Church. These trustees to hold office as such until the local Church affiliated with this church of any of the tribes of Indians shall select and name their successors.

ARTICLE VII.

This corporation shall have no capital stock but it is authorized to levy for the purpose of the support of the Main Church of assessments to be determined by the General Council upon the individual members of the church in the various tribes.

ARTICLE VIII.

The General Council composed of the trustees nominated herein shall, within thirty days after receiving Certificates of Incorporation, from the Secretary of State of the State of Oklahoma meet at El Reno, Oklahoma, and adopt, a Constitution and By-Laws for the government and control of the church.

ARTICLE IX.

At the meeting of the General Council called in pursuance of ARTICLE VIII hereof shall, at such meeting elect a President of the General Council, a Vice-President, and a Secretary and Treasurer of this organization who shall hold office until their successors are elected under the provisions of the Constitution and By-Laws to be adopted by the General Council.

The first officers of the Central Church were Frank Eagle (Ponca), president; Mack Haag (Cheyenne), vice-president; George Pipestem (Oto), secretary; and Louis McDonald (Ponca), treasurer. For the first twenty-five years about thirty people from seven or eight tribes occupied all elected offices and the five or six appointed positions. As well as the member of the original general council, they included Alfred Wilson (Cheyenne), James W.

Waldo (Kiowa), Ned E. Bruce (Kiowa), Edgar McCarthy (Osage), Frank W. Cayou (Omaha), and McKinley Eagle (Ponca). Annual meetings were specified and some were probably held.

The only record of an early meeting available to me is that of 1925, which included a report for 1923 and 1924. Most of those attending the "convention" were from Oklahoma, and all elected to office were Oklahoma residents. Previously unreported Oklahoma tribes to attend were the Yuchi, the Shawnee, the Sac and Fox of Oklahoma, the Caddo, and the Wichita. In 1924, Mack Haag had been elected president and Alfred Wilson secretary and treasurer; both were from the Southern Cheyenne tribe. Alfred Wilson was appointed a special delegate to Washington, D.C., to work with the Oklahoma congressmen to defeat the special appropriation with which the antipeyotists hoped to combat peyote distribution and also to be on guard against peyote prohibition laws. By that time, nine bills had been introduced into Congress. In 1925, President Haag reported that there were twelve hundred to fifteen hundred peyotists. Visitors from outside Oklahoma were welcomed. Orin Curry, a Ute Indian from the Uintah-Ouray Reservation in eastern Utah, probably traveled the greatest distance. Utah's 1917 law against peyote had led to fines and jail terms, and he asked for help. Two Omaha Indians from Nebraska declared peyotism had helped them conquer alcohol. One claimed peyote could not be harmful because he had passed the army physical examination although he had used peyote for years. Clearly, the Native American Church was becoming a truly pan-Indian organization and the legal forum to deal with antipeyotism.

Undoubtedly, incorporation of the Native American Church helped to prevent national legislation against peyote and strengthened the status of peyote in Oklahoma and elsewhere. No serious attempt was made again to prohibit peyote in Oklahoma. Also, since incorporation in one state carries over into all others, unless a state specifically outlaws the organization, the Native American Church became legally incorporated in all states which had not legally prohibited it. In 1918, only Utah, Colorado, and Nevada had done so.

As can be expected, the antipeyotists were not idle. Having failed to get a national prohibition law against peyote in 1918, they redoubled their efforts to try again. In 1919, South Dakota representative H. L. Gandy reintroduced his original antipeyote bill, again without success. The Bureau of Indian Affairs sent out another questionnaire to all reservations, Indian schools, hospitals, and so on, asking for information on all aspects of peyotism, and published the results in a strongly antipeyote pamphlet, entitled *Peyote* (1922), by Dr. Robert E. L. Newberne, chief medical supervisor. Among the data was the information that 13,345 American Indians were considered to be active participants in the peyote religion, or 4 percent of the total of 316,008 Indians at that time on the records of the bureau. Interest in peyote had been stimulated by the congressional hearings, and the first edition of a thousand copies of the pamphlet was exhausted in the first few months after publication, so two thousand more were printed. It was reprinted again in 1925 by the Haskell Indian School and widely distributed to individuals, libraries, and Indian agencies until 1934, when it was withdrawn from circulation by Commissioner John Collier. Another antipeyote document, Bulletin 21 (U.S. Bureau of Indian Affairs 1923), containing some of the same material, was also widely distributed by the bureau.

In 1921 and 1922, Congressman Hayden again introduced bills which would have outlawed peyote, but neither passed. In 1923 no bill was passed, but that year the antipeyotists managed to amend the Indian appropriation bill to designate twenty-five thousand dollars "for the suppression of traffic in intoxicating liquors and deleterious drugs, including peyote, among Indians." Similar wording was retained in appropriation bills for Indian affairs through 1934. Of this Slotkin wrote (1953: 53): "Even though Congress had specifically rejected any prohibition of peyote during the years 1910–1922, the Bureau went counter to Congress and continued to enforce its anti-Peyotist regulations. . . . The anti-Peyote rider passed by Congress during the years 1923–1934 was, from a legal point of view, simply a bluff."

In 1924, Senator Charles Curtis, himself a Kaw Indian from Kansas, introduced the bill to prohibit peyote. In 1926 it was Montana representative S. Leavitt who introduced the antipeyote bill. And so the effort continued.

But if the antipeyotists were unsuccessful in passing an antipeyote law in the U.S. Congress, they met with more success in state legislatures. As has been pointed out, Utah, Colorado, and Nevada had passed state laws against peyote in 1917. The fourth state to prohibit peyote was Kansas, whose Senator E. H. Thompson had sponsored federal legislation to prohibit peyote in 1916. Arvel R. Snyder, superintendent of the Prairie Potowatomi Agency at Mayetta, was mainly responsible for the Kansas legislation. Rabidly opposed to peyote, he had answered the Bureau of Indian Affairs questionnaire, Circular 1522 (U.S. Bureau of Indian Affairs 1919), as follows: "The peyote preachers and leaders, William Skishkee and Oliver Marshall, both of whom are degenerates and apparently worthless beings, make it their business to supply our Indians with the buttons." As soon as the Kansas law was enacted, he arrested a number of peyotists. Twenty-six had served jail terms by January, 1924.

In 1923, Arizona, Montana, and North and South Dakota passed laws prohibiting the use of peyote. Since Arizona senator Ashurst and Arizona representative Hayden had both introduced federal legislation to prohibit peyote, it seems safe to assume that it was they who stimulated the Arizona state legislation. There were no peyote users at the time in Arizona. In Montana it was Superintendent C. H. Asbury who spearheaded the legislation with inspiration and assistance from Congressman Gandy of South Dakota, the commissioner of Indian Affairs, the Indian Rights Association,

Newberne's pamphlet, and the National Indian Association. In less than two months, antipeyote legislation passed the Montana legislature unanimously. No Indian testified.

The legislation in North and South Dakota was engineered by Gertrude Bonnin and Congressman Gandy. Of the South Dakota law we have Sioux Judge Randall's account:

Mrs. Bonnin . . . took special study of this practice [peyotism] and after gathering all the facts about it, she took it before [State] Senator Johnson and there they discussed the whole thing and there was twenty delegates of other reservations went and I was present there. . . . The matter being reached the South Dakota legislature, they enacted this peyote law that the State has now in the book.

Mrs. Bonnin had assembled twenty antipeyotist Sioux to speak for the Indians of South Dakota, avoiding members of the South Dakota Native American Church, who had no idea an antipeyote law was pending. No Indian spoke in defense of peyote.

In 1925 a bill to amend the state narcotic code of Iowa by adding "peyote or the mescale button" to the list of prohibited substances passed the Iowa legislature and was signed into law because of the efforts of Superintendent F. T. Mann, of the Winnebago Agency in Nebraska, just across the Missouri River from Sioux City, Iowa. He wrote to the commissioner of Indian affairs that the bill had been "introduced by the two representatives from Sioux City, at my suggestion, and its passage urged and worked for by Dr. Bried [of the Sac and Fox Sanatorium] and myself."

Antipeyotists were not so successful in Nebraska. Actively organized there for some time, they had attempted to insert into the Nebraska state constitution a ban against peyote during the constitutional convention in 1920. The antipeyote proposal was introduced by H. L. Keefe at the request of C. D. Munro, superintendent of the Winnebago Agency, and E. J. Bost, superintendent of the Omaha Agency. But H. L. Keefe was not unfavorably disposed toward peyote. It was he who had written the strong, favorable letter of introduction for the delegation of Omaha peyotists protesting possible peyote legislation in Washington, D.C., in 1912. He introduced the antipeyote legislation before the Nebraska constitutional convention, but he also invited Omaha and Winnebago Indians to testify before the committee considering peyote in the Nebraska legislature, and the result was that it was omitted from the constitution.

When F. T. Mann replaced Superintendent Munro, he was determined to carry on the fight for antipeyote legislation, and a hearing took place in 1921. Hiram Chase, Omaha peyotist and attorney, testified and arranged for other peyotists to do so. This time the antipeyote bill did not reach the floor. Nebraska has never had an antipeyote bill.

In 1929 peyote was outlawed in New Mexico and Wyoming. The New Mexico law was requested by the Bureau of Indian Affairs to support the

Taos antipeyotists. In Wyoming it was again through the efforts of the inde-
fatigable Superintendent C. H. Asbury, who had stimulated the legislation
in Montana and Nevada. He argued that an antipeyote law in Wyoming
would help enforcement of the law in Montana. In 1933, Idaho passed an
antipeyote law.

The state laws were largely futile. They did little to impede the spread
of peyotism. States and their courts had little jurisdiction on Indian reservations. From the beginning, the U.S. government has considered Indians as
sovereign people to be dealt with only as one nation to another, as it would
deal with, say, Great Britain. States could not engage in legal transactions
on Indian land, and as long as Indians practiced peyote on their reservations, and no federal law or tribal law intervened, they were free to do so.
The states could and did interfere to some extent with the transportation of
peyote. By federal regulation, products outlawed by a state should not be
dispatched into that state by mail, express, or freight. The shippers are
required by law to withhold such materials. But the state laws passed in the
twenties were almost impossible to enforce and were mostly an irritant and
motivation for the game of getting around state laws. The largest shippers—
Aguilares Mercantile Co., L. Villegos and Co., and Wormser Bros.—whose
primary income came from Oklahoma, in which peyote was legal, did not
take chances shipping into states with laws against it. They sent peyote to
Oklahoma, and peyotists from states where it was illegal traveled to Oklahoma to buy peyote or received packages from friends in Oklahoma, where
the post offices and express offices were not on guard against illegal products. And of course peyotists traveled in increasing numbers to Laredo
themselves to bring back peyote. With automobiles and better roads, buying directly from the dealers became the popular thing to do. George
Morgan (1976:84–85) reported that in 1927, Joe Herrara cut and dried
thirty-eight thousand peyote buttons near Oilton and took them to Oklahoma to sell so that while there he could participate in peyote rituals. Joe
said that he sold the buttons for two dollars per thousand.

Occasionally, however, Indians carrying peyote were arrested. In 1933
in northeastern Wyoming a local sheriff, collaborating with federal Indian
police and the superintendent of the Northern Cheyenne reservation, in-
tercepted a trailer full of peyote and arrested the five Northern Cheyenne
Indians who were bringing the peyote from Laredo to Montana for the use
of the Northern Cheyenne. One thousand pounds of peyote were destroyed, and the Indians were put in jail, tried, convicted, and placed on
probation. Usually, however, peyote was brought to its destination without
mishap.

State laws probably discouraged the halfhearted, but at the same time
they challenged the devout, and peyotism continued to flourish. The peyotists responded to the proliferation of state laws by incorporating more
state churches. This was not legally necessary, inasmuch as Oklahoma incorporation covered other states as well. Still, peyotists outside Oklahoma

thought it might help, and, besides, they felt the need for more organization. The first tribe to incorporate a peyote church beyond Oklahoma was the Winnebago of Nebraska. In 1921, the Peyote Church of Christ was incorporated, and a charter was granted to Winnebago, Thurston County, Nebraska. The charter stated: "We recognize all people who worship God and follow Christ as members of the one true church. . . . We believe in the sacrament and the sacramental bread and wine, but in so much as the use of the same is forbidden to Indians, we of the people who cannot obtain or use the same have adopted the use of bread as Peyote and water as wine." There were thirty-eight signatures on the charter, among them those of Albert Hensley and Jesse Clay, which gave representation to both the Cross Fire and the Half Moon sects. Oliver La Mere and Jesse Clay were two of the early presidents. In 1922 the Winnebago charter was amended to change the name to the Native American Church of Winnebago, Nebraska.

The Sioux peyotists were not satisfied with one incorporated church, but felt one in each county would be better. The first was the Native American's Church of Allen, South Dakota, incorporated on October 5, 1922. It was followed by the Native American Church of Charles Mix County on November 28, 1922; the Native American Church of St. Charles, Gregory County, on February 20, 1924; the Native American Church of Rosebud on July 26, 1924; the Native American Church of South Dakota on November 28, 1924; the Native American Church of Washabough County on March 14, 1928; the Native American Church of St. Francis on January 10, 1935; the Native American Church of Buffalo County on July 18, 1935; the Central Council of the Native American Church of South Dakota on October 8, 1935; the Native American Church of Porcupine on March 20, 1936; the Native American Church of Sisseton on January 14, 1939; and the Native American Church of Norris on April 14, 1939.

The word *peyote* is not mentioned in any of the articles of incorporation or charters for the churches in South Dakota. This may have been wise in 1922, when a torrent of antipeyote publicity directed at South Dakota filled the nation's press. A two-column headline in the *Washington, D.C., Evening Star* of June 19, 1922, read: "Peyote Eating New Drug Craze Among Indians of South Dakota." The article went on to say: "Eaten by the Indians under any circumstances, it has demoralizing effects, mentally and morally as well as physically. To complicate the situation in South Dakota, the peyote habit has been coupled with religious ceremonials which combine ancient Indian superstitions with Christian rites, and the craze is now in full sway. . . ."

Most of the articles of incorporation of peyotists in South Dakota were on printed forms provided by the state for the incorporation of churches. When words were added, as in the case of the Native American Church of Charles Mix County, Christian ideas were stressed: "The purpose of this corporation is to foster and promote the Christian beliefs among the Sioux

Indians . . . and to teach among them the scriptures, morality, charity, right living, to cultivate the spirit of self-respect, brotherly love and union among all American Indians. . . ." The right to conduct funerals and maintain cemeteries was covered under the provision to "buy, sell, own and care for property for religious purposes." When the Central Council was incorporated in 1935, it equated itself with other Christian churches when it stated:

This is to certify that the Central Council of the Native American Church of South Dakota has hereby granted to William Black Bear of Allen, South Dakota, the privilege and authority to take up the cause of Religious Extension work within this State as well as in other States where the Indian Tribes reside. He is also granted permission to preach the gospel, baptize, solemnize marriages, and administer the Holy Sacrament of the Church.

The Montana peyotists incorporated themselves March 26, 1925, bringing together two tribes that had been historic enemies. The organization was carried out by nine Crow and three Northern Cheyenne peyotists with the assistance of attorney C. C. Guin, who signed the original articles of incorporation as a witness to the fingerprint signatures of the Indians. Two of the incorporators, who also became trustees, were Thomas Stewart (Crow) and Thaddeus Redwater (Northern Cheyenne), who had attended Carlisle. The other Crow incorporators and trustees were Childs, Big Sheep, Holman Ceasley, Erick Bird Above, Austin Stray Calf, Arnold Costa, Harry Whiteman, and Frank Bethune. Thomas Stewart was the first president and Holman Ceasley was the first secretary. The model for the Native American Church of Montana was that of Oklahoma, but as from the charters of South Dakota, the word *peyote* was omitted.

The election of Franklin D. Roosevelt in 1932 not only brought a "New Deal" to the American people generally but also brought a "new deal" especially to the American Indians. Harold L. Ickes became Roosevelt's secretary of the interior, under whom operated the Bureau of Indian Affairs. Ickes was a liberal activist, interested in civil liberties, conservation, reform, and Indians. He had been involved in the American Indian Defense Association and there had met John Collier, who was its executive secretary. The American Indian Defense Association was an organization formed in the twenties to protect the Pueblo Indians from being deprived of much of their land and water rights without fair compensation. It went on to take up the Indians' cause in many areas: in protecting their religious freedom to engage in their native rituals, their oil and gas royalties, and in a multitude of other cases wherein white Americans were trying to gull Indians one way or another in order to make profitable deals for themselves. Made up of private citizens interested in progressive causes, the association had been opposed to many of the policies of the Bureau of Indian Affairs. Ickes was aware of Collier's dedication to the Indians and his formidable record of achievement in their behalf, and Collier was his choice for commissioner of Indian affairs. He was sworn in as Indian commissioner on April 21, 1933.

Collier and Ickes in charge meant a completely new philosopher for the Bureau of Indian Affairs. Heretofore, the view of the bureau had been that the Indians were somewhat less intelligent than white people and their culture had little, if any, value. The purpose of the bureau had been to encourage Indians to forego everything Indian as soon as possible and strive to be like white people. Collier, on the other hand, felt that in many ways Indian culture was superior to American culture and that white Americans could learn much that was good from the Indians. He felt that the very presence of Indian culture was a great asset to American society:

He said that the government had the duty to bring education and modern scientific knowledge within the reach of every Indian. And, at the same time, the government should reawaken in the soul of the Indian not only pride in being an Indian, but hope for the future as an Indian. It had the obligation to preserve the Indian's love and ardor toward the rich values of Indian life as expressed in their arts, rituals, and cooperative institutions. [Philip 1977:118]

Such a radically different point of view was bound to bring many conflicts. Tenured superintendents, teachers, missionaries, whites generally, and even the Indians themselves, schooled in the old attitude, had difficulty accepting the new philosophy. Nevertheless, Collier brought much-needed assistance, reform, and incentive.

The new attitude toward peyote was expressed in Bureau Circular 2970, (Jan. 3, 1934), entitled *Indian Religious Freedom and Indian Culture,* which said, in part: "No interference with Indian religious life or ceremonial expression will hereafter be tolerated." It would seem that the troubles of peyotists were now over for all time. However, this was not to be. Although John Collier was an experienced administrator, he was also a reformer, and sometimes one of his reforms collided with another. For instance, while he strongly encouraged tribes to maintain their ancient practices in order to govern themselves, he also insisted that they practice religious tolerance, which was not always consistent with ancient Indian culture. At Taos, what was seen as religious persecution of peyotists by the tribal government led to another attempt to secure a federal law against peyote.

The trouble between Taos peyotists and other members of Taos Pueblo, usually the governing body, which had led the Bureau of Indian Affairs in 1927 to ask for a New Mexico state law against peyote, continued in the 1930s. Elsie Clews Parsons (1936:67) wrote:

In recent years the peyote people have been let alone by the hierarchy. . . . But the hierarchy has not relented as the decision of a Council meeting in December, 1931, made quite clear. The blankets and shawls that were confiscated ten years ago had not been distributed among the officers as is usual with confiscated property but had been kept in a bundle and handed on from Governor to Governor. One of the peyote men, their arch fighter, had wanted to appeal the matter to the agent, but the others were afraid. Now, however, a council was called to settle the affair. As the retiring Governor was brother of one of the peyote chiefs, it was probably thought that now the controversy could be amicably settled. At any rate, the peyote men went in a conciliatory spirit to talk peaceably with their "brothers" and "fathers," and offered to pay a fine of $10 if the property was returned and the council would give them a signed agreement to molest them no more. The Council refused to give this assurance and insisted on a payment of $25 a piece for the return of the blankets and shawls. The meeting adjourned without coming to any agreement.

In 1934, peyotist Gerónimo ("Star Road") Gómez was elected lieutenant governor, and at least one other peyotist, Telesfor (usually called Teles) Romero, was elected to the council. Feeling in a stronger than usual position in Pueblo affairs, the peyotists seized the opportunity to hold a peyote meeting openly in the Pueblo. They also returned the shawls and blankets which had been confiscated to their rightful owners and paid only a part of the fine that had been assessed. Mabel Dodge Luhan, a wealthy New Yorker who in 1920 had adopted Taos as her home and had married a Taos Indian and one-time peyotist, sent a frantic telegram to her old friend, the newly appointed Indian commissioner:

In defiance of Council of former Governors and war captains, the present Governor and war captains set up Peyote tepee on reservation Saturday night which was first time any officers ever did this.

Three delegates were sent to this meeting to crash and were not allowed in. Instead they were arrested for alleged drunkenness by war captain and thrown in jail there. There is now overt opposition in Pueblo to war captain and Governor who is his tool. . . .

Long heated meeting last night. Another follows tonight. Fearing a showdown ending in violence . . . I think well to advise you. . . . We wish to avoid catastrophe.

This report resulted in the peyotists being removed from office and the lieutenant governor being put in jail because he had returned the shawls and blankets without collecting the complete fines. The peyotists appealed to the Native American Church in Oklahoma. Alfred Wilson, then president, wired a protest to Collier, and followed it by this letter:

We the members of the Native American Church, chartered in the State of Oklahoma, appeal to you for advice regarding the religious freedom of Indians in the State of New Mexico.

A group of Pueblo Indians affiliated with the Native American Church have been imposed upon by the Governor and Counsel of the Taos Pueblos. They have forbidden the use of their religious sacrament, the earthly herb, peyote. Their meetings have been disturbed by drunks. The governing body has fined and jailed the religious participants rather than the disturbers.

A band of worshippers, who are affiliated members of our organization have appealed to the mother church for aid in their predicament of not being able to worship God as they see fit. In compliance with their request we have had two special conferences to discuss the merits of the case. Rather than go to a big deal of expense and undesiring notoriety the members in conference decided to appeal to you, because you have authority to inform all tribes coming under your guidance, the constitutional rights both civil and religious of all Indians in any state on tribal or federal matter, concerning their individual rights.

Therefore the Native American Church in special conference respectfully request that the Honorable Commissioner of Indian Affairs inform the Governor and Counsel of the Taos Pueblo Indians the constitutional rights of all Pueblos under their control the right to worship God as they see fit. We sincerely believe this will settle the case and any further disturbances of nonadherents of this faith.

We the special committee appointed by the Native American Church to present this appeal and to discuss the case, if you so desire, request your immediate attention in this matter. We know it will be appreciated by the many members of this faith not only in the State of Oklahoma, but other States where Indians hold services according to the Rituals of the Unwritten Code as given to them by their Maker the Creator of the Universe, the Great Spirit, God Almighty (Signed) The Committee, Francis M. Cayou (Omaha), Edward McCarty (Osage).

Collier wired the Indian office in New Mexico for an explanation and received the following from Superintendent C. E. Faris:

For a number of years, may be a decade, there has been shifted from one governor to another some Navajo blankets and other items of value held in trust for security of a fine imposed on the peyote group of the earlier day. Star Roads as lieutenant-governor and the ex-governor [Santiago Martínez] returned these blankets to their rightful owners and paid only in part the fines assessed. When the present acting officials asked Mr. Roads for payment of the balance he became angry and acted in a manner that the council felt warranted his confinement until he could meet them with respect for the council. He was confined for overnight and was visited by a delegation of officials who in short time convinced him of the error of his position and settlement made and all concerned were seemingly happy on our visit there with Dr. Lasswell.

. . . I have not yet been able to see Mr. Gomez, but I am advised that he is satisfied with the settlement made and there seems no reason for any further consideration of that particular and long-standing difficulty. It is better that we appreciate the efforts of the council and the governing officials of the latter half of the calendar year in their successful efforts at a satisfactory solution of a matter that had been more or less troublesome for a decade.

But trouble was not over at Taos, for all of Faris's reassuring words. The peyotists continued to try to hold meetings, and the antipeyotists continued to oppose them. One of the contributing reasons for dissension was the interference into Pueblo affairs of Mabel Dodge Luhan. Since 1920, this rich and sophisticated lady had lived in the shadow of Taos pueblo in a large two-story adobe house which she had had built to harmonize with the idyllic northern New Mexico landscape. She had attracted some of the artistic and intellectual talents of the world to visit her there, and some, notably D. H. Lawrence, stayed to live and work in the area. In 1920, John Collier had come and had there made his first personal contacts with Taos Indians. Mabel Dodge had married a Taos Indian, Tony Luhan, and in a sense one might say she felt that not only he belonged to her, but all of Taos belonged to her. They were "her" people. Certainly she had a proprietary attitude toward them, and what happened at Taos concerned her deeply.

Mabel Dodge Luhan hated peyote. Her attitude began at a party in her New York apartment in 1914, before she ever came to Taos. Peyote was supplied and a pseudo-peyote ritual was directed by ethnologist M. R. Harrington, who had learned about it in Oklahoma among the Delaware. Mabel Dodge was shocked by the ritual, was revolted by the taste of peyote, and was terrified when a guest became disoriented. As she reported it, the group first feared for their sanity and then for their lives. A condition of marriage to Tony Luhan had been that he, a leading peyotist, give it up forever.

Whether or not her negative influence was responsible for the conflict between the antipeyotists and the peyotists from the time she arrived in Taos, I cannot say. However, in the thirties there is no doubt that she influenced the tribal officers to take action against the peyotists and that she supported the punishment of peyotists through her attorney, Henry A. Kiker.

In February, 1936, the governor of Taos reported: "Wednesday night [February 12, 1936] Governor and Officers, also War Chief, met and decided to place all attending the Peyote party in Taos County jail for disturbance and using Peyote, which is against the rule of the Pueblo." The arrests were made at the home of Telesfor Romero just before a peyote meeting was about to begin. Taos officer Antonio Mirabel came to the Romero home looking for a psychotic boy named Alvino, who had shown himself naked and had escaped on the way to the hospital. Upon discovery of the sand altar made in preparation for the peyote meeting, Mirabel asked about it, then threatened John Reyno with his pistol when Reyno refused to turn over his supply of peyote. Fifteen peyotists were arrested that night and were tried before chief judge and arresting officer, the same Antonio Mirabel, in the presence of the governor and pueblo council. Mirabel said he was lenient in fining everyone $100 for using peyote, since the state law authorized a fine of $200. He fined Gerónimo Gómez an additional $125 because he argued with him. Three, John Márquez, Joe Bernal, and Don Márquez, refused to pay fines and were sent to a Santa Fe jail. No one paid money, but signed over land, which was parceled out to Mirabel and other pueblo officials.

After the break-up of the peyote meeting and the fines and imprisonment that followed, the peyotists again sought help from Collier, who came
to New Mexico for a personal interview with the Taos governor. He told
him and his council that he wanted to respect their institutions but that they
must respect freedom of conscience. Under his influence, Mirabel and
Gómez came to an agreement whereby the peyotists were allowed to continue to hold meetings in the pueblo but were cautioned to use peyote judi-
ciously, to make no disturbance, and not to proselytize.

But the trouble did not end. In the National Archives (Record Group
75), the peyote file for Taos for 1936 contains more than two hundred pages
of correspondence, minutes, legal opinions, statements, and reports.
Among them, an official of the United Pueblo Agency wrote Collier that
there were "outside influences" on Antonio Mirabel,

one of my best friends who has made a splendid officer, but I feel that his sense
of loyalty to his own political faction at Taos has overridden his sense of duty
to the Indian administration. . . . In the past three or four months [he] has
changed his whole outlook. I refer to the influence of Tony Luhan and his wife,
Mabel Luhan. Through some investigation made by my department I find that
Tony Mirabel visits the Luhan house daily, and if he does not visit them Mabel
Luhan sends for him.

The peyotists sought aid from the Native American Church and from
legal advisors. Dr. Sophie D. Aberle, the new superintendent of the United
Pueblo Agency, and under fire partly because she was a woman and partly
because she was much disliked by Mabel Luhan, forwarded to Washington a
petition from the Taos Council of the Native American Church and seventy-
five church members. After stating support for Superintendent Aberle, the
petition complained: "The wife of Tony Luhan, Mabel Dodge Luhan [is]
doing a lot of trouble-making in our village. . . . It is only Tony Mirabel and
Tony Luhan who have objection to Dr. Aberle's work. The reason is because
Dr. Aberle won't do what Mabel Dodge Luhan wants her to do." The interference of Mrs. Luhan was a matter for discussion in the Pueblo council on
June 6: "Antonio Luhan explained that his wife . . . never interfered in
matters concerning Taos Pueblo or any other Indian matters unless she
was asked to do so and it was for the good of the Indians. . . ." Finally, in a
memo to Ickes, Collier referred to the trouble Mrs. Luhan was causing
when he reported that his agreement with the governor of Taos and the
peyotists was blocked because "an outside influence" was controlling the
pueblo governor: "This outside influence is Mrs. Luhan, who, in turn, is
being advised by a lawyer named Kiker."

On September 30, Secretary Ickes ordered the governor of Taos to restore to the peyotists the land taken in lieu of cash to pay the fines imposed
in February. The governor's telegram of refusal said, "We have no knowledge of any Native American Church," and he could not allow the peyote

religion because it would be in violation of a New Mexico law. Ickes answered: "It is a matter of regret to me the officers of an Indian Pueblo, led by two white individuals, should do grievous wrong to fellow Indians."

In 1937 there was a new spirit of conciliation in the pueblo of Taos. Following the election in January, the governor reaffirmed the intention of the pueblo council to stop the use of peyote in the pueblo. However, evidence of arrests or other restrictive measures is lacking, while records indicate that the peyotists recovered their land and unobtrusively carried on their peyote meetings. That year a daughter of a well-known peyotist was married to the son of the lieutenant governor by a Catholic priest in a regular Catholic church wedding ceremony, and feelings about peyote one way or another did not color this happy event. As a matter of fact, peyote factionalism had moved from Taos to the national capitol.

In 1936, Mabel Dodge Luhan was no longer a friend of John Collier. She not only sought a federal law to prohibit use of peyote, but also through such a law she sought Collier's removal from office. A report to Superintendent Aberle from Gerónimo Gómez, based on someone listening at the window of the council rooms at Taos, stated:

John D. Concho had a letter and he said: "I am reading a paper which I got from Judge Kiker, saying that we wish to go ahead and fight this Native American Church. . . ." He read the letter which had been written by Judge Kiker to President Roosevelt, saying that they wanted to get rid of Secretary Ickes and have John Collier, Dr. Aberle, Judge Hanna, and Mr. Brophy put out of the Indian Service because they all had gone over to the side of the people of the Native American Church. . . .

In a letter to Ickes, Mrs. Luhan stated her feelings:

Do you really mean that you are defending *self-government* when you take the side of a few drug addicts against the efforts of the pueblo officers to eradicate the usage of the peyote drug? These officers are trying to deliver the Indians from their bondage to narcotic and you try to encourage them in their use of it. The Catholic Church does not recognize the "Native American Church." Would you stand for hashish, cocaine, or morphine and defend them on the grounds of religious liberty?

Through the efforts of Mrs. Luhan and Judge Kiker, on February 8, 1937, Senate bill 1399 was submitted by Senator Dennis Chavez of New Mexico. Its purpose was "to prohibit the interstate transportation of anhalonium, commonly known as peyote." The opening move by Senator Chavez had been made in August, 1936, when he arranged a hearing on affairs at Taos under provisions of a Senate resolution of the Seventieth (1927) and Seventy-first (1928) Congresses to make a *Survey of Conditions of Indians in the United States* (1937). The published hearings on the Taos matter required about 150 pages. The publication begins with a letter from Mabel Dodge Luhan to the Senate Committee on Indian Affairs, dated August 20,

1936. The first fifty pages deal with peyote at Taos, both pro and con. A twenty-page bibliography follows. The remainder is mostly a complete reprinting of documents and testimony published in support of the Hayden bill of 1918. A few reprints of Bureau of Indian Affairs reports for 1935 and 1936 are included. Senators Hayden and Ashurst of Arizona were still in Congress and, of course, supported the bill.

Collier brought expert opinion to defeat the bill. By 1937 there was a wealth of expert knowledge available. Weston La Barre was deep in data for his Ph.D. thesis at Yale, which was published as *The Peyote Cult* (1938). Vicenzo Petrullo's Ph.D. thesis for the University of Pennsylvania had been published as *The Diabolic Root*. H. Scudder Mekeel, bureau field representative in charge of applied anthropology, personally wrote to Professor Franz Boas of Columbia for authority. At the request of Senator Elmer Thomas of Oklahoma, chairman of the Senate Committee on Indian Affairs, the office of the secretary of the interior prepared a report on the Chavez bill. Widely distributed later by the bureau as "Documents on Peyote" (1937), it recommended "that S. 1399 be not enacted." In addition to a covering letter from Charles West, acting secretary of the interior, it included statements against S. 1399 from anthropologists Franz Boas, A. L. Kroeber, Ales Hrdlicka, John F. Harrington, M. R. Harrington, Weston La Barre, Vincenzo Petrullo, and Elna Smith. Opinions against the bill were also contributed by economic botanist Richard E. Schultes of Harvard and Osage tribal chief Fred Lookout. Peyotists on reservations from Oklahoma to Montana were notified of the pending legislation and were ready to go to Washington to testify against the bill. Officials of the Native American Church in Oklahoma sent wires and letters offering their services should they be needed. The great antipeyote publicity campaigns which had accompanied peyote legislation from 1916 to 1926 were not much in evidence in 1937. The Chavez bill, S. 1399, quietly disappeared.

Only once more was there an attempt to get a federal law against peyote. On December 13, 1963, Representative Dante B. Fascell of Florida introduced H.R. 9488 to add peyote to the federal law regulating sale, and so on, of marijuana. Within weeks, congressmen from many states were alerted to oppose the bill. Officials of the Native American Church obtained the support of Commissioner Philleo Nash to oppose the Fascell bill if it should come up for hearings. However, no hearings were held, and H.R. 9488 died quietly in the House Committee on Ways and Means, to which it had been referred for study. Thus ended the congressional battles against peyote, both those led by the Bureau of Indian Affairs bound to fit Indians into the white man's mold with some traditional form of Christianity, and those led by a few patrons of Indians bound to keep Indians in the mold of their ancient fathers, rejecting all innovations of the present day.

CHAPTER 9

An International Church and the Further Spread of Peyotism on the High Plains

BEFORE considering the details of conversion to and practice of peyotism among the tribes who adopted it after 1918, it would be well to look at the progress of the Native American Church and its many subgroups during the years following incorporation. In doing so, it should be noted that the records of the church during its early years are not often available. If they were kept, they were not usually passed on and accumulated by the organization. To be organized, to write things down, to keep records, to delegate responsibility, to conform to a pattern—such things were new to Indian culture and perhaps temperament, and so records were not kept as an organization, or became the personal property of individuals, or were lost. Plain carelessness produced haphazard record-keeping, even after the idea of organization had been generally recognized as necessary and enthusiastically adopted.

Nevertheless, there was much initial success. Although a number of Oklahoma tribes remained aloof for a while, the Native American Church (NAC) in Oklahoma was able to strengthen peyotism in Oklahoma and to help new groups elsewhere by example and by bringing pressure, as it had done in the case of the trouble at Taos. We have noted the chartering of churches in Nebraska, South Dakota, North Dakota, Montana, and Idaho. In 1939 a charter was obtained for an NAC church in Wisconsin, and in 1943 one was granted to the NAC in Iowa. The NAC in Oklahoma continued in the role of the primary church until 1944, holding annual meetings, electing officers according to the by-laws, abetting newly incorporated churches in other areas, and giving help and advice when asked. There had been some fruitless effort as early as 1923 to get a national charter. In 1934 that idea was abandoned and the Oklahoma charter was amended to accept specifically the many state churches as legal affiliates. In 1944, in another attempt to nationalize and broaden the Oklahoma Native American Church, the charter was amended to change the name to the Native American Church of the United States. Clearly, its aim was to be the "mother" church.

For a few years there was uneasiness among Oklahoma peyotists about belonging to the Native American Church of the United States. Although there were those who felt the need to be a national body, there were also others less interested in the national aspect who preferred their old state organization. In the end the latter group prevailed, and the original name the Native American Church was reinstated, retaining the 1918 charter. In 1950 a new charter was obtained for the Native American Church of the United States, and that church, without replacing the Oklahoma state church, has become the official primary church, its name soon being revised to the Native American Church of North America in order to accommodate the peyotists of Canada.

The first officers of the Native American Church of the United States, elected in 1944, were all from Oklahoma except for the vice president, Frank Takes Gun (Crow). That year tribes not previously represented at a convention were the Northern Cheyenne, the Winnebago of Nebraska and Wisconsin, the Seneca, the Menominee, the Potawatomi of Kansas, the Navajo of Utah, the Bannock, and the Shoshone. In 1945, stimulated by the efforts of Frank Takes Gun, the Navajo near the Four Corners area incorporated their church in the state of Utah, and the Taos Indians secured a charter for their church in the state of New Mexico.

In 1946, Allen P. Dale (Omaha) was elected president and Frank Takes Gun was again elected vice president. These two remained in office at the head of the church until 1956. The minutes of the 1946 convention lacked a list of those attending but did include a "Mailing List of the Native American Church" of thirty-one names, eighteen of whom were members of tribes outside of Oklahoma. They were from Montana, Wisconsin, Nebraska, Iowa, New Mexico, Idaho, and Colorado. In 1946, again mainly because of the help and inspiration of Frank Takes Gun, the Colorado and Arizona Native American churches were incorporated.

In 1950 the NAC of the United States met at the home of Apache Ben (Kiowa-Apache) of Apache, Oklahoma, on June 29 and 30. Delegates from nine states outside of Oklahoma were represented. The speakers were Jack [Johnathan] Koshiway (Sac and Fox of Kansas), Robert Yellow-Tail (Crow), and Jess Rowlodge (Southern Arapaho). John Pokibro (Bannock) was named to the board of directors. A long resolution was passed honoring U.S. Senator Elmer Thomas of Oklahoma for his help in protecting peyotism in the U.S. Congress. In 1952 the convention was also hosted by the Kiowa-Apache. Sixteen delegates from Kansas, Iowa, Utah, Idaho, Nebraska, Wisconsin, and New Mexico were registered.

In 1953 the convention of the NAC of the United States was held for the first time outside Oklahoma, at Macy, Nebraska, on the Omaha reservation. Tribes not previously represented were the Rocky Boy's Cree of Montana, the Navajo of Arizona, and three reservations from South Dakota. In 1953 there was some trouble for peyotists in Texas. In 1937 Texas had passed an antipeyote law, but that law had little effect on peyotism, since no Indians lived in Texas and the Texas narcotic agents and officials of the Texas Department of Agriculture allowed peyote to be harvested, sold, transported, and eaten in Texas "for religious services." In 1953, without any known change in the law, Claudio Cárdenas, a *peyotero* of Mirando City,

FIG. 13. First officers of the Native American Church of the United States. Front row, left to right: Mack Haag (Southern Cheyenne), Alfred Wilson (Southern Cheyenne). Back row, left to right: Joe Kaulity (Kiowa), Truman Dailey (Oto), Frank Takes Gun (Crow). Photograph collection of J. Sydney Slotkin in possession of O. C. Stewart.

FIG. 14. Allen P. Dale (Omaha),
1955. Photograph by
Slotkin.

Texas, was arrested and charged with breaking the law. Cárdenas wrote to
his customers in Oklahoma, who came to his aid. Allen Dale, president of
the NAC, retained a well-known attorney and member of the Texas legislature, Manuel J. Raymond, to defend Cárdenas. When Cárdenas was
brought before the grand jury in Laredo in 1954, the grand jury dismissed
him upon recommendation of the district attorney, and, in a special session
of the legislature in April, Mr. Raymond was able to get the Texas Narcotic
Drug Act amended by having the words *peyote* and *mescal bean* removed.

The 1954 NAC convention met at Tama, Iowa, among the Fox tribe.
A number of unusual features distinguish this meeting. A motion was made
by Mitchell Weso, Menominee delegate of Phlox, Wisconsin, to nominate
James Sydney Slotkin to be on the board of trustees. This was unusual,
inasmuch as Slotkin was a white anthropologist from Chicago. The motion
was made in all seriousness, however, since Weso explained that when
Dr. Slotkin was studying the Menominee, he had been made an honorary
member of the NAC by the Menominee tribe. Slotkin was not at the meeting, but anthropologist Sol Tax, also of Chicago, who had been involved in
an extensive study of the Fox of Tama and had come to the meeting hoping
to make a film of the convention and the peyote ritual, was there, and he
made the speech of acceptance for Slotkin. Later, Slotkin, as a member of
the board, offered to publish a quarterly newsletter for the NAC and to distribute and analyze a questionnaire to discover the location and number of
NAC members. Working closely with President Dale, Slotkin soon provided

FIG. 15. Johnathan Koshiway (Sac and Fox), 1955. Photograph by Slotkin.

printed membership cards and "Certificates of Group Affiliation with the NAC" for members of the NAC of the United States.

Early in 1955, using all the names and addresses of present and former officials that he could come by, Slotkin mailed out 154 forms under the title, "Questionnaire of People Using Peyote as a Sacrament." He asked for the names, addresses, tribes, and numbers of men, women, and children peyotists; he also requested the informant's name and the name and address of a responsible official. Sixty-six groups returned the questionnaire and listed 7,218 members, scattered in two Canadian provinces, Alberta and Saskatchewan, and in the following states: California, Idaho, Arizona, New Mexico, Colorado, Wyoming, Montana, N. Dakota, S. Dakota, Nebraska, Kansas, Oklahoma, Texas, Minnesota, and Wisconsin. By the time the results of the questionnaire were published in the first issue of the *Quarterly Bulletin of the Native American Church of the United States*, three more states had contributed to the data—Iowa, Nevada, and Utah—bringing the total number of states to eighteen.

The 1955 annual convention of the NAC of the United States convened in Wisconsin Dells, Wisconsin, on September 8. It was then that the charter was amended to change the name to the Native American Church of North America (NAC of NA). The year before, the NAC of Canada had been incorporated in Saskatchewan. The 1956 annual meeting was held at the home of a Sioux Indian, Joe T. Sierra, of Scottsbluff, Nebraska. Of the twenty-four registered delegates, ten were Sioux from different reservations. In addition, there were three from the Winnebago tribe, two each from the Fox, Omaha, Navajo, and Crow tribes, and one each from the Oto, Menominee, and Shawnee tribes. Officers elected were Frank Takes Gun (Crow), president; Hola Tso (Navajo), vice president; Reuben De Roin (Oto), reelected treasurer; and William Wall (Crow), secretary.

With the election of Frank Takes Gun as president, the relatively peaceful days of the NAC of NA were over. Takes Gun was an unusually able and ambitious man. As vice president for ten years, he had led an almost one-man campaign to stimulate tribes to incorporate under the laws of their states. His help was significant in the incorporation of the churches in Utah, New Mexico, Arizona, Colorado, Canada, and, later in 1958, California and Nevada. He later worked for years to persuade the Navajo Council to legalize peyotism among the Navajo. He was primarily interested in the legal problems involved in peyotism, and he learned the importance of getting charges under state laws moved up from justice or police courts to county or superior courts, thereby getting a more significant ruling. He became acquainted with the American Civil Liberties Union (ACLU), and he was able to solicit their aid in defending Indians in various cases involving peyote.

But if Takes Gun was able, he was also ambitious and unwilling or unable to cooperate within a democratic institution. As soon as he became president, the NAC of NA became a one-man organization. The first annual meeting after he became president was held at Lodge Grass, Montana, in June, 1957. The minutes of the meeting noted a vote to extend the term of office of the president from two to six years, but the procedure was not according to the by-laws. Reubin de Roin, treasurer, complained later in a letter to Takes Gun that "there wasn't even a quorum." William Wall, secretary, wrote to Slotkin that he had been present at the start of the meeting, but when not recognized or asked to serve as secretary, he left after three hours. He listed a half-dozen unconstitutional actions taken by Takes Gun during the start of the meeting and considered the Lodge Grass meeting sufficiently illegal to require an election to name honest officials to guide the NAC. It seemed that President Takes Gun had assumed complete control of the NAC of NA. Other officials became figureheads.

In 1958, Slotkin announced the end of his duties as editor of the *Quarterly Bulletin*. The last issue contained a notice that Takes Gun had called the national meeting for 1958 to be held at Gallup, New Mexico. Several of the older members from the Middle West attended the meeting but were not allowed to speak. Mrs. Marjorie Williams (Winnebago), who had been secretary for a number of years, attended the Gallup meeting and wrote to Slotkin that at Gallup "there were no minutes read nor any financial report. . . . He [Takes Gun] called down the past administration, saying they were a group of school boys. . . . He does not have any use for you or the

Bulletin."* She said further that Angelo La Mere and Allen Dale promised to lead a movement to restore the NAC of NA to proper legal status. There was not much that Slotkin could do, but he did write Hola Tso and Jimmie King, leaders of the two Navajo factions, detailing how Takes Gun had ignored the NAC by-laws, giving seven examples and saying: "Mr. Takes Gun has acted like a dictator." At the time, Takes Gun was spending most of his time among the Navajo.

On May 6, 1958, a registered letter was sent to Takes Gun and a letter to all members of the NAC of NA, inviting everyone to a conference to discuss the need for proper government of the NAC. The meeting was called for May 22, 23, or 24, 1958, by Angelo La Mere at the home of Reubin De Roin, Morrison, Oklahoma. No account of the reorganization meeting has come to me, but on November 19, 1958, I received a letter from Allen P. Dale, stating he had been "put back in" as president of NAC because the officer who replaced him had not functioned properly.

Beginning in 1958, I became involved in an extended research program on the Ute reservation at Ignacio, Colorado, which required most of my attention. Although I attended several peyote meetings and met visiting leaders, I lost track of much that was happening to the Native American Church. I knew that Takes Gun was continuing to act as president in spite of Dale's statement that he, Dale, was president. Takes Gun had arranged for me to testify in 1960 in behalf of Navajo Mary Attakai, and in 1962 he arranged for the ACLU to pay my travel to San Bernardino to testify for Navajo section hands arrested during a peyote meeting near Needles, California. When asked, peyotists seemed loath to criticize Takes Gun and simply said that though he was helping in legal matters, the NAC members were worried because of his illegal behavior in the management of the church. To me, an outsider, it seemed that Takes Gun was still considered to be president of the NAC of NA, but he seemed to be devoting all his time to the Navajo, among whom the fight to legalize peyote was at its height.

In late 1964, I received *Newsletter No. 1* from its author, Angelo La Mere (Winnebago), which contained a report of recent events relating to the NAC of NA. The Omaha tribe had elected a temporary planning committee for the reorganization of the NAC of NA, as follows: chairman, Leonard Springer (Omaha); vice-chairman, Walter Wabaunasee (Fox of Iowa); treasurer, Alfred Gilpin (Omaha); and secretary, Marjorie Williams (Wisconsin Winnebago). In August, 1964, an election conference had been held at Macy, Nebraska, on the Omaha reservation and had elected as offi-

*The year 1958 was also the year of the untimely death at the age of forty-eight of Sidney Slotkin. It was a tragic loss for the Native American Church, for his family, and for social science as a whole.

cers of the NAC of NA: president, Emerson Decorah (Wisconsin Winnebago); vice president, Walter Wabaunasee; treasurer, Alfred Gilpin; secretary, Mary Natani (Winnebago from Chicago). Coeditors of the *Newsletter* were John Greany, Jr. (Omaha), and Angelo La Mere (Winnebago). Allen Dale and Frank Takes Gun had been especially invited to the meeting, but neither had attended. Tribes represented at the reorganization were the Fox, the Potawatomi, the Kickapoo, the Pawnee, the Cheyenne, the Caddo, the Winnebago, and the Omaha. Messages of support had come from Indians in Idaho, Minnesota, South Dakota, and Utah.

On June 25–27, 1965, the Sixteenth Annual Conference of the reconstituted Native American Church of North America was held on the Potawatomi reservation at Mayetta, Kansas. Frank Takes Gun did not take part in this meeting or in others of the reorganized church. Nevertheless, he still considered himself to be president of the NAC of NA, as was evident from an item in the *Navajo Times* of June 8, 1966: "Frank Takes Gun, National President of the Native American Church of North America, was the keynote speaker at the first annual meeting of the NAC held at the Window Rock Civic Center." In the audience there were said to be three thousand Navajos.

In 1967 the Texas legislature outlawed the possession of peyote in the state of Texas. It was not said why this action was taken, but it seems likely that the recent interest of whites in all forms of psychedelic drugs, including peyote, may have been responsible. California had passed an antipeyote law in 1959, and New York had passed one in 1965, both probably more directed against whites than Indians and having little effect on the Native American Church members. But as soon as the new Texas prohibition was known, alarm spread throughout the reservations where peyotism flourished. Indians in increasing numbers were making sacred pilgrimages to the vicinity of Oilton, Mirando City, and Laredo to collect a few of the sacred plants and to purchase supplies for their growing churches. At a special session of the NAC of NA at El Reno, Oklahoma, on January 27, 1968, delegates from nineteen tribal groups met to plot a united effort to have the Texas antipeyote law amended. Peyotists from reservations in Montana, Idaho, Wyoming, Utah, Colorado, New Mexico, Wisconsin, Nebraska, and Oklahoma were present and signed the petition addressed to both the governor and the Texas state legislature, seeking an exemption to allow transportation and use of peyote for religious purposes.

Frank Takes Gun did not join the majority of peyotists in working to persuade Texas to amend its law; instead he directed Navajo David S. Clark to get arrested in Laredo so that there could be a test case; the arrest occurred in March, 1968. Judge E. James Kazan found the Texas prohibition of peyote unconstitutional and dismissed the case against Clark. However, the judge's ruling had force only in his judicial district. It was the large delegation of officials from the NAC of NA, led by Leonard Springer and Fred

Hoffman, with help from Professor J. Gilbert McAllister, anthropologist from the University of Texas, who persuaded the Texas legislature to amend its law by allowing the collection, transportation, and use of peyote in Texas. The exemption reads:

The provisions of this Act relating to the possession and distribution of peyote shall not apply to the use of peyote by members of the Native American Church in bona fide religious ceremonies of the church. However persons who supply the substance to the church are required to register and maintain appropriate records of receipts and disbursements in accordance with rules promulgated by the director. The exemption granted to members of the Native American Church under this section does not apply to a member with less than 25 percent Indian blood.

Thus, it became necessary for dealers to keep sales records, including names of purchasers, and to see proof that the Indians buying peyote were members in good standing of some branch of the peyote religion and were at least one-quarter Indian. All churches of the Native American Church whose members obtained peyote in Texas were required to file names of officers and a roster of its members with the Texas Department of Health Resources. It is with some difficulty that the members of the Native American Church, the peyote dealers, and officials of the state of Texas to this day comply with the Texas Narcotic Law of 1969.

The NAC of NA continued to hold annual conventions without Takes Gun, who nevertheless continued to claim to be president. On November 28, 1968, the *Tribune-Herald* of Hardin, Montana, reported: "Frank Takes Gun was re-elected president of the Native American Church 'by acclamation' at the Native American Church National Convention at Gallup, N.M., Nov. 16." When the twentieth annual conference of the legal NAC of NA was held on the Navajo reservation at Shiprock, New Mexico, in June, 1969, this meeting, like the others, was avoided by Takes Gun and is evidence that he was generally rejected except by the Arizona Navajo.

As the Native American Church of 1918 had grown to become the international NAC of NA of 1955, so had the body of believers in peyotism grown to extend beyond the borders of the United States. In that time more High Plains Indians accepted peyotism and extended it to its northernmost point, well over three hundred miles into Canada. From the late teens through the twenties and thirties peyotism spread to the Bannock and Shoshone Indians at Fort Hall in southeastern Idaho and to the Cree and Chippewa at Rocky Boy's Reservation in northern Montana. It spread to the remnants of the Mandan, Arikara, and Hidatsa tribes gathered on the Fort Berthold Reservation in North Dakota, and it spread beyond the United States to the prairie provinces of Canada to the Cree and Chippewa living in Alberta and Saskatchewan.

The spread of peyotism at this time was characterized by the same phenomena that have been noted from its beginning in Oklahoma. First, and foremost, the initial appeal to converts was for a cure. Generally, knowledge of peyotism preceded the practice of peyotism. Peyotism was always accompanied by opposition. Peyotists continued to participate in and considered themselves members of other religions while remaining active peyotists. Visiting between tribes in order to experience an interchange of leadership was pervasive. Peyotists continued to make an effort to visit the "peyote gardens" near Laredo, Texas, and to perform ritual acts while collecting peyote. Conversion to and support for peyotism was associated with family relationship. Finally, peyotism in most tribes remained a minority religion.

THE BANNOCK AND SHOSHONE OF IDAHO

The Bannock and the Shoshone were established on a reservation at Fort Hall, Idaho, in 1869. The Bannock speak Northern Paiute, related to Shoshone, and some members of the two tribes, who had occupied a broad area over Utah, Idaho, Nevada, and Oregon from early times, came together when they received horses. Fort Hall is one of the most isolated reservations, apt to be missed by even a pan-Indian religious movement. Nevertheless, some Bannock-Shoshone found their way to Oklahoma and learned from the Comanche and Cheyenne the Tipi way, and ever-restless Sam Lone Bear found his way to Fort Hall and taught the Cross Fire cult.

Concerning the first knowledge of peyote at Fort Hall, La Barre wrote (1938: 114): "The Bannock of Idaho used peyote since 1906–1911, apparently against considerable opposition. They formerly met in log-houses in the backwoods, and did not use the plant openly until the Oklahoma Native American Church was organized. The Cheyenne are believed by the writer to be the source of the cult." La Barre does not give the source for this assertion and does not include the Bannock in his "Chronological Outline for the Diffusion of Peyotism." The years 1906–11 seem early for the Bannock, and one is inclined to question those dates.

Robert Lowie, Julian H. Steward, and E. A. Hoebel published their interviews with the Indians at Fort Hall before 1940, but all failed to mention peyotism. In a letter to me dated January 8, 1940, Hoebel wrote:

I did not attend any Peyote meetings at Fort Hall and am in consequence unable to supply you data for that. However, Peyote worshippers at Fort Hall told me that they learned the ritual directly from the Comanche in Oklahoma and that their performances are an exact copy of the Comanche. Inasmuch as the Shoshone at Fort Hall make quite regular visits to participate with the Comanches in Oklahoma this statement is probably true.

There is also indication that the first missionary to Fort Hall may have been Sam Lone Bear. Sven Liljeblad had been studying the Bannock language at Fort Hall for about twenty-five years when he wrote me in 1971:

As a leader of Peyote meetings, Sam Lone Bear apparently visited Fort Hall several times, beginning about 1915. When visiting Fort Hall he stayed, apparently for indefinite periods of time, with Jack (alias John) Edmo, son of Chief Edmo. Jack Edmo (Attedmo) was an influential full-blood Shoshoni Indian for sometime serving as police officer at the Agency. He died in April 1929 seventy-two years old. He was one of the first promoters of Peyote at Fort Hall.

The Indians at Fort Hall must certainly have been circumspect in their early practice of peyotism, even as La Barre suggested, for the officials at the agency denied the presence of peyote when replying to the Bureau of Indian Affairs questionnaires of both 1916 and 1919. In Newberne's tabulation based on the 1919 questionnaire, the whole state of Idaho was declared free of peyote. Unusual as it may seem, the first written record of peyotism among the Bannock and Shoshone of Idaho is in the articles of incorporation of the Native American Church of Idaho, signed before a notary public in Blackfoot, Idaho, on March 19, 1925, and filed a few days later with the clerk of the district court at Blackfoot and a couple of weeks later with the secretary of the state of Idaho at Boise. The articles closely follow those of the Native American Church of Oklahoma, and the incorporators were Eugene Diggie (Bannock), Grant Martin (Bannock), Peter Jim (Shoshone), and Jack Attedmo (Shoshone). The incorporation of the Native American Church of Idaho was followed in 1933 by the enactment of a law prohibiting the possession, etc., of peyote in that state, but the law was repealed in 1937. I am not aware of the details behind these events.

Some of the inconsistencies in the reports of how and from whom the Bannock-Shoshone of Fort Hall learned peyotism were clarified by an interview I had in 1971 with Grant Martin. He was in the hospital because of a sore on his leg which would not heal, but he seemed in good mental health. He said his birth date was 1891, which would make him eighty when I talked with him. He had been recommended to me as an old-time peyotist whom I could find because he could not walk, and I began my interview without the knowledge that he had been one of the incorporators of the Native American Church of Idaho.

To my surprise Grant passed over Sam Lone Bear as the initiator of peyotism at Fort Hall and asserted that the Comanche in Lawton, Oklahoma, were more important to peyotists in Idaho than was Lone Bear. As I reconstruct the situation, it seems that at about the same time that Lone Bear began coming to Idaho to hold peyote meetings, a few Bannock and Shoshone were going to Oklahoma and learning a different style of peyote ritual from their linguistic kin, the Comanche. It was difficult to get exact dates for Grant's first trip to Oklahoma; he was "just traveling around." The first time was "a few years after the death of Quanah Parker," who had died in 1911. A Comanche who had helped him during a two- to three-month visit was "Post Oak Jim, a big tall guy," who was later an informant for Hoebel. On another trip he had taken Eugene Diggie with him, and it was then that the Comanche encouraged them to get an Idaho charter for the Native American Church. Grant said that Wilbur Pewo was their main instructor in how to go about getting a charter. They had stayed at his place, and Wilbur had given them a copy of the Oklahoma charter as an example to follow when they reached home. One can imagine the enthusiasm and "know-how" of Pewo in instructing Martin and Diggie by recalling that Wilbur Pewo was one of the incorporators of the original Native American Church of Oklahoma in 1918. Grant said: "We got the charter for the Native American Church in Boise. I was the main promoter. I had sample articles to show in Boise."

Grant Martin had run peyote meetings at Fort Hall for about thirty years, beginning about 1930, always in the Comanche way. He had known Sam Lone Bear and Sam's friend Sam Nipwater, but he had little good to say about Lone Bear. He knew Lone Bear had conducted peyote meetings at Fort Hall, but added: "You didn't learn anything from him." Moreover, "Sam Lone Bear didn't like the Comanche way to run a meeting. . . . Some Oklahoma Indians didn't like Lone Bear."

Since 1945 members of the Fort Hall Native American Church have been active in the national organization. They began with a letter from John Pokibro, a Bannock from Blackfoot, Idaho, to Allen Dale, who became president of the Native American Church of the United States, inquiring how to obtain peyote. In 1946, Pokibro was a delegate to the national convention at White Oak, Oklahoma, at which Dale was elected president. In 1950 he was appointed to the board of directors at the meeting of the Native American Church at Apache, Oklahoma. In 1954 he welcomed President Allen Dale to Fort Hall as follows:

Dear Friend: Your letter of March 2 to Isaac Sandy has been received here. He is one of my neighbors and he is first cousin of Eugene Diggie, your friend.

My home has been chosen for your stopping place on April 25th. Maybe you remember where I live. One time you and Grace and Frank Takes Gun stopped here—same place. We appreciate your coming here and we will be glad to have you here, Allen.

We are going to invite a few Western Tribes of Indians here (peyote people). Awaiting your arrival.

Among the Fort Hall peyotists who have attended national conventions of the Native American Church are Sam Nevada, who was with Pokibro at White Oak in 1946; Willie Jim and Timothy Miller, who represented the Bannock-Shoshone at The Dells, Wisconsin, in 1955; and Alvin Buckskin and Layton Littlejohn, who were delegates at an NAC conference in Montana in 1968. Peyotists from Fort Hall attended a state convention of the Sioux Native American Church of South Dakota in 1971 and a special intertribal conference at Ashland, Montana, in 1972. This list is by no way complete, and is given simply as an example of the kind and amount of interest.

Peyotism at Fort Hall has been characterized by an interchange of roadmen. Roadmen from Fort Hall who led meetings at Owyhee on the Duck Valley Reservation of Nevada are Ray Crow, George Tendoy, and Raymond D. Warren. In 1939, the Duck Valley Tribal Council wrote to the Bureau of Indian Affairs that Dan Dick of Fort Hall had introduced peyote to Owyhee as early as 1915. A more recent missionary to the same place is Alfred Gould. At McDermit, Nevada, where there is a small group of Northern Paiute peyotists, Woodrow Bat, Joe Winch and Walker Nevada, all from Fort Hall, have served as roadmen. Gilbert Jack and John Pokibro have been missionaries to the Gosiute at Wendover, Utah.

One of the roadmen to visit Fort Hall is Truman Daily (Oto), who said, "I have been to Idaho twice—ran a meeting each time." George Wesaw, a Wind River Shoshone who married on the Fort Hall Reservation and made his home there, has become a very active traveling roadman, and as such he is often host to visiting peyotists and arranger of meetings for the traveling proselytizers. George claims to have made arrangements at Fort Hall for Joe Red Calf (Cree) of Hobbema, Alberta; Bill Denny (Cree) of Rocky Boy's, Montana; Truman Dailey (Oto); Edgar Moore (Oto); Ralph Turtle (Arapaho); Star Weed (Wind River Shoshone); Baldwin Parker (Comanche); and Thomas Black Star (Comanche). Billie Turtle (Arapaho), married to a Washo in Nevada in 1972, and his brother, Wayne Turtle, married to a Navajo in Arizona, have conducted peyote services at Fort Hall. Emerson Spider, follower of the Cross Fire branch of the Native American Church of South Dakota, informed me that he traveled to Fort Hall and conducted a Cross Fire service at the invitation of Johnny Two Eagles, indicating that there is some interest in the Cross Fire sect started by Sam Lone Bear. There is some sign that a split may have existed at one time at Fort Hall between the followers of the Cross Fire way and those of the Tipi way. If so, it probably followed tribal lines, the Shoshone following Sam Lone Bear's form of the ceremony and the Bannock favoring the Comanche version. However, today the Tipi way is by far the dominant form of the ritual at Fort Hall.

Intermarriage, which allows longtime residence in a new tribe, may do more to integrate the modern Indian ritual than the brief visits of missionaries. Consider Mildred (Millie) Brown Pokibro Auck (Wind River Shoshone), who was born at Fort Washakie in 1904. Her parents were peyotists and her uncle was roadman Marshall Washakie. She attended high school with Arapaho peyotists Ben Friday and George Behan. In 1935 she moved to Fort Hall to be housekeeper for the agency superintendent, and in 1940 she married Bannock peyotist and tribal councilman John Pokibro, with whom she lived until his death in 1966. In 1972, I interviewed Millie in her home on the Fort Hall Reservation, and she recalled going with John Pokibro to conduct peyote meetings for the Ute at Whiterocks, Utah; for the Gosiute at Skull Valley, Utah; for the Shoshone at Fort Washakie; and for the Cree at Rocky Boy's, Montana. She had been to Laredo four times to get peyote. In 1972 she was treasurer of the Fort Hall Native American Church and had charge of the reservation supply of peyote. She furnished peyote for each meeting and collected the money to pay for the next car that would go to Laredo for supplies. Peyote was purchased green in Texas, then sliced, dried, and ground to make a tea or paste. Millie had a supply of two thousand buttons on hand.

Another Wind River Shoshone peyotist who married on the Fort Hall Reservation and chose to stay is the aforementioned George Wesaw. Two Sioux men who married members of the Fort Hall peyotists are John Weasel Bear and Johnny Two Eagles. Mrs. Louise Two Eagles was designated to receive mail for the Native American Church and reported to Slotkin in 1955 that there were 360 peyotists in the vicinity of Fort Hall.

CREE, CHIPPEWA, BLACKFOOT, AND ASSINIBOINE
OF NORTHERN MONTANA

In the space of four hundred miles east of the Rockies in Montana near the Canadian border are four Indian reservations: Rocky Boy's (Chippewa-Cree), Blackfoot, Fort Belknap (Gros Ventre), and Fort Peck (Assiniboine). Only the Algonquian-speaking Blackfoot are in their aboriginal territory. The Algonquian-speaking Cree came from Canada, and the Algonquian-speaking Chippewa originated in Minnesota.

Of the four reservations, only Rocky Boy's has a significant group of peyotists today, although peyotism is certainly not unknown on the others. In 1919, Special Officer Alf Oftedal, answering the bureau's Circular No. 1522, wrote from Browning, Montana, on the Blackfoot reservation that he had worked on the northern Montana agencies for four years and had found no use of peyote. The year before there had been one lurid, unlikely report from Fort Peck. One of the items of testimony furnished by Gertrude Bonnin and given to the House of Representatives at the 1918 hearings was that of one Chester Arthur of the Assiniboine tribe at Fort Peck, who said, "One woman . . . became turned against peyote . . . and then confessed it all to me, and told me of their sexual excesses at those times when they took those women out. . . . we have seen it make our people act like dogs, and we hate it and we are opposed to it." Since there is no other mention of peyote at Fort Peck, one suspects this story to be pure fabrication.

Of the Blackfoot, about four hundred miles west of Fort Peck, La Barre (1938: 114) wrote:

The Blackfoot in 1913 were said to lack the peyote religion, but Wissler states that he heard them singing peyote songs within a hundred yards of the very agent who denied the existence of the cult among them. Alfred Wilson (Cheyenne) who as president of the Native American Church has occasion to know, says the Blackfoot have peyote. . . .

In 1961 the Museum of the Plains Indian, Browning, Montana, on the Blackfoot reservation, produced a six-page mimeographed report, *Peyotism and the Blackfeet Indians of Montana,* by Leslie B. Davis. Davis could not find a peyotist on the Blackfoot reservation to interview in 1960, but he learned that a large percentage of Indians on the reservation had heard about peyote. Concerning rituals conducted there, he wrote:

A number of Cree have taken Piegan [Blackfoot] wives, but maintain very strong ties with their friends and relatives on the peyote-using Rocky Boy [*sic*] Reservation some 150 miles to the east. Also, near Starr School on the reservation there was a tightly-knit Cree-Piegan (by marriage) enclave in which Peyotism had previously flourished. Further, a Cree, currently an official in the Rocky Boy [*sic*] peyotist group, lived for a number of years near Starr School.

In 1916, by executive order of President Woodrow Wilson, certain Cree and Chippewa Indians were given a reservation on part of the Fort Assiniboine Military Reserve in northeastern Montana. The reservation was named Rocky Boy's Reservation in honor of Chief Rocky Boy, who had been instrumental in showing the need for a definite place for the local Cree and Chippewa Indians. It was a small reservation, in 1919 numbering 460, and it was there that an on-going peyote cult developed.

The earliest record that peyotism existed at Rocky Boy's is in letters in the Seattle branch of the National Archives dealing with the spread of peyotism from the United States to Canada. A letter of January, 1952, stated that Louis Sunchild (Cree) of the Stony-Sarcee Indian Agency in Alberta, Canada, had lived for a number of years on Rocky Boy's Reservation and upon returning to Canada had introduced the peyote religion. He said that Bill Stanlog and Bill Denny were his principal instructors in the ritual.

Dr. Carl J. Couch and Joseph D. Marino of Montana State University at Bozeman have made available to me a twenty-one-page manuscript on peyotism based on interviews on Rocky Boy's Reservation in 1956 and 1957 (Davis 1979). They found at Rocky Boy's that the acceptance of peyotism was primarily a result of a strong cultural carrier, in this case William Denny (Cree), who had spent two years on the Crow Reservation and returned in 1934 to direct peyote rituals for his people. Except for members of his own family, Denny attracted few Chippewa-Cree from 1934 to 1946. His meetings were sporadic, usually dependent upon a request for a cure or upon the occasion of a visit from a Crow peyotist.

In 1946, change in the peyotism at Rocky Boy's began. The peyotists obtained their own charter and thereby became a branch of the NAC of the United States. That year the Montana State Conference was held at Hardin,

Montana, and Allen Dale, president, and Frank Takes Gun, vice president, of the national church attended and were honored guests. Also attending were Bill Denny (Cree); Harry Brown (Oto), a visitor from Oklahoma; and Mike Brown (Arapaho), a visitor from Wyoming. From that time, William Denny showed greater confidence and aggressiveness in his role as leader, and more Indians joined the Rocky Boy's church. Denny has remained the dominant peyotist at Rocky Boy's and has been regularly elected president of the local NAC.

Although long stays on the Crow reservation helped Denny acquire the skill to direct peyote meetings, as Couch and Marino (1979) and Dusenberry (1962: 176) point out, Denny received inspiration and instruction more widely than from the Crow and the Northern Cheyenne. Three informants at Fort Hall reported that Bill Denny frequently traveled the 540 miles from Rocky Boy's to Fort Hall to attend meetings. Mildred Pokibro Auch was sure that in 1949, Denny had remained at Fort Hall for months, camped beside the Pokibro home. George Wesaw and his mother-in-law reported visits from Bill Denny which they had reciprocated every year by visiting Rocky Boy's to conduct peyote meetings. In 1953 the minutes of the national meeting of NAC show that Denny was in attendance; in 1955 his name was on Slotkin's mailing list to receive the NAC *Quarterly Bulletin,* and in a letter to NAC president Allen Dale, Slotkin recommended that Denny be appointed delegate-at-large. Denny maintained his active interest in peyotism in 1972 when I met and talked with him. He attended the NAC of NA convention in Mirando City, Texas, in 1975 (photograph, *Laredo Times,* February 23, 1975). And Paul Small of Rocky Boy's was delegate in Laredo in March, 1978 (*NAC Newsletter,* June, 1978).

Another person important in the establishment of peyotism at Rocky Boy's is Lawrence P. Murie (Pawnee), married to a "Cree/Blackfoot/Assiniboine" and living on the Rocky Boy's Reservation as a resident alien missionary. He must have come in the 1940s if it is indeed his son Robert who in 1972 is listed on the Texas pharmacy list as a custodian for peyote for Rocky Boy's NAC and who claimed 7-8 Indian blood from the "Pawnee/Cree/Blackfoot/Assiniboine" tribes. George Wesaw said that Lawrence P. Murie "introduced peyote to the Rocky Boy Cree," then married and made his home there. Southern Paiute peyotist Clifford Jake of Cedar City, Utah, knew Murie and said that Murie had stopped with him at Cedar City several times while on his way from his new home in Montana to his old home in Oklahoma. It may be that association and inspiration with an experienced peyotist like Murie was what helped to give confidence to Denny in the early 1940s when his leadership qualities ripened.

At Rocky Boy's there was the usual interchange of leaders and visitors with other peyote using centers. In 1963, Sven Liljeblad wrote that Denny and peyotist Tom Arkinson (Cree) had visited Fort Hall, saying, "Mr. Tom Arkinson, with whom I talked at some length the morning after a meeting at Fort Hall, is Cree and the sharpest brain I know about among the Peyotists." Silas Grant (Omaha living with Sioux) said that Tom Arkinson had attended meetings at Wounded Knee and that he had reciprocated by conducting a meeting at Rocky Boy's. Liljeblad also reported that Pat Chiefstick (Cree) had been at Fort Hall, and John Woodenlegs (Northern Cheyenne) reported that Bill Denny, Pat Chiefstick, and Raining Bird, all of Rocky Boy's, had visited the Northern Cheyenne. Jim Blue Bird (Sioux) said Sam Red Door had come by train from Rocky Boy's to visit him and learn his way of conducting the peyote ritual. Bill Tyner (Shawnee) of Tulsa said he had run meetings at Rocky Boy's and that Bill Denny and others from that reservation stopped in Tulsa from time to time on their way to and from Laredo, Texas. George Wesaw said that Baldwin Parker (Comanche), son of Quanah, had left for Rocky Boy's after a long visit at Fort Hall. Wayne Turtle (Southern Cheyenne) said he conducted meetings at Rocky Boy's. And so the interchange continues. Often the visits resulted from invitations; at other times a visiting missionary presented himself and was accommodated with financial help and hospitality.

As might be expected with so much action, the cult at Rocky Boy's flourished. Whereas in 1919 there were no peyotists, in 1957, according to Couch and Marino (1979), "approximately 60 per cent of the adults living on the reservation actively participate in the peyote rituals."

Peyotists were active both in Christian religions and in aboriginal ceremonies. Dr. Verne Dusenberry (1962: 178–79), who has published the major ethnological work on the Montana Cree, quoted one of his informants, Raining Bird:

There are no conflicts in religion. . . . Since we are all the children of one God, whether it is *Ki-sei-men-to* or the God of the white man, its all the same thing. So a man can be a Catholic and a leader of the Spirit Lodge or the Smoke Lodge or the Sun Dance. He is just following the instructions of the Creator in different ways. He can also be a leader of the Peyote church, for here again, one is just following the Creator who has put all this power in Peyote. You see, he can take part in all three of these ways of doing things, for all the prayers lead to the same place in the end.

Dusenberry further commented:

A man can be a Sun Dance leader or a medicine man or any other kind of leader who possesses power and still be a peyote leader. . . . Sun Dance leaders as well as the Spirit Lodge followers and some Catholics and Lutherans belong. . . . Although the Native American Church is perhaps nearer to Christianity than any other type of observance found on the reservation, the Montana Cree believe that . . . they are practicing a religious belief that is superior to the white man's.

THE MANDAN, HIDATSA AND ARIKARA

The Mandan, Hidatsa, and Arikara tribes had occupied the area of the northern bend of the Missouri River for at least a century before Lewis and Clark visited them in 1805. The Arikara spoke a Caddoan language, whereas the Mandan and Hidatsa spoke related Siouan languages, but all three were peaceful, agricultural people, living in villages of partly subterranean earth lodges and enjoying a similar culture. In 1871, after the tribes had been considerably reduced in numbers by smallpox, they were given a reservation at Fort Berthold, North Dakota. Since the building of dams on the Missouri, their reservation headquarters has been Newtown, North Dakota.

According to the 1919 questionnaire of Newberne (1922), there were no peyotists among the twelve hundred Indians of the Fort Berthold Agency. The only record of a possible peyotist came from G. A. Vinnink, a missionary to both the Crow and Fort Berthold agencies, who wrote that one Indian must be "a heavy user" of peyote because he had "attacked the Agent, deserted his wife, and seemed ready to aggravate anyone when he would come to any gathering."

Shonle (1925) found no peyotists at Fort Berthold, and La Barre (1938) did not mention peyotists at Fort Berthold until the third edition (1969) of *The Peyote Cult,* wherein he cited ethnologist Edward M. Bruner (1961), who wrote: "It has been reported that the Native American Church, the peyote cult, which had a temporary success at Fort Berthold in 1912, has been revived within the last few years." By itself, this statement is hard to evaluate. The truth is that we have very little information concerning the early experience with peyote at Fort Berthold. Wesley Hurt (1960: 23) had this to say: "Informants vary regarding the date of introduction of peyote at Fort Berthold. The range of time given is from 1912 to 1920. . . . According to one informant, an Arikara learned the custom from the Pawnee in Oklahoma." In a personal communication to me in 1957, James Howard wrote that the source of the original Mandan, Hidatsa, and Arikara fireplace was Albert Hensley (Winnebago). Concerning the revival of peyotism, Howard later wrote (personal communication, 1978):

While I was doing archaeological work on the Ft. Berthold reservation in 1951–52, the peyote religion had almost died out. Only Thomas Goodall (Arikara) and Walter Plenty Chiefs (Arikara) claimed membership. Goodall had collected peyote feathers from a number of former members and showed them to me commenting, "I am about the only one left." A few years later, however, in 1958, 1959, and 1960, I found the church reactivated. Prominent members were Alfred Driver and his sons, Robert Cherries, Charles Fox, and Louis Brown. Tom Ross, the Yanktonai from Devil's Lake, was very active in their reintroduction and Alfred Driver apprenticed himself to Tom Ross to learn more about the peyote way. I once visited the combined Ross and Driver families encamped south of Grand Forks where they picked potatoes for white farmers during the days and "tied a drum" and sang each evening. I rather suspect that the Fort Berthold ritual I saw was introduced by Tom Ross.

In 1961, Howard was a professor at the University of North Dakota and used the opportunity while there to visit several Indian reservations to learn more about peyotism. On January 8, 1961, the *Grand Forks Herald* published an interview and his photograph with "ritual objects used" in peyote ceremonies. From the interview and photograph it is clear that the peyote ritual in North Dakota is the Cross Fire ceremony. Describing it, Howard said: "The Christian religion, its teaching and symbols are unmistakably a part of the service. . . . Passages from the Bible are also read, and crosses appear alongside the ancient Indian symbols. . . ."

In answer to the NAC questionnaire sent out by Sidney Slotkin in 1955, Robert Cherries of Newtown reported that there were eleven men and four women who were active members of the Newton NAC, which included members of the Mandan, Hidatsa (Gros Ventre), and Arikara tribes. Slotkin also obtained from the North Dakota secretary of state a copy of the articles of incorporation of the North Dakota NAC, which had been filed January 6, 1956. The board of directors, all of Newtown, were Tom Goodall, Tom Rogers, Robert Cherries, Alfred Driver, and Charles Fox. One of the "purposes" of incorporation read, "To foster and promote the Christian religion, recognizing, adopting, and continuing the use of Peyote for sacramental and religious purposes. . . ," in spite of the fact that there still existed on the books a 1923 North Dakota law prohibiting the use of peyote within the state.

Peyotism continues among a small group at Newtown. In 1968, Alfred Driver (Hidatsa) was a delegate to an NAC conference in Montana. And in March, 1978, James Howard sent me the following information: "[Peyotism] was flourishing in 1972, the occasion of my last visit. One of the pow-wows at Newtown, in fact, was sponsored by Alfred Driver and other Peyotists."

THE CHIPPEWA, SIOUX, BLACKFOOT, AND CREE OF CANADA

In Canada, along the international border, are several Plains Indian tribes similar in language and culture to tribes along the border in the United States. These are the Algonquian-speaking Chippewa (Ojibwa), Cree, and Blackfoot and the Siouan-speaking Assiniboine and Dakota Sioux, some of whom emigrated to Canada with Sitting Bull after the battle against Custer on the Little Big Horn in 1876. Eventually, a few of these Indians learned of peyote from friends, relatives, and missionaries from the United States and developed a local peyote cult, one group of which was incorporated into the Native American Church of Canada in 1958. The Canadian peyotists included Indians from as far west as Rocky Mountain House in Alberta and extended east through Saskatchewan to the Long Plains Reserve in Manitoba. They were proselytized principally by Indians from reservations in the border states of Montana, North Dakota, and Minnesota.

Little is known of the beginning of peyotism in Canada, but there was early opportunity for diffusion from the United States. By 1919, according to Newberne, there were Sioux peyotists at Devil's Lake, North Dakota, about eighty miles from the Canadian border, Chippewa peyotists at Leech Lake, Minnesota, about one hundred miles from Canada, and a large number of Cheyenne and Crow peyotists in southern Montana, 350 miles from the border. When Wissler said that he had heard the Blackfoot singing peyote songs in 1913 (La Barre 1938:114, 122), they could have been Canadian Indians. In a personal letter to me in 1975, anthropologist Ruth Wallis wrote of field work with her husand Wilson: "We couldn't pursue Peyote among 'our' Eastern Dakota because of Canadian law, but I have a photograph taken by Wilson in 1914 in Manitoba of a wide ring of stones which had ashes in the center, which Wilson thought was remains of a Peyote ceremony." This is weak evidence, as is the assertion in 1936 of Alfred Wilson, NAC president, that some Blackfoot, possibly in Canada, were peyotists and the unsubstantiated statement of La Barre (1938:114) that "the Cheyenne are currently a source for peyote among the Blood [Blackfoot] in Canada, who were being organized in the summer of 1936. The Canadian Cree and Chippewa are very recent partial converts, too; the latter received it from the Chippewa of Minnesota."

Better evidence came in 1971 in a meeting with Jim Blue Bird of Allen, South Dakota, who had been a leader of Sioux peyotism for over fifty years (see chapter 7). Jim said that peyotism was introduced to the Devil's Lake Sioux at Fort Totten, North Dakota, in 1926 by Johnson Goodhouse, a Yankton Sioux, who also held peyote meetings that same year at Griswold, Manitoba, for the Canadian Sioux. Bluebird was fairly confident of the date because he himself had worked near Griswold in the fall of 1928 and while there had directed two peyote meetings. My confidence in Jim's memory was strengthened by the discovery that the name of Johnson Goodhouse appeared in reply to both the 1916 and 1919 Bureau of Indian Affairs questionnaires as importer and distributor of peyote, as well as leader of Yankton Sioux peyotism. The missionary at Fort Totten said that the man who received the peyote from Goodhouse was generally one Mibebey, whose name appeared as one of the incorporators in 1922 of the NAC of Charles Mix County and in 1923 as one of the incorporators of the NAC of North Dakota.

Another Devil's Lake Sioux who led early peyote meetings in Manitoba was Tom Ross. In 1973, James Howard wrote me: "In regard to the Canadian Dakota (Sioux), I found that Tom Ross, the Yanktonai leader from Fort Totten, carried peyote to the Oak River (now Sioux Valley) reserve [in Manitoba] in the 1920s." Earlier he had described Tom Ross to me in this way: "He ran a modified cross-fireplace ritual. Well-known in North Dakota,

FIG. 16. Jim Blue Bird (Sioux), 1971. Photograph by author.

Minnesota, South Dakota, and Montana. He was active from *at least* 1930 until 1968. Alfred Driver (Hidatsa) often served as Tom's drum chief. Tom also ran meetings at Edwin, Manitoba." Tom Ross was also on Slotkin's 1955 questionnaire as leader of peyotism at Devil's Lake.

In his third edition of *The Peyote Cult* (1969: 214) La Barre included data from a letter from Ruth Wallis, written in 1963: "Mrs. W. D. Wallis reports that around Griswold, according to Dakota-speaking Father Gontran La Violette, about eight families, including leaders of Catholic and Anglican churches, are peyotists, as are three more families at Oak Lake or Pipestone Reserve." From my telephone call to Alice Kehoe, who La Barre had said (1969: 214) was "working on peyotism among the Canadian Dakota," I learned that the Saskatchewan Dakota (Sioux) did not seem to be peyotists but that there were rumors that the Sioux at Griswold sponsored meetings from time to time, and that the Cree at North Battleford, Saskatchewan, were peyotists. In 1955, Ernest Nicotine (Cree) of Red Pheasant, Saskatchewan, said the Ojibwa (Chippewa) Frank Petters of Edwin, Manitoba, was leader of peyotists in that area.

Regarding the Plains Ojibwa (Chippewa) of Manitoba, James Howard wrote me in 1978:

When I lived in Grand Forks [in early 1960s] peyote "smugglers" frequently stayed at my house en route to Canada. Gunnysacks of green buttons were commonly stowed in car trunks. They usually crossed the border north of Neche or Maida, N.D.

In regard to Plains Ojibwa peyotists, I knew John Beatty, Ross Woods (Wascoup) and his brother Teddy Woods. Tom Ross [Yanktonai Sioux] was active on the Long Plains Reserve (Edwin, Manitoba) as a missionary and the area also received strong influence from the Chippewa near Cass Lake, Minnesota. Teddy Woods was married for a time to the daughter of Clarence and Mary White of Cass Lake.

In 1972, I learned that a group of urban Indians from Winnipeg often came to Long Plains Reserve to attend meetings. This included some persons originally from Long Plains, like Ross Woods, but also other Indians, including one Northern Ojibwa from Berens River. This is probably the northernmost peyotist known.

In the beginning, the attitude of the Canadian government and officials to peyotism seemed to be one of indifference, possibly because so few Indians were involved. Peyote was confiscated, if detected, at the border because it was generally considered to be included in the Canadian law forbidding the importation of narcotics. This was, of course, a problem for peyotists and led to smuggling and to transshipment of peyote.

A report in 1954 in the *Winnipeg Tribune* indicates the attitude of the general public to peyote. Above the picture of a dried peyote button was the headline, "Devil's Brew—or Sacred Potion?" The article was occasioned because customs officials had confiscated seventy peyote buttons, seized because they were not declared, there being no law against importation. The text continued with the usual stories of sexual excesses by peyotists but modified them with, "American anthropologists have come to the defense of peyote . . . as an integral and necessary part of the Indians' worship," ending with, "Until Ottawa decides, the Salteaux [Plains Ojibwa] Indians at Long Plains are finding the peyote 'drunk' colorful and exhilarating."

About seven hundred miles west of the Long Plains and Sioux Valley reserves in Manitoba, another Canadian chapter in the history of peyotism was enacted. Sometime before 1951, peyote was introduced to Indians on the Sunchild Cree Reserve, which is in Alberta north of Rocky Boy's Reservation in Montana. In December, 1951, peyote had come to the attention of the superintendent of the Stony/Sarcee Indian Agency at Calgary. At first he did not know what it was, and he sought information from the superintendent of the Blackfoot Indian Agency, Browning, Montana, as follows:

As you are probably aware, there is quite a bit of visiting done between Indians from Rocky Boy and Indians of the Sunchild Cree Reservation north of Rocky Mountain House, Alberta.

One of these Canadian Indians, Louis Sunchild, returned last summer after having spent several years in Montana. There is now a report circulating throughout the Sunchild Cree Reserve that Louis brought back a supply of a weed which apparently grows in Montana and from which they make a brew or tea that has a pronounced narcotic effect on people who drink it. Our local agent has made a quiet investigation and is quite convinced most of these reports are well founded. He states that the beverage is called "pudy" and that persons who supply it are called "pudy boys" by the Indians.

The local Canadian Mounted Police are carrying out an unofficial investigation. Before we officially ask them to enter the scene, we should like to know a little more about the matter.

Have you ever heard of the existence of such a beverage or narcotic in Montana? If so, we would much appreciate any assistance you can give us in having this matter investigated.

The letter was passed on to Paul L. Fickinger, area director of the Bureau of Indian Affairs at Billings, Montana, while Superintendent Guy Robertson wrote to Mr. Battle that he had never heard of "pudy." The Canadian Agency supplied additional intelligence: "We have found that one of the Indians who is felt to be the principal offender, namely Louis Sunchild, has been in communication with the following people at Rocky Boy . . . Bill Stanlog and Bill Denny."

When Fickinger answered the Canadian agency, he correctly identified "pudy" as an almost certain phonetic corruption of "peyote." He further wrote:

There is much controversy as to whether or not peyote is a drug and apparently no real scientific study has as yet been completed that would classify it in the same category as heroin or marijuana, and similar drugs. It is my understanding that a study is under way and has been for a number of years by the Johns Hopkins University of Baltimore but there are the emotional groups of people who take the position that peyote is part of the native Indian Tradition and therefore should not be disturbed. On the other hand, there are those of us who have to deal with problem every day who know and can see the effects of the use of peyote. We have seen, and see it every day, Indians who have been making good in their efforts to rehabilitate themselves economically and socially but who suddenly join one of the peyote cults and deteriorate rapidly both in their morals and physical being.

I could site many cases of these results but I am enclosing a file on the subject which consists largely of some studies that have been made by one of my Superintendents in the Area that may be of some interest to you. I would like to have the files returned after they have served your purpose. . . . the Sunchild family . . . [which] resided on the Rocky Boy Reservation for a number of years was a member of the peyote cult. . . .

The "studies" referred to were compiled by a persistent antipeyotist, H. E. Bruce, who had tried to stop peyotism while serving as superintendent of the Potawatomi Agency in Kansas from 1935 to 1947. His reports at that time had seemed so biased to Commissioner Collier that Collier had cautioned him to be "rigidly factual" in his study and to "take nothing for granted." Later, as superintendent of the Turtle Mountain Chippewa Agency, 1947–49, he had misguided a team of doctors from the American

Medical Association about peyote and had started a new movement aimed at producing a national law to prohibit peyote. And he continued his work against peyotism at the Winnebago Agency where he was transferred in 1949. His files included every antipeyote argument from 1915 to 1936.

Fickinger's action denigrating peyotism, which had been contrary to BIA policy since 1934, came to the attention of the Washington office when Fickinger's successor as area director, J. M. Cooper, received a request from Mr. Grah, a newspaper reporter, for permission to cite the antipeyote data, especially a report from Bruce to the commissioner of Indian affairs in 1947 (after Collier's resignation). Cooper asked Washington for advice. The BIA's reply reflected the new policy toward peyotism:

The material supplied by Mssrs. Fickinger and Bruce, of course, represents their impressions and opinions as individuals. We do not feel that Mr. Grah should use the material presented by Messrs. Fickinger and Bruce because it is non-scientific and a matter of personal opinion. Other staff members with different training would evaluate the behavior of the tribes differently.

Without having had an opportunity to do either ethnographic or archival research on peyote in Canada, one relies on chance bits of information. At an informal conference of peyotists at Ashland, Montana, in 1972, I had a short conversation with a Cree Indian from Hobbema, Alberta, near Rocky Mountain House, who asserted that the Sunchild family of his Cree group started holding meetings in their home in 1937, but few except the immediate family participated. My informant, Marcel, started attending meetings in 1946 and went regularly for ten years before he quit because of drinking. In 1969 he had returned to peyotism and said he had not used alcohol since, being a strong peyotist in 1972. In that year he estimated there were about two hundred peyotists among the thirty-two hundred Cree in Alberta.

In his first report after his election as president of the NAC of North America in July, 1956, Frank Takes Gun wrote (*Quarterly Bulletin of the NAC*, 2, no. 3 [1956]:4):

In 1953 I visited Canada at Calgary, Alberta Province. . . . I discovered the use of peyote was outlawed by the Canadian government. I was invited by Louis Sun Child, a Canadian Cree Indian, to assist in bringing forth a better understanding of the use of peyote as a religious sacrament. We had roundtable discussions with Head Superintendents, which in the states we call Area Directors, and Chief Inspectors of the Royal Canadian Mounted Police, and Attorneys General of the Province of Alberta, who later ruled, that there were no statutes prohibiting the actual use of peyote and it was established that Peyote was not a narcotic. Their information was from the Narcotic Bureau of the United States.

It is possible that the visit to Alberta by Takes Gun was the stimulation for Canadian peyotists to incorporate themselves into the Native American Church of Canada on October 27, 1954, at Red Pheasant, Saskatchewan,

Canada. Louis Sunchild of Rocky Mountain House, Alberta, was elected president. The other officers, all from Red Pheasant, Saskatchewan, were Paul Stone and Archie Curley, vice presidents; David Stone, treasurer; Tommy Stone, secretary; Ernest Nicotine, assistant secretary; and George Baptiste, Herbie Stone, Mike Bird, Henry Spyglass, George Nicotine, and Mary Whitford, directors.

It will be remembered that in 1954, J. Sidney Slotkin had been elected to the board of directors of the NAC of the United States and had stated his intention to publish a "quarterly bulletin" in behalf of the church. When he received word of the incorporation of the NAC of Canada in 1954, he obtained a copy of the charter and began correspondence with members of the Canadian group and thereby was able to keep the peyotists in the United States informed of peyotism north of the border. In 1955 he and Takes Gun visited the peyotists of Canada, and that year at the national convention the NAC of the United States changed its name to the NAC of North America to include the Canadian church.

The *Quarterly Bulletin* continued to publish information about Canadian peyotism. Volume 2, no. 2 (April–June, 1956), stated that the regional representative of NAC of NA Region 8, Canada, was Ernest Nicotine of Red Pheasant, Saskatchewan, and that the national conference of the NAC of Canada would be held at Red Pheasant on July 5–7, 1956. In the same issue the editor commented:

After reading the article, "Is Peyote a Narcotic?" in the last issue of the *Bulletin,* one of the foremost authorities on the subject wrote to the editor. He was Dr. Humphrey Osmond, Superintendent of the Saskatchewan Hospital, Weyburn, Saskatchewan. In his letter of February 14, 1956, he said, "My colleague, Dr. [Abraham] Hoffer, and I, who have done I suppose more research on the psychophysiological aspects of this than anyone in Canada, frequently express this viewpoint and emphasize that all the evidence that we have suggests that Peyote is wholly beneficial and in no way a drug of addiction. It cannot even be defined in that way since it does not have the essential compelling qualities or the withdrawal symptoms."

Volume 3, no. 1 (1957), of the *Bulletin* contained a news item entitled "White Officials Attend Meeting in Canada." This article referred to a meeting held the night of October 13, 1956, at Fort Battleford, Canada, with Frank Takes Gun as roadman, assisted by Crow tribal judge William Russell. At this meeting Dr. Osmond participated fully, and three others, biochemist A. Hoffer, psychiatrist T. Weckowics, and psychologist D. Blewed, were there as observers without eating peyote. Sixteen photographs had accompanied the two-page story when it appeared in the *Saskatoon Star-Phoenix*.

The peyotists of Canada were included in Slotkin's "Questionaire on People Using Peyote as a Sacrament," and three answers were returned. One was from the Cree living on the Red Pheasant Reservation in Saskatchewan, which claimed a membership of 37, the officers being Ernest Nicotine and George Baptiste; another, also from the Red Pheasant Reservation, was from the Assiniboine living in the town of Stony, who reported 49 members, the officers being George Lightfoot and Paul and Tommy Stone; and the third was from the Cree at Rocky Mountain House, Alberta, who claimed a membership of 41, with Louis Sunchild and Mary Ann Whitford, officers. If this report truly describes Canadian peyotism, it is indeed a minority religion; not counting those in Manitoba, we have 127 out of a total Indian population of 70,000. I do not know the extent of visiting, if any, that has taken place among the peyotists of Alberta, Saskatchewan, and Manitoba. Recently, the officials of the NAC have informed me that peyote is no longer considered a narcotic by the border police of Canada and therefore is no longer subject to confiscation.

CHAPTER 10

The Development of Peyotism in the Far West

THE area of the Great Basin in the western United States is a vast desert area roughly between the Wasatch Mountains and the Sierra Nevada. It includes western Utah and all of Nevada and extends north into Idaho and Oregon and south to include the Mohave Desert in California. It is not a simple basin, as its name suggests, but rather a great geological depression characterized by flat valleys and high mountains. In it many streams and lakes have no outlet to the sea. The region is extremely dry, the average rainfall being three inches in the southern part and ten inches in its northern part. In prehistoric times this inhospitable area was peopled sparsely by Shoshone, Gosiute, Ute, and Paiute Indians. The Gosiute spoke Shoshone and the Northern Paiute spoke a language related to Shoshone, and they all had a similar culture, dictated by the limits of their environment. They were hunters of small game and gatherers of roots, seeds, and berries, moving in small family groups from one subsistence area to another. In this chapter we will consider the diffusion of peyotism to these Indians as well as to one small group of Washo Indians who, although they form a distinct group with a language unrelated to any other, share the same culture.

THE GOSIUTE AND WESTERN SHOSHONE

Tribal headquarters for the Gosiute are at Ibapah and Grantsville in Utah. The Shoshone are located on several reservations and colonies throughout Nevada, sometimes sharing a reservation with the Northern Paiute. The Nevada Shoshone, with one exception, resisted peyotism; the Gosiute, on the other hand, developed a fairly strong church.

No Gosiute Shoshone, Nevada Shoshone, Northern Paiute, or Southern Paiute Indians were reported to be peyotists in 1917, at the time the Utah and Nevada state laws banning peyote were passed, and there were no Shoshone-speaking peyotists in Utah and Nevada in 1919, according to Newberne's report. Although there were doubtless a few Indians who had learned something of peyote through tribal visiting, it was not until 1929 that peyotism really came to the western Great Basin. Sam Lone Bear came to Ibapah that year and conducted peyote ceremonies for several weeks. That was after he had taken the Crow girl Julie to New Mexico, and he was again in trouble with the law. In January, 1927, a warrant had been

265

sworn out against him in Montana, and he was moving about to avoid being arrested. It is like him to have sought refuge and new opportunity in an out-of-the-way place like Ibapah.

In 1972, while on the Gosiute reservation, I had the good fortune to meet three Shoshone Indians who had participated in a peyote service led by Sam Lone Bear at Ibapah in 1929. Each, independently, gave the same data, without any suggestion from me. One was Ivy Black Bear, an elderly Shoshone roadman who said he had been with Sam among the Ute at White Rocks and then had come to Ibapah with Sam. In 1929 he had been chief drummer for Lone Bear when Lone Bear conducted a peyote service during which a little girl was cured. Black Bear described the curing ceremony:

Sam sent me to get four sticks of wild plum wood. He asked me to get a cup of water and then he put hot coals in his mouth. Flames came out of his mouth. He blew the flames on the child's chest and back. He prayed to have God cure her. She is still alive. He called me brother and told me not to try to put hot coals in my mouth until God taught me how to do it.

A few weeks later he had helped Lone Bear "get away in a hurry" when policemen came to Ibapah inquiring after Sam.

Another Indian who remembered the meeting when Sam Lone Bear cured the little girl was Lilly Pete, who had been my interpreter in 1937 and who remembered me well when I returned in 1972. We also discussed peyotism when I visited Ibapah in 1981. She had been only twelve in 1929 when Sam Lone Bear conducted that meeting, but she vividly recalled it. She said, "Lone Bear cured my cousin with peyote and blowing on her after putting hot coals in his mouth. That was when he was here in 1929. I saw it. She was real sick."

Finally, Ethel Moon, the girl's mother, confirmed that it was her daughter who had been cured by Sam Lone Bear at a peyote meeting in Ibapah in 1929.

Another who had attended Sam Lone Bear's peyote meetings at Ibapah was Grover Tom, a Shoshone from Owyhee who had spent most of his life among the Northern Paiutes at McDermit. I met him at a Paiute peyote meeting in 1972 at Fort McDermit, where he was roadman. After some discussion, he admitted that he was really a Shoshone and that during peyote meetings he prayed in Shoshone, although he knew Paiute very well, having lived at McDermit for twenty-three years. He said that in 1929 he was living at Ibapah with his relative, Frank Steele, when Sam Lone Bear arrived, and he had participated in meetings conducted there by Lone Bear.

The form of the ceremony introduced by Sam Lone Bear was, of course, the Cross Fire way, although it has been variously referred to by a number of ethnologists doing research with the Gosiute in Utah as "the old Ute way," "the Sioux way," "the Western Slope way," and even "the Sam

Lone Bear way." No ethnologist has reported participating in a Gosiute Cross Fire ritual, but several have commented on it, clearly depicting its basic characteristics. Alden Hayes (1940: 34) reported that it did not use tobacco, and Carling Malouf (1942: 99–100) said that the Cross Fire ritual "does not require a breakfast, the use of candy or tobacco, and the basic songs are different." Lilly Pete also confirmed that there is no smoking or ceremonial breakfast and added that Sam used a cloth altar.

The Cross Fire cult of Sam Lone Bear has persisted at Ibapah, and though he never returned after those few weeks in 1929, he is remembered there with unusual affection. Or perhaps it is the brevity of his visit which accounts for the respect amounting to reverence in which some people hold him. Lilly Pete is one of these. She said she only attends Cross Fire services. Her father-in-law, Johnny Pete, who claimed to be the first peyotist among the Gosiute, had traveled to the Uintah-Ouray Reservation in 1924 for the purpose of learning more about peyotism, and he had received help from Lone Bear. When Lone Bear had come to Ibapah in 1929, Johnny Pete had welcomed him and "put him up." Because of their close friendship, Lone Bear had entrusted his supply of herbs to Johnny Pete when, on short notice, Sam had had to flee from the law enforcement officers. In 1972, Lilly still had the sack of herbs and curing objects. Considering it an honor and responsibility, she permitted me to see the sack and to examine its contents. It contained no peyote; instead there were half a dozen regular drugs, packaged by Parke Davis and Co., such as chamomile flowers, prickly ash, phosphated iron, mullein leaves, and fourteen little cloth bundles of leaves, seeds, bark, roots, charcoal, minerals, and so on. In addition, there was a small china doll, which Lilly said was to help during childbirth. From the appearance of the sack of medicine, Lone Bear was as much a curing shaman as peyote proselytizer. Lilly said that we were viewing the contents of Lone Bear's bundle of medicine for only the second or third time since it had been entrusted to the Pete family. "He was going to come back to show us how to use the medicines, but Chief Annies Tommy threatened to have him arrested." Lilly was apparently unaware that federal officers had arrested Lone Bear and that he had served about two years in the McNeal Island Federal Prison at Steilacoom, Washington. Lilly claimed still to be caring for the sack of medicine when I visited with her in 1981.

Among the Shoshone of Nevada, Sam Lone Bear's influence is most strongly felt in the village of Lee, Nevada, where ranchland was purchased in the 1930s to establish the Te-moak Indian Reservation so that landless Shoshone from Ruby Valley and Elko could become ranchers if they wished to do so. One who moved into an old ranch house, maintained it, and became a successful rancher was Sam Long, whom I visited and interviewed in September, 1972, and in October, 1978. I had been directed to Sam Long by Shoshone Indians at Owyhee and at Elko when I asked peyotists where I might find Shoshone roadmen. I was given the address of Ethel Moon, a name I was already familiar with, but Ethel was too old, too feeble, and too deaf for much communication. However, she gave me the name of her brother, John Long, of Ruby Valley, who was an early believer and had been the person to take her and her sick daughter to Ibapah for the famous cure in 1929. More importantly, she said that her nephew, Sam Long, was carrying on the Sam Lone Bear way at Lee, Nevada.

Sam Long, or Sammy, as he signed his New Year's letter to me in December, 1972, has developed a ritual patterned after the Cross Fire ritual of Lone Bear, but it has been changed and augmented and in some respects simplified by him through supernatural instruction from peyote. Sam Long was seventeen when Lone Bear held his famous meeting in Ibapah, but he did not attend it and he never saw Lone Bear. He went to his first peyote meeting at Ibapah in 1934; there Jim Clover was the Tipi way roadman. From 1934 to 1937, Sam attended a number of Cross Fire meetings. In Ouray, Utah, John Tabby was the Cross Fire roadman; at Ibapah, the roadman was Frank Steele. Sam also attended some Tipi way rituals—one, for example, with Jim Humpy at Owyhee. By attending meetings regularly, he learned to be a roadman himself, and by 1937 he began to run Cross Fire rituals in Ruby Valley. Attendance was never large, but his father, John Long; his brother-in-law, Willie Tamoak; his aunt, Ethel Moon; and other family members supported him.

Since it is an article of faith of the peyote religion that peyote can teach all who partake of it, every peyotist should hold himself open to enlightenment during rituals. Most peyotists consider themselves instructed by a supernatural spirit—God, Jesus, peyote—during rituals. For most, the revelations are for personal improvement, but Sam Long, like John Wilson, felt that he received supernatural instruction to conduct peyote ceremonies in a different way.

His first requirement is to use a staff patterned after one which Lone Bear had given to Johnny Long, Sam's father, in 1929, when Lone Bear was at Ibapah. The original staff is kept by Sam Long in a soft buckskin sheath in a trunk, and I was told that I was one of the few people to be shown it. Even Sam seldom sees it and does not use it, having made a duplicate which is almost as sacred as the original. This staff is about a yard in length and an inch in diameter, rounded at one end and pointed, not sharply, at the other. The wood is soft and white like aspen or cottonwood, and about three inches from the rounded top a band of red paint encircles it. The space from the red band to the point is roughly divided into three sections, the center section being incised with four lightning symbols, about five inches long and a quarter inch deep, the incisions filled with red paint. Below the lightning is a series of angles pointing up, with open bases, which are similarly incised and filled with red paint. The impression is of a red and white staff.

Sam's altar cloth is a square yard of white cotton sheeting which he believes to be like that of Sam Lone Bear. For decoration he has been inspired to make a blue silk heart outlined with red, white, and blue glass beads. Embroidered across the heart in two lines, also in red, white, and blue beads, are the words "God Bless Our Heart." During the ritual, held in a living room of a dwelling, the leader sits at the west of the room; on the floor in front of him is the white cotton cloth upon which is placed the blue silk embroidered heart, and on the heart, the Chief Peyote. There is no fire or sand altar. Peyote is usually ground fine and mixed with water to make a "gravy." One button or one spoonful of peyote "gravy" is taken each round. A pitcher of fresh water accompanies the peyote so that each participant may take a drink of water after each time he or she consumes peyote.

One of the unusual innovations introduced into the ritual is Sam Long's rule to reverse the ceremonial direction. Everything is passed counterclockwise. But Sam has retained the ceremonial number four. Sam's drum, staff, feathers, and rattle are passed around the circle four times during a ritual. Participants sing four songs each time. With no smoking ceremony, no cedar incensing, no special midnight water ritual, or the like, such a peyote meeting might be greatly reduced in length.

Except when in use, ordinarily four or five times a year, the blue silk heart is stored flat in a red-satin-covered, heart-shaped valentine chocolate box of the same size and is carefully placed in a trunk with the staff and other paraphernalia. It will be brought out if a peyotist asks for a curing ritual or for a few holiday meetings. Generally, only a half dozen followers will be present.

It seems that Sam Long has indeed produced true variation in the peyote service, though it is doubtful that it will survive him. The group is too small and too isolated. The surprise is that Sam Lone Bear should be revered as teacher and guiding inspiration among a small group of Shoshone Indians off the main highway in the middle of Nevada.

The Tipi way ritual appears to have been received and accepted by the Gosiute soon after the Cross Fire was introduced and was performed at Ibapah as a competing ritual by 1934 (Malouf 1942: 93). By 1938, according to a letter to me from A. L. Robertson, a school teacher at Ibapah, out of a total Gosiute population of 158 adults, 87 were peyotists and 71 were non-peyotists. Of the peyotists, 59 followed the Tipi way and 28 followed the "Sioux" way. In 1972, both rituals still survived, and the Tipi way was still the most popular. This was true in 1981.

In spite of the success of peyotism among the Gosiute at Ibapah, there was at one time strong opposition to it. Antipeyote letters from Ibapah to the BIA started on October 25, 1937, when Thomas Mayo, a white man who had lived on the reservation for seventeen years, wrote on behalf of Indians friendly to him. He asked the commissioner to reply either to him or to Gosiute chief Annies Tommy. Although admitting "that they use this peyote in *Religious* form," Mayo asserted that peyote "ruins their lives . . . ruins the health of young people. . . . they use it to kill each other. . . . it is a poison. . . . Because they realize themselves that this peyote is doing away with Indians on this reservation, they had a meeting in regard to this."

Before the BIA could reply, Chief Annies Tommy sent to Dr. E. A. Farrow, superintendent of the Southern Paiute Agency at Cedar City, Utah, a resolution of the council of the Gosiute reservation stating similar objections to peyotism and declaring: "The council are trying to stop the use of this peyote." He also sent a similar letter to Commissioner Collier, adding: "We are notifying you the total amount of death of which are caused by peyote. The people that are died with it. There are 33 died with it. That is total amount and if there are any information ask about this total the council of tribe shall give it." Ten Gosiutes signed the letter with him.

Dr. Farrow replied to Annies Tommy:

I have your letter relative to the use of peyote. I will say that we have worried considerably about the use of peyote at Gosiute. This has been going on for a matter of about eight years and has been on the increase.

I am sorry to be obliged to tell you that there is no federal law that prevents the possession or use of it. The State of Utah makes it an offence to possess peyote, however, the Utah law does not prevail on an Indian reservation. I am sending a copy of your letter to the Commissioner and doubtless he will either write to me or to you about the matter. He will very likely give you his idea.

Some years ago a delegation visited me from Goshiute and asked me to take some action to prevent the use of peyote there. I submitted the matter to the Indian Office and was advised that there was no law under which we could operate.

You will understand that peyote-users use it for sacramental purposes in connection with their church and there is nothing that seems possible to do in the absence of a Federal Law, which would be difficult to obtain because of the fact that the constitution of the United States gives all people the right to worship God according to the dictates of their conscience. I know that this is not the thing that you would like to have me tell you and I am sorry that I can tell you nothing else. There is no means, at present, by which we can prevent the use of peyote.

Collier answered Annies Tommy by asking for more information. In his letter to Dr. Farrow, he asked: "Cannot you find out more about the realities of the situation and then write me . . . (1) what facts as to dead Indians; (2) how recent is peyote there, how being introduced, etc.; (3) is any outside influence being used on the petitioners?"

Before Superintendent Farrow could do the research necessary to answer Collier's questions, a new and mysterious organization entered the scene to the extent of providing a letterhead for Chief Annies Tommy. The letterhead was used January 7, 1938, by Chief Tommy to write to Commissioner Collier, but rather than sending it directly, it was first sent to Joseph Chez, attorney general of the state of Utah, to be typed and sent on to Collier, which Chez did, including the original. The letterhead was that of the "League of Nations of North American Indians," organized "To

Cooperate with the National Government for the Welfare of Indians within the United States and Canada." The council of eight chiefs included three from Canada—a Chippewa, a Micmac, and a Salteaux—and five from the United States: a Sioux from South Dakota; an Iroquois-Mohawk from Stillwater, Oklahoma; a Potawatomi and a Kickapoo from Kansas; and Annies Tommy from Ibapah, Utah. The chairman was Lawrence Two Axe (Iroquois-Mohawk) of Oakland, California.

In his letter, Chief Annies Tommy declared: "One year old child was killed by eating this peyote. . . . Died December 19, 1937. . . . Dr. Farrow told us make sure that the one die or anyone dies make sure that its kill by peyote. He don't help out anyone and I'm writing right straight to you John Collier." Attorney General Chez included a note to Collier: "I suggest that you have the Indian Superintendent, Dr. Farrow of Cedar City, take up this complaint and take diligent steps to protect the Indians from peyote . . . from being subject to its dire consequences." To Chez's note Collier replied: "From what I know of the physiological reactions of peyote, I should be entirely surprized to learn that it had killed anybody. Indeed, such an item would be of great scientific interest."

By January 25, 1938, Dr. Farrow was able to answer Collier's questions:

Replying to your letter . . . relative to the matter of use of peyote on the Goshiute Reservation, I will say that I have talked the matter over with the Goshiutes who are anti-peyote and they expressed the opinion that something will have to be done to stop its use.

Study of the death reports tells us very little. Since the more or less extensive use of peyote covers about six years, we have compared it with a corresponding death record of six years previous. There is nothing in the record that shows an increase in the death rate in one period over another. There have, however, been fluctuations that could be accounted for otherwise.

As to the source of supply I am told that the article is brought in by the Indians themselves. A few years ago a report was made . . . that it came in by registered mail from some place in Oklahoma. I know that in recent years there have been more visits to Oklahoma than formerly.

There is no evidence that outside influence has been active either for or against its use by the Indians, unless we take into consideration frequent visits by other Indians who seem to promote its use.

From the great volume of literature on this subject we draw the conclusion that real evidence of the physiological affect of peyote is lacking. . . .

I asked Annies Tommy to prepare a list of the people believed by him to have died as a result of the use of peyote and in each case to give me the reasons for his belief. So far he has not made the list available. We believe that something more than half of the Gosiutes are users of peyote.

This seems to have ended the controversy at Ibapah, at least for the time being, but similar outcries took place on other reservations, particularly where the majority of Indians were Shoshone. Except for Sam Long's small congregation at Lee, no Nevada Shoshone band accepted peyotism.

A few Shoshone individuals joined Northern Paiute, Washo, or Gosiute meetings, but the Nevada Shoshone remained indifferent, if not downright hostile, to peyotism. In the late thirties on the Owyhee Reservation, which was shared by Shoshone and Northern Paiute, with Shoshone in the majority, there existed an enthusiastic Northern Paiute peyote church, much opposed by the Shoshone residents. When I visited Owyhee in 1972, I found no Shoshone peyotist.

One Shoshone reservation I visited in 1972 was Yomba on the Reese River, at the end of the road forty miles south of Austin. In 1964 an ethnographic study was made at Yomba by Michael D. Lieber, a graduate student at the University of Pittsburgh, who wrote that the Yomba Shoshone made "fundamental assumptions about the nature of peyote . . . [and] interpreted it in terms of the more traditional concept of supernatural power. By taking peyote, one acquires the power of the rattlesnake. . . . Opposition is based fundamentally on traditional concepts of native medicine and myth. . . ." I was curious about such a group. When I visited Yomba on a Sunday afternoon, I asked for the leader whose name I had learned from Fallon Shoshone. It required only five minutes for him to assure me there was no peyotism to be found at Yomba and there was no interest in it whatsoever.

What can be said of the diffusion of peyote generally can be said of its presence among the Gosiute and the Shoshone. Where it was accepted, it was a curing ceremony, spread by missionaries such as Lone Bear and by visiting among tribes. Clifford Jake (Southern Paiute), Gilbert Jack (Bannock), Franklin Mack (Washo), and Grover Tom (Shoshone–Northern Paiute) were some of the visiting roadmen. Ben Lancaster (Washo) visited Ibapah often and helped supply the Gosiute with peyote. Peyotists were often exceptional Indians with more than average education and ability. It was a minority religion, sometimes strongly opposed, and peyotists participated in other religions.

The Mormon church has proselytized the Gosiute since the days of the Pony Express, when a relay station and farm were established on Gosiute land. Church records indicate that the Indians there were all baptized into the Mormon church at least once and probably several times, because baptizing times were gift-giving times. As of 1972, most Gosiute were on the rolls of the Mormon church, but few were active. Only Bob Steele was singled out as a devout Mormon and active peyotist. At the Ibapah trading post operated by white Mormons I provoked a strong antipeyote lecture by saying I was interested in the study of the peyote religion. Notwithstanding the Mormon antipeyote bias, in 1972 the son of Lilly Pete, a peyotist, was a senior at the Brigham Young University School of Education, and when he graduated, he hoped to get a job teaching Indians.

THE WASHO AND NORTHERN PAIUTE

In western Nevada along the California-Nevada border at Lake Tahoe and into California, in the foothills of the Sierras, live the Washo Indians. In the same vicinity are a number of bands of Northern Paiute whose reservations extend northward and eastward into Idaho and Oregon as well as into California. Like the Shoshone and the Gosiute, they were hunters of small game and gatherers of seeds, roots, and berries, traveling in small groups from one subsistence area to another yet having a well-recognized home territory. Today, the Washo occupy several villages south of Carson City, official headquarters for the Indian Service in Nevada—Minden and Gardnerville in Nevada and Woodfords and Coleville in California, to name the most important. The Northern Paiute are more numerous and scattered. Some live near the Washo at Reno and Carson City and in small towns nearby. Other groups live south in Owens Valley, California, and northeast along the Nevada-Idaho border at Owyhee and along the Nevada-Oregon border at McDermit and farther north into Oregon and California. Both groups learned about peyote at about the same time, but independently, in the 1930s.

As has been noted, there seems to have been no knowledge of peyote among the Indians of Nevada in 1917 when the law prohibiting peyote was passed, nor was there knowledge of peyote in 1919, according to Newberne (1922). Although a few Washo–Northern Paiute Indians may have become acquainted with it where it was practiced elsewhere, it seems to have been introduced to them first at Fallon, Nevada, in 1929 by none other than Sam Lone Bear, calling himself "Leo Okio" undoubtedly to confound the law. He probably arrived in Fallon shortly after his hurried leave-taking from Ibapah.

In 1938, in Reno doing field work for my doctoral dissertation on Washo–Northern Paiute peyotism, Joe Green, a Northern Paiute shaman, described Leo Okio's meetings (Stewart, 1956b):

Peyote first came in the fall of 1929. That time a man that I did not know came and stayed with me. He said that he was a doctor and that his name was Leo Okio. After he had been at my place [in Nixon] for a week or so, he saw a woman, my aunt, Annie Davis, who had been paralyzed for four years and who received no help from other Indian doctors or white doctors. He said he thought he could help her, but that it would cost $8.00, and that he would need $4.00 before the treatment so that he could get medicine. . . . He sang, prayed, and gave her medicine two nights a week. At the 7th meeting he told her to walk around the fire with someone helping her. At the 8th she walked around the fire seven times, and at the 9th he told her to walk to the store to get fruit and food, for that would be the last meeting. She has walked since then. The next one he doctored was Willie Hardin who was at Nixon, although he belonged at McDermit, and was dying. . . . Leo made a ball of chewed peyote and gave it to Willie. . . . Then Leo sucked out the disease and Willie got well right away. . . . After that, all the sick people wanted Leo to doctor them and we held meetings all over for three months. I drummed for him and went everywhere with him. I ate a lot of peyote at every meeting and what I saw, the people it cured, made me decide that peyote is a good medicine. At some of the meetings Leo took in a lot of money.

Summarizing my 1938 data, I wrote (1944: 69):

More than a dozen Indians described the 1929 meetings, several as eyewitnesses. The ritual differed in several particulars from the present Washo-Paiute cult, resembling what is known in the Great Basin as the "old Sioux way." As many as seventy Indians attended Leo's meetings, some coming from as far away as Bishop, California, and McDermit, Nevada. Although a number of converts were made, peyotism completely ceased as an active force when Leo Okio left.

In 1938, I did not know that Leo Okio, or as he was sometimes called, "Old Coyote," was really Sam Lone Bear, or "Sam Roan Bear," as I had interpreted the name when it was given me by my 1936 and 1938 informants, nor did I know the history of Sam Lone Bear. It is clear now why such a successful missionary and shaman should suddenly arrive and as suddenly disappear; he was always in trouble with the law. The federal officers finally did catch up with him in 1933 and imprisoned him in a federal prison in the state of Washington. The difference in his ceremony and the 1938 ceremony I observed at Mono Lake was the difference between the Cross Fire and the Tipi way ceremonies, and his success indicated that the old Sam Lone Bear charm was undiminished. After two years in prison, he returned to Fallon a changed man, for there is no evidence that he conducted any peyote ceremonies after his release. He did "marry" again, to Mamie Charley of Fallon, and he took her to South Dakota, where they lived in an abandoned shack on his allotment on the Pine Ridge Sioux Reservation and where a daughter, Ruth May Lone Bear, was born to them in January, 1936. He found little to do in South Dakota, and times were hard. Jim Bluebird, employed at the time by the BIA to distribute food and other supplies to destitute Indians, regularly brought food to Lone Bear's poor dwelling. During the winter of 1936–37, Lone Bear became sick, perhaps with pneumonia, but did not go to the hospital. Rather, he asked for a peyote meeting at his place, and Bluebird, with other Cross Fire peyotists, conducted a service for him. It was no use, and Sam Lone Bear died at age fifty-eight.

Ralph Kochampanaskin (also known as Raymond Lone Bear) was the second missionary to hold meetings in the western Great Basin. A Uintah Ute, he had learned of peyote at Pine Ridge, South Dakota, in 1913. Before marrying a Washo girl and settling with her tribe (where I met him in 1938), he had attended peyote meetings in Wyoming, Montana, Colorado, New Mexico, and with both the Ute and Gosiute in Utah. He came to Nevada in 1932 and was befriended by Sam Dick, a Washo shaman at Minden. Soon he started "Sioux way" meetings and also doctored as an old-time shaman, much as Sam Lone Bear had done among the Paiute and Shoshone of Fallon. Successful with both techniques, for a few months he collected from fifteen to sixty dollars for a single treatment. Nearly all the Washo in the vicinity attended his meetings. Sam Dick learned the peyote songs and made a kettledrum, acting as drummer during the rituals. Eventually, Ralph failed because he could not live up to the ideals he was preaching. He became drunk several times and was jailed.

A third and most important missionary, Ben Lancaster, also called Chief Grey Horse, arrived among the Washo in 1936. He was born about 1880 near Mountain House, Nevada, an old stagecoach station about fifteen miles south of Gardnerville, almost on the Nevada-California state line and, incidentally, almost on the boundary between Washo and Northern Paiute territory. His mother was Washo and his father a white man. He seems to have had no more than one year of formal schooling, but he became fluent in English, Washo, and Northern Paiute, three completely different languages belonging to three unrelated linguistic families. Ben said, "I was raised by the German people near Gardnerville, Nevada."

In 1938, I interviewed Ben at length. During his youth he was a ranch hand. Fair enough to pass for a white man, he deserted his Indian friends and ranch jobs to become "the best bartender in Nevada" and a professional gambler. From Reno he went to San Francisco to "work on the water front." While in that city, he learned to cook opium in a Chinatown den on Dupont Street, and later worked nearby in a "planing mill at the foot of Broadway in Oakland." After mining or prospecting "in every mineral district in Nevada," he caught an eastbound freight train in 1916. He worked in Bingham Canyon, Utah, and during the war, in the Black Hills of South Dakota. Working for Armour and Company in Omaha, "busting bronchos" near Red Rock, Oklahoma (1919), and bootlegging whiskey in Hot Springs, Arkansas, were a few more of Ben's experiences before 1921, when he got a job as a farmhand near Clinton, Oklahoma, and attended a Cheyenne peyote meeting. It was then that he learned the peyote ritual.

Details about Ben's introduction to peyote among the Southern Cheyenne have come to me from the Cheyenne themselves. In 1973, Truman Daily (Oto) of Red Rock, Oklahoma, told me that Ben Lancaster had worked as a cowboy for his father, George Daily, and had attended peyote meetings with his family. Truman said his father had a lot of Cheyenne Indian friends, and the Cheyenne came to Red Rock annually for a big powwow. During one of these visits Ben met a Cheyenne woman he liked, and he decided to come to Clinton, where he married her. Ben became a peyote roadman among the Cheyenne. Truman said, "He got his fire-place from the Cheyenne." Ben was about twenty years older than Truman and impressed him as a sophisticated and able cowhand.

Ben's participation in peyote meetings with the Southern Cheyenne was confirmed by Mack Haag, one-time president of the NAC, in a letter dated December 3, 1938: "You asked me if I knew Ben Lancaster or Gray Horse—Yes—and that if he was a member of the Native American Church—Yes—and if I have seen him in Peyote meetings—Yes. Many times. But I did not know he started peyote meetings in Nevada. However, he is well-qualified man to do that." When I asked Ben for some names of Southern Cheyenne peyote leaders whom he knew, he named Mack Haag, Alfred Wilson, and John P. Heart.

Others knew Ben as a seller of herbs or medicine in Oklahoma. Shortly after he settled in Clinton, he began "traveling for a medicine company," and for the next ten years, letting his hair grow and sporting a fancy feather headdress and beaded buckskin clothes, he trekked throughout the United States selling "Chief Gray Horse's Indian Herbs, a natural laxative." Although he claimed he advertised the medicine for Baker Chemical Company, Cincinnati, and sold it only to stores, he is known widely in Oklahoma as an herb-medicine salesman. He sold his few remaining boxes of medicine to his Nevada converts to peyotism at the regular price of one dollar. The package contained an ounce or two of dry, ground "cascara, mandrake, polk root, gentian, uva ursi, licorice, wild cherry, senna, and other herbs," a medicine "strictly botanical," prepared by "Chief Gray Horse Remedy Company, Cincinnati, Ohio."

Although he traveled widely, he returned to Oklahoma to spend Christmases with the Cheyenne, and in 1930 when John Wright, a Northern Paiute from Fallon, met him there, Ben confided his intent to take peyote to Nevada. Still, he did not do so until October, 1936, when he arrived at the home of his "aunt," Susie Dick, and his "cousin," Sam Dick, in Minden, Nevada. Sam, not unfamiliar with peyote, having learned a good deal from Ralph Kochampanaskin, became Ben's first convert. The second was Mary Creek, a Northern paiute from the Walker Lake Reservation at Schurz, Nevada, who was twenty years younger than Ben and who married him in Indian fashion and provided a home for him at Schurz.

During the first six months Ben was in western Nevada, he held peyote meetings in six Indian communities: Gardnerville (Washo); Coleville, California (Washo-Paiute); Fallon (Shoshone-Paiute); Schurz (Paiute); Wellington (Paiute); and Yerington (Paiute). Almost a hundred miles separated Fallon from Coleville, with Schurz about midway between. Although it was the time of the Great Depression, Ben received enough in free-will offerings at the end of each meeting to purchase a new Ford V-8 to take him to Texas in February, 1937. Returning from Texas in late April with a large supply of dried peyote, Ben continued to hold meetings in Washo and Paiute communities. In Woodfords, California, and in Carson City, Nevada, Washo requested meetings. At Bridgeport, California, it was a Miwok who had lived in the Paiute community for years who sponsored a peyote ritual there.

After a successful second season, in December, 1937, Ben again left his wife Mary with his aunt, Susie Dick, and traveled to Oilton, Texas, where he had a white wife, Sylvia Gray Horse, who ran a restaurant. A Washo devotee who hitchiked to Oilton to assist him in the peyote harvest confirmed in Nevada the rumor of Ben's Texas wife. When he returned to Nevada in the spring, Ben left wife Mary, but soon he had married Shoshone Louise Byers of Fallon, who took the precaution of going with Ben whenever he went to Texas for a supply of peyote. In the 1940s he established himself with Louise in the Paiute-Washo colony at Coleville, where a wooden church was constructed, following the model of the octagonal wooden peyote churches of the Osage.

From the time of his arrival in western Nevada, Ben promoted attention to himself and to peyotism. In Schurz, in November, 1937, at a general meeting called to allow Commissioner John Collier to address the Indians, Ben drew from the commissioner information favorable to peyote. Collier admitted that his son had attended a peyote meeting in Oklahoma and that he had strongly opposed the Chavez bill earlier that year that would have outlawed nationally possession of peyote. After that, Ben was invited to speak before the Minden Rotary Club and was permitted to prepare a peyote exhibit at the Carson Valley Day Fair.

As might be expected, the attention he received did not always produce favorable reactions. By January, 1937, Superintendent Alida C. Bowler of the Carson Indian Agency wrote to Collier concerning peyote:

It has been introduced by Ben Lancaster, Washoe Indian, who, according to reports, left this region with a circus a good many years ago. Eventually he landed in Oklahoma where he remained and presumably became familiar with peyote there. If Ben Lancaster were a different kind of person, I should not feel any particular concern about the situation. However, my contacts with him and my knowledge of his actions convince me that his use of peyote is not that of the sincere religious devotee. It has earmarks of a profitable "racket." Moreover, I very much fear that he may be mixing certain other drugs with it in order to obtain other effects. For example, confidential reports from people who have attended the meetings seem to indicate that some of the potions given to women contain a sexual excitant of some character which is exactly the opposite to the effect of peyote alone.

Miss Bowler asked for more information on peyote and was sent "Documents on Peyote," which the BIA had submitted to Congress on May 18, 1937, to counteract the Chavez bill. The documents contained the testimony of eight anthropologists, a botanist, and an Osage Indian chief.

In June, 1937, at the request of Miss Bowler, Ben's car was searched at the California Quarantine Station by officers of the California State Highway Patrol and in Nevada by BIA special officers. Jars of a "white powder" and a "brown fluffy powdery substance" were taken and analyzed. The local chemists reported something like morphine, but were not sure. In July a special narcotics agent who had worked in Oklahoma and "who knew the real peyote" arrived to help get evidence on Ben. Miss Bowler wrote Collier:

We have been having a number of deaths of persons whom Ben has "doctored," the Indians believing that he is using peyote only. . . I hope that we are going to be able to build a strong case against this man and send him up where he can do no harm for a long time to come. It would appear that his trail should be followed back to Oklahoma where there may be a ring of drug peddlers operating among Indians under the guise of genuine peyote cultists.

The agent from the narcotics bureau was withdrawn when a sample of the brown powder analyzed in Washington, D.C., proved not to be narcotic. Miss Bowler persisted and received an independent analysis from chemists in San Francisco who reported that the brown powder was peyote ground to a fine powder, which, being made of alkaloids, had produced a reaction like that to morphine, but more complete tests "gave results indicating the absence of morphine." Notwithstanding the above, Bowler wrote to Collier: "This report, therefore, shows that we do not yet have a case on the suspect. It in no way convinces us that a case cannot be made. All that it means is that the particular substances we seized did not contain prohibited drugs." And she obtained the services of another BIA special officer and the cooperation of the sheriff of Alpine County to help track down "suspicious clues." She wrote again to Collier:

I feel that it is . . . important to the Indians and to you and your administration that any persons using the peyote religious cult to distribute dangerous narcotics should be exposed and that this case therefore, becomes one of considerable significance. . . . Please do *not* take the matter up with the Federal Narcotics Bureau. They proved entirely useless and might hamper rather than help matters here.

Ben's absences in order to harvest peyote in Texas added to Miss Bowler's suspicions. In December, 1937, she wrote Collier:

Ben Lancaster left Nevada and we have as yet been unable to ascertain where he went or when he is likely to return. My personal opinion is that he will not return until his racket can be more profitable than it would be during the winter months, his profits here come from seasonal agricultural earnings of the Indians.

Although Superintendent Bowler's searches were an irritant to Lancaster, he appeared to ignore them and continued to gain followers. He had started with his "cousin" Sam Dick, whom he had taught to be his assistant and understudy. However, within a couple of years he rejected Sam, probably because he did not want competition if it could be avoided. The same selfishness appears to have motivated the rejection and slander of Ute Ralph Kochampanaskin, Paiute John Wright Harrington, and Gosiute-Shoshone Pat Eagle, all roadmen who made gestures of cooperation but were denied even admittance to Ben's meetings.

Ben emphasized the importance of peyote and the peyote ritual as a means of curing every kind of illness, and most converts cited the cures produced by peyote to justify their initial interest and continued support. Others found in it a conversion in the conventional sense—a recognition of sin, repentance, faith, and a desire for a new and better way of life. Ben was at the height of his popularity when I came to Nevada to study the acculturation of the peyote religion among the Washo and Northern Paiute. After attending a couple of Ben's meetings, I noted that the peyote ceremony was primarily a curing ceremony, but a few adherents joined because it was a satisfying way to worship "the one true God," even though they were active in Protestant churches. All considered peyote a great teacher, and three had received new peyote songs. Visions were merely a part of the religious aspects of the rituals. Some adherents felt that peyote protected them from witchcraft, and some carried Chief Peyote as fetishes.

Only a few Indians opposed peyotism on religious grounds, and they stressed other reasons. Some of the opposition said that peyotism was not really a religion at all; others accused Ben of praying, quoting the Bible, and making moral speeches only to attract Indians to be robbed or raped. Some said that peyote kills. (Those allegedly killed by peyote demonstrably suffered from disease or senility which might at any moment have brought death, and it was so noted in official reports.) Some arguments both for as well as against peyote were based on economic grounds. A few considered a peyote meeting cheaper than, yet equal to, a shamanistic treatment for which a price, from $2.50 to $3.00, was fixed and to be paid in advance.

The peyote ritual changed very little in western Nevada. Perhaps the most unusual feature was the position accorded to women: they led the singing while holding the staff and rattle, beat the drum, and sometimes acted as chief drummers. Ben's ritual also lacked the morning water call. Whistle blowing was omitted. A most surprising feature was dancing. At one meeting the members danced a few times around the Half Moon altar following the ritual and the morning recess. Any changes in the ritual must be attributed to Ben, who undoubtedly made them in the interest of expediency and to maintain complete control for his financial benefit.

Other anthropologists have studied the Washo–Northern Paiute peyote religion. Edgar E. Siskin (1941) spent the summers of 1937, 1938, and 1939 among the Washo. Of interest is his statement: "Peyote . . . arousing great enthusiasm at the outset and giving promise of gaining wide support, it yet failed to become entrenched and was ultimately expelled from Washo territory." Alan P. Merriam and Warren L. d'Azevedo (1957:615) expressed a similar opinion:

In 1936 [Ben Lancaster] . . . started the proselyting which resulted in the creation of an enthusiastic group of Washo and Paiute adherents during the period 1936–39. By 1940, however, the movement had already become defunct, and meetings were no longer held in Washo territory. Ben Lancaster continued to preside over the embittered and secretive remnants of the cult, which consisted of a handful of loyal Paiute and a very few Washo members.

The word *defunct* seems extreme. Because of active duty in World War II following a year of postdoctoral study in eastern universities and at Zuni, my contact with Washo-Paiute peyotism after November, 1938, was limited to letters. These indicated that peyotism had not completely died out among the Washo or Paiute in western Nevada. Ute Ralph Kochampanaskin, although inactive in 1938, wrote me in February and May, 1939, and again in January, 1942, that he was conducting peyote ceremonies on a limited scale. Sam Dick wrote me in March and April, 1942, asking my help in getting peyote by mail from Laredo. In 1944, Grace M. Dangberg, California ethnologist and folklorist of the Washo, on whose family estate at Minden Sam Dick lived most of his life (his mother was a longtime maid in the Dangberg household), wrote me after receiving a copy of my published thesis:

Washo and Northern Paiute Peyotism is a delightful piece of work and tells a story about our Indians here which is, as far as any of us can discover, true in every detail. . . . Sam Dick continues to be the person you knew. He holds his meetings regularly and his sincerity is not to be questioned. Through his mother, Susie, I learned that he is placing more and more emphasis on living according to the rules of Christianity. For example, he insists that Susie observe the Sabbath by not working.

In 1949, Grace Dangberg again wrote: "Sam Dick still continues his work here with spiritual and moral success." Other information about Sam Dick came from informant recall when I visited the area in 1972. Ramsey Walker, then leader of Washo peyotism, who lived and conducted services at Woodfords, told me that Sam Dick "always held meetings" and that he had made trips to Laredo to obtain peyote. Sam had attended his, Ramsey's, meetings at Woodfords and had at other times served as roadman himself. I was also told Sam had led a meeting at Carson City probably in 1966. In 1974, in Cedar City, Utah, Mrs. Clifford Jake (Southern Paiute) remembered being in a peyote meeting at Woodfords when Sam Dick was carried in on a blanket. She thought the year was 1964, and she had heard that Sam died some months after that.

Ben Lancaster, too, continued to hold peyote meetings in the forties, although his lack of cooperation with other leaders and his acquisitiveness must have damped the enthusiasm of many and caused a falling off. He had other problems, too. In May, 1940, he was questioned by District Attorney E. E. Winters at a coroner's inquest into the death of a thirteen-year-old Indian girl who had died after attending a peyote meeting conducted by Ben near Fallon. The verdict was death from tuberculosis, as it had been after two other inquests a few months before. The headline, "Girl Died After Peyote Meeting" in the *Reno Evening Gazette* may have contributed to the

FIG. 17. A peyote meeting in Nevada, Mono Lake, California, 1938. Sam Dick, third from left, is the roadman. Photograph by author.

action in February, 1941, by the Nevada State Legislature to restore peyote as a prohibited substance, the antipeyote legislation of 1917 having somehow disappeared from the Nevada statutes. The new law, which simply added "peyote" to the law prohibiting certain poisons, was soon put to use, and in October 23, 1941, the *Nevada State Journal* reported that Ben Lancaster had been arrested:

Lancaster was charged with possession of Peyote, a cactus which grows near the Mexican border. . . . [He] had in his possession two or three pounds of peyote. . . . [He] told them he made a trip south each year to collect the cactus. . . . [He] gave his occupation as preacher, prospector, and miner. He lives in Coleville, California.

The report of the preliminary hearing provides further description of the case (*Nevada State Journal*):

Ben Lancaster . . . admitted exponent of peyotism, ancient religion of the Aztecs, yesterday was held for district court trial in the first prosecution of its kind in Nevada. Justice of Peace Harry Dunseath at a preliminary hearing ruled that Lancaster, 66-year-old Coleville, Cal., Indian, must be tried on charges of possession of peyote, a little brown button which grows on a species of cactus on the Mexican border. A law enacted by the 1941 legislature classes peyote as a poisonous drug. Lancaster was released on $250 bail. The charge is a gross misdemeanor. Conviction carries a maximum of $1000 fine or a year in prison. Lancaster, appearing in court in a cowboy hat, long hair falling in two braids bound with red twine over his shoulders, did not testify on his behalf. . . . Floyd O. Burnett, regional president of the Nevada-California-Utah National Fellowship of Indian Workers and Indian Missionaries . . . declared he had affidavits from Indians to show that Lancaster conducts three-day peyote "parties" at Fallon in an old brick building.

The U.S. Indian Service, in a booklet, has declared peyote not habit-forming. The Navajos of Arizona and the Schurz Indians of Nevada have voted in tribal council to ban peyote, which is not controlled by federal narcotic laws. Dr. Charles L. Tranter, Reno physician, also testified.

It is necessary to say something about Dr. Tranter, neurologist, who had been for some time, and continued to be, an opponent of peyotism and of John Collier. His interest, if not his antipathy, probably began in 1935 when he attempted to establish an Indian Botanical Institute in connection with the Carson Indian School at Stewart, Nevada. He gained the support of Alida Bowler, agency superintendent, who became secretary of the board of which Tranter was chairman. Commissioner Collier was asked to lead the forces in Washington to obtain $200,000 of federal funds to build offices, library, laboratories, green houses, and animal houses and to establish forty acres of gardens on which Indian medicinal plants would be grown for testing. A University of Nevada botanist was also a collaborator, and he received a small grant to collect Indian medicinal plants in Nevada and published the results of his research, but the grandiose plan of Dr. Tranter produced nothing.

Collier did not cooperate to get the backing in Washington to fund the institute, and in 1939 Bowler resigned her office of superintendent of the Carson Agency. Tranter took out his frustration on Ben Lancaster and the peyotists, who had an evil reputation with him as with Bowler. Using Ben Lancaster's arrest to inform the world of the evils of peyote and the inadequacy of Collier as commissioner, he sent a special article to the *New York News,* which appeared in the Sunday edition, November 30, 1941. A photograph of Ben was explained by a headline, "Ex-Bartender High Priest. Ben Lancaster, Paiute, heads cult employing peyote in rituals. Group crusading against narcotic has caused Ben's arrest under Nevada statute against Peyote." There was a smaller picture of "Crusaders—Dr. Charles Lee Tranter, neurologist, and Malcolm Esterlin, attorney, who are leading movement to outlaw use of peyote, 'Sacred Mushroom of the Aztecs,' among Indians of the West, asserting addiction is spreading."

The article contained antipeyote literature from the BIA files from 1916 onward but concentrated on Ben and the new menace of peyote in Nevada. It was written as sensationally as possible:

Some authorities estimate that a quarter of the Indians in the State have been reduced to a trance-like condition by habitual use of the peyote buttons; others that 50% of them have been rendered incapable of working steadily for a living. . . . [Ben Lancaster] vanished from Nevada, turned up again in this section four years ago, this time as the high priest of a cult centering . . . around the use of peyote. He established a secluded headquarters near Coleville, California, under the towering peaks of the Sierra Nevada. . . . From this refuge, where he conducted his church, he would emerge from time to time to gather adherents from the poverty-stricken Indians living in squalor and hopelessness. . . . While he was gathering a congregation around him, the whites were observing with more and more alarm the growing use of peyote. Chief among these were Dr. Charles Lee Tranter, neurologist and brain specialist, who heads the Association for Prevention of Peyotism, and Malcolm Esterlin, New York and Washington attorney. . . . Lancaster's arrest came at the end of a long investigation. . . . The prosecution seems to be aimed not only at Ben Lancaster, but at Indian Commissioner John Collier, who does not view the use of peyote with much alarm. . . . When he was told about Ben Lancaster's trouble, Collier said, "I have been wondering what Lancaster was doing out there." He may get a chance to find out when the anti-peyotists start testifying at Ben's trial.

After the *New York News* article, one by Malcolm Esterlin appeared in Scribner's *Commentator* (1941: 77–82) which portrayed Collier as the worst possible commissioner of Indian affairs for his policy of protecting "native religion." As for Ben Lancaster, "He started by giving away peyote to those suffering from disease, then he began to arrange the so-called 're- ligious' meetings as an excuse to use it. He now has a number of assistants, calls meetings whenever his pocket-book gets low, and states openly that the Indian Service is behind him. . . ."

In spite of all the publicity, Ben's trouble with the law was soon over. On November 21, 1941, his attorney, Emerson J. Wilson, filed a demurrer contending that the 1941 legislative act under which the charge was brought was faulty in that it was an attempt to amend a repealed and nonexisting former act. The demurrer was argued on November 28, and on March 17, 1942, the judge sustained the demurrer and ordered the charge against Lancaster dismissed and his bondmen released. The *Washington Daily News* of March 19 published a dispatch from Reno with the two-column headline, "Pale Face Judge Frees Indian Whoopee Chief!" The article stated: "Chief Greyhorse went back to his friends today to lead the ceremonials enlivened by a concoction brewed from 'the sacred mushrooms of the Aztecs.'" Actually, Lancaster left for Texas to obtain peyote immediately as soon as his case was dismissed. I received a letter from his former collaborator, Sam Dick, in April, which said: "Gray Horse came back from Texas bringing lots of peyote but he didn't give me some. He never comes to my house. I don't know what is the matter. All those folks said hello to you."

Tranter and Esterlin continued their fight against peyote and Collier for a few years and were joined by others, including Reverend G. Elmer E. Lindquist, then corresponding secretary of the National Fellowship of Indian Workers. Tranter's articles appeared in a variety of media from *PIC*, with photographs showing "Indian Sleeping Off Effects of Peyote Debauch" and "House . . . [where] Several Persons Died after Peyote Orgy" to the *Journal of Nervous and Mental Disease* (May, 1943). The latter was written in collaboration with Walter Bromberg, M.D. Dr. Bromberg also published an article against peyote in *Nature Magazine* (October, 1942). Even though published in scholarly journals, Tranter and Bromberg had no new data or insights to contribute. In a meeting of the House of Representatives Committee on Indian Affairs in December, 1944, Congresswoman Frances Bolton of Ohio proposed a federal law to prohibit the use of peyote and cited Dr. Tranter as her principal source of information to justify such a prohibition. The proposal came to nothing, and after that Dr. Tranter seems to have dropped his campaign against Nevada peyotism.

Collier paid little attention to the fuss in Nevada. He did write to his new superintendent at the Carson Agency, Don C. Foster, for information about Tranter, and Foster obliged by sending him the *PIC* article written by Tranter, with the comment:

One of the most interesting things in this article to me is the two old women who are shown here. These old women do not even use peyote. They are both related to Dewey Sampson, an Indian living on Reno-Sparks Colony. As you may know, Sampson is the fellow that continually writes everybody in the Federal Government, from the President on down about Indian affairs in general. We are having plenty of difficulty with Sampson. He gets the old age pension checks for these two old women who are relatives of his. The old women do not get full benefit of the checks, yet they will not make a complaint because they are afraid of Sampson. On the other hand, the pension people refuse to make a move unless the old women make complaint. I am merely giving you this little side-light as to the type of man Sampson is, as he is working hand-in-hand with Dr. Tranter. . . . I would like to talk to you about some of these situations, particularly this Dr. Tranter and his fealty rantings.

Anthropologist Warren d'Azevedo of the University of Nevada at Reno has studied the Washo in depth. In the summer of 1954 he attended a Washo peyote meeting and wrote me at length about the changes which had occurred since 1938. As was to be expected, Washoes and Paiutes were attending peyote meetings with other tribes. In April, 1954, six had attended a regular NAC ritual at Fort Hall. Beginning about 1940, Washo Roy James had gone to Fort Hall to learn the "real tipi way" and had returned to lead meetings in competition to those conducted in Coleville. d'Azevedo made a comparison of the Washo ritual of 1954 and found it differed from the one I had described in 1938, moving toward the more traditional rituals of Oklahoma tribes. Of the 111 individuals I had named in 1938 to be active peyotists, 36 were still active in 1954, but there were 34 new names making a total of 70 peyotists in 1954.

Ben Lancaster died in 1953, but his widow, Louise, continued to be an active peyotist. On January 18, 1954, she sent the following letter to Allen Dale of Vinita, Oklahoma:

There was a letter received by Harry Sam last week, stating that you are confronted with situation that calls for all of our members to respond to a cause that requires a great amount of money. We here at our church would very much like to know if that is so. . . . We are willing to do that for our church. We realize and know what the peyote has done for each and all of us. You see, we lost our beloved leader here not very long ago. He was well known. . . . His name was "Ben Lancaster" also known as "Chief Gray Horse." . . . Jim Summers . . . operates the meetings for us . . . and we will act soon as possible to get the money to you the best we know how.

When the first issue of the *Quarterly Bulletin of the Native American Church* was published that year, the financial report showed a contribution of one hundred dollars from Louise Lancaster, Coleville, California.

In 1955, d'Azevedo wrote Slotkin a summary of the state of peyotism among the Washo and Northern Paiute:

There are six roadchiefs in the Washo area and three active groups. As you perhaps know, all of these groups stem from the original meetings established by Ben Lancaster some twenty years ago, and described by Omer Stewart (1944). . . . Before Ben Lancaster's death two years ago two groups had already split off from his rather dominating handling of Church matters, and a number of younger men, formerly members of his group, began to conduct meetings of their own. Among these were Harry Sam, Roy James, and Ramsey Walker. All members of the Church continued to respect Lancaster as the man who had brought the knowledge of Peyote to this area, but many could not get along with him. . . . After Lancaster's death, Jimmy Summers carried on the work of his group and maintained his way. In the meantime, the group in Woodfords had grown considerably and most of the Washo church members began to attend those meetings. . . . The largest, most active, and growing group in the area is the one at Woodfords. The Paiute members of the Church have tended to stay with Jimmy Summers in Coleville, California. For many years Harry Sam has been holding meetings for a few people in Woodfords, but recently he has joined forces with Streeter Dick . . . and they are now conducting meetings in Coleville. . . . Despite these problems which have tended to fractionate the Church members, there are no open clashes between the groups and the general attitude is one of tolerance and support of the whole movement.

Slotkin asked d'Azevedo to have the NAC questionnaire-census filled out by local groups, and d'Azevedo himself completed two forms. In a covering letter he wrote: "I consulted Ramsey Walker, Pat Eagle, and Roy James—all roadchiefs—and the data represents only their *active* members. They have not included the much larger number of people who attend meetings only occasionally. The numbers mentioned are those persons who are usually expected at every meeting." The Woodfords group consisted of twenty-nine members: twenty-three Washo, five Paiute, and one Shoshone, the Shoshone being Pat Eagle, roadman. The Coleville group consisted of three Washo, two Washo-Paiute, and two Paiute, with Harry Sam and Streeter Dick those responsible for the group. Louise Lancaster filled out a form for Jimmy Summer's group, giving thirteen Paiutes and Shoshones as members. A fourth form was completed at Bridgeport, California, by Harold Walker (Washo), son of Ramsey Walker. Jack Jasper of Leevining was said to be the person in charge of fifty-one Washoes and Paiutes. If there were no duplications in the four questionnaires, there were then 110 peyotists in the area in 1955.

By 1954, there was considerable interest among the Washo–Northern Paiute in the NAC of NA. Subscriptions to the *Quarterly Bulletin* came from Bridgeport, Woodfords, and Coleville. Reubin Hardin, Northern Paiute of McDermit, and Dewey Charles of Owens Valley subscribed. The NAC of NA likewise showed interest in its Nevada-California outpost. In 1958, president of the NAC Frank Takes Gun came to Coleville and encouraged the peyotists to go with him to Sacramento to file articles of incorporation for the Native American Church of the State of California. Bridgeport, California, was given as the principal place of business; the directors were Levi Dick, Frank Sam, Streeter Dick, and Jimmy Summer, all Paiute peyotists of Coleville, California. The incorporation was accomplished on May 19, 1958. On May 20, 1958, incorporation of the Native American Church in the State of Nevada was accomplished with the assistance of Takes Gun, and the directors were listed as Ray Fillmore of Genoa, Louise Lancaster of Coleville, Leonard Moore of Carson City, and Harry Sam of Gardnerville. In 1959 the state of California amended its narcotics law to prohibit the possession or use of peyote within the state, but there is no evidence that this was done to discourage or stop Washo-Paiute peyotism.

When I was in Nevada in 1972, the only one of my major informants of 1938 whom I was able to find was Harry Sam. He had attended Ben Lancaster's meetings in 1937, but was dropped by Ben in 1938 when only Sam Dick responded to his offer to sponsor meetings at his home in Nixon. By 1939, he was holding meetings himself, getting peyote by mail from Mrs. Amanda Cardenas of Oilton, Texas. Sam said that he has been maintaining the ritual of Ben Lancaster, but d'Azevedo has written that Harry Sam was roadman for a divergent group: "The Tipi Way group say that Harry Sam's way is a curious hodgepodge of ritual and that Sam can't get along with anyone." Sam has made the pilgrimage to Texas four times, first in 1951, and at age seventy-five he expected to go again soon. Nowadays, he frequently attends peyote meetings at Woodfords.

The leader of Washo peyotism for a long time has been Ramsey Walker. In 1972 he welcomed me to his place at Woodfords and talked freely of the history of peyote in Nevada. He had been a peyotist since 1938 and a road-man since 1940. Since 1954, when he attended the regional NAC confer-ence at Fort Hall, he has been as active as possible in NAC affairs. He has been ten times to collect peyote and to pray in the peyote gardens. On his way he visits peyotists in Oklahoma, and he has attended meetings with the Comanche, Cheyenne, and Arapaho and has received visits from many of them, including visits by Ralph Turtle and Joe Pedro. Johnny Two Eagles, a Sioux settled at Fort Hall, comes to meetings at Woodfords, as do the Jakes, Southern Paiutes of Cedar City, Utah. Walker has attended several meetings in Arizona with the Navajo, and several Navajos have attended his meetings in Woodfords. He is often invited to conduct peyote services for Indians of the San Francisco Bay area. National officers of the NAC Frank Takes Gun and Truman Dailey at different times have visited Wood-fords. Walker has cooperated with anthropologist Warren L. d'Azevedo, James F. Downs, John A. Price, and Alan P. Merriam in their studies of Washo peyotism and peyote music, in addition to serving as an informant for me.

Washo and Northern Paiute have not hesitated to attend each other's meetings in the past nor do they today. In 1938 about 10 percent of these two tribes were converted to peyotism. According to Merriam and d'Azevedo, there was some reduction in their numbers by 1957, and the slacking off has continued with variations from place to place and from time to time.

We turn now to the introduction of peyotism on the Duck Valley Reser-vation at Owyhee, Nevada, some 300 miles from Carson City. At about the same time that Ben Lancaster came to Fallon in 1936, with his peyote but-tons and his new religion, Bannock and Shoshone Indians from Fort Hall brought peyote to Owyhee, and it soon became important to a considerable number of Northern Paiute but was heatedly rejected by the Shoshone, with whom they shared the reservation. Owyhee is agency headquarters for one of the most isolated Indian reservations in the United States. Astride the Idaho-Nevada state line, it is about a hundred miles south of the Union Pacific Railroad along the Snake River in Idaho and the same distance north of the Western Pacific railroad along the Humboldt River in Nevada. It is almost 250 miles from Owyhee to Fort Hall; nevertheless, visiting be-tween the Indians of these reservations frequently took place.

I found out about the peyotists of Owyhee only when I visited Owyhee in 1972. I had been there before in 1936, checking a tribal element list for the Northern Paiute band, but at that time I was not informed of peyotism there. When I returned in 1972 to inquire about peyotists, the oldest peyotist I found turned out to be Jessie Little, born in 1887, my Northern Paiute interpreter in 1936, who remembered me. She was glad to tell me of the early history of peyotism in Owyhee because it involved her family.

Although peyote was known as a medicine earlier, Mrs. Little insisted that the first peyote meeting at Owyhee was held in her home in 1937, and it was a curing ceremony for her husband, George Little. The peyote leaders were Raymond Warren, George Tendoy, and Ray Crow from Fort Hall. George Little had attended meetings at Fort Hall, and the visiting leaders were his friends. Jim Humpy attended that first meeting and, like George, became an early Owyhee roadman. When I met Jim Humpy in 1972, he boasted that he had been a peyotist for fifty years, "the oldest Peyotist in Owyhee." Jessie said she had not "packed water" for the midnight or morning water call of the peyote ritual for over fifteen years—"just two or three times after George died" (in 1953). At age eighty-five, she described her religious feelings:

I'm a Christian lady. I go to the Assembly of God church all the time. I prayed to God, worshipped God, worshipped Jesus in the peyote meeting. The Christian church and peyote meetings are the same. I learned of Jesus in peyote meetings. In peyote meeting they said Jesus is going to come back, just the same as they say in the Assembly of God.

Soon after peyotism became noticeable at Owyhee, the usual outcry against it began. This time it was unsympathetic Shoshone Indians on the Duck Valley Reservation who objected. A letter to Commissioner John Collier from the Tribal Council of the Western Shoshone Agency at Owyhee, January 14, 1939, stated:

The matter of the use of Peyote on our reservation was brought to the attention of the Business Council by a member, Raymond Thacker, at our regular meeting . . . and it was unanimously agreed that this letter be written . . . requesting authority to make the use of Peyote on this reservation a criminal offense.

We realize the attitude toward Peyote insofar as it may serve as medicine by our medicine men, or where it may be used under the pretense of religion, and if these were the only uses made of this weed, it possibly would not be endangering the health and future of the members of our Tribe; but we are certain that the only use to which this weed is being made on this reservation is in the form of a stimulant, the effects of which are similar to a person under the influence of opium or marijuana.

Besides the grown people, a number of our smaller children are being given this weed to which we strenuously object. There are no native medicine men on this reservation, and all the Peyote used here is brought in from Indians from the Fort Hall Reservation and, after very close observation by this Council, we are satisfied that a large portion of the money which the members of the Tribes receive, which they should use for groceries and clothing, is given over to these Indians from Fort Hall in payment for Peyote.

Our Superintendent has discussed this matter with us and advised us that, insofar as this weed is used as medicine or in any way connected with our native religion or religious custom, that we should not object to its use. But . . . we are certain it is not used for these purposes . . . and . . . we are certain that each year there are many more members of our Tribes using Peyote, and in an effort to protect the health and future of our tribe, we urgently request your support in this matter."

The letter was signed by Thomas Premo, Louis Dave, George Brady, Gene Grady, John Dick, Bib Harney, and Raymond Thacker.

Collier recommended further study by the Western Shoshone council and told them that peyote was not illegal under federal law. The council replied with a "history" of peyote on the reservation, including:

Three men from Fort Hall visited this reservation at the time our community hall was dedicated and evidently interested the people in the north end of the reservation in the use of peyote. This group, known as the Miller Creek group, have been using peyote continually since that time and have formed a cult or group and meet quite regularly for the use of peyote.

This group . . . regard its use as a form of religion, but because of its effects on different members of this group, we are convinced that the religious connection is not of most importance.

There are about 175 members who use peyote to some extent.

The letter continued, accusing the peyotists of lacking ambition, of parental neglect, and of clanishness, and their children of not doing well in school, concluding:

The Council understands . . . that the Indian Office is not opposed to the use of peyote, and, inasmuch as it is not agaisnt any federal laws to use or transport it, and, as also indicated, it may not be habit-forming, we have decided to handle the situation through a program of education, led by ourselves and other leaders of the tribe, in the suppression of peyote, with the idea of possibly bringing its use on our reservation before the people in a popular referendum rather than for the Council to pass tribal legislation regarding its suppression, which we undoubtedly would find difficult to enforce.

With this letter the council included a letter from a doctor who related the case of a patient suffering from lobar pneumonia who have been given peyote by some visitors and had become extremely sick and nearly died.

The Miller Creek group referred to in the complaint were the Northern Paiute band who shared the reservation with the Shoshone, and the education drive, if there was one, did not discourage peyotists among them. Not only did they continue to hold meetings, but they also began attending meetings elsewhere and receiving visiting roadmen from all over. Jessie Little said that George traveled to Woodfords in California to run meetings for the Washo and the Paiutes of Owyhee. Ramsey Walker corroborated this, saying that Jim Humpy came from Owyhee in about 1940 and "gave" him a new tipi and taught him how to conduct a "true Tipi way meeting." Jessie remembered that George had led peyote meetings at McDermit and that Sam Nipwater of the Wind River Shoshone Reservation came from Wyoming to conduct services at Owyhee, and Sam confirmed this. She remembered that Gosiute peyotists Jimmy Steele, Louis Moon, and Arthur Johnson were visitors at Owyhee meetings.

In 1972, Alvin Sims, one of the new peyote leaders at Millers Creek, claimed peyotism is growing at Owyhee. If his claim is true, that one-third of the reservation is peyotist, many Shoshone must be joining the Paiutes. Ned Yassie, a Navajo working at Mountain Home, Idaho, is a frequent roadman at Owyhee; Washo Ramsey Walker of Woodfords and Arapaho Billie Turtle, who lives at Carson City, Nevada, also are visiting roadmen at Owyhee. Alvin Sims and Tommy Soap, Jr., have made trips to the peyote gardens.

Grover Tom, aged about sixty-five in 1972, Shoshone-Paiute roadman in McDermit, confirmed the history of peyotism at Owyhee as told by Jessie Little and added that Raymond Warren and Ray Crow of Fort Hall, who conducted the first meetings at Owyhee, also conducted the first meetings at McDermit. He acknowledged that he had been influenced by peyotists among the Shoshone, Paiute, and Washo, but emphasized that he ran peyote meetings strictly in the Comanche fashion, which he learned from the Comanche while he lived at Walters, Oklahoma, sometime between 1939 and 1942. That was also the time when he had made three trips to Texas to get peyote.

During the 1950s, Willie, Ross, and Reuben Hardin were the leaders of peyote at McDermit, but by 1960, Stanley Smart was the major spokesman for this band of Northern Paiute. Stanley agreed with Grover Tom that peyotism had come to McDermit from Fort Hall by way of Owyhee and said that his father, Raymond Smart, was the first McDermit roadman and that his father had learned to conduct the ritual in 1935 at Fort Hall. He said, moreover, that in the fifties his father had been invited to conduct peyote services for the Northern Paiute at Burns, Oregon, a hundred miles northwest of McDermit. He had gone to Burns with his father to serve as chief drummer in 1954 or 1955. Charlie Gill had become a local roadman at Burns, but no one had replaced him at his death. Stanley's father was also said to have conducted peyote meetings for the Surprise Valley Paiute at Cedarville, California. Minnie Thompson, aged seventy-two, a Surprise Valley Paiute whom I met at McDermit, confirmed Stanley's statement that peyote meetings had been held among the Surprise Valley Paiute and that peyote services had been available irregularly around Cedarville and Fort Bidwell.

Like many other roadmen, Stanley Smart was a leader on his reservation. In 1968 he had been an official delegate to Washington, D.C., regarding the nutritional needs of Indians, and when I met him in 1972, he was on the McDermit tribal council. Before the Nevada legislature he had been a witness regarding peyote cases six or seven times. He named twenty leaders of peyote from various tribes who had conducted peyote services at McDermit, including Ralph Turtle and Joe Littlehead (Cheyenne) from Oklahoma, and he had been invited to be roadman for the Paiute at Owyhee, the Bannock-Shoshone at Fort hall, the Washo at Woodfords, and the intertribal groups of peyotists around San Francisco Bay who hold peyote services in a hogan built at Healdsburg, California. Stanley attended a recent NAC national convention, at Aneth, Utah, on the Navajo reservation, where he participated in Navajo peyote rituals and became acquainted with many national leaders. On June 29, 1982, he testified in defense of peyote in Superior Court, Yakima, Washington.

THE SOUTHERN PAIUTE

The Southern Paiute are another Great Basin tribe who speak a Shoshonean language and are related to the Ute, Goshiute, Shoshone, and Northern Paiute. In aboriginal times they occupied southern Utah and Nevada and into Arizona south of the Colorado River, becoming the northern neighbors of the Hopi. Like other Great Basin tribes, they were foragers and hunters of small game, traveling in small family groups, although some groups had maize, beans, and squash by 1776. Today they live in the same area in and around a number of Mormon towns—Cedar City, Richfield, and Kanosh, to name a few. Their reservations are small and widely scattered and provide little subsistence. Tribal headquarters is at Cedar City, Utah. Probably all of the Utah Southern Paiute are nominal members of the Mormon church.

When I first visited the Southern Paiute in 1937 (again checking a list of tribal elements), I found no evidence of peyote among them, although peyote was much on my mind, since I had recently attended meetings with the Ute and had talked about peyote with the Gosiute. The next year, collecting data for my thesis on peyotism, I wrote to one of my 1937 informants, asking specifically about it. She answered (Kanosh 1939):

You asked me about the peyote meeting. I have never been to one. Belle [a sister] attended one but we don't believe in it. We went to Deep Creek (Ibapah, Gosiute reservation] to a dance but not to a peyote meeting. The same way we went to White Rocks [Uintah-Ouray Reservation] to a dance. I'm afraid of that stuff.

Obviously, in 1937 the Southern Paiute were sufficiently familiar with peyote to reject it.

It was not until 1971 that I learned (from a Shoshone informant from Wind River) that peyote meetings were held for the Southern Paiute at Cedar City and that Clifford Jake, Southern Paiute of Cedar City, was the peyote leader (Tom Collins, personal communication). Others (Martha Knack and Catherine Fowler, ethnologists, and Lilly Pete and Louis Moon, Gosiute peyotists) confirmed this, and in 1974, I interviewed Clifford Jake and his wife Yetta in their home in the Indian colony at Cedar City.

The history of Southern Paiute peyotism is the history of Clifford Jake. In 1946 his uncle Joe D. Roe, a Southern Paiute married to a Ute and living on the Uintah-Ouray Reservation, gave a curing ceremony for Clifford at Randlett, Utah. Clifford was then twenty-seven years old, a veteran of World War II, and his father, Carl Jake, had requested the meeting especially for him. In the next year or two, Roe traveled twice the four hundred miles from Randlett to the Shivwits Reservation near Santa Clara, in the extreme southwestern corner of Utah, to conduct peyote meetings. Clifford missed the first meeting, but some others who were there were Archie and Will Rogers of nearby Newcastle and Mr. and Mrs. Dan Bullets of Moccasin, Arizona, just south of Kanab, a hundred miles to the east. At the second meeting Clifford was present with the Rogers brothers, Charlie Chasis, Rex and Nora Asket, Edward Rice, Rex Mokee, and Smith Bushhead.

The Southern Paiute incorporated the Native American Church of Southern Utah in 1969, with Archie Rogers as president, and he remained president to the time of my interview in 1974. Clifford Jake became the first, and up to 1974, the only resident roadman, but he had welcomed many visiting leaders. Those he remembered coming to Cedar City were Harvey Goodbear (Southern Cheyenne) from the Ute reservation; Harrison Shoyo from the Wind River Reservation; Lawrence Murie, Pawnee peyotist married to a Cree and living at Rocky Boy's Reservation in Montana; and Ralph Turtle, Arapaho living with the Navajo. Clifford, sometimes accompanied by his wife Yetta, had attended peyote meetings at Woodfords and Coleville, California, and many times with the Navajo at Page, Gap, Bitter Springs, Copper Mine, and Fredonia, Arizona, and at Gallup, New Mexico; he had become acquainted with Navajo roadmen Black Horse; Leland Goatsman; Billy Shaine; and Eddie, Gilbert, and Franklin Yazzie. In 1972, Clifford was invited to Ignacio, Colorado, to be roadman for a peyote service sponsored by Southern Ute peyotist Vincent Grove. And once he stopped with the Ute Mountain Ute at Towaoc, Colorado, to share a Sunday feast following a peyote ceremony at the home of Jacob Lopez.

Clifford has taken his family four times to Texas to the peyote gardens. They visited the fields at Mirando City, Oilton, and Rio Grande City, as well as Laredo. During the last trip, in 1968, a miracle happened. He had searched some time before finding one small plant. He knelt down before it, rolled a cigarette of Bull Durham tobacco, and prayed, blowing smoke over the peyote plant from time to time. When he had finished, he discovered that peyote plants had come up all around him. He need search no more. After cutting some fresh buttons, Clifford bought five hundred dollars' worth of peyote at thirty-five dollars per thousand. In 1974 he still had peyote on hand from that purchase.

The ceremony of the Southern Paiute is, like that of the Ute, the Tipi way. Both Clifford and Archie Rogers said that they had become interested in peyotism because of the cures they and others had received. Family connections, friendliness, and hospitality were important in the spread of peyotism to the Southern Paiute. Clifford Jake said, "You can tell a peyote believer, because they wear a little silver medallion. . . . When you meet another Peyotist . . . you give him a place to stay, food, gas for his journey. It makes you feel good to act right this way" (Martha Knack 1973).

CHAPTER 11

The Navajo

THE Navajo are an Athapascan tribe, linguistically related to the Apaches. In aboriginal times, the Navajo occupied an extensive arid land among the Pueblo Indians in northeastern Arizona and northwestern New Mexico. Because they were becoming aggressive toward their Pueblo neighbors, as well as toward whites, in 1863 the U.S. Army with Ute soldiers rounded up most of the tribe and put them in Fort Sumner on the Pecos River in New Mexico, where it was hoped they would learn to be plow farmers. However, the experiment was not successful, and in 1867 they were allowed to return to their former homes, where the present reservation of almost ten million acres was established for them and where they remain today. The tribe has grown from about 9,000 in the 1860s to about 150,000 today, making it the largest and most homogeneous American Indian tribe. It is estimated that over half the Navajo Nation are today considered peyotists, which means that about one-fourth of the membership in the Native American Church is Navajo. In 1976, Texas officials reported sales of peyote to Arizona to be 38 percent and to New Mexico, 13 percent, making a total of 51 percent, the bulk of which would have been used by Navajos.

Notwithstanding present enthusiasm, the practice of the peyote religion was late in coming to the Navajo, or at least in being officially acknowledged. The early questionnaires of 1916 and 1919 concerning peyote had been sent from the BIA to the Navajo, as they had been to other tribes, and the agents had reported that peyote was not to be found on the Navajo reservation. Nevertheless, off the reservation, the Navajo were beginning to learn about it. The earliest and most important source of knowledge was the Ute Mountain Reservation with headquarters at Navajo Spring, later at Towaoc, Colorado (Aberle and Stewart 1957). The Navajo and Ute Mountain reservations adjoined, in fact overlapped, for a few miles until the boundary was settled in federal court in favor of the Navajo in 1970, and the Navajo living north of the San Juan River in two small communities, Aneth and Mancos Creek, were closer to the Ute than they were to other Navajo. The Navajo at Aneth had to pass through the Ute reservation to travel by automobile from their homes to other parts of the Navajo reservation. Due to this proximity, the Navajo at Aneth and Mancos Creek learned of peyotism at the same time that the Ute of Towaoc learned of it.

It will be remembered that it was the fall of 1914 when Sam Lone Bear brought the Cross Fire ritual to Dragon, Utah, where he soon had a group of followers among the Uncompahgre and White River Ute, one of whom was named Wichits (Superintendent Kneale, Uintah and Ouray Agency 1916). Towaoc informants reported that Wichits (Aberle and Stewart 1957: 19) was the first peyotist to conduct meetings at Towaoc, probably in 1915 or 1916. Wichits was soon followed by John P. Heart (John Peak Heart), the Cheyenne from Oklahoma, who brought to the Ute the more popular Half Moon ritual. Before 1918 and continuing until 1952, when he would have been seventy years old, John P. Heart visited Towaoc each summer, staying with his good friend Walter Lopez and directing peyote meetings (Opler 1940a: 464; Aberle and Stewart 1957b: 20–21). His influence among the Navajo as well as the Ute was considerable. Ute informants reported that Navajo north of the San Juan attended peyote meetings with them and Heart from the beginning. Chester Tso (Navajo) of Shiprock said he first attended peyote meetings with the Ute in 1918 and learned to conduct peyote services from Heart, so that he followed the John P. Heart Way (Aberle and Stewart 1957a). Chester Tso was also said to be the first local Shiprock–Teec Nos Pas Navajo to become a roadman, "slightly less strict" in conducting meetings than was John P. Heart (Howard Nez, personal communication). Raymond Tso, Chester's son, said his father had learned the ritual and received the moon and equipment from Heart and began conducting services about 1930, and after World War II, Chester had accompanied Heart to his home in Oklahoma, where he received a refresher course in peyotism for several weeks (personal communication).

The introduction of peyotism to the Navajo, however, was not to be smooth sailing. To understand the impact of peyotism on the Navajo reservation, it is necessary to bear in mind the size of the reservation, the great distances between villages, the nomadic nature of the culture, and the isolation of many families. These phenomena made it possible for considerable inroads to be made by peyotism among the Navajo without the centers of population becoming aware of what was going on. They also accounted for deep differences in feelings about peyote between Navajo in isolated areas and those Navajo more closely associated with the agencies and the Navajo bureaucracy. They also made it possible for peyotism to continue, and even to flourish, in spite of severe tribal laws, as well as state laws, forbidding its use. Thus it was that peyotism began in one part of the Navajo reservation before 1920 and during the next twenty years was hardly noticed by the official Navajo tribe, and only in 1940 did it meet head-on with the tribal opposition which tried with might and main to stamp it out.

For years BIA officials and Christian missionaries had been educating the Navajo to oppose peyote. Since 1916, antipeyote literature had come in a steady stream. Two BIA officials, H. F. Coggeshall and A. H. Kneale, after serving as superintendents on agencies where they had fought active peyotism, later became superintendents on the Navajo reservation, and they would have warned the Navajo of the evils of peyotism. The Navajo were doubtless influenced by the repeated efforts of Arizona congressmen

H. F. Ashurst and C. Hayden to pass a national bill against peyote, and, when unsuccessful, to pass an Arizona state law against it. In such ways the Navajo Tribal Council had been prepared to be against peyote. Although since Collier's time, in 1933, a more enlightened attitude had prevailed at the bureau, and there were many reasons to look with tolerance on the new religion, still the older attitude was strong among the officials, particularly among those Navajo who had had strong Christian indoctrination.

The first official action concerning peyote on the Navajo reservation was on January 25, 1938, when two peyote priests were arrested and "charged with the offense of possessing dope [peyote] on the Navajo Reservation." The next mention of peyote came in January, 1939, when Anselm G. Davis of Lukachukai wrote to Collier that "the introduction of a new religion is being considered by some Navajos of this section which uses a medicine called peyote." It was in 1940 when real action began. Some time in 1940, Senator Chavez of New Mexico, who had tried to have enacted a federal antipeyote law in 1937 following pressure from Mabel Luhan at Taos, wrote to the superintendent of the Navajo Agency, E. Reesman Fryer, asking for a full investigation of peyote on the Navajo reservation. Reesman passed the request along to Howard Gorman, vice-chairman of the Navajo Tribal Council and liaison officer, who made an investigation during April and May. The council met on June 3, 1940, to consider the results.

The chairman of the tribal council was Jacob C. Morgan, a Navajo Christian missionary educated at Hampton Institute. Some others on the council were practicing Christians, particularly Howard Gorman and Roger Davis. Although the request by Senator Chavez probably was the reason for meeting at that particular time, it was evident when the meeting began that the leaders of the tribal council, Morgan and Gorman, had been concerned about Navajo peyotism for some time and that they had their minds made up against it. They showed familiarity with antipeyote literature, and particularly referred to Newberne's *Peyote: An Abridged Compilation* (1922), which claimed peyote was dangerous. They favored and were well versed in all the early BIA and Christian missionary antipeyote arguments. Even though they knew that the bureau now favored a more lenient viewpoint, they were not convinced that peyote was harmless and had no sympathy for "a new religion." Collier had recently been severely criticized in *The Christian Missionary,* a fundamentalist publication, for allowing the printing in *Indians at Work,* a bureau publication, of an article by Petrullo favorable to peyote. Moreover, there was strong anti-Collier sentiment among the council members for other reasons, such as the bureau's reduction of animals permitted on Navajo grazing lands because of overgrazing. No doubt they were pleased to oppose him on peyotism.

The only peyotist at the meeting, Hola Tso, defended peyote. He asked for more evidence, for an analysis of the plant, and for medical testimony. He informed the council that he had gone to a peyote meeting run by Alfred

Wilson, a respected Cheyenne and president of the NAC, and implied that he spoke with more authority than others present. Nevertheless, the ideas of Morgan and Gorman prevailed. The council adopted the following resolution:

To prevent the introduction in or the use of peyote on the Navajo Reservation WHEREAS, during the last few months great quantities of peyote have been brought into the Navajo Reservation, and
WHEREAS, its use is not connected with any Navajo religious practices and is contradiction to the traditional ceremonies of the Navajo people:
THEREFORE: BE IT RESOLVED that as far as the Navajo people are concerned peyote is harmful and foreign to our traditional way of life;
BE IT FURTHER RESOLVED that the introduction into the Navajo country of the use of peyote by the Navajo people be stamped out and appropriate action be taken by the Tribal Courts to enforce this resolution;
BE IT FURTHER RESOLVED that there be added to the Code of Tribal Offenses, approved by the Secretary of the Interior on June 2, 1937, the following section: "Any person who shall introduce into the Navajo country, sell, or use or have in possession within said Navajo country, the bean known as peyote shall be deemed guilty of an offense against the Navajo Tribe, and upon conviction thereof shall be sentenced to labor for a period not to exceed nine months, or a fine of $100.00, or both";
BE IT FURTHER RESOLVED that any person having a peddlers license who is found trafficking in peyote shall, in addition to the above sentence, have his peddlers license forever cancelled;
BE IT FURTHER RESOLVED that the Tribal Council hereby petitions Congress to enact a law to supplement the above addition to the Code of Tribal Offenses to the end that peyote shall never be permitted in the Navajo Country.
                                CERTIFICATION
I hereby certify that the foregoing resolution was passed this 3rd day of June, 1940, by a 52 to 1 vote of the Navajo Tribal Council in assembly at Window Rock, Arizona, at which a quorum was present.
                                J. C. Morgan
                                Chairman, Navajo Tribal Council
WITNESSED:
Howard Gorman (Sgd.)
Vice-President, Navajo Tribal Council

When the adoption of this resolution reached Commissioner Collier of the BIA, he gave it his approval. Since he had opposed the action of the Taos Tribal Council to outlaw peyote, it is important to review his reasoning in this case, as well as to recall the interference of white people in the affair at Taos. When several Indians were arrested for possession of peyote on the Navajo reservation in December, 1940, Collier sent a long memorandum concerning the "Navajo Resolution" to Secretary of the Interior Ickes, in which he said:

I am transmitting an ordinance concerning peyote adopted by the Navajo Tribal Council on June 3, 1940, and I am recommending its approval.

This ordinance was passed by the Tribal Council after prolonged discussion. While I seriously question the findings of fact contained in a report made to the Council by one of its officers to the effect that peyote is a hurtful and habit-forming drug, I agree that the use of peyote among the Navajos is of very recent origin and is not in keeping with their traditional ceremonial rites. . . .

I am now recommending your approval of this Navajo anti-peyote ordinance, not because peyote is a deleterious, habit-forming drug—which according to the greatly preponderating evidence it is not—but because the authority of the Navajo Tribal Council to prevent the introduction of this substance on the reservation should be respected. . . .

In the case of the Navajo Tribe, the issue concerning peyote is essentially a social one. The peyote cult has never entered into the life or the ceremonial rites of the Navajos. The resistance of the Navajo tribe to its attempted introduction is vigorous. To proselytize is regarded as a duty by the members of the peyote cult. In the opinion of the Tribal Council and of the Superintendent, the effect of peyote-proselytizing among the Navajos would be disruptive. While I am not convinced that peyote would have the anticipated disruptive consequences, I believe that the regulatory authority of the Tribal Council should be upheld because at this stage the civil liberties of a Navajo minority are not yet involved.

I, therefore, recommend your approval of the ordinance, although reiterating that by the preponderance of evidence (a) peyote is not a habit-forming or a deleterious drug, and (b) its ceremonial use is, in the minds of the members of the cult, truly a religious one. I think that the action of the Navajo Tribe falls within its proper police powers, and within its proper authority to legislate concerning social welfare. Approval of the ordinance in the case of the Navajo Tribe, if given, should not be considered as a precedent, indicating future approval of similar ordinances in other tribes. . . .

In the *Navajo Yearbook* (Young 1961: 227) three arrests were reported in 1941 resulting in two convictions. The *Yearbook* editors reported no other arrests of peyotists until 1952, but there were other reports of arrests. In 1941, James Oliver was arrested in November, which caused his wife to write Collier: "James Oliver is mistreated for it [peyote] at the jail, like Jews did Jesus in the past." There was one arrest in 1942, and three in 1944 (Aberle 1966: 110; fnn. 115 and 114). These arrests and a visit from a delegation from the NAC, including Alfred Wilson (Cheyenne) and Jesse Row Lodge (Arapaho), complaining that Navajos were being jailed for their religious beliefs, caused Collier concern. He wrote to the agency superintendent:

The men whom we talked with yesterday believed that the real initiative in this matter had come from one of our own Indian Service people. . . .

They further stated . . . that they had been informed that Chee Dodge had said the Navajo Council was not disposed to be active in the enforcement of the peyote ordinance at this time. . . .

It is our definite policy here that Indian Service personnel shall not be officially or unofficially active in the proscription or prosecution of peyote worship;

certainly not . . . with religious observation. This is a definite policy, and in fact, a stern one. [March 10, 1944]

He added: "The foregoing statement will not, of course, affect the activities of any tribal employees paid out of tribal funds" [April 7].

The prohibition against peyote by the Tribal Council caused a few arrests, as shown, but even then it did not stop the importation of peyote, the proselytizing of the Navajo by peyote missionaries from Oklahoma and elsewhere, or the activities of the NAC on the Navajo reservation. For one thing, at the beginning enforcement of the law was weak. Moreover, the size of the reservation, with long distances between settlements over unimproved roads, made it possible for peyotists to gather for meetings without coming to the attention of officials. Furthermore, once welcomed, dedicated Oklahoma peyote missionaries found the Navajo an attractive group to proselytize.

One of the important peyote missionaries to the Navajo in the early 1940s was Truman Dailey (Oto), who claimed to have received his fireplace from the renowned old Kiowa, Hunting Horse. Truman told me of his trips to the Navajo: "I first went to the Navajo during World War II, about 1943, Enforcement of the Navajo anti-peyote ordinance was very lax. Some Navajo came to see me and said they needed help. I put up a peyote meeting for them. I was Secretary of the NAC of Oklahoma."

Probably it was Hola Tso who had asked Dailey for help, for in 1943 he had attended a peyote meeting run by Dailey at Red Rock, Oklahoma (interview, September 11, 1959, Denver, Colorado). Responding to the invitation, Truman went to New Mexico and conducted his first peyote meeting for the Navajo at Divide Store, just off the reservation east of Window Rock. There he met Mike Kiyaani, who became his disciple, and Mike told David Aberle about it (1966: 140):

He [Kiyaani] went to Oklahoma to visit Truman Dailey, his teacher, and learn how. Truman came to Piñon for a visit, and then Mike went back to Oklahoma again to learn. He learned how to run a meeting during meetings that he attended, and then Truman watched him run a meeting and told him that he knew how. Truman ran a meeting for his benefit. He plans to go back to Oklahoma to learn more. Instruction is given to people bit by bit. Truman has told Mike the main part of the ceremony. You have to rise toward it.

Truman named Ambrose Lee, Hola Tso, and Clarence Yazzie as his earliest hosts, but said that since 1943 he has returned to the Navajo reservation for about three weeks every year. He said of his visits: "My association with the Navajo is like a baseball coach, to lecture them, to help them. I have seen young Navajo grow up good."

Some Navajo traveled beyond Oklahoma to find experience and instruction in peyotism. Robert Shorty said he had traveled to the Pawnee, Ponca, Oto, Washo, Winnebago, Sac and Fox, and Sioux to learn about peyote.

I myself have attended meetings along with visiting Navajo with the Sac and Fox, the Shoshone, the Northern Paiute, the Ute of White Rocks, and the Taos. Two who studied the peyote ritual off the reservation were David Sam Clark and Andrew Pete, who were taught by Teles Romero at Taos. Clark and Pete were students at New Mexico Highlands College at Las Vegas who wished to learn about peyotism at Taos. Teles informed them by mail whenever a peyote meeting was scheduled, and the two college students regularly traveled the eighty miles from Las Vegas to Taos to attend services. Teles asserted: "I taught peyote to those two Navajo."

Navajo peyotists began to learn about the NAC and to become members. In May, 1942, a handwritten document containing testimonials from new Navajo peyotists was sent by Della C. Oliver (Navajo from the Four Corners area) to the commissioner of Indian affairs. From its content, it was obviously intended for Alfred Wilson, president of the NAC, to whom it was forwarded and later returned. Della Oliver wrote: "It has been two years James and I became Native American Church members." Arthur Little said: "We became members of this Native American Church and kept on going up. This spring I became a real singer and prayer. Now I can run big meetings. I thank God and Oklahoma Indians for the great peyotes. I will hold it for my whole tribe. *Thank God.*" John Harvey said, "I thank God for he had given us his great medicine peyote and I thank Oklahoma Indians and Native American Church people." Evan Harvey said, "I thank Peyote and James Oliver and I thank John P. Hart from Oklahoma. . . ." Mary Harvey said: "I wish all of our friends belongs to Native American Church to help us to worship God with Peyote . . . and the headmen of the Native American Church. I thank you all."

The NAC was equally interested in its new converts. In 1944 Frank Takes Gun was elected vice president of the NAC, and his particular interest in peyotism was in the legal problems encountered in establishing and maintaining religious freedom for the church. In June, 1944, he went to Salt Lake City with James Oliver, president; Sam Capitan, vice president; and Della Oliver, secretary of the NAC of Utah, to file the articles of incorporation of the Native American Church of Utah. Aneth, the Navajo reservation village, was named as the "principal place of business of said corporation." Although the resolution authorizing the incorporation specified that NAC members of the Ute tribe were to be included, all the trustees and officers were Navajo. Besides the officers, the trustees were James Tapohah, Toney Claw, Chester Chilley Begay, Mary Harvey, Herbert Lansing, Frank Lansing, Edward Lansing, Thomas Billy, Myron Poyer, Jason Wallace, Arthur Little Hat, and Chester White.

On February 28, 1946, "at the request of Frank Takes Gun," the office of the Arizona Corporation Commission at Phoenix, Arizona, accepted the articles of incorporation of the Native American Church of the State of Arizona, with Arthur Little Hat, president; David Claw, vice president; and

FIG. 18. Takes Gun helps the Navajo of southern Utah incorporate the Native American Church of Utah in Salt Lake City, 1944. Left to right: Takes Gun (Crow), Sam Capitan, Della Oliver, James Oliver (Navajos). Photograph given to O. C. Stewart by Frank Takes Gun.

Sam Capitan, secretary. Other trustees were Aida Begay, Billy Odell, Tom Shiprock, Stuart Etsitty, Hosteen Cedar, Holly [Hola] Tso, Hohtele Zonni [Hatati Zhoni], Keeyaoni Bedagaili, Anselm G. Davis, and Thomas Peters. The principal place of business for the first year was St. Johns, Arizona, a town about fifty miles south of the Navajo reservation boundary which traditionally had no Indian population.

The Native American Church of New Mexico had also been reorganized and incorporated by Frank Takes Gun in 1945, all officers being from Taos Pueblo. As has been said, it was not necessary to file articles of incorporation in each state in order to carry on the business of the NAC, but Takes Gun and a number of other Indians thought to gain protection and status by being incorporated in all states where peyotists held meetings, and in several states, including Utah, Washington, Wisconsin, and South Dakota, the NAC has been incorporated several times under slightly different names.

At the annual meeting of the NAC of the United States at White Oak, Oklahoma, on May 24, 1946, Takes Gun reported that he had been in Washington, D.C., to help a Navajo delegation gain religious freedom. He said: "The Department of the Interior recognized the Native American Church. . . . We had undertaken to help the controversy States. . . . The only thing that saved the day for the Navajos was the establishing and organizing of the Church on that reservation." Navajos present at that meeting were Mike Kiyaani (no address), Ambrose Lee (Divide Store, New Mexico), Sam Capitan and James Oliver (Aneth, Utah), and Hola Tso (Saw Mill, Arizona), who made the motion to establish membership cards and a fee system, which was approved.

In 1946 there was a rash of arrests as well as complaints from some that the law was not being enforced. Antipeyotism was never far from the surface, and now it erupted, with white doctors, scholars, and organizations getting involved. An article in the *Journal of the American Medical Association* (Braasch et al. 1949: 2251) condemned peyote severely, which worried peyotists and nonpeyotists alike because they believed it was the judgment of the entire prestigious AMA. I asked for and received a reprint of the article from Dr. Braasch of the Mayo Clinic. It was obvious from the article that Braasch and his fellow authors were completely unaware of the long history and extensive literature on the legal struggle over peyotism. There were no new data presented in the article. One source was hearsay: "In conversing with Indian agents, with physicians in the neighborhood of Indian settlements and with other people, the evidence is quite unanimous that the use of Peyote causes deterioration in the morale of the Indians" (no peyotists were questioned). His other source was the Council of Pharmacy and Chemistry of the AMA, which placed peyote in the category of narcotics. Dr. Austin Smith, secretary of the council, cited Stollman (*Manual of Pharmacology,* 1948): ". . . mescaline . . . produces peculiar psychologic disorientations, with hallucination. . . . Mescaline and its related compounds produce a number of *other effects,* including fall of blood pressure . . . motor paralysis by depression of the central nervous system, and death by respiratory failure."

In the autumn of 1949, the National Fellowship of Indian Workers, which was dedicated to the struggle to outlaw peyotism, used the Braasch article as authority for a pamphlet announcing "a new effort being made to have Congress outlaw the use of peyote." The article was written by H. E. Bruce, former superintendent of the Potawatomi reservation, where he had fought unremittingly against peyotism. He had lost neither his hatred of peyotism nor his taste for battle. To understand the true situation, the Bureau of Indian Affairs hired David Aberle, anthropologist, to make a complete, unbiased history of peyotism on the Navajo reservation.

Articles against peyote continued to appear in the press. Dr. Clarence Salisbury, medical missionary to the Navajo and head of Ganado Presbyterian Mission (Navajo), was one of those who provided antipeyotist statements to the press, and in 1951 he became commissioner of public health in the state of Arizona. An article in *Time* magazine based on his views appeared on June 18, 1951. Immediately anthropologists concerned with peyote refuted the article. Weston La Barre, David McAllester, and I sent letters to the editors of *Time,* and they were published in the issue of July 9. J. Sydney Slotkin prepared a statement favorable to peyote which was signed by us and Sol Tax, and it appeared in the November 30, 1951, issue of *Science* (114:582–83). Former commissioner John Collier seconded the statement of the anthropologists with another short but strong expression of support for peyote in 1952, also in *Science* (115:503–504).

The Navajo law against peyote began to be prosecuted with more vigor. The number of arrests and convictions for use of peyote by Navajos from 1946 to 1951 was not recorded, if they occurred. Records for 1952 showed 25 arrests. In 1953, there were 88, and in 1954, 102 arrests.

In 1954 the Navajo Tribal Council voted to reconsider its 1940 antipeyote ordinance. For two and one-half days, June 1 to 3, 1954, it listened to reports from anthropologist David Aberle, pharmacologist Maurice H. Seevers, M.D., and Navajo tribal attorney Norman M. Littell and then questioned them. Former councilman and peyotist Hola Tso was offered five minutes to defend peyote, but he refused to speak because five minutes would not be time enough. The council denied NAC president Allen Dale (Omaha) the privilege of speaking because he was not a Navajo. Navajo peyotists James Oliver and Clifford Beck were allowed time to make statements and were questioned. Oliver reported he had been jailed five times for peyote. He testified that he did not mix the peyote ritual and equipment with the ritual and paraphernalia he used as an old-time Navajo medicine man. After the long statements and questions, the tribal council took no action, and the antipeyote ordinance remained in force and arrests continued. Aberle (1966:118–19) summarized the meeting:

Thus the 1954 Council, few of whose members had been present in 1940, refused to act or to override the 1940 Council. It would seem that the Council wanted more evidence of damage from peyote before it would vote to reaffirm, and more assurances than could be supplied that peyote had positive effects religiously and medically before it would reconsider.

Although the peyotists were disappointed by the council's action—or inaction—they were not entirely discouraged. The council hearings had stimulated a good deal of publicity favorable to peyotism, both local and national, including articles in the *Santa Fe New Mexican* (1954), the *Arizona Republic* (1954), and *Time* (1954).

The arrests continued. In 1955 there were ninety-nine; in 1956, eighty-six; in 1957, ninety-one; in 1958, ninety-seven; in 1959, seventy; and in

1960, thirty-eight. And not all the publicity was good. A news item in the *Arizona Republic,* February 20, 1956, headed "24 Nabbed Sniffing Cactus-Button Drug!" suggests intensified activity against peyote by non-Indians. Seldom has so much misinformation been attached to a report of a raid on a church:

Williams AP—Twenty-four Navajo Indians were sentenced early yesterday for using peyote after officers broke into a hogan filled with smoke from the cactus-button drug.

Two men described by the group as ringleaders, Kee Mitchell and Junior Thomas, were sentenced by Justice of the Peace Thomas Way to Williams jail for 60 days.

The other 22 were given 30 days suspended sentences "because the jail is too small to hold all of them," Way said. . . .

Peyote is a drug made from a small cactus which grows throughout the Southwest. It is used . . . in a Mexican liquor known as pulque. Users are left in a stupor often lasting as long as a week, Cole said.

The party was the first report of off-reservation use of the drug in Arizona within recent years. Last week, officers broke up a party at Houck, Deputy Cole said, and took 46 Indians to Fort Defiance for action.

Navajo peyotists continued periodically to petition the tribal council to amend the 1940 antipeyote ordinance to allow peyote for religious services. In June, 1955, J. Sydney Slotkin, having been elected to the board of the NAC of NA, helped to compose one such petition during a visit to Saw Mill, Arizona. It was signed June 20, 1955, by Hola Tso, Edward Damon, Ambrose Lee, and Billy O'Dell and was presented to the council on July 5, 1955. A shorter petition was signed in October by Sam Capitan, Lucy P. King, Taft Blackhorse, and Thomas Peters, the elected officers of the "Northern Navajo Four Corners Area Chapter of the Native American Church of North America," and the next month it was filed with the tribal council. Nothing but continued discussion followed these two formal petitions.

Navajo peyotists had become increasingly active in the NAC, sending delegates to the conventions of 1950 and 1952 through 1956. When Slotkin began publishing the *Quarterly Bulletin of the NAC* in 1955, it contained many items concerning the Navajo. The first issue, which listed contributions, recorded the names of four Navajos who had sent in a total of over one hundred dollars. In the next issue, Mr. and Mrs. Jimmie King of Shiprock, New Mexico, reported:

A petition has been presented to the Navajo Tribal Council to repeal the anti-Peyote ordinance. . . . The following spokesmen were elected to represent our side of the issue to the Tribal Council: Hola Tso . . . Jimmie King . . . Hatatlhshonee [Hatati Zhoni] from Red Rocks, Arizona; Joe Yazzie from Lower Greasewood, Arizona; Taft Blackhorse from Shiprock; Raymond Arviso from Crownpoint, New Mexico; and Mike Kiyaani from Black Mountain, Arizona. . . .

If the religious persecution should be continued, the resources of the Department of Justice should be used to protect the religious liberty of our people, which seeks to establish us in the public opinion of the country as a dignified, permanent, and important unit in the life and culture of the U.S. and with our humble prayers on our lips, and thru the grace of our Lord and God, we carry the banners forward. Onward, Christian soldiers of the NAC everywhere thruout this land of ours and unto all the world.

It was at the NAC annual convention in 1956 at Scottsbluff, Nebraska, that Frank Takes Gun (Crow) was elected president of the NAC of NA, and Hola Tso (Navajo) was elected vice president. As has already been shown, immediately following his election, Takes Gun began to manage the NAC as he wished without concern for the NAC constitution and by-laws, and when the 1958 convention at Gallup was not conducted according to the rules, and when Winnebago delegates were not allowed to speak, the traditional leaders of the NAC—Plains Indians—ignored Takes Gun and his meetings and set in motion procedures to restore the NAC to its former democratic and legal condition. Takes Gun likewise ignored them, holding meetings when and as he saw fit that were attended mainly by Navajos. Thus began the deep and far-reaching schism between most Navajo peyotists and other members of the Native American Church.

Meanwhile, Frank Takes Gun concentrated his attention on the affairs of the Navajo. In his first communication to the members of the NAC in the *Quarterly Bulletin,* July–September, 1956, he reviewed the history of the Navajo antipeyote ordinance and vowed the resources of the NAC to obtain freedom of religion for the Navajo. He soon demonstrated skill and energy in getting legal help to test the Navajo prohibition. The first case came during his first year as president. On December 31, 1956, Mike Kiyaani was arrested for possession of peyote and jailed in Fort Defiance. Under Takes Gun's direction, Hola Tso, representing Navajo peyotists, consulted with attorneys Neil V. Christensen and Jack M. Anderson of Flagstaff, who took the case and appealed for a writ of habeas corpus to free Kiyaani. The hearing was in Prescott, Arizona, on February 9, 1957. Takes Gun and J. Sydney Slotkin were witnesses for Kiyaani. The lawyers attacked the ordinance as a bar to religious freedom and therefore unconstitutional. Federal judge James A. Walsh denied the request and kept Kiyaani in jail, thus upholding the Navajo council's 1940 ordinance against peyote. To pay the court costs, Takes Gun solicited funds from all members of the NAC of NA, but most costs were met by the American Civil Liberties Union (ACLU) and by the Navajo themselves.

The next effort was also unsuccessful. On April 14, 1958, a Native American Church service at Shiprock, New Mexico, was raided, and Shorty Duncan, William F. Tsosie, and Frank Hanna, Jr., were arrested and assessed a fine and jail penalty by Joe Duncan, judge of the Navajo Tribal Court. Again directed by Takes Gun, the peyotists took their complaints to the U.S. district court of New Mexico, and the judge, Waldo H. Rogers, dismissed the complaints. This time a notice of appeal was filed, and when the U.S. Court of Appeals met in September, 1959, in Denver, Colorado, and considered the appeal, Judge Walter A. Huxman also denied it, saying: "It follows that neither under the Constitution or the laws of Congress, do the Federal Courts have jurisdiction of tribal laws or regulations, even though they may have an impact on forms of religious worship" (272 F. 2nd 131; 10th Cir. 1959).

At Takes Gun's request I had been a consultant to attorney Fred M. Standley, the lawyer who presented the appeal. Hola Tso, Stewart Etsitty, Dudley Yazzie, and David Sam Clark had come to Denver as resource persons, and I had an opportunity to interview these Navajo peyotists in depth regarding Navajo peyotism. It was evident that the Navajo appreciated the efforts being made in their behalf. From that time, the fall of 1959, I was involved in many of the legal maneuvers engineered by Takes Gun to help the Navajo peyotists.

At that time an effort was made to modify the New Mexico state anti-peyote law to allow peyote to be used in a bona fide religious ceremony. The bill had passed the state legislature but was in danger of being vetoed by the governor. Takes Gun asked me to do what I could to strengthen the inclination of the governor of New Mexico, John Burroughs, to sign the bill or to allow it to take effect without his signature. I talked to him by telephone, wrote a letter, and sent literature favorable to peyote to him. A favorable article in *Time* with a photograph of Frank Takes Gun (1959) may have helped Governor Burroughs resist strong pressure to veto the bill. Burroughs allowed the amendment to become law, and the peyote religion became legal in New Mexico for Taos and Navajo peyotists. It was Takes Gun's first real victory, and he became a hero to the Navajo peyotists.

In 1960, Takes Gun requested Carling Malouf of the University of Montana, J. Verne Dusenberry of Montana State College, and me to supply ACLU attorneys in Washington, D.C., with data to help them prepare a suit to require the secretary of the interior to rescind the approval of the 1940 Navajo ordinance against peyote. We did so, but the attempt to have the approval reversed, or canceled, failed. Assistant Commissioner Selene Gifford wrote: "Because the resolution was enacted by the Navajo Tribal Council, this Bureau has no authority to rescind or eliminate it. Such action would have to be taken by the Navajo Tribal Council" (letter to NAC president Allen Dale, May 14, 1954).

In 1960, another test case was underway in Arizona. It was the Mary Attakai case, and Takes Gun asked me to serve as an expert witness. Mary Attakai had been arrested in Williams, Arizona, on October 29, 1959, following the arrest of her brother, Jack Attakai, upon the complaint of Mary because her brother was drunk and disorderly in her home. In retaliation, Jack informed the arresting officer that Mary had peyote in the house. The peyote was found, and Mary was taken to jail for possession of peyote, and Jack for disorderly conduct. The trial was set for July 25 and 26, 1960, in Flagstaff, Arizona, and I went to Flagstaff a day early to meet with Herbert L. Ely, the ACLU lawyer from Phoenix, who was handling the case. David Sam Clark, then an official representative of the NAC, served as interpreter for Mary before Judge Yale McFate, who usually sat in Phoenix but who came to Flagstaff because the local Superior Court judge had disqualified himself.

Mary Attakai, who had worked in the Williams laundry for about five years, was a convincing witness as she described her faith in God as creator of peyote to help the Indians worship. Frank Takes Gun testified that there were 225,000 members of the NAC of NA, a figure which often has been repeated but never proven and sometimes doubted. He also said that he had never attended a Navajo peyote meeting.

In court Ely directed me to describe the peyote religion, to give in some detail its history and ritual. He asked me to recall my personal experiences as a participant observer in peyote meetings. I was on the stand about three hours. Psychiatrist Bernard C. Gorton, M.D., who had studied the affects of mescaline at the New York Psychiatric Institute with Dr. Paul Hoch, an early researcher of peyote, was also a witness. Gorton maintained that peyote was not harmful, not addictive, and not dangerous.

The opinion of Judge McFate freed Mary Attakai, and moreover, when appealed to the Arizona Supreme Court, the opinion was not reversed and therefore became a sound legal precedent. The opinion reads:

The defendant admits the possession . . . and she is therefore guilty of the crime of illegal possession of peyote unless the statute under which she is charged is unconstitutional. Council for defendant strongly urges that it is in violation of the Fourteenth Amendment of the United States Constitution and Article II, Section 4, 8, 12 and 13 of the Arizona Constitution.

The Fourteenth Amendment of the United States Constitution prohibits any state from enacting any law which abridges the privileges and immunities of the citizens of the United States. Nor shall any state deprive any person of liberty without due process of law, or deny to any person the equal protection of the laws. The Arizona Constitution, Article II, Section 4, 8, 12 and 13 covers substantially the same subject matter. . . . Freedom of religious worship is guaranteed by these fundamental constitutional provisions.

The State of Arizona, under the police power, may regulate or prohibit the use or possession of substances, even though used in religious rites, if reasonably necessary to protect the public health or safety. Liberty of conscience secured by the provisions of our Constitutions may not be construed to excuse acts of licentiousness or to justify practices inconsistent with the peace and safety of the public.

The precise question before this court, therefore, is this: Is this statute prohibiting possession of peyote reasonably necessary to protect the public safety?

The evidence in this case establishes that peyote is a small cactus which grows along the banks of the Rio Grande. When taken internally it produces— especially when the eyes are closed—extraordinary physiological and psychological effects such as bright colors and so-called visions, as though one were witnessing an actual scene; yet, while these effects are being produced, the subject is completely aware of his actual environment and in possession of all his mental faculties. And there are no harmful after-effects from the use of peyote.

Peyote is not a narcotic. It is not habit-forming. It is actually unpleasant to take, having a very bitter taste.

There is no significant use of peyote by persons other than Indians who practice peyotism in connection with their religion. There are about 225,000 members of the organized church, known as the Native American Church, which adheres to this practice. The peyote rite is one of prayer and quiet contemplation. The doctrine consists of belief in God, brother love, care of family and other worthy beliefs. The use and significance of peyote within the religious framework is complex. It is conceived of as a sacrament, a means of communion with the Spirit of the Almighty—and as an object of worship, itself, as having been provided for the Indian by the Almighty.

The Indians use peyote primarily in connection with their religious ritual. When thus consumed, it causes the worshipper to experience a vivid revelation in which he sees or hears the spirit of a departed loved one, or experiences other religious phenomenon; or he may be shown the way to solve some daily problem, or reproved for some evil thought or deed. Through the use of peyote, the Indian acquires increased powers of concentration and introspection, and experiences deep religious emotion. There is nothing debasing or morally reprehensible about the peyote ritual.

The use of peyote is essential to the existence of the peyote religion. Without it, the practice of the religion would be effectively prevented.

From the foregoing it follows:

First, the only significant use made of peyote is in connection with Indian rites of a bona fide religious nature, or for medicinal purposes.

Second, there are no harmful after-effects from the use of peyote.

Third, it is not a narcotic, nor is it habit-forming.

Fourth, the practical effect of the statute outlawing its use is to prevent worship by members of the Native American Church, who believe the peyote plant to be of divine origin and to bear a similar relation to the Indians—most of whom cannot read—as does the Holy Bible to the white man.

The manner in which peyote is used by the Indian worshipper is not inconsistent with the public health, morals, or welfare. Its use, in the manner disclosed by the evidence in this case, is in fact entirely consistent with the good morals, health and spiritual elevation of some 225,000 Indians.

It is significant that many states which formerly outlawed the use of peyote have abolished or amended their laws to permit its use for religious purposes. It is also significant that the Federal Government has in nowise prevented the use of peyote by Indians or others.

Under these circumstances, the court finds that the statute is unconstitutional as applied to the acts of this defendant in the conduct and practice of her religious beliefs.

There will therefore be an order dismissing this complaint, exonerating the bond, and releasing the defendant.

Thus, though the Arizona state law outlawing peyote still remained the law, a legal precedent had been set which freed peyote's use for religious purposes. Its use for bona fide religious purposes by Indians has not since been questioned by the state of Arizona. It was questioned at a later date involving some whites who wished to celebrate their wedding in a peyote ceremony, but again, when the ceremony was shown to be an authentic NAC ceremony, permission to use peyote was upheld. However, peyote was still illegal on the Navajo reservation.

With the Mary Attakai case, Takes Gun had won an important victory for Navajo peyotists, and they were grateful. They bought him a house in Albuquerque, provided him with an automobile, and took care of all his needs. Even the Plains Indian peyotists whom he had offended in his high-handed administration of the NAC of NA and who were involved in setting up a new national NAC recognized the value to all peyotists of his legal successes for the Navajo. It tempered their criticism of him, but it did not stop their reorganization.

The next victory for the Navajo peyotists because of Frank Takes Gun's efforts in their behalf began in 1962 in the desert near Needles, California, when Jack Woody, Leon B. Anderson, and Dan Dee Nez, Navajo section hands employed by the Santa Fe Railroad, were arrested in a hogan during a peyote meeting being conducted by Truman Dailey. The Navajo were charged with violating the California antipeyote law because they had purchased the peyote, sponsored the meeting, and owned the hogan, constructed of discarded used railroad ties.

I learned of the case first by means of a letter from Joan Ablon, an anthropology graduate student from Chicago, who was doing research on urbanization of Indians in the San Francisco Bay area. Local Navajo peyotists had appealed to her for help, and upon advice from Sol Tax she wrote to me. When Frank Takes Gun learned of the arrest, he went to San Bernardino and arranged to have the case transferred to the Superior Court of the county and made contact with the ACLU of Los Angeles, who accepted the case. The Association of American Indian Affairs of New York City offered financial aid (San Bernardino, *Evening Telegram,* May 12, 1962).

On May 13, Takes Gun telephoned me and requested that I testify for the NAC as an expert witness in the case. I agreed, and on November 12, 1962, I went to San Bernardino for pretrial conferences with the attorneys and Frank Takes Gun. On November 13, I testified most of the court session. The following day, Dr. Gordon A. Alles, professor of pharmacology at the University of California, Los Angeles, testified that peyote was neither habit-forming nor dangerous as used by the Indians. The trial received wide newspaper coverage, from the *San Bernardino Daily Sun* to the *New York Times,* and it was generally favorable to the Indians. Nevertheless, the decision rendered by Judge Carl B. Hilliard in San Bernardino on November 29, 1962, was not favorable. It read:

The Attorney General of this state, by opinion No. 62/93 rendered May 18,

FIG. 19. Navajo peyotists on trial before the Superior Court of California for the County of San Bernardino, November, 1962. Front row, left to right: Jack Woody, Dan Dee Nez, Leon B. Anderson. Back row: A. L. Wirin, ACLU attorney; Rufus Johnson, defense attorney. Courtesy Dick Oliver, *Los Angeles Times* photo.

1962, has effectively summarized the position adopted by this Court. Both the reasoning and conclusions of that opinion are incorporated in this memorandum decision, and this Court could not improve upon the final statement of such opinion: "Thus in California, the Native American Church must forsake its peyote rituals in deference to the unqualified legislative command of prohibition. Any plea that might be advanced in behalf of less restrictive treatment of peyote should be addressed to a legislative rather than a judicial remedy."

The Court finds and determines that the defendants, and each of them are guilty.

As a matter of fact, a "legislative remedy" was already being sought, but it was not successful. Some Navajo peyotists in the San Francisco Bay area, under the leadership of Philip Jackson of Tuba City, Arizona, who was working in Oakland, were seeking legal help to amend the California law to permit use of peyote for religious purposes, and they had engaged the help of Fred F. Cooper, attorney of Oakland. On January 11, 1963, the Honorable Nicholas C. Petris, a law partner of Cooper and member of the California State Assembly, introduced a bill to legalize the Native American Church's use of peyote. The bill passed the assembly but was killed in the Senate's Committee on Public Health and Safety.

The *Woody et al.* case was appealed to the District Court of Appeals in Los Angeles, where again the conviction was upheld. A further appeal to the California Supreme Court was accepted, and this time an opinion favorable to peyotism freed Jack Woody, Leon Anderson, and Dan Dee Nez. The opinion delivered on August 24, 1964, was written by Justice J. Tobriner and was concurred in by five of the six other justices. Justice Tobriner wrote:

On the other hand, the right to free religious expression embodies a precious heritage of our history. In a mass society, which presses at every point toward conformity, the protection of a self-expression, however unique, of the individual and the group becomes ever more important. The varying currents of the subcultures that flow into the mainstream of our national life give depth and beauty. We preserve a greater value than an ancient tradition when we protect the rights of the Indians who honestly practiced an old religion in using peyote one night at a meeting in a desert hogan near Needles, California."

Since the California law remained unchanged in spite of the California Supreme Court ruling, Navajo Indians and others discovered transporting peyote in California are at times arrested and held until the local district attorney learns of the *Woody et al.* case and of the exemption given by the court when peyote is used in a bona fide religious ceremony.

In March, 1967, for the first time the Navajo Tribal Council formally accepted the Bill of Rights of the U.S. Constitution, the first amendment of which guarantees freedom in the practice of religion, and the next week the council met to consider peyotism in the light of the new tribal law. Even so, it took nearly two days of debate before the controversial issue passed by a vote of twenty-nine to twenty-six. The amended ordinance read: "Provided that it shall not be unlawful for any member of the Native American Church to transport peyote into Navajo country, or buy, sell, possess, or use Peyote in any form, in connection with the religious practices, sacraments or services of the Native American Church." The *Navajo Times,* October 19, 1967, reported:

Only 55 councilmen (of 72) were recorded as voting on the issue. Some were absent and some apparently did not want to vote on it.

Vice Chairman Nelson Damon presided throughout the first week of the full session. Chairman Nakai and General Council Harold Mott appeared in the Council briefly. . . . Mott told the Council that the resolution appeared unnecessary, since a Navajo Bill of Rights guaranteeing religious freedom had been passed on the previous Monday.

However, the Council went ahead and voted on the issue.

Following the amendment of the Navajo ordinance against peyote, the importance of Frank Takes Gun to the Navajo quickly diminished. They no longer needed him. He was a Crow, not a Navajo, not even married to a Navajo. He was expensive, and he was controversial. Although he had claimed to be president of the NAC of NA for the past ten years and had held "annual meetings," few except the Navajo had supported these meetings and all Navajo were aware of that fact. Already most Navajo of the northern Four Corners Area had joined with the Plains and Basin Indians in the reconstituted NAC of NA, which was holding its own annual conventions with widespread representation.

The break with Takes Gun was described in the *Navajo Times* of November 21, 1968:

There seems to be confusion over whether or not Frank Takes Gun, a Crow, has been re-elected president of the Native American Church of North America.

Takes Gun . . . announced that he was re-elected following a meeting in Gallup Saturday.

But Robert Shorty, Jr., Secretary of the Native American Church of Navajoland, charges that proper election procedures were not followed during the Gallup meeting and there were not enough delegations present to elect new officers.

[He] said that for one thing Takes Gun declined to step down as presiding officer while the vote was being taken. He asked for the "ayes," . . . and about half of those presented voted for him, but then did not ask for the "nays."

A question was raised from the floor that there were not enough delegations present to elect officers. . . . [Shorty] said that out of some 320 different tribes in the U.S., the representatives of only four tribes were present—the Navajo, . . . the Crow, the Northern Cheyenne, and one representative from the Sioux. "There was nobody there from the Oklahoma tribes, and nobody from Wisconsin, or Nebraska, or even from Colorado." Shorty . . . believes the meeting, which lasted only a half day, was poorly attended because the membership probably had not been "properly informed" by Takes Gun.

Obviously, Takes Gun was still incorrigible when it came to working in the framework of a democratic organization and had given the Navajo reason to disassociate themselves from him. While he had been useful to them, they had supported him as president of the NAC of NA as well as with gifts, but there seemed to be no reason to do so any longer. The *Navajo Times* article continued:

The officers of the Native American Church of Navajoland [the Southern Arizona Peyotists] issued a statement to the news media Tuesday disputing Takes Gun's announcement that he had been reelected. The statement said: "During the recent half-a-day meeting, an alleged election of officers was held against the wishes of the majority present. The majority decided, by vote, that due to a lack of delegations present all action taken be forfeited. It was further decided that the convention for reelection of officers be postponed until early spring 1969. Therefore, the majority of the Native American Church of Navajoland and its executives do not recognize nor do they accept the alleged election of officers of the Native American Church of North America. It is the desire of the executive officers of the Native American Church of Navajoland that as many as possible different tribes of Indians be represented to participate in the election of officers of the Native American Church of North America."

The statement was signed by the officers of the NAC of Navajoland: David S. Clark, president; James Notah, vice president; Anson C. Damon, Sr., treasurer; and Robert Shorty, secretary.

The Southern Arizona Navajo peyotists, those around Window Rock, had organized themselves as the NAC of Navajoland in 1966. They were the Navajo peyotists who had most supported Takes Gun and were most supported by him. While closely allied with Takes Gun and feeling somewhat dependent upon him, they had shunned the reconstructed national church, only supporting Takes Gun's meetings. Now they felt allegiance neither to him nor to the reconstructed church. Contrary to the suggestion in the *Navajo Times* that they might desire to be part of an NAC of NA in which "as many as possible different tribes of Indians be represented to participate in the election of officers," the NAC of Navajoland did not affiliate with and have never affiliated with the NAC of NA. Being the largest group of Navajo peyotists, they are also the strongest group, and they have made a point of remaining independent of the NAC of NA. They have, in effect, become a rival church.

In 1970 they attempted to incorporate in the state of Arizona under the name Native American Church of Navajoland, but they were refused. A similar attempt in 1971 met the same fate. Finally, in 1973 they were incorporated in the state of New Mexico. The officers applying for incorporation were those who signed the statement in the *Navajo Times* repudiating Frank Takes Gun. To the credit of the NAC of Navajoland, Frank Takes Gun has frequently been requested to speak at their conventions, and on June 17, 1975, he was honored with a special plaque.

In contrast to the Southern Arizona peyotists, the Navajo peyotists in the Four Corners area remained strongly allied with the reorganized NAC of NA, often providing leadership for that organization. Jimmie King, Taft Blackhorse, and Howard Nez have been leaders of the Four Corners branch, giving way eventually to the present leaders, James Atcitty and Emerson Jackson.

As well as these two large groups of Navajo peyotists, there are many other small functioning groups with independent leaders and organizations, sometimes more or less affiliated with the large groups, sometimes not at all. One such group in 1969 was known as the Northern Native American Church Association. It was organized and apparently completely controlled by Raymond Tso of Shiprock, New Mexico, who had a ceremonial hogan and house near Teec Nos Pas, Arizona. I attended one of his meetings in September, 1972, and was given a membership card good for life. Raymond Tso insisted he maintained carefully the ritual of John P. Heart. Members of the NAC of NA in the Four Corners area sometimes attend Raymond's meetings, but generally ignore him. Nevertheless, he is a dedicated road-man who has a loyal and devoted following of a few dozen peyotists who ask no more than to be directed and inspired by him.

A different group which I visited in 1969 was at Parks, Arizona, just south of the Navajo reservation line on old U.S. Highway 66 between Flagstaff and Williams, Arizona. Parks is not much more than a crossroads with gas stations and a trading post. In 1960, peyote meetings had been held in a building with a sand floor near the trading post owned by Andrew Scott, a Cherokee mystic. Later, in 1964, Scott had built a special peyote hogan, thirty feet in diameter, beside his trading post to accommodate the many Navajo peyotists who came to his place before peyote was legalized on the reservation. Andrew Scott attracted many Navajo peyotists as well as traveling roadmen from other tribes and a few non-Indians.

In 1969, Scott described his group in a letter to a fellow peyotist, Fred Hoffman (Cheyenne) of Hammon, Oklahoma, from whom he sought advice:

From time to time some people who are part Indian came, some Indians were married to non-Indians and they too were allowed to attend by the Road Chief and Crew. Since then, a precedent has been established so non-Indians who wish to attend are not excluded. . . . At no time has a non-Indian conducted the Ceremonies in our Church. . . . We have thought many times we should affiliate with the Mother Church nationally, just somehow we hadn't taken the action. We had been getting membership cards from Navajo Church until two years ago, [i.e., 1967] then for no reason or explanation, no more cards were mailed to us. When we applied for them, the executive who received the money did not return our money we sent for cards.

We have always used the Ceremony in proper ritual in the right way. The following are some of the Roadchiefs and Crews that have run meetings here in this Church: Nelson Franklin, Cheyenne from Ignacio, Colorado; Leslie Long, Navajo Reservation from Aneth, Utah; Enoch Smith, Navajo Reservation from Red Lake, Arizona; Tya Shaw, Navajo from Flagstaff—now residing in Holbrook, Arizona; Ralph Turtle, Cheyenne from Cortez, Colorado; Eugene Black Bear, Cheyenne, from Watonga, Oklahoma; Paul Tosie, Navajo, Tuba City, Arizona; Harvey Good Bear, Cheyenne, from Oklahoma; Lester Boone, Navajo from Red Lake, Arizona; Tony Beyal, Navajo from Red Lake, Arizona; Matthew Nelson, Navajo from Jeddito, Arizona; Harrison Begay, Navajo, Jeddito, Arizona; John Fowler, Navajo, Tonalea, Arizona; Dan Conejo, Navajo, Ganado, Arizona; Joe Charlie, Navajo, from Winona, Arizona; Tom Mike Marshall, Navajo, Tonalea, Arizona; Ned Johnson, Navajo, Tuba City, Arizona; Sam Boone, Navajo, Red Lake, Arizona; Chee Yabney, Navajo, Kayenta, Arizona; and many others. . . .

Also, what steps may we take to become affiliated with the Mother Church. . . . We have a membership of approximately one hundred and twenty people of which 60% are Indian, 20% part Indian, and 20% non-Indians, some married to Indians. . . .

Last election: Held in Parks, Arizona, July 6, 1969; Native American Church of North America, Parks, Arizona, Division; Officers of the Church:

Andrew E. Scott, President and Trustee (Cherokee); Dr. Bruce Jewell, Clinical Psychologist (of Los Angeles) (Cherokee); Wanda Jewell, Secretary (non-Indian); Mary J. Scott, Treasurer (Cherokee); Sam Boone, Director and Trustee (Navajo); Tony Beyal, Director and Trustee (Navajo).

Another independent group was the one at Needles, California, led by Truman Dailey. It was in 1959 when Truman, after making extended visits to the Navajo reservation every year for almost twenty years, decided to move there for good and settle down among some of his converts. However, just at that time he was hired to be an Indian chief in the Disneyland Indian village in Anaheim, California, an acting job he accepted and maintained for the next ten years. During those years at Anaheim he kept in touch with the Navajo on the reservation by spending most of his vacations there, and during the winter, by frequent short visits. During the winter months he worked only two days a week, so he could drive the five hundred miles to the Navajo reservation, direct a peyote meeting, and then drive back to Anaheim in any three- or four-day period, with his wife or other drivers taking turns at the wheel. Also during this time, for ten years Truman regularly and almost singlehandedly conducted meetings for the Navajo workers on the railroads of southern California, where Navajo had become the favored section hands. It was Truman Dailey who stimulated the organization and construction of the peyote church in the hogan near Needles, California, by Jack Woody, Dan Dee Nez, and Leon B. Anderson, and he regularly drove three hundred miles from Anaheim to the hogan in the desert to be roadman for peyote worshipers in the region and was in charge of the services the night that Woody, Nez, and Anderson were arrested. In 1972, Truman estimated that he was roadman for peyote rituals in California on an average of over thirty times a year, and one year when he kept a careful record of his activity, he found the total was forty-five weekends that he had served as roadman for Navajo Indians in California or on the reservation. Wide Ruins, Tuba City, and Greasewood were the Navajo communities on the reservation which he visited most often. At the same time, Truman was an active member of the NAC of NA, elected time after time to various offices.

Typical of the practice of peyotism on the Navajo reservation, as it was everywhere, was the even more informal community group which did not "belong" to the NAC of NA or any other organized group but who enjoyed the services from time to time of a home-grown roadman, a resident alien roadman, or just a temporary visiting roadman. Resident alien roadmen, that is, Indians from another tribe who visited the Navajo to proselytize and teach and then stayed for extended periods, were characteristic of Navajo peyotism. There were many. Most married into the tribe for a time and settled with the bride's people and regularly conducted meetings in the vicinity. Gus Hayes (Southern Cheyenne) was one of these. There were others: Southern Arapaho Ralph Turtle and his two sons, Winston and

Wayne Turtle; Otoes Edgar and Clarence Moore and Edward Tohee; Kiowas Emmett Tsatigh and Horace Daki; Winnebagos Vannert Dick and Stacey Mitchell; Sac and Fox Johnathan Koshiway and his son George and Brigham Minthern, to name a few.

Johnathan Koshiway was "the Grand Old Man of peyote" by the time he visited the Navajo and more or less settled down among them. He would have been nearly sixty years old in 1949 when his son-in-law, Truman Dailey, first introduced him to the Navajo. Privy to the mysteries of peyotism before 1910, he had been spreading "the gospel" for forty years in Oklahoma, Kansas, Wisconsin, Nebraska, Utah, and other states. It was his mission in life, and he was never known to have worked at anything else. After 1949, Koshiway stayed with different Navajo for long periods and eventually died among them, in 1971, at the age of eighty-six. Howard Nez, Navajo peyotist of Shiprock, said Koshiway had large followings at Canyoncito, Winslow, Page, Kayenta, Ganado, Shiprock, and Wide Ruins. Nez said it was about 1960 when Johnathan Koshiway visited him in Shiprock and stayed for five years. After he left Shiprock, he went to live with his son George, who had married a Navajo woman and was living with her near Steamboat, Arizona, in the south central part of the reservation.

Ethnologist Roland Wagner, whose research centered on the western section of the Navajo reservation from 1966 to 1970, wrote me about the Koshiways:

Franklin Yazzie from Bodaway told me that he was traveling around the reservation as apprentice for George Koshiway and his father, Jack Koshiway, who was supposed to be a "very old man" by 1970. The Koshiways are "Oklahoma Indians." At the time (1970) George and Jack were staying near Gallup, New Mexico, and Yazzie traveled to Texas with the Koshiways to pick peyote. Reportedly, the Koshiways know nothing of Navajo songs and preach that they shouldn't be "mixed" with peyote (no syncretism). As Franklin put it, George Koshiway preaches "only God, and peyote, and Jesus Christ. He also preaches one wife, one fireplace, one fire, one smoke stick." Some of these doctrines are distinctly different from the Navajo form of Peyotist doctrine.

The occasional visiting peyotists from Oklahoma and elsewhere with supplies of dried peyote for the Navajo, who stay a short time on the reservation to direct meetings and receive free-will offerings to pay expenses, are, of course, legion. And there are many successful home-grown Navajo roadmen who provide leadership for the thousands of Navajo worshipers. The typical ceremony is the Half Moon ceremony, although the Cross Fire ceremony is not unknown. For example, Robert Shorty of the NAC of Navajoland has become a skilled Cross Fire roadman.

There are many accounts of the Navajo peyote ceremony. An early one published in *Time* magazine on August 9, 1954, was a meeting conducted by Davis Anselm with Hola Tso in charge of arrangements. Reporters were permitted to observe and photograph the ceremony, and Dave Weber, a newspaper man from Santa Fe, prepared a manuscript of fourteen pages accompanied by eighteen pictures, from which *Time* based its article. Ethnologists David Aberle (1957; 1966; 1971; 1973; 1983) and Roland M. Wagner (1974: 1975*a,b,c,d*) and Dr. Robert L. Bergman, chief of the mental health program among the Navajo during 1971 and 1972 (1971, 1972, 1975), are among those who have attended many Navajo peyote meetings and who have described and commented upon them. All scholars agree, with minor differences, that the Navajo peyote ceremony is essentially the same ceremony that it is elsewhere. Elements of Navajo syncretism, when noted, are rare.

Aberle compared the ritual on several Navajo locations with the rituals of other tribes. He wrote (1966: 173): "The ritual of Navajo peyotism resembles very closely that of various Oklahoma peyotist groups. It is the identity of Navajo ritual with what might be called standard peyote ritual which should be stressed." Roland M. Wagner spent nearly a full year on the Navajo reservation collecting material for his Ph.D. dissertation, "Western Navajo Peyotism: A Case Analysis," at University of Oregon. He stated (1974: 2): "The similarities in modern-day Peyotism are more marked than the differences, and if one attended peyote meetings throughout the reservation or even on different reservations the rituals would probably be almost indistinguishable." Robert L. Bergman (1971: 696), too, participated in many peyote ceremonies also and described the typical Half Moon service. Moreover, he confirmed my own impression with the following:

The hallucinogenic effects of peyote used during meetings seem to vary. I have interviewed approximately 200 Peyotists on this subject, and most report that they seldom experience hallucinations. The most frequently reported effects are seeing beautiful colors. . . . Frightening experiences are almost never reported.

My own experiences in Navajo peyote meetings have been the same. Variations in the ceremony of the Navajo with others I have attended have been minor. In August, 1964, near Lupton, Arizona, I attended a peyote meeting in the hogan peyote church of Albert L. Lewis. The roadman was a Kiowa peyote missionary, Emmett Tsatigh, who was married to a Navajo and living at Lupton. Tsatigh recognized me as the anthropologist who had helped the NAC in court cases and seated me to the right of the chief drummer so that he could speak to me during the ceremony. He remarked several times during the night that he let pass some error of procedure because "these people are just learning." Except for such ritual slips, the ceremony was similar to other Half Moon meetings I had attended in Colorado, Utah, and Nevada.

Again in 1972, at the meeting directed by Raymond Tso, I found a traditional Half Moon ceremony. Raymond Tso was strict and formal in the management of the ceremony. Except for a metal hood over the fire in the center of the hogan, blowers to force out the smoke, and a louvered door to better adjust the temperature, one could have been in a tipi. As I had experienced with the Oto, Raymond provided a meal in a modern frame house near the hogan church for all who arrived for the ceremony, which may have caused the start of the ritual to be delayed until about 11 P.M. Other unusual features I noted might have occurred in any peyote meeting: invitations to a number of white physicians to attend the services, membership cards, and Raymond's sermons following the formal ritual.

As has been noted on other reservations, Navajo peyotists are at ease with two or three religions at the same time. Wagner cited Aberle (1966: 396) to the effect that a peyotist refused to state a preference for either peyotism, Navajo ceremonies, or white men's medicine: "I like all three. I have used them all." Wagner recorded the religious preferences of 208 Navajo families. Thirty preferred peyotism; 42 preferred Christianity; 60 preferred traditional Navajo religion; 47 preferred peyote-traditional; 29 preferred Christian-traditional; and 7 family heads said they did not have any kind of preference (1974, Table 17, pp. 235–27).

An obituary of Jim Sears McRaw in the *Navajo Times,* November 3, 1966, reads: "He strongly believed in the Native American Church, Navajo traditional religion, and was a Mormon. People had great trust in him." Another obituary in the *Navajo Times,* March 1, 1973, reported the death of Mrs. Lillie C. Johnson: "Born 102 years ago . . . at Two Gray Hills, she was a medicine woman, housewife, and a member of the Mormon Church."

Finally, in summary, what can be said about the motives and practice of peyotism on other reservations can be said equally of the peyotism of the Navajo. Its main appeal was as a curing ceremony, but its appeal was also social and spiritual. It was spread by dedicated missionaries. It survived a good deal of persecution. Although late in coming, peyotism today finds its strongest expression among the Navajo.

CHAPTER 12

Recent Developments

SINCE the publication in 1966 of N. Scott Momaday's *House Made of Dawn,* which contains a description of a peyote meeting held in the basement of the "Los Angeles Holiness Pan-Indian Rescue Mission," many people have assumed there are urban peyote meetings. Indeed, the service was so accurately described that I wondered, too, if there might be such a store-front peyote church in Los Angeles. I asked Truman Dailey about it, and he assured me that there was no such church, and that Momaday's church was purely imaginative. So far as Truman knew, all peyotists in southern California traveled out into the desert for peyote meetings, especially to the hogan peyote church built near Needles, where he was the principal roadman.

There is evidence, however, that Indians in the San Francisco Bay area have established a firm peyote group, although the meetings are not held in a city. The group began about 1955, and the leader was Phillip Jackson (Navajo) of Oakland, formerly of Tuba City, Arizona. In 1972, Truman Dailey confirmed my informants in Nevada, who had said that Jackson was in charge of a northern California branch of the NAC and that the group met in a hogan church in Healdsburg, California. By 1972, Stanley Smart, Northern Paiute roadman of McDermit, Nevada, had directed meetings at Healdsburg four times. Ramsey Walker (Washo) of Woodfords, California, said he had run meetings at Healdsburg six or seven times. Karl James (Washo) of Carson City said he had run meetings at Healdsburg "a few times." These informants also maintained that the Bay area peyotists sometimes attended peyote meetings at Woodfords and Carson City.

Peyote meetings have also been held from time to time in the vicinity of Denver, Colorado, to accommodate urban Indians. One meeting was held in 1959, and Philip Eagle Bear (Sioux) of Rosebud, South Dakota, was roadman. It was a regular Half Moon service in a tipi that had been put up on city park land in front of Coloraw's Cave near Red Rocks at the start of the hills west of Denver. Members of the Denver Westerners, a group of historians, mostly amateur, interested in western history, had been invited to attend, and during an interruption in the meeting, photographs were taken. I was able to show some of the photographs of this meeting to Sioux peyotists at Pine Ridge when I was visiting there in 1971 and was surprised to have several identify themselves in the pictures. Sam Kills Crow Indian of Porcupine, South Dakota, said the meeting had been called to doctor his mother, a very old woman sitting beside him. He also said that two or three peyote meetings a year were put up in the Denver area during the twenty years that he lived and worked there. "We had a peyote meeting whenever someone needed it," he said.

An opportunity to attend a peyote meeting in the Denver area came in the fall of 1972. Knowing that peyote meetings sometimes occurred in the area, I had asked Richard Tall Bull (Cheyenne), peyotist and longtime guard at Rocky Flats Atomic Energy Facility, to have me invited to a peyote meeting sometime. Years had passed since my suggestion, and then one Saturday afternoon I received a phone call telling me there was to be a meeting that evening. It was to be held on a farm at Firestone, Colorado, where Wilford Arapahoe (Sioux) was employed, and he thought I would be welcome. Firestone is a small agricultural village about twenty-five miles northeast of Boulder and thirty miles north of Denver. Wilford had been employed on the farm for some time and lived in an old, commodious farmhouse. His employer and landlord approved of his holding peyote meetings, and it was an ideal place, since the property was isolated and there was plenty of parking space.

It was a cold night, and the Cross Fire ritual was held in the living room. A special thick tray of sand, raised about four inches above the floor, provided a safe place for the hot coals for the crescent, carried in from the fire built outside. It was a birthday meeting in honor of Wilford Arapahoe, sponsored and paid for by his wife and sister. The roadman was from Scottsbluff, Nebraska, and several guests were from the Pine Ridge Reservation. Others were about equally divided between Navajo and Sioux. I estimated that two-thirds of the participants were from Denver, but a few came from Wyoming, Kansas, and Nebraska. I have heard that Wilford still lives at Firestone and peyote meetings continue to be held in his house.

With the ease of movement in the United States today and the habit of traveling by Indians as well as the entire population, it is to be expected that the Native American Church should be well known in all areas of the Indian population, among those who have left the reservation for the cities and also in new areas. The newest place where peyotism seems to be gaining a foothold is in the state of Washington. In 1977, in that state, articles of incorporation were filed by three independent and apparently mutually unknown peyote groups on three different reservations: the Yakima reservation on July 8, the Tacoma reservation on September 20, and the Colville reservation on October 3. I am not aware of the details of diffusion which led to the information about the Tacoma branch of the NAC, but only that articles of incorporation of the Native American Church of North America were filed on September 20, 1977, with Tacoma, Washington, listed as the main place of business and that Don Matheson (Puyallup), John Chiquiti (a Pueblo Indian residing on the Suquamish reservation), Bob Olney (Yakima), and Sid Mills (Yakima) living in Olympia, Washington, were the incorporators.

More is known of the Yakima group, which was incorporated as the Native American Church of the State of Washington of Toppenish, Washington (Yakima Reservation). Theodore Strong of Yakima had filed the petition, and in 1978 he provided me with the details of his conversion to peyotism and of the formation of the Yakima church. Theodore recalled that in 1970 while in Arizona he had traveled with Truman Dailey to attend a peyote meeting conducted by Truman. During the meeting he had had a vision of Mount Adams, a 12,307-foot peak on the western edge of the Yakima reservation in southwestern Washington. The next day when Theodore told Truman of his vision, Truman interpreted it as signifying that peyotism would someday be established in the state of Washington.

After that, Theodore Strong had visited Truman frequently in Red Rock, Oklahoma, to learn from Truman the Old Kiowa Hunting Horse way of conducting peyote meetings. Then in 1977, in order to fulfill Truman's prophecy, he had filed the articles of incorporation for the NAC in the Washington state capital at Olympia. Not unnaturally, Truman Dailey was one of the first to be notified of the incorporation, and he volunteered to come to Yakima to conduct a meeting, which he did on July 30, 1977. He and his wife arrived with a large tipi as a gift for Theodore. Thus it was in his own tipi at Yakima that Theodore received the Hunting Horse moon from Truman and was assured he could thenceforth conduct meetings in the correct Half Moon style. From July, 1977, to our interview in December, 1978, Theodore had conducted five Half Moon rituals at Yakima. He also told me that he considers himself an adopted son of the Truman Daileys.

Almost exactly at the same time that these two groups were becoming organized, another group was seeking incorporation on the Colville reservation some 250 miles from Yakima. Knowledge of this group came to me in 1978 when I was asked by Emerson Jackson (Navajo), then president of the NAC of NA, to go to Nespelem, Washington, to testify at the trial of some young peyotists of the Colville reservation who had been arrested for possession of peyote. While there, I was able to learn the complicated events that led to the organization of this particular group of peyotists.

Peter B. ("Sonny") George, a member of the tribe, claimed to be the first Colville Indian to attend a peyote meeting. That had occurred in 1964 at Parks, Arizona, in the hogan church of Andrew Scott, the Cherokee trader who had built his church just off the Navajo reservation to accommodate Navajos at the time when the Navajo police were vigorously enforcing the Navajo prohibition against peyote on the reservation. Sonny George had come to Scott's peyote hogan from Los Angeles with Bill Jefferies (Cherokee), a chiropractor and religious leader who directed peyote services and other ceremonies in an orange grove near Whittier, California. It was said that urban Indians from South Dakota, New Mexico, and Oklahoma as well as Washington and elsewhere, several of whom worked as actors at Knott's Berry Farm amusement park, were organized by Bill Jefferies as the "Black Elk Two Group." Sonny George had joined this interracial and intertribal group of about forty men and women to form a religious commune near Tahlequah, Oklahoma.

A friend of Sonny's from the Colville reservation, George ("Zomber")

Nanamkin, joined him in the commune near Tahlequah, where they both lived for about five years. Sonny returned home to Nespelem in 1970, and Zomber returned in 1973, on his way visiting the Andrew Scott hogan in Arizona. (In 1972 I had asked Scott to name and identify by tribe as many as possible of the peyotists who had attended meetings at his trading post. Among others, he had spelled out for me the name "Nanamkin" of Tahlequah, Oklahoma. When I wrote "Cherokee" after the name, Scott had corrected me, saying Nanamkin was from Washington—he thought Flathead. He then supplied the first name George and the Indian name of Going Snake. After meeting George Nanamkin in Colville, I was pleasantly surprised to find this information in my earlier notes from Arizona.) In 1976 a third Colville Indian, Vance Robert Campbell, Sr., also attended peyote meetings with the Navajo Indians, his interest having been aroused by Sonny George and Zomber Nanamkin.

A Native American Church Drafting Document was prepared about June, 1977, by Sonny George, and at the same time Vance Robert Campbell wrote to a recently incorporated NAC in Montana (probably the Cree of Rocky Boy's), who sent them "all forms and applications they used in establishing their church," including copies of the articles of incorporation of the Native American Church of North America which had been filed in Oklahoma in 1950; articles of incorporation of the Native American Church of the State of Nevada, dated 1958; and minutes of the meeting of the Native American Church of North America of January 27, 1977, Austin, Texas.

Under the direction of attorneys of the Colville tribal legal office, on August 15, 1977, an organizational meeting of the board of directors of the proposed Native American Church of the State of Washington was called together by Vance Robert Campbell, who presided over the meeting and appointed Alex C. Moomaw to act as secretary. Also present were Donny Moomaw and Sonny George. This meeting led to the filing of articles of incorporation in the office of the secretary of state. The officers given were Vance Robert Campbell, Sr., president; Peter B. George, Jr., vice president; Alex C. Moomaw, secretary; and Danny Moomaw, treasurer. The purposes of the incorporation were the same as those of the first charter in Oklahoma in 1918: "To foster and promote religious beliefs in Almighty God . . . with the sacramental use of peyote for religious purposes." To the surprise of all, the articles of incorporation were returned by the Office of the Secretary of State for the reason that "an identical corporation" was already on file in that office. It was only then that the Colville group learned of the other Washington peyotists. The Colville peyotists then changed the name of their organization to the First Native American Church (FNAC) of the Colville Tribes, and as such they were duly incorporated on October 20, 1977.

As soon as the FNAC of the Colville Tribes was legally established, friends among the Sioux peyotists were notified, and Leonard Crow Dog and Gilbert Stewart of the Rosebud Reservation and Rufus Kills Crow Indian of the Pine Ridge Reservation came to Colville with peyote to conduct the first peyote meeting on that reservation, using the Cross Fire ritual.

From the beginning the Colville peyotists were obviously concerned with following all correct procedures in the practice of their new religion. In December, 1977, Vance Robert Campbell used the title "Minister of the First NAC of the Colville Tribes" when he applied to the U.S. Fish and Wildlife Service for a "permit" to acquire eagle feathers for religious use." In order to legally gather peyote in Texas, a letter was sent to Helen Holloway, the Texas official in charge of enforcing the Texas law regulating the possession and transportation of peyote in that state, asking for information necessary to comply with the law. In response to this, the Colville tribe printed in four colors a four-page form to be distributed as follows: white to the Texas Department of Public Safety; yellow to the FNAC secretary; pink to the authorized person collecting peyote; and gold to the local FNAC file. The form provided the following information: the name of "bona fide member of FNAC of Colville," his membership card number, his chapter, his tribal enrollment number, his social security number, the effective dates of certification, the date of issue, and the signature and telephone number of the authorizing FNAC official. In addition, it contained the declaration: "That this individual member will comply with Federal and the State of Texas regulations, that the said peyote will be used for religious purposes only, and that this individual is one-fourth or more degree Indian blood."

The Colville church continued to be very legal, in 1978 sending to the Washington secretary of state an annual report with a one-dollar filing fee and the names of current officers, which included some new officials: Andrew Elwell, Jr., secretary, and John W. James, treasurer.

In February, 1978, Sonny George, as "Legal Assistant," sent letters to Paul Small, Sr., of Rocky Boy's, Montana, and to Larry Butler, Sr., of Cushing, Oklahoma, requesting guidance in becoming affiliated with the Native American Church of North America, and when the Twenty-ninth Annual Conference of the NAC of NA was held on March 10–12 at Laredo, Texas, Robert Vance Campbell and Andrew Elwell were delegates from the Colville tribes. That year Paul Small (Cree) and Joe Stanley (Cree) came to Nespelem several times to direct meetings and to teach the local leaders the order of service of the Half Moon ritual. Soon both Sonny George and Vance Robert Campbell were accepted as local roadmen. Zomber Nanamkin estimated that there were about thirty local members of the FNAC and that there was a peyote meeting someplace on the Colville reservation almost every weekend.

The local roadmen and those from Montana followed the Half Moon ritual, which is somewhat simpler than the Cross Fire ceremony. However, there was considerable interest in the Cross Fire ritual, probably because of the particular interest of Leonard Crow Dog, who not only was a dedicated Cross Fire proselytizer, but also an active leader in the American Indian Movement (AIM), an intertribal activist group of "Indians for Indians." He and others from the Rosebud Reservation, eleven hundred miles away, were important proselytizers to the peyotists of Colville.

We come now to the arrests of Kenneth Little Brave (Sioux), Roger Eagle Elk (Sioux), and Robin Gunshows (Colville) for possession of peyote on August 30, 1978. It was to testify at their trial that I had been summoned to Colville. At the time of their arrest, the three young Indians were traveling to a peyote meeting and were stopped by police for a traffic violation. They were found to be also in possession of peyote, the arresting officers considering this to be a violation of the law. They were jailed and held because they could not put up the bail of five thousand dollars required for each. The officers who arrested them and the judge who held them did so under a bill passed by the U.S. Congress in 1965, entitled the Drug Abuse Control Acts, which listed peyote as forbidden along with other psychedelic drugs. This law, when passed in 1965, was not aimed at peyotists, but was rather an effort to control the increased use of psychedelic drugs of many kinds in American society. It had not alarmed peyotists, and indeed they were hardly aware of it. Moreover, in the interpretation of the law by the Drug Enforcement Administration, peyote was specifically exempted when used in a bona fide religious ceremony, and most states, especially those used to dealing with peyotism, adjusted their state laws, as well, to exempt peyote when used for religious purposes. However, the Washington state law had not been so adjusted. When the federal exemption was pointed out in court, Ferry County Superior Court judge B. E. Kohls dismissed all charges for illegal possession of peyote by the defendants, ordered the return of the one hundred peyote buttons which had been confiscated, and expressed his regret that the three defendants were jailed for thirteen days.

The trial had taken place on October 11, 1978. That night a peyote meeting was held to "thank the Lord" for the success of the Colville tribal attorneys to free Robin Gunshows of Colville and for the success of the public defender, who had represented the visiting Sioux Indians. Although not present for the trial, Leonard Crow Dog and an automobile full of family members arrived in time to participate all night in the peyote service. About half of the twenty-six participants were Sioux; the other half were residents of Colville reservation. Four others were present: NAC president Emerson Jackson and three non-Indians—Spokane newspaper staff writer Deborah McBride, Public Defender John G. Burchard, and myself.

The tipi had been put up in a field near the summit of a pine-covered hill about fifteen miles from Nespelem. What appeared to be a semipermanent sheep camp was not far away, and the participants gathered there before going together in a body to the peyote meeting. The roadman was Edward Jess Eagle Elk (Sioux), the father of one of the Sioux Indians who had been arrested. That it was to be a Cross Fire ritual was made manifest when he stood the ritual staff upright instead of laying it on the ground in front of him. No cigarettes of Bull Durham tobacco were hand-rolled and smoked during the introductory prayers, as would have been done in the event of a Half Moon ritual. The form of the altar also fit the Cross Fire mode; it was large and in the shape of a horseshoe. As the night passed, the hot coals and ashes were arranged and rearranged into several different designs within the altar. Emerson Jackson (Navajo) served as cedar chief, Kenny Little Brave (Sioux) performed as chief drummer, and Zomber Nanamkin was fire chief. As always, the roadman carefully directed the ritual, requesting and receiving advice and help from a number of participants. His wife blessed the ceremonial breakfast of water, corn, meat, and fruit. Whether the prayers were said in English, Sioux, or one of the Indian languages spoken on the Colville reservation, one heard frequently the names of the attorneys, witnesses, and the judge in the prayers of the peyotists. In his prayer, Zomber Nanamkin said that he was pleased that peyotism had reached the state of Washington, for this partly fulfilled the "dream of old peyote leaders in Oklahoma that someday the Peyote Religion would reach the four corners of the United States of America."

The state of Washington did not amend its drug law to exempt peyote for religious purposes as a result of the *State* vs. *Little Brave, Eagle Elk, and Gunshows,* and Indians are still likely to be arrested for possession of peyote, although usually they will be freed later when the exemption for religious purposes in the federal law is pointed out. In fact, such another case happened in the city of Yakima in 1982.

It might be pointed out here that the federal legal system allows each state to interpret independently the federal law and to test the federal law in state courts, and while the opinion of one state court may be taken into consideration in arriving at a judgment by other state courts, the opinion is not binding. The Drug Abuse Control Acts have been tested a number of times in a number of states and in relation to other religions than peyotism. One of these involved the Neo-American Church, a church which was organized and incorporated by Art Kleps when he and Timothy Leary were promoting the general use of all psychedelic substances. The earliest of these cases involved William Robert Bullard III at the University of North Carolina, Chapel Hill. Bullard admitted possession of peyote and marijuana in his apartment but claimed exemption because he had recently become a convert to and had been named a regional official of the Neo-American Church. He was convicted by the trial court on December 13, 1965, and after review by the North Carolina Supreme Court, his conviction was affirmed.

The United States vs. *Kuch* was a more sophisticated and deliberate test of the Marijuana Tax Act of 1937, as amended, and of the Drug Abuse Control Act of 1965. Judith H. Kuch, of Washington, D.C., was indicted under the Food, Drug, and Cosmetic Act for unlawfully obtaining and transporting marijuana and for the unlawful sale, delivery, and possession of LSD. One of her contentions was that granting the Native American Church a limited exemption for use of peyote while denying her, as a member of the Neo-American Church, the alleged religious use of LSD constituted a denial of equal protection under the law. The defendant failed to establish the Neo-American Church as a religion, in part because the "church" included among its paraphernalia a Chief Boo Hoo as its head, a three-eyed toad as its symbol, and "Victory over Horseshit!" as its motto. There appeared clear evidence that the desire to use drugs and to enjoy drugs for their own sake, regardless of religious experience, was the coagulant of the organization and the reason for its existence. Motion to dismiss the indictment was denied.

In 1972, in the case of *Kennedy* vs. *the Bureau of Narcotics and Dangerous Drugs,* the court upheld a denial of the exemption to use psychedelics to the Church of the Awakening, which had been organized and incorporated in Socorro, New Mexico, in 1963, by a sincere religious mystic John W. Aiken. On May 15, 1969, in Kent County, Michigan, Aiken petitioned the Narcotics Bureau for an exemption from the antidrug laws covering psychedelics. The rejection was based in part on the finding that Aiken's group was only "a loose confederation of kindred souls whose purpose is to explore the mystical boundaries."

Although New Mexico had legalized the use of peyote for religious purposes in 1959, in 1970 one Robert Dan Pedro was arrested and convicted for possession of peyote, the conviction later reversed by the Court of Appeals when Pedro was found to be a peyotist in good standing. In the state of Oregon, one Roland Soto was arrested for possession of peyote, but the outcome of his trial was disappointing. At a pretrial conference the judge forbade the defendant to present any evidence pertaining to his religious beliefs. In this case, the judge of the Oregon Court of Appeals affirmed the conviction. Usually, however, religious beliefs have been considered and members of the Native American Church have been permitted to possess peyote. In 1982–83, a case similar to those in the state of Washington occurred, with similar results, in San Diego, California.

A case still pending as of December 6, 1984, is that of the *Peyote Way Church of God, Inc.,* vs. *the Attorneys General of the United States and of Texas* in the U.S. District Court in Dallas, Texas. Mana Paradeahtan, a man of questionable Indian parentage, who won a case in Denver in 1967 which enabled him to carry on a regular form of the Native American Church, is suing, as "Immanuel Paradeahtan Trujillo," for the right of Indians with less than one-quarter Indian blood and non-Indians to obtain peyote in Texas to use in his newly organized Peyote Way Church of God, which also adheres to the dietary laws of the Mormons' sacred book, *The Doctrine and Covenants.* The case was dismissed late in the fall of 1983, but has been appealed and awaits another chance for a hearing.

PEYOTE TODAY

It will soon be a hundred years since James L. Mooney first described the peyote ceremony of the western United States. During those hundred years we have witnessed the growth and spread of peyotism beyond Oklahoma to most of the western states. Its adherents have been found among Indians as widely separated in habits and language as the Plains Comanche and the Pueblo Taos, the desert Navajo and the northern Cree. From a few Indians formerly living on the Rio Grande in southern Texas, the practicers of peyotism have increased to embrace possibly as many as two hundred thousand Indians from the Mississippi to California, although the exact number is impossible to determine, inasmuch as no complete records of members and participants are maintained. It has crossed tribal as well as geographical boundaries, bringing an integrating force unique among Indians. Except for the Indian powwow, it is the most pan-Indian institution in America.

As has been pointed out in the course of this history, the ceremony itself has not changed in any fundamental way over the years, and this is assurance that the ceremony as first observed had been set in practice and tradition over many years. Just when and how this happened, we can only speculate, but that it took place in the area of natural growth along the Rio Grande is more certain, and it seems probable that the Carrizo were the source and the Lipan Apache were the principal early missionaries to the wild Indians of the Plains as they were assembled in Oklahoma in the last part of the nineteenth century. It is remarkable that the ceremony as described by Mooney is so typical of the peyote ceremony in dozens of different settings today that it could be one of them.

Nevertheless, it would be wrong to say that the changes in Indian circumstances and indeed in all of American life in the last one hundred years have not been felt by peyotism. The most important change in the ceremony was made early in its introduction into Oklahoma when John Wilson inaugurated the Big Moon variation, later to be further developed and expanded as the Cross Fire ritual by the Osage, Winnebago, and Sioux. Some other changes have been brought about by the changes in reservation life. Today special peyote churches, homes, and other shelters have often replaced tipis and brush enclosures as meeting places, necessitating changes in the construction of the altar and the use of fire and ashes. Usually a specially built peyote church will be constructed directly on the ground so it is possible to have a fire, and the service is little changed. In such peyote churches the altar is of concrete and therefore permanent. If a house or other structure with a wooden floor is used, of course it is not possible to have a fire, and there are several alternative actions. Sometimes the half moon or horseshoe-shaped altar and that part of the ceremony concerned with fire are dispensed with entirely. At other times sand is brought inside the house in a large box or on a metal sheet, and an altar of sand is constructed on or above the floor. A fire is kept outside, and the fireman brings in hot coals, which he puts before the altar of sand, and during the night he pushes the ashes against the inside of the Half Moon altar to form a Half Moon of ashes or, in the case of the Cross Fire ritual, he arranges and rearranges the ashes inside the Horseshoe-shaped altar according to the symbolism preferred by the roadman. If there is to be no sand altar or fire inside a house, peyotists sometimes spread an altar cloth on the floor and sit around it. The cloth may be embroidered with a "moon" or other symbols of peyotism along with some sacred words, and the Chief Peyote will be placed upon it. Although such changes are accepted as necessary, it is still greatly to be desired to hold meetings in the original tipi setting with altar and fire.

Except for the changes described above, the ritual remains the same. It generally begins about nine o'clock on a Saturday night. Today the participants are both men and women, although men are usually the leaders. They come dressed in their best clothes, having clean shirts and dresses. Many men wear a silk handkerchief around the neck, folded in a particular way and held together with a silver bola in the form of some peyote symbol—a button, a peyote bird, a cross. Some may wear red bean necklaces or other Indian jewelry, and some will have decorated cases which hold ceremonial feather fans handsomely beaded and tasseled with buckskin, to be used for incensing themselves with cedar smoke, and small gourd rattles similarly decorated. Some will wear blankets and shawls, for things Indians are the preferred dress. Some, especially women, will wear moccasins.

Even if the ceremony is held in a house, the peyotists sit on the floor in a circle, the roadman facing east, the chief drummer to his right and the cedarman to his left. The ceremony begins when the roadman takes from a special case his ceremonial paraphernalia consisting of a staff, usually carved or ornamented with beads and dyed horsehair (it will be placed in front of him in a Half Moon ceremony, stood upright in a Cross Fire ceremony); a decorated rattle; a special fan, probably of eagle feathers; and an eagle bone or reed whistle. He also produces a large peyote button to be the Chief Peyote, which he places on the moon altar. He also brings forth a sack of peyote buttons and usually a container of peyote tea to be consumed during the night, and, in the case of a Half Moon ceremony, two sacks of Bull Durham tobacco and papers or corn husks for the prayer cigarettes.

The cedarman throws a quantity of cedar on the fire, producing a dense aromatic smoke, and all the ritual objects, including the drum, are passed through this smoke in order to purify them. In the case of the Half Moon rite, the sacks of tobacco and papers are then circulated clockwise, and when all have prepared a cigarette, the roadman prays aloud and smokes his cigarette in concert with the others, who pray silently, all directing their smoke toward the fire and altar where rests the Chief Peyote. The sacks of peyote and tea are then passed clockwise around the circle, and each partakes either of tea or four buttons. The prayer and cigarettes finished and the first four peyote buttons eaten, the roadman, holding the staff and fan in one hand and vigorously shaking the rattle with the other, accompanied by the quick beat of the chief drummer, sings the ceremonial Opening Song, "Na he he he na yo witsi nai yo," syllables which go back to the Lipan Apache, to the songs of the first U.S. peyotists. He sings the hymn four times. He sings three more songs four times, and then the staff, fan, and rattle are passed clockwise to the next participant and the drum to that person's next neighbor. The person receiving the staff, fan, and rattle then sings four songs four times, and passes it on to the next participant, and so the staff, rattle, fan, and drum go around the circle, each participant singing four songs four times. Before midnight, the singing continues in this way only interrupted a few times when the peyote is circulated again.

At midnight, the roadman sings another ceremonially determined song, the Midnight Water Call. Then the fireman brings in a pail of water, which the cedarman passes through cedar smoke and blesses while smoking a prayer cigarette. After pouring a little on the ground "for Mother Earth," the water is passed around the circle to all participants. Today, instead of a common dipper as was used in the past, paper cups are often used. Sometime during the Midnight Ceremony, the roadman usually goes outside and blows the whistle to the four directions; this, however, is one of the more variable elements of the ceremony and may be dispensed with or changed. At the end of the Midnight Ceremony, there is a recess lasting ten to thirty minutes when everyone goes outside to relieve himself or to stretch. It is a quiet time with little talking.

When the meeting resumes, the singing begins again and continues. One-half to two-thirds of a peyote meeting is occupied in singing. Peyote may also be circulated. At this time the participants may take from their cases their own ceremonial rattles and fans for use during singing. Also, individuals may request a prayer cigarette from the roadman, and the singing will stop while all listen to the prayer. These prayers are sometimes confessionals, sometimes testimonials, sometimes supplications for help and guidance. This is also the time for a special curing ceremony, if such has been planned.

As the first rays of sunrise appear, the roadman sings another special song, the Dawn Song. He may also blow his whistle again to the four directions. This is followed by the entrance of the peyote woman, usually the wife of the host, who brings in water which is again blessed and circulated. She also brings the ceremonial breakfast of corn, meat, and fruit, which is circulated, with each person taking a bit of each food. Following the ceremonial breakfast, the roadman may give a little talk. If this has been a Cross Fire service, the roadman may read a text from the Bible and interpret its meaning to the congregation. In full daylight the roadman sings the last of the ceremonially determined songs, the Quitting Song. Then he and the others carefully put away the ceremonial paraphernalia, wrapping the fans, rattles, and any other ceremonial objects in silk handkerchiefs and depositing them in their special boxes and cases. It is then that the meeting is over and all go outside to "welcome the sun."

Now the congregation begins to visit with one another, and the women begin preparation for breakfast. This will be the best meal that the host, assisted by his friends, can offer. There will be a good deal of talk concerning the feelings and experiences of the previous night. In the afternoon the peyotists will begin to leave for home, which for some could be a considerable distance. It is not unusual for peyotists to travel more than a hundred miles to attend a meeting.

Thus ends a typical ritual. Except for a few changes because of the circumstances of modern life and a few additions from Christian lore, the ceremony is the same as that observed by Mooney. It should be borne in mind that the roadman is expected to use his judgment in the conduct of each ceremony, and he may make some variations, such as dispensing with the eagle bone or reed whistle ceremony, or, for convenience, the fire and altar, if need be. But these are temporary, one-time variations, and all are aware of them. Anthropologists have recounted the ceremony many times, but peyotists themselves or the NAC have never fully written down the ceremony in order to study it or establish its exact form. The ritual is always learned by one man from another and by repeated attendance at many meetings for the purpose of learning how it should be done.

It should be pointed out that among peyotists their religion is more than a ritual to attend from time to time, generally about once a month. It is a part of everyday life. Peyote singing is enjoyed at home. Most peyote homes will have a peyote rattle hanging on the wall. It is easy to take it down, fashion a drum from a piece of inner tube stretched over a coffee can, and do some singing. Children use rattles and drums in play and try to imitate the peyote singing of their elders. Adults more formally practice hymns at night. I was asked to participate in such a home practice session at the residence of Fred Hoffman (Cheyenne-Arapaho) of Hammon, Oklahoma, in April, 1972, after a peyote drum was tied and a space was cleared so that two could kneel side by side and perform as if in a meeting. The drummer was at the right of the singer, and from time to time the two would change sides and thus change roles. Albert Hoffman, Fred's father and well-known missionary to the Ute, and I were invited to take a turn as singers. Fred's wife and his son's wife, who sat at a table beading the handles of rattles, joined in the singing. Also, peyotists often share peyote music with nonpeyotists, and it is not uncommon to see nonpeyotists in a group of peyotists in informal hymn singing.

Peyote continues to be used sometimes as a home medicine, and many believe it has helped them. And it continues to be used as a fetish. Angelo

La Mere (Winnebago) carried a small bundle of peyote tied into a sack and hung around his neck when he enlisted in World War II. It was the gift of his anxious mother. Later, when he was on a destroyer in the Pacific, it was noticed by his commander as well as himself that he could see in a blackout better than others, and therefore he was asked to take the watch during blackouts. He felt that it was his mother's gift of peyote that gave him this extra power.

The theology of peyotism, like the ritual, is rooted in the past in a belief in the supernatural origin of the sacred cactus. To all, peyote is a divine plant given to Indians by divine revelation to help them; it can and does work miracles. Sven Liljeblad, ethnologist-linguist of Idaho State University, at Pocatello, has written a most eloquent and judicious statement on peyote theology and practice which deserves to be given here at length. His principal informant was John Pokibro (Bannock), a leader of the peyotists at Fort Hall and his long-time friend. In 1960, Liljeblad wrote:

The all-embracing view is that of a personal God in a monotheistic sense, and Peyote has come to the Indians to lead them to Him as Christ came to the whites. As God reveals Himself in Peyote, it becomes a sacrament whereby communion is established with Him or with the spiritual world in general. In prayers, sermons, and confessions at the meetings, there are frequent references to the Christian Trinity in terms of "Our Father" and "Our Brother Jesus" given in the vernacular, and "The Holy Ghost" given in English. As a meaningful and expressive pantheistic symbol, "Our Mother Earth" sometimes enters, all depending on the individual theory of life. Many a Peyote follower displays in private conversation a great deal of biblical knowledge. His tentative attempts at exegesis may sometimes seem strange, but no more so than the entangled conceptions in Christian scholasticism and sectarian amendments. He may take a quotation from the white man's Scriptures at its face value, and it is often amazing what he can do with it in support of his own opinion. Most people to whom Peyote affords consolation, many of whom can neither read nor write, have no need of theological proofs in matters of faith. In conformity with traditional religious aspect, faith is sanctioned for each one according to his own psychic experiences relating to the supernatural, and today Peyote affords the means of direct revelations. Rather than being a weakness, this non-commital attitude in confession of faith is a great strength of the Peyote religion. It satisfies any demand for denominational and even secular individual freedom. The partaker may beside his adherence to the Peyote movement be a member of any other church, or of none, and yet feel in harmony with the group.

The religious conceptions in the sphere of belief which the Peyotist applies are imperative only to the extent that they guide him in his never-ceasing search for righteousness and in his prayers for health. His piety resolves itself in ethnical norms based essentially on Christian moral values. But there is, also, in his ethics, a considerable freedom of thought and conscience. In his observances, he has to take the road Peyote tells him to follow. Abstinence from alcohol occupies a prominent place in his code or mores, evidently because alcohol consumption has caused so much trouble on the reservations. Chastity and family obligations are also of great concern, apparently for similar reasons. In general, one must try hard to do one's best as a self-supporting citizen and strive to become a respected member of the community. Friendliness and helpfulness between members of the group are much stressed. One must entertain friendly feelings toward one's neighbors and live in peace with all men. Coming as a novice to a meeting and asking the leader what to pray for, since you are neither sick nor troubled—which will surprise him greatly—would evoke the answer: "You should pray for peace, for those who are sick, and for your relatives." Consideration for other persons' problems justifies the Peyotist in disclosing his own grievances to other members of the group. Personal worries and shortcomings may be confessed. A statement during the testimonial period of a meeting may end with an appeal for moral support. Desire to help and to be helped in conforming to the moral standard of the group has a psychotherapeutic function which certainly comes to actual want in the present time of frequent individual maladjustment among the reservation people.

Yet the curative power of Peyote is the vital point. Presumably most converts join for this reason. By following the Peyote Road, health and advanced age would be secured. In most cases, a meeting is sponsored by a person troubled about his health or a case of illness in his family. He appointed the leader and defrays the cost. The Indians themselves may refer to the Peyote cactus as a medicine. But to them "medicine" is not merely a pharmaceutical product of the kind bought in drugstores. In their language there are two ways of verbalizing the notion of medicine, and both may be applied to Peyote. One of these terms refers collectively to the great and varied number of botanical items which the Indians have used therapeutically for colds, rheumatism, sore eyes, toothaches, and for all kinds of ailments, and most of which are known and used in modern pharmacology. The other term refers to something much more subtle which even a very intelligent speaker of the language has a hard time defining. And no wonder, since it leads straight into mysticism. White writers have tried to catch the underlying idea with such contradictory terms as "medicine," "supernatural power," and "the Great Spirit," none of which is sufficiently significant to cover the meaning. It may refer to an immaterial force which manifests itself in Nature's realm. The healing Peyote is conceived by the great majority as a divine panacea and by the sophisticated few as spiritual power of healing through mental effort. While Peyote ethics are saturated with Christian ideology and represent the acceptance of new social values, the rituals which remain the core of the cult are entirely native. The number of ceremonial elements, except for the spoken word, to which a Christian meaning may be attributed is limited to one: the cross on the Peyote drum. [Liljeblad 1972: 103–105].

Peyotism today echoes the longstanding problem of its opposition by the dominant population—the Spanish in Mexico and other Americans in the United States, government officials, Christian missionaries, educators, and U.S. senators and representatives, among others. Legally, peyotists today have won their fight for religious freedom in the United States. Since 1978, with the passage of the American Indian Religious Freedom Act (42 USC

1996, P.L. 95–341), the practice of peyotism by American Indians is protected by law. This act orders all federal agencies to be aware of American Indian sacred sites, objects, plants, materials, etc., and to protect them from destruction, if possible, and to make their use available to Indians. Peyotism is one of the several American Indian religions named as needing protection. But there is still the possibility of harrassment of peyotists under the Drug Abuse Control Act of 1965, which includes peyote among prohibited narcotics, and many state laws which have similar restrictions. While a test in court will clear anyone of arrest for possession of peyote if it is shown that the peyote is for use in a ceremony of the NAC and that the possessor is a member of the NAC, the arrest and detainment can be discouraging. NAC members are learning to be careful not to carry peyote around with them, to carry identification of membership in some NAC congregation, and to know the law. While the efforts to enforce the Drug Control Act where it involves peyote may be an annoyance, most Peyotists are willing to conform to the law.

An unusual case of harrassment under the Drug Control Act took place in Grand Forks, North Dakota, in October, 1984, when a white couple, Mr. and Mrs. John D. Warner, were arrested by the FBI for possessing peyote, a controlled drug. The two were members of the NAC of Tokio, North Dakota, and had been for a number of years, and Mrs. Warner was custodian of the supply of peyote for the Tokio congregation. The FBI had learned of the possession of peyote by the Warners from the president of the NAC of NA, Emerson Jackson (Navajo), so it was he who brought them to trial. Jackson said that they were not bona fide members of the NAC because they were not Indians. He maintained that in 1982 a motion had been passed by the NAC of NA to the effect that membership in that organization be limited to persons with one-quarter Indian blood, thereby excluding this white couple. A jury trial in Grand Forks Federal Court found the defendants innocent of breaking the law, since they were able to prove that although they were not Indians, nevertheless they were members in good standing of the local congregation of peyotists. The charges were dismissed.

This case not only illustrates harrassment under the Drug Control Act, but it also brings up the legality of non-Indians as bona fide members of the NAC. From the beginning, attendance of non-Indians to peyote meetings has been a somewhat personal or tribal matter. For instance, very early in Oklahoma some Caddo refused to allow non-Indians to attend any of their meetings. But others, such as the Kiowa and Comanche, welcomed non-Indians, black or white, as long as they were seriously interested. With the formation of the NAC, the same attitude has generally prevailed, and the presence of non-Indians has been no problem. It was in the sixties when the hippie generation became interested in peyote and became a nuisance in the peyote gardens of Texas, bringing about the Texas law which forbids possession of peyote by persons not having one-quarter Indian blood and proof of membership in the NAC, that race became an issue in membership. Since then, if non-Indians wish to be allowed to possess peyote, they must show that their involvement in the peyote religion is genuine—that it is not just a recreational, frivolous, or passing interest but a real commitment. Then, as the case against the Warners shows, race is not an issue. Still, it is especially important for non-Indians to carry identification of membership in the NAC if they have occasion to carry peyote, and even so, non-Indians possessing peyote violate Texas law.

The ruling of the NAC of NA that only Indians should be enrolled in the Native American Church is new and is not shared by most peyotists. The NAC of NA does not speak for all peyotists, much as it would like to do so. All peyotists consider themselves members of the Native American Church, but most are not affiliated with the NAC of NA. Each congregation makes its own rules, just as each meeting is conducted by its own roadman.

The internal strife within the NAC from 1956 to 1972 which swirled around Frank Takes Gun did not end with his eclipse. Divisiveness has become as much a characteristic of the peyote religion as it is of other religions. Today there are many peyote churches which have little to do with the NAC of NA. Some are large with wide jurisdiction; others are a single congregation. The Native American Church of Navajoland is now the largest body of peyotists. It counts as members most of the peyotists of the southern Navajo reservation in Arizona. This church body competes in Arizona with the Northern Navajoland Native American Church Association and the Native American Church of the Four Corners. In Oklahoma, most peyotists are content with their state organization, the Native American Church of Oklahoma. In South Dakota, there is the Ancient Native American Church of South Dakota (Half Moon) and the Native American Church of Jesus Christ at Porcupine (Cross Fire). These churches are loosely affiliated, if at all, with the Native American Church of North America, and there is rivalry, jealousy, competition, and many differences among them.

This is not to say that the NAC of NA is not important. It has the widest scope and its adherents range geographically from Iowa to Washington. It holds annual meetings and considers problems which seem to be common to all peyotists. When peyotists have legal problems, help is usually sought of and given by the NAC of NA. The current president of the NAC of NA, Emerson Jackson (Navajo of the Four Corners area), has been an official in the organization for over ten years and president since 1978, except for one term. Recently, he went to Mexico to visit the Huichol Indians to learn first-hand about their peyote beliefs and practices. Following his visit, he arranged for a party of Huichol peyotists to come to Tucson, Arizona, where they participated in a peyote meeting conducted by him and other NAC of NA officials.

The main problem today facing the Native American Church in whatever manner of organization is the present reduction in the supply of peyote. The original peyote gardens which furnished such a plentiful and inexpensive supply to the Indians of Oklahoma in the last century are becoming depleted. This reduction has resulted from a number of changes which have taken place in the limited area of peyote growth in Texas. In the early years of peyotism in Oklahoma, the peyote trade was in the hands of the *peyoteros* who lived amidst the peyote fields. After the Texas-Mexican Railway was built, crossing the border at Laredo and connecting with points near Indian reservations in Oklahoma, these enterprising Mexican families saw opportunity for a steady income in the expanding peyote market. They became familiar with the characteristics of peyote and learned that in order to keep plants producing, it was necessary to harvest them properly, cutting the top neither too deeply nor too shallowly. They found that properly cutting the plant actually increased the plant's growth, one root supplying many "buttons" where only one had been. They also dried the peyote to reduce spoilage and to reduce weight for shipping. Thus, the Indians of Oklahoma received a good product cheaply, and the *peyoteros* kept the peyote fields flourishing and made a good living. The *peyoteros* were well behaved, and the ranchers who owned the land saw no harm in this activity and usually charged the *peyoteros* nothing. It is possible that the ranchers found the *peyoteros* useful as caretakers and ranch hands.

In the thirties there was an oil boom in Texas, and the ranchers rented out land for oil exploration. Oil was discovered in the heart of peyote country, and this upset peyote harvesting to some extent. A sign of the times was the changing of the name of the little peyote town of Torrecillos to Oilton. The influx of people brought new harvesters of peyote. When they were not otherwise busy, oil workers became part-time *peyoteros.* Not viewing peyote harvesting as a lifetime occupation, they were not as careful as the traditional *peyoteros,* and the peyote gardens suffered.

In the sixties there was another invasion of people—the hippies, strangers associated with the drug culture from throughout the country. They were looking for peyote, and when they were not able to buy it from licensed dealers because it was a controlled substance, they trespassed and cut their own, and they, too, were not careful. Moreover, they angered the ranchers, some of whom locked their gates forever against anyone seeking peyote. Indians, too, began coming in greater numbers to harvest peyote, and though they worshiped the plant, they were often careless in cutting it. In some of the old peyote growing areas, alteration of the land by root-plowing to remove brush and improve grazing reduced the amount of peyote. There is still a lot of peyote in Texas, but the gardens are not what they once were, and now the demand for peyote is greater than ever because of the recent increase of peyotists among the Navajo.

Occasional shortages and increased demand have resulted in substantial price increases. In 1955 the price paid for one thousand peyote buttons was $9.50 to $15.00. Today the price is $100.00 for a thousand buttons. Increased prices have resulted in lower levels of consumption of peyote at peyote meetings, and many tribes now use only one-half to one-third the amount that they used a few years ago.

Peyotists are beginning to eye with envy the largely untouched peyote fields in Mexico. However, also alarmed by the hippies in the sixties, the Mexican government passed a law forbidding possession and exportation of peyote. It would take the cooperation of the U.S. government and the government of Mexico to alter the Mexican law in favor of peyotists, and it would probably take the cooperation of all branches of the Native American Church to bring about the cooperation of those governments. Perhaps it can be done. The Canadian government finally revised its law objecting to peyote and made it legal for peyote to be imported into Canada for religious purposes.

Another way to increase the supply of peyote would be to cultivate it. This would be expensive, necessitating greenhouses if it were not cultivated in the area of natural growth. Again, this would necessitate changes in the law, for at present it is unlawful to cultivate it, even in a greenhouse. As for the area of natural growth in Texas, all of the land is privately owned. Generally it is used for ranching, but there is still some oil activity. Recently viticulture has been attempted in the area with some success. And so the future of the little cactus, the essential ingredient of peyotism, its sacrament, is still in doubt.

APPENDICES

APPENDIX A

Peyote Ritual

THE peyote ceremony provides objective and concrete data which can be observed over and over again and therefore can be studied in detail and compared in the ritual's many settings. I began to do this in 1937 in my study *Ute Peyotism* by preparing a list of ritual elements and checking the reports of ethnologists who had studied different peyote groups to see how often the same ritual elements appeared. Fortunately, I have since been able to have many of the ethnologists themselves check my element list and supply helpful notes. To all of those who have given time and knowledge to do this, I am extremely grateful.

My first element list appeared in 1948 in *Ute Peyotism* and contained reports from seventeen peyote groups; the list contained herein has been enlarged to twenty-nine lists. Only two are unchanged, and most new material comes from participant observation. The list of elements has also been increased. My new data reinforce my earlier conclusion that the peyote ritual in its two variations—Cross Fire and Half Moon—is everywhere the same throughout the United States and Canada. The theological rule that the ceremonial leader of each peyote service is free to conduct the meeting as he wishes allows for minor variations; nevertheless, nearly all rituals fit into either the Half Moon or Cross Fire pattern.

Many of the differences between the two sects are related to smoking. Besides not using tobacco in the peyote meeting, the Cross Fire ritual is distinctive by greater reference to the Bible, by displaying a Bible in the peyote meeting, and by ending the all-night ceremony with a sermon based on a text taken from the Bible. These features go along with more frequent use of Christian words in prayers and songs in Cross Fire meetings, although such words are also common in Half Moon meetings. Deviations from the norm of each sect are most evident in the forty-two new elements in the present list, which generally reflect the characteristics of the Cross Fire variation. For example, Winnebago and Sioux Cross Fire rituals do not use tobacco at all, while the Osage and Caddo-Delaware permit the roadman to smoke a little.

Several elements have been added concerning differences in the ritual fire and altar. From the time of John Wilson, differences in altars or moons have been said to distinguish the two main sects. Speck (1933:543) recorded the origin of the Wilson moon from George Anderson:

Each day while under the spiritual guidance of Peyote during his seclusion, Wilson worked out the instructions given him in regard to the construction and furnishings of the peyote tent and the "moon" made of earth and markings on its floor. At first he said he made a small "moon," increasing its size day by day symbolical of his progress in spiritual knowledge. By the end of his sojourn . . .

he came to make the so-called large "Moon," the Wilson 'Moon' which has become typical of his followers.

This report of Anderson to Speck in 1932 of events which took place a half century earlier might best be considered as idealized legend. I believe the peculiarites of the Wilson moon had a parallel development in the Kiowa and Comanche Half Moon. Statements about construction and shapes of early altars force me to the conclusion that there was considerable variation from the beginning and that the method of constructing the altar, often dependent on circumstance, was an important factor in the size and shape of the altar. As time has passed, the Cross Fire altar has become the more elaborate altar, with additional markings and structures supplementing the moon; also, the variable treatment of ashes during the night characterizes the Cross Fire ceremony.

Column Abbreviations and Sources

The sources for the data in both the list and the notes to the list, and the abbreviations at the heads of columns, are as follows:

Mex: Mexico in general. Sources are Lumholtz (1891–1904); Mason (1912); Bennett and Zingg (1935); Zingg (1938); Furst (1969–1976); Benzi (1972; 1977); Benitez (1975).

L-A: Lipan Apache. Morris E. Opler (1938).

*K-A:*Kiowa-Apache. List filled in and notes supplied by J. Gilbert McAllister from information obtained during ethnographic fieldwork performed 1933–34 (eleven months) under the sponsorship of the University of Chicago. Other sources are K. Beals (1967); Bittle (1954); Jordan (1967–68).

Kio: Kiowa. List filled in and notes supplied by Weston La Barre. When returning the list, La Barre wrote: "I believe that in peyotism tribal affiliation in this intertribal religion is far less important than leadership, i.e., what the particular leader's 'way' is, and from what leader he got his meeting." La Barre did fieldwork in Oklahoma under the auspices of the Laboratory of Anthropology (1935), Yale University, and the American Museum of Natural History (1936). Howard (1967); Marriot (1942 and 1954); Earle (1968). I was fortunate to be able to make personal observations at a Kiowa peyote meeting near Fort Sill, Oklahoma, in April, 1972, at the home of Nelson Big Bow.

Com: Comanche in Oklahoma. List filled in and notes supplied by E. Adamson Hoebel, supplemented from Wallace and Hoebel (1952) and Jones (1972).

Kic: Kickapoo in the vicinity of McLoud, Oklahoma. List filled in and notes supplied by John A. Noon, who attended a meeting during the summer of 1932. The Kickapoo leaders recognized that they "followed the Kiowa-Comanche 'way.'"

AbS: Absentee Shawnee of central Oklahoma. List filled in and notes supplied by Erminie W. Voegelin; meeting attended in 1933.

Del: Delaware. Cult of the Kiowa-Comanche type among the Delaware. List filled in by James C. Webber, a Delaware informant recommended by Frank Speck, supplemented from Petrullo (1934).

S&F: Sac and Fox. Personal observation during a peyote meeting in April, 1972, near Stroud, Oklahoma, when the roadman was Carl Butler, son of one of the original peyote leaders in the area with his sons, Larry and George, assisting. Additional data from George and Mabel Harris, interviewed by Boyce Timmons for the University of Oklahoma Oral History Project (1967).

Iowa: Meeting described and illustrated by four drawings by Murray (1972), who also filled in the peyote element list and supplied additional notes.

Oto: Originally from Curtis (1930) and presented in Stewart (1948). Additional data by me after I participated in a meeting with Truman Dailey, Red Rock, Oklahoma, April, 1972.

NoC: Northern Cheyenne of Montana. List filled in and notes supplied by E. Adamson Hoebel in 1949. A few additional notes added by me after I attended a meeting at Ashland, Montana, in 1972, when a Northern Cheyenne was roadman.

Cro: Montana Crow. List filled in and notes furnished by Fred Voget, of Yale University, in the course of ethnographic fieldwork in 1939.

Ara: Arapaho. Originally from Kroeber (1907), but completed according to data from Underhill (1950) and from observations I made while attending a peyote meeting with the Arapaho in Wyoming in 1971.

WRS: Wind River Shoshone. List filled in and notes supplied by D. Shimkin from observation and inquiry in the course of ethnographic fieldwork sponsored by the University of California in Wyoming in 1939. Additional information from my personal observation of a peyote meeting in 1971 and from Day (1938), Stenberg (1946), and Moore and Schroer (1950).

Ute: Ute of Utah and Colorado. Observation and inquiry by me in 1937–38 when doing fieldwork sponsored by the University of California. Additional Ute Half Moon data from peyote services seen from 1960 to 1972.

Gos: Gosiute of Ibapah, Utah. List filled in and notes supplied by Carling Malouf, who attended a Tipi way meeting in 1939 and talked with Arthur Johnson, an official in the cult. Malouf's information was supplemented by an official "Program of the Native American Church" procured by A. L. Robertson while he was subagent at Ibapah in 1937.

W-P: Washo–Northern Paiute. Observation and inquiry by me in 1938 during work sponsored by the University of California. Notes added after participating in a meeting with the Paiute at McDermitt, Nevada, in 1972 and from information furnished in a letter from d'Azevedo to me, November 5, 1954.

Taos: Taos of New Mexico. List abstracted from published accounts by Curtis (1926) and Parsons (1936). A Ph.D. thesis, "Peyotism at Taos Pueblo and the Problem of Ceremonial Descriptions" (1969), and two articles by John J. Collins provided additional information. After attending a meeting at Taos in July, 1976, I was able to add details. T. Romero, informant, 1972, host and roadman of Taos peyote meeting I attended in 1976.

WHM: Winnebago Half Moon. I attended such a ritual at Wittenburg, Wisconsin, in 1972, and those observations were supplemented from Radin (1923), Densmore (1932), Lurie (1944), and Pelletiere (1963*a–e*).

SHM: Sioux Half Moon. George Morgan and Father Paul Steinmetz, S.J., marked the element list 1973 and 1974. This was supplemented by Ruby (1962).

Nav: Navajo. List filled in from personal observation of meetings near Teec Nos Pos, Arizona, conducted by Raymond Tso, and of one conducted by Emmitt Tsatigh near Lupton, Arizona. Other sources are Aberle (1966); Bahti (1970); Underhill (1963); Nabokov (1969); and Anderson (1980).

Osa: Osage. Information for list supplied by Garrick Bailey, October, 1978 and by his informant, LeRoy Logan, Osage roadman. Bailey also wrote: "There are several important points which you have to remember concerning the Osage Peyote Church. 1) The round houses were organized as churches with memberships. The staff, the rattle, and the drum belong to the round house, not Roadman. 2) Only the Roadman can smoke tobacco in the meeting. 3) Osage meetings last until noon of the following day and cedar is used only at the very end of the meeting. 4) The Osage have no 'cedarman,' but have a 'tobacco man.' 5) There is a chief fireman and two assistant firemen." Information on Osage peyotism is also found in Maker (1968); Mathews (1932; 1945; 1961); and La Barre (1938).

C-D: Caddo-Delaware. "Wilson way" among the Delaware (La Barre's Caddo-Delaware). Abstracted from Petrullo (1934) with additional data supplied by James C. Webber. The list does not adequately bring out the degree of divergence which the cult has attained, which could only be done by devising a list based on the Wilson way. The altar is greatly changed from the Kiowa-Comanche prototype and at times becomes extremely elaborate (see Petrullo 1934: pls. 3–6).

WCF: Winnebago of Nebraska. The Winnebago Cross Fire ritual is apparently a variant of the Wilson way, although Alexis A. Praus, who filled in the list and supplied the notes, did not designate it as such. Praus attended a meeting in 1939 "sponsored by two Winnebago women . . . 'to thank Jesus' for their recovery from a recent sickness." A visiting Oglala Sioux was chief drummer. Additional data is available in Radin (1914; 1923) and in Densmore (1932).

SCF: Sioux Cross Fire. List filled in from observations of a meeting near Allen, South Dakota, in 1971, when Reverend Emerson Spider, chief priest of the NAC of South Dakota, was roadman. Father Paul Steinmetz, S.J., who had attended Sioux Cross Fire rituals, also filled in an element list.

Men: Menominee. The publications of Slotkin (1952) and the Spindlers (1952–1971) provided the data to fill in this list.

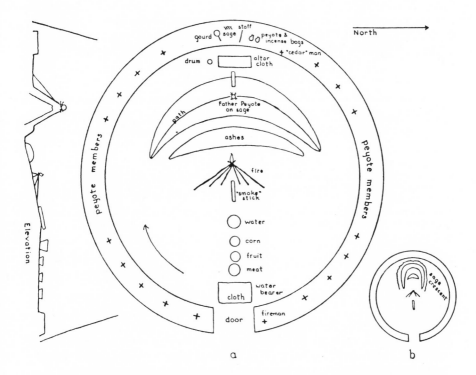

FIG. 20. "Arrangement of interior of tipi for peyote meeting. (a) Kiowa 'standard' peyote meeting; (b) Comanche horseshoe moon variant." From La Barre (1938:44, fig. 1).

MHA: Mandan, Hidatsa, and Arikara. Data on the list supplied by James H. Howard (1978).

Col: Colville reservation, state of Washington. List filled in from personal observation of a Cross Fire meeting conducted by Edward ("Jess") Eagle Elk (Sioux) of Rosebud, South Dakota. The special Wednesday night ritual was hurriedly arranged to celebrate and "thank the Lord" for the freedom of three "Peyote boys" tried October 11, 1978, for unlawful possession of peyote, according to Washington State law.

PEYOTE ELEMENT DISTRIBUTION LIST

Symbols Used in the Element List

+ Element present
− Element absent
A blank indicates information
   is lacking.

( ) Exactness of data doubtful
R Recent development
* Indicates a note to the element is appended at the end of the list.

PEYOTE ELEMENT DISTRIBUTION LIST

(See notes at end of list.)

*+

Element	Mex	L–A	K–A	Kio	Com	Kic	Ab S	Del
* 1. Staff of authority of leader	*+	+	+	+	+	+	+	*+
2. "Cane" 3–5 feet long	+	+	+	+	+	+	*+	+
3. Tufts of hair at top			*+	+	+	+	*+	*+
4. *Artemisia* tied near top or held along with cane			+	+	+	−	*+	−
5. Passed around		+	+	+	+	+	*+	+
6. Always passed between drum and altar			(+)	+		(−)	+	
7. Person holding staff leads singing		+	+	+	+	+	+	+
8. Rattle of leader	+	+	+	+	+	+	+	+
9. Gourd	+	+	+	+	+	+	+	+
10. Decorated	+	+	+	*+	+	+	*+	+
11. Handle beaded			+	+	+	+	+	+
12. Tufts of hair on top			+	+	+	+	+	+
13. Rattle passed around		+	+	+	+	+	+	+
14. Person singing shakes rattle	+	+	+	+	+	+	+	+
15. Individual rattle also used	+	+	+	+	+	−	−	+
16. Only after midnight			+	+		−	−	+
17. To accompany singer holding staff			+	+		−	−	+
18. Fan of leader (eagle tail feathers)	+	+	+	+	+	+	*+	+
19. Each feather tied separately	+		+	+	+	(−)	+	+
20. Binding decorated	+		+	*+	+	+	+	+
21. Passed around			+	−	+	(−)	−	+
22. Held with staff while singing			+	*+	+	+	−	+
23. Individual fans also used	+		+	+	+	+	+	+
24. Only after midnight			+	+	−	(+)	−	+
25. All fans used to draw smoke over head, body			+	(+)	+	+	+	+
26. Eagle-wingbone whistle of leader		+	+	+	*+	+	+	+
27. Used at special midnight ritual			+	+	+	+	+	+
28. At special morning ritual			+	+	+	(+)	+	
29. Placed near altar in front of leader			+	+	+	+	+	+
30. Only leader uses whistle			+	+	+	+	+	+
* 31. Paraphernalia satchel	+		+	+	+	+	+	+
32. Cloth upon which to place paraphernalia	+		+	+	+	+	*+	+
33. Drum of leader (or chief drummer)	+	+	+	+	*+	+	+	+
34. Water drum		*+	+	+	+	+	+	+
35. Iron kettle		+	+	+	+	+	+	+
36. Pottery jar			−	−			−	+
37. Charcoal in water		+	+	+	+	(−)	+	+
38. Head of deerskin	+	+	+	+	+	+	+	*+
39. Skin tied on before meeting		+	+	+	+		+	+
40. 7 stones or sticks used in tie			+	+	+	*−	*−	*+
41. 7 stones represent days			*+	+	−	*+	−	−
42. Rope forms star on bottom of drum			+	+	+	+	+	
43. Star significant			+	+			*(+)	
44. Skin removed at end of meeting			+	+	+	+	+	+
45. Only one drum used	+	+	+	+	+	+	+	+
46. Drumstick of leader			+	+	+	+	+	+
47. Individual drumsticks also used			+	+	+	(−)	+	+
48. Only after midnight				+	+		*−	+
49. Drum and drumstick passed around			+	+	+	+	+	+

Occurrence

S&F	Iowa	Oto	No C	Cro	Ara	WRS	Ute	Gos	W–P	Taos	WHM	SHM	Nav	Osa	C–D	WCF	SCF	Men	MHA	Col
+	+	+	+	*+	+	+	+	+	+	+	*+	+	+	*+	+	*+	*+	+	+	+
+	+	+	+	+	+	+	+	*+	+	+	+	+	+	*+	+	+	+	+	+	+
+	+	+	+	*+	+	+	+	−	*+	+	+	+	+	*+		*+	*−	−	+	+
+	+	+	+	*+	+	*+	+	+	+	*+	+	+	+		+	−	−	+	+	+
+	+	+	+	+	+	*+	+	+	+	+	+	+	+	+	+	+	+	+	+	+
+		+	+	(+)	+	+	+	+	+	+	+	+	+	+			+		+	+
+	+	+	+	+	+	+	+	+	+	+	+	+	+	+	+	+	+	+	+	+
+	+	+	+	*+	+	+	+	+	+	+	+	*+	+	+	+	+	+	+	+	+
+	+	+	+	+	+	+	+	+	+	+	+	+	+	+	+	+	+	+	+	+
+	+	+	+	+	+	+	+	+	+	+	+	*+	+	+	+	+	+	+	+	+
+	+	+	+	+	+	+	+	*+	*+	+	+	+	+	+	+	+	+	+	+	+
+	+	+	+	*+	+	+	+	+	+	+	+	+	+	+	+	+	+	+	+	+
+	+	+	+	+	+	+	+	+	+	+	+	+	+	+	+	+	+	+	+	+
−	+	+	−	+	+	+	+	−	+	*+	+	*+	*−	*−	+	−	*−	+	+	+
−	+	+	−	+	+	*−	+	−	+	−	+	+	−	−	*−	−	−	+	+	+
−	+	+	+	+	+	+	+	−	+	+	+	*+	−	+	+	−	−	+	+	+
+	+	+	+	*+	+	*+	+	+	*+	+	+	*+	*+	*+	*+	+	+	+	+	+
−	+	+	+	+	+	−	+		+	+	+	+	+	+	+	+	+	+	*+	+
+	+	+	+	+	+	−	+		+	+	+	+	+	+	+	+	+	+	+	+
−	+	+	+	+	+	+	+	+	*+	+	+	+	+	+	+	+	+	+	+	−
*−	+	+	+	+	+	+	+	+	+	+	+	+	+	+	−	+	*+	+	+	+
*+	+	+	+	+	+	+	+	+	+	+	+	+	*+	+	+	+	−	+	+	+
−	+	+	−	+	+	+	+	+	+	−	+	+	*+	−	*−	+	+	+	+	+
+	+	+	+	*+	+	+	+	+	+	+	+	+	+	−	+	−	+	+	+	+
*+	+	+	+	*+	+	+	+	+	*+	+	+	+	+	−	*−	−	+	+	+	+
+	+	+	+	+	+	+	+	*+	+	+	+	+	+	−	−	−	+	+	+	+
+	+	+	+	+	+	+	+	*+	+	+	+	+	+	−	−	−	+	+	+	+
+	+	+	+	+	+	*−	+	+	+	−	+	*+	+	−	−	−	*+	+	+	−
+	+	+	+	+	+	+	+	+	+	+	+	+	*+	−	+	+	+	*+	+	+
+	+	+	+	+	+	+	+	+	+	+	+	+	*+	+	+	+	+	+	+	+
+	+	+	+	*+	+	+	+	+	+	+	+	*+	+	+	+	+	+	+	+	+
+	+	+	+	+	+	+	+	+	+	+	+	+	+	+	+	+	+	+	+	+
+	*+	+	+	*+	+	+	+	*+	+	+	+	+	*+	*+	+	+	+	*−	+	+
−	*+	*−	−	−	+		+		−	−	+	−	−	+	*+		−	−	−	−
+	+	+	+	*+	+	+	+	*+	+	+	+	+	+	+	+	+	+	+	+	+
+	+	+	+	*+	+	+	+	+	+	+	+	*+	+	+	+	(+)	+	+	+	+
+	+	+	+	+	+	+	+	+	+	+	+	+	+	+	+		+	+	+	+
+	+	+	+	*+	+	+	+	+	+	+	+	+	+	*−	−	+	+	*+	+	+
−	+		−	+	+	+	+	+	*+	*+			+	−	−					
+	+	+	+	*+	+	+	+	+	+	+	+	+	+	+			+	+	+	+
−	+			*+	+	+	+	*+	+	*+	+	+		−					−	+
+	+	+	+	+	+	+	+	*+	+	+	+	*+	+	+	+	+	*+	+	+	+
+	+	+	+	+	+	+	+	+	+	+	+	+	+	+	+	+	+	+	+	+
+	+	+	+	*(+)	+	+	+	+	+	+		*+	+	+	+	+	+	+	+	+
+	+	+	−	+	+	+	+	−	+	+		+	+	+	+	−	+	+	+	+
−	+	−	−	+	−	−	+	−	+	−		−	−	−	−	−	−	+	+	+
+	+	+	+	+	+	+	+	+	+	+	+	+	+	+	+	+	+	+	+	+

Peyote Element Distribution List (*Continued*)

Element	Mex	L–A	K–A	Kio	Com	Kic	Ab S	Del
			Occurrence					
50. Separate drummer accompanies singer		+	+	+	+	+	+	+
51. Drummer usually at right of singer		+	*–	+	+	+	+	+
52. Only men drum	+	+	+	+	+	–	*–	+
53. Bag of cedar (juniper) leaves of leader		+	+	+	+	*	+	+
54. Cedar sprinkled on fire			+	+	+	+	+	+
55. Usually by cedarman			*–	+	+	+	*–	+
56. Only one bag of cedar used			+	+	+	+	+	+
57. Tobacco furnished by leader	+	+	+	+	*+	+	*+	+
58. Rolled in maize husks	+	+	+	+	+	+	+	+
59. In oak leaves		+	*–	+	+	–	*(+)	–
60. In paper			–	–	–	–	–	–
61. Only leader's tobacco used		+	+	+	+	+	–	+
62. Tobacco lacking from ritual	–	–	–	–	–	–	–	–
63. Peyote furnished by leader		+	+	+	+	+	+	+
64. Chief Peyote, an extra large button	+	+	+	*+	+	+	+	+
65. Decorated with white lines		*+	–	–		(–)		–
66. Placed on altar in front of leader	+	+	+	+	+	+	+	+
67. Is not eaten	+	+	+	+	+	+	+	+
68. *Artemisia* leaves under Chief Peyote		+	+	+	+	(–)	+	+
69. Form cross			*+	*+	+		+	+
70. Peyote for eating passed around	+	+	+	+	+	+	+	+
71. Only leader's used until after midnight			*+	+		(+)	*–	+
72. Leader	+	+	+	+	+	+	+	+
73. Called chief or peyote chief		+	+	*+	+	(+)	*+	*+
73a. Called Roadman			+	+	+		+	+
74. Sits west of altar or shrine or fire	+	+	+	+	+	+	+	+
75. Has complete charge of meeting	+	+	+	+	+	+	+	+
76. Assistants	+		+	+	+	+	+	+
77. 2 assistants	+		+	*–	–	–	–	–
78. 3 assistants			–	+	+	+	–	–
79. 4 or more assistants			–	*–	–	–	+	+
80. Chief drummer		+	+	+	+	+	+	*+
81. Sits at leader's right		+	+	+	+	+	+	+
82. Drums for leader		+	+	+	+	+	+	+
83. Drums for each singer in turn			–	–	–	–	–	
84. Cedarman or cedar chief			–	+	+	+	*+	+
85. Sits at leader's left			–	+	+	+	+	+
86. Sprinkles cedar leaves on fire			–	+	+	+	+	+
87. Offers prayers at specified times			–	+	–	(–)	+	+
88. Fire chief or fire tender	+	+	+	+	+	+	*+	+
89. Sits at north side of entrance		+	*+	+	+	+	+	+
90. Starts fire before meeting		–	+	+	+		+	+
91. Replenishes fire		+	+	+	+	+	+	+
92. Cleans up and arranges ashes			+	+	+	+	+	+
93. Conducts people in and out			–	+	+	+	+	+
94. All bathe before attending meeting		+	+	*+	*–		(–)	
95. Meeting place arranged (house, hogan, tipi)	+	+	+	*+	+	+	*+	+
96. In open	+	+		*–	–	–	(–)	–
97. Entrance or opening toward east	+	+	+	+	+	+	+	+
98. Altar is (crescent) mound of earth			+	*+	+	+	+	+
99. Concave side toward east			+	+	+	+	+	+

									Occurrence											
S&F	Iowa	Oto	No C	Cro	Ara	WRS	Ute	Gos	W–P	Taos	WHM	SHM	Nav	Osa	C–D	WCF	SCF	Men	MHA	Col
+	+	+	+	*+	+	+	+	+	+	+	+	*+	+	*+	*+	+	+	+	+	+
*+	+	*+	+	*+	+	+	+	+	+	+	+	+	+	+	+	+	+	+	+	+
+	+	+	+	*+	+	+	+	+	*+	+	+	+	+	+	+	+	+		+	−
+	+	+	+	*+	+	+	+	+	*+	+	+	+	+	*+	+	+	+	+	+	+
+	+	+	+	+	+	+	+	+	+	+	+	+	+	+	+	+	+	+	+	+
+	+	+	+	+	+	+	+	+	+	*+	+	+	+	*−	−	+	+	+	+	+
+	+	+	+	+	+	+	+	+	+	+	+	+	+	+	+	*−	+	+	+	+
+	+	*+	+	+	+	*+	+	+	+	+	*−	*+	+	*+	+	*−	*−	−	−	−
+	+	+	*+	+	+	+	−	*−	*−	+	−	*+	−	+	+	−	−	−	−	−
+	−	+	−	−	−	+	−	−	−	−	−	−	−	−	−	−	−	−	−	−
−	−	+	+	*+	−	+	+	+	+	+	−	*+	+	−	−	−	−	−	−	−
+	+	+	+	*+	+	+	+	(+)	+	+	−	+	+	+	+	−	−	−	−	−
−	−	*+	−	−	−	−	*+	*+	−	−	+	−	−	−	−	+	+	+	+	+
*+	+	+	+	+	+	*+	+	+	+	+	*+	*+	+	+	+	*−	*−	*+	+	+
+	+	+	+	*+	*+	+	+	+	+	+	+	*+	+	+	+	+	+	+	+	+
−	+	+	+	*+	+	*−	+	*(+)	*−	+	+	+	+	−	*+	−	+	+	+	+
+	+	+	+	+	+	+	+	+	+	+	*+	+	+	+	+	+	+	+	+	+
−	−	−	+	*+	+	*+	+	*	+	+	+	*−	+	+	*+	−	−	+	−	
+	+	+	+	+	+	+	+	+	+	+	+	+	+	+	+	+	+	+	+	+
+	+	+	+	+	+	+	+	+	+	+	+	+	+	+	+	+	+	+	+	+
+	+	+	+	+	+	+	+	+	+	+	+	+	+	+	+	+	+	+	+	+
+	+	+	−	−	−	−	−	−	−	−	−	−	−	−	−	−	+			
−	+	*+	+	−	+	−	+	+	+	+	+	*+	+	−	*+	−	+	+	+	−
−	+	+	+	−	+	+	−	−	*+	+	+	+	−	+	*+	−	+	−	−	+
+	+	+	+	+	+	+	+	+	*+	+	*+	+	+	+	*+	+	+	+	+	+
+	+	+	*−	+	+	+	+	+	+	+	+	+	+	+	+	*−	+	+	+	+
+	+	+	+	+	+	+	+	+	+	+	+	+	+	+	+	+	+	+	+	+
*−	−	*+	−	*+	*−	*−	*+	−	*−	*−	−	*+	−	*+	*+	*−	+		*−	−
*−	+	+	+	*+	+	+	+	+	+	+	*+	+	+	−	−	*+	+	+	−	+
−	+	+	*−	*+	+	+	+	+	+	+	+	+	+	−	−	*−	+	+	−	+
−	+	+	−	+	+	+	+	+	+	+	+	+	+	−	−	+	+	+	−	+
+	+	+	+	+	+	+	+	+	+	+	+	+	+	*+	+	+	+	+	+	+
+	+	+	+	+	+	+	+	+	+	+	+	+	+	+	*+	+	+	+	+	+
+	+	+	+	*+	+	+	+	+	+	+	+	+	+	+	+	+	+	+	+	+
+	+	+	+	+	+	+	+	+	+	+	+	+	+	+	+	*+	+	+	+	+
+	+	+	−	*+	+	+	+	−	+	+	+	+	+	+	+	−	+	+	+	+
−	*+	+	*−	*+	+	+	+	+	*+			+	+	*+	*−	−	−	+	−	
+	+	+	+	*+	+	+	+	*+	+	+	+	+	+	*+	+	+	+	+	+	+
−	−	−	+	+	−	−	+	−	+	+	−	−	−	−	−	−	*+	−	+	−
+	+	+	+	+	+	+	+	+	+	+	+	+	+	*+	*+	+	+	+	+	+
+	*+	+	+	+	*+	+	+	*+	*+	*+	+	*+	*+	*−	*−	*−	*−	+	+	+
+	+	+	+	+	+	+	+	(+)	+	+	+	+	+	+	*+	*+	−	+	+	+

Peyote Element Distribution List (*Continued*)

Element	Mex	L–A	K–A	Kio	Com	Kic	Ab S	Del
					Occurrence			
100. Line on top of moon			+	+	+	+	(−)	+
101. Fire east of leader's place	+	+	+	+	+	+	+	+
102. East of moon			+	+	+	+	+	+
103. Sticks placed to form right angle			+	+	*−	+	+	+
104. Old methods used to start fire		+	−	*+	−		+	+
105. 4 sticks on fire				(+)	*−	(−)	+	*−
106. Special fire stick (poker)			+	+	+	+	+	+
107. Worshipers congregate outside			+	+	+	+	+	+
108. Indian dress, moccasins, etc., preferred	+	+	+	+	+	+	*+	+
109. Meeting starts in evening	+	+	+	+	+	+	+	+
110. Leader prays before entering meeting			+	*+	+		*(−)	
110a. Ceremonial circuit outside of tipi	+		*+	*+	*+			
111. Order of entrance: chief first			+	+	+		+	+
112. Chief drummer second			+	+	+		+	+
113. Cedarman third			−	+	+		−	+
114. Men (before women and children)	+		−	+	+	+	(+)	
*115. Women and children allowed	+	*−	*+	*+	*+	*+	+	+
116. Fire chief last			+	+	+		+	+
117. Seating: leader west of altar or shrine	+	+	+	+	+	+	+	+
118. Men, either side, near leader		+	−	+	+	+	+	+
119. Women, either side, near entrance			−	*+	+	+	+	−
120. Separation of men and women	+		−	−	+	(−)	−	*+
121. An assistant on each side of leader	+		−	+	+	+	+	+
122. Women sit behind men			−	−	−	*−	−	−
123. All pass to south of moon			+	+	+	+	+	+
124. Sit on blankets, straw, etc.			+	+	+	+	+	+
125. *Artemisia* (sagebrush) [126. Missing.—O.C.S.]		+	+	+	+	+	*+	+
127. Prayer or speech or both at start of meeting	+		+	+	+	+	+	+
128. Tobacco passed, all roll cigarettes		+	+	+	+	+	+	+
129. Cigarettes lit with fire stick, clockwise			+	+	+	+	+	+
130. Leader prays aloud during smoking		+	+	+	+	+	*−	+
131. Others pray silently			+	+	+	+	+	+
132. Smoke blown toward altar	+		+	+	+	+	+	
133. All motion toward altar or Chief Peyote		+	+	+	+	+	*−	+
134. Cigarette butts placed against altar	+		+	+	+	+	+	+
135. *Artemisia* (sage) leaves passed clockwise			*−	+	+	+	+	−
136. Leaves rubbed on hands, clothes			*+	+	+	+	+	−
137. Chewed			−	+	+	+	−	−
138. Peyote incensed before passing			+	+	+	(+)	−	
139. Peyote passed round circle	+	+	+	+	+	+	+	+
140. Clockwise		+	+	+	+	+	+	+
141. All take 4 buttons at start			*+	+	+	−	*−	+
142. Each button chewed, spit into hands, rolled, offered to altar, and swallowed			*+	*+	+	+	−	
143. Chest patted during swallowing of button				*+	+	(−)	−	
144. First peyote eaten before singing starts		+	+	+	+	(+)	+	+
145. Paraphernalia brought out by chief			+	+	+	+	+	+
146. Laid on ground between leader and altar			+	+	+	+	*−	+
147. Cedarman throws cedar leaves on fire				+	−	(+)	*+	+
148. Paraphernalia incensed	+		+	+	−	+	+	+
149. 4 times			+	+	−		+	+

									Occurrence												
S&F	Iowa	Oto	No C	Cro	Ara	WRS	Ute	Gos	W–P	Taos	WHM	SHM	Nav	Osa	C–D	WCF	SCF	Men	MHA	Col
+	+	+	+	+	+	+	+	+	+	+	+	+	+	+	*−	*−	−	+	+	+
+	+	+	+	+	+	+	*+	*+	+	+	+	+	+	+	+	+	+	+	+	+
+	+	+	+	+	+	+	+	+	+	+	+	+	+	+	+	+	−	+	+	+
+	+	+	−	*+	+	*−	+	+	+	*−	+	+	+	*−		−	*+	+	+	+
*+	*+		−	*−	+	−	+	+	−	−	−	−	−	+	+	−	−	−	−	−
+	+	+	*−	*+	+	−	+	+	+	*−	+	−	+	+	*−	−	+	−		+
+	+	+	+	+	+	*+	+	+	+	+	−	+	+	+	+	+	−	*+	+	−
*+	+	+	+	+	+	+	+	+	+	+	+	*+	−	−	+		−	+	+	−
+	+	+	−	*−	+	−	+	−	+	*+	+	−	−	*+	*+	−	−	−	+	+
+	+	+	+	*+	+	+	+	+	+	+	+	*+	*−	+	+	+	+	+	+	+
−	+	+	+	*+	+	+	+		+	+	+	*+	−	−	−		*−	+	+	−
+	−	+	+	+	+	+	+		*+	+	+	*+	+	−		*+	−		−	
−	+	+	+	+	+	+	+	*+	+	+	+	+	−	+	*+		−	+	+	−
−	+	+	+	+	+	+	+	+	+	+	+	+	−	+	*+		−	+		
−	+	+	+	+	+	+	+	+	+	+	+	+	−	−			−	+		
−	+	+	+	*+	+	+	+	+	+	*−	+	*−	−	+	−		−	−		
*+	+	*+	+	+	+	*+	+	+	+	+	+	+	+	+	+	+	+	+		
+	+	+	+	+	+	+	+	+	+	+	+	+	−	+	+		−	+		
+	+	+	+	+	+	+	+	+	*+	+	+	+	+	+	*+	+	+	+	+	+
−	+	+	+	+	+	+	+	+		+	+	*−	+	−	+	+	+	+		+
−	−	−	+	+	−	+	+	+		+	+	−	+	−	−	+	+	−		+
−	−	−	+	*+	−	*+	+	−	−	−	−	−	−	+	*+	+	−	+		+
−	+	+	+	+	+	+	+	+	+	+	+	+	+	+		+	+	+		−
−	+	−	−	+	−		+		+	−	−	−	−	+	−	−	−	+		+
+	+	+	+	+	+	+	+	+	+	+	+	*+	+	−	+	+	−	+		+
+	+	+	+	*+	+	*R	+	+	+	+	+	*+	+	+	*+	+	+	+	+	+
−	+	+	+	+	+	*+	−	−	*−	+	+	+	−	−	+	+	+	−		+
+	+	+	+	*+	+	+	+	+	+	+	+	+	+	+	+		+	+	+	+
+	+	*+	+	*+	+	+	+	*+	+	+	−	+	+	−	*−	−	−	−		−
+	+	+	+	+	+	+	+	+	+	+	−	+	+	+	−	−	−	−		−
+	+	+	+	*+	+	+	+	+	+	+	−	+	+	*+	+	−	−	−		−
−	+	+	+	+	+	+	+	+	+	+	−	*+	+	+	+	−	−	−		−
+	+	+	+	*+	+	+	+	+	+	+	−	−	+	+		−	−	−		−
+	+	+	−	+	+	+	+		−	+	−	−	+	+	+	−	−	−		−
*+	+	+	+	*+	+	*+	+	+	*+	*+	−	*−	+	*+	*−	−	−	−		−
+	+	+	−	*+	+	+	+	+	+	*+	+	+	+	+	+	−	*+	−	+	−
+	+	+	−	+	+	+	+	+	+	+	+	+	+	+	+	−	+	−	+	−
−	−	+	−	*−	+	+	+	+	+	+	+	+		+	+	−	+	−	+	−
+	+	+	+	+	+	+	+	+	+	+	+	+	+	+		+	+	+	+	+
+	+	+	+	+	+	+	+	+	+	+	+	+	+	+		+	*+	+	+	+
*+	+	+	+	+	+	+	+	+	+	+	+	+	+	+	+	+	+	+	+	+
−	+	+	+	+	+	*+	+	+	+	*+	+	*+	*−	*−	+	+	−	+	+	+
−	+	+	−	*+	+	*+	+	+	+	+	−	−	−	−				+	+	−
−	+	−	−	*+	+	+	+	+	+	+	−	+	+	−			+	−		−
+	+	+	−	*+	+	+	+	+	+	+	+	*+	+	+	+		+	+	+	+
+	+	+	+	+	+	+	+	*+	+	+	+	+	+	*+	+		+	+	+	+
+	+	+	+	+	+	+	+	+	+	+	+	+	+	−	+	+	*+	+	+	+
*−	+	+	−	*+	+	+	+	+	+	+	+	+	+	−	−		+	+	+	+
+	+	+	−	+	+	+	+	*+	+	+	+	+	+	−	+	*+	+	+	+	+
+	+	+	−	+	+	*−	+	+	+	+	+	*+	+	−	+		+	−		+

Peyote Element Distribution List (*Continued*)

Element	Mex	L–A	K–A	Kio	Com	Kic	Ab S	Del
					Occurrence			
150. Worshipers incensed			*+	+	−		+	+
151. 4 times				+	−		+	
152. Whistle placed near altar			+	+	+	+	+	+
153. Leader starts singing, 4 songs		+	+	+	+		+	+
154. Sings fixed opening song			+	+			+	+
155. Holds staff in front of him		+	+	+	+	+	+	+
156. Another beats drum			+	+	+	+	+	+
157. Chief drummer beats drum		+	+	+	+	+	+	+
158. Drum, rattle, etc., passed round clockwise		+	+	+	+	+	+	+
159. Each man sings 4 songs		+	+	+	+		*+	+
160. Each man drums for 4 songs of man to his left		+	+	+	+		+	+
161. Rule against women singing			*+	+	+		(+)	+
162. Drumming, singing all night (except for midnight water call)	+	+	+	+	+	+	+	+
* 163. Midnight water call and recess		*−	*+	+	+	+	+	+
164. Leader recalls drum, staff, etc.			+	+	+	+	*+	+
165. Fire chief forms ashes into crescent			+	+	+	+		*+
166. Fire replenished			+	+	+	+		+
167. 4 sticks added								−
168. Altar and floor carefully cleaned by fire chief	+		+	+	+	+		+
169. Cedar sprinkled on fire			+	+	+	+	+	−
170. Whistle blown by leader			+	+	−	+	+	−
171. 4 times			+	+	−	+	+	
172. Leader sings fixed water song			+	+			+	+
173. Bucket of water brought in by fire chief			+	+	*+	+	+	+
174. By women			−	−	*+	*−	−	−
175. Water bearer kneels east of bucket			+	+	+	+	+	−
176. Cedarman prays, sprinkles cedar on fire			+	+	+	+	+	−
177. Water bearer draws incense to water			+	+	+	+	*+	+
178. Water bearer prays, blesses water			+	+	+	+	+	+
179. While smoking cigarette			+	+	+	+	+	
180. Leader given butt of same cigarette, smokes, prays			+	+	+	+	+	
181. Water bearer spills water on ground			*−	+		+	+	+
182. Bucket passed clockwise, all drink			+	+	+	+	+	+
183. Devotees rub, sprinkle ("baptize") selves with water			−	+	+	−	−	−
184. Chief Peyote, paraphernalia sprinkled			−	*+	+			−
185. Water bearer takes water outside			+	+	+	+	+	+
186. Makes circuit of altar before removing water				+	+	+	+	+
187. Drum, staff returned to place they occupied before midnight			+	+	+	+	*	−
188. After paraphernalia placed, leader goes outside			+	+	+	+	+	+
189. Blows whistle to cardinal directions			+	+	+	+	+	+
190. Prays to cardinal directions			+	+	+	+	+	+
191. Leader incensed upon return			+	+			+	+
192. Replaces whistle near moon			+	+		+	+	+
193. After midnight individual fans, rattles, etc., used				+	+	*+	−	+
194. All urged during meeting to eat as much peyote as possible	*+	+	*−	*+		+	+	+
195. Urged not to eat too much			*+	−			−	−
196. Individual prayers aloud, by men		+	+	*+	+	+	−	+
197. By women			+	*+	−	*+	−	+
198. Suppliant first gets tobacco from leader		+	+	+	+	+	−	+
199. Cigarette lighted with fire stick			+	+	+	+	−	+
200. 4 puffs of smoke blown toward altar at start			+	+	+	+	−	+

Occurrence

S&F	Iowa	Oto	No C	Cro	Ara	WRS	Ute	Gos	W–P	Taos	WHM	SHM	Nav	Osa	C–D	WCF	SCF	Men	MHA	Col
+	+	+	−	+	+	+	+	+	+	+	+	+	+	−	+		+	+		+
+	+	+	−	*−	+	*−	+		+	+	+	+	+	−			+			+
+	+	+	+	*+	+	+	+	+	−	+	+	+	+	−		−	+	+		+
+	+	+	+	+	+	+	+	+	+	+	+	+	+	+	+		+	+	+	+
+	+	+	−	+	+	*+	+	*+	+	+	+	+	+	+	+		+	+	+	−
+	+	+	+	+	+	+	+	+	+	+	+	+	+	+	+		+	+	+	+
+	+	+	+	+	+	+	+	+	+	+	+	+	+	+	+		+	+	+	+
+	+	+	+	+	+	+	+	+	+	+	+	+	+	+	+		+	+	+	+
−	+	+	+	+	+	+	+	+	+	+	+	+	+	+	+	+	+	+	+	+
*−	+	*+	+	+	*+	+	*+	+	*+	−	−	*−	*−	*+	*+	+	*−	+	+	+
*−	+	−	+	*−	*+	+	−	*+	*−	*−	+	*−	−	−	+	−	*−	−	−	−
+	+	+	+	+	+	+	+	+	+	+	+	+	+	+	+	+	*−	+	+	+
*+	+	+	+	+	+	+	+	*+	*+	+	+	+	+	*+	*−	+	*−	+	+	+
+	+	+	+	*+	+	+	+	+	+	+	+	+	+	*+		+	−	+	+	+
−	+	+	−	*+	+	+	+		*+	+	+	+	+	−		−	*−	*+	+	+
+	+	+	+	+	+	*+	+		+	+	+	+	+	−		−	*−	*+	+	+
+	+	+	+	+	+	+	+	+	+	+	+	+	+	−	*−		−	+	+	+
+	+	+	*+	+	+	+	+	+	+	+	+	+	+	+	−	+	−	+	+	+
−	+	−	*+	−	−	−	−	−	−	−	−	−	−	−	−	−	−	−	−	−
−	+	+	+	+	+	+	+	+	+	+	+	+	+	−	−	+	−	+	+	+
−	+	+	+	+	+	+	+	+	*−	+	+	+	*+	−	−	+	−	+	+	+
−	+	+	+	+	+	+	+	+	+	+	+	+	+	−	−	+	−	+	+	+
+	+	+	+	+	+	+	+	+	+	+	−	+	+	−	−	−	−	+	+	+
+	+	+	+	*+	+	+	+	+	+	+	−	+	*+	−	−	−	−	+	+	+
+	+	+	+	+	+	+	+	*+	+	+	−	+	+	−	−	−	−	+	+	+
+	+	+	+	+	*+	+	+	+	+	+	+	*+	+	+	−	+	−	+	+	+
+	+	+	+	+	+	+	+	+	+	+	+	*+	+	−	−	−	+	+		
+	+	+	+	+	+	+	+		+	−	+	+	+	+	−	−	−	−	−	+
+	+	+	+	+	+	+	+	+	+	+	+	+	+	−	−	+	−	+	+	+
+	+	+	+	*+	+	−	+	+	+	+	+	+	+	−	−	−	−	−	+	+
+	+	+	+	+	+	+	+	+	+	+	+	+	+	+	−	*+	−	+	+	+
+	+	+	+	+	+	+	+	+	+	+	+	+	+	−	−	*−	−	+	+	+
+	+	+	+	+	+	+	+	+	+	+	+	+	+	−	−	−	−	+	+	+
+	+	+		+	+	+	+	+	+	+	+	+	+	*−	−	−	−	−	−	+
+	+	+	+	+	+	+	+	+	+	+	+	+	+	−	−	−	−	+	+	+
*+	+	+	+	+	+	+	+	+	+	+	+	+	−	−	+	*+	−	+	+	+
+	+	+	*(+)	+	−	+	*(+)	+	+	+	+	+	+	−	+	*−		*−	+	+
−	−	−	−	(+)	−	−	*+	−	−	−	−	−	−	−	−	−	−	−	−	−
+	+	+	+	+	+	+	+	+	+	+	+	+	+	+	*+	+	+	+	+	+
+	−	+	−	+	+	+	+	−	+	+	+	+	+	+	+	−	+	+	+	+
+	+	+	+	+	+	+	+		*+	+	−	*+	+	−	+	−	−	−	−	−
+	+	+	+	+	+	+	+		+	+	−	+	+	−	+	−	−	−	−	−
+	+	+	+	+	+	+	+		+	+	−	+	+	−	+	−	−	−	−	−

Peyote Element Distribution List (*Continued*)

Element	Occurrence							
	Mex	L–A	K–A	Kio	Com	Kic	Ab S	Del
201. Butt handed to leader				+	+	(−)	−	
202. To cedarman, who blows 4 puffs toward altar				+	−	(−)	−	
203. To chief drummer, who blows 4 puffs toward altar				+	−	(−)	−	
204. Handed back to leader, who blows 4 puffs toward altar				+	−	(−)	−	
205. Prayer by individual followed by one by leader			*+	+	(−)	−		−
206. No one leaves meeting while anyone is singing, praying, or eating peyote	+		+	*+	+	+	+	+
207. Morning water call (similar procedure to midnight ritual)		+	+	+	+	(+)	+	+
208. Water brought in		+	+	+	+	+	+	+
209. By woman			+	+	+	+	+	+
210. Who blesses water			+	+	+		+	+
211. Woman makes circuit of altar before taking water outside			+	+		(+)	+	
212. Woman returns immediately with food and water			+	+	+	+	+	+
213. "Peyote breakfast"	+	+	+	+	+	+	+	+
214. Lined up in front of door, in order (from fire toward door)		+	+	+	+	+	+	+
215. Order: water, maize, fruit, meat	+	+	*+	+	+	−	−	+
216. Water, rice, fruit, meat			−	*−	−	−	−	−
217. Water, maize, fruit, candy							*+	
218. Water, maize, meat, fruit						+	−	−
219. Parched maize	+	+	+	*+	+	+	+	+
220. Candy also included in the breakfast			−	+	−	+	*+	−
221. Food blessed			+	+	+	+	+	+
222. Wash before eating	+	+	−	−	−		−	
223. Paraphernalia put away after blessing			+	+	+	+		
224. Before eating			+	−		+		
225. Drum untied		+	+	+	+	+	+	+
226. Water from drum drunk			+	+	+	−	+	+
227. Water touched to body with stick, hands—"baptism"		*+	+	+	+	−	−	+
228. Any remaining poured on or between crescents			+	+	−	+	*+	
229. Objects used to tie on drumhead touched to body			+	+	+		−	+
230. All parts of drum passed, handled			+	+	+		−	+
231. Leader's outfit taken out by fire chief				+			+	
232. Food passed clockwise			+	+		+	+	
233. Replaced on floor between fire and door				?	+		+	
233a. Order before passing reversed				+			+	
234. Taken out by fire chief			+	*+	+		+	
235. After food taken out, all go outside, about 9 A.M.		·	+	+	+	+	+	
236. Sun greeted	+		*−	−	(−)	−		
237. Return to tipi to lounge, talk, smoke			+	*+	−		(−)	+
238. Tipi dismantled, altar destroyed following meeting		+	*−	*+	+		+	
239. Feast follows meeting	+	+	+	+	+	+	+	+
*240. Aligned between leader and door starting at west: Bible			−	−	−	−	*−	−
241. Staff, rattle, and feathers	+		+	+	+		+	+
242. Whistle			+	+	+	+	+	+
243. Chief Peyote	+	+	+	+	+	+	+	+
244. Crescent of earth			+	+	+	+	+	+
245. Crescent of ash			+	+	+	+	−	+
246. Fire	+	+	+	+	+	+	+	+
247. Fire stick			+	+	+	+	+	
248. Water	+		+	+	+	+	+	+
249. Person blessing water			+	+	+	+	+	+

Occurrence

S&F	Iowa	Oto	No C	Cro	Ara	WRS	Ute	Gos	W-P	Taos	WHM	SHM	Nav	Osa	C-D	WCF	SCF	Men	MHA	Col
−	+	+	−	*+	+	+	+	+	+	+	−	+	+	−	*+	−	−	−	−	−
−	+	+	*−	+	+	+	+	+	−	−	−	+	+	−	−	−	−	−	−	−
−	+	+	−	+	+	+	+	+	−	+	−	+	+	−	+	−	−	−	−	−
−	+	+	+	+	+	+	+	+	−	+	−	+	+	−	+	−	−	−	−	−
−	+	+	+	+	+	+	+	+	*−	−	−	+	+	−	+	−	−	−	−	−
*+	+	+	+	*+	+	+	+	*+	+	+	+	*+	−	+	+	+	+	+	+	+
+	+	+	+	+	+	+	+	*+	*+	+	+	+	+	−	*+	*−	*+	+	+	+
+	+	+	+	+	+	+	+	+	+	+	+	+	+	−	+	−	*−	+	+	−
+	+	+	+	+	+	+	+	+	+	+	+	+	+	−	*−	−	*−	+	+	+
+	+	+	+	+	+	+	+	+	+	+	+	+	+	−	*−	−	*−	−	+	+
+	+	+		+	+	+	+	+	+	+	+	+	+	−	−	−	−	+	+	+
+	+	+	+	*+	+	+	+	+	+	+	+	+	−	−	*−	*−	−	+	+	+
+	+	+	+	*+	+	−	+	+	+	+	+	*+	+	+	*−	*−	*−	+	+	+
+	+	+	+	+	+	+	+	+	+	+	+	+	+	+	−	−	−	+	+	+
+	+	+	*+	+	+	*+	+	*+	*+	*+	+	+	+	+	−	−	*−	+	+	+
−	−	−	*−	−	*−	−	−	*+	*+	+	−	−	−	−	−	−	−	−	−	−
−	−	−	−	−	−	−	−	−	−	−	−	−	−	−	−	−	−	−	−	−
−	−	−	−	*−	*−	−	−	−	−	−	−	−	−	−	−	−	−	−	−	−
+	+	−	−	*+	+	*+	+	+	−	*+	+	−	*+	+	−	−	−	−	+	−
*+	+	+	−	*−	+	*+	−	−	−	*+	+	−	*+	+	*+	−	*−	+	−	−
+	+	+	+	*+	+	+	+	+	+	+	+	+	+	+	−	−	−	+	+	+
+	+	+	+	+	+	+	+	*+	+	*−	+	+	+	−	*+	*+	*−	+	+	+
+	+	+	−	+	+	+	+	+	+	*−	+	+	−	*−	+	+	*−	+	+	+
+	+	+	+	+	+	+	+	+	+	+	+	+	+	+	+	+	*−	+	+	+
+	+	+	*−	+	+	−	+	+	+	+	−	−	+	+	−	−	−	+	−	
+	+	+	−	+	+	*+	+	+	+	+	+	+	*−	+	+	*−	*−	+	+	+
+	+	+	−	+	+	+	+	+	−	+	−	−	+	+	+	−	−	−	+	−
−	+	+	+	+	+	−	+	+	−	+	−	−	+	+	+	−	−	−	+	−
+	+	+		+	+	+	+	+	−	+	+	*+	+	+			−	+	+	+
+	+	+	+	+	+	+	+	+	+	+	+	+	+	*−			−	+	+	+
+	+	+	+	+	+	+	+	+	+	+	+	+	+				−	+		+
*−	+	+	+	+	+	+	+			+	+	+	+	−			*−		+	+
+	+	+	+	+	+	+	+	+	+	+	+	+	*−	+	*−		*−	+	+	+
−	+	+	−	*−	+	+	+	+	+	*+	+	−	−	+	*+		−			−
+	+	+	−	+	+	+	+	+	+	+	−	+	+				*−	+	+	+
−	+	−	+	*−	+	−	−	−	−	+	−	+	+				*−	*+	+	−
+	+	+	+	+	+	+	+	+	+	+	+	+	+	+	+	+	*−	+		+
−	*+	*+	−	*−			−	−	−	−	*+	−	−	−		*+	+	−	−	−
+	+	+	+	+	+	+	+	+	+	+	+	+	+	+			+	+	+	+
+	+	+	+	+	+	+	+		−	+	+	+	+	−			+	−	+	+
+	+	+	+	+	+	+	+	+	+	+	+	+	+	+	+	+	+	+	+	+
+	+	+	+	+	+	+	+	+	+	+	+	+	+	*+	+		*+	+	+	+
+	+	+	+	+	+	*+	+	+	+	+	+	+	+	−			*+	+	+	+
+	+	+	+	+	+	+	+	+	+	+	+	+	+	−	+	+	+	+	+	−
+	+	+	+	+	+	+	+	+	+	+	+	+	+	−	−	−	+	+	+	
+	+	+	+	+	+	+	+	+	+	+	+	+	+	−		+	+	+	+	
+	+	+	+	+	+	+	+	+	+	+	+	+	+	−	−	+	+	+	+	

Peyote Element Distribution List (*Continued*)

Element	Mex	L-A	K-A	Kio	Com	Kic	Ab S	Del
250. Peyote breakfast	+	+	+	*+	+	+	+	+
251. Beliefs connected with peyotism: belief in a Great God (Great Spirit)	+			+	−	+	+	+
252. Belief in spirit forces subservient to the Great God	+			+		(−)	+	+
253. Peyote is a spirit force chosen to guide the Indians	+		+	+	+	+	*+	+
254. Peyote's function is medicinal	+	+	+	+	+	+	+	+
255. Peyote's function is particularly ethical-religious			+	*+	+	+	+	+
256. Peyote's doctrines can be understood only through peyote intoxication	+		+	+	+	+	(+)	+
257. Ultimate goal of intoxication is enlightenment and physical betterment	+		+	+	+	+	+	+
258. Individual can be helped by concerted prayer			+	+	−	+	+	+
259. Individual must attain purity before approaching spirit forces	+		+	+	+	+		+
260. An important function of peyote meeting is to purify	+	+	+	+	+	(+)	*+	+
261. Modifications permitted by new revelations				+				−
262. Approach to spirit forces should be humble			+	*+	+	+	*+	+
263. Concept of the peyote road as ethical-religious			+	*+	+	+	+	+
264. Identification of the peyote road with the Creator's road			+	*+	−		−	+
265. Identification of the peyote road with Jesus' road			+	*+	+	*+	−	−
265a. (See note)								
266. Jesus named in songs	+		+	+	+			
267. Jesus named in prayers	+		+	+	+		+	
268. Ritual number four	+	+	+	+	+	+	+	+
269. Cardinal directions important	+	+	+	+	+	+	+	+
*270. Salt taboo while consuming peyote	+	*+		*+	*+	+		
271. Sacred water	+		+	+	+	+	+	+
272. Peyote helps foretell future	+			+	+	+		+
273. Peyote helps influence future	+		*+		+		+	
274. Dancing during ritual regularly	+							
275. Dancing during ritual rare, occasional		*+	*+	*+	*+			
*276. Pilgrimage to harvest peyote	+	+	*+	*+	+	+	+	
277. Prayer before harvest of peyote	+	+	+	+	+	+	+	
278. Offering before harvest of peyote	+		+		+		+	
279. Tobacco smoke blown toward peyote	+	+	+	+	+	+	+	
280. Peyote protects from witches	+	+			+			
281. Peyote teaches	+	+	+	+	+	+	+	+
282. Peyote called medicine	+	+	+	+	+	+	+	+
283. Peyote ground or powdered	+	+	+	+	+			
284. Peyote made into paste or mush	+	+	+	+	+			
285. Peyote tea	+	+	+	+	+	+	+	+
286. Staff stood in hole when not circulating								
287. Altar shaped like horseshoe				+	+			
288. Mound or circle east of altar								
289. Mound called Mount Sinai								
290. Wooden peyote church building								
291. Concrete altar in building								
292. NAC cemetery								
293. Concrete altar in cemetery								
294. Mescal bean necklace or bandolier		+	+	+	+	+	+	+
295. Meal served before meeting				*+				
296. Whistle sometimes accompanies singing			+					

										Occurrence										
S&F	Iowa	Oto	No C	Cro	Ara	WRS	Ute	Gos	W–P	Taos	WHM	SHM	Nav	Osa	C–D	WCF	SCF	Men	MHA	Col
+	+	+	+	+	+	+	+	+	+	+	+	+	+	–	–	–	*–	+	+	+
+	+	+	+	+	+	*+	+	+	+	+	+	+	+	+	+	*+	+	+	+	+
+	+	+				+	*+	*+	+	+	+	+	+	–	+	+			+	+
+	+	+	+		+	+	+	+	+	+	+	*+	+	+	+		+	+	+	+
+	+	+	+	+	+	+	+	+	+	+	+	+	+	+	+	*+	+	+	+	+
+	+	+	+	+	+	+	+	(+)	+	+	+	+	+	+	+		+	+	+	+
+	+	+	+			+	+			+	+	+	+	+	+	+	+	+	+	+
+	+	+	+		+	+	+	+	+	+	+	+	+	+	+	+	+	+	+	+
+	+	+	–		+	+	+		+	+	+	+	+	+	+	+	+	+	+	+
+	+	+	+		+	*+	+		+	+	+	*+		+	+	+	+	+		+
+	+	+	+		+		+	+	+	+	+	+	+	+	+	+	+	+		+
+	+	+			+	–	+		*–	+	+	+	+	–	+		+			+
+	+	+	+		+	+	+		+	+	+	+	+	+	+	+	+	+	+	+
+	+	+	+		+	+	+		+	+	+	+	+	+	+	+	+	+	+	+
+	+	+	+		+	+	+		+	+	+	*–	+	+	+		*+		+	+
+	+	+	–		+	+	+		+	+	+	*+	+	+	+	+	+		+	+
								*+												
+	*+	+	+	+	+	+	+	+	+	+	*+	+	+	*+	+	*+	+	*+	+	+
+	+	+	+	+	+	+	+	+	+	+	+	+	+	+	+	+	+	+	+	+
+	+	+	+	+	+	+	+	+	+	+	+	+	+	*+	+	+	+	+	+	+
					+									+		+				
+	+	+	+	+	+	+	+	+	+	+	+			+	+	+		+	+	+
					+				+					–	+	+	+		+	+
					+				+					–	+	+	+		+	+
														–						–
				*+					*+					+						–
+	+	+	+	+	+	+	+	+	*+		+	+	*+	+		+	+			+
*+				+							+	+	+	+						
				+								+	+	–		+	+			
+				+							+	+	+	+						
		+											+	+			+			
+	+	+	+	+	+	+	+	+	+	+	+	+	+	+	+	+	+	+		+
+	+	+	+	+	+	+	+	+		+	+	+	+	+	+	+	+	+		+
+	+	+	+	+	+	+	+		+	+	+	+	+	+		+	+			+
+		+	+	*+	*+				+	+	+	+	+	+		+	+			+
+	+	+	+	+	+	+	+	+	+	*+	+	+	+	+	+	+	+	+	+	+
														*+		*+	+			+
														+	+	+	+			+
	*+										*+			+	*+	*+	*+			–
														–		*+				–
								+			+		*+	*+		*+				–
											*+			*+		+				–
											+	+		–			+			–
														–			+			–
+	+	+	+		+	+				+	+	+	+	+	+	+	+		+	–
+		+	+		+	+				+	+	+	+	+		+				–
										*+				–						+
																				–

Peyote Element Distribution List (*Continued*)

Element	Occurrence							
	Mex	L–A	K–A	Kio	Com	Kic	Ab S	Del
297. Water served to anyone anytime		*+						
298. Water available to anyone after midnight								
299. Ashes shaped into heart, star, piles								
300. Cloth altar								
301. Person reentering meeting incensed								
302. Morning star important	+			+			+	+
303. Peyote strung to preserve, carry	*+	+						
304. Sucking shamanism during rituals		*+						
*305. Crucifix displayed during ritual	+			+	+			

Notes to Element List

1. *General:* The Osage call the staff "arrow," as do the Delaware, Quapaw, and Oto. It is called "bow" by the Ponca (La Barre 1938: 67). *Mex:* "The Rods of Power preside over all rites during the Peyote Pilgrimage. . . . a peyote-seeker goes at the head of the column carrying the Brazil-wood batons wrapped in their red kerchiefs" (Mata Torres 1973: 26, 31). *Cro:* Straight stick of any kind or collapsible cane, beaded at the joints (Voget). *WHM:* "Represents Moses staff, undecorated" (Densmore 1931:5). *Osa:* "The 'arrow' referred to here is the staff which is owned by the roadman and passed around in the meeting and held by each man as he sings" (Maker 1968:5). "The staff, the rattle, and the drum belong to the round house, not the roadman" (Bailey). *WCF:* "+" called by Rave the "shepherds crook" (Densmore 1931:5). *SCF:* Special hole in ground to stand staff upright before and after meeting and during recess. See note 286, below. A catalog card regarding the staff names it "Peyote spear" and adds "reminds the people of the congregation of the spear with which the side of Christ was pierced" Rosebud Catholic Museum. Menominee: Crosses carved a long staff (Slotkin 1952: 588; Spindler and Spindler 1971: 102).

2. *AbS:* "The staff represents a walking cane" (Voegelin). *Gos:* Made of mountain mahogany by leader himself (Malouf). *Osa:* called "arrow" (Bailey).

3. *K-A:* Not necessarily (McAllister). *AbS:* Deer's tail dyed red (Voegelin). *Del:* Staff decorated with feathers, ribbon, and otter skins (Petrullo 1934: 49). *WCF:* Tufts of hair around two joints about a foot from each end of cane. An oval celluloid device five inches long with feathers attached around its edge was suspended from the upper joint. Staff was walking stick with crook (Praus). *Cro:* Horsehair among the Crow. Sometimes hair of different animals is used. "People wish for the same type of animal as the hair. It is a sort of wishbone." Crow prefer white horsehair to black. "The old-time Indians say white is the cleanest thing on earth; that is why they use that" (Voget). *W-P:* (Stewart 1944). *WCF:* +, based on a photograph (Radin 1923: 388, pl. 54, and text p. 389). *SCF:* Cross on top of staff (Stewart 1972c). *Osa:* deer tail (Bailey).

4. *AbS:* Held by person giving the meeting, at opening of meeting only (Voegelin). *Cro:* Four pieces of sage used; held along with staff. Silvery wide-leafed variety of sage is employed (Voget). *WRS:* Four pieces of *Artemisia* are tied on (Shimkin). *Taos:* Sage held separately with staff (Stewart 1975).

5. *AbS:* Bunch of sage passed around separately at beginning of meeting (Voegelin) *WRS:* Clockwise, "the same as the world" (Shimkin).

														Occurrence						
S&F	Iowa	Oto	No C	Cro	Ara	WRS	Ute	Gos	W–P	Taos	WHM	SHM	Nav	Osa	C–D	WCF	SCF	Men	MHA	Col
														*+	*+					
														+	+	*+				−
										*+				+	*+		+			+
		*+				+	*+	*+						+		*+	+			−
									*+					*+	*+					+
	+			+			+							+	+					−
				*+										+						−
				*+			*+		*+					*+	+					−

8. *SHM:* Not always leader's rattle. Sometimes the rattle of the sponsor is used (Morgan 1973).

9. *Cro:* Man who has his own rattle which suits the pitch of his voice holds leader's rattle in his left hand and rattles his own with his right hand. "Each man does as he wishes in worship." But note that individual rattles are not employed until after midnight, apparently out of deference to the position of the leader. That would be impolite (Voget).

10. *Kio:* Decoration of gourd proper doubtful. But I have seen "Jesus talk" written on a Comanche gourd (La Barre). *AbS:* Gourd itself is stained dark brown with walnut bark [*sic;* more likely from husk of nut] dye; undecorated otherwise. But handle and projecting end are beaded, tasseled, etc. (Voegelin).

11. *SHM:* Sometimes handle has plastic strips. (Morgan 1973).

12. *Gos:* White horsehair at end of handle is not dyed (Malouf). *W-P:* Feathers also used.

13. *Cro:* "Passed with cane" (Voget).

15. *SHM:* Usually only ceremonial rattle used; after midnight water call individual rattles may be used. If a member uses his own, he usually cedars it first. Reg. ceremonial rattle is held in left hand with staff, while right hand shakes owner's rattle (Morgan 1973). *Taos:* Only to replace rattle passed with staff by leader of a song (Stewart 1975). *Nav:* At a meeting I attended in 1964 directed for Navajo by a resident Kiowa roadman, individual rattles were used, but at a meeting directed by a Navajo they were not (Stewart 1972c). Aberle wrote "Sometimes." *SCF:* No individual rattles used during Cross Fire ceremonies I attended, but their use was affirmed by Steinmetz (Stewart 1972c). *Osa:* "today they do" (Bailey).

16. *C-D:* In "Wilson way" meeting members can rattle own rattles any time (Webber). Prohibition on using rattles other than ones used by road chief until midnight (Petrullo, 90, 158). *WRS:* After drum goes around once, individual rattles may be used (Shimkin). Used before midnight (Moore and Schroer 1950).

17. *SHM:* Often other men will shake their own rattles to help the singer—usually after midnight (Morgan 1973).

18. *SHM:* Feathers often of hawk, scissortail (Morgan 1973). *Nav:* Fan of leader passed only after midnight (Stewart 1972c). *Osa:* Old photographs and paintings show two types of fans—feathers tightly bound together and feathers tied separately (Stewart 1972c). *AbS:* Eagle, chicken hawk, parrot, "any kind of bird." Leader did not have special fan that was passed around; each person, including leader, brought and used own fan all night (Voegelin). *C-D*: Fans and single feathers used in meeting (Webber). See note 3. *Cro:* Any feathers

used. Usually eagle tail feathers come out in set of twelve; that is, twelve good feathers found naturally in tail of each bird. "The twelve-feather set represents months of the year; we do not change that" (Voget). *WRS:* Eagle-wing fan with feathers bound together is most common. Fan is same style as other ceremonial fans (Shimkin). *Ara:* Several types of feathers (Trenholm 1970: 299). *WRS:* May not be eagle (Day 1938: 5). *W-P:* At McDermitt, leader did not use fan but only two large eagle feathers (Stewart 1972c).

19. *MHA:* Multiple feathers only by leader after midnight (Howard 1978).

20. *Kio:* Buckskin feather sockets not decorated or beaded, but handle is beaded (La Barre).

21. *W-P:* Leader's fan passed only after midnight.

22. *Kio:* Leader holds own fan with staff when singing; other men do likewise with their fans when singing (La Barre). *S&F:* A single feather passed and held with staff (Stewart 1972c). *SCF:* Also baton one and half feet long beaded at places (Stewart 1972c).

23. *S&F:* At about two hours before midnight the roadman announced he was going to put cedar on the fire, and individual fans might be used to draw cedar smoke to participants (Stewart 1972c). *Nav:* Photographs in Aberle (1966) show individual participants holding fans. At the meeting I attended with Raymond Tso, no personal fans used (Stewart 1972c).

24. *C-D:* Anyone having single feathers or fans can use them anytime they wish (Webber). *Nav:* Exceptions made at times (Aberle 1966: 170).

25. *Cro:* "Used to draw smoke to inhale" (Voget).

26. *C-D:* Whistle not used in "Wilson way" meeting (Webber). *Cro:* Sometimes used four times in course of meeting. Midnight: strong, sharp, long blasts four times. "We make these four long calls in order that the Creator might hear us. That is the way I understand it among the Crows." Right after the water call, leader goes outside tipi, usually whistles in order toward east, south, west, and north, the four parts of the earth. Four blasts are given to each direction, and a prayer is offered. Type of prayer depends upon the leader, "but each corner has something of its own." East: prayer to rising sun, which brings daylight, and to wind, which comes from east, about which all peoples, Indian and white, know. "I do not know what other countries have, but the Montana east wind is harmless." South: prayers offered to those things of the south, for instance, warmth and food. West: setting of the sun brings darkness. Also, certain foods come from the west. "Whatever property is needed from the west [the leader asks for]." North: the same holds for the north; but north wind usually cold, so leader usually asks Creator to control it, keep it not too cold so that animals will not die (Voget 1944). *Com:* "Most roadmen use an eagle bone whistle. The use of the cane whistle in this ceremony is Comanche style" (Brito 1975: 37fn.). *W-P:* Not used by Sam Dick in 1939, but recognized proper and used later (d'Azevedo 1954; Stewart 1972c). *S&F:* A wooden, cane, whistle used to make two notes. It was explained that anciently, and still usually, an eagle bone whistle was used (Stewart 1972c).

27. *Gos:* Also used before meeting, while all are lined up outside (Malouf).

28. *Gos:* See note 265a, below.

30. *WRS:* Leader allows others to blow whistle as special privilege—to show thanks to Creator (Shimkin). *SHM* and *SCF:* Cedarman also uses whistle sometimes (Steinmetz).

31. *General:* Many peyotists have wooden equipment boxes, which are especially made and decorated. From the full range of the peyote religion, these boxes are sought after as museum pieces (Stewart). *Men:* Tackle box (Slotkin 1952: 588); tool box (Spindler and Spindler, 1971: 102). *Nav:* San Diego Museum made a special publication about a Navajo paraphernalia box and its contents (Fintzelberg 1969).

32. *AbS:* Square of purple velvet (Voegelin). *Nav:* None used by Tso (Stewart 1972c).

33. *Com* and *NoC:* Chief drummer does not necessarily provide or tune drum. Best drum available used (Hoebel). *Cro:* Leader has complete outfit, and if drummer, whom he selects, has no drum, leader lends his (Voget). *SHM:* Drum often someone else's (Morgan 1973).

34. *L-A:* Originally Lipan did not use water drum, according to Pinero (Quoetone

in Stewart 1972*c*). "Kettle drum" untied at end of meeting in Lipan story (M. E. Opler 1940: 58). Use of metal drum with and without charcoal recorded by M. E. Opler (1938: 277).

35. *Cro:* Can be copper, gold, aluminum, or "anything of iron" (Voget). *Gos:* 1½-gallon size used, although 1-gallon (No. 6) size desired (Malouf). *Men:* Copper (Spindler and Spindler 1971: 101); cast brass (Slotkin 1952: 588). *Iowa:* +1920 to 1973 (Murray 1973). *Nav:* Iron, brass, or aluminum (Aberle 1966: 170). *Osa:* Also "brass kettle" (Maker 1968: 5).

36. *C-D:* Among Caddo (La Barre). *Iowa:* Used before 1920s (Murray 1973). *Oto:* "Sometimes use a crock" (La Barre 1938: 68fn.).

37. *Cro:* Charcoal obtained from leader's stove (Voget). *Gos:* Fourteen pieces; Goshute don't know what they represent (Malouf).

38. *Del:* Otter skin sometimes used (Webber). *Cro:* Usually deerskin best, but any soft skin may be used (Voget). *SHM:* Sometimes elk hide, but deer skin preferred (Morgan 1973).

40. *Kic:* Six pebbles used (Noon). *AbS:* Eight small round pebbles (Voegelin). *Del:* Four small stones used (Petrullo 1934: 50). *Cro:* Seven stone "marbles" or "small ball-like rocks" (Voget). *Men:* Seven marbles (Slotkin 1952: 588). *Osa:* "use eight marbles" (Bailey).

41. *K-A:* Seven stones to tie drumhead represent the seven days of creation (K. Beals 1967). *Kic:* + (La Barre 1938: 68). *W-P:* + (d'Azevedo 1954). *Taos:* + (Collins 1968).

43. *AbS:* I suspect it is significant, but my informant did not comment on this (Voegelin). *Cro:* Symbolized stars in the sky; later the people observed that law officers carried such, and so "we use it to signify living within the law" (Voget). *Gos:* Represents Morning Star (Malouf). *Taos:* + (Collins 1968: 429).

44. *Gos:* See note 265*a*, below. *SHM:* For Memorial Day or funeral the last four songs are at the cemetery where drum is untied—meeting ends in cemetery (Morgan; Steinmetz). *SCF:* For Memorial Day meeting drum dismantled only after service continuation at cemetery, to which everyone repairs from tipi (Stewart; Steinmetz).

46. *Cro:* Chief drummer's used if he has one (Voget). *SHM:* Often drumstick of someone else also. Often two drumsticks passed around, one heavy, one light (Morgan 1973).

48. *AbS:* Used only after drum had passed halfway around tipi, as far as door; then individual drumsticks smoked in cedar, and permission given to use them—but this long before midnight (Voegelin).

50. *C-D:* See note 83, below. *Cro:* Man asks permission of drum chief to pick out drummer (Voget). *SHM:* One either has the chief drummer or calls upon his own special one (Steinmetz). *Osa:* "one drummer each round" (Bailey).

51. *K-A:* Each person participating drums. Feeling is strong that one should have a peyote partner, and singing and drumming occur in couples. First man sings, his partner drums; then first man drums, other sings. Singing occurs in regular order. Drum skips and then goes back; then skips again, etc. (McAllister). *Cro:* If man on right (A) wishes man on left (B) to drum, B circles room clockwise and sits to right of staff held by A (Voget). *Oto* and *S&F:* Drummer usually at right of singer, but frequently at left. Convenience seemed to be enough to have drummer at left. Singer asked special person to serve as drummer. Old friends, relations, honored guests, and notably skilled drummers were asked to move to anyplace in the circle. Individuals exchanged places if there was not room to accommodate the drummer by squeezing other participants closer together (Stewart).

52. *AbS:* "Women sometimes drum at a peyote meeting," but mainly men, I noticed (Voegelin). *Cro:* "There is no law against women (drumming), but they just don't" (Voget). *W-P:* Women drummed in 1939 (Stewart 1944) but not in 1954 (d'Azevedo) or in 1972 (Stewart).

53. *Kic:* My information not definite on this point. My recollection is that the bag of cedar belonged to the cedarman—this may be a confused impression because of the fact that the cedarman alone threw the cedar on the fire (Noon). *Cro:* Members also have some for their own use (Voget). *W-P:* At McDermitt, Nevada, cedar sprinkled more times and more people were incensed more completely than I have observed elsewhere (Stewart). *Osa:* "just at Sunday noon by firechief" (Bailey).

55. *K-A:* No "cedarman"; drummer usually puts cedar on fire (McAllister). *AbS:* Usually cedar sprinkled by leader (Voegelin). *Taos:* In August, 1975, as an honored guest at the peyote meeting in Taos Pueblo, I was seated at the left of the roadman, who was also host and sponsor, in the place usually occupied by the cedarman. A number of the functions usually performed by the cedarman were assigned to other elders (Stewart). *Osa:* "by firechief" (Bailey).

56. *WCF:* Both assistants to right and left of leader have cedar bags and sprinkle it on fire at different times. Man on left did so at midnight ceremony (Praus).

57. *AbS:* This tobacco is mixed with sage (Voegelin). See note 198 *W-P,* above. *WRS:* Person calling meeting, or sponsor, gives tobacco to leader before meeting, unless sponsor also leader (Shimkin). *SCF:* No smoking in ritual, and evils of tobacco mentioned in a speech (Stewart). *Oto:* Under Church of the First Born, 1914, there was no smoking, but the prohibition had nearly disappeared by 1972 when I observed smoking (Stewart). *Com:* "The smoking of tobacco is a distinctive Indian rite and is observed with great solemnity" (Simmons 1913: chap. 3:2). *SHM:* Tobacco furnished by host. Although the leader passes the tobacco out. (Morgan 1973). *WCF* and *WHM:* Tobacco is not used in either ritual among Winnebago (Stewart; Brito 1975; Radin 1923). *Osa:* "Nobody smoked in there, but he [roadman] himself, the man who is conducting from the start. Only he makes smoke . . . and he goes to make that tobacco and prays" (Fred Begman, Kiowa-Apache, describing Osage meeting, Oklahoma University Oral History, 1967). "Only Roadman smokes" (Bailey).

58. *Gos:* See note 265*a,* below. *NoC:* Although Hoebel reported the Northern Cheyenne used paper for rolling Bull Durham tobacco into cigarettes in 1939 (Stewart 1944), later he wrote: "From the depths of his black satchel he produced dried corn husks and Bull Durham for the making of the sacred smoke. Paper cigarettes are tabu" (Hoebel). *W-P:* Cornhusks used sometimes (Alvin Sims, Paiute of Duck Valley, to Stewart). *SHM:* Tobacco and maize husks used only by a few men wanting to make a special prayer during the meeting (Morgan). *SHM:* Maize husks used for second, third, and fourth smokes by anyone. Paper for first smoke by everyone (Steinmetz).

59. *AbS:* Perhaps—but I never heard of it for peyote meetings, although Shawnee use oak leaves sometimes for ordinary cigarettes (Voegelin). *K-A:* For prayers Bull Durham "wrapped in cornhusks or blackjack [oak] leaves" (K. Beals 1967:6).

60. *Cro:* Paper not "proper"; only when no husks available (Voget). *SHM:* See note 58 (Steinmetz), above.

61. *Cro:* If leader has no tobacco on hand, others may offer their own (Voget).

62. *Ute and Gos:* Tobacco not used in "old Sioux way" sects among Ute and Goshute. *Oto:* Some Oto retain the no-smoking rule of 1914 Church of the First Born (Stewart).

63. *WCF:* Cost of peyote defrayed by persons sponsoring meeting; I received buttons from fire chief, assistant at right of leader, and various men in the group (Praus). *WRS:* Sponsor gives peyote to leader. Names for peyote: (1) hus, (2) w gʷe i-a, Comanche word for "cactus" (Shimkin). *S&F:* Leader announced that he would furnish "medicine" and "tobacco" (Bull Durham) on demand at any time. Other participants also brought peyote tea to share with friends (Stewart). *SHM:* Peyote furnished often by host, often by friends—seldom by leader (Morgan 1973). *SHM:* Peyote usually furnished by the sponsor and other people who help out (Steinmetz). *WHM:* Sponsor provides peyote to leader to control (Pelletiere 1963*b*). *Men:* Usually (Slotkin 1952:582). *WRS:* Leader may hold other's peyote (Day 1938:5). *WHM:* At Wittenberg, Wisconsin, the Half Moon group of NAC has an organized church corporation which supplies peyote, manages a building and a store, and supervises a cemetery (Stewart).

64. *Cro:* Represents the original peyote which the woman found, as recounted in the legend which purports to account for the discovery and subsequent use of peyote (Voget). *Kio:* "The other leader now produced a package of mescals and selecting the largest one deposited it carefully upon the top of the mound upon a bed of fragrant herbs arranged in the form of a cross" (Mooney 1892*a*). *Ara:* "The pouches used to contain the peyote-plant have

room for only one of the disks, which is usually carried more or less as a personal amulet in addition to being the center of worship during ceremonies" (Kroeber 1907). *SHM:* Often small—the size of a regular button (Morgan 1973).

65. *Cro:* Lines "grow" on the peyote naturally; that is, peyote is not redecorated, the lines (white) being natural products (Voget). *L-A:* "He sprinkled piñon pollen on one of the peyote 'buttons.' . . ." (Opler 1946: 140). *SHM:* Tufts of hair in a straight line (Morgan 1973). *Taos:* "Fetish" peyote decorated (Collins 1968: 431).

66. *WCF:* Chief Peyote placed on open Bible during meeting (Densmore 1931: 7 second section).

67. *Cro:* Informant thought the Chief Peyote could be eaten, but did not know of any instance (Voget).

68. *Taos:* placed on top of rock (T. Romero in Stewart 1972c). *W-P:* − (Stewart 1944). *SCF:* After the meeting the *Artemisia* is given to someone as a special valued gift (Stewart 1972c).

69. *K-A:* Called a star rather than a cross (McAllister). *Cro:* Represents four corners of earth and also sun's rays (Voget). *WRS:* At times four, eight, or twelve leaves used to produce different forms (Shimkin). *Kio:* Cross or rosette (La Barre 1938: 79). "Herbs arranged in the form of a cross" (Mooney 1892a). *Ara:* "The leader . . . carefully smoothes a little space at the middle point of the crescent. . . . Breaking eight short stems of sage, he lays them on this spot in the form of two superimposed crosses, the ends of the stems pointing in the cardinal directions and between" (Kroeber 1907: 401).

70. *WCF:* See note 63, above. *SCF:* Ground, mixed with warm water, eaten with spoon; only one spoon used (Stewart).

71. *K-A:* Not necessarily. Depends upon supply and generosity of leader (McAllister). *AbS:* People urged to eat their own peyote, if they had brought any, early in evening (Voegelin). *C-D:* Peyote other than leader's may be eaten before midnight if leader's supply runs out (Webber). *Cro:* One's own peyote can be used from the start (Voget). *WRS:* Leader's peyote required only for "first round" (Shimkin). *Gos:* All peyote in one bag (Malouf). *W-P:* No individual supplies of peyote used in meeting.

72. *WHM:* Represents God in Trinity (Densmore 1931: 7).

73. *Kio:* Called "road chief" or "road man" from the "peyote road" on symbolic altar; leader tells them the "road" to go (La Barre). *AbS:* "Boss man" or "road man" (Voegelin). *Del and C-D:* "Road man" (Webber; Petrullo 1934). *Cro:* Usually just plain "chief" (Voget). *WRS:* tegwahin (Shimkin). *Gos:* See note 275a, below. *SCF:* Priest or Chief Priest or Peyote Priest or High Priest (Stewart, 1972c; Steinmetz). *WRS:* Called road chief (Moore and Schroer). *SHM:* Almost always called "road man" or "leader" (Morgan 1973).

74. *C-D:* In one "Wilson way" meeting, the roadman sat at east end of moon, faced west (Webber). In one Big Moon variant, road chief to east of altar (Petrullo 1934: 182). See note 97, below.

77. *Kio:* "The old man [Clyde Ahtape] said Cedarman a new position, added to honor a friend. In old days and at Big Bow meeting only three officials—Roadman, Drummer and Fire Chief" (Nelson Big Bow to Stewart).

78. *Oto:* Cedarman not essential. Frequently there may be two firemen (Stewart). *SHM:* Frequently two firemen (Steinmetz).

79. *Kio:* Four assistants if peyote woman, water and food bringer, is included (La Barre). *C-D:* See note 83, below. *W-P:* − (Stewart 1944).

80. *Del and C-D:* Called "drum chief" (Webber). *W-P:* Leader's wife often chief drummer. *WHM:* "Represents Jesus Christ in Trinity" (Densmore 1931: 7).

81. *WCF:* Chief drummer sits at leader's left (Prause). *NoC:* At leader's left.

83. *C-D:* "In some Caddo Delaware 'Big Moons'" the drum chief accompanies the drum around the circle, drumming for each singer (La Barre 1938: 69). At start the fireman drums not only for road man, but for everyone completely around the circle; they have as many as five assistant firemen and they drum in turn until end of meeting (Webber). *WCF:* May be

chosen by anyone (Praus). *Cro:* Any man can drum if picked out by the singer (Voget). *WRS:* May drum for beginner (Shimkin). *Ute:* Chief drummer drums for each singer in turn once during meeting. *W-P:* May drum for anyone who asks him, or he may offer to drum for individuals. Singer may ask anyone to drum for him; leader often asked. *Taos:* Singer may ask anyone to drum for him (Parsons). *Ara:* Could do as special honor, but not general (Stewart 1972c). *Oto:* May drum for all, but not required (Stewart 1972c). *S&F:* Frequently invited to drum for others (Stewart 1972c). *SHM:* Chief drummer drums for each in turn unless the person calls for his own drummer (Steinmetz). *MHA:* Chief drummer may drum for everyone, if asked to do so (Howard 1978). *Osa:* Drummer or one of the firemen: "He goes drum for each man in the row, for all . . . goes plumb around" (Fred Bigman, K-A, describing Osage meeting, University of Oklahoma Oral History Project, 1967).

84. *AbS:* At meeting I attended, a visiting Arapaho filled all the functions you note for cedarman. But he was not explicitly referred to as cedarman (Voegelin). *WCF:* See note 56, above. *Cro:* Apparently selected by leader for each meeting. There might be a different one before and after midnight (Voget). *WHM:* "Represents Holy Ghost" (Densmore 1931:7). *S&F:* In neither the Kiowa nor Sac and Fox ceremony I observed in April, 1972, was there a cedarman to the left of the roadman. In the Sac and Fox meeting, that place was occupied by the new Pawnee wife of the Sac and Fox roadman. She was a member of a renowned Pawnee peyote family (Stewart).

85. *WCF:* Sits a leader's right (Praus). *NoC:* Sits at leader's right (Hoebel). *Cro:* "Just chance" (Voget).

88. *AbS:* Also second fire chief (Voegelin). *Osa:* Duties of fireman (Maker 1968:2).

89. *K-A:* Yes, but theoretically fire chief should sit on south side (McAllister). *C-D:* Firemen sit on both sides of door (Webber).

90. *Cro:* "He builds the fire, it commences" (Voget).

92. *WCF:* See note 162, below.

93. *Cro:* "Well, he lets them come in, he lets them go out. If sick or helpless, he has to help"; otherwise people find own seats. Conducts late arrivals to their seats (Voget).

94. *Kio:* In theory; not rigidly adhered to (La Barre); + Marriot 1954). *C-D:* Bathing not always before, sometimes after meetings (Webber). *NoC:* Only chief and assistants by requirement, others may (Hoebel). *Cro:* The people clean up. Could be viewed as a purification (Voget). *W-P:* Bathing recommended; often done in hot springs. *Com:* "All prepared for the meeting; they bathed and returned to camp to get painted up" (Wallace and Hoebel (1952:335). *Iowa:* Usual, not required (Murray 1973): *Osa:* "The attendants usually purify themselves by sweat baths the Friday preceding the Saturday-Sunday meeting, and by drinking hot water" (J. Collier 1935:695); "Sweat lodge is an integral part of the Osage peyote round house plan" (La Barre 1938:86).

95. *AbS:* Tipi, sometimes in house (Voegelin). *Cro:* House or tipi may be used, latter more proper (Voget). *Gos:* Although tipi preferable, house used at meeting attended. All good peyote members have houses facing east for that reason (Malouf). *Kio:* "Tipi poles: each pole represents a different denomination tied together for one God. Gospel covers all [canvas]. I used 18 around and two flap poles and one to help construction" (Nelson Big Bow to Stewart). *Osa:* West opening peyote churches built by Wilson to please Osage chiefs Black Day and Claremore (Mathews 1961:744–746).

96. *Kio:* In old days; not now (La Barre). *SCF:* Many meetings end in NAC cemetery, where cement altar is prepared at base of large wooden cross, seen at Allen, South Dakota (Stewart 1972c).

97. *C-D:* One Big Moon variant has entrance to west (Petrullo 1934:182). Sometimes door to west (Webber). See notes 74 above, 99 below. *Osa:* "In the case of the number of leaders is further limited by the number of permanent 'churches' available; Murphy, lists eighteen. 'East Moon' on the reservation and three 'West Moons'" (La Barre 1938:62–63).

98. *C-D:* Most usual; Big Moon crescent altar is drawn on ground, instead of being made in a mound. Numerous other innovations in type of altar were introduced by Wilson and

his followers (Petrullo 1934:80, 179–84). However, Anderson's Big Moon altar, consisting of crescentic mound with a line on its crest, is described and shown in picture (Petrullo 1934: 48, 101). *WCF:* Altar consists of pit inside of horseshoe incised on floor. Lines extended beyond altar in the cardinal directions (Praus). Altar resembles that of the Delaware Big Moon variant shown by Petrullo (1934:79, pl. 3). *Gos:* Inasmuch as meeting held in dwelling, special altar constructed. In addition to crescent, apron of earth extended toward the east from concave side of moon which protected the wooden floor from hot embers carried in from fire outside (Malouf). *Kio:* Half moon altar higher in summer to protect from heat. Lower in winter to allow heat for roadman (Stewart). *Ara:* The Half Moon altar is of red clay, brought in by Felix Grossbeck in a tub. It has a sort of base wider than the Half Moon itself. Near center on the west side was a small projection. *W-P:* A Northern Paiute of McDermitt, Nevada, Roadman Grover Tom, made the crescent altar of prepared red earth after participants had seated themselves in room of dwelling where meeting was held. A small shelf, one inch high and an inch wide, constructed on east, concave, side of crescent (Stewart). *SCF:* Altar made for Half Moon ritual allowed to remain in tipi for Cross Fire ritual but was not functional (Stewart). *Taos:* Feathers stuck in ground near altar (T. Romero). *Iowa:* Half Moon (Murray 1973). *Nav:* Frank Duncan runs meeting without moon—just ashes made into star, according to Jacob Lopez, Ute, and Tsatigh. Sand crescent very long (about 12 feet) and high (8 inches in center), yet with nearly vertical sides. It was only about 2 inches thick on top. A line of ashes extended from fire to ash crescent (Stewart 1972c). *SHM:* Howard Red Bear had cloth Half Moon in 1922 for peyote meeting altar. No sand Half Moon (Walker to Stewart, Wounded Knee, June, 1971). *Osa:* "dug out" (Bailey).

99. *C-D:* End toward west in one Big Moon variant (Petrullo 1934:182). See notes 74, 97, above. *WCF:* See note 98, above.

100. *C-D:* See note 98, above. *WCF:* See note 98, above.

101. *Gos:* Kerosene lamp, four sticks, and hot coals used in place of fire impossible in house (Malouf). *Ute:* Meeting in house, ashes carried in from fire maintained outside; oil lamp on floor, near north tip of crescent (Stewart).

103. *Com:* Sticks from tipi (Hoebel). *Cro:* Point or "face" west (Voget). *WRS:* Must be neat is only rule (Shimkin). *SCF:* In a dwelling near Denver, Colorado, no altar. Hot coals brought in from fire outside and placed in single pile on tray of earth raised four inches on legs resting on tiles. Hot coals only to burn cedar for incense (Stewart 1972c). *WRS:* Geometric crossing (Moore and Schroer). *Taos:* Sticks cleaned (T. Romero). *SHM:* Sticks crossed near one end to make v-shape. (Morgan 1973). *Osa:* – (Bailey).

104. *Kio:* In theory; not rigidly enforced. One leader insists fire be lit with one match (La Barre). *Cro:* "Matches is the quickest, or they could use 'clinkers'; that is the Indian way. But that is all past, you know" (Voget). *Iowa:* Flint and steel, if available (Murray 1972). *S&F:* Both Kiowa and Sac and Fox designated the fire "flint fire" because of the rule followed to ignite it with flint and steel (Stewart).

105. *Com and NoC:* Seven sticks on fire (Hoebel). *C-D:* Twelve sticks at start (Petrullo 1934:50, 101). *Cro:* Number varies with weather, but usually at least four (Voget). *Taos:* Seven sticks (Parsons).

106. *WRS:* Sometimes carved (Shimkin). *Men:* Two pokers (Slotkin 1952:591).

107. *SHM:* Worshipers congregate outside only at tipi meetings—not house meetings (Morgan 1973). *S&F:* Participants were encouraged to enter the tipi and mark place by leaving cushions, blankets, etc., at chosen places. Just before start of service all went outside and were soon directed to reenter without further ceremony. The roadman indicated order of reentry, which appeared something of a mark of importance. I was asked to enter immediately after some aged Pawnee and the roadman's new wife. My name was recognized as that of a friend of NAC (Stewart).

108. *AbS:* Not obligatory, except for female. "Should wear moccasins." Several men wore blankets; "depended upon whether they owned one or not" (Voegelin). *Cro:* "They put on the best they have; they doll up, just as the whites when they go to church" (Voget). *Taos:*

"Peyote boys" wear American shoes and hats, contrary to the rule of going in Indian habit while at the pueblo. Peyotists refuse to cut seats from trousers (Parsons). *Osa:* "About five years ago [i.e., ca. 1903] I was informed, a Southwestern Indian named [John] Wilson, came to the Osage, introducing the mescal religion. . . . Pictures of Wilson are in demand among devotees, who kiss them on sight. The man has been deified since his death. The agent states that the mescal religion has the beneficial effect of causing the Osage to give up whiskey drinking. The younger Osage and those who have embraced the mescal rites, may be distinguished from the old conservative element by their manner of wearing the hair in two braids supplemented with ribbons and yarn hanging down on their chests" (Speck 1907: 171). *C-D:* "They paint and dress in blankets when they go in to eat [peyote]" (Ijams 1895: 2).

109. *Cro:* When dark (Voget). *Nav:* The roadman arranged hogan for meeting from about 8:00 PM to 11:00, when service actually began (Stewart 1972c).

110. *Kio:* Varies with leader (La Barre). *AbS:* Leader offered prayers when putting up tipi, putting the sage(?) cross on moon, etc., but I do not think he prayed just before going in, except when he made the peyote tea just before the meeting (Voegelin). *SHM:* Only if tipi meeting (Steinmetz). *Cro:* Example meeting in Canada conducted by NAC president Frank Takes Gun (Sagi 1956).

110a. *Com:* "When we pray before the entrance of the tipi, it is to ask God to purify everything inside the tipi. We all walk around the tipi to make a complete circle which will serve as a shield around the tipi. . . ." (Brito 1975: 33–34). *W-P:* Group walks around tipi (Alvin Sims, Duck Valley Paiute to Stewart); also observed with Washo (d'Azevedo 1954). *Kio:* + (Marriot 1954); + (Earle, 1968). *K-A:* "Everyone had to circle the tipi completely on the outside before entering" (Jordan 1968). *WCF:* A ceremonial circuit of the lodge was at one time associated with the peyote cult (Radin 1914: 21).

111. *C-D:* Chief enters alone and is seated when others enter (Petrullo 1934: 89; Webber). *Gos:* Chief enters alone and blows whistle for others to enter (Malouf). See note 265a, below.

112. *C-D:* Drum chief led worshipers into tipi (Petrullo 1934: 96).

114. *Cro:* "Each family goes together; women could precede men" (Voget). *SHM:* No special order for men, women and children. *Taos:* No special order (Stewart 1975).

115. *General:* "In the early days the Kiowa, Comanche, Tonkawa, Sauk and Oto prohibited women from attending" (La Barre, 1938: 60). *Kic:* Women attend, but no children except when meeting given to heal child (Noon). *WRS:* Children allowed only if ill (Shimkin). *L-A* and *K-A:* Originally women and children excluded (M. E. Opler 1946: 148). Female exclusion relaxed (Penaro, Lipan-Apache, 1918; Blackbear, Kiowa-Apache, 1968). At first peyote meeting of Carrizo observed by a Lipan woman present (Opler 1938: 278). *K-A:* "Until about fifty years ago, women were completely excluded from meetings" (K. Beals 1967: 30). *Com:* "In those days, they didn't let young boys into meetings or even women" (Brito 1975: 125).

117. *C-D:* See notes 74, 97, and 99, above. *W-P:* Rules for seating not fixed. When room, husband and wife sit together in inner circle; when crowded, wife and children sit back of husband.

118. *SHM:* Women often near husband (chief drummer, etc.) (Morgan 1973).

119. *Kio:* Varies with leader; some on south side; some near door; some anywhere (save officials' places) (La Barre).

120. *Del and C-D:* Women south of altar, men north of altar (Petrullo 1934: 57; Webber). *Cro:* Single line used so no one sits between anyone else and the Creator's gift. Segregation would be result of chance (Voget). *WRS:* Theoretically proper, often disregarded (Shimkin).

122. *Kic:* All worshipers sit in single row save when more worshipers than can be thus accommodated (Noon).

123. *SHM:* Often pass to north. Varies considerably depending on roadman and fire chief. Must find out anew each time (Morgan 1973).

124. *Cro:* Blankets, or each has his own cushion (Voget). *WRS:* Canvas-covered straw (Moore and Schroer 1950). *SHM:* Blankets—especially in house meetings (Morgan 1973).

125. *AbS:* Sage underneath blankets (Voegelin). *WRS:* Sage formerly required (Shimkin). *W-P:* − (Stewart 1944).

127. *Cro:* Instructions first as to teaching or belief, followed by prayer (Voget).

128. *C-D:* Leader prepares first prayer cigarette, which is passed around to all (Webber). *Cro:* Cigarette rolled before prayer (Voget). *Gos:* See note 265*a*, below. *Oto:* No tobacco in few remaining meetings of Peyote Church of the First Born (Stewart).

130. *AbS:* Leader prayed silently while smoking (Voegelin). *Cro:* Tells about purpose of meeting so they may pray (Voget). *Osa:* "The leader makes a cigarette out of 'corn shucks', lights it, and 'prays for all of the people—everybody in the world.' When the prayer is finished he places the cigarette in the 'road'; the attendants place their hands on their foreheads and breasts, and stretch their hands to the peyote and 'fire', and they feel themselves with the warmth'" (Collier 1935: 695).

131. *SHM:* Often many pray aloud (Morgan 1973).

132. *Cro:* To "peyote chief," but "just the same as moon." Smoke blown toward "chief peyote" (Voget).

133. *AbS:* Prayed with bowed heads, eyes closed, men must kneel (Voegelin).

134. *C-D:* In original Wilson moon, cigarette butts placed at left side of altar, in front of road chief, but in other Big Moon ceremonies left in front of smoker to be gathered by fire chief (Webber). *Cro:* Those sitting facing convex surface of moon place their cigarette butts against moon; those facing concave side place their butts at point of horns of moon; those north of line between leader and entrance place theirs on north side of altar, and vice versa (Voget). *WRS:* Butts placed against moon by fire chief and assistant (Shimkin). *Taos:* Roadman placed butts standing against moon in front of him. Others collected and laid neatly at points of crescent. Fireman noted if burned ends pointed out; he carefully turned them to have burned ends point towards fire (Stewart 1975). *Osa:* See note 128, above. "Placed under altar cloth" (Bailey). *W-P:* Remains of roadman's four "main smokes" placed on shelf built into east side of altar. Cigarette butts from other participants collected at each end of crescent (Stewart). *SHM:* Butts placed at tips of horns (Morgan 1973). *S&F:* On north side of crescent cigarette butts stood aligned along side of altar; on south side butts together at tip of crescent altar (Stewart).

135. *Cro:* "Some take sage from seat and rub this on hands" (Voget). *K-A:* "When the chief has prayed, he passes the sage. Each participant takes a piece, rolls it between his hands, smells it, and rolls it over himself" (K. Beals 1967: 10). *Taos:* Instead of taking sage from bundle passed around, each participant took leaves from under blanket where he sat (Stewart 1975). *SCF:* Participants instructed to take sage from under seat or extending from blanket under each participant (Stewart).

136. *K-A:* Sage leaves placed under blankets and each person uses his own (McAllister).

137. *Cro:* Informant did not remember any chewing, but it may have happened a long time ago (Voget).

139. *SCF:* First time around the roadman carried bowl of ground and moistened peyote and spooned four spoonfuls to each participant; after first time, bowl passed (Stewart).

140. *S&F:* Only initial round of roadman's peyote required to go clockwise; after that passed back and forth (Stewart).

141. *K-A:* Yes, but at the meetings I attended they "cut the dose," as they termed it, to two, out of consideration for my presence, for they thought I would find it difficult to eat four; and I would have at one time (McAllister). *AbS:* At the meeting we attended each was told to take two buttons (Voegelin). *WRS:* Some take two (Shimkin). *K-A:* "The common amount consumed is around ten, but anyone is free to eat whatever he chooses in addition to the ceremonially required first two (K. Beals 1967: 7). *Taos:* Green peyote pieces and tea furnished by sponsor. Individuals brought dried buttons. Most took four pieces of peyote first serving; took four sips of tea (Stewart 1975). *SHM:* Often only peyote paste or "peyote tea"

used (Steinmetz). *Osa:* Peyote pounded in wooden mortar before meeting and powdered peyote moistened and formed into pellets. Four taken at start of meeting (Maker 1968:8). *SHM:* Supposed to take four (Morgan 1973).

142. *K-A:* Optional: some do, most do not. *Kio:* Mode of eating depends on each individual (La Barre). *Cro:* Some. Most simply take it and eat (Voget). *WRS:* As special sign of respect to Creator (Shimkin).

143. *Kio:* Mode of eating depends on each individual (La Barre). *Cro:* Optional (Voget).

144. *Cro:* First four peyote buttons eaten before singing starts (Voget). *SHM:* Singing usually starts when peyote reaches fireman (Morgan 1973); only partial round (Steinmetz).

145. *Gos:* See note 265*a*, below. *Osa:* "by fireman" (Bailey).

146. *AbS:* Leader held paraphernalia in hands; drum chief likewise (Voegelin). *SCF:* Placed on altar cloth (Stewart).

147. *AbS:* Leader sprinkled cedar (Voegelin). *Cro:* Chief does the incensing at this point (Voget). *S&F:* Roadman sprinkles first cedar and does so most often thereafter, but sometimes he asks others to do it (Stewart).

148. *Gos:* See 265*a*, below. *WCF:* "Cedar is placed on the fire early in the ceremony and the staff, gourd rattle, drum, drumstick, and eagle feather fans are incensed in the smoke" (Densmore 1931, second edition:7).

149. *WRS:* More than once; number not fixed (Shimkin). *SHM:* Sometimes three times (trinity?) (Morgan 1973).

150. *K-A:* When cedar is placed on the fire, each person symbolically washes himself with it (McAllister).

151. *Cro:* "Just once; so everyone can smell the smoke" (Voget). *WRS:* Number not fixed (Shimkin).

152. *Cro:* In front of leader (Voget).

154. *WRS:* Either Shoshone or Arapaho starting song may be used (Shimkin). *Gos:* See note 265*a*, below.

159. *AbS:* "The usual number is four, but sometimes men feel so good that they may sing as many as twelve songs (Voegelin).

160. *C-D:* Each man sings, then drums for his neighbor (Petrullo 1934:91). In Wilson moon the drum chief and different fire chiefs do all the drumming (Webber). See note 83, above. *W-P:* See note 83, above. *Ute:* Singer invites special drummer (Stewart 1972*c*). *SHM:* Most people have their special drummer; often friend (Morgan 1973). *Oto:* Special drummer usual (Stewart 1972*c*). *S&F:* Frequently so, but not set rule (Stewart). *Nav:* Special drummers usually invited by singer to drum (Stewart 1972). *SCF:* Usually singer invites special person, friend to drum (Stewart). *Taos:* Singer asks special people to drum (Stewart 1975). *Ara:* Unless a special drummer invited by singer (Stewart 1972*c*). *Osa:* "Chief Drummer may drum for each song leader or the drum is passed and each person drums for one to his left" (Maker 1968:9).

161. *K-A:* Women attend, but I never saw them participate. I do not know if there is a rule; probably merely a feeling that they should not (McAllister). *Cro:* No rule against women singing (Voget). *Gos:* I inquired about this especially and they said women used to sing but do not do so any more (Malouf). *W-P:* Women hold staff, lead singing, drum. *Taos:* Women sing in meeting at Taos (La Barre 1938:6); Navajo present. No woman held staff to lead song (Stewart 1972*c*). *Ara:* Women did not hold staff. Sang in unison with men leaders (Stewart 1972*c*). *SCF:* Both Sioux and Navajo women held staff and led songs (Stewart 1972*c*). *SHM:* Rule, but not enforced—some sing, but very few (Morgan 1973; Steinmetz). *S&F:* One Navajo woman had told the roadman before the meeting that she liked to hold staff and lead songs. The roadman mentioned this to group and encouraged the Navajo woman to lead a song when the staff reached her. She did so, only once. No other women lead songs, but just joined with others (Stewart 1972*c*). *SCF:* Most women did not hold staff and sing, but after midnight about half of women did lead singing (Stewart 1972*c*). *W-P:* + (d'Azevedo 1954).

162. *SCF:* No midnight water call (Stewart). Midnight water call present (Steinmetz).

163. *C-D:* No midnight recess (Petrullo 1934:42). Midnight water call and recess present in Big Moon cult (Petrullo 1934:158). Recess only to burn cedar incense for everyone to fan over themselves while standing. Water in meeting all night and can be used anytime, but is used with restraint (Webber; Petrullo 1934:93). *Gos:* See note 265a, below. *W-P:* No fixed song for water calls, or any time. *General:* "The midnight water call is kind of new to the old peyote way. . . . Some people say that the Comanche introduced it (the midnight water call) around 1870. . . . They say that water has always been used in the meetings. But that in the old way, it was brought in at the beginning of the meeting. . . . Today the best idea that we have about the old way is the way the Caddo ran their meetings. In their way, water is brought in when the meeting begins. It's not brought in at midnight or in the morning either. If you want a drink of water, you ask the fire-man for it. . . . Most of them try not to drink water throughout the whole meeting. But if someone needs water bad, then it's okay to ask for it" (Brito, citing Michael White, 1975:159–60). *L-A:* "The Lipan have no midnight water ceremony. The Hoag (Caddo) rite has no water ceremonies . . . but water is brought in for visitors who might call for it or provided outside to be drunk at recesses" (La Barre 1938:85); Pinero, Lipan Apache, told Guy Quoetone, Kiowa, that ancient Lipan Apache did have a midnight water call (Stewart 1972c). *K-A:* and *L-A:* In report that Chiwat, Lipan Apache, taught Apache Ben, Kiowa-Apache, Roy Blackbear, Kiowa-Apache, said "Ben . . . don't stop at midnight" (University of Oklahoma Oral History Project, 1968); no water during night in old way, according to Joe Blackbear (McAllister, MS, 1938, p. 47). *S&F:* Midnight water call and recess was a major interruption in the ceremony. The water was brought in and placed before the roadman, who marked a cross on the top of the water with his whistle and with a single large eagle tailfeather. The feather then was used to touch himself and "companion" (wife) at his left. The senior sponsor, Bill Tyner, Shawnee–Delaware–Sac and Fox from Tulsa, made a speech in English asking for special prayers for various people. The roadman then prayed at length in the Sac and Fox language. He was followed by his son, the chief drummer, who pronounced a long, emotion-charged prayer in English, frequently punctuated with "Heavenly Father." It was a Christian prayer with reference to "Your only begotten Son sent as a sacrifice to save us," "faith in Jesus," "the Second Coming," "heal as you did when Jesus walked the earth," "this Peyote is the comforter you promised," "forgive us our sins," "we are weak and pitiful and need your help, O Lord," and ending with "In the name of the Father, the Son, and the Holy Ghost, Amen." (Stewart 1972c). *Osa:* "In the southwest corner [of the octagonal wooden peyote church] are three buckets of water for the thirsty [during the entire Peyote meeting]" (Information from Chief Lookout in J. Collier 1935:695). "And as the people prepare themselves for the meeting, the 'Road Man' then instructs his firemen to go get the water that they are supposed to use for the night and the three firemen go out and get the water and bring it in [before the ritual starts]" (Maker 1968). + (Bailey). *SCF:* No midnight water call in Cross Fire ritual observed by Stewart (1972c), yet reported present by Steinmetz.

164. *AbS:* Recalls and lays them down (Voegelin). *Cro:* "Chief has to put outfit in front of himself" (Voget). *Osa:* + (Bailey).

165. *Del:* Ashes formed into an eagle in one small-moon variant (Petrullo 1934:78). *C-D:* Ashes piled on each side of fire to represent the lungs of Jesus. Also formed into a heart (Petrullo 1934:101, 181). *WCF:* Ashes formed into a moon twice during the ritual and, in addition, formed into a heart twice, the "Morning Star" twice (the second time with lines across two points), a cross (by filling with embers the interspaces of the cross incised on floor), and finally a sun (Praus). *SCF:* Although the ashes were once formed into a crescent, later the ashes forming the crescent were reshaped into a heart; the heart was changed into a five-pointed star; all ashes then divided into four piles in the four quarters formed by the cross incised into the packed earth of the cross (Stewart 1972c). *SHM:* Often fire chief makes design of ashes—that is, a heart or the like. Proper way—crescent (Morgan 1973).

WRS: Done by assistant fire chief (Moore and Schroer 1950). *Ara:* Into shape of "Spread Eagle" (Trenholm 1970:301). *Men:* Ellipse (Slotkin 1952:596). *Osa:* "after every round" (Bailey).

168. *S&F:* Only the space between ashes and altar was swept regularly. Neither altar-moon nor space in tipi cleaned. In the morning the roadman explained to me that some tribes sweep and clean all the free space in the tipi, but the Butlers, Sac and Fox, follow "the old way" and do not. Cigarette butts not burned at end of meeting (Stewart 1972c).

169. *C-D:* See note 163, above. *Cro:* By cedarman (Voget).

170. *Cro:* Four blasts on the whistle, then two songs are sung, the first being "fixed" (Voget). *SCF:* Whistle blown four times near midnight, although no water ritual, at meeting near Denver (Stewart 1972c). *W-P:* Not used by Sam Dick, 1939, but became regular (Stewart 1972c). *Men:* By cedar chief (Slotkin 1952:596).

171. *WRS:* Sometimes twice (Shimkin). *Men:* Four long, four short (Slotkin 1952:596).

172. *C-D:* Special water song used to call for fresh water in morning (Petrullo 1934:93).

173-74. *Com and NoC:* Water handed into lodge by women; put in position by fire chief (Hoebel). *Kic:* Woman once observed blessing water at midnight (Noon).

176. *W-P:* Cedarman only sprinkles cedar on fire; no prayer. *Nav:* Cedarman makes long prayer, about fifteen minutes, before sprinkling cedar (Stewart 1972c).

177. *AbS:* Swings water bucket four times over fire on which cedar has been sprinkled. (Voegelin).

180. *Cro:* Drummer both smokes and prays (Voget). *Nav:* Leader prayed for over an hour following long prayers by cedarmen and fireman (Stewart 1972c).

181. *K-A:* + (Jordan 1968). *Gos:* To moisten "mother earth" (Malouf).

182. *Ara:* Four sips (Underhill).

184. *Kio:* + (Marriot 1954).

186. *Cro:* Makes circuit of room after removing water (Voget).

187. *AbS:* Drum and staff were lying beside the leader; he picks up staff at this point and hands it to man on his left, while he goes outside with whistle (Voegelin). *WCF:* During drinking of water at midnight, staff placed upright in hole just west of incised horseshoe, in front of leader (Praus).

188. *WCF:* Drummer goest outside after paraphernalia placed (Praus).

191. *Osa:* Fan people when reenter house (La Barre 1938:70). − (Bailey).

193. *WCF:* Only individual's fans used after midnight (Praus). *Kic:* Only fans (Noon). *S&F:* A few used individual rattles as they led singing, but only one old Pawnee rattled an accompaniment. Individual fans in use halfway through period before midnight and after (Stewart 1972c).

194. *K-A:* No urging; each is expected to be his own judge (McAllister). *Kio:* Depends on leader and age of those to whom he is talking (La Barre). *Cro:* "Chief tells them to eat all they wish, but it is up to the individual. Free will, you know. He does not coax to fill them up, or not to" (Voget). *Gos:* Urged to eat as much as desired (Malouf). *SCF:* Amount eaten seemed very personal. No one seemed to pay attention (Stewart 1972c). *Mex:* As in film "To Find Our Life" by Furst (1969); "eat a lot" (Mata Torres 1973:20).

195. *Kio:* Depends on leader and age of those to whom he is talking (La Barre). *Ute:* In "old Sioux way" devotees urged not to eat too much; usually eat only four buttons.

196. *Kio:* As designated by leader (La Barre). *C-D:* Roadman usually announces that anyone wishing to pray through a cigarette may do so after midnight, but some leaders do not approve of individual prayers (Webber).

197. *Kio:* As designated by leader (La Barre). *Kic:* Exceptional. Only when woman is close friend of family of person being treated. Spiritual value of prayers of friends is great (Noon).

198. *W-P:* For special individual prayers, leader rolls the cigarettes, to which he adds ground sage leaves. See note 57 *AbS,* above.

201. *C-D:* Road chief lighted and puffed cigarette before handing it to individual for his

prayer, then this chief puffed it and prayed following individual (Petrullo 1934:93). *Cro:* It might be handed to anyone (Voget).

202. *NoC:* Instead of to cedarman, butt handed to fire chief, who blows four puffs toward altar (Hoebel).

205. *Kio:* Procedure not rigid. Leader may run this differently at each meeting (La Barre). *W-P:* Leader occasionally but not usually prays following individual prayers.

206. *Kio:* May leave between a man's four songs, if get leader's permission. Prescribed etiquette for passing before smokers and eaters (La Barre). *Cro:* Permissible to leave any time, if necessary (Voget). *Gos:* No one left during songs, but several went outside during prayers in early morning (Malouf).

207. *C-D:* Fixed water call in morning for fire chief to bring pail of fresh water, replacing that which had been in meeting all night (Petrullo 1934:93, 102). All blessings by road chief in Big Moon variant (Webber; Petrullo 1934:102). *WCF:* No water brought into meeting in morning (Praus). *Gos:* See note 265a, below. *W-P:* Absent in 1938, but observed in 1972 (Stewart); + (d'Azevedo 1954). *SCF:* meeting near Denver no separate morning water call. Food and water brought together (Stewart 1972c).

208–10. *SCF:* Woman brought in food and water then took bag of cedar and stood holding it while she prayed. After prayer she sprinkled cedar and with one eagle feather incensed food, water and the congregation (Stewart 1972c).

209. *C-D:* See note 207, above.

210. *C-D:* Road chief blesses water (Webber).

212. *C-D:* No peyote breakfast (Petrullo 1934:94). Peyote breakfast present in all Big Moon variants (Petrullo 1934:157). As a rule, at "Wilson way" meeting no peyote breakfast served; instead candy, refreshments served, especially if among rich Oklahoma Indians (Webber). *WCF:* Food eaten outside without special ceremony after meeting (Praus). *Cro:* "If breakfast ready, she [woman water carrier] brings it in; if not, fire chief brings it in later" (Voget).

213. *SCF:* Stewart observed only water brought into tipi, but Steinmetz reported no separate water call, but water and food brought in to meeting at Allen, S.Dak.; large meal served at dawn outside of tipi and Cross Fire ritual. Everyone traveled in cars to the cemetery for the closing ritual act of meeting. No noon feast (Stewart). *SHM:* "Morning breakfast" (Morgan 1973).

215. *NoC:* In absence of corn, Cracker Jack [a brand of candied popcorn] used. Boiled raisins and rice used as fruit (Hoebel). *WRS:* Order varied; fruit sometimes last (Shimkin). *Gos:* See note 265a, below. *Taos:* Rice sometimes used in place of maize (Parsons 1936). Strawberries used (Stewart 1975). *K-A:* Ceremonial breakfast described by Julie Jordan after a Kiowa-Apache peyote meeting at home of Alfred Chalepah, James Silverhorn, Roadman (Jordan 1968). *SCF:* Near Denver order was water, dry pemmican, dry pounded maize, cherries in Jello, candy and cookie mix (Stewart 1972c). *NoC:* Cracker Jack for corn peyote breakfast (Llewellyn and Hoebel 1941:85). *W-P:* At McDermitt, Nevada, ceremonial breakfast consisted of water, sweetened Cream of Wheat cereal, canned corned beef as taken from can, canned fruit cocktail, soda crackers. Crackers got in front of other food (Stewart 1972c).

216. *NoC:* See note 215, above, for use of rice. *Gos:* According to my Washo-Paiute informants, Gosiute boiled rice instead of corn at times. *W-P:* Fruit (canned peaches, salad mixture) sometimes served before boiled rice. *Ara:* Food: Stewed corn, rice, stewed beef (Underhill 1950:6). *Kio:* At closing of ceremony group served "rice or other boiled grain" (Mooney 1896b:8).

217. *AbS:* Fruit was home-canned blackberries (Voegelin).

218. *WRS:* + (Day 1938:9). *Ara:* "Fruit gravy" (Underhill 1950).

219. *Cro:* "Just cooked corn; if do not have it, used canned corn" (Voget). *WRS:* May be canned corn (Shimkin). *Taos:* + (Stewart 1975). *Nav:* + (Nabakov 1969:132); not at Teec Nos Pos (Stewart 1972c).

220. *AbS:* Red and white striped peppermint stick candy, broken into inch pieces (Voegelin). *C-D:* See note 212, above. *Cro:* "Not here, but I hear those south boys use it" (Voget). *WRS:* For special ceremonies—Christmas, Easter, etc. (Shimkin). *Nav:* Candy included (Nabakov 1969: 132); not at Teec Nos Pos (Stewart). *Taos:* No candy in 1975 (Stewart 1975). *SCF:* + (Steinmetz).

221. *Cro:* Individual selected especially for blessing food (Voget).

222. *C-D:* Exit from tipi at dawn to wash and greet sun, then return to tipi until dinner (Petrullo 1934: 93). *Osa:* "continue singing until noon dinner" (Bailey).

223. *C-D:* Drum untied and paraphernalia put away after blessing and before eating dinner at noon (Petrullo 1934: 94). *WCF:* Paraphernalia put away after blessing of dinner at noon (Praus). *Gos:* See note 265*a*, below. *Taos:* After breakfast, singing continues until paraphernalia reach chief (Parsons 1936). *SCF:* The Cross Fire ritual I attended at Allen, S.Dak., June, 1971, was part of the S.Dak. State Convention of NAC, and the ritual did not end until the ritual acts in the peyotist cemetery; consequently elements 223 to 236 are all negative or absent. According to Steinmetz, there are several of these present in a regular Cross Fire ritual (Stewart).

224. *SCF:* + (Steinmetz). *Taos:* Paraphernalia put away after ceremonial breakfast (Stewart 1975). *Osa:* "After dinner" (Bailey).

225. *SCF:* + (Steinmetz).

226. *NoC:* Water tasted on drumstick (Hoebel).

227. *WRS:* Recently discontinued (Shimkin). *SCF:* + (Steinmetz). *L-A:* Baptism in peyotism is "thoroughly doubtful" of Christians origin "since it occurs in pre-white Peyotism (e.g. Lipan)" (La Barre 1983: 43fn.). Baptism is Lipan (La Barre 1938: 91). *Com:* "In this Sacred Peyote Society, they have a form of Baptism, and they baptize with the tea made from stewing the Peyote, and they baptize you in the name of the Father and the Son and the Holy Ghost, the Holy Ghost being the Peyote. Then you drink some of the tea and they make signs on your forehead with the tea, and then they take an eagle's wing and fan you with it" (Semans 1911: 4); similar to Sioux Cross Fire baptisms (Stewart 1972*c*). *WCF:* Rave baptized: "dips his fingers in infusion and then passes them over the forehead of the new members, prays to 'God, the Son, and the Holy Ghost'" (Radin 1923: 389).

228. *AbS:* poured on west side of moon (Voegelin). *WCF:* Water from drum sprinkled on four interspaces of cross (incised on floor of fireplace) which had been filled with live embers by the fire chief (Praus). *SCF:* + (Steinmetz). *Nav:* Water poured on ground on convex side of altar—i.e., between altar and officials (Stewart 1972*c*).

231. *SHM:* Remains in tipi or room (Steinmetz).

232. *SCF:* + (Steinmetz).

233. *Osa:* "Placed in front of Roadman" (Bailey).

234. *Kio:* Usually handed by fireman to woman or women helpers (La Barre). *S&F:* Only first receptacle carried out by fire chief. Other participants, in order, took a pan or dish. Being fourth from the door I carried out dish of remaining candy and cookies. Dish was taken from me by children waiting at the door (Stewart 1972*c*). *SCF:* + (Steinmetz).

235. *C-D:* Meeting continues until noon (Petrullo 1934: 94; Webber). *Nav:* Ceremony ended about 6:00 A.M. so that laborers could leave. Those staying remained in hogan informally or went outside. Free passage in and out (Stewart). *SCF:* + (Steinmetz).

236. *Kio:* No formal lining up to greet sun. May be individual wordless "greetings" (La Barre). *C-D:* Devotees file out of tipi and line up facing sun, at dawn (Petrullo 1934: 93, 97). At exactly noon, leader gazes at sun and worships sun and blesses food (Webber). *Taos:* − (Stewart 1975). *Cro:* + (Takes Gun 1957).

237. *Kio:* May or may not return to tipi. Those with photophobic eyes seek shade either in tipi, under "shade," or under "tree" (La Barre). *SHM:* Seldom return to tipi. If house meeting, especially if cold—yes. During the course of the year there are few tipi meetings (Morgan 1973). *SCF:* + (Steinmetz).

238. *K-A:* Tipi dismantled, but altar is simply left; no longer sacred, but not intentionally

destroyed (McAllister). *Kio:* Depends on leader (La Barre). *Cro:* "Tipi might be taken down in evening, leaving altar way it is" (Voget). *SCF:* + (Steinmetz). *Men:* Occurs late in day (Slotkin 1952: 603).

239. *SCF:* + (Steinmetz); also at Denver meeting where participants did not travel to cemetery to conclude meeting (Stewart 1972c).

240. *General:* "The Omaha placing of an open Bible near the father peyote may indeed have been influenced by the Winnebago (who put the peyote directly on the open book), and so to the Iowa, but the Oto use of the Bible in the Church of the First Born probably preceded it in Oklahoma . . ." (La Barre 1938: 73); "We accept Jesus Christ and the Bible. We are Christians" (Allan Dale, President of NAC of North America as quoted in *Time,* Aug. 9, 1954, p. 50); the Prairie Potawatomi of Kansas use Bible and mention God and Jesus Christ in peyote meetings (Landes 1970: 114, 302, 311ff.). *AbS:* Bible not used, but I was told that it is used among the "Loyal" or Cherokee Shawnee of northeastern Oklahoma. Some among the Cherokee Shawnee take peyote "according to the Bible way . . . like those Iowas." The "Bible way" peyote takers are "against" old native religious ceremonies and dances, which is not the case among the Absentee Shawnee (Voegelin). *Iowa:* In 1916, Indian agent reported the Iowa read from the Bible during peyote meetings (1916 questionnaire); "Before them [the roadman] rests the open Bible. . . . The Peyote chief . . . leads in the preaching and Bible reading" (Skinner 1915a: 724–25). *Cro:* "Some of the priests are 'returned students' and in Christian communities they claim that the Indian's religious road differs from that of the white man and that peyote is the Indian road; that Peyote is the Indian's way of knowing God and seeing Christ; that Peyote is the Indian way of observing communion and learning God's will for him. At some of these services prayers and offerings to God and Christ, testimonies and exhortations are given, and the Bible is read and occupies a prominent place on the altar" (Kinney 1921: 4). *WHM:* Yellow Bank informant for "half moon sect of Winnebago placed a Bible beside the altar near the 'chief Peyote' in a sketch of the Peyote meeting" (Densmore 1931). *Oto:* "Charles Whitehorn allowed Bible in Peyote meeting before Koshiway organized First Born Church in 1914. . . . James Arkeketah wanted to bring Bible into Peyote meeting first. He read from the Bible in there. Everything was Jesus Christ" (Truman Dailey to Stewart). "Evidently the Bible was included in the Peyote rite among the Oto, ca. 1900 . . ." (Slotkin 1956b: 119, fn. 8). *WCF:* "When we first commenced to use the peyote the Government police were sent out to arrest us. . . . We went to work (to) buy a Holy Bible to shield our peyote lodge. A man by the name of Harry Rave was sent out to buy a Bible. This man, Harry Rave, have testify to same once before" (Tebo 1917: 31). "Upon the small earth mound are placed the two 'chief' peyote, the Bible, and the staff" (Radin 1914: 4; 1923: 389). "Albert Hensley calls upon twelve educated members to translate and interpret certain portions of the Bible for the nonreading members. He arranges with the leader to have the singing stop at certain places so that some of these young men can speak" (Radin 1914: 5; 1923: 395). "During the early hours, before the peyote has begun to have any appreciable effect, a number of apparently intrusive features are found. These, for the most part, consist of speeches by people in the audience, and the reading and explanation of parts of the Bible" (Radin 1914: 3; 1923: 389). "John Rave liked the Bible" (Peter Rave to Stewart 1972c).

244. *SCF:* − (Steinmetz). During Sioux Cross Fire ritual observed in a house near Denver, Colorado, no crescent made, but one was constructed for meeting in Allen, S.Dak. (Stewart). *Osa:* "concrete" (Bailey).

245. *SCF:* − (Steinmetz). During the Sioux Cross Fire ritual I observed at Allen, S.Dak., the ash crescent was made once, but ashes changed to several other shapes later (Stewart). No ash crescent at Denver (Stewart 1972c). *WRS:* Possibly − eagle too (Stenberg 1946: 117).

250. *Kio:* Before the blessing of the water takes place, the food is outside the tipi back of the prayer. When it is set up for "peyote breakfast" it is between prayer and water (La Barre). *SCF:* + (Steinmetz).

251–65. These elements are thus defined by Petrullo (1934: 154–58). *Win:* Jesus mentioned in all prayers (Praus). *WRS: dame ape* (Our (inclusive) father). One informant used the exclusive form *ni me ape* (Shimkin).

252. *Gos:* Prayers addressed to God, Jesus Christ, Mary, and Peyote (Malouf). Also among Ute (Stewart 1948).

253. *AbS:* "God sent the peyote for man to worship" (Voegelin). *SHM:* Peyote is a mediator between God and man (Morgan 1973).

254. *WCF:* Meeting I attended was held to thank Jesus for the recovery of two women (Praus).

255. *Kio:* Some say so, some not (La Barre).

259. *WRS:* + sage used before meeting (Day 1938: 7). *SHM:* Individual can be purified by peyote (Morgan 1973).

260. *AbS:* Purification not stressed, but in line with all I heard about peyote (Voegelin).

261. *W-P:* Modifications were made, but there was no claim that they were based on revelations.

262. *Kio:* True of all American Indian religions about which I know, possibly of all approaches to all gods and spirits in all religion (Maybe this is one of the definitions of religion!) (La Barre). *AbS:* I should say so! "We are pitiful people" (Voegelin).

263. *Kio:* Like Calvin Coolidge's preacher, the Kiowa are "against sin" too; I don't know what else this element means (La Barre).

264. *SCF:* ? (Steinmetz). *SHM:* "Road of life—birth death" (Morgan 1973).

265. *Kio:* Depends on the individual and his special life history (La Barre). *Kic:* The informant said the incised line on the crescent was "the line toward Christ" (Noon). *Gos:* Simply called the path of life (Malouf). *SHM:* Often identification is with one's self (Morgan 1973).

265*a*. A copy of the following program was given to the Ibapah Gosiute by an Oklahoma Indian. When the copy was badly worn, the Indians asked subagent A. L. Robertson to make a new one, which he did, sending me the carbon copy in January, 1940:

PROGRAM: NATIVE AMERICAN CHURCH

Part 1—Enter Tepee about 7 or 8 o'clock P.M. in file viz., first, the leader, second drummer or assistant chief, third, audience follows, all taking seats, fourth, last man to enter fire chief.

Part 2—First let [place] peyote on moon, second, pass tobacco and corn husks to right to man next to door south, third fire chief passes cigarette lighted [cigarette-lighting] stick to first man south side of door going around the fire. Man places stick in fire. The chief or leader offers prayer for purpose of meeting it of 5—finish prayer out. Everybody put down stubs around base of moon.

Part 3—Pass sacks of medicine [peyote] to first man south of door and everybody take 4 peyote each and chew and eat medicine.

Part 4—Leader, lay rattler, staff, feathers, and whistle before you, and smudge outfit with cedar leaves by putting in fire and pass over the smudge whole outfit 4 times. Motion forward and back and drummer follows same motion. Lay whistle vertical along side of moon, under chief peyote. Start singing first song follow with any other 3 songs. Pass rattler, staff to left—going around.

Part 5—Midnight. Fire chief fix fire clear up. Gather [place] cigarette stubs to each end of moon [tips of crescent].

Leader recalls outfit to him, puts cedar in fire smudge outfit, drum also and sing midnight song, smudge the water sitting before fire, and fire man behind it and pass to leader and drummer will take cigarette puff. A few times and pass to leader to finish, lay cigarette down between base of moon and whistle and spill a little water on the ground, pass some where outside and return into tepee. Go around the place and leader then passed the outfit back to the man where the outfit was recalled for taking out water. Leader steps outdoors to offer prayer to four corner points of wall facing, east, south, west, north, blow whistle facing east and going to south side and blow the whistle south and going to west blow whistle to west and going to the north side blow whistle to the north and then return inside and drummer will make cedar smudge to you and take your seat as before. Lay whistle back in the same place and proceed as before.

Part 5—Morning. Fix ashes along side of moon and clean up. Fire man hands you whistle and smudge feathers and whistle. Sing morning song and follow with 3 songs and lay everything to right and leader may ask anyone to offer prayer with cedar to smudge water and meantime drummer rolls smoke for woman and when through smudging water pass cigarette to fireman. He lights it and gives to woman, she offers prayer. When through she takes her seat and smokes, then gives to leader. He offers prayer, finishes, puts stub down as usual. Woman spills little water on ground, drinks and passes water to one south side of door and going around as before. Woman rises, going around and picks up bucket before stepping out. As soon as possible have breakfast delivered, water, corn, fruit, meat. Recall outfit.

Sing 3 songs. Last one quitting song. Lay outfit before you. Offer as blessing for all. Take off chief peyote. Untie drum and pass around the circle.

Fire man takes outfit outside and comes in, goes around and pass breakfast to man south side door in position. Go out as soon as through.

266. *Iowa:* Songs and prayers to Jesus (Skinner 1915a: 727). *WHM and WCF:* Data from Densmore (1931). *Osa:* "The singers sang about Jesus" (La Flesche 1915: 115). — (Bailey). *Men:* Other names too (Slotkin 1952: 579).

267. *Osa:* "called 'Son of God' in prayers" (Bailey).

270. *L-A:* "eat no salt, chili or pepper" during ritual (Mooney n.d. *b,* MS 1930, n.d., BAE). *General:* Salt taboo widespread (La Barre 1938: 21); No salt (Paffrath 1887). *Com:* "No salt was used on food eaten during the peyote ceremonies" (Lucy Wahkahquah 1966). *Kio:* "I was forbidden to eat salt all day Friday. 'Peyote doesn't like the salt,' Wilma said" (Marriot 1954); "no salt in food until after ceremony" (Mooney 1896a: 8).

273. *K-A:* + (K. Beals 1967: 8).

275. *L-A:* "When one man sings, another may get up and dance. Anyone who wants to can get up and dance" (Morris E. Opler 1938: 281). *K-A:* "Tennyson Berry asserts that there is occasional dancing in a meeting—by the men only, and that the whistle is sometimes used with the singing" (Aberle 1955). *Kio:* "It was said very earnestly that 'sometimes toward morning it might be danced in the Peyote tent if a man had much reverence, but only if he had very great reverence'" (Ida Lone Wolf, in Tsa Toke 1957: 57); "he [the leader] began to get up and dance" (Geo. Hunt to La Barre, field notes Aug. 26, 1935). *Com:* About 1954, NAC president Allen Dale said: "They still see dancing occasionally during the Peyote rite among the Comanche and Kiowa" (Slotkin 1956b: 110); "Once without warning Comanche danced in a meeting. It was like God sent Holy Ghost to influence people" (Mihcoby to Stewart 1972c). *Ara:* "The fire-tender scrapes the ashes into a crescentic shape, inside the crescent of earth, and then stands and dances" (Kroeber 1907: 403). *W-P:* + (Stewart 1948).

276. *General:* Although non-Indians have sold peyote to Indians since 1870s (E. L. Clark 1888), often transporting it to reservations, since 1909 it has been known Indians from reservations in the U.S. have made pilgrimages to harvest some peyote themselves (William E. Johnson 1909b). G. Morgan (1976) documents such trips. From seven hundred in 1966 to thirteen hundred in 1957 visited one supplier (p. 113) from fifteen states and Canada (Stewart). On February 22, 1975, the *Corpus Christi Caller* published a photograph of Indians drying peyote and wrote: "Some 1,200 Indians make the pilgrimage to a camp outside Mirando City near Laredo, at this time each year." On February 3, 1975, the *Laredo Times* published a photograph of Cree William Denny from Rocky Boy's, Montana, and two Sioux from Yankton, South Dakota (Stewart). *K-A:* Annual trips to vicinity of Laredo, Texas, to collect peyote. "A ritual accompanies the collection" (K. Beals 1967). *Com:* ". . . was making pilgrimages to the peyote fields of Texas two or three times a year and bringing back 'peyote buttons' for

Comanche use" (McAllester 1949: 47). *W-P:* Karl James, Washo, of Carson City, Nevada, reported trips to Texas to collect peyote in 1967 and 1968 (Stewart). *Kio:* "As I have long known, it is a part of the ceremony of the Native American Church to make a pilgrimage to secure the peyote" (Letter to White Horse, Kiowa Agency, from John Collier, 1943). *Nav:* A Navajo I met among the Sac and Fox reported he sprinkled "corn pollen" on the first peyote he found, where he also smoked a Bull Durham cigarette, blew smoke on the peyote, and prayed (Stewart).

277. *S&F:* Account of pilgrimage and smoking and praying from George and Mabel Harris (1967).

283. *Mex:* "When traveling, they take a gourd in which is mixed water and powdered Peyote" (Benzi 1972: 339). *Nav:* Peyote ground into coarse powder, bottle of ground peyote passed (Underhill 1963). *Osa:* "The Peyote was ground nearly to the fineness of flour and mixed with water and kneaded into dough. This dough was distributed among the members, and each member arranged his portion in little pellets about the size of a hazelnut, which he swallowed one at a time" (La Flesche 1915: 115). "Duties of Fireman's wife: Pounding Peyote and Praying" (Msker 1968: 6).

284. *WRS:* Peyote paste (Moore and Schroer). *Ara:* Peyote paste (Trenholm 1970: 300).

285. *Taos:* "Peyote tea" seldom made (Collins 1968: 431).

286. *Osa:* Osage roadman, Ed Red Eagle, told me of this practice when I visited Pawhuska, Oklahoma, April, 1972 (Stewart). *WCF:* On outline of arrangement of meeting place (Densmore 1931).

288. *Oto* and *SCF:* Charles Whitehorn, Oto, directed Cross Fire ritual at Lake Andes, South Dakota, for Sioux. He built a mound east of the fire (Louis Stacker to Stewart). *C-D:* Mound east of altar (La Barre, 1938: 75, fig. 4). *WHM:* Drawing by member of Jesse Clay Half Moon sect of Winnebago, Jesse Yellowback, shows circle east of altar designated "the earth" (Densmore 1931). *WCF:* Whenever the ceremony is performed in the open, a fire-place in the shape of a horseshoe is made. At one end of this fireplace is placed a very small mound of earth, called by Rave 'Mount Sinai'" (Radin 1923: 389).

290–91. *Nav:* Special peyote hogans (Aberle photo; Stewart; Underhill). *Osa:* The peyote houses, or churches, are approximately twenty to twenty-two feet in diameter, octagonal in shape. . . . The floor is of dirt; the altar and apron of cement (U.S.–BIA 1935: 695). They sat in a circular house. . . . You will notice a little cross on top of it (La Flesche 191: 115). "The Osage adherents, instead of a temporary lodge, have well constructed buildings, circular in form, with concrete floors and altars, and the accompanying sweat-lodges are provided with similar floors. Such permanent buildings for the performance of the ceremony are invariably termed Peyote churches" (Curtis 1930: 211). *WCF:* Peyote wooden church building (Radin 1923: 388). The ceremony is generally held in a building, called by the peyote worshippers a church, although frequently it likewise takes place in the open (Radin 1914: 2; 1923: 388).

295. *Kio:* There is no preliminary preparation, such as by fasting or the sweatbath, and supper is eaten as usual before going in" (Mooney 1896*b*: 8).

296. *K-A:* + (Aberle 1955). *Taos:* + By old Taos peyotist, not roadman (Stewart 1972*c*).

297. *Osa:* Water in church all night (Fred Bigman, Kiowa-Apache, re. Osage meeting, University of Oklahoma Oral History Project, 1967). *L-A:* "They say in the old way [water] was brought in at the beginning of the meeting" (Brito 1975: 159). *C-D:* Water at any time (Petrullo 1934: 92).

298. *SCF:* At Cross Fire ritual observed near Denver directed by Sioux, midnight water left in room and a cup given to anyone upon request. Roadman asked for and received an extra cup during morning hours (Stewart).

299. *C-D:* Ashes in two piles (La Barre 1938: 78).

300. *Cro:* Cloth altar. Black felt painted white border, two white stars at top, eagle, "Jesus only," cross, U.S. flag across bottom, "Love one another" (attributed to Sam Lone Bear; owned by Chester Medicine Crow) (photographed by Stewart 1972, Lodge Grass,

Montana). *Gos:* "Jimmy Steele keeps the cloth altar given him by Sam Lone Bear in 1929." Another Shoshone, Sam Long of Tamoak Reservation, south of Elko, Nevada, also has a Sam Lone Bear cloth altar (Stewart 1972c). *WCF:* ". . . I have seen a few Winnebago leaders use a silk altar cloth" (Brito 1975:98). *Ute:* At some meetings conducted by Lone Bear, 1914–29 (Stewart 1972c). *SHM:* See note 98, above.

301. *Osa* and *C-D:* Fanning each person at reentry (La Barre 1938:70). *C-D:* Purified upon reentry (Petrullo 1934:92). *W-P:* + At Peyote meeting observed at McDermitt (Stewart 1972c).

303. *Mex:* Huichol string Peyote on cord to transport and preserve (Peter Furst, personal communication, July 1978). *L-A:* Lipan and Carrizo string peyote to "make a sort of rosary of it, and keep it by them" (Berlandier 1969:22). *Ara:* "String of Peyote buttons" from Clinton, Oklahoma (Photographed in the *Pawhuska Daily Journal-Capital,* Sept. 26, 1934; also in Densmore 1936).

304. *L-A:* Morris Opler reported shaman during peyote ritual: "sometimes he sucks right away without singing" (M. E. Opler 1938:284; also La Barre 1938:86). *Ara:* Roadman served as sucking shaman during a declared break in ceremony after midnight which I observed (Stewart 1972c). *Ute* and *W-P:* Sucking shamans also peyotists, but not observed sucking during ritual (Stewart 1956b).

305. *General:* "At all meetings a fine selected specimen of peyote is placed upon the crescent altar, and if the leader should be a Catholic, there rests across the peyote a crucifix (Curtis 1930:19, 201)." Also Curtis photograph showing above for Osage.

Program of the Native American Church State Convention, Allen, South Dakota, July 3–7, 1948

Author's note:
This is an example of the conduct and content of a peyote convention. It was given to me by Jim Bluebird in 1971; at that time he was president of the NAC of South Dakota.

Saturday, July 3rd Program—First Day
9 A.M.   Invocation by Rev. Solomon Red Bear
   Welcome Address by Dave Arapahoe
   Respond, George Gapp
   Address by Mrs. Alice Richard
   Reading of the minutes of last convention
10 A.M.   Business Council
   General Reports
   State Chairman Sam High Hawk
   Vice Chairman Dick Fool Bull
   Secretary, Vacancy
   Executive Committee, Women's Auxiliary
   General Director, Delegates Reports, Etc.
12 M.   Noonday Prayer by the Clergy
1 P.M.   Short Prayer by Leo Plenty Arrows
   Memorial Hour in honor of the late Schuyler Crow,
      by the Council
   Jeremiah 15: 16, by Henry Crow Dog
2 P.M.   Business Council
5 P.M.   Council Adjourned
   Recreation
      Master of Ceremonies and General Director:
      Jim Blue Bird

Sunday, July 4th—Second Day
9 A.M.   Invocation by Rev. Paul Spider
   Declaration of Independence, by Dick Fool Bull

St. John 15:13 by Ed. J. Red Feather, veteran W.W.I

"Jesus Christ is your friend. It makes no difference who you are, where you are, or what you have done! Jesus is your friend," by Mr. John Sully of Wagner, South Dakota.

10 A.M.   Business Council

12 M.   Noonday Prayer, by the Clergy

1 P.M.   Short Prayer, by John Bird Head

"Where are the Dead?" by Isaac White Crane

St. John 3:1 to 16, by Rev. Paul Spider

2 P.M.   Business Council

5 P.M.   Council Adjourned

Master of Ceremonies. General Director:
    Jim Blue Bird

Monday, July 5th—Third Day

9 A.M.   Invocation by Rev. Moses Holy Eagle

"Ashes to Ashes," by Mr. Alex Ice

St. Mark 16:15 to 20, by Mr. Tom Bullman

10 A.M.   Business Council

12 M.   Noonday Prayer, by the Clergy

1 P.M.   Short Prayer, by Lester Fool Bull

St. John 4:24, by Rev. Joe Good Breast

Advancement of the N.A.C. of South Dakota
by Sam High Hawk

2 P.M.   Business Council

Election of New State Officers

Inauguration, Testimony

5 P.M.   Council Adjourned

Recreation

Master of Ceremonies. General Director:
    Jim Blue Bird

Tuesday, July 6th—Fourth Day

9 A.M.   Invocation, by Rev. Jim Bush

St. Matt. 18:20, by Tom Big Owl

1 John 4:1 to 3, by the General Director

10 A.M.   Business Council

12 M.   Noonday Prayer by the Clergy

1 P.M.   Short Prayer by Dave Little Brave

"The sign of the Times," by Chas. Spotted Eagle

Rev. 2:17, by Rev. Joe White Face

2 P.M.   Unfinished Business

Calling of the 1949 Convention

Farewell Address
Benediction, by the High Priest
5 P.M.   Council Adjourned
7 P.M.   Prayer Meeting
Master of Ceremonies. General Director:
Jim Blue Bird

Church Canons for Native American Church of South Dakota, 1948

INTRODUCTION

The Native American Church of Allen, South Dakota, which is the central organization of the State of South Dakota was based on the Holy Scriptures and Herbs, Romans 14:2. The Constitution of the United States guarantees this right, therefore the Indians of the United States so chose accordance with their way of life and costume, as God has given them, in worshiping God.

SECRETARY

PREFACE

In persuant to Article 11, amended Article 11 of Articles of Incorporation of Charter No. 1583 and by request of the General Council, Native American Church, Central Organization of Allen, South Dakota, the Secretary has codified the Church Canons. Ordained Ministers, ministers of the church with their duties and powers, church services, and otherwise the general usage and practice thereof shall hereafter be defined and codified in adherence to the above Articles of Incorporation and request of the General Council.

Canon One

High Priest—Duties and Powers

Section I
Duties

Clause (a) There shall be a High Priest.
     (b) Whose duties will be to ordain,
     (c) To administer all Sacraments of the Church,
     (d) To teach the Gospel and various church services to his subordinates,
     (e) To bless cemeteries,
     (f) to conduct all services,

Section II
Powers

    (a)   He shall have powers to send proclamations to all local branches, enforce the church Canons, and otherwise propagate and promote the welfare of his church body and congregation.

Canon Two

Assistant High Priest—Powers, Duties
Section I
Powers

    There shall be an assistant High Priest whose powers shall be:

    (a)   Powers conferred upon him by the High Priest.
    (b)   To teach Gospel and enforce church canons.
    (c)   To teach his subordinates the teachings of the church.

Section II
Duties

    Whose duties shall be;

    (a)   Conduct services,
    (b)   To administer all Sacraments,
    (c)   To bless cemeteries
    (d)   To teach his subordinates the teachings of the church,
    (e)   To preach the word of God.

Canon III

Priest—Powers, Duties
Section I
Powers

    There shall be a ordained priest in each Local Branch or District,

    Clause (a)   Whose powers shall be as prescribed by the Canons and consistant with State and Federal laws.
    Clause (b)   To investigate the circumstances of all matters pertaining to law in relations to the church before administering Sacraments and blessings thereto, such as minors wishing to get married must have consent from proper authority, parents, and etc.

Section II
Duties

    Clause (a)   Whose duties are to preach the Gospel.

    (b)   To conduct prayer services, especially important church holidays.

    (c)   To administer Sacraments,

    (d)   To teach his subordinates all the services, the teaching of the church.

    (e)   To go to homes, to bless and baptize, to visit the sick.

Canon IV

Chief Leader—Powers and Duties, Jurisdiction

The Chief Leader has the jurisdiction of all local branches or districts

Section I

Powers,

Jurisdiction.

Clause (a)   He has the power to teach the conduct of all services of the church,

Clause (b)   To enforce the church canons,

Clause (c)   Who shall baptize and conduct funeral services on emergency only, or upon orders of superiors.

Section II

Duties

Duties of the Chief Leader.

Clause (a)   To conduct prayer services.

Clause (b)   May upon request offer prayers.

Clause (c)   May by request make peace and bliss of family troubles or grievances.

Canon V

Leaders—Powers and Duties

There shall be a leader in each district.

Section I

Powers

Clause (a)   Whose powers will be to enforce the church canons.

Clause (b)   To protect, propagate and powers conferred upon them by superiors.

Section II

Duties

Clause (a)   Whose duty will be to conduct prayer services and prayers requested.

Clause (b)   Who shall baptize and conduct funeral services on emergency only or upon request by superiors.

Clause (c)   To teach the word of God.

Canon VI

Ass't Leaders, Candidate Leaders
Section I

> This Order of Leaders is Candidates and must take instructions and studies. However they must be given consent by High Priest or by his assistant to conduct prayer services and by emergency may conduct funeral services, and baptism.

Canon VII
Chief Drummer—Powers and Duties Each Dist.
Section I
Powers

   Clause (a)   Chief drummer of each district is the director and has charge of the hymns.
   Clause (b)   He has the power to teach drumming and songs to all members, which is the integral part of worshiping God.

Section II
Duties

               Chief Drummer—Duties
   Clause (a)   It is his duty to prepare the drum for prayer service.
   Clause (b)   Must be his duty to encourage the making of the outfits, bead works, feathers, etc.

Canon VIII
Chief Cedarman—Duties, Powers, Each Dist.
Section I
Powers, Duties

   Clause (a)   Chief Cedarman of each district must make efforts to procure cedar and have a supply on hand.
   Clause (b)   It is his duty to make cedar offering for prayer.
   Clause (c)   Cedar offering for Herbs.
   Clause (d)   Cedar offering for outfit.

Canon IX
Chief Fireman—Powers, Duties
Section I
Powers, Duties

   Clause (a)   The chief fireman must prepare the fireplace in case of tepee fireplace.

Clause (b)   Must prepare his outside fire in event of non-tepee worship.
Clause (c)   He has the power to enforce the church canon.
Clause (d)   His assistant is the waiter.

Canon X

Gospel, Sacraments, Herbs and Prayers
Section I
Clause (a)   This word of God must be preached.
Clause (b)   It must be explained.
Clause (c)   This clause authorizes the High priest to form religious and Biblical classes for young and older people.
Section II

Sacraments, Baptism
Clause (a)   If a baby is to be baptized, the parents must have two sponsors, a man and a woman.
Clause (b)   They must be properly questioned.
Clause (c)   Baptismal certificates must be issued.
Clause (d)   No baptism performed during lent.
Section III

Sacraments, Matrimony
Clause (a)   If one of both parties to be married are minors, they must show a written consent from parents.
Clause (b)   Blood test must be shown.
Clause (c)   They must have sponsors.
Clause (d)   Announcement must be made and reasonable time must be allowed before the marriage.
Clause (e)   The officiating minister must ask his congregation if there is any objection, before administering or proceeding with the ceremony.
Clause (f)   No marriage performed during lent.
Section IV

Sacraments, Confession
Clause (a)   Confession may be heard by a Priest only.
Clause (b)   His subordinates cannot hear confession but may in the absence of a Priest offer a prayer until such time as a Priest may be present.
Section V

Herbs—(Medicine) (Peyote)
"Another who is weak, earth Herbs," Romans 14:2
Clause (a)   The herb must be blessed before partaking.
Clause (b)   This is used as a Sacramental purpose only for all.
Clause (c)   For illness, must be administered by Faith.

Canon XI

Lord's Prayer, Ten Commandments, prayers by request
Section I
> Lord's Prayer is used for our Leading prayers and closing our service.

Section II
> The Ten Commandments must be taught and practiced.

Section III
> Prayers by request are taken up at a given station.

Canon XII

Tepee Fireplace Service of Variations
Section I
   Clause (a) Announcements by the sponsors, others by the conductor of the prayer meeting.
   Clause (b) Lord's prayer and blessing of the Herbs, partaking of herbs.
   Clause (c) Cedar offering for the outfit.
   Clause (d) Four evening songs.
   Clause (e) First Station
   Clause (f) Second Station
   Clause (g) Third Station
   Clause (h) Special station here for baptism.
   Clause (i) Fourth Station.
   Clause (j) Water (Breakfast spiritual offering)
   Clause (k) Sunday offering
   Clause (l) Word of thanks
   Clause (m) Four morning songs
   Clause (n) Lord's Prayer
Section II
> House prayer service

   Clause (a) Announcements
   Clause (b) Cedar offering, Lord's Prayer.
   Clause (c) Distribution of Herbs
   Clause (d) Cedar offering, outfit, four evening songs.
   Clause (e) Midnight station for Gospel
   Clause (f) Prayer requested
   Clause (g) Station reserved for administering Sacraments
   Clause (h) Thanksgiving
   Clause (i) Four morning songs
   Clause (j) Lord's Prayer
Section III
> Tent fire place service

Clause (a)   This is the same as tepee only fire is brought from outside fire place.
Clause (b)   Midnight station—Gospel
Clause (c)   Prayers requested
Clause (d)   Time reserved for Sacraments.
Clause (f)   Thanksgiving
Clause (g)   Four songs—Lord's Prayer
Section IV

Funeral Service
Clause (a)   Announcements
Clause (b)   Cedar offering
Clause (c)   Distribution of Herbs
Clause (d)   Four evening songs.
Clause (e)   Midnight songs, Gospel
Clause (f)   Prayer, blessings
Clause (g)   No Baptism, Marriage.
Clause (h)   Thanksgiving
Clause (i)   Cedar offering—songs, Lord's Prayer.

[No *Canon XIII*—O.C.S.]

Canon XIV

Church Rules
Clause (a)   No one must be excused ahead of the going staff.
Clause (b)   Nor while anyone is partaking of the Herbs.
Clause (c)   Nor while singing is in progress.
Clause (d)   Nor while someone is praying.
Clause (e)   There shall be strictly no talking while the service is in progress.
Clause (f)   No speech, complaints must be made by interrupting the staff (Speech belongs in the business meeting) and complaints to the Gen. Council, quarterly meetings and Executive Committee.
Clause (g)   Proper songs must be taught and used.

Canon XV

Cemeteries, Church grounds
Section I—Cemeteries
Clause (a)   All cemeteries of Native American Church must be blessed and recorded.
Clause (b)   It must be taken proper care of such as fencing, etc.
Section II—Church grounds
Clause (a)   Tepee fireplace is the regular place of worship according to

               our general usage of Native American Church, the others its variations.

Clause (b)   If financial condition warranted a meeting house would be constructed.

Canon XVI

Certificates, ordination
Section I—Certificates

Clause (a)   The Highest Priest in charge must sign all certificates of ordination; issued by Secretary and sealed thereof.

Clause (b)   Also all certificates of Leader, Assistant Leader, or permits relating to the Native American Church.

Clause (c)   Certificates of Baptism, Marriage shall be signed by officiating Priest and issued thereof.

Clause (d)   Upon issuance of Certificate or ordination it shall be recorded same at their respective County seat. Attest by Sec'y and own sealed applied.

Section II—Ordination

Clause (a)   The ordination of Priest should take place at a designated place and date of General Convention.

Clause (b)   All candidates for Priest, Leaders, Ass't. Leaders must be presented to Gen. Convention for approval.

Clause (c)   Leader is disqualified upon conviction of any court.

Canon XVII

Holy Orders
Section I—Powers, Authorization

Clause (a)   The Canon is constructed to be powers and authorization granted to the High priest to propagate and strengthen his church body and members according to general usage and practice of the church or worshiping God and in relation to Legal aspects.

Canon XVIII

Amendment, Repeal
Section I—Amendments

Clause (a)   Any part of the foregoing canons of the Native American Church State of South Dakota, may be amended at General Convention quarterly meetings and shall be effective by ratification by a majority of the Local Branches or District.

Section II—Repeal
Clause (a)   Any part of the foregoing canons, of the Native American Church, State of South Dakota may be repealed at General Convention of quarterly meeting and shall be effective upon ratification by majority of the Local Branches or Districts.

Ratified by Local Branches

Local Chairman	Districts	Date
Porcupine		
Allen		
Kyle		
Potatoe Creek		
Norris		
St. Francis		
Ogalala Black Pipe		
Parmlee		
Wounded Knee		

The foregoing Church Canons of the Native American Church, Central organization of Allen, South Dakota upon ratification of all Local Districts were approved and signed by Convention and church officials.

(Signed)   OLIVER SPIDER
                    High Priest in charge
(Signed)   SAMUEL KILLS CROW INDIAN
                    State Chairman
(Signed)   JAMES BLUE BIRD
                    Gen. Director
(Signed)   CHRISTOPHER EAGLE THUNDER
                    Acting Executive Committee Chairman
Attest: SCHUYLER CROWE
                    Secretary

Bibliography

Aberle, David F.
1955   Letter to J. S. Slotkin, Feb. 4. In possession of O. C. Stewart.
1966   *The Peyote Religion Among the Navajo.* 2d ed. Viking Fund Pub-
            lications in Anthropology, vol. 42. Chicago: University of Chi-
            cago Press, 1982.
1971   Deposition on Interrogatories of the Defendant, Arizona Cor-
            poration Commission, in No. Civ 70-401-PHX-WEC. NAC of
            Navajoland. Plaintiff, Feb. 18. U.S. District Court for Arizona.
1973   "Navajo Religion: Peyote." Manuscript for *Handbook of North
            American Indians.* Washington, D.C.: Smithsonian Institution.
1983   "Peyote Use and the Native American Church." Report to
            International Congress of Americanists. Manchester, En-
            gland, Sept. 8, 1982.
———, and O. C. Stewart
1957*a*   Field notes. In possession of O. C. Stewart.
1957*b*   *Navajo and Ute Peyotism: A Chronological and Distributional
            Study.* University of Colorado Studies, Series in Anthropology,
            no. 6. Boulder: University of Colorado Press.
Adovasio, J. M., and G. F. Fry
1976   "Prehistoric Psychotropic Drug Use in Northeastern Mexico
            and Trans-Pecos Texas." *Economic Botany* 30(1): 94–96.
Aguirre Beltrán, G.
1963   *Medicina y Magia.* Mexico City: Instituto Nacional Indigenista.
Aiken, John W.
1970   "The Church of the Awakening." In *Psychedelics,* ed. B. Aaron-
            son and H. Osmond. New York: Doubleday and Co.
Alegre, Francisco Javier
1763   *Historia de la Compañía de Jesús en Nueve-España.* 3 vols.
            Vol. 2, bk. 6, p. 1219. New edition, Mexico City, 1841–42.
Alva, Bartholomé de
1634   *Confessionario mayor y menor en lengua mexicana . . . y plati-
            cas contra las supersticiones de idolatria.* Mexico City.
American Indian Magazine
1916   Report on Sioux Conference at Mitchell, S.D. 700 Opposed Al-
            cohol and Peyote. 4(4): 344–45.
Anderson, Edward F.
1969   "The Biogeography, Ecology, and Taxonomy of *Lophophora*
            (Cactaceae)." *Brittonia* 21: 299–310.
1970   See Boke and Anderson, 1970.
1980   *Peyote: The Divine Cactus.* Tucson: University of Arizona
            Press.
Angier, Roswell P.
1918   Letter to Robert Hall. In U.S. Congress, Senate, Committee
            on Indian Affairs, 1918, p. 185.

Anonymous
1954   "Members of the U.S. Native Indian Church Convene at Tama."
            Cedar Rapids Gazette (Iowa), July 25, sec. 1, p. 1; sec. 2,
            pp. 1, 4.
1960   "Peyote Not Habit-forming Drug, Judge Rules; Ban on Use
            Voided." *Phoenix Gazette,* July 27, sec. 2, p. 1.
1962   "Trial of Navajo Members of the North American Church."
            Arizona Daily Star, Nov. 15.
1965   "Nevada Indians Assured Continued Use of Peyote." *Nevada
            State Journal,* Mar. 13, p. 23. Also *Inter-Tribal Council of Ne-
            vada, Inc. Newsletter* 2(1): 10–11.
1967   "Freedom for a Church Ritual." *Des Moines Register,* May 22,
            p. 6.
Apekaum, Charles E.
1949   "Indians for Indians." Text for broadcast, University of Okla-
            homa radio station WNAD, Norman, Oklahoma. Copy pre-
            sented to O. C. Stewart by David Apekaum in 1972.
Arias y Saavedra, Antonio
1672   *Información acerca del estado de la Sierra del Nayarit, 1672.* In
            Santoscoy, 1900, pp. 7–35.
Arizona Republic
1954   "Peyotism and the Peyote Ceremony," July 11.
1956   "24 Nabbed Sniffing Cactus-Button Drug," Feb. 20.
1971   "Trial Hears of Deadly Peyote Test," March 22 [Citing Maurice
            H. Seevers, M.D. and D.Pharm.].
1974   "Court Refuses to Review Peyote Ruling." Associated Press
            report from Washington, D.C., regarding Whittingham case.
Arizona Superior Court
1960   *Flagstaff State* v. *Mary Attakai,* no. 4089. See McFate, 1960.
Arleguí, José
1737   *Crónica de la Provincia de Zacatecas.* Bk. 2, chap. 6, pp. 154–
            55. 2d ed., Mexico City, 1851.
Arreguí, Domingo Lazaro de
1621   *Descripción de la Nueva Galicia.* Estudios Hispano-Americanos
            de la Universidad de Sevilla, no. 24. Sevilla: Padura, 1946.
Bahti, Tom
1970   "Peyote." In *Southwestern Indian Ceremonials,* pp. 58–61.
            Flagstaff, Ariz.: KC Publications.
Bailey, Garrick A.
1973   *Changes in Osage Social Organization, 1673–1906.* University
            of Oregon Press, Anthropological Papers, no. 5.
———, and LeRoy Logan
1978   List of elements of peyote ritual for Osage for this book.
Baker, Fred
1964   "Father Peyote's 'Disciples.'" *Empire Magazine, Sunday Den-
            ver Post,* July 26, pp. 4–5.
Baldwin, F. D.
1896   Letter to the Commission of Indian Affairs, September 3.

                    Manuscript, Kiowa, vol. 51, pp. 370–72. Oklahoma Historical
                    Society, Oklahoma City.
Bancroft, H. H.
    1883   *The Native Races of the Pacific States of America,* vol. 10. *North-
                    ern Mexican States,* vol. 1. San Francisco: A. L. Bancroft.
Bass, Althea
    1954   "James Mooney in Oklahoma." *Chronicles of Oklahoma* 22(3):
                    246–62.
    1966   *The Arapaho Way: A Memoir of an Indian Boyhood.* New York:
                    Clarkson N. Potter.
Bautista, Juan
    1600   *Advertencias para los Congesores,* fol. 112, Mexico City.
Beals, Kenneth L.
    1967   "The Dynamics of Kiowa-Apache Peyotism." Master's thesis,
                    University of Oklahoma.
Beals, Ralph L.
    1932   "Comparative Ethnology of Northern Mexico Before 1750."
                    Ibero-Americana 2: 94–225.
    1933   "The Acaxee, a Mountain Tribe of Durango and Sinaloa."
                    Ibero-Americana 6.
Bee, Robert L.
    1965   "Peyotism in North American Indian Groups." *Transactions
                    of the Kansas Academy of Sciences* 68(1): 13–60. Lawrence,
                    Kans.: Department of Microbiology, University of Kansas.
    1966   "Potawotami Peyotism: The Influences of Traditional Patterns."
                    Southwestern Journal of Anthropology 22: (2): 194–205.
Beede, Cyrus
    1877   "Osage." *Annual Report of the Commissioner of Indian Affairs,*
                    p. 90.
Bender, George A.
    1968   "Rough and Ready Research—1887 Style." *Journal of the His-
                    tory of Medicine and Allied Sciences* 23(2): 159–66.
Benitez, Fernando
    1968   *En la tierra mágica del peyote.* Mexico City: Biblioteca Era
                    Ensayo.
    1975   *In the Magic Land of Peyote.* Intro. Peter T. Furst. Trans. John
                    Upton. Austin: University of Texas Press.
Bennett, Wendell C., and Robert M. Zingg
    1935   *The Tarahumara: An Indian Tribe of Northern Mexico.* Chi-
                    cago: University of Chicago Press.
Benzi, Marino
    1972   *Les Derniers adorateurs du peyotl.* Paris: Editions Gallimard.
    1977   *A la quête de la vie.* Paris, Éditions du Chêne.
Bergman, Robert L.
    1971   "Navajo Peyote Use: Its Apparent Safety." *American Journal of
                    Psychiatry* 128(6): 695–99.
    1972   Dr. Bergman Replies. *American Journal of Psychiatry* 129(1).

1975   "Learning from Indian Medicine." *Diversion Magazine* 3(1):
                8–9, 34–35.

Bergmans, J. J.
1921   Letter to Charles H. Burke, Commissioner of Indian Affairs.
                Aug. 2. Regarding Taos peyotism. Record Group 75, Ed.—L.
                and O. Taos, File nos. 66245–21, National Archives, Washing-
                ton, D.C.

Bergquist, Laura
1957   "Peyote: The Strange Church of Cactus Eaters [Lodge Grass,
                Montana]." *Look,* Dec. 10, pp. 36–41.

Berlandier, Jean Louis
1969   *The Indians of Texas in 1830.* Ed. John C. Ewers. Washington,
                D.C.: Smithsonian Institution Press.

Bittle, William E.
1954   "The Peyote Ritual: Kiowa-Apache." *Bulletin of the Oklahoma
                Anthropological Society* 2: 69–78.

1967   Interview of Fred Bigman, Kiowa-Apache, peyotist. Oral His-
                tory Project, Western History Collections, University of Okla-
                homa Library, Norman.

Blackbear, Ray
1968   "Kiowa-Apache: Oral History of the Native American Church."
                Manuscript, Western History Collections, University of Okla-
                homa Library, Norman.

Black Dog
1908   Statement in Oklahoma legislature, House, 1908.

Blair, Emma Helen
1912   *The Indian Tribes of the Upper Mississippi Valley and Region of
                the Great Lakes.* Vol. 2. Cleveland: Arthur H. Clark Co.

Blessing, Fred K.
1961   "Discovery of a Chippewa Peyote Cult in Minnesota." *Min-
                nesota Archaeologist* 23: 1–8.

Boas, Franz
1937   Statement on Senate Bill 1399. In U.S. Bureau of Indian Af-
                fairs, 1937.

Boke, N. H., and E. F. Anderson
1970   "Structure, Development, and Taxonomy in the Genus Lopho-
                phora." *American Journal of Botany* 57(5): 569–78.

Bolander, Walter L.
1922   Letter to A. W. Leech, Supt. Northern Pueblos, Espanola,
                N.Mex., Taos, May 3. Report of arrest of peyotists and seizure
                of peyote drum, blankets, etc. Files 62343–21 and 75423–21,
                Ed.—Law and Order, Taos, Record Group 75, National Ar-
                chives, Washington, D.C.

Bollaert, William
1850   "Observations on the Indian Tribes in Texas." *London Ethno-
                logical Society Journal* 2: 277.

1956   *William Bollaert's Texas.* Ed. W. Eugene Hollon and Ruth Lap-
                ham Butler. Norman: University of Oklahoma Press.

Bolton, Frances
    1944   Statement in *Hearings to Investigate Indian Affairs.* 78th Cong., 2d sess., Dec. 13, pt. 4, pp. 299–343.13.

Bolton, Herbert E.
    1910   "Texas, Tonkawa, etc." In Hodge, 1907–10, pt. 2, pp. 738–41, 778–83.

Bonnicastle, Arthur
    1915   Statement in U.S. Congress, House, Committee on Indian Affairs, 1918*a,* pt. 1, pp. 79–80.

Bonnin, Gertrude
    1918   Letter to Rev. Bruce Kinney re Mooney, Oct. 21. R. H. Pratt Papers, series 1, box 16, folder 391, Rare Book and Manuscripts Library, Yale University, New Haven, Conn.

    1924   Cited by Utah Rep. Colton, *Congressional Review* 65(2): 1421.

    1937*a*   Letter to Hayden, Society of American Indians, Against Peyote. In U.S. Congress, Senate, Committee on Indian Affairs, 1937, p. 18283.

    1937*b*   Statement of Jan. 29, 1918 in "Hearing on Appropriation Bill." In U.S. Congress, Senate, Committee on Indian Affairs, 1937, pp. 18258–59, 19274–76.

————, and Raymond T. Bonnin
    1916   Letter to S. M. Brosius, Oct. 12. *Annual Report of the Indian Rights Association* 34: 39–40.

Bowler, Alida C.
    1937   Letter to Commissioner of Indian Affairs, Washington, D.C., Jan. 22. Central Correspondence files 1907–39, file 22312-37-126, Carson, Record Group 75, National Archives, Washington, D.C.

Boynton, Paul
    1918   Statement in U.S. Congress, House, Committee on Indian Affairs, 1918*a,* pt. 1, pp. 182–86.

Braasch, William F.; B. J. Branton; and A. J. Chesley
    1949   "Survey of Medical Care Among the Upper Midwest Indians." *Journal of the American Medical Association* 139(4): 20–26 (also circulated in mimeographed form, for release Nov. 26, 1948, by the Office of Indian Affairs).

Brannon, C. C.
    1910   Letter to M. Russell, February 17. File Education-Liquor 66110-1910, Record Group 75, National Archives, Washington, D.C.

Brant, Charles S.
    1963   "Joe Blackbear's Story of the Origin of the Peyote Religion (Kiowa-Apache)." *Plains Anthropologist* 8(21): 180–81.

    1969   *Jim Whitewolf: The Life of a Kiowa Apache Indian.* New York: Dover.

Bravo, H. Halia
    1937   *Las cactaceas de México.* Mexico City: Universidad Nacional de México.

1967   Unva revision del genero *Lophophora. Cact. Sucul. Mex.* 12(1): 8–17.

Briggs, J. R.
1887   "Mescale Buttons—Physiological Effects." *Medical Register* 1: 276–77. Also *Druggist's Bulletin* 1(5): 78.
1896   Letter to D. W. Prentiss and F. P. Morgan, Aug. 24. Manuscript 2537, Bureau of American Ethnology, Washington, D.C.

Brito, Silvester John
1975   "The Development and Change of the Peyote Ceremony Through Time and Space." Ph.D. diss., Indiana University, Bloomington.

Bromberg, Walter
1942   "Storm over People." *Nature Magazine* 35: 410–12, 444.
———, and C. L. Tranter
1943   "Peyote Intoxication: Some Psychological Aspects of the Peyote Rite." *Journal of Nervous and Mental Disease* 97(5): 518–27.

Brosius, S. M.
1916   "The Ravages of Peyote." *Annual Report of the Indian Rights Association* 34: 37–41.

Browning, D. M.
1896   Letter to F. D. Baldwin, Aug. 4. Kiowa-Indian Celebrations and Dances, Oklahoma Historical Society, Oklahoma City.

Bruce, Harold E.
1935   Antipeyote letter to BIA, June 6 and June 25. Files 31793 and 356621, Potawatomi Agency, Record Group 75, National Archives, Washington, D.C.
1947   Antipeyote letter to BIA, from Potawatomi Agency, May 20, plus report using material back to 1919. File 027, Record Group 75, Billings Area, Federal Record Center, Seattle, Wash.
1949   "Your Religion: A Frank Discussion on Some Aspects of the Peyote Drug." *Newsletter of the National Fellowship of Indian Workers,* no. 40.

Bruner, Edward M.
1961   "Mandan." Chap. 4 in Spicer, 1961, pp. 187–277.

Bull Bear, Jock
1911   Letter to J. Mooney, Nov. 13. In U.S. Congress, House, Committee on Indian Affairs, 1918a, pt. 1, p. 86.
1912   Letter to J. Mooney, Feb. 12. In U.S. Congress, House, Committee on Indian Affairs, 1918a, pt. 1, p. 106.
1918   "Arapahoe Indian Chief Explains About an Indian Religious Society." In U.S. Congress, House, Committee on Indian Affairs, 1918a, pt. 1, pp. 104–106.
1926   Letter to C. Washakie, Feb. 2. In Stenberg, 1946, p. 147.

California State Senate
1970   Senate Bill 946, sec. 11. Amends sec. 11540 of the Health and Safety Code. Original prohibition, 1959 (see Mosk 1962, pp. 276–79).

California Supreme Court
1964   *People* v. *Woody et al.* See Tobriner, 1964.
Campbell, Thomas N.
1958   "Origin of the Mescal Bean Cult." *American Anthropologist*
            60(1): 156–60.
Cárdenas, Juan
1591   *Primera parte de los segretos marvilosos de los Indios.* Mexico
            City, 1591. 2d ed., Museo Nacional de Arqueología, Historia y
            Etnología, no. 17 (1913), pp. 145–208. Facsimile: Colección
            de incunables americanos, no. 9. Madrid: Cultura Hispanica,
            1945.
Carrigan, M.
1961   "Hallucination-producing 'Button' Feature of Little-Known Reli-
            gion" [featuring James H. Howard]. *Grand Forks Herald,* Jan. 8,
            p. 26.
Carson City Daily Appeal
1938   "Claim Drug Used by Washoe Tribe Makes Bad Indians Good
            and Good Indians Better," Oct. 22. Copy in possession of
            O. C. Stewart.
Carter, Robert Goldthwaite
1961   *On the Border with Mackenzie.* New York: Antiquarian Press.
Casey, Lee
1948*a*   "But Why Defend Peyote Cults?" *Rocky Mountain News,*
            Oct. 22.
1948*b*   "Is Peyote Harmful?" *Rocky Mountain News,* Oct. 25.
Castetter, E. F., and Morris E. Opler
1936   *The Ethnobiology of the Chiricahua and Mescalero Apache.* Uni-
            versity of New Mexico Bulletin 297. Ethnobiological Series
            4(5): 54–55, 61. Albuquerque: University of New Mexico
            Press.
Chalapan, Alfred
1968   "Kiowa-Apache: Oral History of the Native American Church."
            Manuscript in Western History Collections, University of
            Oklahoma Library, Norman.
Chavez, Dennis
1937   "Documents on Peyote." See U.S. Bureau of Indian Affairs,
            1937.
Clark, David
1967   "The Peyote Religion." *Navajo Times,* June 22, p. 4.
Clark, E. L.
1888   Letter to E. E. White, June 10. Letters Received, 1888,
            no. 17455, Fort Sill, Record Group 75, National Archives,
            Washington, D.C.
Cline, J. H.
1904   "The Mescal Feast." *Western World* 4(1): 5–29. Also *Western
            World* 5(5).

Cohen, Sidney
    1964   *The Beyond Within: The LSD Story* [peyote, pp. 21–22]. New York: Atheneum.
Cohoe
    1964   *A Cheyenne Sketchbook*. Commentary by E. A. Hoebel and K. D. Petersen. Norman: University of Oklahoma Press.
Collier, Donald
    1935   Interview with Kuiton, July 19. Copy in possession of O. C. Stewart.
    1937   "Peyote, a General Study of the Plant, the Cult, and the Drug (1931)." In U.S. Congress, Senate, Committee on Indian Affairs, 1937, pp. 18234–58.
Collier, John
    1923   Statement in U.S. Congress, House, Committee on Indian Affairs, *Pueblo Land Titles: Hearings on H.R. 13, 452 and H.R. 13, 674*, 67th Cong., 4th sess., pp. 202–203.
    1924   *The Indian and Religious Freedom*. New York: American Indian Defense Association.
    1934   *Indian Religious Freedom and Indian Culture*. Circular 2970. Washington, D.C.: Bureau of Indian Affairs. Reprinted in U.S. Congress, Senate, Committee on Indian Affairs, 1937, pp. 18319–20.
    1937   "Statement on Peyote at Taos." In U.S. Congress, Senate, Committee on Indian Affairs, 1937, pp. 18170, 18319–20.
    1940   Memorandum (on Navaho antipeyote ordinance) for Secretary Ickes, Dec. 6 (mimeographed). Document nos. 129020–21. Bureau of Indian Affairs, Washington, D.C.
    1947   *The Indians of America*. New York: Norton
    1952   "The Peyote Cult." *Science* 115(2992): 503–504.
Collings, Ellsworth
    1965   "Roman Nose: Chief of the Southern Cheyenne." *Chronicles of Oklahoma* 42: 448–49, 454–57.
Collins, John J.
    1967   "Peyotism and Religious Membership at Taos Pueblo, New Mexico." *Southwestern Social Science Quarterly* 48: 183–91.
    1968   "A Descriptive Introduction to the Taos Peyote Ceremony." *Ethnology* 7: 427–49.
    1969   "Peyotism at Taos Pueblo and the Problem of Ceremonial Description." Ph.D. diss., State University of New York, Buffalo (University Microfilms 69-20591).
Collins, Thomas W., and Clifford Duncan
    1971   "The Changing Role of the Native American Church on the Northern Ute Reservation." Paper presented at meeting of the Rocky Mountain Social Science Association, Fort Collins, Colo., May 7.
Colton, Don E.
    1922   Statement at congressional hearing against peyote. *Congressional Record* 64(2): 1069.

1924   Statement against peyote. *Congressional Record* 65(2):1421.
Connell, R. S.
1906*a*   Letter to Bryon E. White, July 24. Cheyenne and Arapaho—
             Vices. Oklahoma Historical Society, Oklahoma City.
1906*b*   Letter to Commissioner of Indian Affairs, July 31. File 2989-
             1908-126, pt. 1-C, Ponca, Record Group 75, National Ar-
             chives, Washington, D.C.
1907   Letter to BIA, copy to William E. Johnson from Rosebud,
             S.Dak. File 2989-1907-126, Record Group 75, National Ar-
             chives, Washington, D.C.
Conner, Stuart, and Roger Stop
1970   Interview about Crow peyote, August 23. MS 569, Ameri-
             can Indian Research Project, University of South Dakota,
             Vermillion.
Corwin, Hugh D.
1958   *The Kiowa Indians.* Lawton, Okla.
1959   *Comanche and Kiowa Captives in Oklahoma and Texas.* Guth-
             rie, Okla.: Cooperative Publishing Co.
1968   "Protestant Missionary Work Among the Comanches and
             Kiowas." *Chronicles of Oklahoma* 46: 41–47.
Couch, Carl J., and Joseph D. Marino
1979   "Chippewa-Crow Peyotism at Rocky Boy's." In *Lifeways of In-
             termontane and Plains Montana Indians,* ed. Leslie B. Davis.
             Bozeman: Montana State University.
Coulter, John M.
1891   "Botany of Western Texas." *Contributions to the U.S. National
             Herbarium* 2: 129.
1894   "Preliminary Revision of the North American Species of Cac-
             tus, Anhalonium, and Lophophora." *Contributions to the U.S.
             National Herbarium* 3: 128–32.
Cozio, A. V.
1720   "Proceso contra un indio de Taos que había tomado peyote y
             alborotado el pueblo." In Slotkin, 1951.
Cunningham, D. K.
1902   Letter to the Commissioner of Indian Affairs, March 21. Let-
             ters Received, 1902, no. 17150, Record Group 75, National
             Archives, Washington, D.C.
1907   Letter to C. E. Shell, Feb. 11. Cheyenne and Arapaho—
             Vices. Oklahoma Historical Society, Oklahoma City.
Curry, Orin
1925   Statement regarding peyotism of Ute. Minutes of 6th Annual
             Convention, Native American Church, Calumet, Okla.
Curtis, Edward S.
1907–30   *The North American Indian,* 20 vols. Cambridge, Mass.: Har-
             vard University Press. Includes *Taos-The Tiwa,* vol. 16 (1926),
             pp. 46–47, and *The Peyote Cult (Oto),* vol. 19 (1930), pp.
             199–219.

Curtis, Natalie
    1907   *The Indians' Book.* New York: Harper & Brothers. Reprints,
                New York: Dover Publications 1968.
Daiker, F. H.
    1914   "Liquor and Peyote, a Menace to the Indians." In *Report of the
                32nd Annual Lake Mohonk Conference on the Indian,* pp. 62–
                68. Lake Mohonk, N.Y.
Dale, Allen
    1946   Minutes of the Convention of the Native American Church of
                the United States, White Oak, Okla. Copy in possession of
                O. C. Stewart.
Dart, B. L.
    1936   Letter to Alfred Wilson, Native American Church, regarding
                dismissal of case against John Harper, Nick, Jim Wash, and
                Robert Colorow for possession of peyote. Fourth Judicial Dis-
                trict Court, Duchesne County, Utah.
Davis, Leslie B.
    1961   *Peyotism and the Blackfeet Indians of Montana: An Historical
                Assessment.* Museum of the Plains Indian Studies in Plains An-
                thropology and History, no. 1. Browning, Mont.: U.S. Depart-
                ment of the Interior, Office of Indian Affairs.
———, ed.
    1979   *Lifeways of Intermontane and Plains Montana Indians: In
                Honor of J. Verne Dusenberry.* Bozeman: Montana State
                University.
Day, Gilbert
    1938   "Statement on Peyote Church Among Shoshone," Jan. 21.
                Manuscript. U.S. Bureau of American Ethnology, Smithsonian
                Institution.
d'Azevedo, Warren
    1954   Letter to Omer C. Stewart regarding Washo-Northern Paiute
                peyotism, especially ritual, Nov. 5.
Deadwood Daily Pioneer-Times (Black Hills, S.Dak.)
    1916   [Peyote Protected by the Courts] summarized Sept. 8. Also in
                American Indian Magazine 4(4): 345–46.
DeCredico, Al
    1948   "CU Prof Performs Rites of Banned 'Peyote' Cult." *Rocky
                Mountain News* (Denver, Colo.), Oct. 21.
Deer, James H.
    1898   Letter to W. J. Walker, Anadarko, Okla., Sugar Creek, Aug.
                29. Oklahoma Historical Society, Oklahoma City.
Densmore, Frances
    1931   "The Peyote Cult and Treatment of the Sick Among the Win-
                nebago Indians." Manuscript no. 3205. U.S. Bureau of Ameri-
                can Ethnology, Washington, D.C.
    1932   "Winnebago Songs of the Peyote Ceremony." Manuscript no.
                3261. U.S. Bureau of American Ethnology, Washington, D.C.
    1936   "Cheyenne and Arapaho Music." *Southwest Museum Papers*
                (Los Angeles) 10, pp. 15–23, 82–93.

1938   "The Influence of Hymns on the Form of Indian Songs." *American Anthropologist* 40: 175–77.
1941   "Native Songs of Two Hybrid Ceremonies Among the American Indians." *American Anthropologist* 43: 77–82.
n.d.   "Winnebago Songs." Manuscript no. 1971. U.S. Bureau of American Ethnology, Washington, D.C.

Denver County Court
1967   *The People of the State of Colorado* v. *Mana Pardeahton*. Criminal Action no. 9454. [Hearing: May 24; finding: June 27].

Dick, Sam
1942   Letter to Omer C. Stewart, March 22.

Dickens, Walter F.
1917   Letter to Supt. O. J. Green, Shawnee Indian School, Shawnee, Okla., from Red Lake Indian Agency, Red Lake, Minn., Jan. 24. Indian Archives Division, Oklahoma Historical Society, Oklahoma City.

Diguet, L.
1907   Le Peyote et son usage ritual chez les indiens du Nayarit. *Journal de la Societé des Americanistes de Paris,* n.s. 4(1): 21–29.

Dorrington, L. A.
1917   Inspection report regarding Ghost Dance and peyote. Nevada Agency and School, Education Division, Law and Order, May 12–13. Reno, Nev. Letters Received, 70737, July 24, Record Group 75, National Archives, Washington, D.C.

Dorsey, G. A.
1905   The Cheyenne, II—The Sun Dance. Field Columbian Museum, *Anthropological Series* 9(2): 177–78.

———, and Alfred L. Kroeber
1903   *Traditions of the Arapaho.* Field Columbian Museum, Publication 81. Anthropological Series, vol. 5. Chicago.

Driver, Harold E.
1969   *Indians of North America.* Chicago: University of Chicago Press.

Duncan, John
1916   Letter to Standing Bear, Feb. 20. Peyote Correspondence, file 2989-1908-162, pt. 4, Record Group 75, National Archives, Washington, D.C.

Dusenberry, J. Verne
1962   *The Montana Cree: A Study in Religious Persistence.* Stockholm: Almquist and Wiksell.

Earle, Jane.
1968   "White Woman at Peyote Ceremony." *Oklahoma Orbit,* Sept. 15.

Easterlin, Malcolm
1941   "Peyote-Indian Problem #1." *Scribner's Commentator* 11: 77–82.

Edwards, F. Henry
1924   *History of the Reorganized Church of Jesus Christ of Latter Day*

Saints. Vol. 7, Independence, Mo.: Reorganized Church of Jesus Christ of Latter Day Saints.

Eggan, Fred
1959   "James Sydney Slotkin, 1913–1958." *Economic Development and Cultural Change* 7(2): 189.

Elkin, Henry
1940   "The Northern Arapaho of Wyoming." In Linton, 1940, pp. 207–55.

Erdoes, Richard
1971   *Crow Dog's Paradise. Songs of the Sioux* (album note and photographs). Album EKS-74091, New York: Elektra.

Espinosa, Isidro Felix de
1709   "Diario." In *Viajes de misioneros franciscanos a la conquista del Nuevo México.* Seville. Reprint, San Antonio, 1915. Also in *Preliminary Studies of the Texas Catholic Historical Society,* vol. 1, no. 3. Austin, Texas: Saint Edwards University, 1930.

Estrada y Flores, Andrés de
1659   *San Pedro Teocaltiche.* Mexico City: Vargas Rea, 1946.

Ewers, John C., ed.
1969   See Berlandier, 1969.

Fallers, Lloyd A.
1960   The Role of Factionalism in Fox Acculturation. Documentary History of the Fox Project, 1948–1959. Exhibit 14, pp. 62–84. Directed by Sol Tax. Ed. Fred Gearing, Robert M. Netting, and Lisa R. Peattie. Chicago: University of Chicago.

Fascell, Dante B.
1963   "Federal Law to Curb Possession of Peyote." *Congressional Record—House,* Dec. 13, p. 23394.

Fickinger, Paul L.
1952   Letter to Superintendent, Stony/Sarce Indian Agency, Calgary, Alberta, Canada, Jan. 11. Record Group 75, Billings Area Federal Records Center, Seattle, Wash.

Finney, Frank F.
1957   "The Osage Indians and the Liquor Problems Before Statehood." *Chronicles of Oklahoma* 34: 462–64.
1962   "Progress in the Civilization of the Osage." *Chronicles of Oklahoma* 40: 8–9.

Fintzelberg, N. M.
1969   "Peyote paraphernalia." *Ethnic Technology Notes,* no. 4 (October). San Diego: Museum of Man.

Firstborn Church of Christ
1914   Articles of Incorporation, filed Dec. 8. Oklahoma Secretary of State, Oklahoma City.

Furst, Peter T.
1968   "Endo-cannibalism Among the Huichols?" *Review of Ethnology,* no. 3 (Sept. 2), p. 7.
1969   *To Find Our Life: The Peyote Hunt of the Huichols of Mexico.* Film. Latin American Center, University of California, Los Angeles.

1972   "To Find Our Life: Peyote Among the Huichol Indians of Mexico." In *Flesh of Gods*, ed. Peter T. Furst, pp. 136–84. New York: Praeger.

1976   *Hallucinogens and Culture*. San Francisco: Chandler and Sharps.

———, ed.

1972   *Flesh of the Gods: The Ritual Use of Hallucinogens*. New York: Praeger.

Gaitán, José Manuel

1816   Correspondence from Refugio Mission near Corpus Christi, Texas. Spanish Archives of Bexar (San Antonio). Furnished to O. C. Stewart by Elizabeth A. H. John, 1979.

Gandy, Harvey L.

1920   "The Nation Should Be Aroused to the Danger of Peyote." *Appendix to the Congressional Record* 59(9): 9149–51.

García, B.

1760   *Manual para administrar los santos: Sacramentos, etc.* Mexico City.

Gardenerville (Nev.) *Record-Courier*

1938   "Washoe Indians Are Still Using a Drug Known as Peodi." Oct. 21. In possession of O. C. Stewart.

Gassaway, B. F.

1903*a* Letter to W. A. Jones, Jan. Letters Received, no. 6842, Record Group 75, National Archives, Washington, D.C.

1903*b* Letter to W. A. Jones, April 16. Letters Received, no. 33469, Record Group 75, National Archives, Washington, D.C.

Gilmore, Melvin R.

1912   "Uses of Plants by the Indians of the Missouri River Region." *Bureau of American Ethnology Annual Report* 33 (1911–12): 43–154.

1913   "A Study of the Ethnobotany of the Omaha Indians." *Collections of the Nebraska State Historical Society* 17: 318–20.

1919   "The Mescal Society Among the Omaha Indians." *Publications of the Nebraska State Historical Society* 19: 163–67.

Gorman, Howard

1940   "The Growing Peyote Cult and the Use of Peyote on the Navajo Indian Reservation." Navajo Tribal Council, May 18, no. 131287. Also in *Proceedings of the Meeting of the Navajo Tribal Council*, June 3, pp. 11–42. Window Rock, Ariz.

Gorton, Bernard E.

1961   "Peyote and the Arizona Court Decision." *American Anthropologist* 63(1961): 1334–35.

Grand Forks Herald

1961   Interview with James H. Howard regarding Cross Fire ritual at Fort Berthold Reservation, Jan. 8.

Greene, A. C.

1972   *The Last Captive: The Lives of Herman Lehman*. Austin, Texas: Encino Press.

Haag, Mack, and Alfred Wilson
    1925   Report of the President and Secretary of the Native American
                Church, Oklahoma, Jan. 1, 1912, to Jan. 1, 1925. Typescript.
                Submitted June 8, Calumet, Okla.
Hagan, William T.
    1958   *The Sac and Fox Indians.* Norman: University of Oklahoma
                Press.
    1962   "Quanah Parker, Indian Judge." In *Probing the American West:
                Papers,* ed. K. Ross Toole et al., pp. 71–78. Conference on the
                History of the American West, vol. 1. Santa Fe: Museum of
                New Mexico Press.
Hall, J. Lee
    1886   "Report of the Kiowa, Comanche, and Wichita Agency." *U.S.
                Bureau of Indian Affairs, Annual Report,* p. 130.
Hall, Robert D.
    1912   Letter to F. H. Abbott, Assistant Commissioner of Indian Af-
                fairs, concerning the effects of peyote on the Indians at Win-
                nebago, Neb., Jan. 30. Affidavits by John Semans and Harry
                Rave against peyote. File 2989-08-126, pt. 3, Record Group
                75, National Archives, Washington, D.C.
    1914   Statement on peyote. In Report of the 32d Lake Mohonk Con-
                ference on the Indian, pp. 74–76. Lake Mohonk, N.Y.
    1923   "Affidavit on Peyote." In *Peyote.* Bureau of Indian Affairs Bul-
                letin no. 21. Mimeographed. Washington, D.C.: U.S. Bureau
                of Indian Affairs.
    1937   "Affidavit on Experience, Nov. 10, 1911. In U.S. Congress,
                Senate, Committee on Indian Affairs, 1937, pp. 18271–72.
Harrington, John P.
    1937   Statement on Senate Bill 1399. In U.S. Bureau of Indian Af-
                fairs, 1937.
Harrington, M. R.
    1921   *Religion and Ceremonies of the Lenape.* Indian Notes and Mono-
                graphs no. 19, pp. 185–90. New York: Museum of the Ameri-
                can Indian.
    1937   Statement on Senate Bill 1399. In U.S. Bureau of Indian Af-
                fairs, 1937.
Harris, George, and Mabel Harris
    1967   Informants for Sac and Fox, Oral History Project. Western
                History Collections, University of Oklahoma Library, Norman.
Harris, Jack S.
    1940   "The White Knife Shoshoni of Nevada." In Linton, 1940,
                pp. 39–116.
Hatfield, S. M.; L. J. J. Valdes; W. J. Keller; W. L. Merrill; and V. H. Jones
    1977   "An Investigation of *Sophora secundiflora* Seeds (Mescal-
                beans)." *Lloydia* 40(4): 374–83.
Havard, Valery
    1885   "Report on the Flora of Western and Southern Texas." *Pro-
                ceedings of the U.S. National Museum* 8: 449–533.

1896   "Drink Plants of the North American Indians." *Bulletin of the Torrey Botanical Club* (Lancaster, Pa.) 23(2): 33–46.

Hayden, Carl
1921*a*   "Statement Against Peyote." *Congressional Record* 61(5): 4681–91.
1921*b*   "The Alleged Peyote Religion." Speech in House of Representatives, Aug. 4. In U.S. Congress, Senate, Committee on Indian Affairs, 1937, p. 18278.

Hayes, Alden
1940   "Peyote Cult on the Goshiute Reservation at Deep Creek, Utah. *New Mexico Anthropologist* 4(2): 34–36.

Hennings, Paul
1888   "Eine giftige Katee." *Anhalonium Lewini. mu. sp. Gartenflora* 37: 410–11.

Hensley, Albert
1908   Letter to Commissioner of Indian Affairs. In Peyote Correspondence, file 2989-1908-126, pt. 3, Record Group 75, National Archives, Washington, D.C.
Ca. 1909   "Account of the Peyote." In Radin, 1923, pp. 397–400.
1916   Letter to Miss M. V. Gaither, re role of Alice Fletcher in helping Albert get to Carlisle in 1888. Record Group 75, National Archives, Washington, D.C.

Hernández, Fernando
1628   "Historia, 1577." Abridgment: *Rerum medicarum Novae Hispaniae thesaurus, seu(nova) plantarum, animalium, mineralium Mexicoanorum historia.* Rome: Mascardi.
1900   *De Historia Plantarum Novae Hispaniae.* Reprinted in *Anales del Instituto Medico Nacional* 4(11): 204. 1790 ed. 3 vols. Madrid: Ibarra.

Hidalgo, Francisco
1716   "Letter to the Viceroy of Mexico." In Swanton, 1942, pp. 265–71. See *Southwestern Historical Quarterly* 1927–28 (31): 53–62.

Hoag, Enoch
1923   "Statement in Favor of Peyote." *Congressional Record* 65(2): 1424.

Hodge, Frederick Webb, ed.
1907–10   *Handbook of North American Indians North of Mexico.* 2 vols. Bureau of American Ethnology Bulletin no. 30. Washington, D.C.: U.S. Government Printing Office.

Hoebel, E. Adamson
1944   "Lists of Elements of Peyote Ritual of the Comanche and the Northern Cheynne." In Stewart, 1944, pp. 103–21.
1950   "The Wonderful Herb: An Indian Cult Vision Experience." *Western Humanities Review* 3: 126–30.
1952   See Wallace and Hoebel, 1952.
1964   See Cohoe, 1964.

Hollon, W. E., and R. L. Butler, eds.
 1956   *William Bollaert's Texas.* Norman: University of Oklahoma Press.
Hough, Walter
 1907   "Mescal." In Hodge, 1907, 1:845.
Howard, James H.
 1950   "Notes on Omaha Peyote Cult." *University of South Dakota Museum News* 11(2):1–3.
 1951*a* "A Tonkawa Peyote Legend." *University of South Dakota Museum News* 12(4):1–4.
 1951*b* "Omaha Peyotism." *Hobbies—The Magazine for Collectors* 56(2):142.
 1956   "An Oto-Omaha Peyote Ritual." *Southwestern Journal of Anthropology* 12(4):432–36.
 1957   "The Mescal Bean Cult of the Central and Southern Plains: An Ancestor of the Peyote Cult?" *American Anthropologist* 59:75–87.
 1960   "Mescalism and Peyotism Once Again." *Plains Anthropologist* 5:84–85.
 1962*a* "Peyote Jokes." *Journal of American Folklore* 75(295):10–14.
 1962*b* "Potawotami Mescalism and Its Relationship to the Diffusion of the Peyote Cult." *Plains Anthropologist* 7(16):12–35.
 1965*a* *The Ponca Tribe.* Bureau of American Ethnology Bulletin no. 195. Washington, D.C.: U.S. Government Printing Office.
 1965*b* "Half Moon Way: The Peyote Ritual of Chief White Bear." *University of South Dakota Museum News* 28(1–2):1–24.
 1978   "List of Elements of Peyote Ritual of Mandan, Hidatsa, and Arikara." Manuscript prepared at request of O. C. Stewart.
———, ed.
 1966   "Possible Threat to Native American Church." *University of South Dakota Institute of Indian Studies Bulletin,* May.
Howard, Richard P.
 1974   Letters to O. C. Stewart regarding Oto, Iowa, and Omaha Indian missionaries of the Reorganized Church of Jesus Christ of Latter Day Saints. Church Historian, Independence, Mo.
Hrdlicka, Ales
 1937   Statement on Senate Bill 1399. The U.S. Bureau of Indian Affairs, 1937.
Humphreys, Ray M.
 1916   "Peyote Replaces Whiskey on Reservation: Indians Get 'Jags' With the Mescal Bean." Interview with Henry A. Larson, BIA Chief Special Officer. *Denver Times,* Dec. 2.
Hurt, Wesley R.
 1960   "Factors in the Persistence of Peyote in the Northern Plains." *Plains Anthropologist* 5(9):16–27.
Ickes, Harold L.
 1936   "Letters to S. Sandoval," Sept. 30, Oct. 23. *Indians at Work* 7(4):9–13. Reprinted in U.S. Congress, Senate Committee on Indian Affairs, 1937, pp. 18231–34.

Ijams, J. W.
    1895   Letter to W. T. Walker, Aug. 29. Kiowa and Comanche—
                   Vices. Oklahoma Historical Society, Oklahoma City.
    1898   Letter to W. T. Walker, Oct. 12. Kiowa and Comanche—
                   Vices. Oklahoma Historical Society, Oklahoma City.

Indian Helper [Carlisle Indian School]
    1899   "Another Habit That Kills." 14(25): 7.
    1909   "An Indian Stock Raiser" [Leonard Tyler]. N.d.
    1913   "Obituary for Leonard Tyler." Jan. 2.

Jackson, C. L., and G. Jackson
    1963   *Quanah Parker: Last Chief of the Comanches.* New York: Ex-
                   position Press.

Jacobs, Jan
    1969   "I-See-O, 'Stone-Age Product' Bridged White, Indian Gap."
                   Lawton Constitution Morning Press, Jan. 5.

Joffe, N. F.
    1940   "The Fox of Iowa." In Linton, 1940, pp. 259–331, 294–96,
                   302–21.

Johnson, Horace J.
    1918   *To the Indians* (handbill against peyote and alcohol). Stroud,
                   Okla.: Privately printed.

Johnson, William E. ("Pussyfoot")
    1907*a*   Letter to C. E. Shell, April 29. Cheyenne and Arapahoe—
                   Vices. Oklahoma Historical Society, Oklahoma City.
    1907*b*   Letter to C. E. Shell, December 23. Cheyenne and Arapa-
                   hoe—Vices. Oklahoma Historical Society, Oklahoma City.
    1909*a*   Circular Letter, June 10, and replies. Questionnaire on peyote.
                   Peyote Correspondence, file no. 2989-1908-126, Chief Special
                   Officer, pt. 1C, Record Group 75, National Archives, Washing-
                   ton, D.C.
    1909*b*   Documents relating to a campaign for the suppression of pey-
                   ote. Peyote Correspondence, file no. 2989-1908-126, Chief
                   Special Officer, pt. 1C, Record Group 75, National Archives,
                   Washington, D.C. Also Cheyenne and Arapaho—Vices, Okla-
                   homa Historical Society, Oklahoma City.
    1910   Letter to Commissioner of Indian Affairs, September 13. Edu-
                   cation and liquor, file no. 66110-1910, Record Group 75, Na-
                   tional Archives, Washington, D.C.
    1912   "History, Use and Effects of Peyote." *Indian School Journal*
                   12(7): 239–42; (8): 289–93.
    1918   Letter to W. B. Wheeler, April 10. *Congressional Record* 61(5):
                   4681–82. Also U.S. Congress, Senate, Committee on Indian
                   Affairs, 1937, pp. 18281–82.

Jones, David E.
    1972   *Sanapia: Comanche Medicine Woman.* New York: Holt, Rine-
                   hart and Winston.

Jordan, Julia
    1967–68   Interviews with Kiowa-Apache peyotists. Oral history project.

Western History Collections, University of Oklahoma Library, Norman.

Kanosh, Nancy
1939   Letter to O. C. Stewart discussing peyote among the Southern Paiute, Jan. 19.

Kappler, Charles J., and Charles B. Merillat
1912   Letter to BIA for clients, the Osage Tribe, Jan. 18. Ed.—Law and Order, file 5527-1912, Letters Received 5527, Record Group 75, National Archives, Washington, D.C.

Keefe, Harry L.
1912   Letter to BIA from Attorney Keefe, Walthill, Neb., Mar. 19, to introduce a delegation of Omaha and stating good results of peyotism. Ed.—Law and Order, file 2989-08-126, pt. 3, Liquor Traffic, Record Group 75, National Archives, Washington, D.C.

Kelly, Isabel
1965   *Folk Practices in North Mexico.* Institute of Latin American Studies Monograph no. 2. Austin: University of Texas Press.

Ketcham, William H.
1912   Memorandum to Board of Indian Commissioners against peyote, Mar. 1.
1918   Letter to J. N. Tillman, Feb. 26. Bureau of Catholic Indian Missionaries Against Peyote. In U.S. Congress, Senate, Committee on Indian Affairs, 1937, pp. 18307–309. Also Newberne, 1925, pp. 14–15.
1919   Letter to BIA, Aug. 7. Peyote for sale in Ashland, Montana, store. Ed.—Law and Order, file 62985-19. Letter received, no. 68145, Record Group 75, National Archives, Washington, D.C.

Kiker, H. A.
1937   Testimony at Santa Fe. In U.S. Congress, Senate, Committee on Indian Affairs, 1937, pp. 18164–70.

Kingfisher County, Okla., District Court
1907   *Territory of Oklahoma* v. *Taylor et al.* For possession of mescal, arrested Feb. 9. Manuscript, case no. 1021. Reuben Taylor, Howling Wolf, Percy Kable found not guilty. Copies of documents dated June 22, 1907–Apr. 13, 1908, from district court clerk in possession of O. C. Stewart.

Kinney, Bruce
1921   "A Drug Peril Under Religious Guise." *Native American* 22: 3–5, Jan. 1.

Knack, Martha
1973   Field Notes on Southern Paiute Peyotism. Copy in possession of O. C. Stewart.

Kneale, Albert H.
1911   Letter to R. D. Hall, Nov. 23. In U.S. Congress, House, Committee on Indian Affairs, 1918a, pt. 1, pp. 43–46.
1916   Reply to BIA Peyote Questionnaire, Oct. 28, for the Uintah

and Ouray Reservation. File 2989-08-126, Letters Received 125925, Dec. 9, Record Group 75, National Archives, Washington, D.C.

1950   *Indian Agent.* Caldwell, Idaho: Caxton Printers.

Kochampanaskin, Ralph

1942   Letter to Omer C. Stewart.

Kohlenberg, W. C.

1906   "Report of Superintendent in Charge of Sac and Fox Agency." *U.S. Bureau of Indian Affairs, Annual Report,* pp. 322–24.

Koshiway, Jonathan

1955   Letter to J. S. Slotkin, April 12. Copy in possession of O. C. Stewart.

Kroeber, Alfred L.

1907   *The Arapaho.* American Museum of Natural History Bulletin no. 18, pt. 4, pp. 320–21, 398–410.

1937   Statement on Senate Bill 1399. In U.S. Bureau of Indian Affairs, 1937.

———, and G. A. Dorsey

1903   See G. A. Dorsey.

La Barre, Weston

1935   Interview with Charles Apekaum, and Observations, Aug. 21. Copy in possession of O. C. Stewart.

1937   Statement on Senate Bill 1399. In U.S. Bureau of Indian Affairs, 1937.

1938   *The Peyote Cult.* Yale University Publications in Anthropology, no. 19. New Haven, Conn.: Yale University Press.

1939   "Notes on Richard Schultes' 'The Appeal of Peyote.'" *American Anthropologist* 41: 340–42.

1944   "List of Elements of Peyote Ritual of Kiowa as of 1935." In Stewart, 1944.

1946   Review of Stewart, 1944. *American Anthropologist* 48: 633–35.

1947   "Primitive Psychotherapy in Native American Cultures: Peyotism and Confession. *Journal of Abnormal and Social Psychology* 42(3): 294–309. Bobbs-Merrill Reprint Series in the Social Sciences, A-316.

1957   "Mescalism and Peyotism." *American Anthropologist* 59: 708–11.

1960   "Twenty Years of Peyote Studies." *Current Anthropology* 1(1): 45–60.

1964   *The Peyote Cult.* Enlarged ed. Hamden, Conn.: Shoestring Press.

1969   *The Peyote Cult.* Enlarged ed. New York: Schocken Books.

1972   "Hallucinogens and the Shamanic Origins of Religion." In *Flesh of the Gods,* ed. Peter T. Furst. New York: Praeger.

1975   *The Peyote Cult.* 4th ed., enlarged. New York: Schocken Books.

La Flesche, Francis

1915   Statement. U.S. Congress, House, Committee on Indian Affairs, 1918*a*, pt. 1, pp. 80–82.

1963   *The Middle Five: Indian Schoolboys in the Omaha Tribe.* Fore-
                word by David A. Barreis. Madison: University of Wisconsin
                Press.

Lake Mohonk Conference on the Indian and
    Other Dependent Peoples
1961   Copy of resolution against peyote passed by National Indian
                Student Conference. Estes Park, Colo., June 18.

Lamere, Oliver
ca. 1910   "Description of the Peyote Cult." In Radin, 1914, pp. 4–6.
                Also in Radin, 1923, pp. 394–96.

Landes, Ruth
1970   *The Prairie Potawatomi: Tradition and Ritual in the Twentieth
                Century.* Madison: University of Wisconsin Press.

Laredo Press
1975   Photograph of Bill Denny while attending Native American
                Church of North America convention in Mirando City, Texas,
                Feb. 23.

Larson, Henry A.
1916   Letter to superintendents, Oct. 28, and replies. Peyote Corre-
                spondence, file 2989-1908-126, Chief Special Officer, pt. 1b,
                Peyote Questionnaire, Record Group 75, National Archives,
                Washington, D.C.
1919   Letter to H. J. Holgate, Deputy Special Officer from Chief Spe-
                cial Officer, Denver, May 21. Ed.—Law and Order, file 31721-
                19, Peyote File, Record Group 75, National Archives, Washing-
                ton, D.C.

Lasswell, Harold D.
1935   "Collective Autism as a Consequence of Culture Contact:
                Notes on Religious Training and the Peyote Cult at Taos."
                Zeitschrift für Sozialforschung 4: 232–47.

La Torre, Felip A., and Dolores L. La Torre
1976   *The Mexican Kickapoo Indians.* Texas Pan American Series.
                Austin: University of Texas Press.

Laurence, M.
1953   "A Trip to Quapaw in 1903." *Chronicles of Oklahoma* 31:
                145–52.

Lehman, Herman
1899   Autobiography. In *A Condensed History of the Apache and Co-
                manche Indian Tribes,* comp. J. H. Jones. San Antonio, Texas:
                Johnson Brothers Printing Co.
1927   *Nine Years Among the Indians, 1870–79.* Ed. J. M. Hunter.
                Austin, Texas: Von Boeckman-Jones.

León, Alonzo de
1909   "Relación, 1649." In *Docmentos inéditos o muy raros para la
                historia de México,* vol. 25, pp. 9–188.

León, M.
1911   *Camino del cielo en lengua mexicana.* Mexico City: López.

Leonard, Irving A.
1942   "Decree Against Peyote, Mexican Inquisition, 1620." *Ameri-can Anthropologist* 44:324–36. [AGN, Inquisición: 333.35: 1620. Edicto impreso del Santo Oficio contra el uso del *peyote*, p. 1. Mexico City. In Aguirre Beltrán, 1963:371.]

Lesser, Alexander
1933   "The Pawnee Ghost Dance Hand Game." *Columbia University Contributions to Anthropology* 16:76, 117–18, 123.

Leupp, Francis E.
1903   "Kiowa Indian Agency." U.S. Congress, Document and Report, ser. 4587, no. 26, p. 23. Washington, D.C.: U.S. Government Printing Office.

Lewin, Louis
1888   "Anhalonium Lewinii." *Therapeutic Gazette* 4(4):231–37.
1924   *Phantastika.* Berlin: Stilke.
1931   *Phantastica: Narcotic and Stimulating Drugs.* Trans. P. H. A. Wirth. New York: Dutton.

Liljeblad, Sven
1963   Letter to O. C. Stewart naming peyotists in Idaho, Nevada, Montana, and Wyoming. March 10.
1972   *The Idaho Indians in Transition, 1805–1960.* Special Publication. Pocatello: Idaho State University.

Lindquist, G. Elmer E.
1912   "Report on Mescalero Apache Peyotism from Personal Experience." In report to BIA by Robert D. Hall, Jan. 30. File 2989-08-126, pt. 3, Liquor Traffic, Record Group 75, National Archives, Washington, D.C.
1919   "Editorial: Pernicious Camouflage." *American Indian YMCA Bulletin* 8(8):2.
1923   *The Red Man in the United States.* New York: Doran.
1937   "Preliminary Report on Peyote." Home Missions Councils. File 2989-1908-126, pt. 5, Record Group 75, National Archives, Washington, D.C.
1939   "Statement on Peyote." *Chronicles of Oklahoma* 17:348.

Linton, Ralph
1940   *Acculturation in Seven American Indian Tribes.* New York: D. Appleton-Century.
1943   "Nativistic Movements." *American Anthropologist* 45:230–40.

Little Hand
1918   Statement in U.S. Congress, House, Committee on Indian Affairs, 1918a, pt. 2, pp. 169–71.

Lizarraras, Luis de
1770   Report to Governor Don Jacobo Ugarte y Loyola. Archivo General de la Nación, Provincias Internas, Mexico City. Copy in Bancroft Library, University of California, Berkeley; cited in Stewart, 1948, p. 34.

Llewellyn, K. N., and E. Adamson Hoebel
    1941   *The Cheyenne Way: Conflict and Case Law in Primitive Juris-prudence.* Norman: University of Oklahoma Press.
Lone Wolf, Chief
    1918   Statement. U.S. Congress, House, Committee on Indian Affairs, 1918a, pt. 1, pp. 149–59.
    1937   Statement on Senate Bill 1399. U.S. Bureau of Indian Affairs, 1937.
Lorenzo de la Peña, Antonio
    1770   Letter to Jacobo Ugarte y Loyola. Archivo General de la Nación, Provincias Internas, Mexico City, vol. 24, fols. 28v–29v. Copy in Bancroft Library, University of California, Berkeley; cited in Stewart, 1948, p. 34.
Lowie, Robert H.
    1917   "Peyote Rite." *Encyclopedia of Religion and Ethics,* 9:815. New York: Scribners.
    1922   "The Religion of the Crow Indians." *American Museum of Natural History, Anthropological Papers* 25:309–444.
    1924   "Minor Ceremonies of the Crow Indians." *American Museum of Natural History, Anthropological Papers* 21:323–65.
    1925   *Primitive Religion.* London: George Routledge and Sons.
    1935   The Crow Indians. New York: Holt, Rinehart and Winston.
    1959   *Ethnologist: A Personal Record.* Berkeley and Los Angeles: University of California Press.
Luhan, Mabel Dodge
    1936   *Movers and Shakers.* Vol. 3 of *Intimate Memories.* New York: Harcourt, Brace & Co.
    1937   *Edge of Taos Desert.* Vol. 4 of *Intimate Memories.* New York: Harcourt, Brace & Co.
Lumholtz, Carl
    1891   "Report of Explorations in Northern Mexico." *American Geographical Society Bulletin* 23:386–402.
    1894a   "The American Cave Dwellers." *American Geographical Society Bulletin* 26:299–325.
    1894b   "Tarahumari Life and Customs." *Scribners Magazine* 16(1):32–39.
    1894c   "Tarahumari Dances and Plant Worship." *Scribners Magazine* 16(4):438–56.
    1898   "The Huichol Indians of Mexico." *American Museum of Natural History Bulletin* 10:7–13.
Lyon, Harry; Silas Wood; and Noah Leming
    1916   Omaha peyotists testify before Chief Special Officer Henry A. Larson, Washington, D.C., April 1. Interpreter Francis LaFlesche. Transcript. File 2989-1908-126, pt. 4, Record Group 75, National Archives, Washington, D.C.
McAllester, David P.
    1949   *Peyote Music.* Viking Fund Publications in Anthropology 13. New York: Viking Fund.

1951*a*   "Peyote Music." *American Journal of Sociology,* Jan.

1951*b*   "Pro-Peyote." In Slotkin, 1952.

1971   Letter to O. C. Stewart on similarity between Apache music and peyote music.

McAllister, J. Gilbert

1938   "Peyote Among the Kiowa Apache." Manuscript. Austin, Texas. Copy in possession of O. C. Stewart.

1944   "List of Elements of Peyote Ritual Among Kiowa-Apache." In Stewart, 1944, pp. 103–21.

1952   "Peyote." In *The Handbook of Texas,* 2:369–70.

1970   *Daveko, Kiowa-Apache Medicine Man.* Bulletin no. 17. Austin: Texas Memorial Museum.

McCarthy, Edgar

1912   Petition to BIA to protect peyote for supply of Osage, 23 signatures, Feb. 12. Ed.—Law and Order, file 20619-1912, Record Group 75, National Archives, Washington, D.C.

————, ed.

1923   *Peyote, as Used in Religious Worship by the Indians.* Hominy, Okla.: Privately published. Copy in possession of O. C. Stewart.

McClung, Paul

1971   "Kiowa-Apache "Old Man" Joins History." *Prairie Lore* 8(2): 89–93.

McCormick, T. F.

1929   Letter to State Senator Ed. Safford requesting a New Mexico state law against peyote, Jan. 14. Ed.—Law and Order, file 66245-29; 63215-29, Record Group 75, National Archives, Washington, D.C.

McDonald, Louis

1920   Address to meeting of Otoe Branch of the Native American Church. Minutes, May 9. Copy presented to O. C. Stewart by Fred Hoffman, president of Native American Church of Oklahoma, 1972.

————, and Frank Eagle

1923   Letter to G. A. Hoyo, Oct. 8. In Shonle 1923.

McFate, Y.

1960   "Decision of the Honorable Yale McFate in the Case of the *State of Arizona* vs. *Mary Attakai,* no. 4089, Superior Court, Coconino County, Flagstaff, Arizona, July 27, 1960, 3:30 P.M." *American Anthropologist* 73:1135–37.

McNickle, D.

1943   See Reh and McNickle, 1943.

Maker, Leonard

1968   Information on Osage Peyotism. Oral History Project. Western History Collections, University of Oklahoma Library, Norman.

Malouf, Carling

1940   "A History of the Gosiute Indian Relationship with the White

Man." M.S. thesis, University of Utah, Salt Lake City. Copy in possession of O. C. Stewart.

1942   "Gosiute Peyotism." *American Anthropologist* 44:93–103.

1944   "List of Elements of Peyote Ritual of the Goshute as of 1939." In Stewart, 1944.

1977   Letter and three pages of notes. Missoula, Mont., Sept. 15. In possession of O. C. Stewart.

Marriott, Alice

1940   Field notes on Peyote, 1936–40. Western History Collections, University of Oklahoma Library, Norman.

1942   Metal Jewelry of the Peyote Cult. *Material Culture Notes,* no. 17. Denver Art Museum.

1945   *The Ten Grandmothers.* Norman: University of Oklahoma Press.

1954   "The Open Door" (Kiowa). *New Yorker* 30(32):80–91.

———, and Carol K. Rachlin

1971   *Peyote.* New York: Thomas Y. Crowell.

Maryott, G. C.

1912   Letter to the Commissioner of Indian Affairs from G. C. Maryott in behalf of the Omaha Indians who were members of the "Mescal Society." File 2989-08-126, pt. 3, Letters Received 28368, Record Group 75, National Archives, Washington, D.C.

Mason, J. Alden

1912   "The Fiesta of the Pinole at Azqueltan." *Museum Journal* (University of Pennsylvania) 3(3):44–50.

Mata Torres, Ramón

1973   "Vida y arte de los Huicholes, segunda parte, el arta." *Artges de México,* no. 161, año 19.

Mathews, John J.

1932   *Wah-Kon-Tah: The Osage and the White Man's Road.* Norman: University of Oklahoma Press.

1945   *Talking to the Moon.* Chicago: University of Chicago Press. Reprint. Norman: University of Oklahoma Press, 1981.

1961   *The Osages: Children of the Middle Waters.* Norman: University of Oklahoma Press.

Mayhall, Mildred P.

1962   *The Kiowas.* Norman: University of Oklahoma Press.

Mead, Margaret

1932   *The Changing Culture of an Indian Tribe.* Columbia University Contributions to Anthropology, no. 15. New York: Columbia University Press.

Meeker, Louis L.

1896   "The Mescal Bean." Manuscript no. 2537, U.S. Bureau of American Ethnology, Washington, D. C.

Meritt, E. G.

1919   *Concerning Peyote.* U.S. Bureau of Indian Affairs, Circular no. 1522, March 28.

Merriam, Alan P., and Warren L. d'Azevedo

1957   "Washo Peyote Songs." *American Anthropologist* 59:615–41.

Merrill, William L.
   1977*a*   *An Investigation of Ethnographic and Archaeological Specimens of Mescalbeans* (Sophora Secundiflora) *in American Museums.* Technical Report No. 6, Research Reports in Ethnobotany. Contribution 1, Museum of Anthropology. Ann Arbor: University of Michigan Press.
   1977*b*   See Hatfield et al., 1977.

Methvin, J. J.
   1892   Letter to George D. Day, Anadarko, Agent of Kiowa, Comanche, and Wichita. *Report of the Commissioner of Indian Affairs, 1892,* p. 390. Washington, D.C.: U.S. Government Printing Office.
   1899   *Andele, or the Mexican-Kiowa Captive.* Louisville, Ky.: Pentecostal Herald Press.
   1927   "Reminiscences of Life Among the Indians." *Chronicles of Oklahoma* 5: 177–78.
   1931   "Apheahtone, Kiowa: A Bit of History." *Chronicles of Oklahoma* 9: 334–37.

Michelson, Truman
   1915   Statement. U.S. Congress, House, Committee on Indian Affairs, 1918*a*, pt. 1, pp. 74–79.
   1932   *The Narrative of a Southern Cheyenne Woman.* Smithsonian Miscellaneous Collections, vol. 87, no. 5. Washington, D.C.: Smithsonian Institution.
   N.d.   "Sauk-Fox Peyote Myths" (field notes). Manuscript no. 2736, pp. 1–5. Bureau of American Ethnology, Washington, D.C.

Miller, Merton Leland
   1898   *A Preliminary Study of the Pueblo of Taos, New Mexico.* Chicago: University of Chicago Press.

Mirabel, A.
   1937   Testimony at Santa Fe, Aug. 21, 1936. U.S. Congress, Senate, Committee on Indian Affairs, 1937, pp. 18175–92.

Mitscher, O. A.
   1900*a*   Letter to J. F. Randlett, June 21, 1900. Kiowa and Comanche—Vices. Oklahoma Historical Society, Oklahoma City.
   1900*b*   "Report of Agent for Osage Agency." *U.S. Bureau of Indian Affairs, Annual Report,* p. 339.

Momaday, N. Scott
   1966   *House Made of Dawn.* New York: Harper & Row.

Monaghan, James
   1935   Interview with Charlie Wash . . . Uncompagre, near Randlett, Utah. CWA File—"Moffat Co." Colorado State Historical Society, Denver.
   1937   "The Cult." Civilian Work Administration Pamphlet 356/13. Colorado State Historical Society, Denver.

Montana Supreme Court
   1926   "*State* v. *Big Sheep.*" *Montana Reports* 75: 219–40.

Mooney, James
   1891*a*   "The Kiowa Mescal Rite." Report of speech to Anthropological

Society of Washington. *Washington, D.C., Evening Star,* Nov. 4, p. 6.

1891*b*   "The Sacred Formulas of the Cherokee." *Bureau of American Ethnology Annual Report* 7: 303–97.

1891*c*   Notes in J. W. Powell, "Introduction to the Study of Indian Languages," pp. 230–37. Manuscript no. 347, U.S. Bureau of American Ethnology, Washington, D.C.

1892*a*   "Eating the Mescal." *Augusta* (Ga.) *Chronicle,* Jan. 24, p. 11.

1892*b*   "A Kiowa Mescal Rattle." *American Anthropologist* 5: 64–65.

1893   "After the Mescal Ceremony, Kiowa." Photograph no. 1460. U.S. Bureau of American Ethnology, Washington, D.C.

1896*a*   "The Ghost Dance Religion and the Sioux Outbreak of 1890." *Bureau of American Ethnology, Annual Report* 14: 641–1110.

1896*b*   "The Mescal Plant and Ceremony." *Therapeutic Gazette* 12(11): 7–11.

1897*a*   "The Kiowa Peyote Rite." *Der Urquell* 1: 329–33.

1897*b*   "Mescalero and Lipan Apache Notes." Manuscript no. 425. U.S. Bureau of American Ethnology, Washington, D.C.

1898*a*   "The Mescal Plant and Ceremony." *Bureau of American Ethnology, Annual Report* 17 (1895–96): 1.

1898*b*   "Calendar History of the Kiowa Indians." *Bureau of American Ethnology, Annual Report* 17 (1895–96): 129–445.

1898*c*   "Taramari-Guayachi, January 21." Manuscript no. 2537. U.S. Bureau of American Ethnology, Washington, D.C.

1899   *Annual Report of the Bureau of American Ethnology* 18 (1896–97): xxviii, xliv–xlv.

1900   *Annual Report of the Bureau of American Ethnology* 19 (1897–98): xv–xvii.

1907*a*   "The Cheyenne Indians." *Memoirs of the American Anthropological Association* 1(6): 357–418.

1907*b*   "Arapaho." In Hodge, 1907–10, 1: 72–74.

1907*c*   "Musicians, Peyote Ceremony, Kiowa" (photograph). In Hodge, 1907–10, 1: 959.

1907*d*   Letter from Paul Mouse Road, Cheyenne peyotist, requesting Mooney's assistance in continuation of peyote, May 20. Manuscript no. 2537. Bureau of American Ethnology, Washington, D.C.

1910*a*   "Peyote." In Hodge, 1907–10, 2: 237.

1910*b*   "Wichita." In Hodge, 1907–10, 2: 947–49.

1915   Statement. In U.S. Congress, House, Committee on Indian Affairs, 1918*a*, pt. 1, pp. 69–74.

1918*a*   Statement in U.S. Congress, House, Committee on Indian Affairs, 1918*a*, pt. 1, pp. 54–113, 145–47.

1918*b*   Letter to J. B. Prentiss, July 29. File 11552-1919-126, Record Group 75, National Archives, Washington, D.C.

N.d. *a*   "Miscellaneous Notes on Peyote." Manuscript no. 1887. U.S. Bureau of American Ethnology, Washington, D.C.

N.d. *b*   "Peyote Handbook." Manuscript no. 1930. U.S. Bureau of American Ethnology, Washington, D.C.

Moore, Joe, and Blanche Schroer
1950   The bitter paste of DOm APUA. *Denver Post Rocky Mountain Empire Magazine*, April 30, pp. 3–4.

Moorhead, Max L.
1968   *The Apache Frontier: Jacobo Ugarte and Spanish-Indian Relations in Northern New Spain 1769–1791.* Norman: University of Oklahoma Press.

Morgan, George R.
1966   "Half-Moon Peyotists of the Pine Ridge Indian Reservation." Manuscript. Chadron, Neb. Copy in possession of O. C. Stewart.
1973   List of elements in peyote ritual of Sioux Half Moon. Manuscript.
1976   "Man, Plant, and Religion: Peyote. Trade on the Mustang Plains of Texas." Ph.D. diss., University of Colorado.
———, and O. C. Stewart
1984   "Peyote Trade in South Texas." *Southwestern Historical Quarterly* 87(3):270–96.

Mosk, Stanley
1962   "Subject: Religion-Use of Peyote." Opinion No. 62-93. *Attorney General's Opinions* 39:276–79.

Motta Padilla, Matías de la
1870   *Historia de la conquista de la provincia de la Nueva Galicia.* [Written in 1742] Mexico City.

Muñoz Camargo, Diego
ca. 1590   *Historia de Tlaxcala.* Mexico City: Oficina Tipográfica de la Secretaría de Fomento, 1892.

Murie, James R.
1914   "Pawnee Indian Societies." *American Museum of Natural History, Anthropological Papers,* no. 11, pp. 636–38.

Murray, Daniel
1972   "The Peyote Ceremony." *The Raven Speaks* 4(10).
1973   List of elements of peyote ritual of the Iowa, with extensive historical notes. Manuscript.

Myers, Harry L.
1975   "Peyote: Interpretation Under Federal Law." *Drug Enforcement* 2(3):40–41. Washington, D.C.: U.S. Department of Justice.

Nabokov, Peter
1969   "The Peyote Road." *New York Times Magazine,* Mar. 9, pp. 30–31, 129–34.

Natani, M. W. E., ed.
1970–71   *NAC Newsletter.*

National Cyclopaedia of American Biography
1949   Johnson, William Eugene, 1862–1945. Vol. 35, p. 161.

Native American Church, Otoe Branch
1920   Minutes of Meeting on the Otoe Indian Reservation, Noble County, Oklahoma, May 9. Copy presented to O. C. Stewart

by Fred Hoffman, president of NAC of Oklahoma, 1972.

Navajo Times
1966   "Frank Takes Gun, National President NAC of NA." June 6.
1967   "Resolution Allowing Peyote in NAC Rites Passed by Tribal
              Council Balloting." Oct. 19.

Navajo Tribal Council
1940   "Proceedings of the Meeting . . . June 3–6." Navajo Service,
              Window Rock, Ariz.
1954   Minutes of the Meeting. Window Rock, Ariz., June 1–10,
              pp. 17–96, 146.

Nettl, Bruno
1953   "Observations on Meaningless Peyote Song Texts." *Journal of
              American Folklore* 66: 161–64.
1954   "North American Indian Musical Styles." *Journal of American
              Folklore* 67: 305–307.
1958   "Historical Aspects of Ethnomusicology." *American Anthro-
              pologist* 60: 518–30.

Nevada State Journal (Reno)
1965   "Nevada Indians Assured Continued Use of Peyote." March 13.

Newberne, Robert E. L.
1918   "Peyote, an Insidious Evil." *Annual Report of the Indian Rights
              Association* (Philadelphia), no. 36, pp. 47–49.
1922   *Peyote: An Abridged Compilation from the Files of the Bureau of
              Indian Affairs.* Washington, D.C.: U.S. Government Printing
              Office.
1923   *Peyote: An Abridged Compilation,* 2d ed. Chilocco, Okla.: Chi-
              locco Indian Agricultural School.
1925   *Peyote: An Abridged Compilation from the files of the Bureau of
              Indian Affairs.* 3d ed. Lawrence, Kans.: Haskell Institute
              Printing Department.

Newcomb, William W., Jr.
1956a   "The Culture and Acculturation of Delaware Indians." *Museum
              of Anthropology, Anthropological Paper,* no. 10, pp. 113–122.
              University of Michigan.
1956b   "The Peyote Cult of the Delaware Indians." *Texas Journal of
              Science* 8: 202–11.
1961   *The Indians of Texas.* Austin: University of Texas Press.
1970   "Summary of Kiowa-Apache History and Culture." In McAl-
              lister, 1970.

Newcomer, E. D.
1953   "Peyote People." *Phoenix* (Ariz.) *Republic,* July 11, 1954, sec.
              2, p. 14.

New Mexico Courts
1720   "Proceedings Against Indians Who Took Peyote." Manuscript.
              Santa Fe, School of American Research Museum of New Mex-
              ico. In Slotkin, 1951, pp. 421–27. See Valverde.

New York Sunday News
1941   "Sacred Mushroom of the Aztecs—Drive to Outlaw Dream
              Buttons." Nov. 30.

New York Times
1962   "Trial of Navajo Members of the Native American Church."
            Nov. 30.
1964   "Coast Navajos Win Right to Use Peyote in Religious Rights."
            Aug. 25.
Nickels, Anna B.
1885   Letter to Parke Davis and Company, Detroit, Michigan, re-
            garding supplying "Piotes" (*Anhalonium Williamsii*), July 11.
            Copy of letter supplied by G. A. Bender.
Noon, John A.
1944   "List of Elements of Peyote Ritual of Kickapoo of Oklahoma as
            of 1932." In Stewart, 1944, pp. 103–21.
Oklahoma, Constitutional Convention
1907   Hearings before Medical Committee. Photograph and catalog
            notes. Museum, Fort Sill, Okla.
Oklahoma, Legislature
1899   Session Laws, sec. 2651, pp. 122–23. "Mescal bean"
            prohibited.
1908   Hearings on Mescal Bean Bill. Cheyenne and Arapaho—vices,
            Oklahoma Historical Society, Oklahoma City.
Oklahoma, Legislature, House
1908   Report of Indian pow-wow considering the Mescal Bean Bill,
            Jan. 21. Cheyenne and Arapaho—Vices, Oklahoma Historical
            Society, Oklahoma City.
1909   *Journal* 2: 118, 126, 180–81, 211, 353. [Failure to pass anti-
            peyote law.]
Oklahoma, Legislature, Senate
1927   *Journal* 11: 573, 594, 907. [Failure to pass antipeyote law.]
Olivares, Antonio de San Buenaventur
1709   "Carta." In J. A. Pichardo. *Treatise on the Limits of Louisiana
            and Texas,* ed. and trans. C. W. Hackett et al., 2: 396–98.
            Austin: University of Texas Press, 1931–46.
Omaha Indian Peyote Society
1915   "A Petition by the O.I.P.S. . . . to the Honorable Cato Sells,"
            Feb. 20. File 2989-08, pt. 3, Letters Received 20895, Record
            Group 75, National Archives, Washington, D.C.
Opler, Marvin K.
1940*a*   "The Character and History of the Southern Ute Peyote Rite."
            American Anthropologist 42(3): 463–78.
1940*b*   "The Southern Ute of Colorado." In Ed. R. Linton, *Accultura-
            tion in Seven American Indian Tribes,* pp. 190–95. New York:
            Appleton Century.
1942   "Fact and Fancy in Ute Peyotism." *American Anthropologist*
            44: 151–59.
Opler, Morris E.
1936*a*   See Castetter and Opler, 1936.
1936*b*   "The Influence of Aboriginal Pattern and White Contact on a
            Recently Introduced Ceremony, the Mescalero Peyote Rite."
            Journal of American Folklore 49(191/192): 143–66.

1938   "The Use of Peyote by the Carrizo and Lipan Apache Tribes."
           American Anthropologist 40(2): 271–85.

1939   "A Description of a Tonkawa Peyote Meeting Held in 1902."
           American Anthropologist 41(3): 433–39.

1940   "Myth and Legends of the Lipan Apache Indians." *American
           Folklore Society Memoir,* no. 36.

1945   "A Mescalero Apache Account of the Origin of the Peyote
           Ceremony." *El Palacio* 52(10): 210–12.

1946   "Cultural Anthropology: An Application of the Theory of
           Themes in Culture." *Journal of the Washington Academy of Sci-
           ences* 36(5): 137–65.

1969   *Apache Odyssey.* New York: Holt, Rinehart and Winston.
Oregon Court of Appeals
1975   *State of Oregon* v. *Reginald Roland Soto.* June 23. 537 *Pacific
           Reporter,* 2d ser., p. 142.
Orozco y Berra, M.
1864   *Geográfica de las lenguas y carta etnográfica de México.* Mexico
           City.
Ortega, José de
1751   *Historia del Nayarit, Sonora, Sinaloa, y ambas Californias.*
           Barcelona, 1751. Reprint. *Raíz Diabólica.* 1887.
1754   *Apostólicos afanes de la Companía de Jesús.* Reprint. *Historia
           del Nayarit.* Mexico City: Abadiano, 1887.
Osmond, Humphrey
1956   Letter to J. S. Slotkin. Feb. 14. Reporting "peyote in no way a
           drug addiction."
1957   "A Review of the Clinical Effects of Psychotomimetic Agents."
           Annals of the New York Academy of Sciences 66: 418–34.
1961   "That Night in the Tipi." *Twentieth Century* 170: 38–50.
           Slightly edited in *Tomorrow* 9(2).
Paffrath, E. A.
1887   Letter to Parke, Davis, and Co., Aug. 24, Vernon, Texas. In
           files of Parke, Davis, and Co., Detroit, Mich. Copy in posses-
           sion of O. C. Stewart.
Parker, Quanah
1908   Statement in Oklahoma Legislature.
Parsons, Elsie Clews
1936   *Taos Pueblo.* General Series in Anthropology, no. 2. Menasha,
           Wis.: Banta.
1939   *Pueblo Indian Religion.* Chicago: University of Chicago Press.
1941   "Notes on the Caddo." *Memoirs of the American Anthropologi-
           cal Association* 57: 50–53.
Parsons, James, and Mike Zerby
1917   "Sioux Peyote Ceremony." *Minneapolis Tribune Picture Maga-
           zine,* Aug. 1.
Pelletiere, Stephen C.
1963*a*   "Reporter Joins Indian Peyote Eaters." In "All-Night Tepee
           Quest for a Vision." *Milwaukee Journal,* May 27. Photographs
           by George P. Koshollek, Jr.

1963*b*   "You Have to Suffer with Peyote to Achieve the Indian's Vision."
           Milwaukee Journal Green Sheet, May 28, p. 1.
1963*c*   "Reporter Seeks Truth of Peyote." *Milwaukee Journal,* May
           29.
1963*d*   "Reporter, in Seeking 'Vision,' Fights to Keep Peyote Down."
           Milwaukee Journal, May 30.
1963*e*   "Peyote Gave Reporter Feeling of Serene Confidence in Faith."
           Milwaukee Journal, May 31. Photograph by George P. Koshol-
           lek, Jr.

Pe-na-ro
1918   Statement. *American Indian YMCA Bulletin* 8(4).

Perea, Estevan de
1631   Avisa. Manuscript. Inquisición, vol. 372, expedientes 16, 19,
           Archivo General de la Nación, Mexico City.
1632   Avisa. Manuscript. Inquisición, vol. 304, fols. 18–98, Archivo
           General de la Nación, Mexico City.

Perez de Ribas, Andrés
1645   *Historia de los triumphos de nuestra Santa Fe en los misiones de
           la provincia de Nueva España.* Madrid.

Petersen, Karen Daniels
1964   "The Writings of Henry Roman Nose." *Chronicles of Okla-
           homa* 42(4): 460–78.
1968   *Howling Wolf: A Cheyenne Warrior's Graphic Interpretation of
           His People.* Palo Alto, Calif.: American West Publishing Co.

Petrullo, Vincenzo
1934   *The Diabolic Root: A Study of Peyotism, the New Indian Reli-
           gion, Among the Delawares.* Philadelphia: University of Penn-
           sylvania Press.
1937   Statement on Senate Bill 1399. In Report to U.S. Bureau of
           Indian Affairs, 1937.
1940   "Peyotism as an Emergent Indian Culture." *Indians at Work*
           8(8): 51–60.

Petter, Rodolphe
1934   Letter to Commissioner John Collier from Lame Deer, Mont.,
           Feb. 1, File 2593-15, Record Group 75, National Archives,
           Washington, D.C.

Peyotists, Omaha
1912   Hearing . . . before Assistant Commissioner Abbott, in Re-
           gard to the Use of Mescal, March 19. Arranged by H. L.
           Keefe. File 2989-08, Record Group 75, National Archives,
           Washington, D.C.
1915   Petition and Appended Statements. See Omaha Indian Peyote
           Society, 1915.

Peyotists, Osage
1912   Resolution, Feb. 12. Ed. Law and Order, File 20619-1912,
           Record Group 75, National Archives, Washington, D.C.
1918   Letter to C. D. Carter, Feb. 7. In U.S. Congress, House,
           Committee on Indian Affairs, 1918*a*, pt. 1, pp. 160–61.
1923*a*   Petition to Congress. In McCarthy, 1923, pp. 1–7.

1923*b*   Petition to Senate Committee on Indian Affairs. In McCarthy, 1923, pp. 64–67.

Philip, Kenneth R.
1977   *John Collier's Crusade for Indian Reform, 1920–1954.* Tucson: University of Arizona Press.

Piawo, W.
1918   Statement in U.S. Congress, House, Committee on Indian Affairs, 1918*a*, pt. 1, pp. 172–81.

Pokibro, John
1954   Letter to Allen Dale, Mar. 7, regarding Dale's visit to Fort Hall, Idaho. Original in possession of O. C. Stewart.

Pollock, W. J.
1899*a*   "Report of Agent for Osage Agency," *U.S. Bureau of Indian Affairs, Annual Report,* pp. 294–97.
1899*b*   Letter to the Commissioner of Indian Affairs, Sept. 22. Manuscript. Letters Received, 45717, Record Group 75, National Archives, Washington, D.C.

Poor, Henry V.
1876–90   *Poor's Manual of Railroads.* Vols. 9 to 23. New York: H. V. and H. W. Poor.

Post Enquirer (Oakland, Calif.)
1938   "Indians in Strange Peyote Rite." [March 24.] Copy in possession of O. C. Stewart.

Powell, Peter J.
1969   *Sweet Medicine: The Continuing Role of the Sacred Arrows, the Sun Dance, and the Sacred Buffalo Hat in Northern Cheyenne History.* 2 vols. Norman: University of Oklahoma Press.

Powers, W. H.
1962   Ogalala Sam (regarding Sam Lone Bear, 1908). Manuscript. Presented to Sven Liljeblad, Idaho State College, Sept. 25.

Pratt, Richard Henry
1964   *Battlefield and Classroom.* New Haven, Conn.: Yale University Press.

Praus, Alexis A.
1944   "List of Elements of Peyote Religion of Winnebago of Nebraska as of 1939." In Stewart, 1944, pp. 103–21.

Preston, R. C.
1906   "Report of Superintendent of Seger School." *U.S. Bureau of Indian Affairs, Annual Report,* pp. 326–38.

Price, Hirman
1883   *Rules Governing the Court of Indian Offenses* (at request of Secretary H. M. Teller). Washington, D.C.: U.S. Department of the Interior, Office of Indian Affairs, Mar. 30.

Prieto, A.
1873   *Historia y estadística del Estado de Tamaulipas.* Mexico City.

Primeras Misiones de la Viscaya
1598   In *Documentos para la historia de México,* ser. 4, vol. 3 (1857), pp. 15–60.

Putt, E. B.
    1911   *Mescal.* Bureau of Indian Affairs Report no. 2288. Fargo:
                North Dakota Agricultural College and Government Experi-
                ment Station.
    1916   Witness. *U.S.* v. *Harry Black Bear.* U.S. District Court,
                Deadwood, S.Dak., Sept. 8.
    1918   "Mescal." In U.S. Congress, House, Committee on Indian Af-
                fairs, 1918*a*, pt. 1, pp. 32–35.
    1923   "Mescal." *Bureau of Indian Affairs Bulletin* 21: 7–12.
Questionnaires of Bureau of Indian Affairs Regarding Peyote
    1909   June 10. Sent to twelve agencies in Oklahoma, Nebraska, Wy-
                oming, and New Mexico, one each.
    1912   Jan. 18. Circular 598. Sent to "all reservations."
    1916   June 12. Questionnaires to 136 agencies; 26 reported peyote
                use.
    1919   April 4. Circular 1522. 115 western agencies questioned; 302
                replies received, representing 28 agencies, 13,345 peyotists.
                See Newberne, summary of results in each of three editions,
                1922, 1923, 1925.
Radin, Paul
    1914   "A Sketch of the Peyote Cult of the Winnebago: A Study in
                Borrowing." *Journal of Religious Psychology* 7(1): 1–22.
    1920   *The Autobiography of a Winnebago Indian.* University of Cali-
                fornia Publications in American Archaeology and Ethnology,
                no. 16, pp. 430–49. Berkeley: University of California Press.
                Reprinted as Radin, 1926.
    1923   "The Winnebago Tribe." *Bureau of American Ethnology An-
                nual Report* 37(1915–16): 69, 73, 388–426.
    1926   *Crashing Thunder: The Autobiography of an American Indian.*
                New York and London: Appleton.
    1950   "The Religious Experiences of an American Indian." *Eranos-
                Jahrbuch* 18: 249–90.
Randall, William
    1937   "Remarks of Committee of [Oglala Sioux] Indians with Refer-
                ence to the Use of Peyote." Henry Standing Bear, Interpreter.
                Letters Received, 10776 Pine Ridge, Feb. 20, Record Group
                75, National Archives, Washington, D.C.
Rave, Harry
    1911   Affidavit, Oct. 11. Peyote Correspondence, File 2989-08-126,
                pt. 3, Winnebago, Record Group 75, National Archives, Wash-
                ington, D.C.
Rave, John
    1912   "Account of the Peyote Cult and His Conversion." In Radin,
                1923, pp. 989–94.
Reh, Emma, and D'Arcy McNickle
    1943   "Peyote and the Indian" [Idaho]. *Scientific Monthly* 57: 220–29.
Reko, Victor A.
    1928   *La flora diabólica de México.* Mexico City.

Reynolds, T.
1970   "Two Reports on Peyote." Letters. *Navajo Times,* Jan. 15,
              p. 2.
Ribas, A. P.
1645   *Historia de los triumphos de nuestra Santa Fe.* Madrid.
Road, Paul Mouse
1907   Letter to J. Mooney, May 20. Manuscript no. 2537, Bureau of
              American Ethnology, Washington, D.C.
Roddy, T. R.
1909*a*   "The Winnebago Mescal-Eaters." In *The Indian Tribes of the
              Upper Mississippi Valley,* ed. E. H. Blair, 2:281–83.
1909*b*   Letter to E. H. Blair, May 14. Blair Collection, Wisconsin His-
              torical Society, Madison.
Roe, Walter C.
1908   Letter to W. F. Crafts, Nov. 21. Peyote Correspondence,
              Chief Special Officer, File 2989-08-126, pt. 1-C, Record Group
              75, National Archives, Washington, D.C.
1911   "Mescale, Peyote, or *Anhalonium Lewinii.*" In U.S. Con-
              gress, House, Committee on Indian Affairs, 1918*a*, pt. 1,
              pp. 44–45.
Rouhier, Alexandre
1925   "Phénomènes de metagnomie expérimentale observés au
              course d'une experience fait avec le peyotl." *Revue Metapsy-
              chique,* May–June, pp. 144–54.
1926   "Monographie du peyotl." Thesis, Doct. Pharm., Faculté de
              Pharmacie de Paris.
1927*a*   La Plante qui fait les yeux émerveilles—Le Peyotl. Paris:
              Doin. Reprint. 1975.
1927*b*   *Les Plantes diviniatoires.* Paris: Doin et Cie. Reprint. 1975.
Ruby, Robert H.
1962   "Indian Peyote Cult. *Frontier Times* 36(19):30–39.
Rucker, A.
1932   "The Spirit in the Peyote." *Daily Oklahoman,* Sept. 25, sec.
              C, p. 7; Oct. 2, sec. C, p. 7.
Ruiz de Alarcón, Hernandez
1629   "Tratado de las supersticiones y costumbres Gentilicas, 1629."
              Anales del Museo Nacional de México 6 (1898, 1900):123–223.
Russell, R. L.
1909*a*   Letter to E. Stecker, June 23. Reply to questionnaire. File
              2989-08-126, pt. 1-C, Letter 3986 attached, Record Group 75,
              National Archives, Washington, D.C.
1909*b*   Letter to Ernest Stecker, Anadarko, Okla., June 23, for-
              warded to W. E. Johnson, June 24. File 2989-08-126, pt. 1-C,
              Letter 3986, Record Group 75, National Archives, Washing-
              ton, D.C.
1916   Reply to letter from Chief Special Officer Henry L. Larson,
              Denver. File 2989-1908-126, pt. 1-B, Record Group 75, Na-
              tional Archives, Washington, D.C.

Safford, William E.
1915   "An Aztec Narcotic." *Journal of Heredity* 6(7): 291–311.
1916   "Narcotic Plants and Stimulants of the Ancient Americans." *Annual Report of the Smithsonian Institution*, pp. 387–424.
1918   Testimony Before House Committee on Peyote. In U.S. Congress, House, Committee on Indian Affairs, 1918*a*, pt. 2, pp. 186–90.
Sagi, D.
1956   "White Men Witness Indian Peyote Rite." *Saskatoon Star-Phoenix*, Oct. 13, pp. 14–15.
Sahagún, Bernardino de
1830   *Historia general de las cosas de Nueva Espana.* 3 vols. Ed. C. M. de Bustamante. 2: 366; 3: 118, 241. Mexico City. [Sahagún, 1499–1590, cited by Safford, 1916.]
San Bernardino Evening Telegram
1962   "Financial Aid from Assoc. of American Indians." May 12.
Santa Fe New Mexican
1954   "Peyotism and the Peyote Ceremony." July 11.
Santoscoy, Alberto, ed.
1900   *Arte de la lengua mexicana que fue usual entre los indios del obispada de Guadalajara . . . ,* pp. 7–35. Guadalajara: Ancira y hno. A. Ochoa.
Schultes, Richard Evans
1936   "Peyotl Intoxication: A Review of the Literature on the Chemistry, Physiological and Psychological Effects of Peyotl." Thesis, Harvard University.
1937*a*   "Statement on Senate Bill 1399. In U.S. Bureau of Indian Affairs, 1937.
1937*b*   "Peyote and the American Indian." *Nature Magazine* 30: 155–57.
1937*c*   "Peyote and Plants Confused with It." *Harvard University Botanical Museum Leaflets* 5(5): 61–88.
1937*d*   "Peyote and Plants Used in the Peyote Ceremony." *Harvard University Botanical Museum Leaflets* 4(8): 129–52.
1938   "The Appeal of Peyote (*Lophophora Williamsii*) as a Medicine." *American Anthropologist* 40(4): 698–715.
1972   "An Overview of Hallucinogens." In *Flesh of the Gods,* ed. Peter T. Furst. New York: Praeger.
1984   "Foreword." In *Peyotism in the West,* ed. Omer C. Stewart and David F. Aberle, pp. vii–viii. *University of Utah Anthropological Papers,* no. 108.
———, and Albert Hofmann
1979   *Plants of the Gods.* New York: McGraw-Hill.
Science
1951   Statement on peyote. signed by Weston La Barre, David P. McAllester, J. S. Slotkin, Omer C. Stewart, and Sol Tax. 114 (2970): 582–83.

Scott, Andrew
    1969   Letter to Fred Hoffman, president of Native American Church
                of Oklahoma, Hammon, Okla. Nov. 4.
Scott, Hugh L.
    1928   *Some Memories of a Soldier.* New York: Century.
Semans, J.
    1911   Affidavit, Oct. 11. U.S. Bureau of Indian Affairs, Peyote Corre-
                spondence, File 2989-08-126, pt. 3, Record Group 75, Na-
                tional Archives, Washington, D.C.
Serna, Jacinto de la
    1626   "Manual de ministros para el conocimiento de idolatrias y ex-
                tirpación de ellas." July. In *Documentos inéditos para la historia
                de España,* 104: 61, 159–60. Madrid, 1892.
    1656   "Manual de ministros de Indios." In *Anales del Museo Nacional
                de México* 6(1900): 261–480.
Shell, C. E.
    1907*a*   Letter to C. C. Brannon, Feb. 15. File 2989-07-126, Record
                Group 75, National Archives, Washington, D.C.
    1907*b*   Petition to Congress and letter sent to thirteen other Indian
                agents in Oklahoma requesting support of antipeyote legisla-
                tion, Sept. 7. Cheyenne and Arapaho—Vices; Kiowa and Co-
                manche—Vices. Oklahoma Historical Society, Oklahoma City.
    1909   Letter W. E. Johnson, March 10. U.S. Bureau of Indian Affairs,
                Peyote Correspondence, Chief Special Officer, File 2989-08-
                126, Record Group 75, National Archives, Washington, D.C.
    1917   Letter to Hayden, April 16, against peyote. U.S. Congress,
                Senate, Committee on Indian Affairs, 1937, p. 18284.
    1923   "Experience of Charles E. Shell While Under Influence of Pe-
                llote (Peyote) on June 21, 1909." *Bureau of Indian Affairs Bul-
                letin* no. 21, pp. 27–29.
Shimkin, Demitri B.
    1944   "List of Elements in the Peyote Ritual of the Wind River Sho-
                shone as of 1939." In Stewart, 1944, pp. 103–21.
    1953   "The Wind River Shoshone Sun Dance." *Bureau of American
                Ethnology Bulletin* no. 151, pp. 437–43, 467–71.
Shonle, Ruth
    1923   Letters to Agent, Ponca Agency, and replies. Ponca and Oto—
                Vices. Oklahoma Historical Society, Oklahoma City.
    1925   "Peyote: The Giver of Visions." *American Anthropologist* 27:
                53–75.
Simmons, C. S.
    1913   "The Peyote Road." Manuscript no. 2537, U.S. Bureau of
                American Ethnology, Washington, D.C.
Simon, Barbara
    1968   Interviewer, American Indian Reservation Project, Vermillion,
                S.Dak. Manuscript no. 245, Leech Lake Reservation, Minn.
                Also manuscript no. 246A.

Siskin, Edgar E.
1941   "The Impact of the Peyote Cult upon Shamanism Among the
            Washo Indians." Ph.D. diss., Yale University.
1983   *Washo Shamans and Peyotists: Religious Conflict in an Ameri-
            can Indian Tribe.* Salt Lake City: University of Utah Press.
Skinner, Alanson
1910   "Wisconsin Winnebago Collection." *Anthropological Papers of
            the American Museum of Natural History* 4: 289–97.
1915a   "Societies of the Iowa." *Anthropological Papers of the American
            Museum of Natural History* 11: 679–741.
1915b   "Kansa Organizations." *Anthropological Papers of the American
            Museum of Natural History* 11: 741–77.
1915c   "Ponca Societies and Dances." *Anthropological Papers of the
            American Museum of Natural History* 11: 777–801.
1915d   "Associations and Ceremonies of the Menomini Indians." *An-
            thropological Papers of the American Museum of Natural History*
            13: 167–215.
1923   "Observations on the Ethnology of the Sauk Indians." *Bulletin
            of the Public Museum of Milwaukee* 5: 8–10, 51, 85.
1924   "The Mascoutens or Prairie Potawatomi Indians." *Bulletin of
            the Public Museum of Milwaukee* 7(1): 12–15, 232–46.
1926   "Ethnology of the Ioway Indians." *Bulletin of the Public Mu-
            seum of Milwaukee* 5: 181–354.
Sloan, T. L.
1915   Statement. U.S. Congress, House, Committee on Indian Af-
            fairs, 1918a, pt. 1, pp. 82–84.
Slotkin, J. Sydney
1951   "Early Eighteenth Century Documents on Peyotism North of
            the Rio Grande." *American Anthropologist* 53: 420–27.
1952   "Menomini Peyotism: A Study of Individual Variation in a Pri-
            mary Group with a Homogeneous Culture." *Philosophical So-
            ciety* 42(4): 565–700.
1954a   "Mescalin—An Answer to Cigarettes?" *Saturday Review* 37
            (6): 14–15.
1954b   "The Church and the Cactus." *Time,* Aug. 9, pp. 49–50.
1955a   Ed. *Quarterly Bulletin of the Native American Church* 1(1)–
            5(2). Chicago.
1955b   "Peyotism, 1521–1891." *American Anthropologist* 57: 202–30.
1956a   "The Peyote Way." *Tomorrow: Quarterly Review of Psychical
            Research* 4(3): 64–70.
1956b   *The Peyote Religion: A Study in Indian-White Relations.* Glen-
            coe, Ill.: Free Press.
Smith, Elna
1934   "A Negro Peyote Cult." *Journal of the Washington Academy of
            Sciences* 24(10): 448–53.
1937   Statement on Senate Bill 1399. In U.S. Bureau of Indian Af-
            fairs, 1937.

Smith, Miss ——
    1909   Letter regarding Harry Davenport's suicide. File 2989-08-126,
                    Record Group 75, National Archives, Washington, D.C.
Smith, Ralph A.
    1916   "The Comanche Bridge Between Oklahoma and Mexico,
                    1843–44." *Chronicles of Oklahoma* 39: 54–69.
Society of American Indians
    1916   "Resolutions of the Annual Conference." *American Indian
                    Magazine* 4: 223–24.
Sonnichsen, C. L.
    1958   *The Mescalero Apaches.* Norman: University of Oklahoma
                    Press.
Sorre, Max
    1928   *Mexique et Amérique Centrale.* Vol. 14. Paris: Geographie Uni-
                    verselle, Armond Colin.
Speck, Frank G.
    1907   Notes on the Ethnology of the Osage Indians. *Transactions of
                    the University Museum* (University of Pennsylvania) 2(2):
                    159–171.
    1933   "Notes on the Life of John Wilson, the Revealer of Peyote, as
                    Recalled by his Nephew, G. Anderson." *General Magazine and
                    Historical Chronicle* (Philadelphia) 35: 533–56.
Spicer, Edward H., ed.
    1961   *Perspectives in American Indian Culture Change.* Chicago:
                    University of Chicago Press.
Spindler, George D.
    1952   "Personality and Peyotism in Menomini Indian Acculturation."
                    Psychiatry 15: 151–59.
    1955*a*   "Menomini Research." *American Anthropologist* 57: 864–65.
    1955*b*   *Sociocultural and Psychological Processes in Menomini Ac-
                    culturation.* University of California Publications in Culture and
                    Society, no. 5. Berkeley: University of California Press.
    1956   *Personal Documents in Menomini Peyotism: Primary Records in
                    Culture and Personality.* Vol. 2. Ed. B. Kaplan. Lawrence,
                    Kans.: Microcard Foundation Publications.
——, and W. Goldschmidt
    1952   "Experimental Design in the Study of Culture Change." *South-
                    western Journal of Anthropology* 8: 68–83.
——, and Louis S. Spindler
    1971   *Dreamers Without Power: The Menomini Indians.* New York:
                    Holt, Rinehart and Winston.
Spindler, Louise S.
    1952   "Witchcraft in Menomini Acculturation." *American Anthropol-
                    ogist* 54: 593–602.
Steinmetz, Paul B.
    1974   Manuscript of list of elements in peyote religion, Sioux Half
                    Moon. In possession of O. C. Stewart.

Stenberg, Molly Peacock
    1945   "The People Cult Among Wyoming Indians." Master's thesis, University of Wyoming.
    1946   "The Peyote Culture Among Wyoming Indians." *University of Wyoming Publications* 12(4): 85–156.

Stern, T.
    1950   *The Rubber Ball Games of the Americas.* Monographs of the American Ethnological Society, no. 17. New York: J. J. Augustin.

Stewart, Omer C.
    1938*a*   "Field Notes—Washo and Northern Paiute." Manuscripts. In possession of the author.
    1938*b*   "Cactus Christianity." Berkeley: University of California Radio Service. Mimeographed. In possession of the author.
    1939*a*   "Washo-Northern Paiute Peyotism: A Study in Acculturation." Ph.D. diss., University of California, Berkeley.
    1939*b*   "Washo-Northern Paiute Peyotism." *Proceedings of the Pacific Science Congress* 6(4): 65–68.
    1941*a*   "Culture Element Distribution: 14—Northern Paiute." *University of California Anthropological Records* 4: 361–446.
    1941*b*   "The Southern Ute Peyote Cult." *American Anthropologist* 43 (2): 303–308.
    1942   "Culture Element Distributions: 18—Ute-Southern Paiute." *University of California Anthropological Records* 6: 231–360.
    1944   "Washo-Northern Paiute Peyotism: A Study in Acculturation." *University of California Publications in American Archaeology and Ethnology* 40: 3. Berkeley: University of California Press.
    1948   "Ute Peyotism." *University of Colorado Studies, Anthropology Series,* no. 1, pp. 1–42.
    1951   "Pro-Peyote." *Time* 58(2): 6–8.
    1954*a*   "Peyotism: A Modern Indian Religion." *Delphian Quarterly* 37(2): 7–8, 37.
    1954*b*   "Peyote." In *Encyclopedia Americana,* 21: 700. New York: America Corp.
    1956*a*   "Peyote and Colorado's Inquisition Law." *Colorado Quarterly* 5(1): 79–90.
    1956*b*   "Three Gods for Joe." *Tomorrow: Quarterly Review of Psychical Research* 5(3): 71–76.
    1961*a*   "The Native American Church (Peyote Cult) and the Law." *Denver Westerners Monthly Roundup* 18(1): 5–18.
    1961*b*   "The Native American Church and the Law, with Description of Peyote Religious Services." *Westerner's Brand Book* 17: 4–47.
    1961*c*   "Peyote and the Arizona Court Decision." *American Anthropologist* 63(6): 1334.
    1963   *Constitutional Rights of the American Indians: Hearings Before the Subcommittee on Constitutional Rights of the Commit-*

tee on the Judiciary United States Senate, 87th Cong. 2d sess., pt. 3, pp. 524–70.

1970   "Peyotism." In *Encyclopedia Britannica,* pp. 790–91.

1972*a*   "The Peyote Religion of the Ute Indians." *Vernal* (Utah) *Express,* Oct. 26.

1972*b*   "The Peyote Religion and the Ghost Dance." *Indian Historian* 5(4):27–30.

1972*c*   Field notes based on interviews and observations of peyote meetings with Taos, Comanche, Kiowa, Cheyenne, Sac and Fox, Oto, Osage, Winnebago, Ute, Navajo, Crow, Shoshone, Omaha, Northern Paiute, Washo, and Sioux Indians. In possession of author.

1973   "Anthropologists as Expert Witnesses for Indians: Claims and Peyote Cases." In *Symposium on Anthropology and the American Indian,* ed. James E. Officer. San Francisco: Indian Historian Press.

1974   "Origin of the Peyote Religion in the United States." *Plains Anthropologist* 19(65):211–23.

1984   "Taos Factionalism" [over peyote]. *American Indian Culture and Research Journal* (University of California, Los Angeles) 8(1):37–57.

1986   "The Peyote Religion." In *Handbook of North American Indians—Great Basin,* 11:673–81, 142–43. Washington, D.C.: Smithsonian Institution.

In Press   "Peyote and the Law." In *Handbook of North American Indians,* vol. 20. Ed. D'Arcy McNickle and Vine Deloria, Jr. Washington, D.C.: Smithsonian Institution.

———, and David F. Aberle

1957*a, b*   See Aberle, David F., and O. C. Stewart, 1957*a, b.*

1984   *Peyotism in the West.* University of Utah Anthropological Papers, no. 108.

Sturtevant, William C.

1971   Letter to O. C. Stewart re peyotism of Seneca and Delaware. In possession of O. C. Stewart.

Swanton, John R.

1940   "Linguistic Material from the Tribes of Southern Texas and Northeastern Mexico." *Bureau of American Ethnology Bulletin,* no. 127, p. 142. Washington, D.C.: U.S. Government Printing Office.

1942   "Source Material on the History of Ethnology of the Caddo Indians." *Bureau of American Ethnology Bulletin,* no. 132, pp. 51–52, 120–21, 210, 265–71. Washington, D.C.: U.S. Government Printing Office.

Takes Gun, Frank

1957   "Explanations Concerning Rites of Peyotism." Manuscript prepared for *Look* magazine. In possession of O. C. Stewart.

Tax, Sol, et al.

1956   "The North American Indians: 1950 Distribution of Descen-

dants of the Aboriginal Population of Alaska, Canada and the
United States." Map. Copy in possession of O. C. Stewart.

1959   "James Sydney Slotkin, 1913–1958." *American Anthropologist*
        61(5): 844–47.

Taylor, Norman

1944   "Come and Expel the Green Pain." *Scientific Monthly* 58: 174–
        84. Reprinted in Taylor, 1966, pp. 128–49.

1966   *Narcotics: Nature's Dangerous Gifts.* New York: Dell Publishing
        Co.

Tebo, H.

1917   Letter to Gertrude Bonnin, July 6. In U.S. Congress, Senate,
        Committee on Indian Affairs 1918, pp. 31–32.

Texas Department of Public Safety.

1976   *Texas Drug Laws.* Austin.

Thackery, Frank A.

1909   Reply to William E. Johnson questionnaire re use of peyote by
        Kickapoo, July 17. File 2989-08-126, pt. 1-C, Record Group
        75, National Archives, Washington, D.C.

Thurman, Melburn D.

1973   Supplementary Material on the Life of John Wilson, "the Re-
        vealer of Peyote." *Ethnohistory* 20: 279–87.

Tilghman, Z. A.

1938   *Quanah, the Eagle of the Comanches.* Oklahoma City: Harlow.

Tillman, John H.

1921   "Statement Against Peyote." *Congressional Record* 61(5): 4686.

Time

1951a   "Comments of Dr. Salsbury's on Peyotism." June 18.

1951b   "Button, Button." June 18.

1954   "The Church and the Cactus." Aug. 9.

1959   "God and Peyote." Feb. 16.

1964   "Button Eaters." Sept. 11.

Timmons, B.

1967   Interview of the Sac and Fox George and Mable Harris. Uni-
        versity of Oklahoma Oral History Report, Western History
        Collections, University of Oklahoma Library.

Tippo, Oswald, and William Louis Stern

1977   *Humanistic Botany.* New York: W. W. Norton and Co.

Tobriner, J.

1964   Opinion of the Supreme Court of the state of California in
        Criminal Case no. 7788: *The People* v. *Jack Woody et al.* Con-
        firming the Right to Use Peyote in Religious Services of the
        Native American Church. Aug. 24. Copy of opinion can be ob-
        tained from the Supreme Court of the State of California. Copy
        in possession of O. C. Stewart.

Tranter, Charles L.

1942   "New Dope Menace Threatens U.S.—*PEYOTE.*" *PIC*, Dec.
        8.

1944   Article from *PIC* (1942) inserted in Hearings of House of Rep-

resentatives Committee on Indian Affairs by Mrs. Bolton of
Ohio, pt. 4, Dec. 13, 78th Cong. 2d sess., pp. 318–31.

Trenholm, Virginia Cole
1970   *The Arapahoes, Our People.* Norman: University of Oklahoma
            Press.
Tribune-Herald (Hardin, Mont.)
1968   "Frank Takes Gun Was Reelected President." Nov. 28.
Troike, Rudolph C.
1962   "The Origin of Plains Mescalism." *American Anthropologist*
            64: 946–63.
Tsa Toke, Monroe
1957   *The Peyote Ritual.* San Francisco: Grabhorn Press.
Tunnell, Curtis D., and W. W. Newcomb, Jr.
1969   *A Lipan Apache Mission: San Lorenzo de la Cruz, 1692–1771.*
            Texas Memorial Museum Bulletin, no. 14. Austin: University
            of Texas Press.
Ugarte y Loyola, Don Jacobo
1770   Correspondence. Manuscript, Archivo General de la Nación,
            Provincias Internas, vol. 27. From incomplete collection in
            Bancroft Library, University of California, Berkeley.
Underhill, Ruth M.
1950   "Biography of Frank Sweezy (White Wolf). So. Arapaho of
            Greenfield, Oklahoma." Manuscript. July. In possession of
            O. C. Stewart.
1952   "Peyote." *Proceedings of the 30th International Congress of
            Americanists,* London, pp. 143–48. Reprint. *San Vincente
            Foundation Publication,* no. 2, pp. 1–14.
1963   "Navaho Peyotism." Manuscript. In possession of O. C.
            Stewart.
1965   *Red Man's Religion.* Chicago: University of Chicago Press.
1969   "Peyote, the Vegetable Savior of the Indian." Manuscript. In
            possession of O. C. Stewart.
U.S. Bureau of Indian Affairs
1877   Report by Osage Agent Cyrus Beede, p. 90.
1888   Report of Acting Osage Agent Carrol H. Potter, p. 101.
1889   Report of Osage Agent L. J. Miles, pp. 192–93.
1890a   Letter from Commissioner BIA T. J. Morgan to Sac and Fox
            Agent S. L. Patrick, July 31. Record Group 75, Letter Book
            154, Letters Sent—Education, National Archives, Washing-
            ton, D.C.
1890b   Report of the Commissioner of Indian Affairs to Secretary of
            the Interior, Sept. 5. "Wild West Shows and Similar Exhibi-
            tions," pp. lvii–lix.
1905   Report for fiscal year. 59th Cong., 1st sess., Doc. no. 5 [Con-
            gressional Series no. 4959]. Employees of BIA, p. 527.
1909   Letter to C. F. Hauke to W. E. Johnson, Dec. 6. Education-
            Administration, File 93273-1909, Record Group 75, National
            Archives, Washington, D.C.

1910*a* Letter Valentine to Johnson, Nov. 18. Education-Liquor, File 2989-1908, Record Group 75, National Archives, Washington, D.C.

1910*b* Letter Wadsworth to W. E. Johnson, Dec. 28. Peyote sellers from Oklahoma on Wind River Reservation, Wyoming. Education-Liquor, File 2989-1908, Record Group 75, National Archives, Washington, D.C.

1912 Report by Commissioner Robert G. Valentine of intention of BIA to seek a law prohibiting peyote. Ed.—Law and Order, File 26120-1913, Record Group 75, National Archives, Washington, D.C.

1918–23*a* Documents relating to the Native American Church. File 11552-1919-126, Record Group 75, National Archives, Washington, D.C.

1918–23*b* Documents relating to the Native American Church. Oklahoma Historical Society, Indian Archives Division, Oklahoma City. See card index, "Native American Church."

1919 *Peyote*. March 28. Circular 1522, and replies. Replies to circulars [fifth peyote questionnaire], Record Group 75, National Archives, Washington, D.C. Summary in Newberne, 1922.

1923 *Peyote*. Bureau of Indian Affairs Bulletin, no. 21. Mimeographed. Washington, D.C.

1934 John Collier. *Indian Religious Freedom and Indian Culture*. Jan. 3. Circular 2970. Washington, D.C. Reprinted. U.S. Congress, Senate, Committee on Indian Affairs 1937:18319–20.

1935 "Discussion Concerning Peyote." April. Reprinted from *Hearings of the Subcommittee of the House Committee on Appropriations in Charge of Interior Department Appropriation Bill for 1936*, 74th Cong. 1st sess., pp. 689–96.

1937 "Documents on Peyote." Document no. 137817, pt. 1, Feb. 8. Mimeographed Bureau Report on S. 1399, 75th Cong., 1st sess. Washington, D.C.: Bureau of Indian Affairs.

U.S. Congress, House, Committee on Appropriations
1935 *Discussion Concerning Peyote*. Hearing on H.R. 6223, April. 74th Cong., 1st sess., pp. 687–96.

U.S. Congress, House, Committee on Indian Affairs
1918*a* *Peyote*. Hearings on H.R. 2614, pt. 1, Feb. 21–25; pt. 2, March 23. 67th Cong., 2d sess.

1918*b* *Prohibition of Use of Peyote*. U.S. Congress, Documents and Reports, 65th Cong. 2d sess., May 13, ser. 7308, no. 560.

1944 *Investigate Indian Affairs*. Hearings. Part 4 (final volume), Dec. 13. Article from *PIC* inserted by Rep. Frances Bolton. 78th Cong., 2d sess., pp. 299–343.

1965 *Congressional Record*, March 10, pp. 4571–75.

U.S. Congress, Senate
1971 *Biographical Directory of the American Congress, 1774–1971*. 92d Cong., 1st sess., S. Doc. 92–98.

U.S. Congress, Senate, Committee on Indian Affairs
1908   *Affairs of the Mexican Kickapoo Indians.* 3 vols. 60th Cong.,
          1st sess., S. Doc. 215, vols. 14–46 (serial 5247–49).
1918   *Indian Appropriation Bill, 1919.* Hearings on H.R. 8696, 65th
          Cong., 2d sess., Jan. 29–Feb. 13.
1937   *Survey of Conditions of Indians in the United States.* Hearings,
          Aug. 31, 1936; Dec. 14, 1936. 75th Cong., 1st sess., pt. 34,
          pp. 18164–329.
U.S. Congress, Senate, Judiciary Committee
1965   *Constitutional Rights of the American Indian.* Hearings on S.
          961, 89th cong., 1st sess., June 22, 29, and appendices.
U.S. Department of Commerce
1899   Eleventh U.S. Census. Vol. 10, p. 247. Quapaws.
1900   U.S. Census Worksheet for the Sac and Fox and Iowa Reserva-
          tion, State of Kansas, County of Brown, "Koshiway, Johnathan,"
          sheet A-10, p. 241. Photocopy of sheet from microfilm, Fed-
          eral Records Center, Denver, Colo.
1974   Federal and State Indian Reservations and Indian Trust Areas.
          Washington, D.C.: U.S. Government Printing Office.
U.S. Department of Education and Welfare
1960–78   *Cumulated Index Medicus.* National Library of Medicine, Be-
          thesda, Md. Washington, D.C.: U.S. Government Printing
          Office.
U.S. Department of the Interior
1912   Board of Indian Commissioners voted, March 6, a law to pro-
          hibit peyote. File 26120-1912, Record Group 75, National Ar-
          chives, Washington, D.C.
1936   "Secretary Ickes Moves to Protect Minority Religious Groups
          at Taos Pueblo." *Indians at Work* 4(7): 8–13.
1973   "Exemption Allowing Use of Peyote on Navajo Reservation in
          Religious Services of Native American Church." *Federal Regis-
          ter* 38(142): 19909–10.
U.S. Department of Justice, Bureau of Narcotics
1971   "Regulations Implementing the Comprehensive Drug Abuse
          Prevention and Control Act of 1971. Special Exempt Persons
          307.31 Native American Church." *Federal Register* 36(80).
1975   "Peyote: Interpretation Under Federal Law." *Drug Enforce-
          ment* 2(3): 40–41.
U.S. District Court, North Dakota, Northeastern District
1984   *USA* v. *John D. and Frances Warner.* Cr. No. C2-84-51, memo-
          randum and order. Sept. 27. Verdict: not guilty. Oct. 29. Cop-
          ies in possession of O. C. Stewart.
U.S. District Court, South Dakota, Western District
1916   *U.S.A.* v. *Harry Black Bear.* Summary of testimony in *Dead-
          wood* (S.Dak.) *Daily Pioneer-Times,* Sept. 7, 1916, p. 1;
          Sept. 8, 1916, p. 1.
U.S. District Court, Wisconsin, Eastern District
1914   *U.S.A.* v. *Mitchell Neck, alias Nah-qua-tah-tuck.* Manuscript,

Milwaukee. Crim. F, no. 280. Transcript of testimony not located; summary given in Safford, 1915, pp. 306–307.

U.S. Indian Claims Commission
    1961   *Opinions of the Commissioner.* Cheyenne-Arapaho Tribes of Indians of Oklahoma. Docket nos. 329 and 348. 10 Ind. Cl. Comm. 1.

U.S. Statues at Large
    1906   Prohibit sale of liquor to Indians (34th Stat. L. 328).
    1929   *Narcotic Addict Farm Act,* 45: 1085.

U.S. Treasury Department
    1910   Letter, C. D. Hilles to Senator T. P. Gore of Oklahoma, May 20. No law against importation of peyote from Mexico. Copy of letter in C. S. Simmons, manuscript, 1913, appendix, BAE manuscript no. 2537. Washington, D.C.: Smithsonian Institution.

Urbina, Manuel
    1900   "El peyote y el ololuihqui." *Annals of National Museum of Mexico* 7: 25–48.

    1912   "El peyote y el ololuihqui." *La Naturaleza,* 3d ser., 1: 131–54.

Valentine, R. G.
    1909   Letter to Rep. John J. Esch of Wisconsin re obtaining peyote, Jan. 20. File CC86618-1908, Record Group 75, National Archives, Washington, D.C.

Valverde
    1720   Proclamation. Spanish Archives of New Mexico, vol. 2, no. 306, State Records Center, Santa Fe.

Voegelin, Erminie Wheeler
    1933–34   "Shawnee Field Notes." Section on peyote. Manuscript. In possession of O. C. Stewart.

    1944   "List of Elements of Peyote Ritual of the Oklahoma Shawnee as of 1933." In Stewart, 1944.

Voget, Fred W.
    1944   "List of Elements in Peyote Ritual of the Montana Crow as of 1939." In Stewart, 1944.

Wadsworth, H. E.
    1908   Letter to Commissioner of Indian Affairs, Aug. 21. U.S. Bureau of Indian Affairs, Peyote Correspondence, Chief Special Officer, File 2989-1908-126, pt. 1-C, Record Group 75, National Archives, Washington, D.C.

    1910   Letter to William E. Johnson re confiscating peyote, Dec. 10. File 101853—1903, 4689—1910, Record Group 75, National Archives, Washington, D.C.

Wagner, Roland M.
    1974   "Western Navajo Peyotism: A Case Analysis." Ph.d. diss., University of Oregon. Ann Arbor: University Microfilms. Copy in possession of O. C. Stewart.

    1975a   "Some Pragmatic Aspects of Navajo Peyotism." *Plains Anthropologist* 20(69): 197–206.

    1975b   "Pattern and Process in Ritual Syncretism: The Case of Peyotism Among the Navajo." *Journal of Anthropological Research* 31(2): 162–81.

1975*c*   "Pattern and Process in Ritual Syncretism: The Case of Peyotism Among the Navaho." Manuscript in possession of O. C. Stewart.

1975*d*   "'Double-Meetings': A Paradigm for Syncretism in Navaho Peyotism." Manuscript. Copy in possession of O. C. Stewart.

Wahkahquah, Lucy
    1966   "Cavayu, Comanche Indian [Peyotist]." *Prairie Lore* 2(4): 158–59.

Wallace, Anthony F. C.
    1956   "New Religions Among the Delaware Indians, 1600–1900." *Southwestern Journal of Anthropology* 12(1): 1–21.

Wallace, Ernest, and E. Adamson Hoebel
    1952   *The Comanches: Lords of the South Plains.* Norman: University of Oklahoma Press.

Wallis, Mrs. Wilson D.
    1975   Letter re Sioux in Canada, 1914. Sept. 23.

Wallis, Wilson D.
    1929   "Magnitude of Distribution, Centrifugal Spread, and Centripetal Elaboration of Culture Traits." *American Anthropologist* 31: 755–71.

Warden, Cleaver
    1918*a*   Letter to J. Mooney, Feb. 25. In U.S. Congress, House, Committee on Indian Affairs, 1918*a*, pt. 1, pp. 106–107.

    1918*b*   Statement. In U.S. Congress, House, Committee on Indian Affairs, 1918*a*, pt. 2, pp. 191–92.

Washington Daily News
    1942   "Pale Face Judge Frees Indian Whoopee Chief." March 19.

Webber, James C.
    1944   "List of Elements of Peyote Ritual of the Delaware as of 1939." In Stewart, 1944.

Webster, Daniel; Harry Lyon; and Parrish Sansouci
    1912   "Omaha Delegation to BIA to Testify as to the Value of Peyote, March 12." Testimony of 22 pages recorded by Assistant Commissioner F. H. Abbot and sent to Omaha and Winnebago Agent A. H. Kneale, March 28. File 2989-08-126, pt. 3, Record Group 75, National Archives, Washington, D.C.

Weeks, P.
    1962   "Indian Use of Peyote to Face Test in Court." *Los Angeles Times,* Nov. 13, sec. 3, p. 7.

Wells, Otto
    1915   Statement (received by Board of Indian Commissioners, 1915). In U.S. Congress, House, Committee on Indian Affairs, 1918*a*, pt. 1, p. 79.

West, Charles
    1937   "Report to the Secretary of the Interior on Senate Bill 1399," May 18, no. 136514. In U.S. Bureau of Indian Affairs, 1937.

White, E. E.
  1888*a*   Order [prohibiting peyote at the Kiowa, Comanche, and Wichita Agency], June 6. Manuscript. Kiowa and Comanche—Vices. Oklahoma Historical Society, Oklahoma City. Final Copy, Letters Received, 1888, no. 15508 inclos., Record Group 75, National Archives, Washington, D.C.
  1888*b*   Letter to the Commissioner of Indian Affairs, June 9. Letters Received, 1888, no. 15508, Record Group 75, National Archives, Washington, D.C.
  1888*c*   Letter to Commissioner of Indian Affairs, July 6. Letters Received, 1888, no. 17455, Record Group 75, National Archives, Washington, D.C.
  1888*d*   Report of the Kiowa, Comanche, and Wichita Agency, Aug. 18. *U.S. Bureau of Indian Affairs, Annual Report*, pp. 95–101.

Whitehorn, C.
  1923   Letter to G. A. Hoyo, Oct. 1. In Shonle, 1923.

Whitman, W.
  1937   *The Oto.* Columbia University Contributions to Anthropology, no. 28, pp. 127–30. New York: Columbia University Press.

Wiley, H. W.
  1923   Statement. *Bureau of Indian Affairs Bulletin* 21: 15–19.

Wilkinson, J. B.
  1975   *Laredo and the Rio Grande Frontier.* Austin, Texas: Jenkins Publishing Co.

Wilson, Alfred
  1925   See Haag and Wilson, 1925; also Collier, John, 1947, pp. 140–42.

Wilson, Tom
  1960   "Professor Defends Peyote." *Durango Herald,* Apr. 10, pp. 1, 3.

Winnebago Antipeyotists
  1906   Petition to Prohibit Peyote. Letters Received, 111329, Record Group 75, National Archives, Washington, D.C.

Winnipeg Tribune
  1954   "Devil's Brew—Or Sacred Potion." Dec. 2.

Wissler, Clark
  1912   "Societies and Ceremonial Associations in the Oglala Division of the Teton-Dakota." *Anthropological Papers of the American Museum of Natural History* 11(1): 99.
  1913   "Societies and Dances of the Blackfoot Indians." *Anthropological Papers of the American Museum of Natural History* 11: 436.
  1926   *The Relation of Nature to Man in Aboriginal America.* New York: Oxford University Press.

Wolbach, A. B., Jr.; Harris Isabell; and E. J. Miner
  1962   "Cross Tolerance Between Mescaline and LSD-25." *Psychopharmacologia* 3: 1–14.

Woodson, A. E.
    1896*a*   Letter to David Day, Southern Ute Agency, from Cheyenne and Arapaho Agency, July 13. Federal Records Center, Denver, Colo.
    1896*b*   "Report of Cheyenne and Arapaho Agency." *U.S. Bureau of Indian Affairs, Annual Report,* p. 250.
    1899   "Report of Agent for Cheyenne and Arapaho Agency." *U.S. Bureau of Indian Affairs, Annual Report,* pp. 282–86.

Wright, M. H.
    1951   *A Guide to the Indian Tribes of Oklahoma.* Norman: University of Oklahoma Press.

Wyman, F. W., and H. J. Johnson
    1918   "To the [Iowa and Sac and Fox] Indians." Privately printed. [Handbill against peyote.]

Young, J. R.
    1895   "Report of Pima Agency." *U.S. Bureau of Indian Affairs, Annual Report,* p. 122.

Young, R. W., comp.
    1954   *The Navajo Yearbook of Planning in Action.* Report no. 4. Window Rock, Ariz.: Navajo Agency.

————, ed.
    1957   *The Navajo Yearbook.* Report no. 6. Window Rock, Ariz.: Navajo Agency.
    1958   *The Navajo Yearbook.* Report no. 7. Window Rock, Ariz.: Navajo Agency.
    1961   *The Navajo Yearbook.* Report no. 8. Window Rock, Ariz.: Navajo Agency.

Zaehner, R. C.
    1954   *The Menace of Mescaline.* London: Blackfriars Press.
    1957   *Mysticism, Sacred and Profane.* London: Oxford University Press.

Zimmerly, David
    1969   *On Being an Ascetic: Personal Document of a Sioux Medicine Man.* Pine Ridge Research Bulletin, no. 10, August. Mimeographed. Pine Ridge, S.Dak.

Zingg, Robert M.
    1935   See Bennett and Zingg, 1935.
    1938   "The Huichols: Primitive Artists." *Denver University Contributions to Ethnography* 1:1–826.

Index of Personal Names

General Index

Note: For Indian tribes see under Indian tribes, Mexico, *and* Indian tribes, U.S. and Mexico

Aguas Calientes, Mexico: 19
Aguilares, Tex.: 9
Aguilares Mercantile Co., Aguilares, Tex.: 177, 229; *see also* peyote, commerce in
Albert Lea, Minn.: 173
Allen, S.Dak.: 181, 182, 230, 258
American Association of Indian Affairs of New York City: 308
American Civil Liberties Union (ACLU): 244, 304, 305, 308
American Indian Defense Association: 231
Anadarko, Indian Territory (Oklahoma): *see* Kiowa, Comanche, and Wichita Agency
Anaheim, Calif.: 314
Aneth, Utah: 293, 299, 301, 313
Anthropological Society of Washington, D.C.: 7
Apache, Okla.: 240, 250
Arapaho, Wyo.: 190
Ashland, Mont.: 186, 251, 262

Berens River, Manitoba, Canada: 260
Billings, Mont.: 261
Bishop, Calif.: 274
Bitter Springs, Ariz.: 292
Black Elk II Group: 321
Black Foot, Idaho: 249, 250
Black Mountain, Ariz.: 303
Black River Falls, Wis.: 160
Board of Indian Commissioners, U.S.: 213
Boise, Idaho: 249, 250
Bolsón de Mapimi (Durango, Mexico): 25, 26, 46, 52
Bridgeport, Calif.: 276, 286
Browning, Mont.: 252–253
Bureau of American Ethnology, U.S.: 34, 219–22
Bureau of Catholic Indian Missions: 213
Bureau of Indian Affairs: U.S. (BIA): opposition of, to peyote: 128–42 (Oklahoma); 157, 163, 164, 174, 184, 192, 203–207 (Taos), 213–22; change of, in favor of peyote, 231–38 (Taos),

269–71 (Gosiute), 277–84 (western Nevada—Ben Lancaster), 288–89 (Owyee), 294–97 (Navajo)
Burns, Oreg.: 290

Cache Mission School of Religious Education, Cache, Okla.: 73
"Calendar History of the Kiowa" (Mooney): 81
Calgary, Alberta, Canada: 262
Calumet, Okla.: 175, 180
Canyoncito, Ariz.: 315
Carlisle Indian School, Carlisle, Pa.: 64, 82, 85, 101–107, 126, 221
Carrizo Springs, Tex.: 46
Carson City, Nev.: 273, 276, 280, 286, 287, 318
Carson Indian Agency, Carson City, Nev.: 277, 282
Casper, Wyo.: 194
Cedar City, Utah: 254, 270, 271, 280, 287, 291–92
Cedarville, Calif.: 290
Chadron, Nebr.: 197
Cheyenne-Arapaho Agency and Reservation, Indian Territory: 55, 99, 101–102, 104, 116, 131, 193, 195, 202
Chichimec: 16, 19, 30
Chief Peyote: 37, 70, 91, 163, 209, 269, 279, 328; *see also* peyote ceremony in U.S.
Chihuahua, Mexico: 31, 46, 52, 72
Chilocco Indian Industrial School, Okla.: 65, 167
Churches, Indian peyote: *see* Native American Church
Churches, non-Indian peyote: Church of the Awakening, Socorro, N.Mex.: 326; Neo-American Church, 325–26; Peyote Way Church of God, 326
Coahuila, Mexico: 27–29, 46, 52, 139
Coleville, Calif.: 273, 276, 277, 281, 284–86, 292

449